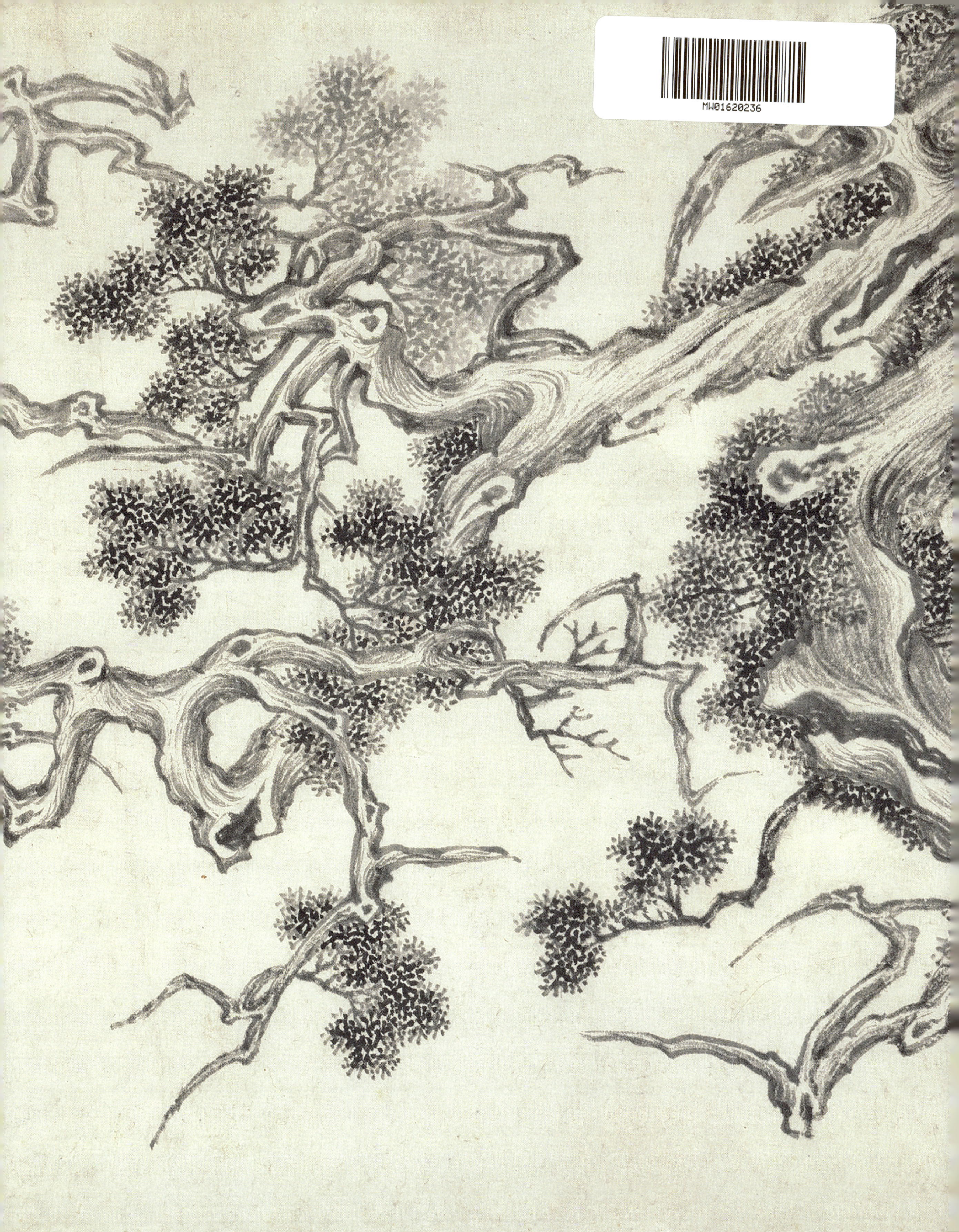

WOMEN ACROSS ASIAN ART

David A. Cofrin Asian Art Manuscript Series

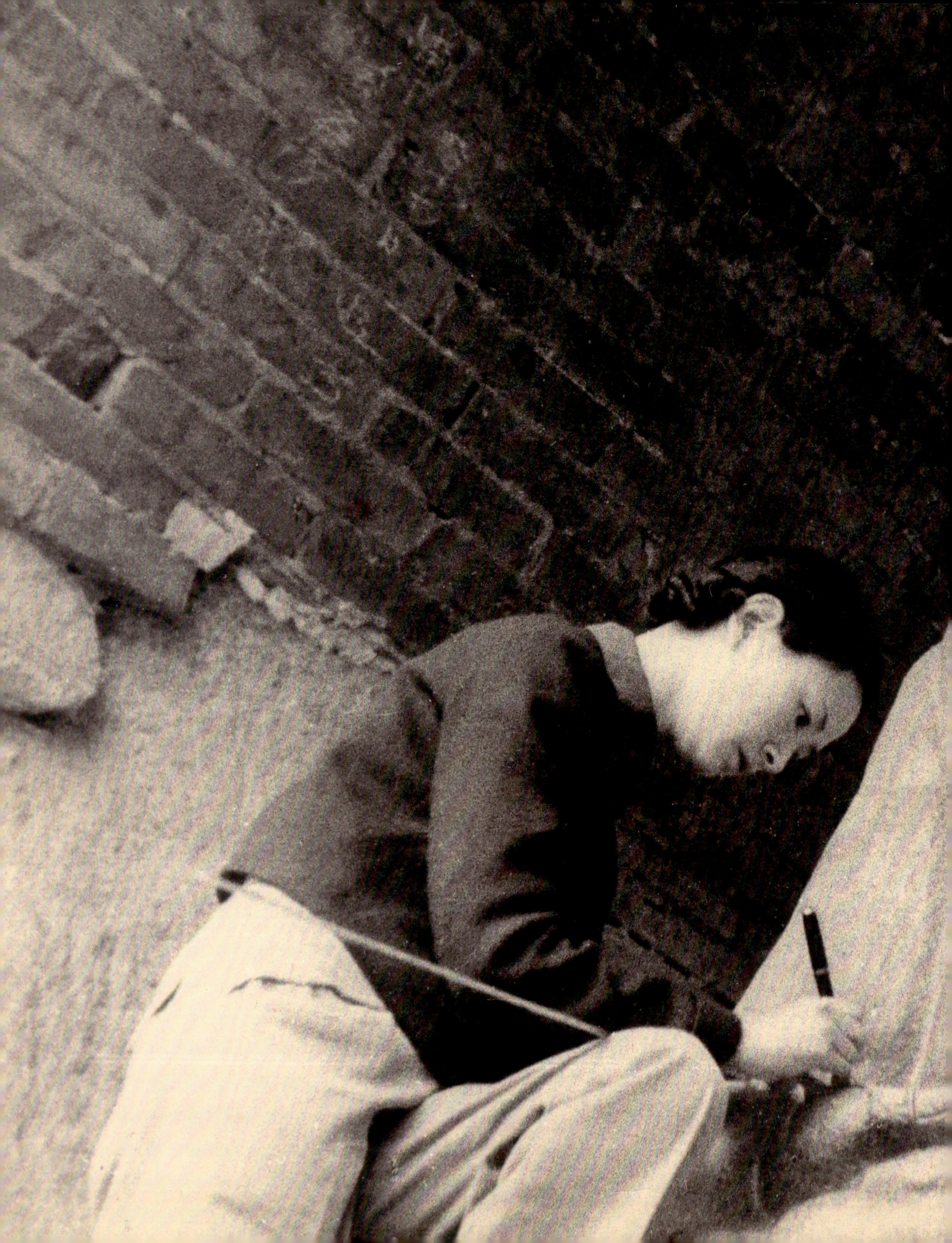

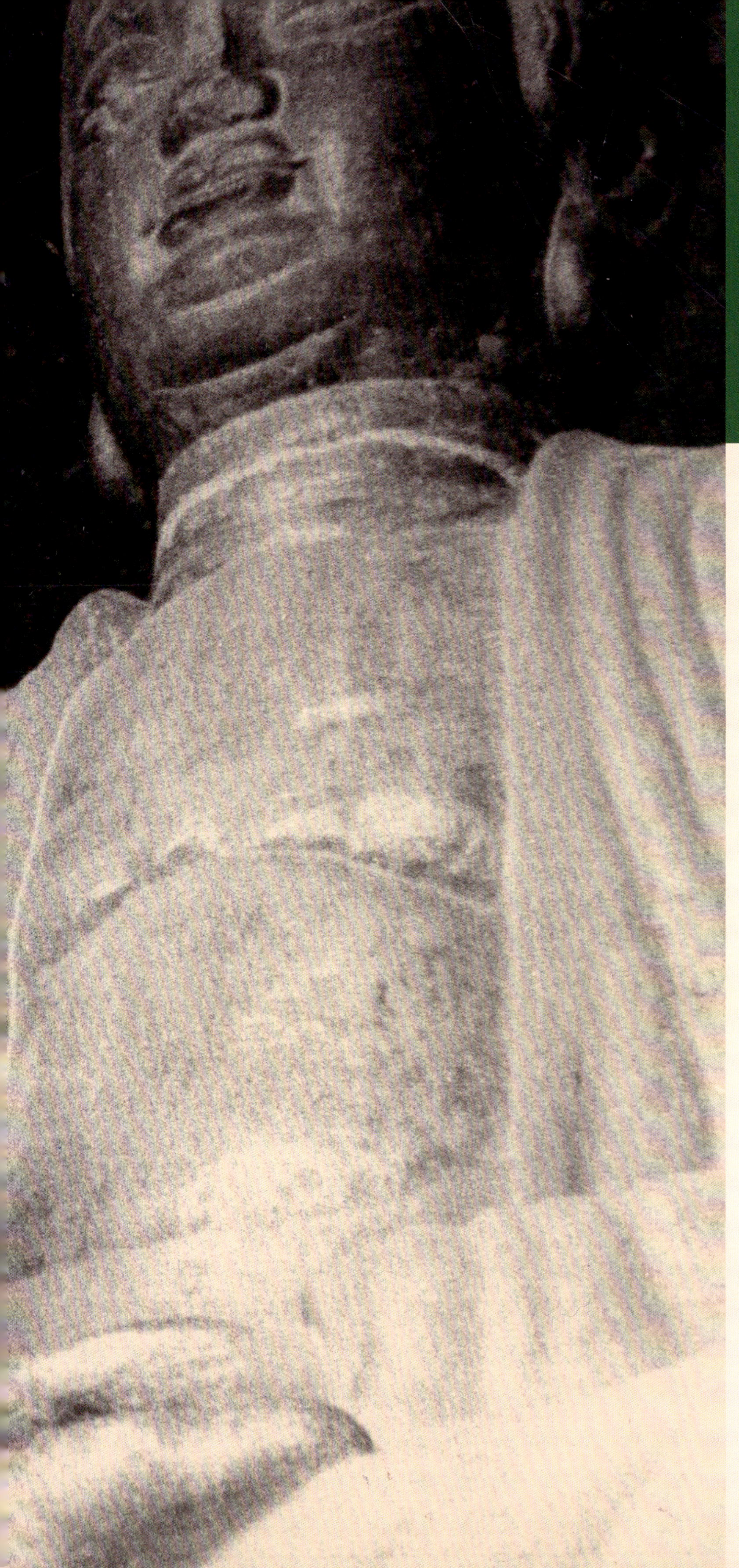

Women across Asian Art

Selected Essays in Art and Material Culture

Edited by
Ling-en Lu and
Allysa B. Peyton

University of Florida Press
Gainesville

Published in the United States of America. Printed in Canada.

28 27 26 25 24 23 6 5 4 3 2 1

Design and typesetting by Louise OFarrell

Endpapers: Wen Zhengming (1470–1559) (detail), *Seven Junipers*, Ming dynasty (1368–1644), dated 1532. Handscroll, ink on paper, 11 9/16 × 389 3/16 in. Gift of Mrs. Carter Galt, 1952. Honolulu Museum of Art (1666.1a).

Title page: Lin Huiyin working at a local temple outside Xi'an, Shaanxi, 1936. From Qinghua daxue jianzhu xueyuan, *Jianzhushi Lin Huiyin* (The Architect, Lin Huiyin) (Beijing: Qinghua daxue chubanshe, 2004), 167. Photograph by permission of School of Architecture, Tsinghua University.

Table of contents: Anonymous, *List of Wedding Gifts Given by Queen Sunwon to Princess Deogon*, 1837, ink on paper, 32.8 × 541.5 cm. National Hangeul Museum, Seoul.

Spread following contents: Wonyi's mother, *A Letter by Wonyi's Mother to Her Husband*, 1586, ink on paper, 34 × 58.5 cm. Andong National University Museum, Andong.

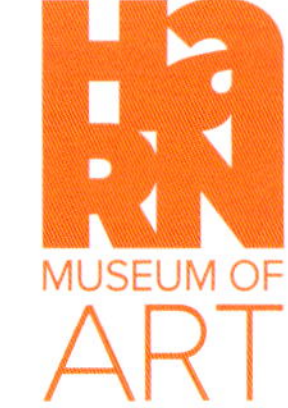

Library of Congress Cataloging-in-Publication Data
Names: Lu, Ling-En, editor. | Peyton, Allysa B., editor.

Title: Women across Asian art : selected essays in art and material culture / edited by Ling-en Lu and Allysa B. Peyton.

Other titles: David A. Cofrin Asian art manuscript series.

Description: 1. | Gainesville : University of Florida Press, 2023. | Series: David A. Cofrin Asian art manuscript series | Includes bibliographical references and index. | Summary: "Filled with exquisite color illustrations, this volume examines an underserved aspect of Asian art history by discussing women artists, collectors, archaeologists, and architects. The essays in Women across Asian Art cover a wide geographical area, from Japan to Pakistan, as they draw attention to people whose efforts have largely been left out of scholarship"—Provided by publisher.

Identifiers: LCCN 2023002880 | ISBN 9781683403586 (cloth)

Subjects: LCSH: Art, Asian—History. | Women artists—Asia—History. | BISAC: ART / Asian / General | HISTORY / Women

Classification: LCC N7260 .W66 2023 | DDC 709.5—dc23/eng/20230331

LC record available at https://lccn.loc.gov/2023002880

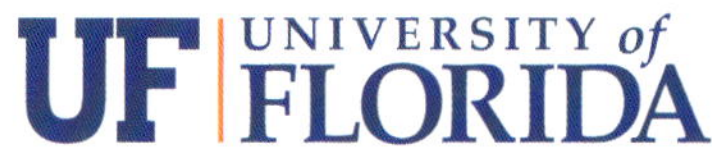

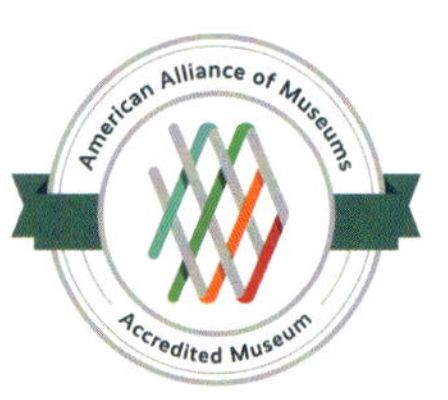

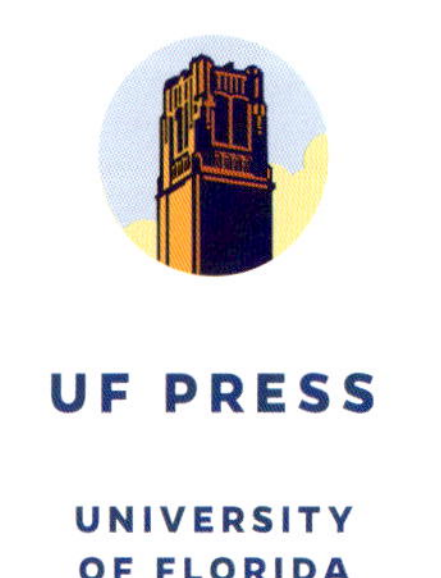

UF PRESS

UNIVERSITY OF FLORIDA

University of Florida Press
2046 NE Waldo Road
Suite 2100
Gainesville, FL 32609
http://upress.ufl.edu

David A. Cofrin Asian Art Manuscript Series

The David A. Cofrin Asian Art Manuscript Series embodies the determination and drive that Dr. David Cofrin (1923–2009) brought to Asian art. Dr. Cofrin was a serious collector of Asian art, acquiring works not only from China but also from regions as far west as Persia, as far east as Japan, and as far south as India. His broad range of interests reflected his investigative spirit and love of learning new things from various places and periods. Dr. Cofrin and his family were responsible for the formation and growth of the Samuel P. Harn Museum of Art and its many collections, especially those of Asian art. From the founding gift that created an art museum on the University of Florida campus to subsequent donations that funded the addition of the Mary Ann Harn Cofrin Pavilion and the David A. Cofrin Asian Art Wing, the Cofrins have been the heart and soul of the Harn Museum of Art since before its inception. Donations that support the work of the museum in perpetuity include not only the establishment of the Cofrin Curator of Asian Art endowment and the David A. Cofrin Fund for Asian Art, but also many others.

Special thanks are due to Ling-en Lu, who agreed to coedit this volume and was instrumental in the shaping and refinement of its contents. Thank you to Jason Steuber, founder of the Cofrin Asian Art Manuscript Series, for planting the seed for this book's development and supporting its growth. The authors of this volume deserve my enduring gratitude not only for their inspiring research and diligent work, but also for doing so during a global pandemic.

I would also like to thank Samuel P. Harn Museum of Art director Lee Anne Chesterfield for intrinsic support; Bryan Yeager for image calibration; the peer reviewers for their insightful suggestions and critique; and Romi Gutierrez, Michele Fiyak-Burkley, Louise OFarrell, and Rachel Walther of the University of Florida Press for their assistance, guidance, and vision during book production. Finally, sincere thanks are given to individuals and institutions that provided images, research, and materials for this manuscript's production—their acknowledgments are located in the photograph credits section.

Special thanks for the funding of this volume are due to the Henry Luce Foundation, the E. Rhodes and Leona B. Carpenter Foundation, and the Tang Research Foundation in memory of Roger E. Covey.

It is with great pleasure that the Samuel P. Harn Museum of Art presents this volume in the David A. Cofrin Asian Art Manuscript Series.

Allysa B. Peyton
Series Editor

CONTENTS

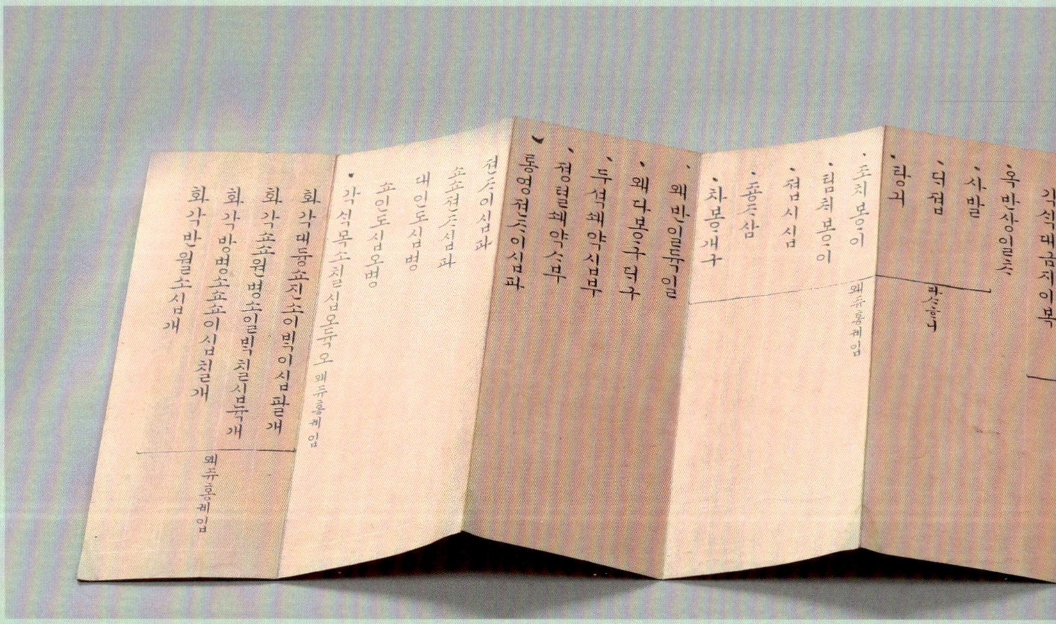

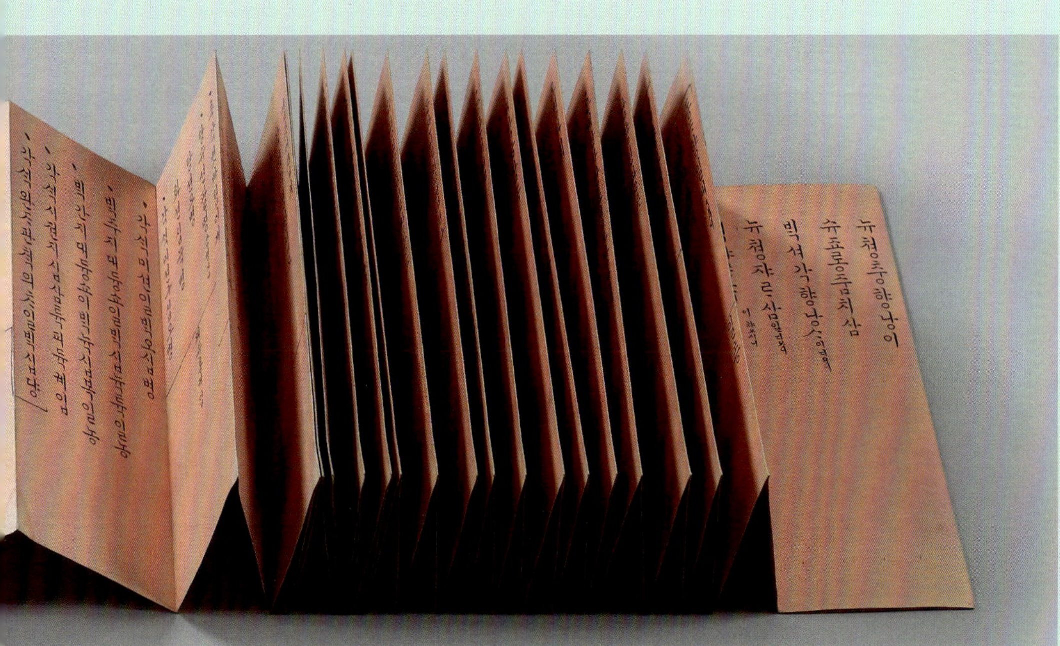

가시ᄂᆞᆫ고 자내 여ᄒᆡ고 아ᄆᆞ려 내 살 셰 업
ᄉᆞ니 수이 자내ᄒᆞᆫᄃᆡ 가고져 ᄒᆞ니 날 ᄃᆞ
려 가소 자내 향ᄒᆡ ᄆᆞᄋᆞᄆᆞᆯ ᄎᆞᄉᆡᆼ 니ᄌᆞᆯ 주
리 업ᄉᆞ니 아ᄆᆞ려 셜운 ᄠᅳ디 ᄀᆞ이 업
ᄉᆞ니 이 내 안ᄒᆞᆫ 어ᄃᆡ다가 두고 ᄌᆞ식
ᄃᆞ리고 자내ᄅᆞᆯ 그려 살려뇨 ᄒᆞ노
다 이 내 유무 보시고 내 ᄭᅮ메 ᄌᆞ셰 와 니
ᄅᆞ소 내 ᄭᅮ메 이 보신 말 ᄌᆞ셰 듣고져 ᄒᆞ야
이리 서 년뇌 ᄌᆞ셰 보시고 날ᄃᆞ려 니
ᄅᆞ소 자내 내 ᄇᆡᆫ ᄌᆞ식 나거든 보고 사롤 일
ᄒᆞ고 그리 가시ᄃᆡ ᄇᆡᆫ ᄌᆞ식 나거든 누ᄅᆞᆯ
아바 ᄒᆞ라 ᄒᆞ시ᄂᆞᆫ고 아ᄆᆞ려 ᄒᆞᆫᄃᆞᆯ
내 안 ᄀᆞᄐᆞᆯ가 이런 텬디 ᄌᆞ온 ᄒᆞᆫ이라

원니 아바님ᄭᅴ 샹ᄇᆡᆨ

병슐 뉴월 초ᄒᆞᄅᆞᆫ날 지븨셔

자내 샹해 날ᄃᆞ려 닐오ᄃᆡ 둘히 머리 셰도록 사다가 ᄒᆞᆫᄭᅴ 죽쟈 ᄒᆞ시더니 엇디ᄒᆞ야 나ᄅᆞᆯ 두고 자내 몬져 가시노 날ᄒᆞ고 ᄌᆞ식ᄒᆞ며 뉘긔 걸ᄒᆞ야 엇디ᄒᆞ야 살라 ᄒᆞ야 다 더디고 자내 몬져 가시ᄂᆞᆫ고 자내 날 향ᄒᆡ ᄆᆞᄋᆞᄆᆞᆯ 엇디 가지며 나ᄂᆞᆫ 자내 향ᄒᆡ ᄆᆞᄋᆞᄆᆞᆯ 엇디 가지던고 ᄆᆡ양 자내ᄃᆞ려 내 닐오ᄃᆡ ᄒᆞᆫᄃᆡ 누어셔 이보소 ᄂᆞᆷ도 우리ᄀᆞ티 서ᄅᆞ 에엿ᄢᅵ 녀겨 ᄉᆞ랑ᄒᆞ리 ᄂᆞᆷ도 우리 ᄀᆞᄐᆞᆫ가 ᄒᆞ야 자내ᄃᆞ려 니ᄅᆞ더니 엇디

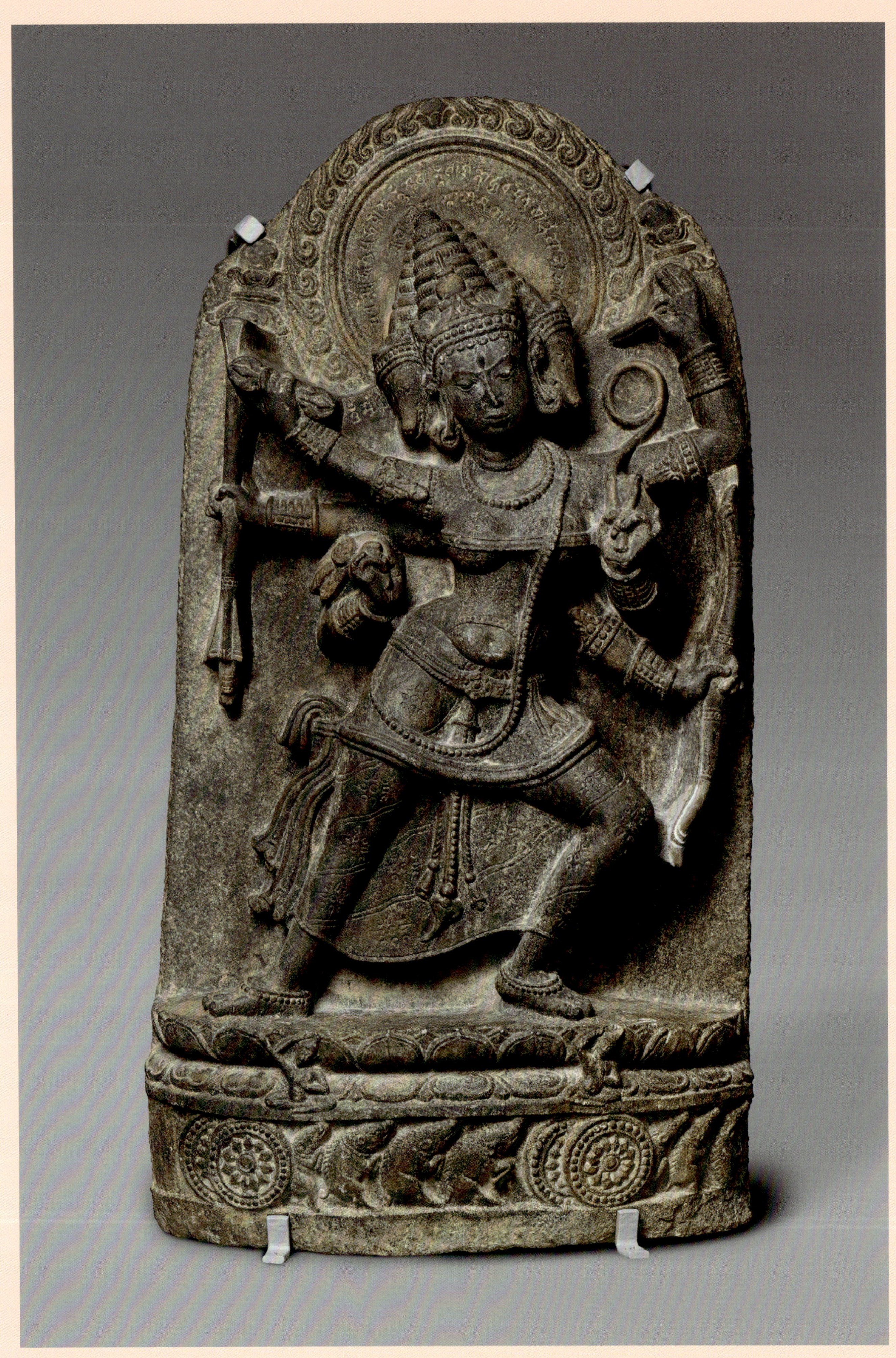

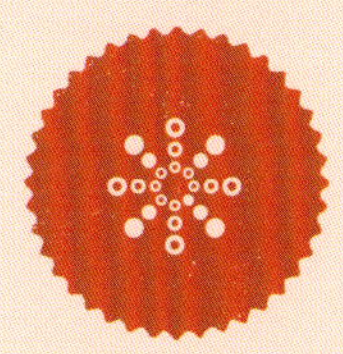

Introduction

LING-EN LU AND ALLYSA B. PEYTON

THE ASIAN ART in this volume purposely covers a wide geographical area and temporal period, from Japan in the east of the continent to Pakistan in the south. Asian art is recognized globally for its complex cultural and artistic traditions. The interpretation of Asian art, similar to interpretations of art in other geographical areas dating back to at least the fifteenth century, was constrained by a dominating narrative that emphasized limited categories defined primarily by male artists and scholars. Only in the late twentieth century did discussion in museums and academia gradually shift—a change generated by the momentum of women's studies.[1] The feminist momentum has led and continues to lead to more exhibitions of marginalized artists and to greater opportunities in research and publications.[2]

In Asian art, a field benefited from the development of feminist studies, attention to women artists began in the museum world through focused exhibitions. In 1988, two groundbreaking exhibitions took place in the US Midwest: Marsha Weidner's *Views from Jade Terrace: Chinese Women Artists, 1300–1912* (fig. Intro.01) and Patricia Fister's *Japanese Women Artists, 1600–1900* (fig. Intro.02). These exhibitions were accompanied by scholarly catalogs that are still influential today.[3] Monographs and papers generated from conferences, forums, and seminars continue to add weight to the discussion.

Entering the twenty-first century, women's roles in inspiring, collecting, researching, and making Asian art are becoming central to increasingly complex discourse. The study of women's roles in art is also reaching farther, expanding into a broader range of historical periods and cultures. Academic and museum professionals in feminist studies and art history should be credited for advancing a more equitable and complete understanding of all documented artists.[4] Their efforts promote active discussion of women's roles in art and society today; as a result, encouraging the recognition of women and marginalized cultures has become a broader trend in America and worldwide.

Facing: Marīcī, the Buddhist deity of the dawn. See figure Intro.05.

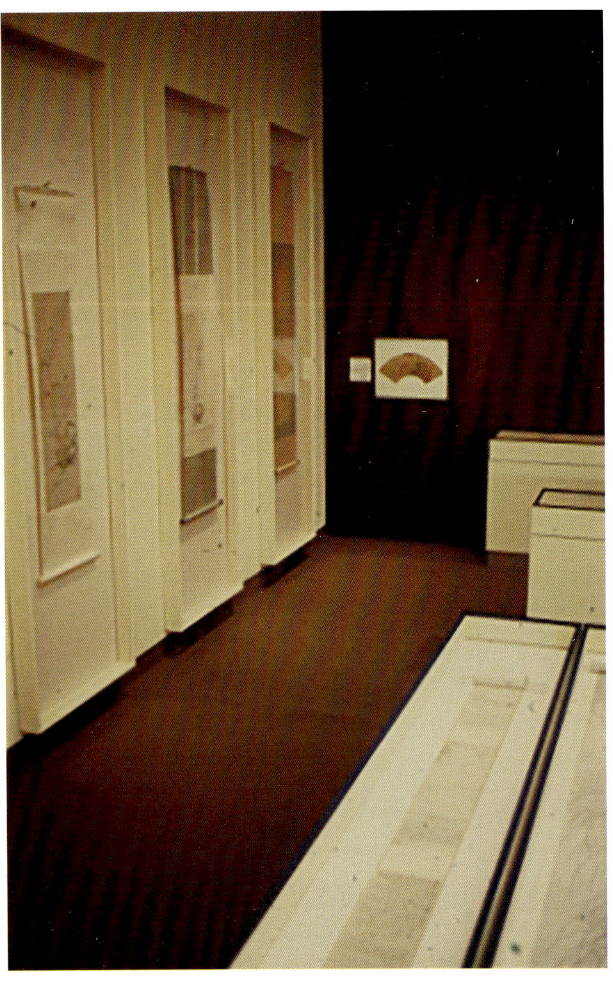

Figure Intro.01. Installation view from *View from Jade Terrace: Chinese Women Artists, 1300–1912*. Image courtesy of the Indianapolis Museum of Art Archives.

As an example of these intersections and exchanges, the US activist group the Guerrilla Girls has been combatting racism and sexism in the art world since the group formed in 1985. By the mid-1990s the group was actively addressing discrimination of all kinds that exists outside of the art world, and it diversified to address inequities in the world at large, including contemporary Asian art. Within the art world, the group's analysis of display and collecting practices has been a force for institutional global reform. Their force, stronger than ever in the twenty-first century, continues to be influential in women's studies and in the field of contemporary and global art (fig. Intro.03).

Throughout the long history of Asian art and archaeology, extant works of art show evidence of women's participation. Many Asian women desired to pursue intellectual and artistic activities, yet because of the constraints of societal traditions their roles in art history are more difficult to see. Opportunities were fettered by societal conventions—being confined to the private realm, the obstacles to a public presence, economic inequality, and even naming conventions in some cultures make women's contributions invisible. The seeming absence of women's participation, along with gender depictions in visual art, transmitted the traditional ideal of Asian women as fragile and submissive that continues to inform Western stereotypes today.

There is a persistent need for book-length assessments of the roles of women in the arts of Asia. It is imperative to examine women's involvement in visual art as creators, curators, collectors, scholars, archaeologists, and indeed subjects, not only because this field is still evolving but also because the thoughtful analysis of gender and identity continues to inform our understanding of the visual arts. Starting with innovative institutions but continuing with the more traditional and conservative galleries, museums

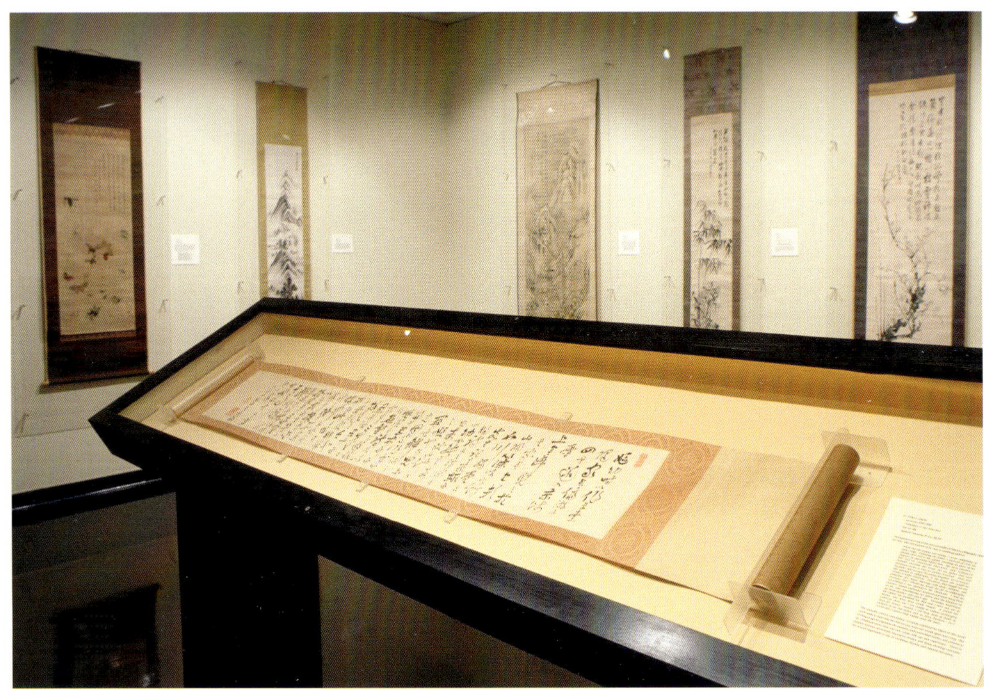

Figure Intro.02. Installation view from *Japanese Women Artists, 1600–1900*, exhibition held in 1988. Image courtesy of the Spencer Museum of Art, University of Kansas.

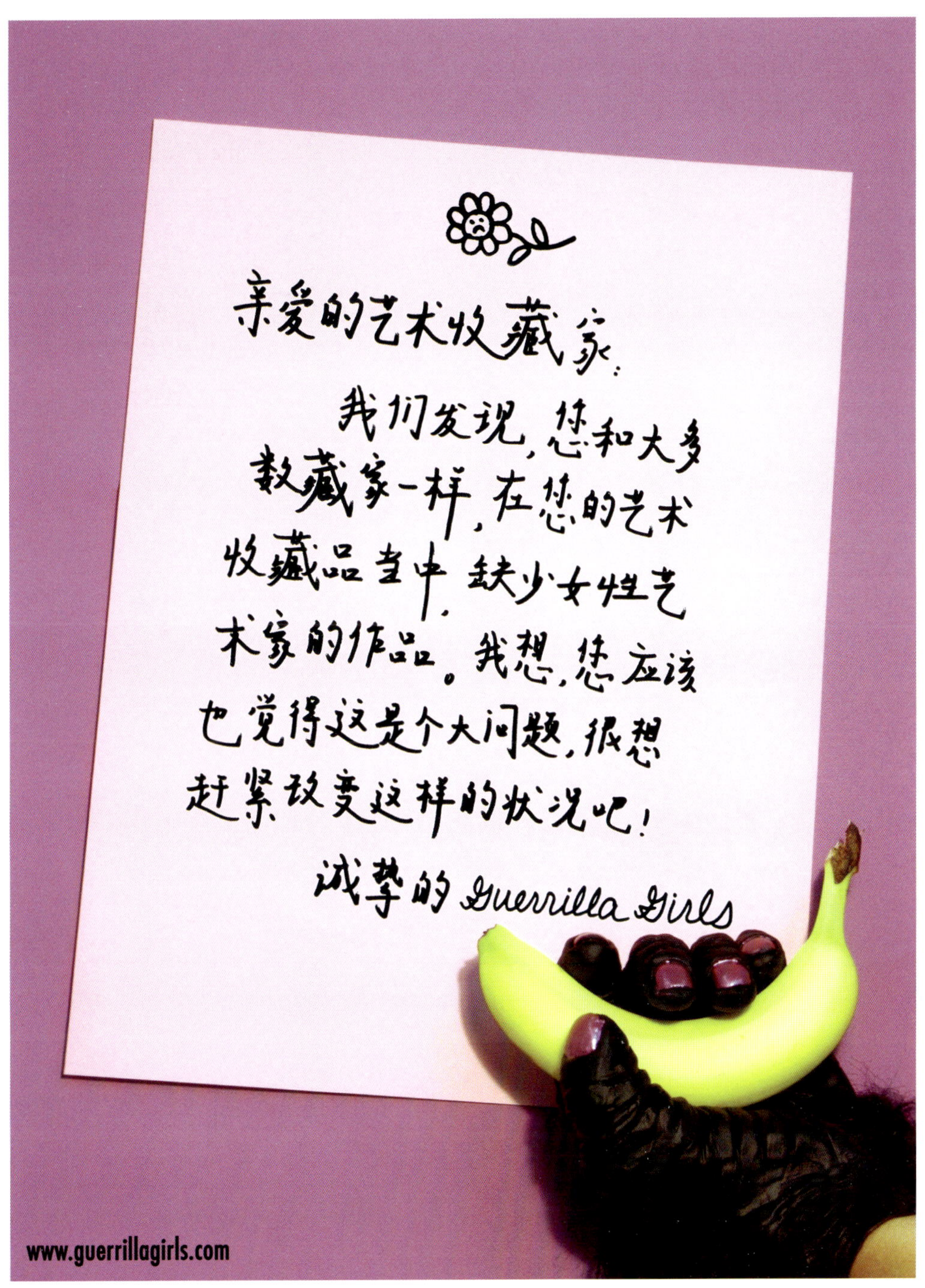

Figure Intro.03. Guerrilla Girls, *Dear Art Collector (Chinese)* print, 17 × 22 in. Harn Museum of Art Collection, Museum Purchase, funds provided by the Caroline Julier and James G. Richardson Acquisition Endowment (2015.47.78). Copyright © Guerrilla Girls, courtesy guerrillagirls.com.

worldwide are intentionally increasing the number of women artists in their collections and considering those who have been excluded. Focusing on qualifiers that infer difference—labels such as gay artist, Black artist, lesbian artist, Asian American artist, Latinx artist, and woman artist—may seem to base identity solely on what is treated as separate from the larger culture. While museums make repeated reparations through collection-building and exhibitions that affirm diversity,[5] inclusion and equality for those previously seen as "other" must be emphasized as the loftier and long-term goal. Until then, studies of historical and contemporary art are critical in uncovering overlooked

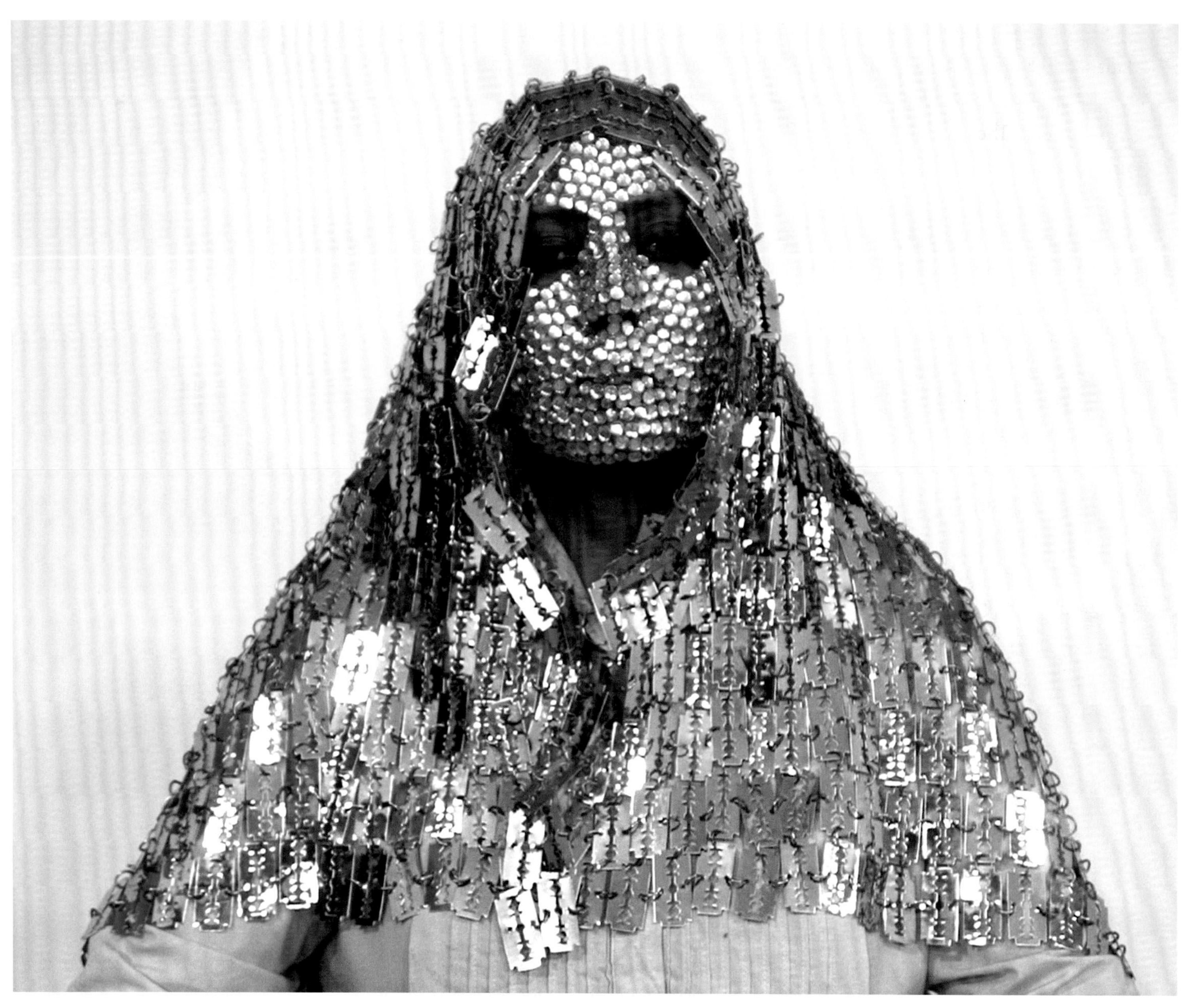

Figure Intro.04. Tayeba Begum Lipi, *Unveiling Womanhood*, single-channel video projection, *This Is What I Look(ed) Like* installation at Sundaram Tagore Gallery, 2019. Image courtesy of the artist.

narratives within Asian art history and methods of display. A recent example of how the narrative is being reframed is the Harn Museum of Art's devotion to acquiring historical and contemporary works of art created by Asian women.[6] As another example, Laurie Barnes at the Norton Museum of Art curated a yearlong series of exhibitions, *The Other Half of the Sky: Twentieth-Century Chinese Women Painters*. And an international webinar, *Untold Stories: Women and the Asian Art Trade*,[7] brought together scholars and museum professionals who shared their research about women's roles in the market circulation of Asian art, institutional collecting of Asian art, and contributions to academic writings.

Women across Asian Art: Selected Essays in Art and Material Culture, a volume in the David A. Cofrin Asian Art Manuscript Series,[8] includes such narratives by eleven authors either hailing from or residing in the United States, Canada, the United Kingdom, Taiwan, Japan, and Korea, who offer original research from their respective fields to fill in the gaps of the broad topic under investigation, namely the acknowledgment of women in the arts of Asia. The contributors include emerging and established scholars, all of whom bring a fresh or original approach to their subjects and themes. Each of them currently performs one or more roles as professor, curator, researcher, educator, or "arbiter of taste" in academies, museums, or research institutions or as independent researchers. These authors' academic training and backgrounds offer a wide range of scholarly viewpoints. Each of them was given the freedom to choose for their focus an understudied area, but one that was important to the visibility of women in Asian art.

Because of the breadth of the contributions, the volume is divided into three parts: "The Feminine and the Goddess," "Pioneers and Trailblazers,"[9] and "Modern and Contemporary Makers." Organized in this way, the chapters move from genders depicted in art to women makers of art, roughly traveling forward in time from the distant past to contemporary activism. Despite a wide geographical and chronological reach, the volume mainly addresses two broad fields within art historical studies of Asia: women's role as muse, and their positions as creators, collectors, and pioneers. The eleven authors explore subjects ranging from the concept of femininity as communicated through religious iconography and symbols to women as creators, scholars, and collectors, and lastly, to the intensely personal reflections of present-day artists, an excellent example of which is Bangladeshi artist Tayeba Begum Lipi (fig. Intro.04). As diverse as these topics are, an overarching theme that emerges is how women have, with varying degrees of success, navigated spheres traditionally dominated by men. Many of the chapters in this volume provide evidence that women were active in more social circles than was previously realized.

Part 1. The Feminine and the Goddess

A thread running through the two chapters in part one is adaption. They address the feminine in Chinese art, but across disparate mediums and chronographies. Although both chapters focus on artworks from a single geographical region, the reception of gender characteristics evolving through centuries and geographies (India to China and Japan) pose profound questions: How is the feminine defined? How do art objects transmit ideas about femininity over the centuries? How do the images speak to the different audiences about the feminine, in comparison to the muscular and nonbinary characteristics? Through their analysis of bronzes, calligraphy, and painting, the authors underscore these issues in their case studies of a cross-cultural iconography and gender symbols.

Starting with the goddess, the first chapter sets the tone of the volume; it uses iconographic and stylistic analysis to read a painting, *The Mandala of Marīcī*, by depicting multiple manifestations of Marīcī, the Buddhist goddess who derived from a pre-Buddhist deva in India[10] (fig. Intro.05). Ling-en Lu, coeditor of this volume and curator of East

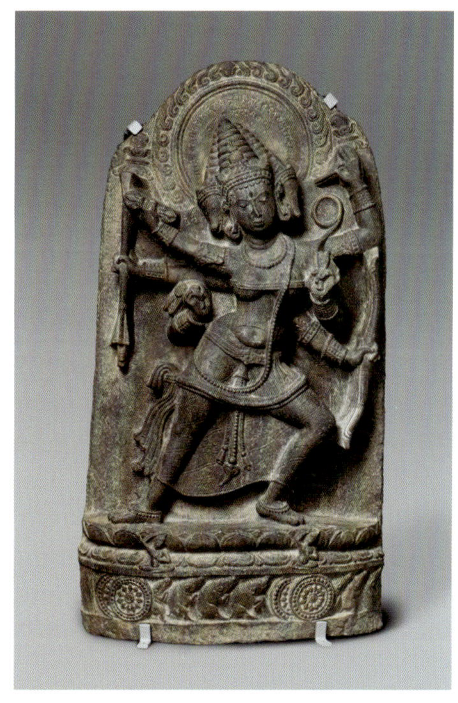

Figure Intro.05. Marīcī, the Buddhist deity of the dawn, approx. 800–850. Bodhgaya, Bihar, India. Stone (mica schist). Asian Art Museum of San Francisco, The Avery Brundage Collection, B63S10+. Photograph © Asian Art Museum of San Francisco.

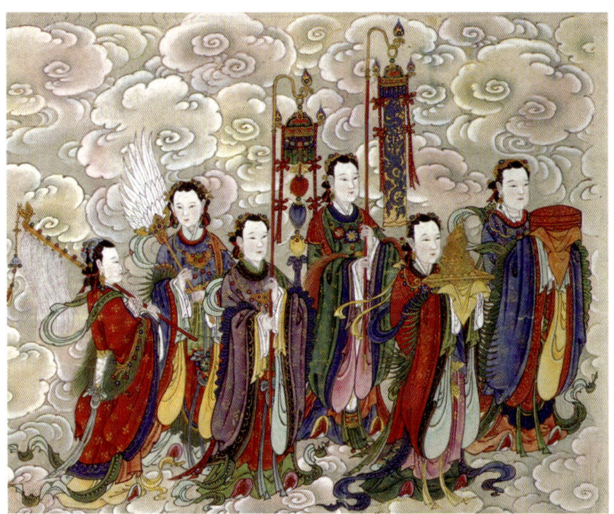

Figure Intro.06. *Ordination of Empress Zhang* (detail) © San Diego Museum of Art / Gift of Mr. and Mrs. John Jeffers / Bridgeman Images.

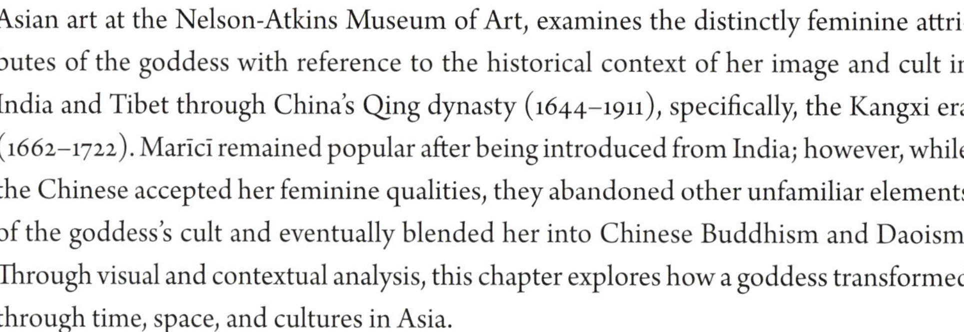

Asian art at the Nelson-Atkins Museum of Art, examines the distinctly feminine attributes of the goddess with reference to the historical context of her image and cult in India and Tibet through China's Qing dynasty (1644–1911), specifically, the Kangxi era (1662–1722). Marīcī remained popular after being introduced from India; however, while the Chinese accepted her feminine qualities, they abandoned other unfamiliar elements of the goddess's cult and eventually blended her into Chinese Buddhism and Daoism. Through visual and contextual analysis, this chapter explores how a goddess transformed through time, space, and cultures in Asia.

Junko Uchida, of the Institute of History and Philology at the Academia Sinica in Taiwan, continues the assessment of social context in chapter 2, but in this case looking at its relation to woman as subject matter in Chinese bronzes. Ambitious in scope, her chapter relates how archaeological evidence from Shang-dynasty (1600 BCE–1046 BCE) bronzes and their inscriptions provides clues to the ways gender roles were established and perpetuated. Focusing on Fu Hao tomb, Uchida describes the development of the megalopolis of Yinxu during the Shang dynasty as a period of continuity and change in which some gender roles shifted while others remained constant. While the artifacts of the archaic period are compared with those as recent as the court paintings of the fifteenth century (fig. Intro.06), the examination of women's roles within ancient Confucian society is also relevant to the study of social systems and their evolution regarding women in other chapters of this book.

Part 2. Pioneers and Trailblazers

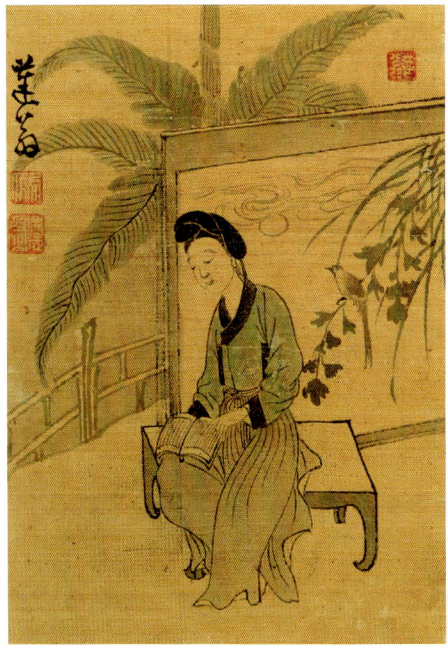

Figure Intro.07. Yun Deokhui, *A Woman Reading a Book*, eighteenth century, ink and color on silk, 20 × 14.3 cm. Seoul National University Museum, Seoul.

Chapters in this section reveal the commonality of the challenges encountered by women with vision and the obstacles they overcame. The chapters in this part cohere around ideas of adumbration, where women as professionals in their own right have been overshadowed by either their better-known husbands or male peers. They honed their self-identities and professional development through the limited opportunities for training, at a time when they faced various social and educational barriers that prevented their equal participation.

Insoo Cho, professor in the School of Visual Arts at the Korea National University of Arts, tackles the investigation of the more ephemeral practice of the calligraphic arts in chapter 3. During Korea's Joseon dynasty (1392–1910), calligraphy was a highly respected form of artistic expression—although access to higher learning and Chinese classics was largely confined to men and the higher classes. With the rise in popularity of a new Korean script, *hangeul*, gender dynamics surrounding writing and scholarship evolved. Cho focuses his inquiry on the royal correspondence of elite women in the Joseon dynasty, challenging conclusions made by previous scholarship and advocating for a more nuanced history of Korean women calligraphers among the court (fig. Intro.07).

Similarly, the adoption of *hangeul* as the vernacular writing system in Korea allowed women access to a form of expression largely shunned by men, while for educated Chinese women, the scholar-amateur tradition in painting as an elite pastime (as opposed to a professional practice) afforded them similar opportunities to men, with success measured by reputation rather than by sales.

In chapter 4, Janet C. Chen, an independent scholar, introduces Luo Qilan (1755–1813) through multiple references to her in paintings, inscriptions, and scholarly records. As the subject of and collaborator with male contemporaries, Luo Qilan led an unconventional life. Despite receiving criticism for operating outside of social norms, she was an active female disciple in the circles of Qing-dynasty scholars Yuan Mei (1716–1797) and Wang Wenzhi (1730–1802). Through careful research of extant paintings (fig. Intro.0.8) and textual references, Chen gives a fuller account of the multifaceted life of this woman scholar and explicates the process by which her many roles contributed to her identity.

In chapter 5, Shana J. Brown, associate professor and department chair of history at the University of Hawai'i at Manoa, delves into previously overlooked contributions of women in modern Chinese archaeology. Archaeology as a field in China developed as it did because of the participation of women, and archaeologist Zheng Zhenxiang (b. 1929) has rightly been lauded as a "trowelblazer" in China after the Cultural Revolution for her discovery of the tomb of Lady Fu Hao at Anyang under testing conditions.[11] Zheng's celebrity has nevertheless obscured the work of an earlier generation of

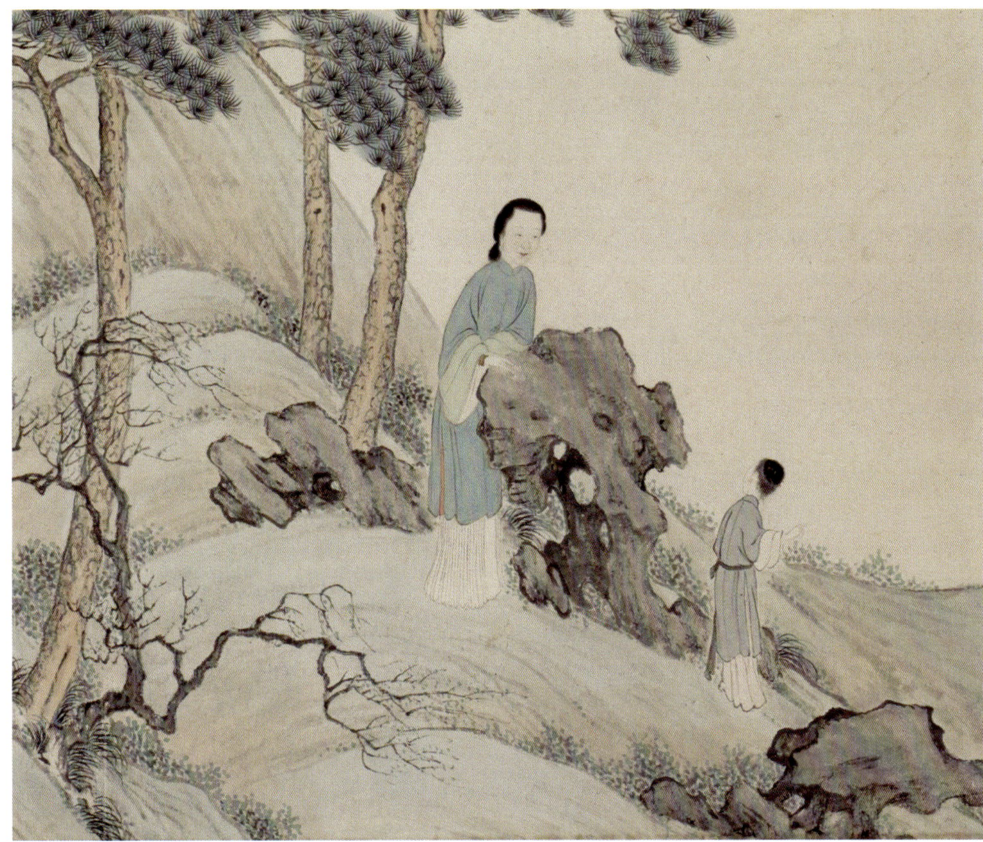

Figure Intro.08. Detail showing Luo Qilan from Pan Simu, *Record of Dreams from the Tingqiu Studio*. Image courtesy of Sotheby's.

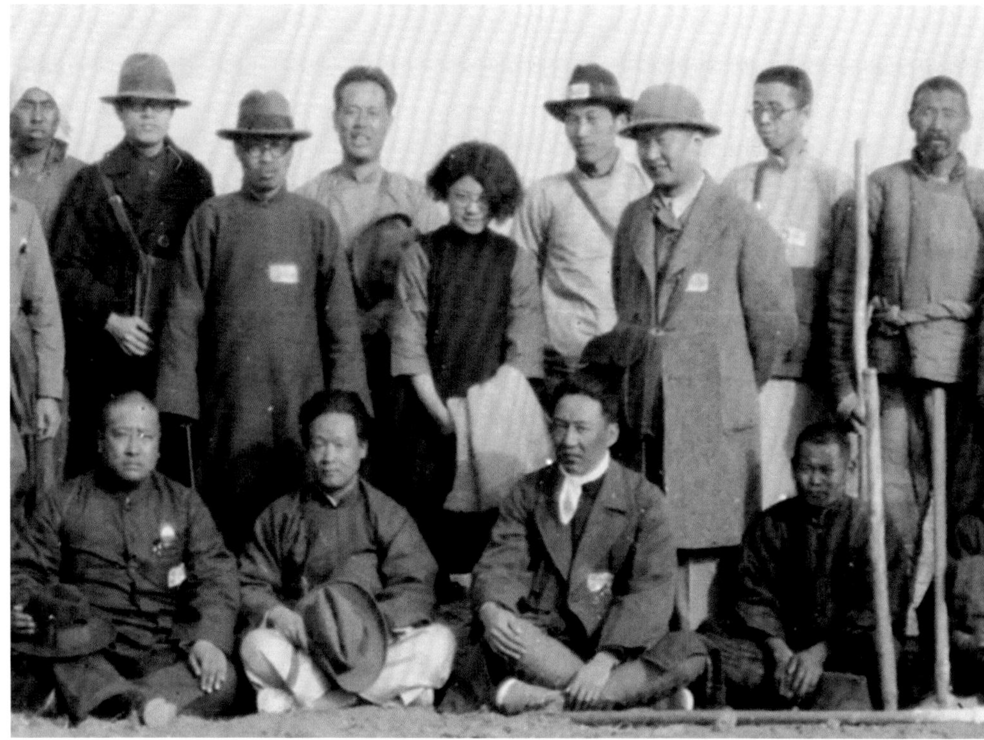

Figure Intro.09. Zhou Yingxue and the excavation team at Anyang, 1931. Institute of History and Philology at the Academia Sinica, Republic of China.

women archaeologists, historians, and folklorists, with the implication that Zheng and her achievements were as unique as her discovery, a situation addressed here with the celebration of not only Zheng but also her immediate forerunners, including Rong Yuan (1899–1996), Zhou Yingxue (1911–?) (fig. Intro.09), and Zeng Zhaoyu (1909–1964). Women in the first half of the twentieth century faced significant barriers to participation in archaeology. To outline the achievement of these pioneers, Brown specifies the professional experiences of these modern archaeologists, their educational backgrounds, and the obstacles they overcame.

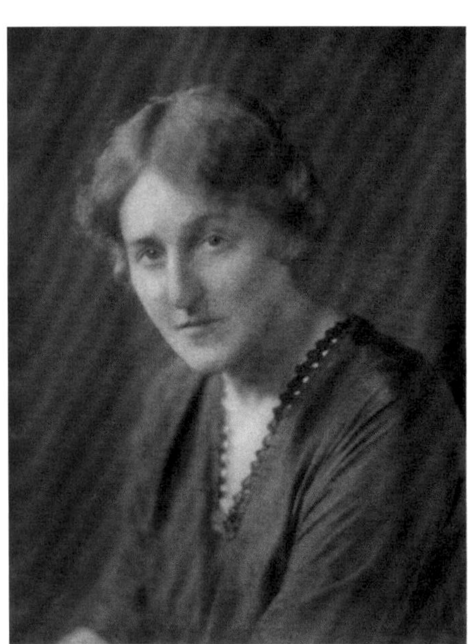

Figure Intro.10. Portrait of Brenda Zara Seligman as a young woman. Reproduced in *Man*, January 1961.

In the field of Asian art collecting in the United States and Europe in the early twentieth century, women are again not so much underrepresented as obscured. The recent book *Great Women Collectors* featured no major collectors of Asian art, and yet it could easily have included some well-studied names. Chapter 6, by Nick Pearce, Richmond Chair of Fine Art at the School of Culture & Creative Arts, University of Glasgow, sheds light on one of these undervalued women collectors of Chinese art in the twentieth century, Brenda Zara Seligman (née Salaman, 1882–1965) (fig. Intro.10), whose collecting activities and skillful custodianship have long been underestimated.[12] She and her husband, Charles, were at the forefront of Chinese collection building during the 1920s and 1930s, but his role in this endeavor has very much overshadowed hers. The chapter details her role in the establishment and reshaping of a significant collection of Chinese art and its eventual bequest to the British Museum and the Victoria and Albert Museum in London.

Similarly, women working as architects in modern China faced significant challenges. In chapter 7, Wei-Cheng Lin, associate professor of art history at the University of Chicago, focuses his essay on the pioneer woman architect of modern China, Lin Huiyin (1904–1955), also known as Lin Whei-yin and Phyllis Lin (fig. Intro.11). Although she was rejected by institutions of architecture where the selections were based on gender preference, Lin Huiyin was able to devote herself to the preservation of traditional Chinese architecture and define the styles of modern architecture without formal training. By highlighting her individual accomplishments and separating her work from that of her husband and collaborator, Liang Sicheng, Lin emphasizes Lin Huiyin's importance in a male-dominated field. His research elucidates the ways in which her work was obscured and how her literary work and aspirations offer insight into her nascent feminist philosophy.

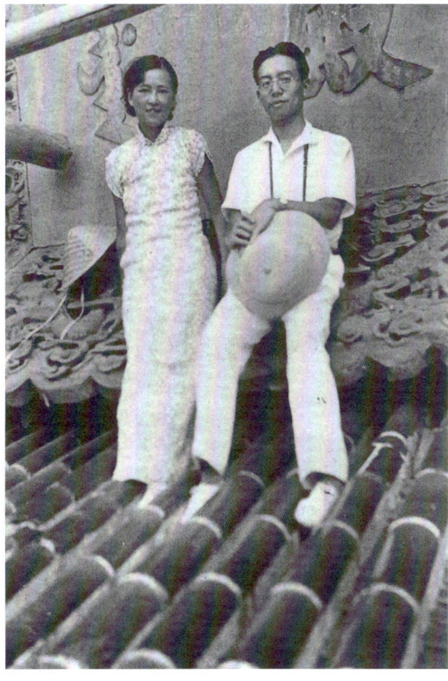

Figure Intro.11. Lin Huiyin and Liang Sicheng on the roof of the Hall of Prayers for Good Harvest. Photograph by permission of School of Architecture, Tsinghua University.

Part 3. Modern and Contemporary Makers

The content of the final part of the volume includes East and South Asian artists and their works, addressing complex issues of gender inequality through the lens of Asian art history and contemporary societies in their home or expatriate countries. The chapters in this part ask difficult questions about East and West, challenge stereotypes about art by and about women, and, most importantly, advocate for the transformation of patriarchal systems.

The influential Saison culture of 1980s Japan likewise emerged from a patriarchal society during a period of economic growth and consumerism, creating a new generation of women artists confident of their own worth. Midori Yamamura, assistant professor of art history at the City University of New York, Kingsborough Community College, examines this powerful force of influence and legacy in chapter 8. While Japanese artists like Yoko Ono (b. 1933) and Yayoi Kusama (b. 1929) were enjoying recognition abroad, Japanese women artists in the mid- to late twentieth century faced intense bias at home. The artists highlighted in this chapter include Masayo Koizumi (b. 1959), Mayumi Terada (b. 1958), and Mika Yoshizawa (b. 1959) (fig. Intro.12), along with Rei Naito (b. 1961), Mio Shirai (b. 1962), Hiroko Ohno (b. 1956), and Yurie Nagashima (b. 1973). Yamamura outlines the unique phenomenon of Saison culture and the exhibitions held at the Seibu Department Stores, a retailer turned artistic tastemaker and trendsetter in Japan. She describes the profound influences that these exhibitions had on emerging women artists and how their work was able to become more gender self-referential over time with commercial support. Although the movement began through small gestures within Japan, Professor Yamamura documents the rise of internationally acclaimed contemporary artists in a global sphere.

While contemporary Asian women encounter inequality, visual art practices in Bangladesh and Pakistan offer an additional focus for gender-based art historical inquiry, challenging gender norms and identities. In chapter 9, Saleema Waraich, associate professor of art history at Skidmore College, focuses her critique on the genre of South Asian illustrated manuscript painting tradition, noting the contemporary shift to a

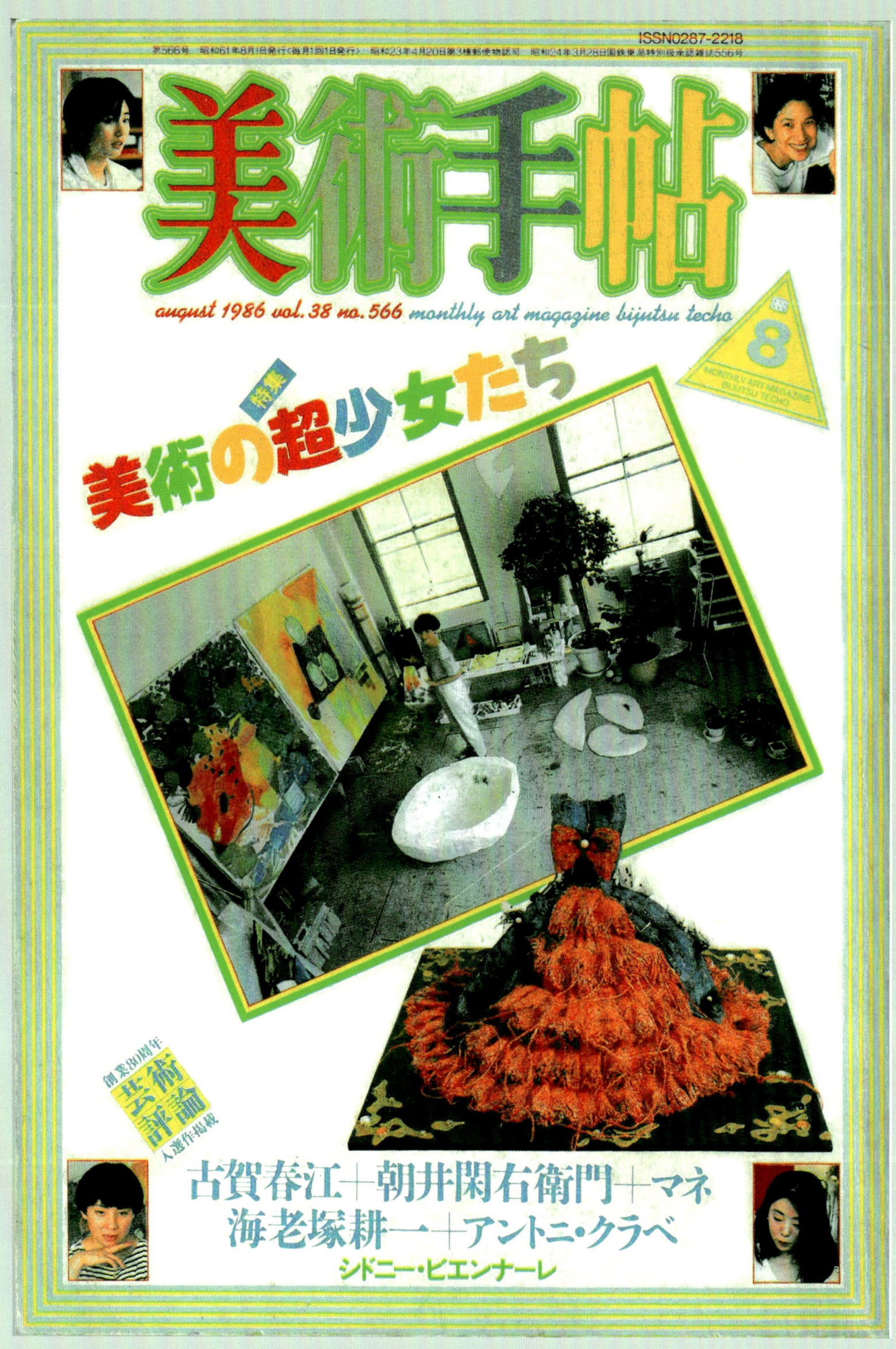

Figure Intro.12. Cover from "*Bijutsu no Chōshōjo tachi* (Super Girls of Art)." *Bijutsu Techō*, August 1986. Design by Nobuo Nakagaki, Bijutsushuppansha.

more inclusive environment for women artists with an examination of the systems that fell along the way. The main focus of her chapter is the Pakistani neo-miniaturist Saira Wasim (b. 1975) (fig. Intro.13) and her use of satirical social and political critiques that subvert and disrupt the status quo. Professor Waraich herself challenges stereotypes of high and low art by including prints by Wasim in cartoon and fashion-magazine formats.

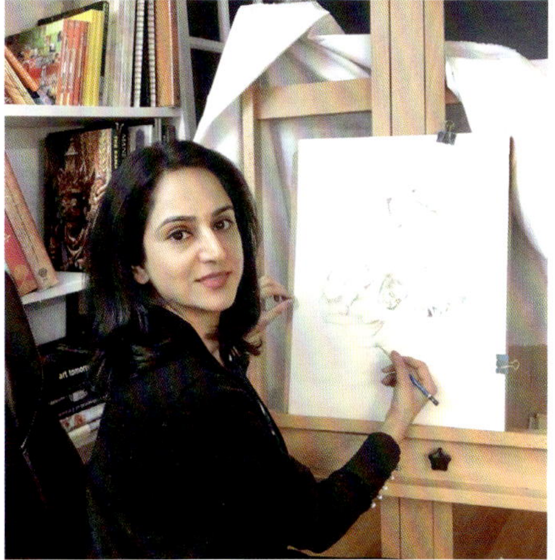

Figure Intro.13. Saira Wasim. Image courtesy of the artist. Photograph by Mahbubur Rahman.

In chapter 10, Sati Benes Chock, Asian art department editor at the Honolulu Museum of Art, rightly reexamines a Chinese-born artist living in the United States who expresses her cosmopolitan sensibilities through a newly invented form of contemporary painting. Tseng Yuho (1925–2017), who preferred to use her original name as her artist name but was better known as Betty Ecke during her married life (fig. Intro.14), challenged conventional wisdom by pushing painting to new forms, celebrating tradition when she desired and abandoning the rules when needed. During their lifetime, she was occasionally under the shadow of her husband, art historian and collector Gustav Ecke (1896–1971). However, as Sati's research suggests, not only was Tseng a vital force of scholarship and connoisseurship behind the family's collection and publications, but she also demonstrated her own brilliance as a painter and scholar. Chock traces the path of the artist's development while also measuring the legacy she left through her roles at the University of Hawaiʻi and the Honolulu Academy of Arts.

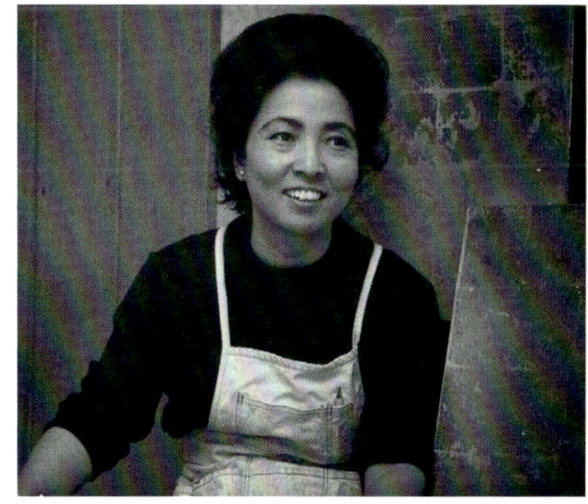

Figure Intro.14. Portrait of Tseng Yuho, 1966. Photograph by Francis Haar. © Francis Haar, courtesy of the Francis Haar Collection, University of Hawaiʻi Library.

Finally, in chapter 11, Melia Belli Bose, associate professor of South Asian art history at the University of Victoria, unapologetically plunges readers deep into the most pressing concerns of our present day. Her chapter highlights the work of Bangladeshi artist Tayeba Begum Lipi (b. 1969) (fig. Intro.15), an artist whose work holds a mirror to Bangladeshi society and actively advocates for political change. Through both an examination of gender and an exposure of class issues, Lipi confronts viewers with matters of inequality, agency, marginality, and structural violence. Her work focuses primarily on sculpture that addresses the female domestic sphere, and the artist exposes taboo subjects and dangerous topics for all to see.

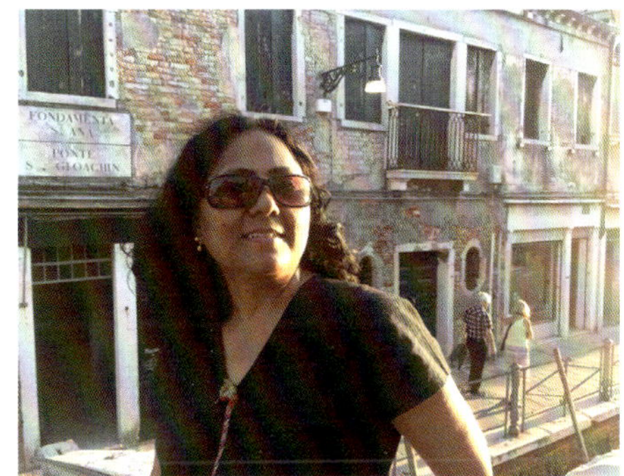

Figure Intro.15. Tayeba Begum Lipi. Image courtesy of the artist.

In conclusion, this selection of case studies will continue to shed light on women's roles as subjects, artists, scholars, and collectors across time and geography. Each author dives deeply into the questions of whether images convey femininity, how women pursued artistic creation in innovative ways, how women earned a reputation in their respective patriarchal societies, and finally, how artists advocated for their work by breaking the glass ceiling. These studies advance the continued scholarly exploration of why gender matters in art, and why these studies are needed for women to be seen and heard. This volume is a committed effort to pave avenues for future women museum professionals, scholars, and artists so that their stories are voiced and incorporated into the next chapters of inclusive academic canons, museum collections, and material culture. This volume, and future work in this area, will increase our collective understanding of how a more equitable representation of scholars in academic publications can ensure a more equitable representation of women's historical contributions.[13] This scholarship is needed to facilitate new connections and reveal hidden subtexts within larger narratives.

Acknowledgments

The authors would like to thank Nick Pearce, Liz Smith, and Jason Steuber for their contributions and review of this introduction.

Notes

1. The academic journal *Feminist Studies* (University of Maryland) was the first peer-reviewed publication covering women's studies. It began in 1972, just a year after Linda Nochlin's famous essay "Why Have There Been No Great Women Artists?," which was first published in Vivian Gornick and Barbara Moran, eds., *Women in Sexist Society: Studies in Power and Powerlessness* (New York: Basic Books, 1971), and was revised for inclusion in the January 1971 edition of *ArtNews*. The opening page of *Women in Sexist Society* addresses the institutional obstacles that face women in a patriarchal society: "THE FAULT LIES NOT IN OUR STARS, OUR HORMONES, OUR MENSTRUAL CYCLES OR OUR EMPTY INTERNAL SPACES, BUT IN OUR INSTITUTIONS AND OUR EDUCATION." Also see Janet Wolff, *Feminine Sentences: Essays on Women and Culture* (Berkeley: University of California Press, 1990), and Tseng Yuho, "Women Painters of the Ming Dynasty," *Artibus Asiae* 53, no. 1/2 (1993): 249–61.

2. For an early example, see Laurel Kendall and Mark Peterson, eds., *Korean Women: View from the Inner Room,* proceedings of a symposium presented at the Association for Asian Studies in Los Angeles in 1979. For a more recent example, see the multi-authored volume edited by Vidya Dehejia, *Representing the Body: Gender Issues in Indian Art* (New Delhi: Kali for Women in association with the Book Review Literary Trust, 1997).

3. Marsha Weidner et al., *Views from Jade Terrace: Chinese Women Artists, 1300–1912* (Indianapolis: Indianapolis Museum of Art, 1988). The book accompanied an exhibition at the Indianapolis Museum of Art that then toured to the Virginia Museum of Fine Arts, the Asian Art Museum of San Francisco, the National Museum of Women in the Arts in Washington, DC, and the Hong Kong Museum of Art. Patricia Fister and Fumiko Y. Yamamoto, *Japanese Women Artists 1600–1900*, exhibition catalogue (Lawrence: Spencer Museum of Art, University of Kansas; New York: Harper and Row, 1988). The exhibition traveled to the Honolulu Academy of Arts. Also see Lucy Lim et al., *Contemporary Chinese Painting: An Exhibition from the People's Republic of China* (San Francisco: Chinese Cultural Foundation, 1983), and Yasumura Toshinobu, *The Exhibition on the Women Painters of the Edo Period*, held at the Itabashi Art Museum, Tokyo, in 1991.

4. Noted examples in this field include Marsha Weidner, ed., *Flowering in the Shadows: Women in the History of Chinese and Japanese Painting* (Honolulu: University of Hawai'i Press, 1990); Aida Yuen Wong, *Visualizing Beauty: Gender and Ideology in Modern East Asia* (Hong Kong: Hong Kong University Press, 2012); Melia Belli Bose, *Women, Gender and Art in Asia c. 1500–1900* (London: Routledge, Taylor and Francis Group, 2018); Kristen L. Chiem and Lara C. W. Blanchard, *Gender, Continuity, and the Shaping of Modernity in the Arts of East Asia* (Leiden, the Netherlands: Brill, 2018); Elizabeth A. Bacus and Kurt F. Anschuetz, *A Gendered Past: A Critical Bibliography of Gender in Archaeology* (Ann Arbor: University of Michigan Museum of Anthropology, 1993).

5. One example of this continued commitment by a museum is that of the Aldrich Contemporary Art Museum. In 1971, Lucy Lippard curated the exhibition *26 Contemporary Women Artists* at the Aldrich. In the summer of 2022, the museum is revisiting the landmark exhibition with an expansion to include emerging women and nonbinary artists that will be titled *52 Artists: A Feminist Milestone.* For more information and a list of the artists who will be included, see

the Aldrich's website, https://thealdrich.org/exhibitions/52-artists-revisiting-a-feminist-milestone, accessed October 15, 2021.

6. For example, Okuhara Seiko, Toshiko Takaezu, Aphrodite Désirée Navab, Sachiko Fujino, and Asuka Tsuboi were all featured in the cross-collection exhibition *Breaking the Frame: Women Artists in the Harn Collections*, held from September 24, 2020, to May 9, 2021, at the Samuel P. Harn Museum of Art.

7. The webinar, which was the third in a series titled *Hidden Networks: Trade in Asian Art*, was co-organized by the Freer Gallery of Art and Arthur M. Sackler Gallery, the Smithsonian's National Museum of Asian Art; Museum für Asiatische Kunst, Staatliche Museen zu Berlin; and the Harvard Art Museums.

8. The David A. Cofrin Asian Art Manuscript Series is leading the field in new directions and providing a much-needed arena in which to bring overlooked subjects to the forefront of twenty-first-century Asian art scholarship.

9. We accept that "pioneer" can be a problematic term, as arguably women have always been involved in the arts of Asia, only less visibly than men. However, it is also true that institutional and societal hurdles made success for a woman more unconventional. Defying convention requires bravery, strength of character, and persistence that inspire admiration in the editors and call for a heroic term, hence the use of the word "pioneer." In some cases, it is also possible that the women being discussed *were* the first women in their field, and "pioneer" would therefore be used in its standard definition.

10. For more on Marīcī in India, see Miranda Eberle Shaw, *Buddhist Goddesses of India* (Princeton, NJ: Princeton University Press, 2006); Mandakranta Bose, *Faces of the Feminine in Ancient, Medieval and Modern India* (New York: Oxford University Press, 2000); and Susan L. Huntington and John C. Huntington, "Marici (Shining), Buddhist Goddess of the Dawn," in *Leaves from the Bodhi Tree: The Art of Pala India (8th–12th Centuries) and Its International Legacy* (Seattle: Dayton Art Institute in association with the University of Washington Press, 1990).

11. "Zheng Zhenxiang," TrowelBlazers, accessed January 22, 2021, https://trowelblazers.com/zheng-zhenxiang/.

12. For more on women collectors, see Charlotte Gere and Marina Vaizey, *Great Women Collectors* (London: Philip Wilson, 1999). The first book to examine a significant number of women collectors, it focuses primarily on those collecting Western art.

13. For other essays in the David A. Cofrin Asian Art Manuscript Series that highlight the accomplishments of women, see Jeannie Kenmotsu, "Prints for Portland: The Mary Andrews Ladd Collection," in Natsu Oyobe and Allysa B. Peyton, eds., *Great Waves and Mountains: Perspectives and Discoveries in Collecting the Arts of Japan* (Gainesville: University of Florida Press, 2022); Katherine Anne Paul, "Masterworks of South Asian Art at the Newark Museum: From Missionaries, Merchants, and Medical Women and Men," in Allysa B. Peyton and Katherine Anne Paul, eds., *Arts of South Asia: Cultures of Collecting* (Gainesville: University of Florida Press, 2019); and Hyeyoung Cho, "Contemporary Korean Ceramics: Its Heritage and Advancement into the Twenty-First Century," in Jason Steuber and Allysa B. Peyton, eds., *Arts of Korea: Histories, Challenges, and Perspectives* (Gainesville: University of Florida Press, 2018).

PART 1

The Feminine and the Goddess

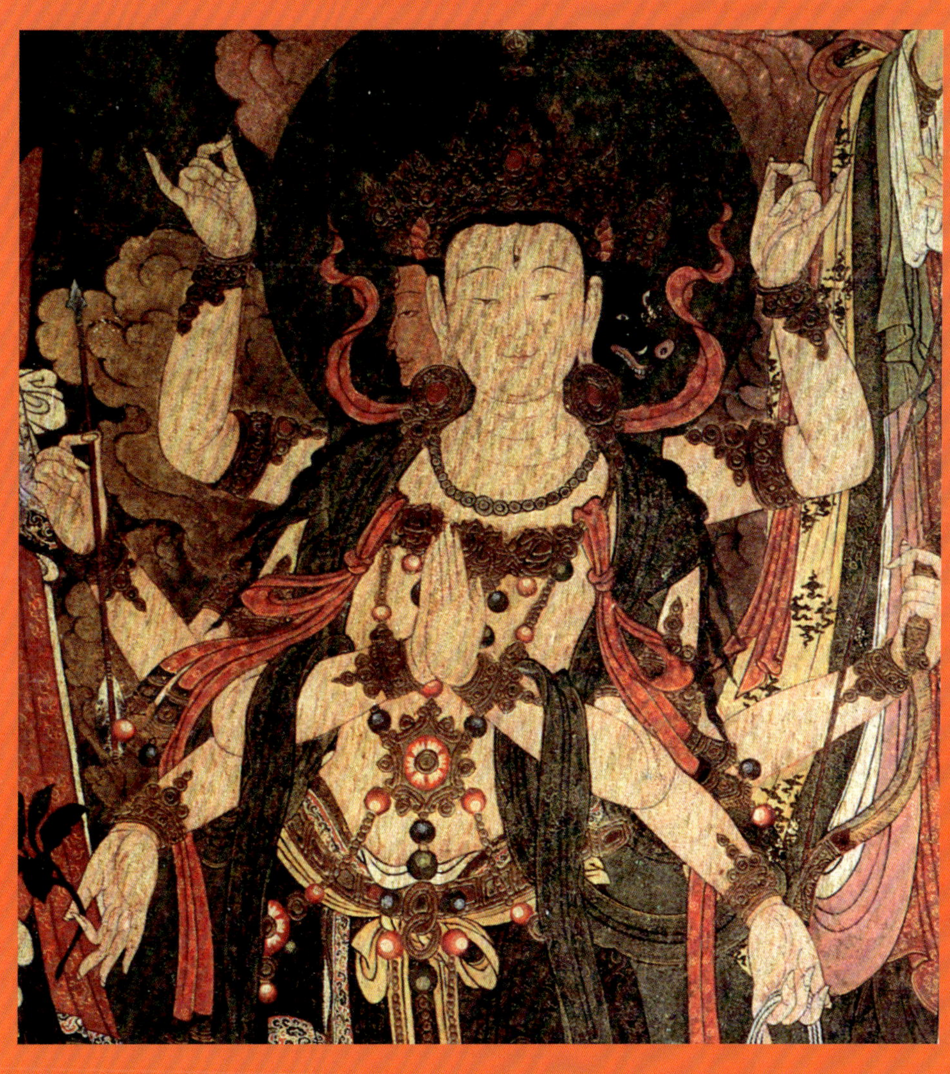

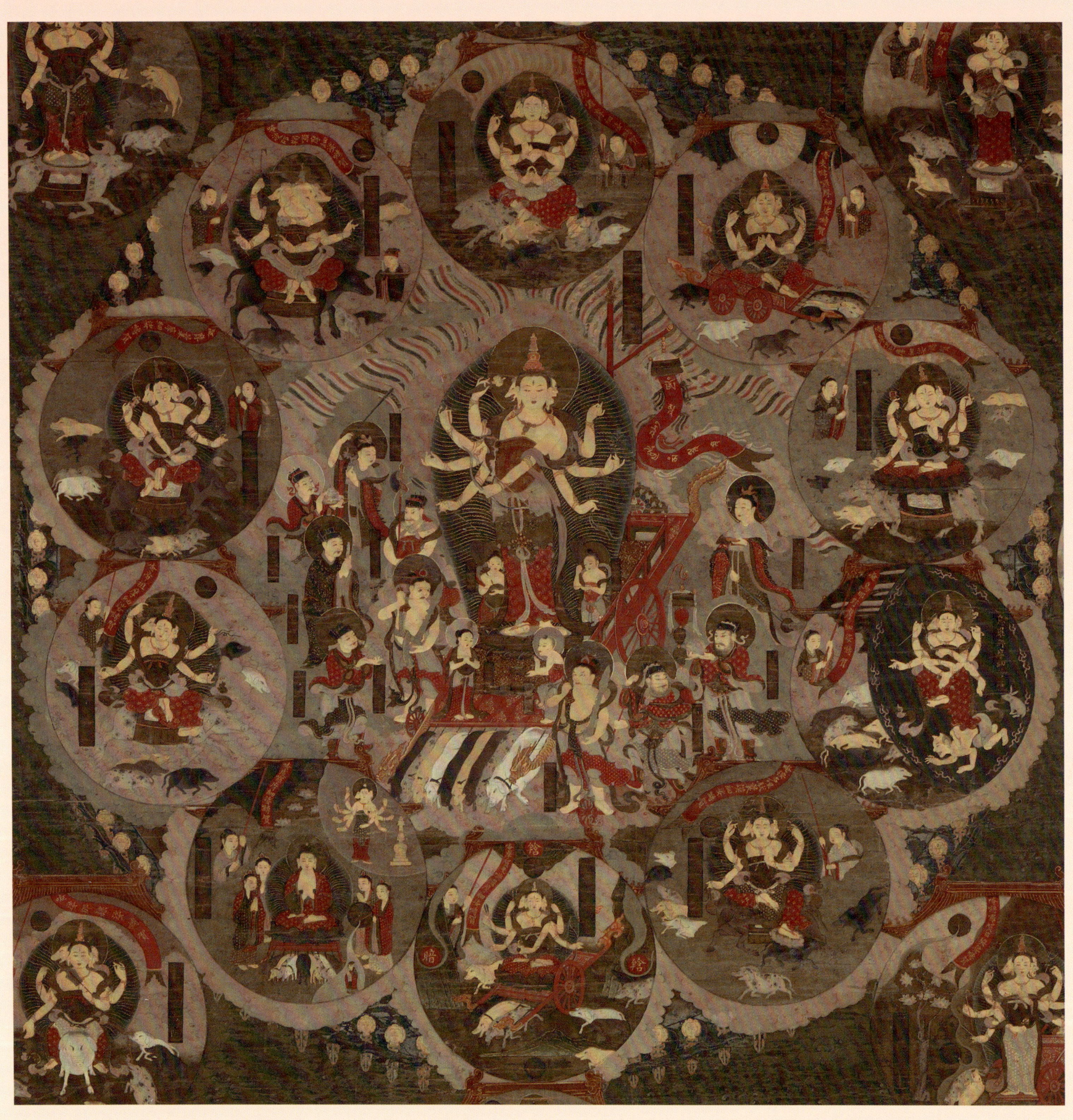

The Mandala of Marīcī

A Goddess of Chinese Buddhism, Tibetan Buddhism, and Daoism

Ling-en Lu

The Goddess Marīcī

Marīcī (Sanskrit: "Ray of Light") emerged in India as a deva who emanates light at dawn and subjugates enemies in battle. Notions of her protective powers originated in ancient Vedic and Hindu beliefs, and these attributes were sustained when she joined the vast pantheon of deities in Vajrayana (Diamond Vehicle), or Esoteric Buddhism, which arose in India in the seventh to eighth centuries.[1] Through the spread of Buddhism, Marīcī was introduced into a wide range of cultures throughout greater Asia. Each culture, in turn, transformed her to suit local religious needs and aspirations. In China, Marīcī is one of the few Buddhist goddesses who enjoyed long periods of worship as deities in Chinese Buddhism, Tibetan Buddhism, and indigenous Daoism. The Esoteric Buddhist deity from India who offered protection during battle and peril evolved over time in China into a popular goddess with broad appeal.

The Mandala of Marīcī

Despite societal, cultural, and religious shifts, the image of Marīcī as a multifaced and multiarmed deity associated with the boar, or pig, changed little over several hundred years. Her esoteric look remained constant and iconic for adherents of her cult in China, as exemplified in the painting *The Mandala of Marīcī*, in the collection of the Nelson-Atkins Museum of Art, Kansas City, Missouri (fig. 1.1). Mounted as a hanging scroll in Chinese style, the painting on silk measures 134.62 centimeters in height and 107.95 centimeters in width and features an ambitious composition with painstakingly rendered

Facing: detail of *The Mandala of Marīcī* 摩利支天曼荼羅. See figure 1.1.

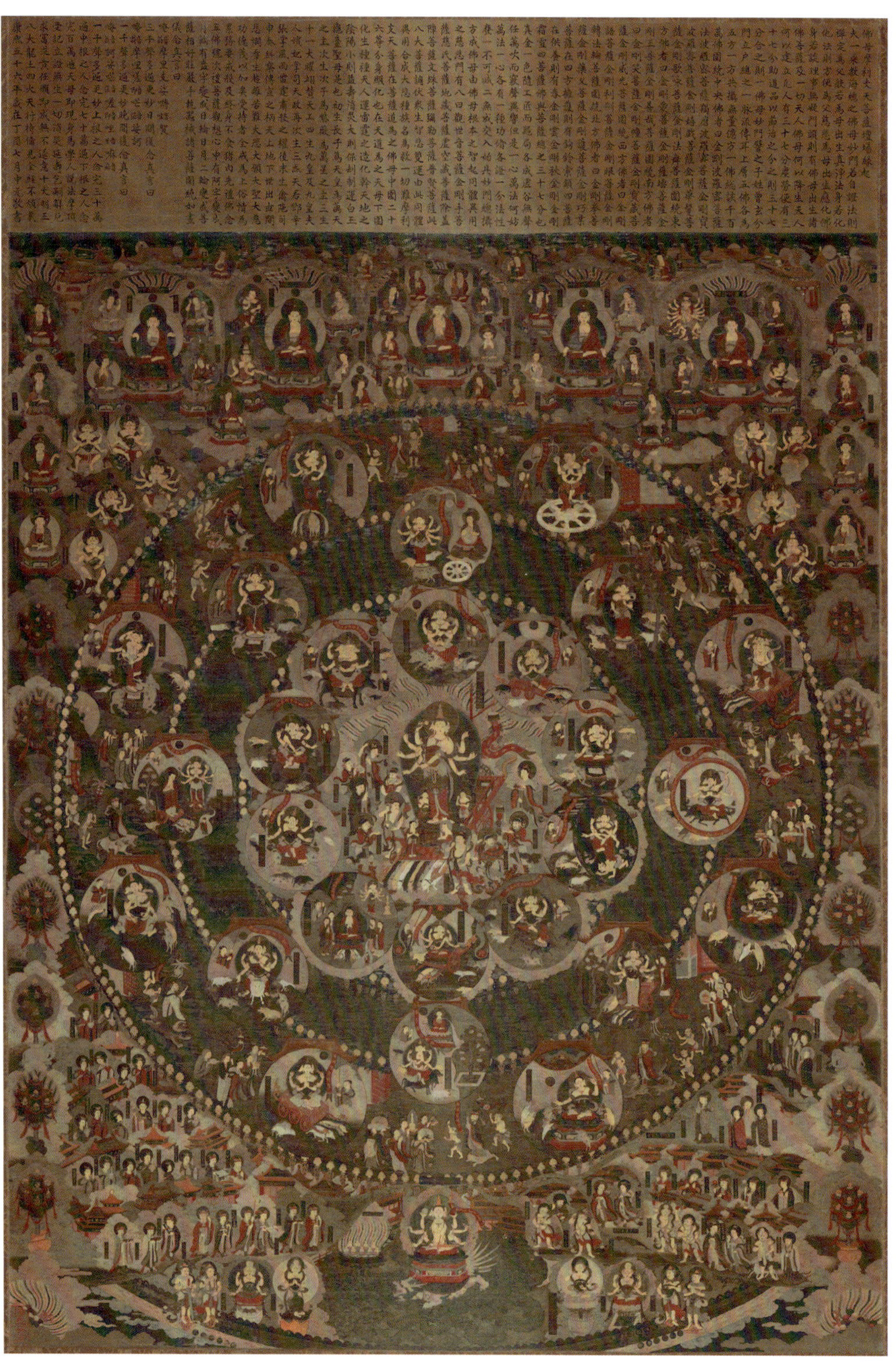

Figure 1.1. *The Mandala of Marīcī* 摩利支天曼荼羅, before 1717. Hanging scroll; ink, color, gold, and silver on silk, 134.62 × 107.95 cm (53 × 41.5 in). Collection of the Nelson-Atkins Museum of Art, 35–172.

details.[2] The brushwork varies stylistically, suggesting that more than one artist worked on the painting. A colophon at the top provides a lengthy description of the deity and the painting. It is dated to the Zhongyuan (Middle Primordial) Festival, commonly known as the Ghost Festival, on the fifteenth day of the seventh month in the fifty-sixth year of the Kangxi era (1717) in the Qing dynasty, which is when the painting was likely completed.

The rich imagery in the painting offers a visual record for the transformation of the cult of Marīcī in China. In this essay, I begin with a brief survey of the cult of Marīcī in history in relation to *The Mandala of Marīcī* before examining the iconography and style of the painting and its place as a work of Buddhist art during the Kangxi era (1662–1722) of the early Qing dynasty. The painting is unsigned, but it was likely created by Chinese painters, who were influenced by two developments at that time: the patronage of Tibetan Buddhist art in the imperial court and the appreciation of the cult of Marīcī by Daoist practitioners. I demonstrate how the art associated with Chinese Buddhism, Tibetan Buddhism, and Daoism enriched and then expanded the depiction of the goddess, and I use the representations of her in the Nelson-Atkins scroll to show how these three prevailing faiths redefined and deepened the layers of complex femininities that Marīcī embodied. Specifically, the representations show that Marīcī as a goddess not only protects Buddhist believers but also commands Daoist constellation deities to repel maladies.

Early Development of the Cult of Marīcī in China

Marīcī became known to Chinese Buddhists during the Six Dynasties period (220–589 CE) and gained fame in the Tang dynasty (618–960 CE), when several short scriptures were translated from ancient Indian texts by Amoghavajra (Chinese: Bukong 不空, 705–774 CE).[3] The early translations introduced the goddess in Chinese as Molizhi 摩利支/摩里支 (transliteration of her Sanskrit name), and often attached the suffixes *tian* 天 (deva, or divine being) and *pusa* 菩薩 (bodhisattva). The scriptural texts inspired a Chinese image of the goddess as a court lady with a fan in her hand.[4] This early form of Marīcī gradually faded from fashion after the introduction of a new Vajrayana scripture in the following Song dynasty.

The scripture that prescribes Marīcī as a multifaced and multiarmed goddess is *Foshuo da Molizhi pusa jing* 佛說大摩里支菩薩經 (Sutra of the Great Marīcī Bodhisattva). It was translated from a now lost text in Sanskrit into Chinese during the Northern Song dynasty (960–1127 CE) by Tianxizhai 天息災 (Sanskrit: probably Devaśānti or Dharmabhadra), a Kashmiri monk who immigrated to China in 980 and died there in 1017.[5] This seven-chaptered sutra, longer than any previously translated scripture, contains Vajrayana Buddhist teaching developed in India before the tenth century. It gives a vivid account of the esoteric spells and incantations associated with Marīcī, and it prescribes contemplation of her various manifestations.

As we understand now, many texts written in the Northern Song and Southern Song (1127–1279) dynasties have laid the foundation for the cult of Marīcī. Zhipan 志磐 (fl. 1258–1269) in *Fozu tongji* 佛祖統紀 (Records of Lineages of Buddhas and Patriarchs) recounts several miracle tales of Marīcī, which suggest the worshippers of the goddess were primarily members of the upper classes. For example, one tale tells the story of how the Song empress dowager Longyou 隆祐 escaped in 1127 from the Jurchen invaders who

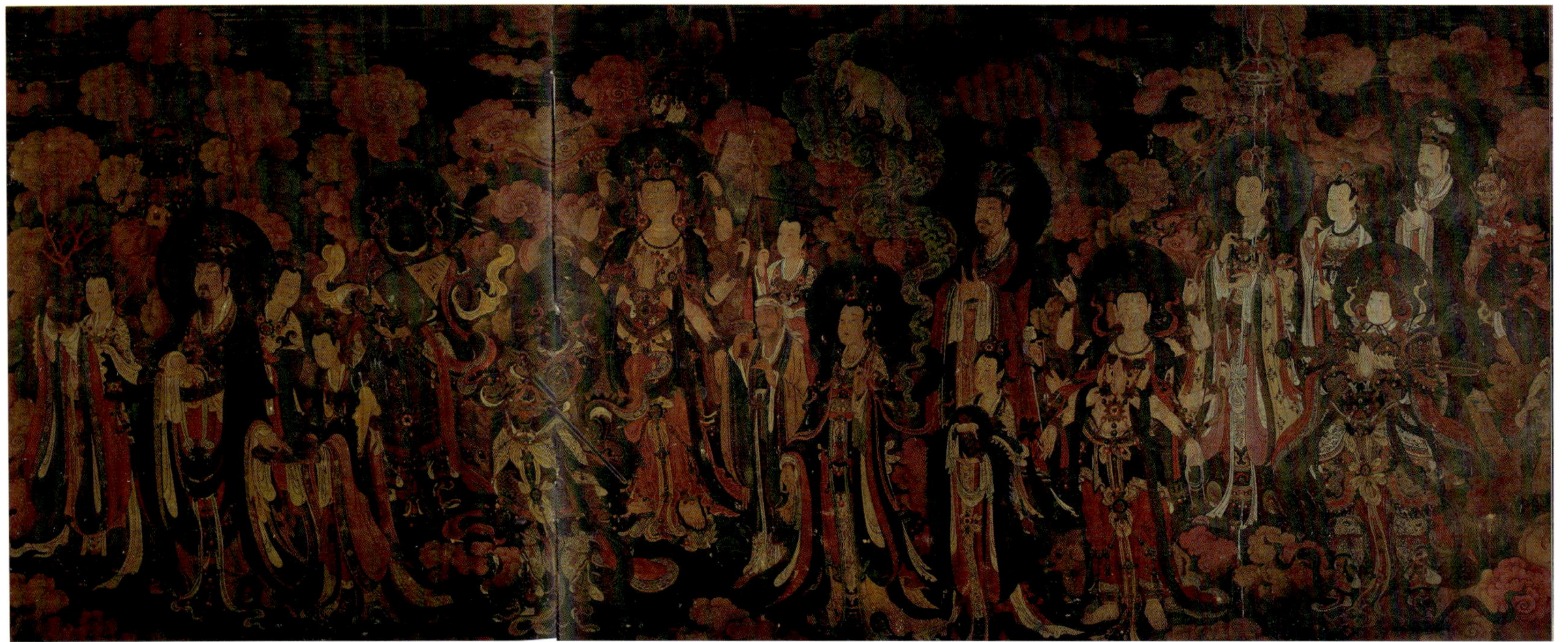

Figure 1.2. *The Dharma Guardians* 護法諸天, 1443. Mural painting, east side of the rear (northern) wall, main hall, Fahaisi 法海寺 temple, Beijing. From *Fahaisi bihua* (Beijing: Zhongguo luyou chubanshe, 1995), fig. 53, unpaged.

established themselves in northern China as the Jin dynasty (1115–1234). The empress was advised by a Buddhist monk to make offerings to Marīcī. Upon reaching the safety of the Southern Song capital at Hangzhou, she commemorated the merciful goddess by commissioning an image of Marīcī on a stele erected in the Middle Tianzhusi temple 中天竺寺 on West Lake.[6]

The role of Marīcī in the Chinese Buddhist pantheon is defined in another Southern Song–dynasty ritual text, titled the *Chongbian zhutian zhuan* 重編諸天傳 (Newly Compiled Biographies of Dharma Guardians), by the monk Xingting 行霆, who wrote in 1173 drawing on previous textual sources. Xingting's text offers Marīcī a role in a unique Buddhist assembly, where she joins some twenty dharma guardians led by Brahma and Indra. The guardians in the assembly were either Hindu or pre-Buddhist deities appropriated as dharma protectors in Buddhism as part of its vast pantheon of worshipful deities, and as *upaya*, or guides for believers on the path of the Buddha. Referencing scripture to specify each guardian's role, Marīcī is the savior and protector of warriors.[7] This text became the inspiration for the image making of Marīcī and her fellow guardians in painting, sculpture, and other forms. Whether the assembly image was erected in the Song temple remains to be determined, but examples from later periods are plenty. One example of a Buddhist assembly is found on the rear wall mural of the main hall of Fahaisi temple, built in 1443 in Beijing (fig. 1.2).[8] The dharma guardians of the assembly are pictured in hierarchical order, conforming to the description of Xingting's text. The portrait of a multiarmed and multifaced Marīcī on the Fahaisi temple mural shows the goddess attired in the fashion of an Indian Buddhist bodhisattva and accompanied by a tusked boar (fig. 1.3), indicating that Chinese artists had knowledge of the Song-dynasty scripture *Foshuo da Molizhi pusa jing*.

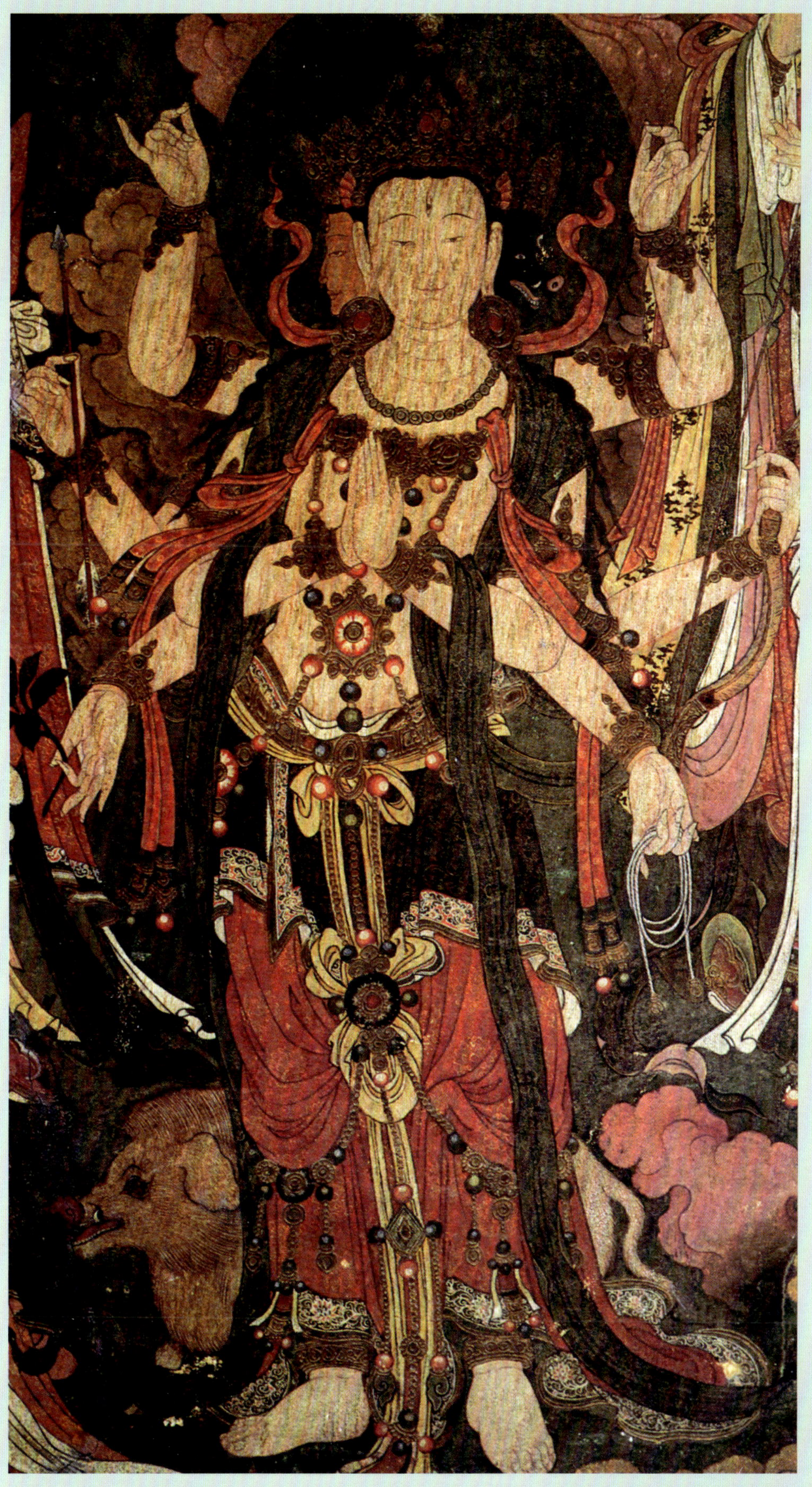

Figure 1.3. *Marīcī* 摩利支天, 1443. Mural painting, rear wall of the main hall, Fahaisi 法海寺 temple, Beijing. From *Fahaisi bihua* (Beijing: Zhongguo luyou chubanshe, 1995), fig. 106, unpaged.

Marīcī in Tibetan Buddhism and Its Visual Arts

Marīcī enjoyed more prominence in Tibet than elsewhere in Asia because she was deemed an important deity in many of Tibet's Buddhist orders.[9] Her Tibetan images have several scriptural bases as compiled in the *Sādhanamālā* (A Garland of Means for Attainment, Ch: *Chengjiu faman* 成就法鬘), a later Vajrayana text composed sometime in the eleventh to twelfth century.[10] The descriptions in her Tibetan scriptures are similar, but not completely identical, to the Song text *Foshuo da Molizhi pusa jing*, and therefore both may have shared the same Sanskrit textual origin.[11] Representations of multifaced and multiarmed Marīcī in the fifteenth-century murals of mandalas are painted on the walls of the Kumbum, a three-dimensional mandala that portrays the Buddhist cosmos, at Palcho Monastery at Gyantse (江孜白居寺吉祥多門塔), in Central Tibet. Here, the goddess is not part of an assembly of dharma guardians, as she had become in China. Instead, she is worshipped in her own right in a separate chapel (fig. 1.4). The images of

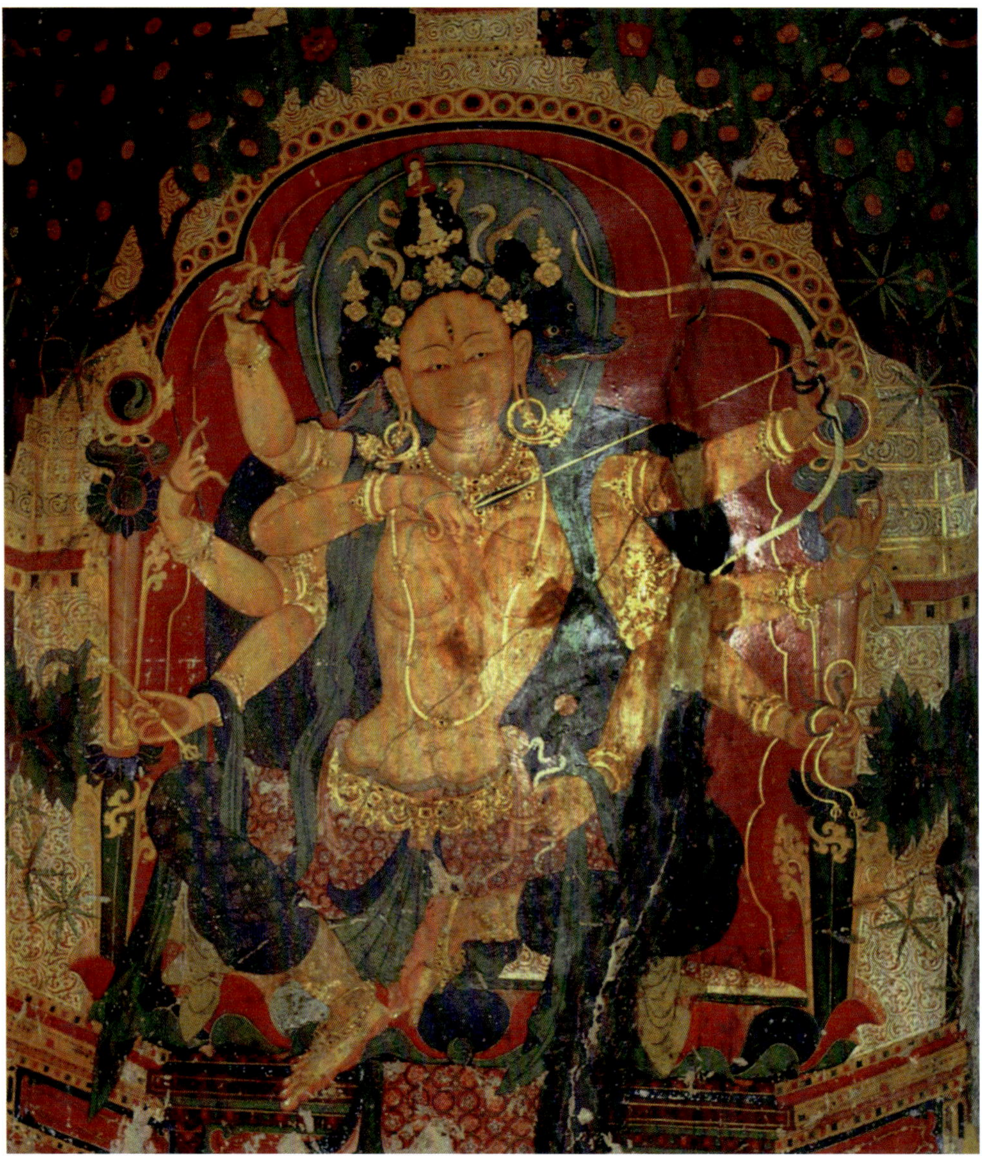

Figure 1.4. Detail of *Marīcī Mandala*, 15th century. Wall paintings at Kumbum, Palcho monastery, Gyantse, Tibet. From Franco Ricca and Erberto F. Lo Bue, *The Great Stupa of Gyantse: A Complete Tibetan Pantheon of the Fifteenth Century* (London: Serindia, 1993), color plate 89.

Marīcī on the walls of Gyantse Kumbum chapel display superb craftsmanship and style with a rich array of diverse iconography, representing Central Tibetan art in the fifteenth century.[12]

In China, the Yuan dynasty (1271–1368) established a relationship with Tibet and honored Tibetan Buddhism and its art. This state of affairs continued to the Ming (1368–1644) and Qing (1644–1911) dynasties, as did the imperial patronage of Tibetan art. The images of Marīcī created in these periods reveal that the cult of the goddess was revitalized in China during several waves of Tibetan influence. With the acquisition of feminine attributes from the Tibetan Buddhist pantheon, the cult of Marīcī grew steadily in China. Moreover, her worship in China seems to have spread from the narrow confines of the upper classes and into the general population. By the fifteenth century, in China as in Tibet, portrayals of Marīcī frequently appeared in Buddhist temples and sutra illustrations.

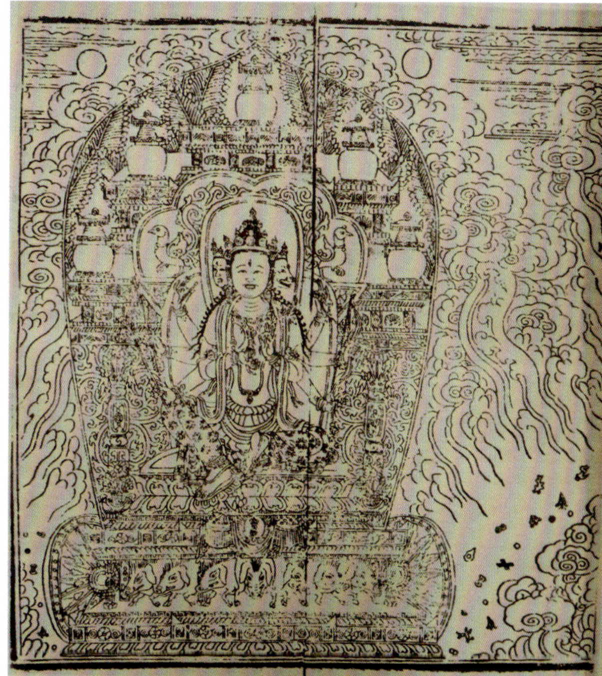

Figure 1.5. *Marīcī* 摩利支天. Printed illustration to the *Foshuo Molizhi tian jing* (Sutra of Marīcī), 1403. From Zheng Zhenduo, ed., *Zhongguo gudai mukehua xuanji* (Beijing: Renmin meishu chubanshe, 1984), vol. II, unpaged.

At this time there was an artistic trend, now known as the "Sino-Tibetan" or "Tibeto-Chinese" style, that blended Chinese and Tibetan elements. This stylistic blending appears, though at times subtly, in the creation of many Chinese images of Marīcī. The Sino-Tibetan trend can be found in two sutra illustrations of Marīcī that are datable to the Yongle era (1403–1424). The first is a miniature *baimiao*, or fine-line drawing, in gold ink on indigo-blue paper that illustrates the *Foshuo Molizhi tian pusa tuoluoni jing* (Sutra of Marīcī Dharani) produced in the court of the Yongle emperor.[13] The second is a woodblock-printed illustration from the *Foshuo Molizhi tian jing* (Sutra of the Divine Being Marīcī), which was reportedly commissioned by Zheng He (1371–1433 or 1435), the imperial admiral and eunuch who led expeditions across the Indian Ocean (fig. 1.5). Although these two sutra texts are transcribed from Tang-dynasty translations made by Amoghavajra, both show in their illustrations the presence of Tibetan artistic elements, as evident in the frontal view of the narrow-waisted goddess seated on a chariot pulled by seven boars. Furthermore, the Tibetan influence on the artworks of Fahaisi temple, which has been widely addressed by scholars, also appears in the mural portrait of Marīcī—it is evident in her swaying posture, narrow waist, and drooping eyelids, although she retains her Chinese role as a dharma guardian in the assembly (see fig. 1.3).[14]

After the Qing dynasty established Tibetan Buddhism as its court religion, the religious art of China experienced its third wave as well as its highest degree of stylistic and iconographic influence from Tibet. Although the courts of Shunzhi (r. 1644–1661) and Kangxi (r. 1661–1722) left fewer works of art than did the later court of Qianlong (r. 1736–1795), the patronage and artistic practices of the early Qing court shaped what was to come for subsequent years of the dynasty. Grand Empress Dowager Xiaozhuang 孝莊 (1613–1688), an ardent patron of Tibetan Buddhism, commissioned a large number of Buddhist projects for the court. Her foremost project was a reproduction of the whole Kanjur section of the Tibetan Tripitaka. This hand-copied manuscript with exquisite illustrations was completed in the eighth year of her grandson Kangxi's reign (1669).[15] As in many Buddhist projects commissioned by the early Qing court, the illustrations to this Kanjur compilation include an image of Marīcī.[16] It was during this time that Marīcī also received from the Qing court a new title translated from Tibetan, Jiguang fomu 積光佛母

(Mother Buddha of Bright Light), sometimes rendered as Juguang fomu 具光佛母or Guangming fomu 光明佛母. The title identifies the source of her power as emanating light and also denotes her nature as *fomu* 佛母, translated from Tibetan with the variable meanings of "matron," "female Buddha," and "mother of Buddhas." Under court patronage, this is but one of the many images created of the goddess. There are numerous bronze sculptures and paintings of Marīcī now in private collections and museums around the world that attest to the lasting legacy of Tibetan Buddhism in China.

Sino-Tibetan Vitality in *The Mandala of Marīcī*

The Mandala of Marīcī in the Nelson-Atkins Museum of Art depicts Marīcī as a principal deity of a mandala and many forms of a multifaced and multiarmed goddess (fig. 1.6). The Chinese scripture *Foshuo da Molizhi pusa jing*, translated by Tianxizhai in the Song dynasty, provided the iconographic elements, the various forms of the esoteric goddess, and the cardinal directions for installing the deities in a mandala. However, most extant paintings and sculptures before the Qing dynasty in China feature the single form of Marīcī. This early Qing painting is exceptional for the depiction of rich and diverse forms of her.

The mandala is divided into an upper, a middle, and a lower section equivalent to the Chinese divisions of celestial, terrestrial, and subterrestrial realms (see fig. 1.6). In the upper section are the Five Cosmic Buddhas flanked by the Eight Great Bodhisattvas and *Mingwang* (Radiant Kings or Vidyarajas). They have always reigned at the cosmic apex of Vajrayana Buddhism; here, they preside over the universe of Marīcī. In the lower section, two groups of deities (which I discuss later) pay homage to the goddess at the center. All the deities are carefully named in the cartouches, although half of the inscribed identities have worn away.

The middle section features the primary mandala, rendered as a large circle that occupies two-thirds of the painting composition. The circular diagrammatic design, differing from the palace-style mandalas commonly seen in Tibet, retains the so-called constellation mandalas typically found in extant mandala paintings of Japan and Korea.[17] It coincides with Marīcī's astrological aspect, in which the goddess manifests herself through the celestial light of the sun and the moon. The circle also recalls the Buddhist wheel, which might be why the writer of the colophon describes Marīcī as the origin of *yicheng* 一乘, or the One Vehicle that carries all sentient beings to Buddhahood (fig. 1.7). Furthermore, the circular mandala places east on the right side of the composition and west on the left side; this can be understood through, for example, the figures of the Eight Great Dragon Kings, who are placed in accordance with their orientations as specified in the *Foshuo da Molizhi pusa jing* (see figs. 1.6 and 1.8).

At the center of the Nelson-Atkins Museum's circular mandala, the principal deity is the eight-armed and three-faced Marīcī, shown standing on a chariot pulled by nine boars, governing over a vast universe (fig. 1.9). She emanates twenty-six manifestations, each enclosed within a small roundel, arrayed from inner to outer circles in three radiating rings (see fig. 1.6). Each roundel features an individual form of Marīcī, an incantation

Figure 1.6. (*facing*) *The Mandala of Marīcī*, showing the entire image of the painting.

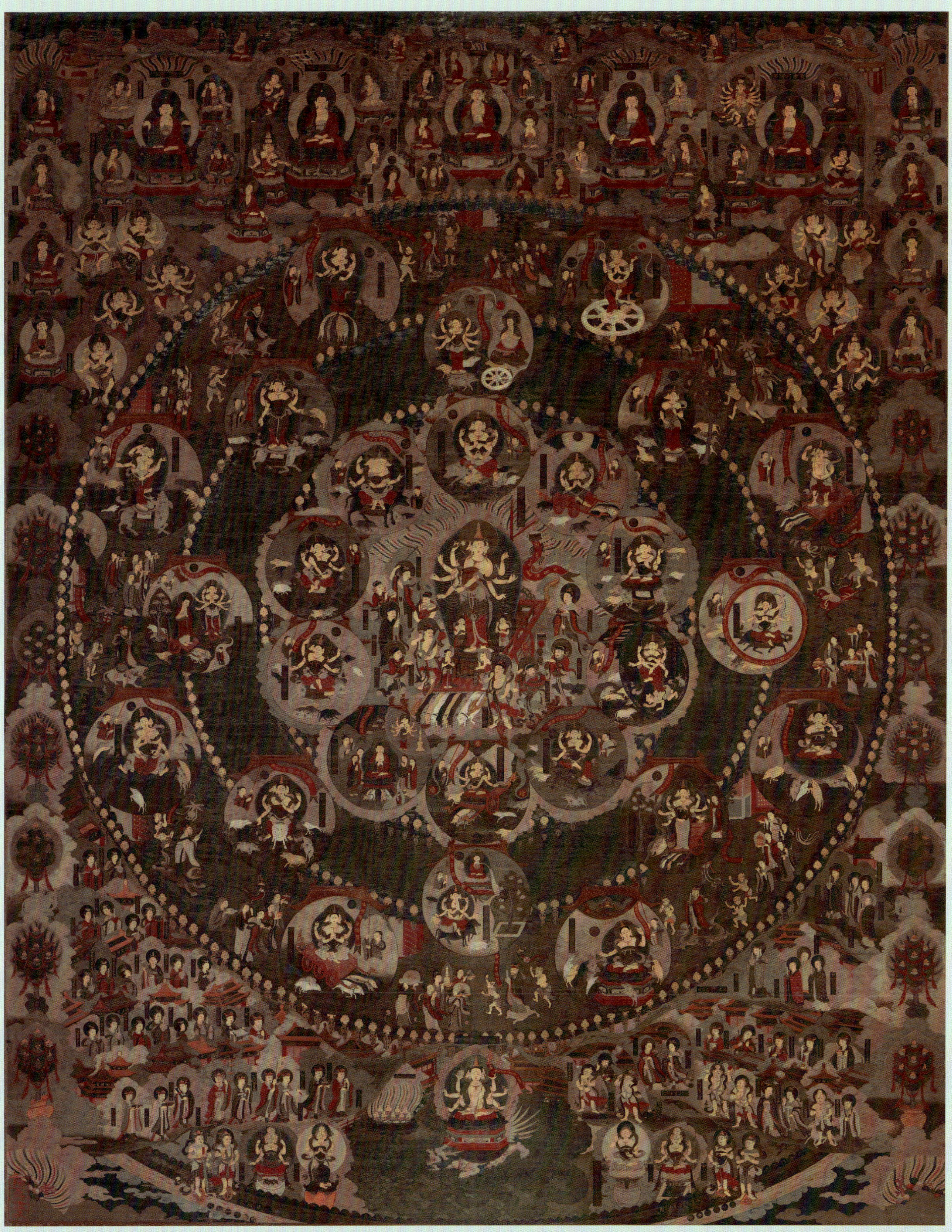

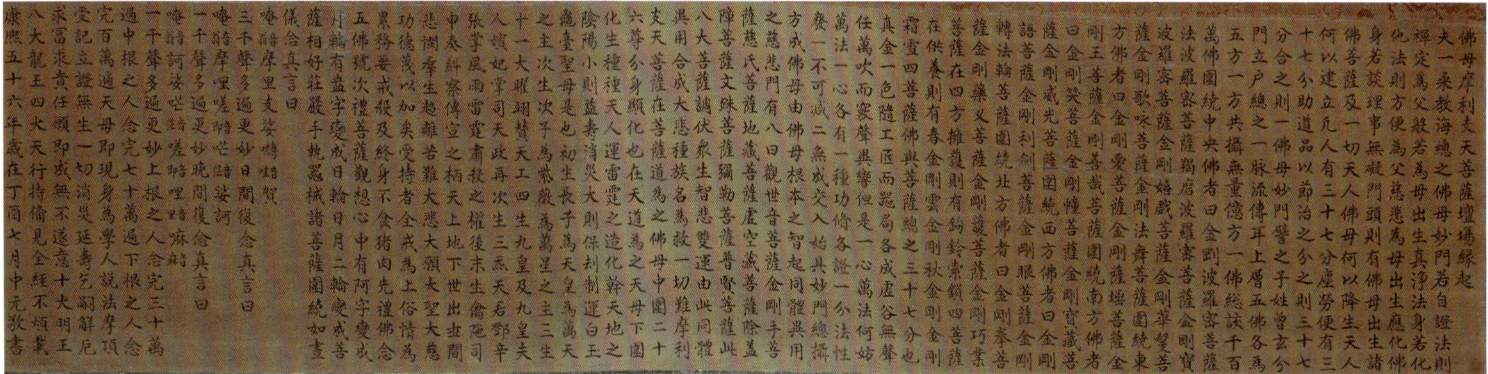

Figure 1.7. Hanging scroll detail of *The Mandala of Marīcī*, showing the colophon.

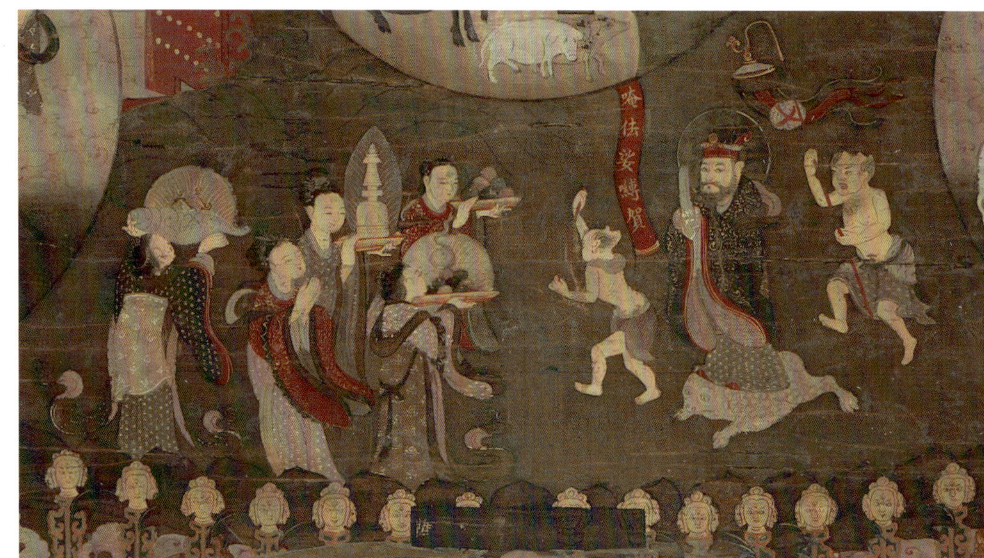

Figure 1.8. Detail of *The Mandala of Marīcī*, showing the Dragon Kings and attendants.

inscribed on a red banner carried by a maid, and a cartouche, in which the faded inscription would have given more identity of the particular form. Another of her manifestations is seated on a dragon throne underneath the outermost circle, as if reigning over the lower realm. All of Marīcī's manifestations in the mandala display three faces—one youthful, one wrathful, and one in the guise of a boar—viewed in various combinations as referenced in the *Foshuo da Molizhi pusa jing.*

Essential to Marīcī's identification is the association with the boar, or pig, manifest both as an additional boar face and by the presence of an accompanying animal. Modern scholars suggest that the boar is derived from Vedic or Hindu astronomical origins and held special meaning in ancient India.[18] This original symbolism was much reduced by the time the multiarmed Marīcī made her debut in China, where the animal served as her identification. The numerous pigs in the Nelson-Atkins Museum's painting are depicted with a variety of hides, including dark, white, brown, and spotted. Buddhist texts describe the boar's sharp tusks to emphasize the viciousness of the goddess.[19] However, the animals depicted here have no tusks, or canine teeth, which genetically grow from the jaws of male hogs in most species. They unquestionably represent sows, serving to denote the gender and also fertile age of the goddess. For the first time in China, the multifaced and

Figure 1.9. (*facing*) Detail of *The Mandala of Marīcī*, showing the principal deity.

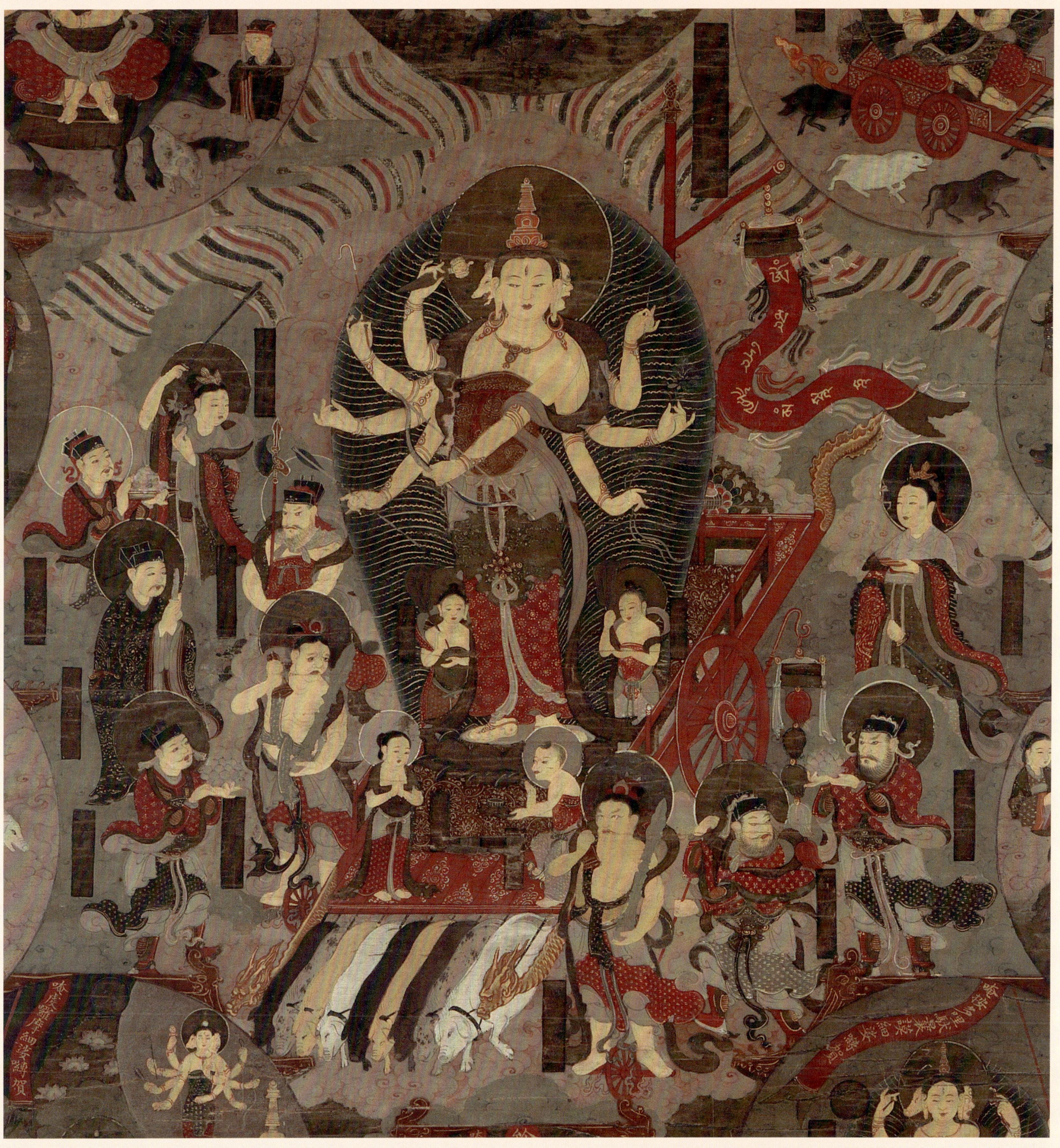

multiarmed Marīcī confirms her female nature, instead of presenting herself as a genderless bodhisattva as in the mural of the Ming dynasty Fahaisi temple.

Her many hands, appearing in sets of two, four, six, or eight, hold sacred weapons, including a bow and arrow, a *vajra* thunderbolt, and a branch of the sacred ashoka tree. A sewing needle paired with thread, which was the standard attribute of Marīcī as she emerged in China from India, serves as her peculiar weapon for binding the eyes and mouths of evildoers (see fig. 1.9). This seemingly innocent tool actually speaks to her complex femininity in greater Asia. In India and Tibet, as Miranda Shaw has demonstrated, Marīcī embodies a fierce and conquering power that is essentially feminine in nature.[20] In China, however, such qualities would not naturally be assigned to a female deity. Chinese goddesses usually embody more gentle qualities, such as motherliness, benevolence, and purity. Yet the Chinese indisputably accepted all of her foreign iconographic traits. Of all the iconic symbols associated with Marīcī, her needle and thread were perhaps the easiest for the Chinese to identify with, as they were essential items found in the women's quarters of most Chinese households. Traditional Chinese poems and secular paintings often portray a woman in her boudoir working with needle and thread as a way to cultivate her femininity or to pass the lonely hours while waiting for the return of a distant lover. Perhaps because of Marīcī's foreignness and protective power, for centuries her fierce femininity coexisted with the needle-and-thread image that under other circumstances would mean gentle femininity.

The rich iconographic program in the Nelson-Atkins Museum's *Mandala of Marīcī* was probably inspired by the sources used by Tibetan lamas to guide their Chinese disciples and students during the early Qing dynasty. The *Nishpannayogavali* (The Garland of Perfection Yoga, Ch: *Jiujin yujiaman* 究竟瑜伽鬘), originally written in Sanskrit by Abhayakaragupta (active late eleventh–early twelfth century) and translated into Tibetan slightly later, provides the textual basis for the twenty-five manifestations depicted in Tibetan mandalas of Marīcī. Although the *Nishpannayogavali* was not translated into Chinese until the twentieth century, this text and the Tibetan images derived from it may have inspired the creation of *The Mandala of Marīcī*. However, not only does the Nelson-Atkins Museum's painting contain more than twenty-five manifestations of the goddess; its depictions of them are more diverse than those found in many extant Tibetan mandalas.[21]

The visual representations of many of Marīcī's manifestations in the Nelson-Atkins Museum's painting rely on Tibetan pictorial precedents, despite the description in the Song-dynasty scripture *Foshuo da Molizhi pusa jing*. One example is a manifestation of Marīcī that shows the goddess drawing a bow and arrow and aiming at the sky (fig. 1.10). This posture recalls the fifteenth-century Tibetan depiction of Marīcī on a mural at the Gyantse Kumbum (see fig. 1.4). Two other manifestations of Marīcī in the Nelson-Atkins Museum's painting, each with one foot raised while the other foot stands on a demon or a prayer wheel (figs. 1.11 and 1.12), perform the dancing posture commonly seen in Tibetan depictions of *dhakini* or *vajrayogini* deities. Another example is a wrathful manifestation of Marīcī, curiously depicted with a ferocious face that rolls its eyes and grinds its teeth and has a boar face emerging from either side of her head (fig. 1.13). This

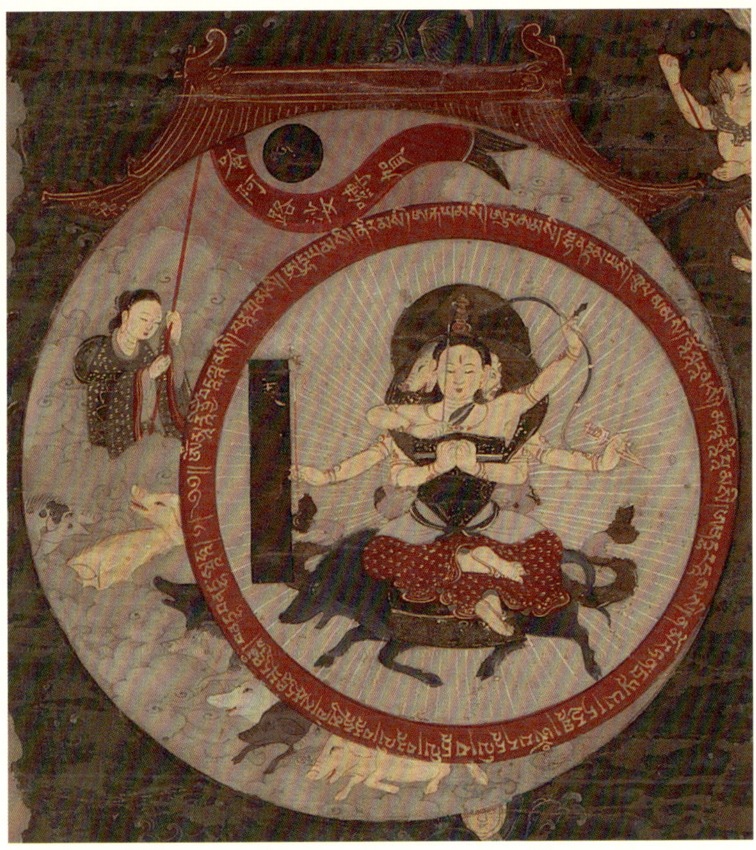

Figure 1.10. Detail of *The Mandala of Marīcī*, showing a manifestation of Marīcī.

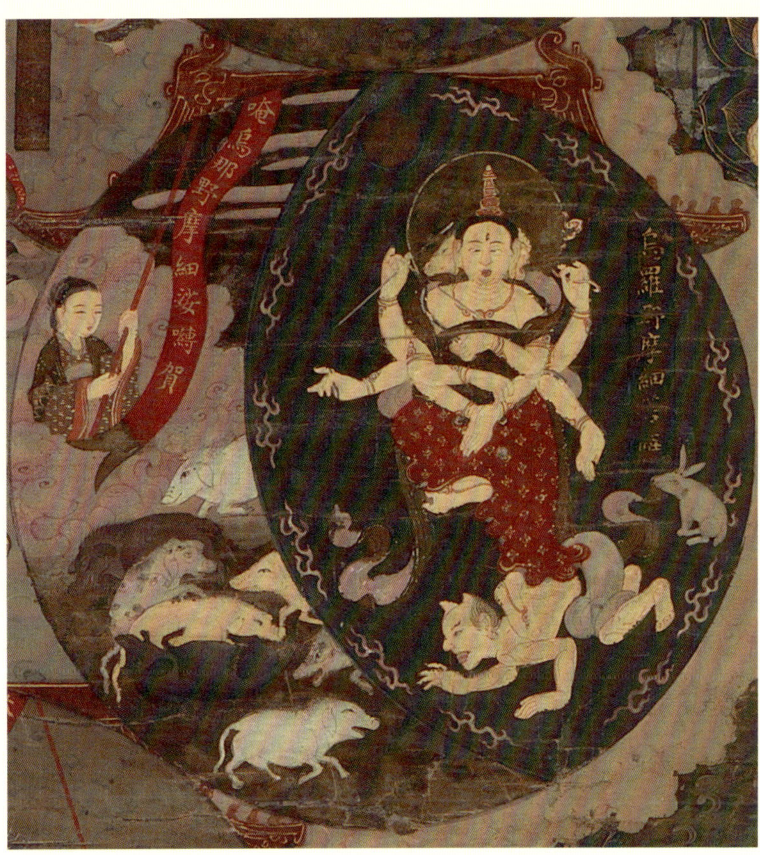

Figure 1.11. Detail of *The Mandala of Marīcī*, showing a manifestation of Marīcī in a dancing posture.

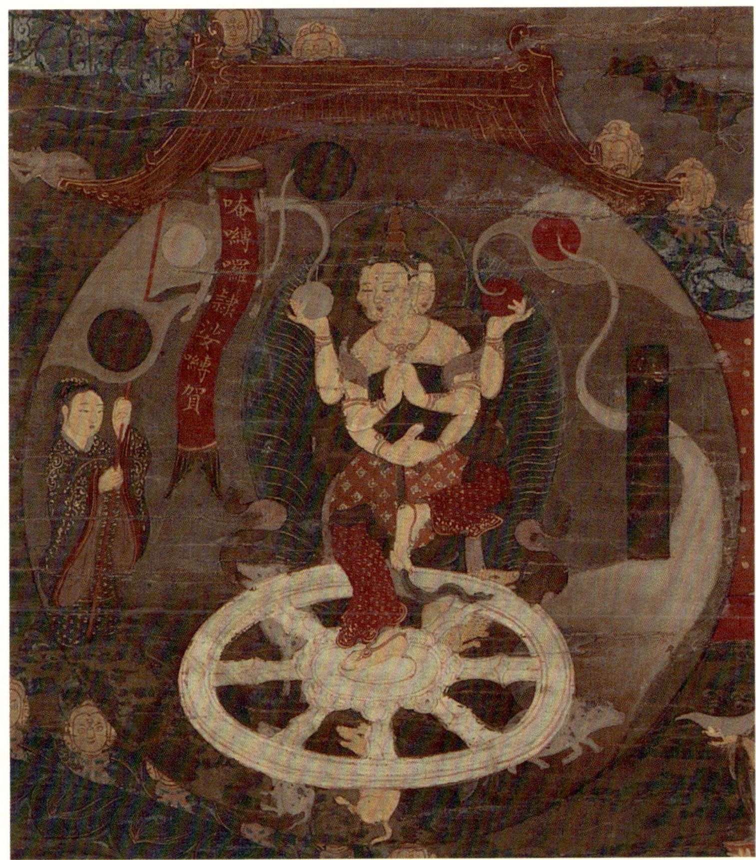

Figure 1.12. Detail of *The Mandala of Marīcī*, showing a manifestation of Marīcī in a dancing posture.

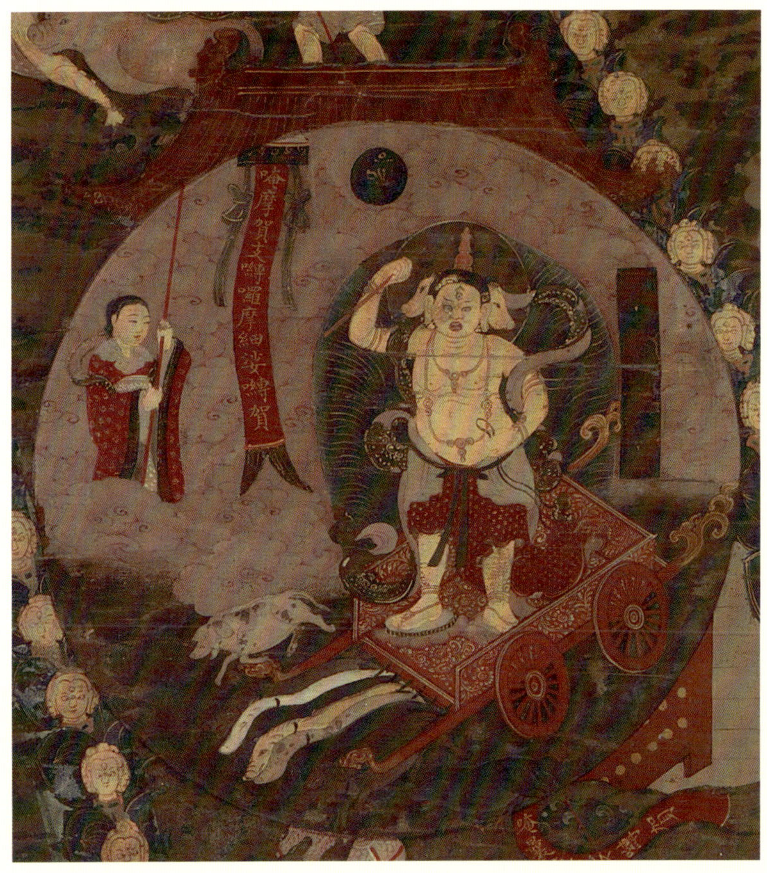

Figure 1.13. Detail of *The Mandala of Marīcī*, showing a wrathful manifestation of Marīcī.

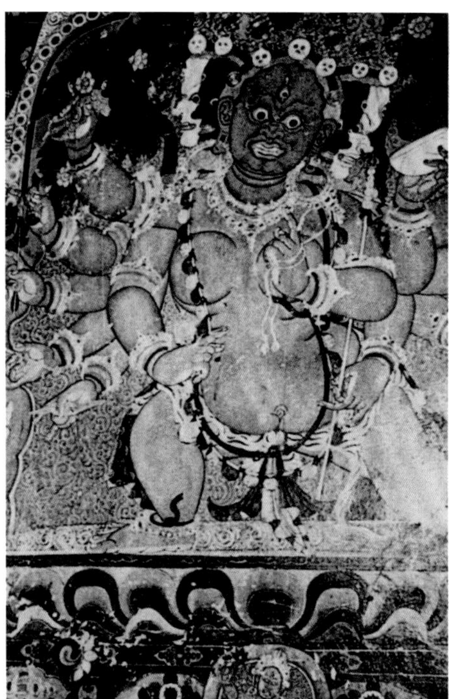

Figure 1.14. Fierce form of Marīcī, 15th century. Wall paintings at Kumbum, Palcho Monastery, Gyantse, Tibet. From Giuseppe Tucci, *Gyantse and Its Monasteries*, part 3, plates. English version edited by Lokesh Chandra (New Delhi: Aditya Prakashan, 1989), fig. 123.

wrathful Marīcī has a precedent on the mural at the Gyantse Kumbum, which is known as the Oddiyana Marīcī in Indian and Tibetan art (fig. 1.14). The Oddiyana Marīcī most likely provided the prototype for this uncommon Chinese version, which has an angry face, a potbelly, and a dwarfish body displaying a U-shaped pendant on its bare chest. The Tibetan-derived wrathful Marīcī seems to have been popular in court art from the Kangxi to Qianlong periods, although the female bodies of these court images of the goddess in her warrior aspect differ from the Nelson-Atkins Museum's image.[22]

A more immediate stylistic inspiration for the artists of the Nelson-Atkins Museum's painting may have been Tibetan Buddhist images created at the imperial court during the Shunzhi and Kangxi eras. A dated example of early Qing court painting from this period is the set of illustrations for the Kanjur section of the Tibetan Tripitaka commissioned by Grand Empress Dowager Xiaozhuang in 1669. It is known that the court workshop for the Kanjur illustrations recruited both Tibetan and Chinese painters, and therefore the Tibetan stylistic practices may have spread from the court to private workshops.[23] The Chinese artists thus adopted the court style for *The Mandala of Marīcī*, and a closer look bears this out. The principal image of the goddess in the mandala (see fig. 1.9) appears as flat in form as the figures found in the Kanjur illustrations, and both lack the three-dimensionality of figures in earlier Chinese depictions of Marīcī, such as the 1443 murals at Fahaisi temple (see fig. 1.3). Resembling the facial features of the Kanjur figures, the Nelson-Atkins's figure has a full face with a short, wide-bridged nose and drooping eyelids.[24] Also like the courtly standing deities, the Nelson-Atkins's Marīcī stands with feet splayed apart symmetrically at hip width. Other details that resemble those in the Kanjur illustrations can be seen in Marīcī's crown, which is topped with a Tibetan-style pagoda, and her mandorla, or aureole of light, which features a delicately rendered nimbus composed of a series of radiating rippled gold lines alternating with smooth silver lines enclosed by a band of pink auspicious clouds.

The Chinese artists of the Nelson-Atkins Museum's image depart from their Tibetan-style counterparts in their treatment of the female body. As Marīcī's gender is noted, Marīcī in both the Kanjur illustration and the Nelson-Atkins Museum's painting demonstrates female character.[25] Whereas the former visibly exposes her breasts, in most cases in the Nelson-Atkins Museum's painting the figure's body is covered with voluminous drapery and a bandeau across the torso. The assimilation of the foreign Tibetan style is therefore modified to fit Chinese decorum.

Nevertheless, the adoption of Tibetan features in a unique Sino-Tibetan stylistic genre as exemplified by the Kanjur images from the early Qing court, and to a lesser extent by the Nelson-Atkins's Marīcī mandala, sets these depictions of the goddess figures apart from depictions of other Buddhist figures that were more fully assimilated into the Chinese tradition, such as the Eight Dragon Kings and their female retinues located in the eight directions throughout the outer ring of the wheel. It is telling that these more Sinicized deities are garbed in traditional Chinese attire (see fig. 1.8). Such juxtaposition of foreign and Chinese elements serves to retain the mystery and sanctity of the goddess at the center of the innermost circle.

Tibetan motifs, appearing throughout this flat, highly detailed mandala, not only contain Buddhist meaning but also embellish Marīcī's universe. A Tibetan mantra is inscribed in gold on a red ground around the edge of the roundel, in which a manifestation of Marīcī sits on her boar vehicle (see fig. 1.10). Tibetan mantras were commonly inscribed as designs on objects during the Qing dynasty, and here the purpose may be to reinforce the power of the Chinese mantras during prayers and invocations. Other motifs, familiar to viewers of Tibetan art, include the garlands festooned with human-headed *vajras* that encircle the three rings of the wheel, components of the Seven Gems (*qizhen* 七珍) and Eight Treasures (*babao* 八寶), and the sea waves finely delineated in gold.

Finally, the physical condition of the Nelson-Atkins Museum's painting suggests that it may not have been mounted as a hanging scroll in the Chinese manner; instead, it may have been originally created for mounting as a *thangka*, the Tibetan-style hanging scroll. Three aspects of the painting indicate this: First, as in thangka paintings, its background is brushed with a thick layer of pigment, which can be glimpsed from the loss of a chunky patch of blue-green pigment from the scroll (fig. 1.15). Examination under a microscope reveals that, along with the mineral-green pigment, many inscriptions on the cartouche have been lost over time rather than scratched out intentionally. Second, tiny horizontal breaks, evenly distributed along the edges of the scroll, suggest the painting may have been mounted in a stretcher, like those used for thangkas (fig. 1.16). Third, the colophon is written on a separate piece of silk that exhibits a fresher and better condition than the painting (see figs. 1.1 and 1.7). It must have been either written or copied after the completion of the painting and then mounted to it to form a hanging scroll.

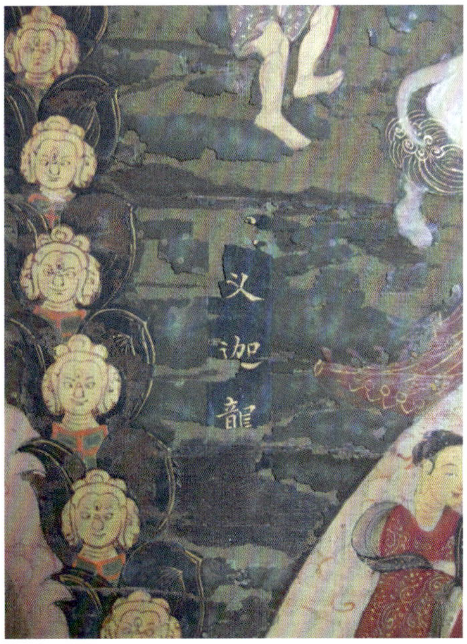

Figure 1.15. Detail of *The Mandala of Marīcī*, showing the loss of pigment. Photograph by the author.

Marīcī as a Universal Chinese Goddess

Although Buddhist iconography dominates the Nelson-Atkins Museum's *Mandala of Marīcī*, Daoist elements can also be found in the painting. These Daoist deity images pay homage to the goddess in the mandala and are identified in the inscribed cartouches (see fig. 1.6). Their incorporation in the mandala indicates that the cult of Marīcī crossed the boundary between Buddhism and Daoism.

Daoism as a religion in China grew steadily after the introduction of Buddhism in China in the second century CE. The growth was achieved through the assimilation of popular Buddhist practices and the incorporation of a large number of Buddhist deities into the Daoist pantheon. Multiarmed Buddhist deities were especially favored, because of the belief in their possession of magical powers. As such, over time indigenous Daoism incorporated Marīcī into its pantheon as a goddess called Doumu 斗母/斗姆, or Mother of the Great Northern Dipper. By the early Qing dynasty, Marīcī was frequently both fused and confused with Doumu in art and literature, as modern scholars have often noted. Deng Zhao has convincingly argued that the Daoist Doumu, because of the similar protective function, borrowed the esoteric body of Marīcī but altered her character.[26] Deng furthermore noted that when the cult of Marīcī was formally proclaimed in the

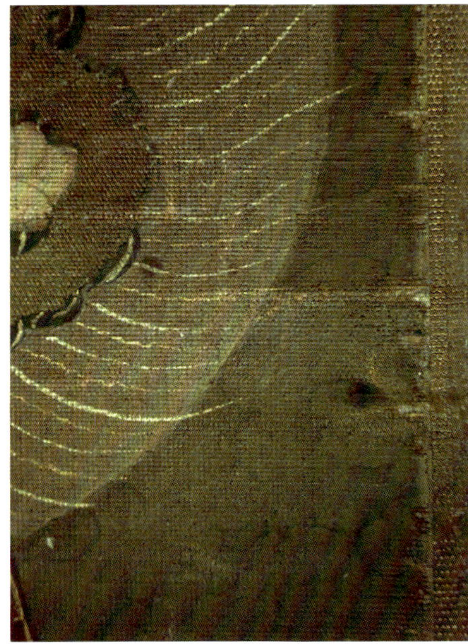

Figure 1.16. Detail of *The Mandala of Marīcī*, showing horizontal breaks along the painting's edge. Photomicrograph by Kate Garland, senior conservator, The Nelson-Atkins Museum of Art.

Ming dynasty, both the Daoist and Buddhist forms of the goddesses were named side by side in the Daoist text *Daofa huiyuan* 道法會元 (Collected Sources on Daoist Ritual). Later, Marīcī was formally incorporated into a lengthy ritual text titled *Xiantian Doumu zou gao xuan ke* 先天斗母奏告玄科 (Mysterious Codes of Petitioning the Dipper Mother before Heaven), which places her in the category of *leifa* 雷法, or Thunder Department, for offering healing and protection to devotees.[27]

The visual arts may have greatly contributed to the dual identities of the goddess from the late Ming to the early Qing period. Shifting notions regarding the goddess came into play during this transitional period, and this is evident in a handscroll painting in a *baimiao* (fine-line drawing) by Zheng Zhong 鄭重 (active first half of the seventeenth century) dated to 1641 of the late Ming period and now in the Bei Shan Tang collection at the Art Museum of the Chinese University of Hong Kong. In the painting, the multi-armed and multifaced esoteric goddess leads a parade consisting of various Daoist deities (fig. 1.17). The esoteric goddess, Marīcī, identified through her boar face on the side and the needle and thread she holds in her hands, is reminiscent of the finely drawn frontal images of the goddess against a mandorla from sutra illustrations of the Yongle period (see fig. 1.5). The handscroll format of Zheng Zhong's painting made it convenient for the owner to solicit the writings of noted Chinese scholars, to whom the Buddhist goddess was not a stranger.[28] After the handscroll passed from the Ming to the Qing dynasty, two scholars added colophons to the handscroll that reveal they were not only aware of but also comfortable with her dual identities. Zhu Yizun 朱彝尊 (1629–1709) inscribed Marīcī's transliterated Chinese Buddhist name, Molizhi tian 摩利支天 (The Divine Being Marīcī), on the frontispiece to the handscroll (fig. 1.18). Zhu's associate Zha Sheng 查昇 (1650–1707), in a colophon dated to 1687, copied a Daoist scripture and addressed the goddess by her dual titles of Doumu and Marīcī, referring to both her adopted Chinese divinity and her Indian origin as the source of emanating light.

During the esoteric goddess's transition from Marīcī to Doumu, the Sino-Tibetan stylistic characters, which would have been transmitted across religions by workshop

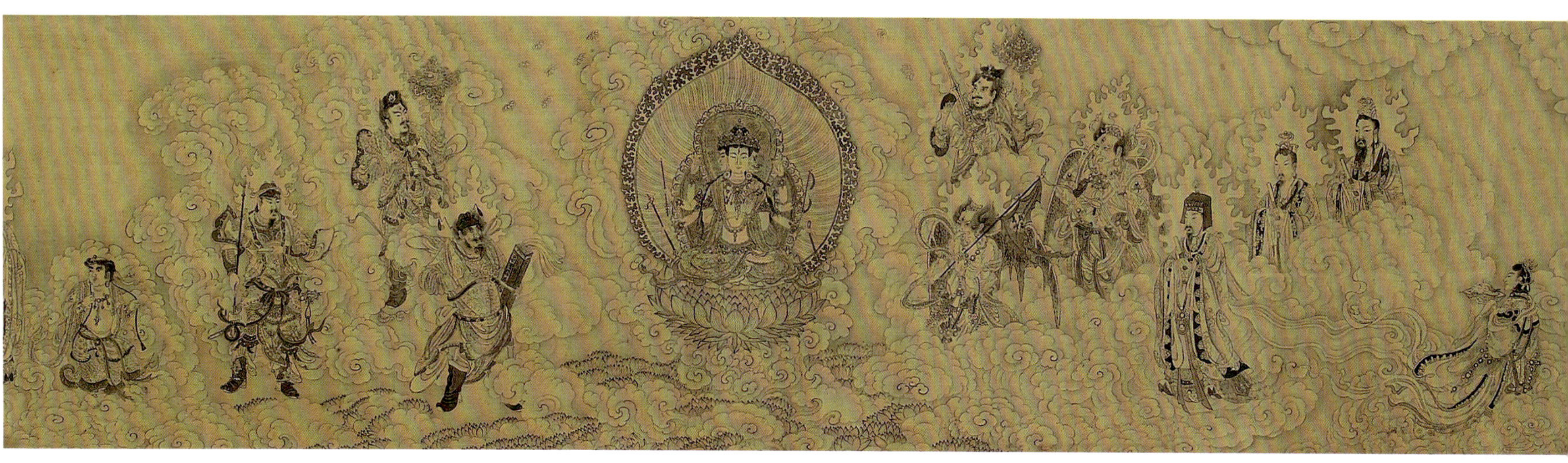

Figure 1.17. Zheng Zhong 鄭重 (act. first half of the 17th century), *Marīcī and Attendants* 摩利支天圖卷, detail, 1641. Handscroll; ink on silk, 30.8 × 561 cm. Collection of the Art Museum, The Chinese University of Hong Kong, 1995.0548, Gift of Bei Shan Tang 北山堂惠贈.

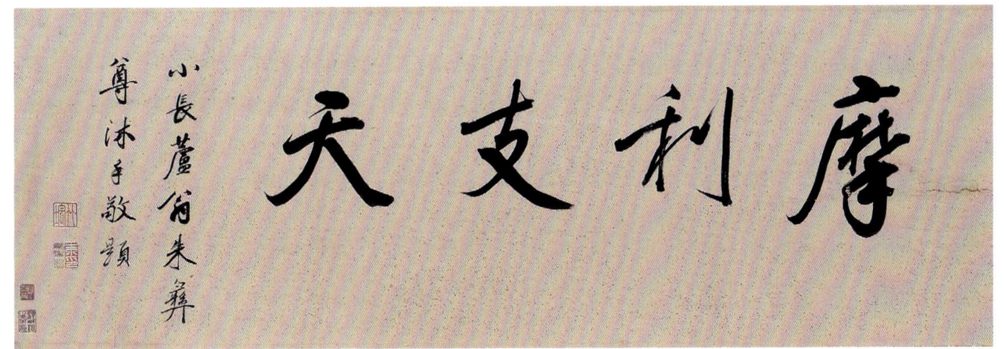

Figure 1.18. Frontispiece by Zhu Yizun 朱彝尊引首. Zheng Zhong 鄭重 (act. first half of the 17th century), *Marīcī and Attendants* 摩利支天圖卷, detail, 1641. Handscroll; ink on silk, 30.8 × 561 cm. Collection of the Art Museum, The Chinese University of Hong Kong, 1995.0548, Gift of Bei Shan Tang 北山堂 惠贈.

artists, likely increased her appeal to Daoist followers and practitioners. Furthermore, when the esoteric goddess was finally incorporated into Daoist worship, as Deng Zhao has observed, her original attribute of needle and thread disappeared from her iconography. Instead of the needle and thread, she holds two discs representing the sun and moon.[29] The transformation can be viewed as the reconciliation of the contradictions between her foreign and Chinese femininities. This is seen in a bronze relief table screen, now in the collection of the Asian Art Museum of San Francisco, depicting the eight-armed goddess seated in the center of the six Daoist celestial warriors (fig. 1.19). The artist not only borrowed the esoteric form but also followed the Sino-Tibetan style, as seen in the goddess's large circular earrings, her narrow waist, and the seven boars underneath her throne. Instead of a needle and thread to shut the eyes and mouths of evildoers, she holds up two round indentations that were once inlaid with semiprecious stones representing the sun and moon.

The frontal-facing image of Marīcī in *The Mandala of Marīcī*, appearing as the principal deity occupying the center of the painting, coincides with the iconic, cult representations of Daoist goddesses in paintings from the late Ming to the Qing dynasty. The visual representation of cult images was commonly seen in the depictions of male deities but had not prevailed for images of goddesses until that period. This iconic image of Marīcī is attended by a large number of celestial divinities of Daoism. In the lower realm under the outer ring of the wheel, two groups of Daoist constellation deities (see figs. 1.6 and 1.20) radiate from the pagoda-shaped crown of the seated Marīcī. This placement suggests that they were generated from her nimbus to occupy the lower subterrestrial realm of the Buddhist universe. To the lower right of this seated subterranean Marīcī, the ensemble includes the celestial deities of Thunder Department: the Celestial Sovereign (Tianhuang 天皇), the Purple Tenuity (Ziwei 紫薇), the Eleven Luminas (Shiyi yao 十一曜), the twin stars Qingyang 擎羊and Tuoluo陀羅, and heavenly messengers (shizhe 使者). To the left of Marīcī, the group is composed of female Daoist deities, the Northern Dipper, and deities of the minor stars (xingjun 星君). Their titles in written cartouches next to the images match those named in Daoist scriptures such as *Daofa huiyuan*, suggesting the iconographers were familiar with Daoist texts.

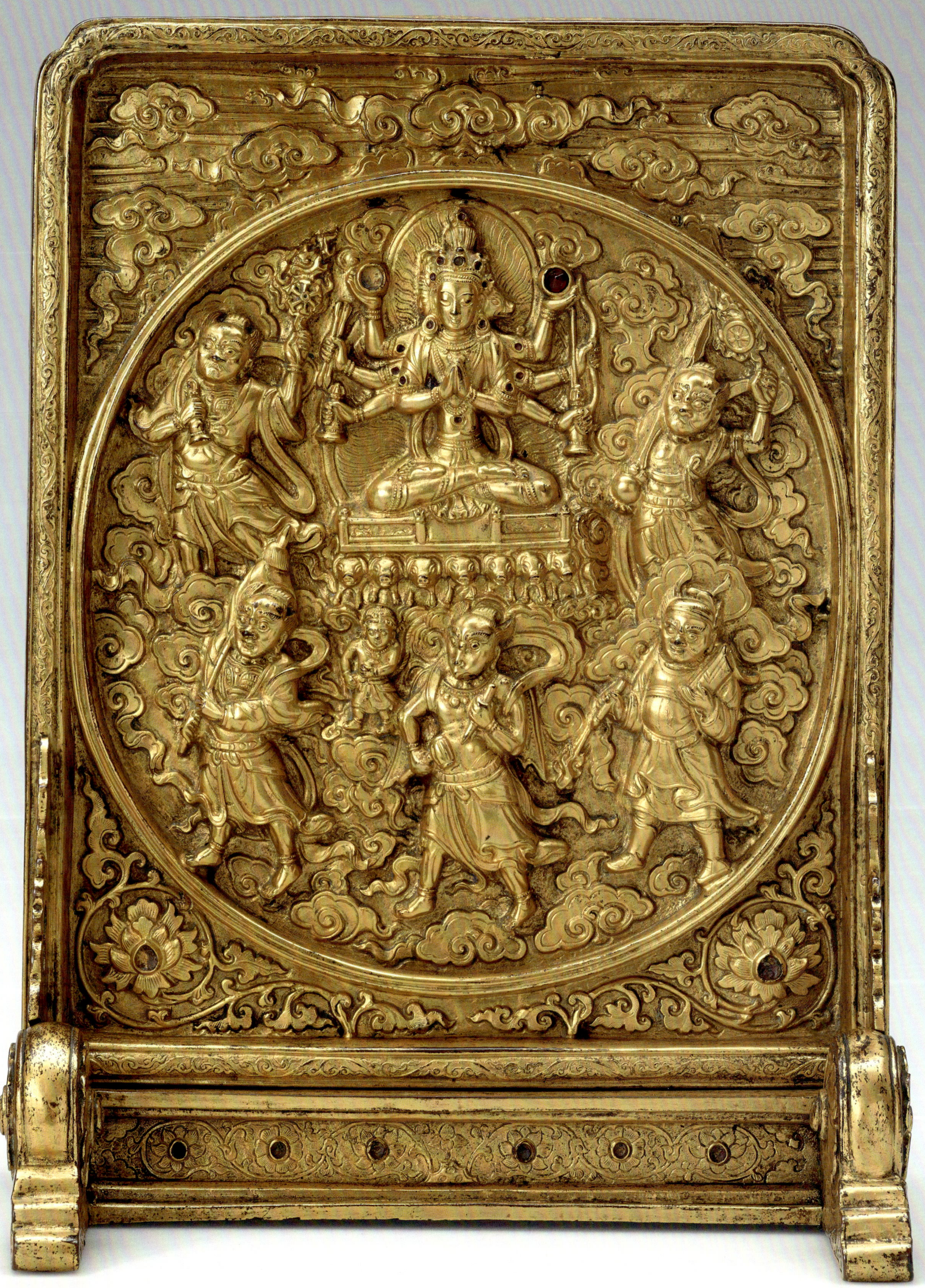

Daoist deities also appear on the throne of the principal deity at the center of the mandala. On either side of Marīcī stands a female celestial who holds up a sword in her right hand and an offering in her left hand (see fig. 1.9). Although the inscriptions in the cartouches next to both figures have faded, this entourage pair is still recognizable because of its inclusion in many paintings of Daoist Doumu. They are the dark twin stars, Qingyang and Tuoluo, who could cause catastrophe if they were put in the wrong positions, but when restored to the right positions, could offer great help to their devotees.[30] In the compositional scheme, Marīcī, or Doumu, has subdued the twin eclipse stars who now flank both sides of her throne as adoring attendants bearing tribute and protection. Viewed as a conventional triad, Marīcī at center has been elevated to a supreme deity, and the sword-bearing twin reinforces the martial character of her shield.

Another syncretic image is that of the nine boar steeds pulling Marīcī's chariot. In Indian, Tibetan, and early Chinese art, there are always seven boars. The expansion to nine boars here may represent the seven stars of the Northern Dipper plus two invisible stars, an addition made sometime during the fusing of Marīcī's identities.[31]

Figure 1.19. (*facing*) Table screen depicting the Daoist deity Doumu and her entourage, approx. 1500–1700, China. Gilded bronze; H. 26.7 cm × W. 19.4 cm × D. 13 cm. Courtesy of Asian Art Museum of San Francisco, Gift of Frances Campbell and the Society for Asian Art, 1991.83. Photograph © Asian Art Museum of San Francisco.

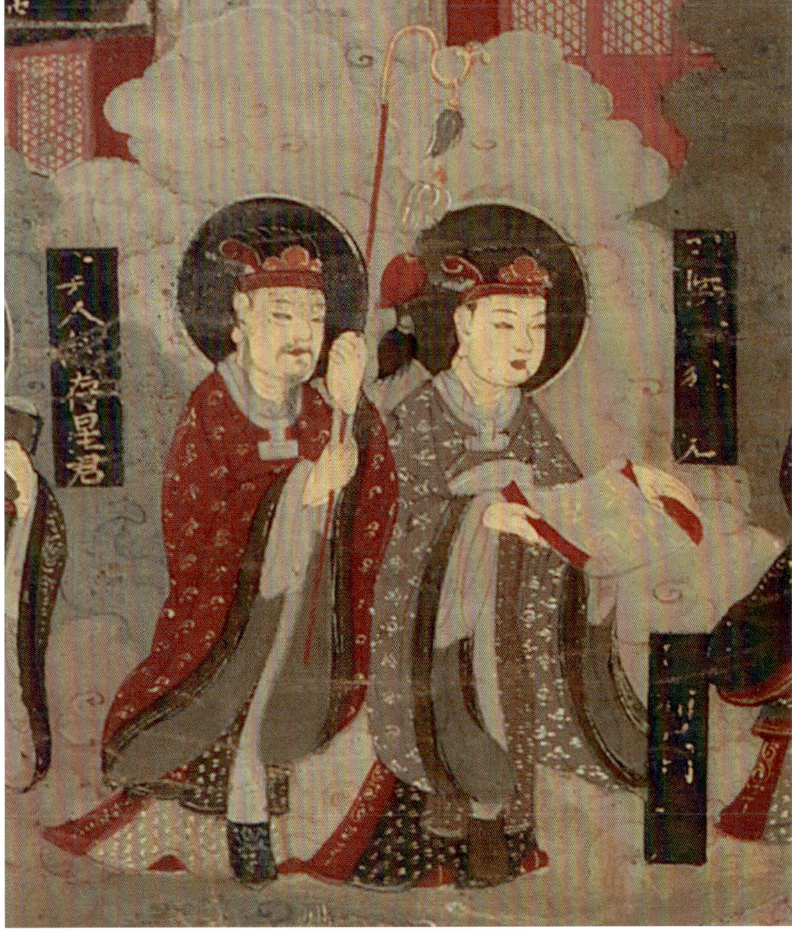

Figure 1.20. Detail of *The Mandala of Marīcī*, showing two Daoist deities. Photograph by the author.

The dual identities of the goddess are described at length in the colophon to the painting with the heading *Fomu Molizhi tian pusa tanchang* 佛母摩利支天菩薩壇場 (The Sacred Space of Marīcī Bodhisattva, the Begetter of All Buddhas) (see fig. 1.7). This title addresses her as *fomu*, which can be understood either as a female Buddha or as the mother/originator of all Buddhas. Following a detailed listing of Buddhist supreme beings and the Daoist celestial sons of the goddess, the text describes the multiple roles she plays as an originator:

> When Marīcī Bodhisattva presides in the bodhisattva path, she is *fomu*. In the central precinct, when she manifests herself as twenty-six divinities, she is *tianmu* (heavenly mother) in the heavenly path. In the nether precinct, when she generates multitudes of celestial beings . . . she is titled Baiyu guitai shengmu 白玉龜台聖母 [the Holy Mother of the White Jade Tortoise Terrace].[32] (see fig. 1.7)

What the colophon does not cite is the horrifying spells used for crushing enemies, as described in the aforementioned Buddhist texts from Song times. In the colophon, the deity is perceived not only as a protector or expeller from peril but also as the originator of cosmic powers that generates the Northern Dipper and a host of other celestial beings.

Like any mandala, the Nelson-Atkins Museum's painting was likely created as a visual aid to guide devotees into the realm of the deity during ritual practices, referred to in the colophon as a sacred space (*tanchang* 壇場). At the end of the colophon, the inscriber dates the work to the Zhongyuan Festival, commonly known as the Ghost Festival, observed by both Buddhists and Daoists. The purposes served by the ritual are also stated: "To assure the release of all beings from rebirth, to avert catastrophe and prolong life, to plead for descendants and their freedom from hardship, and to fulfill the wish of wealth and nobility" (see fig. 1.7).

How Marīcī became part of the artistic program for celebrating the Zhongyuan Festival can be traced to a scripture translated in the Tang dynasty that contains a story about Mulian, a monk who was a filial son. With the help of the Buddha, Mulian is able to travel to the distant Realm of Marīcī (*Molizhi tian shijie*摩利支天世界) to look for his mother, who was reborn as a young woman. There, the Buddha preaches the Dharma law to Mulian's mother so she can be released from the cycle of rebirth. Although this story is lesser known, it nonetheless gives Marīcī a scriptural basis to oversee a paradise.[33]

The ritual use of the painting likely explains the inclusion of yet another syncretic motif that appears to the right of the seated Marīcī underneath the outermost circle of the wheel. Here, seated on lotus blossoms, are nine souls pictured as naked babies (fig. 1.21). The number nine may be significant. Do they represent the nine grades of rebirth as in the Western Paradises of Amitabha Buddha? Or do they recall the nine sons of the Northern Dipper in the realm of Doumu? In either case, this mandala opens up the visual wonders of a Pan-Chinese paradise presided over by Marīcī to those taking part in the religious rituals of the Zhongyuan Festival.

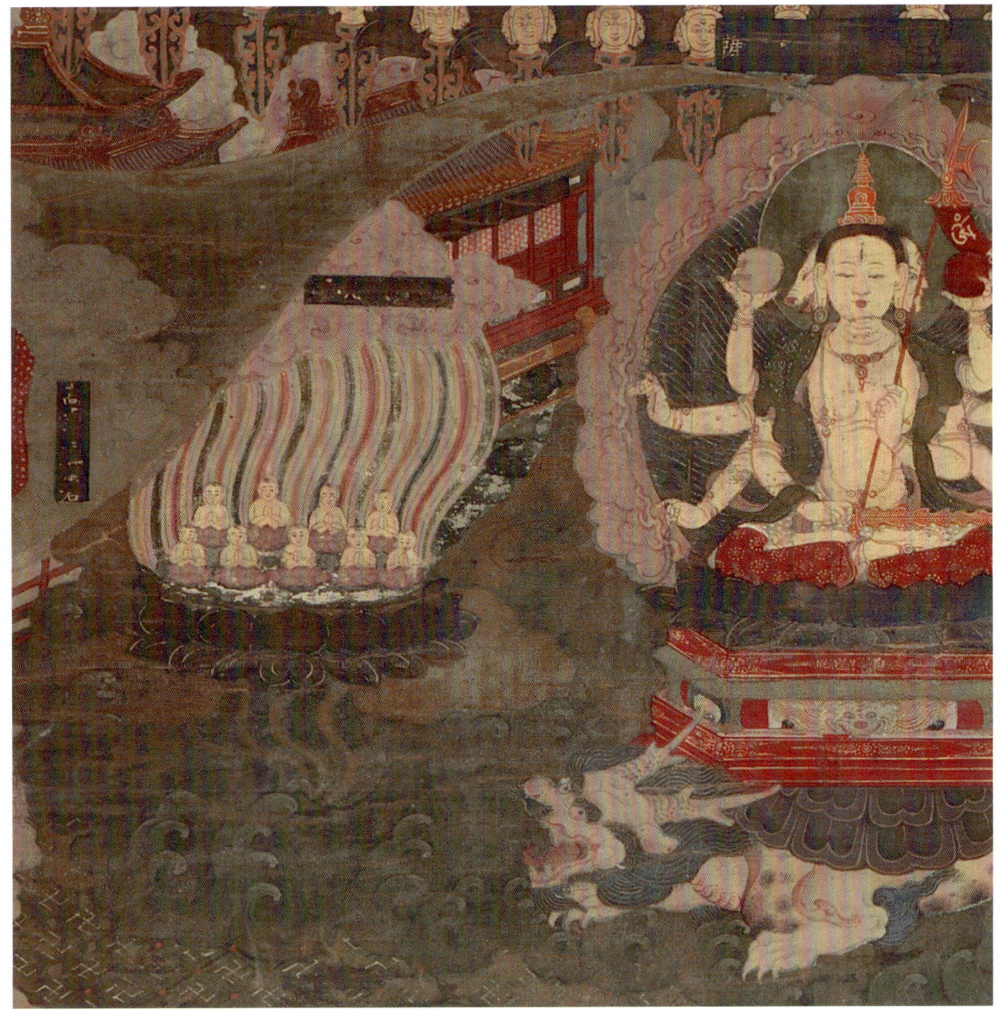

Figure 1.21. Detail of *The Mandala of Marīcī*, showing nine souls. Photograph by the author.

Conclusion

The Mandala of Marīcī in the collection of the Nelson-Atkins Museum of Art was created during the transformative Kangxi era of the early Qing dynasty, when there was a confluence of Chinese Buddhism, Tibetan Buddhism, and Daoism in Chinese society. Detailed analysis of its iconography and style shows the depictions of the multifaced and multiarmed Marīcī continued to depend primarily on the scriptural descriptions of her in the *Foshuo da Molizhi pusa jing*, translated into Chinese by Tianxizhai during the Song dynasty. At the same time, the iconographic innovations of a full universe and many forms of Marīcī show the influence of a more recent text like the *Nishpannayogavali*, as well as knowledge of the Tibetan Buddhist art introduced to China. As I have tried to demonstrate in my analysis, *The Mandala of Marīcī* was likely created by Chinese artists, as it not only retains Chinese stylistic formulas but also incorporates the Sino-Tibetan mode that was currently in fashion at the early Qing court. The analysis also shows Marīcī asserting her femininity through her sow attendants, her attribute of needle and thread, and her female body hidden under the costume. Despite these female characteristics, with the help of imported Tibetan elements she is able to remind the audience that she still holds mystically fierce power. Such melding promoted the goddess to a more far-reaching position than any previous depiction of her in Chinese painting.

This analysis furthermore notes the inclusion of an array of celestial divinities from the native religion of Daoism. Their inclusion can be read as a visual reconciliation of the goddess's dual identities as both the Marīcī of Buddhism and the Doumu of Daoism, debated by scholars and Daoist practitioners of the time. The syncretic universe of Marīcī as represented in the Nelson-Atkins Museum's mandala completes the worship of her across the boundary between Buddhism and Daoism. This had the advantage of attracting a wider audience to the cult of the goddess. The painting, which may have once been formatted as a thangka, found a new ritual use in the Chinese festival of Zhongyuan, observed in both Buddhism and Daoism. The existence of this mandala therefore reveals that by mid-Qing times, Marīcī as a powerful goddess not only protects Buddhist believers with her force and twenty-six manifestations but also commands Daoist constellation deities to repel malady.

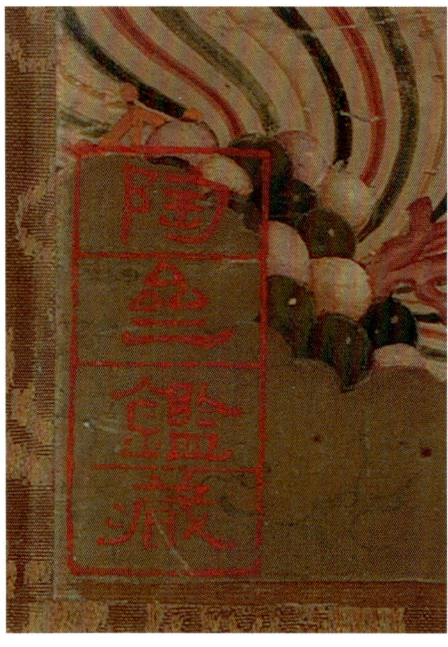

Figure 1.22. Detail of *The Mandala of Marīcī*, showing the seal impression. Photograph by the author.

Postscript

After this mandala ended its life in ritual service to the temple sometime during the nineteenth century, it was preserved as a work of art. Before the Qing dynasty ended, it may have been in the collection of the Manchu official Duanfang (1861–1911), as the lower left corner bears his seal inscribed with *Tao zhai jian cang* 陶齋鑒藏 (Appreciating and Collecting in the Pottery Studio) (fig. 1.22). The painting was acquired in 1935, along with a number of thangkas and other Buddhist paintings, from a shop called Yung Ku Chai in Beijing by Laurence Sickman (1906–1988), a young scholar who later became the curator and director of the Nelson-Atkins Museum. Since entering the museum, the exquisite painting has continued to charm museum audiences and scholars alike.

Acknowledgments

I wish to give my sincere appreciation to Xie Jisheng and Liao Yang of the Sino-Tibetan Association. My gratitude is extended to Marsha Haufler and Jason Steuber, who kindly offered rewarding feedback for this article. An initial study of this topic was presented in a workshop at the Department of Art History, University of Chicago, in 2013. I thank Wu Hung, Annie Feng, and their colleagues for the valuable suggestions.

Notes

1. For pre-Buddhist and Indio-Tibetan developments of Marīcī, see Miranda Shaw, *Buddhist Goddesses of India* (Princeton, NJ: Princeton University Press, 2006), 205–13.

2. *The Mandala of Marīcī* in the collection of the Nelson-Atkins Museum of Art was first published in Denise Patry Leidy and Robert A. F. Thurman, *Mandala: The Architecture of Enlightenment* (New York: Asia Society Galleries, 1997), cat. 48, 125.

3. For scholarship regarding Marīcī and her imagery during the Tang and Song dynasties, see Liu Yongzeng 劉永增, "Dunhuang shiku Molizhi tian Mantuluo tuxiang jieshuo" 敦煌石窟摩利支天曼荼羅圖像介紹, *Dunhuang yanjiu*, no. 5 (2013): 1–11; Li Yumin 李玉, "Tang Song Molizhi pusa xinyang yu tuxiang kao" 唐宋摩利支菩薩信仰與圖像考, *Gugong xueshu jikan* 31, no. 4 (2014): 1–46; David A. Hall, *The Buddhist Goddess Marishiten: A Study of the Evolution and Impact of Her Cult on the Japanese Warrior* (Boston: Brill, 2014), chapter 4, 77–120. Also see Ling-en Lu, "Marīcī: Buddhist Images in the Ming Dynasty," a paper I presented in 1996 to the annual conference of the Midwest College of Art Association at Urbana-Champaign, Illinois.

4. Li Yumin argues that the court-lady form (*tiannü*) has no precedent in India but was likely invented in Tang China by Amoghavajra or his associates. Examples can be seen in the Dunhuang manuscripts in the Aurel Stein and Paul Pelliot collections. See Li, "Tang Song Molizhi," 14; for the Indian images of Marīcī, see Li's figs. 5–6 and 10–12.

5. In *Taishō sinshū Daizōkyō* (repr., Taipei: Xinwenfeng chubangongsi, 1983), T1257, vol. 21, 262–85.

6. Zhipan's text is compiled in *Taishō sinshū Daizōkyō*, T2035, *juan* (section) 47, 423.

7. The names of dharma guardians in assembly appear in the Northern Song–dynasty ritual text *Jinguangming zuisheng canyi* 金光明最勝懺儀, compiled by Zhili 知禮 (active 960–1028). See *Taishō sinshū Daizōkyō*, T1946, 961–63. This text was later revised and compiled in the ritual text by the Southern Song monk Xingting行霆. See Xingting, *Chongbian zhutian zhuan*重編諸天傳 [Newly compiled biographies of dharma guardians], in *Xuzangjing* 續藏經 (repr., Taipei: Xinwenfeng chubangongsi, 1977), vol. 150, 253–85; 275–76 for Marīcī.

8. Fahaisi temple was commissioned by the imperial eunuch Li Tong and constructed in 1443. See Karl Debreczeny, "Ethnicity and Esoteric Power: Negotiating the Sino-Tibetan Synthesis in Ming Buddhist Painting" (PhD diss., University of Chicago, 2007), chapter 2, 97–148; Xie Jisheng 謝繼勝, ed., *Zangchuan fojiao yishu fazhanshi* 藏傳佛教藝術發展史 (Shanghai: Shanghai shuhua chubanshe, 2010), vol. 2, 553–66.

9. Images of Marīcī are ubiquitous in Tibetan art, and she is a major deity in the pantheon of the Kagyupa, one of the four main schools of Tibetan Buddhism. See Karl Debreczeny, *The Black Hat Eccentric: Artistic Visions of the Tenth Karmapa* (Seattle: University of Washington Press, 2012), 188; see also Shaw, *Buddhist Goddesses of India*, 218–23.

10. The *Sādhanamālā* contains sixteen texts of *sādhanas*成就法 (means for attainment), which are partially translated by Benoytosh Bhattacharyya in *The Indian Buddhist Iconography, Mainly Based on the Sādhanamālā and Cognate Tāntric Texts and Rituals* (Calcutta: Firma K. L. Mukhopadhyay, 1958), 207–14.

11. For comparisons between the Chinese and the Tibetan scriptures, see Liu, "Dunhuang shiku Molizhi," 1–11. Another scholar of this subject is Li Yumin, who argues that Tianxizhai's translation of *Foshuo da Molizhi pusa jing* in the Song dynasty is based on an older source than those in the *Sādhanamālā,* and that therefore it conserves more forms of iconography. See Li, "Tang Song Molizhi," 22.

12. See Debreczeny, "Ethnicity and Esoteric Power," 101–2, 113.

13. This sutra and its illustration were compiled in a four-volume set of Vajrayana Buddhist scriptures, titled *Dacheng jingzhou* 大乘經咒. The set contains a preface by the Yongle emperor dating to 1411–12 and an inscription of the Qianlong emperor (r. 1736–1795). For the image and description, see the volume in the digital archive of the National Palace Museum, https://digitalarchive.npm.gov.tw/.

14. The Tibetan elements in the artworks and patronage of the Fahaisi temple have been well addressed in many scholarly studies. See note 9 above.

15. *Longzangjing: Qing Kangxichao neifu nijin Zangwen xieben. Tuxiang zhi bu* 龍藏經: 清康熙朝內府泥金藏文寫本. 圖像之部, vol. 1 (Taipei: Guoli gugong bowuyuan, 2007), introduction, 18–35.

16. For the image, see *Longzangjing*, vol. 1, fig. 014–1.

17. A Japanese example can be seen in a twelfth-century painting in the collection of Horyu-ji temple. See *Kokuhō Hōryūji te: Hōryūji Shōwa shizaichō chōsa kansei kinen* 国宝法隆寺展：法隆寺昭和資財帳調査完成記念 (Tokyo: Henshū Tōkyō Kokuritsu Hakubutsukan, NHK, 1994), 174, plate 117.

18. Shaw, *Buddhist Goddesses of India*, 212–13.

19. The Chinese single word for pig, *zhu* 豬, has no gender implication, but the *Foshuo da Molizhi pusa jing* describes the pig as having "sharp teeth protruding from its face." See T1257, vol. 21, 265.

20. Shaw, *Buddhist Goddesses of India*, 218.

21. The *Nishpannayogavali* is collected in the Tenjur section of Tibetan Tripitaka. It is partially translated into Chinese. See Zhong Ziyin [Chung Tzu-yin] 鍾子寅, "Chongtan Qinghai Qutansi zhi Qutandian (II): Zangchuan fojiao 'Jingangman' (Vajrāvali; rDo rje phreng ba) jiaofa zai mingchu Anduo diqu chuanbo de xinfaxian" 重探青海瞿曇寺之瞿曇殿（二）藏傳佛教《金剛鬘》教法在明初安多地區傳播的新發現, *Gugong xueshu jikan* 32, no. 4 (2015): 191–92. A well-known example of Marīcī's mandala with twenty-five entourages or manifestations is the Four Mandalas of the Vajravali Circle, in the collection of the Rubin Museum of Art, New York. See the Rubin website, accessed July 28, 2019, https://rubinmuseum.org/collection/artwork/four-mandalas-of-the-vajravali-cycle.

22. Shaw, *Buddhist Goddesses of India*, 212–13.

23. For a classification of the labor force in the imperial workshop for the production of the Kanjur illustrations, see Li Baowen 李保文, "Xiaozhuang taihuangtaihou yu Kangxichao 'nijin xieben zangwen longzang jing'" 孝莊太皇太后與康熙朝《泥金寫本藏文龍藏經, *Gugong wenwu yuekan*, no. 2 (2011): 16.

24. For a comparable image, see the Avalokiteshvara in *Longzangjing*, vol. 2, fig. 016–1.

25. For the Marīcī in the Kanjur section, see *Longzangjing*, vol. 2, fig. 014–1.

26. Deng Zhao 鄧昭, "Daojiao Doumu dui mijiao Molizhi tian xingxiang de jieyong" 道教斗母對密教摩利支天形象的借用, *Guoli Taiwan daxue meishushi yanjiu jikan*, no. 3 (2014): 59–108.

27. Many scholars consider that both of these Daoist scriptures were written during the late Yuan to the early Ming era. However, Deng contends that the text of the *Xiantian Doumu zou gao xuan ke* appears in a more mature format than the *Daofa huiyuan*. Moreover, the *Daofa huiyuan* was included in the compilation of the Daoist canon, Daozang, in the early fifteenth century, whereas the *Xiantian Doumu zou gao xuan ke* (HY 1440, DZ 1452) was collected some two hundred years later in the supplement to the Daoist Canon, or Xu Daozang 續道藏, compiled in 1607 during the Wanli era. See Deng, "Daojiao Doumu dui mijiao Molizhi," 70–77.

28. Su Shi, the Northern Song scholar and artist, reportedly created the calligraphy of the sutra, *Molizhi tian jing*, and inscribed a colophon to the scroll. See Li, "Tang Song Molizhi," 16.

29. Deng, "Daojiao Doumu dui mijiao Molizhi," 79. Also see Li, "Tang Song Molizhi," 28, for an interpretation of the small sun and moon discs in the early painting of Marīcī as evidence of Daoist influence.

30. For examples of Daoist paintings of Doumu, see Deng, "Daojiao Doumu dui mijiao Molizhi," 105, fig. 7; 106, fig. 8.

31. See Stephen Little with Shawn Eichman, *Taoism and the Arts of China* (Chicago: Art Institute of Chicago, 2000), 248, 253n6.

32. The title is recorded in Doumu jing 斗姆經 [Classic of Doumu], compiled during the Southern Song period. See Deng, "Daojiao Doumu dui mijiao Molizhi," 66–67. My translation.

33. The lesser-known story is found in *Genbenshuo yiqieyoubu binaiye yaoshi* 根本說一切有部毘奈耶藥事 (T1448, vol. 24, *juan* 4, 16a–b), an early eighth-century Sanskrit scripture that was translated into Chinese by Yijing 義淨 (635–713 CE). The story differs from the more popular version based on the Ullambana Sutra (Yulanpenjing 盂蘭盆經). See also Chen Fangying陳芳英, *Mulian jiumu gushi zhi yanjin jiqi youguan wenxue zhi yanjiu*目蓮救母故事之演進及其有關文學之研究 (Taipei: Guoli Taiwan daxue chubanshe, 1983), 14–15; Stephen F. Teiser, *The Ghost Festival in Medieval China* (Princeton, NJ: Princeton University Press, 1988), 131; Ding Min丁敏, "Han yi da xaio chen fodian zhong 'shenzu feixing' de kongjian xushi" 漢譯大小乘佛典中神足飛行的空間敘事," *Foxue yanjiu zhongxin xuebao*, no. 12 (2006): 30–33.

Bibliography

Bhattacharyya, Benoytosh. *The Indian Buddhist Iconography, Mainly Based on the Sādhanamālā and Cognate Tāntric Texts and Rituals*. Calcutta: Firma K. L. Mukhopadhyay, 1958.

Chen Fangying陳芳英. *Mulian jiumu gushi zhi yanjin jiqi youguan wenxue zhi yanjiu*目蓮救母故事之演進及其有關文學之研究. Taipei: Guoli Taiwan daxue chubanshe, 1983.

Debreczeny, Karl. "Ethnicity and Esoteric Power: Negotiating the Sino-Tibetan Synthesis in Ming Buddhist Painting." PhD diss., University of Chicago, 2007.

Deng Zhao 鄧昭. "Daojiao Doumu dui mijiao Molizhi tian xingxiang de jieyong" 道教斗母對密教摩利支天形象的借用. *Guoli Taiwan daxue meishushi yanjiu jikan*, no. 3 (2014): 59–108.

Ding Min丁敏. "Han yi da xaio chen fodian zhong 'shenzu feixing' de kongjian xushi" 漢譯大小乘佛典中神足飛行的空間敘事. *Foxue yanjiu zhongxin xuebao*, no. 12 (2006): 1–42.

Hall, David A. *The Buddhist Goddess Marishiten: A Study of the Evolution and Impact of Her Cult on the Japanese Warrior*. Boston: Brill, 2014.

Kokuhō Hōryūji te: Hōryūji Shōwa shizaichō chōsa kansei kinen 国宝法隆寺展：法隆寺昭和資財帳調査完成記念. Tokyo: Henshū Tōkyō Kokuritsu Hakubutsukan, NHK, 1994.

Leidy, Denise Patry, and Robert A. F. Thurman. *Mandala: The Architecture of Enlightenment*. New York: Asia Society Galleries, 1997.

Li Baowen 李保文. "Xiaozhuang taihuangtaihou yu Kangxichao 'nijin xieben zangwen longzang jing'" 孝莊太皇太后與康熙朝《泥金寫本藏文龍藏經. *Gugong wenwu yuekan*, no. 2 (2011): 8–17.

Little, Stephen, and Shawn Eichman. *Taoism and the Arts of China*. Chicago: Art Institute of Chicago, 2000.

Liu Yongzeng 劉永增. "Dunhuang shiku Molizhi tian Mantuluo tuxiang jieshuo" 敦煌石窟摩利支天曼荼羅圖像介紹. *Dunhuang yanjiu*, no. 5 (2013): 1–11.

Li Yumin 李玉珉. "Tang Song Molizhi pusa xinyang yu tuxiang kao" 唐宋摩利支菩薩信仰與圖像考. *Gugong xueshu jikan* 31, no. 4 (2014): 1–46.

Longzangjing: Qing Kangxichao neifu nijin Zangwen xieben. Tuxiang zhi bu 龍藏經: 清康熙朝内府泥金藏文寫本. 圖像之部, vol. 1. Taipei: Guoli gugong bowuyuan, 2007.

Shaw, Miranda. *Buddhist Goddesses of India*. Princeton, NJ: Princeton University Press, 2006.

Taishō sinshū Daizōkyō. Reprint, Taipei: Xinwenfeng chubangongsi, 1983.

Teiser, Stephen F. *The Ghost Festival in Medieval China*. Princeton, NJ: Princeton University Press, 1988.

Xie Jisheng 謝繼勝, ed. *Zangchuan fojiao yishu fazhanshi* 藏傳佛教藝術發展史. Shanghai: Shanghai shuhua chubanshe, 2010.

Xuzangjing 續藏經. Reprint, Taipei: Xinwenfeng chubangongsi, 1977.

Zhong Ziyin [Chung Tzu-yin] 鍾子寅. "Chongtan Qinghai Qutansi zhi Qutandian (II): Zangchuan fojiao 'Jingangman' (Vajrāvali; rDo rje phreng ba) jiaofa zai mingchu Anduo diqu chuanbo de xinfaxian" 重探青海瞿曇寺之瞿曇殿（二）藏傳佛教《金剛鬘》教法在明初安多地區傳播的新發現. *Gugong xueshu jikan* 32, no. 4 (2015): 143–218.

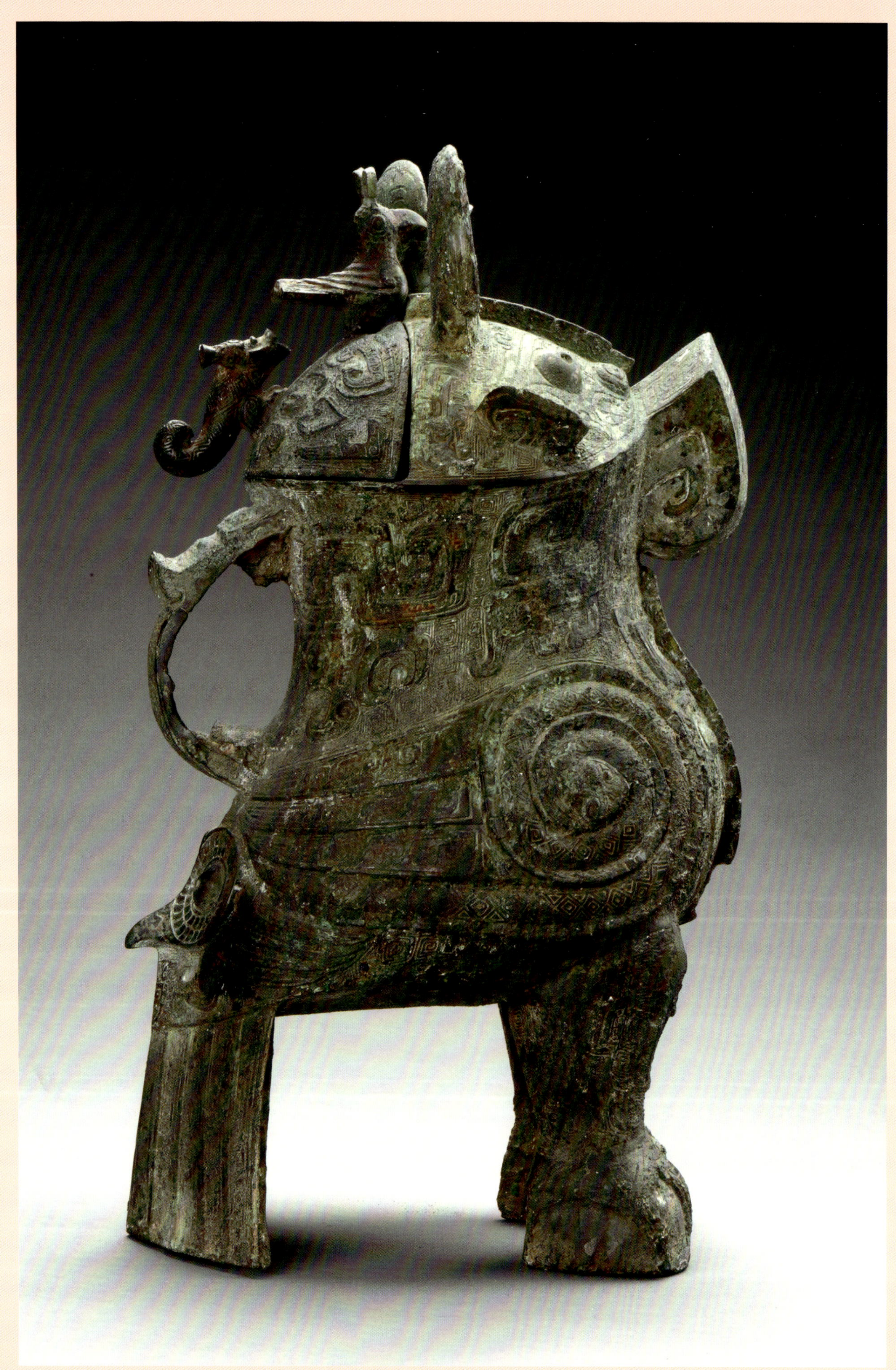

Gender Roles in Bronze Age China

When and Why the Broom Inscription Became the Female Symbol

JUNKO UCHIDA

THE SHANG DYNASTY (1300–1050 BCE), a significant era in Chinese history, is renowned for its construction of huge cities such as Zhengzhou Shangcheng 鄭州商城 and Anyang Yinxu 安陽殷墟 and the development of civilization around them. It is the earliest dynasty to appear in written historical records of China, and it was during this period that the original form of Chinese characters, pictographs, were developed. Shang society seems to have begun to accumulate knowledge in early eastern Asian history. The kings ruled through divination using oracle bones and tortoise shells; bureaucracy and the army were established synchronously, forming the early Chinese state. Yet Shang kings consolidated their supremacy and political regime through ancestor worship.

Various bronze ritual vessels of the Shang period are notable for their fascinating artifact casting techniques; these vessels were often engaged in ancestral rituals and ceremonies. Many Shang bronze vessels have complex and magnificent shapes, thought to have been created by unique casting techniques using segmented molds. There are also primitive Chinese characters cast on some of the bronze vessels' inner walls.

The ancient Chinese characters of the Shang dynasty inscribed on oracle bones and bronze vessels are hieroglyphs, which represent how people conceive of the shapes of objects and offer a key to reconstruct the sociocultural, political, and economic roles that archaeological artifacts played and the concrete meanings that they were given. By examining contextual details of gender-related inscribed ancient Chinese characters, therefore, we can investigate how gender roles in Shang society were established.

Women in China have suffered under patriarchy for more than 3,000 years because of the Confucian ideology, with many women being locked in the home to do domestic work. When and why this gender-based role was placed specifically upon women

Facing: Bronze eagle-shaped *Zun* vessel. See figure 2.4c.

is an interesting and complicated question. Extant historical texts and unearthed inscribed objects arguably have influenced subsequent recorded histories, studies, and their canonical interpretations. Discernable themes, derived from and privileging patriarchal, Confucian, and other gendered social constructs, reinforced gendered ideologies and conceptual frameworks. These then relegated women, and histories of women, to domestic roles, maternal duties, and limited socioeconomic and political accomplishments. One way to examine this issue is through the archaeological record, especially the study of the Shang dynasty, when the megalopolis Anyang Yinxu 安陽殷墟 (or Dayishang 大邑商, as it was known during this period) was established, and when urbanization, as a consequence of increasing social complexity, deeply affected gender construction.

To consider gender roles and gender construction in this era, I focus here on the *Fu* 婦 and *Ge* 戈 characters. The *Fu* 婦 character, which denotes a "lady," is composed of a woman 女 with a broom *zhou* 帚. This composition dates back to the Shang dynasty, when it had the same meaning it does today. The Shang-dynasty character of the woman represents a person sitting upright with hands crossed in front of their chest. The character of the broom has three curved, bristlelike strands at the end of a stick. Why is it that the woman with a broom represents "lady"? A comparative analysis of the shape of the Shang inscription with some relevant archaeological artifacts unearthed in Anyang can shed light on the gender issues surrounding the *Fu* character, the context in which female labor became confined to the domestic realm in particular.

In contrast, one of the most important archaeological artifacts representing the male status is the *Ge* dagger (halberd blade). In this essay I aim to show that the *Ge* 戈 and the broom *zhou* 帚 symbolized the male and female status and their social roles or meanings, respectively, and that their meanings and significance derived from the actual gendered division of labor and how the material items, the dagger and the broom, were used to undertake gender-specific work. By studying the process through which the link between the material items and gender roles and statuses was established, I hope to reveal how patriarchal Confucian ideology originated.

The *Fu* Inscription on the Fu Hao Grave Bronzes

Before investigating the *Fu* character and related items, I will introduce the ancient capital of the Shang dynasty, originally called Dayishang, where the oracle bones inscribed with primitive Chinese characters and related artifacts were unearthed. Dayishang, the capital city of the later phase of the Shang dynasty, was located at Anyang Yinxu in Henan province. The Institute of History and Philology (IHP), Academia Sinica, began to excavate on the terrace of the Huan River 洹河 at the back of Xiaotun 小屯 village in 1928, and the Xibeigang 西北岡 royal cemetery at Houjiazhuang 候家莊 village on the opposite shore was discovered and excavated between 1935 and 1937.[1] The initial objective of the excavation at Xiaotun was to find oracle bones with ancient Chinese pictographs. During the ten-year excavation, the IHP discovered three groups of the remains of large buildings, which are now thought to be a palace and shrine complex.

The Chinese government changed in 1949, which led to the relocation of the institute to Taiwan. In 1976, just after the end of the Cultural Revolution (1966–76), the Anyang Excavation Team, Institute of Archaeology of the Chinese Academy of Social Sciences, excavated the Fu Hao tomb 婦好墓 located near the Xiaotun palace complex.[2] The tomb has a middle-sized chamber measuring 5.6 by 4 meters. The team excavated an extremely rich assemblage of artifacts from the relatively undisturbed chamber and the upper layer, including 468 bronze implements, such as vessels and weapons (190 vessels with inscriptions; 90 percent of the total vessels), and 755 jade items, ivory cups, and cowrie shells. The bronze vessels were of spectacular quality, ornately decorated and large in size, indicating they were owned by a high-status individual. Since many of those excavated bronze vessels of various types have the same inscription, "Fu Hao" 婦好 or "Queen Mother Xin" 司母辛 (or Houmuxin 后母辛), and the name of one of the wives of the twenty-third Wu Ding 武丁(23rd King of Shang 商) was inscribed as "Fu Hao" on some oracle bones, it can be inferred that the tomb's occupant is the king's consort.[3] The artifacts are dated to Phase II of the Yinxu chronological scheme (BCE twelfth century). Studies of the oracle inscriptions and archaeological evidence indicate that the reign of King Wu Ding was extremely prosperous, and the practice of burning turtle plastrons or oxen scapulae to reveal oracles was established and frequently carried out.[4]

The characters *Fu* and *Hao* 婦好 as inscribed on the bronze vessels comprise two women (or two mothers) 女, a broom 帚, and a child 子. These four characters are, intriguingly, placed randomly and differently among Fu Hao inscriptions (fig. 2.1a, 2.1b).

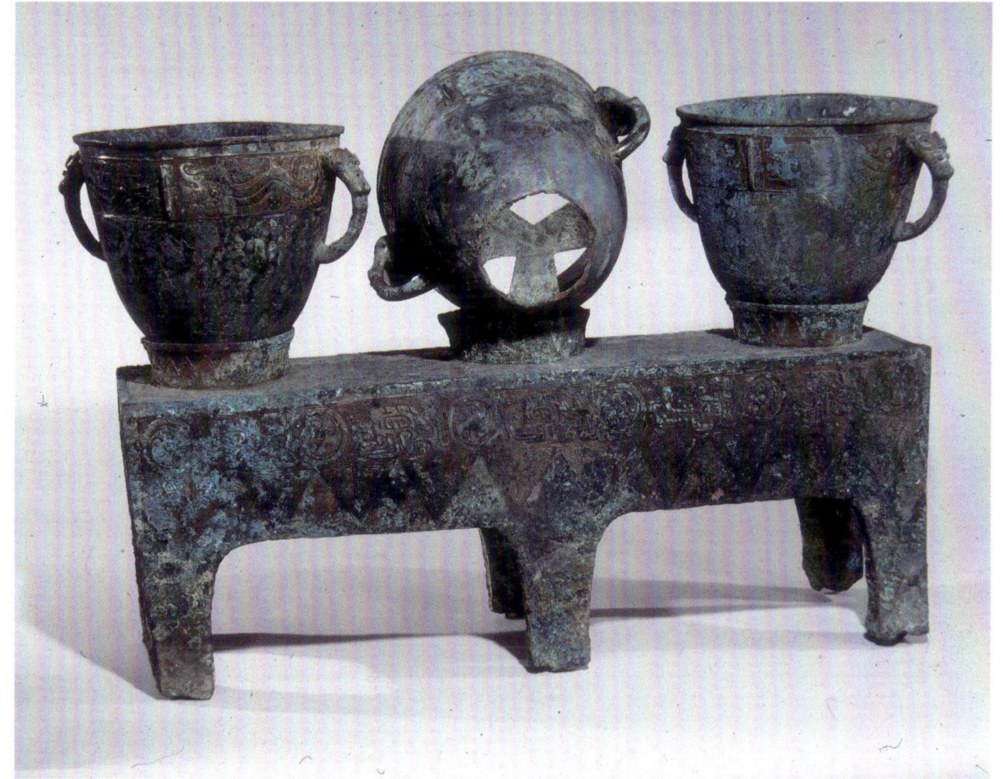

Figure 2.1a. Bronze steamer unearthed from Fu Hao grave in Anyang. Image by Shehuikexueyuan Kaoguyanjiusuo.

Figure 2.1b. Fu Hao inscription. From Yanjiusuo, *Yinxu Fu-Hao Mu* 殷墟妇好墓 (Beijing: Wen-wu chu-ban-she, 1980), figure 23.

Generally, as mentioned earlier, *Fu* is a pictograph consisting of a woman 女 and a broom 帚, a composition that is still in use today. As an individual character, *Fu* is usually joined by other characters to form a name, as in "Fu-someone." Such inscriptions on bronzes or oracle bones are considered to be the names of women of a relatively high social class.

Comparing the Shapes of the Broom and *Ge* Dagger Inscriptions

Why does the *Fu* character (a noble lady) comprise the combination of a woman and a broom? It could be understood that sweeping was an important task for women. However, why should sweeping be associated with a high-ranked woman? After all, sweeping is, and probably was, generally considered to be menial work, and it is unlikely that high-status women such as Fu Hao undertook sweeping as a daily chore. An analysis of the elements of the *Fu* inscription and of certain artifacts unearthed from the Yinxu site may enable us to solve this question by revealing the roles played by *Fu* during the Shang dynasty.

As mentioned, several variations of *Zhou* 帚 are inscribed on the Fu Hao bronze vessels. Each *Fu* inscription, which is believed to represent a broom, generally has three or four carved lines on the top of the shaft. On the other end of the shaft are the following four variations (fig. 2.2):

1. no addition
2. a short horizontal bar
3. a fork
4. a fork and an H-shaped bar

Of the brooms with one end shaped like a fork, the fourth variation (a fork and an H-shaped bar) is considered to be the most faithful depiction of how the *Fu* appeared; the *Fu* inscription with a fork and an H-shaped bar attached to its middle part and the broom that appears to lean against the rack.[5] This pattern appears to be the most sophisticated and complete, realistically reflecting how the broom appeared to Shang women. The other three patterns are simplified versions.

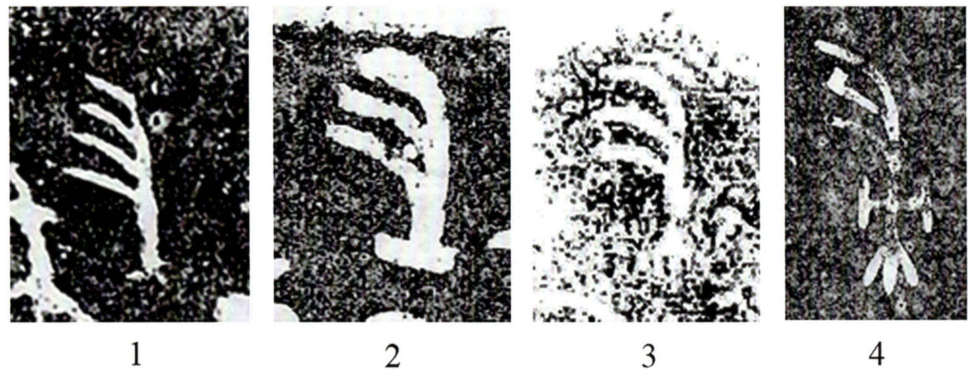

Figure 2.2. Four variations of *Fu* inscription from *Yin-xu Fu-hao Mu*, located at the Museum of Asiatic Art, State Museum, Amsterdam. From Minao Hayashi, *Inshu Jidai Seidouki No Kenkyu* 殷周時代青銅器の研究 (図版編) (Tokyo: Yoshikawa Koubunkan, 1986), 83.

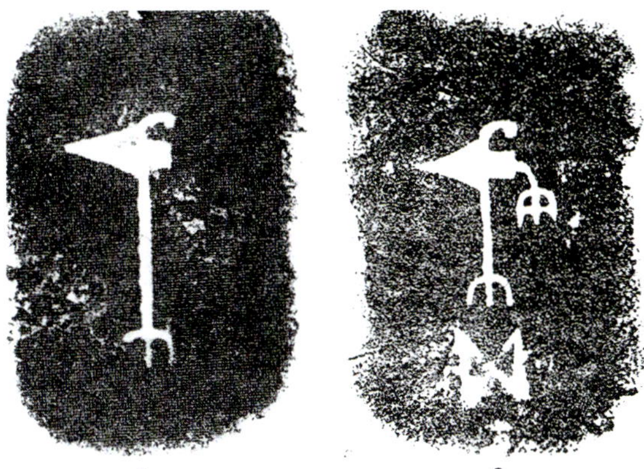

Figure 2.3. *Ge* 戈 inscription of Shang—Zhou dynasty. In the first image, the end of the shaft is attached to a fork-shaped fixture. In the second image, the decoration attached to the backside of the dagger is a tassel, different from the "fork." From Zhen-yu Luo 羅振玉, *Sandai Jijin Wencun*三代吉金文存 (Beijing: Zhonghua Shuqu中華書局, 1936; repr. 1983), vol. 6.

To further investigate the significance of the H-shaped bar in the *Fu* character, I will now study *Ge* daggers. *Ge* daggers are often excavated from Shang tombs, and they were common weapons during the Shang dynasty. They were made from jade during the Neolithic period, but the bronze *Ge* became common during the Erlitou 二里頭 (possibly Xia 夏 dynasty) period.[6] The overall shape resembles a sickle, and it is usually attached to a long shaft at a right angle. Figure 2.3 is an example of the inscription of the character *Ge* on the *You* vessel unearthed from Gaojiabao tomb 1 and there are similar instances in many other inscriptions (see fig. 2.3).[7] A fork-shaped fixture is attached to the tip of the shaft in the many inscriptions of *Ge* during the Shang and Zhou 周 (BCE 1046–771) dynasties.

To our modern thinking, it seems strange that the similarly shaped forklike part is fitted to the tip of both the broom for a domestic chore (i.e., cleaning) and the *Ge*, one of the most advanced weapon types of the era. However, it suggests that the broom and the *Ge* dagger are handled in a similar manner, with the fork-shaped component functioning similarly for the different tools. I argue that this similarity gives us an important clue with which to reconstruct the social positions and roles occupied and played by their user-owners.

The Fork-Shaped Component and Its Significance

What exactly is the purpose of the fork-shaped part attached to the end portion of the dagger shaft? One of the curious-looking bronze objects unearthed from tomb 5 of Fu Hao's grave is a bronze "hand" (M5: 847). Measuring 13.8 cm in height, the hand has four fingers and is socketed (see fig. 2.4a). Its surface is decorated with simple triangle patterns of recessed lines. The artifact is not part of a pair, and it was probably placed in the outer chamber of the Fu Hao tomb, together with magnificent bronze vessels and other grave goods. It may well have been Fu Hao's personal belonging, because those bronze vessels were for her own use. In that regard, the artifact may seem a little peculiar, because it is not as beautiful and sophisticated as other bronze items placed around it.

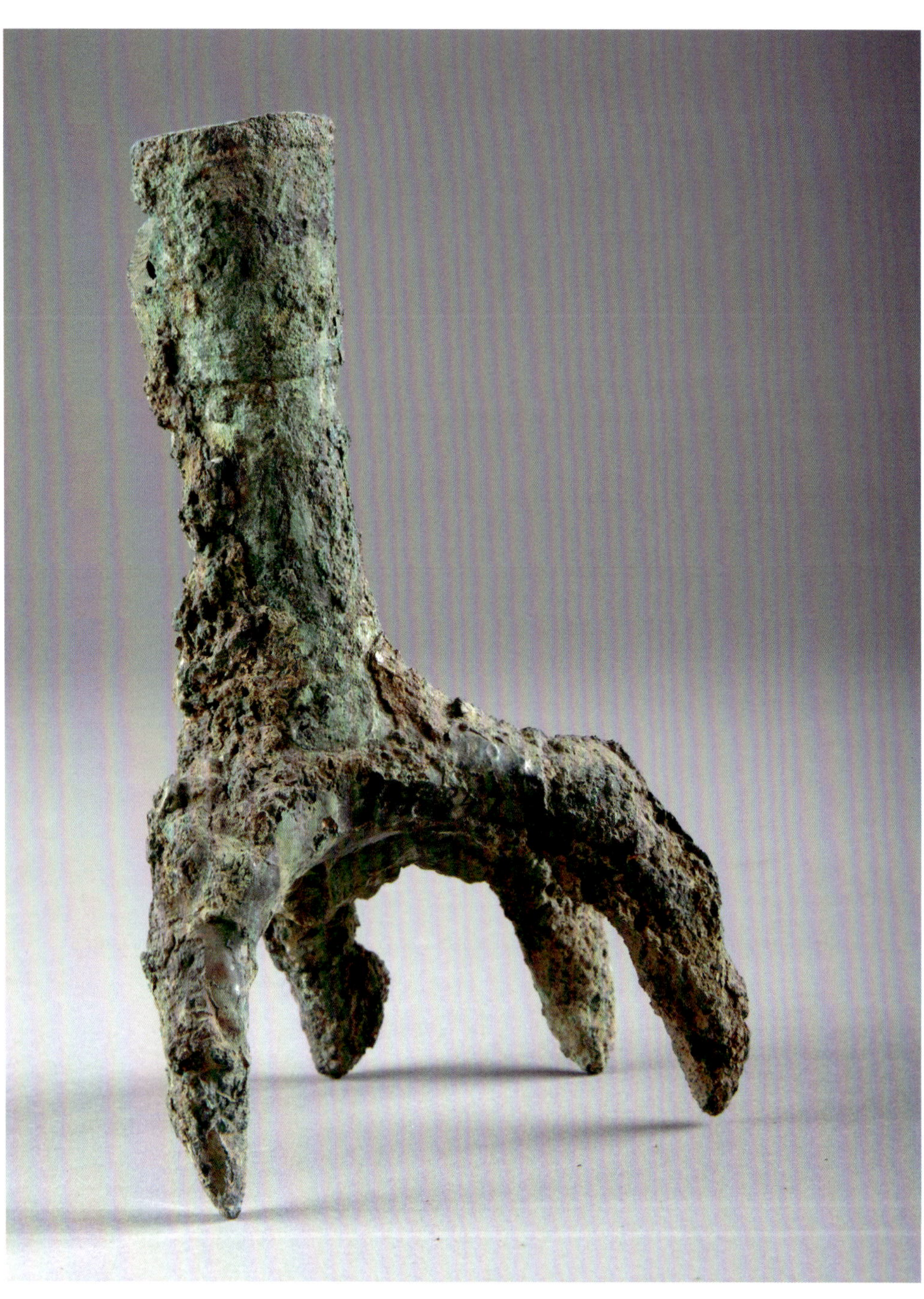

Figure 2.4a. Bronze "hand" from the Fu-hao grave. The bronze hand from the Fu-hao grave looks very similar to the feet of the *Zun* vessel. Image by Shehuikexueyuan Kaoguyanjiusuo.

The bronze hand looks more like a bird's foot than a human hand because the thumb is attached across from the other three fingers. In addition, it appears very similar to the feet of the bird-shaped *Zun* 尊 vessel (see figs. 2.4b, 2.4c) unearthed from HPKM1885 (a small grave beside the HPKM1001 royal grave at the Xibeigang cemetery). The lid, which may have been shaped like a bird's head and possibly made from wood, was unfortunately lost when the vessel was excavated. Hayashi Minao 林巳奈夫 remarked that there are two main types of bird designs among ancient Chinese artifacts: the golden eagle and the owl. Both have hooklike beaks, representing the raptor. A similarly shaped

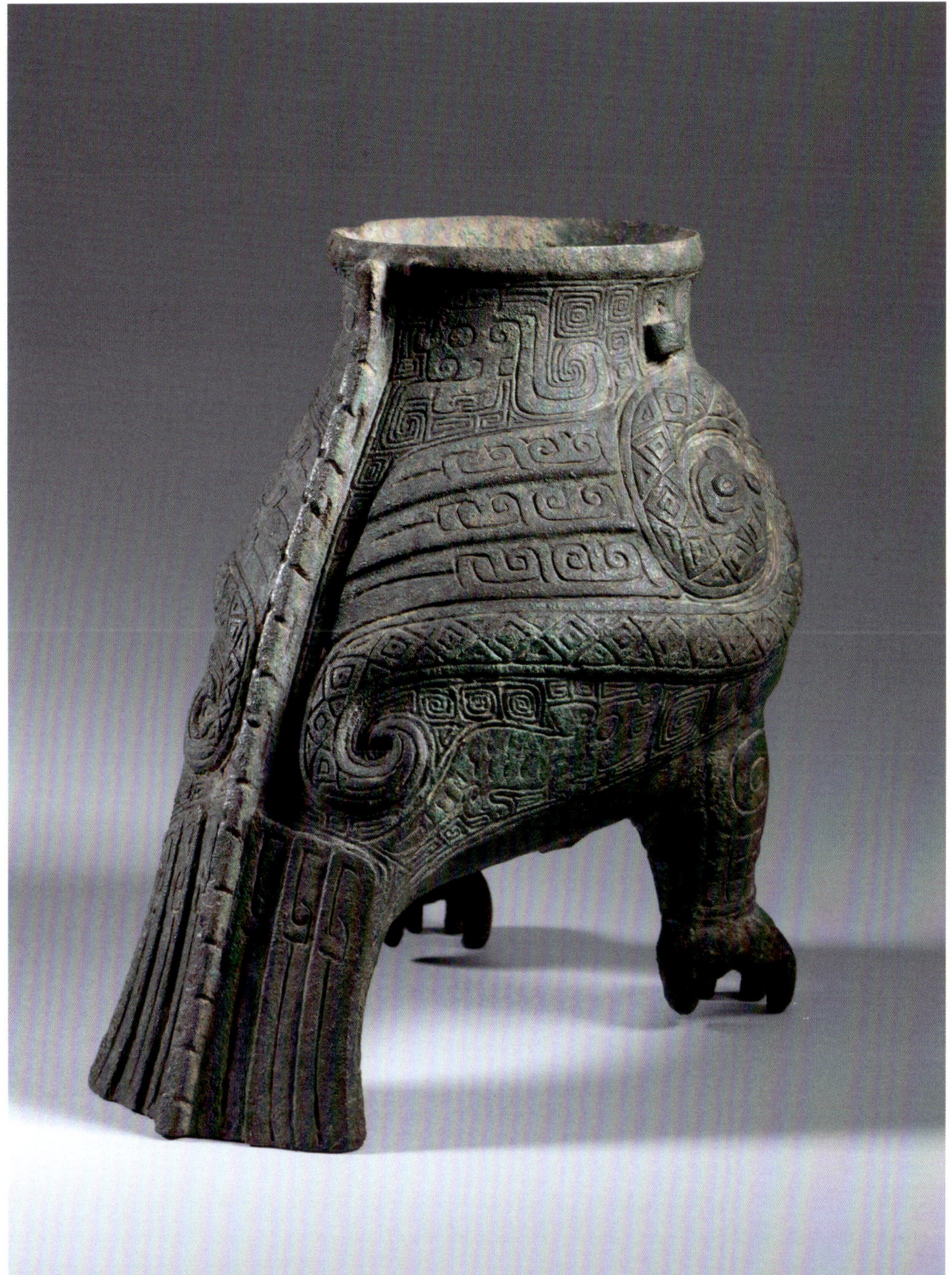

Figure 2.4b. Bronze eagle-shaped *Zun* vessel. The vessels (fig.2.4a and 2.4b) are very similar in shape and represent the golden eagle. Image courtesy of the Institute of History and Philology, Academia Sinica.

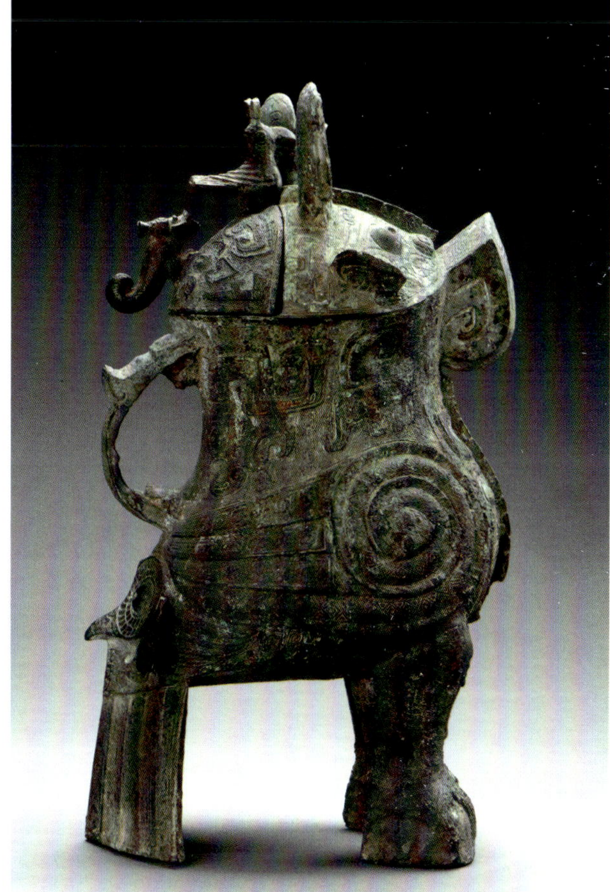

Figure 2.4c. Bronze eagle-shaped *Zun* vessel. The vessels (fig.2.4b and 2.4c) are very similar in shape and represent the golden eagle. Image by Shehuikexueyuan Kaoguyanjiusuo.

vessel (Tomb 5:784) from the Fu Hao grave has both an owl and an eagle design on the same vessel body.[8] The owl on the back of the vessel has only flight feathers, but on the main body there is an eagle that has a large whorl with a snake design at the base of its feathers. R001074 is contemporary with HPKM1001 (Yinxu Phase I), while the Fu Hao grave belongs to the early Yinxu Phase II, and chronologically the two graves are very close. Hayashi describes R001074 as an "owl-shaped *Zun*."[9] However, it is clear that it represents an eagle. The feet of this eagle-shaped *Zun* also have four digits, with the thumb placed across from the other three digits.

Another very similar object (M54:392) was discovered in tomb 54, the grave of a nobleman in the Huayuanzhuang 花园庄 cemetery, placed near the occupant's knee. This object is also shaped like a human hand, measuring 13 cm long and 5.6 cm wide, with five fingers. The patterns on the back of the hand resemble the hooked beak and feathers carved on bone spatulas from the Xibeigang royal tombs (see figs. 2.5a–2.5e). The recessed lines that cover the surface of the object are the result of bronze casting. These lines depict motifs that I interpret as eagle feathers.

Miao Xia 苗霞 compared the bronze hand with the fork cutlery Bi 畢 of the Warring States (戰國) period (475–221 BCE), and Xie Yinling 谢银玲 interpreted it as the top of a ceremonial stick.[10] In terms of shape, however, the bronze hands are quite different from the fork. In addition, there is a huge temporal gap between the items of Yinxu and the forks of later dynasties.

Comparison of the Yinxu bronze "hands" suggests that the human hand-shaped object from tomb 54 of the Huayuanzhuang cemetery evolved stylistically from the bird's-foot-shaped object from the Fu Hao tomb. According to the typochronology of the bronze

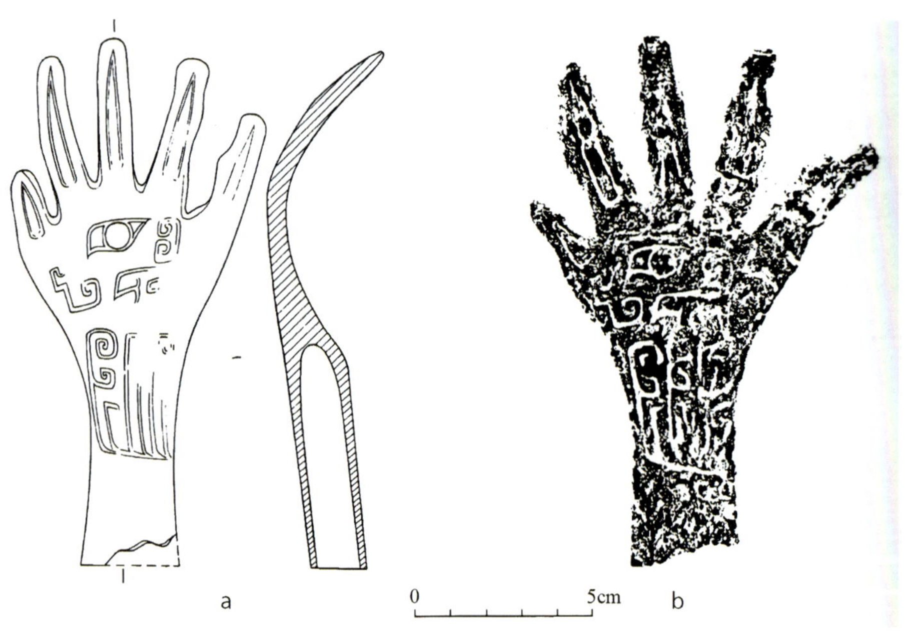

Figure 2.5a and b. Bronze "hand" (M54:392) from Hua-yuan-zhuang M54 (*a*: drawing, *b*: rubbing). Figure 2.5c. (*right*): photograph. This hand has five fingers and its shape is like that of a human hand, with a recessed eagle motif. Figure by Shehuikexueyuan Kaoguyanjiusuo.

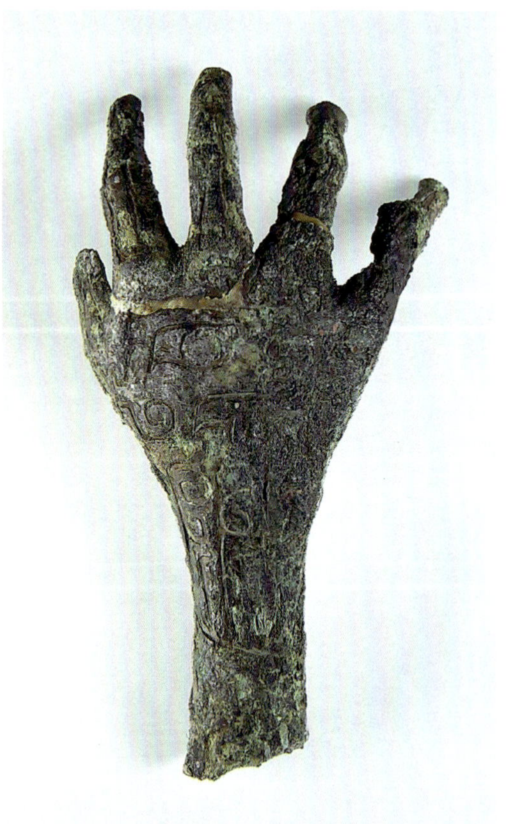

vessels, the Fu Hao grave (the first half of Yinxu Phase II) is dated earlier than tomb 54 (the second half of Yinxu Phase II), supporting this conclusion. Furthermore, there is a raptor pattern on the back of the hand-shaped object, which suggests the connection of the tomb 54 human hand-shaped object to the bird. (The similar "hand" shaped object from the Fu Hao tomb, as argued, is the foot of the bird.)

These hand-shaped objects are socketed, implying that the hands were attached to the ends of shafts and used as ferrules. This inference fits well with the fact that the hand-shaped object of tomb 54 was discovered near the right knee of the deceased and in an upside-down position.

Let us now look again at the broom shape of the *Fu* inscription. The fork-shaped end of the shafts in the inscriptions of the *Ge* dagger represent the ferrule attached to the tip of the shaft. We can thus infer that the broom has a shaft fitted with a hand-shaped ferrule and that the bronze bird's foot from the Fu Hao grave is actually a ferrule. It is therefore possible that the item to which the ferrule is attached functions as a broom in the Fu Hao grave.

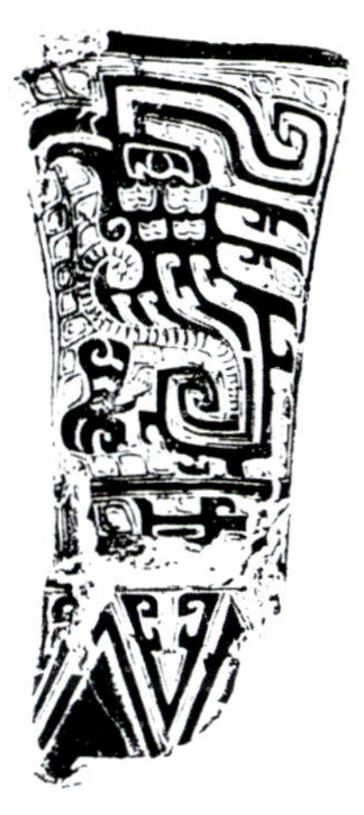

Figure 2.5d. Referring to the curved eagle on the bone spatula R007651 (*d*: rubbing) from HPKM1001 of Yinxu I, the parts of this motif are following the layout of the eagle pattern. Photograph © Institute of History and Philology, Academia Sinica.

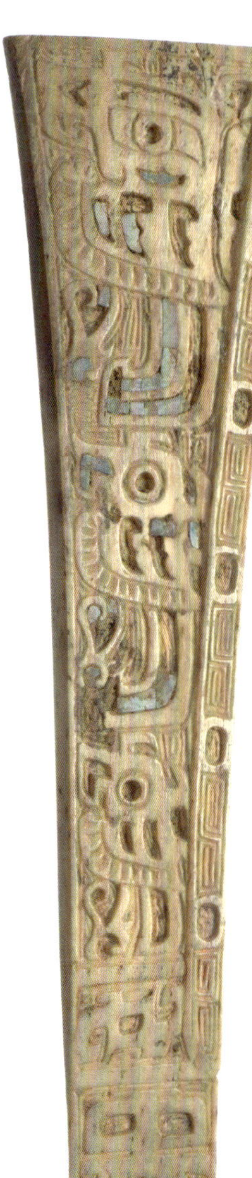

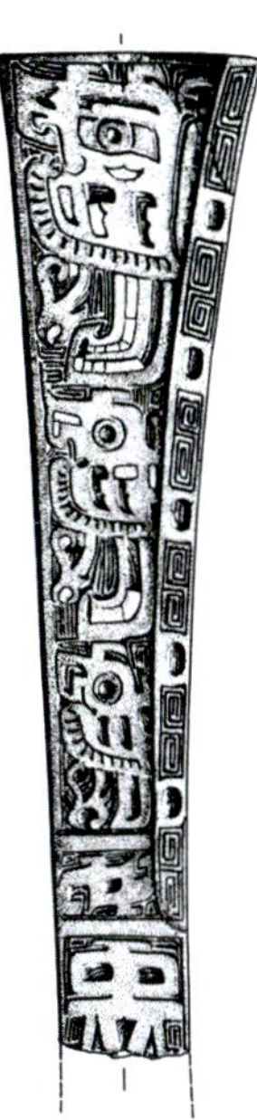

Figure 2.5e and 2.5f. Referring to the curved eagle on the bone spatula R018293 (*e*: photo, *f*: drawing) from HPKM1003 of Yinxu III, the parts of this motif are following the layout of the eagle pattern. Photographs © Institute of History and Philology, Academia Sinica.

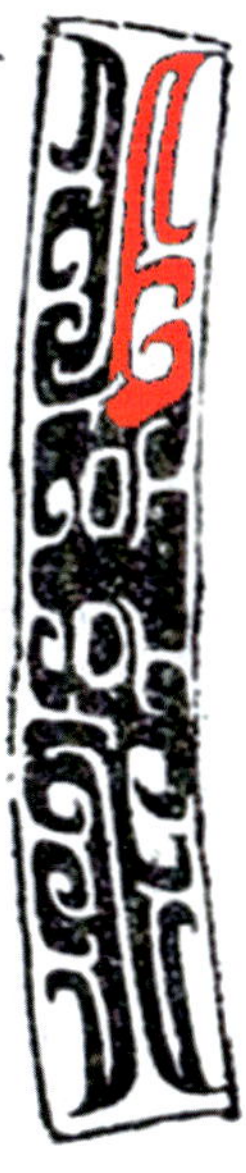

Figure 2.5g. The pattern of f-shaped feather originally appeared in the body of a Taotie design in the Er-li-gang period, on the Ding tripod unearthed from Min-gong-lu, Zheng-zhou, Henan prefecture. Photograph © Institute of History and Philology, Academia Sinica.

Ge as the Symbol for Royal Soldiers

Hayashi has remarked that the raptors with hooklike beaks appearing on many ancient Chinese artifacts symbolized the constellation of the fire bird Zhuniao 朱鳥 and served as the retainer of the Divine, a belief hailing back to the Hemudu 河姆渡 culture (5000–4500 BCE). In the early phase of the Erligang 二里岡 period (early Shang dynasty), bronze vessels were decorated with simpler Taotie 饕餮 patterns, and bird patterns were situated alongside the Taotie motif.[11] Before the Erligang period, the birds' eyes (probably those of eagles) are always sharp-cornered, whereas the eyes in Taotie patterns are not.[12] Sharp-cornered eyes are characteristic of raptors (see fig. 2.6), whereas the owl has circular eyes. Interestingly, in later dynasties the modern Chinese character *Chen* 臣, which means retainer of the royal court, was developed from the pictograph of the sharp-cornered eyes of raptors (fig. 2.7). The bird with eyes similar to those of an eagle was identified as a retainer of the Divine in the Shang dynasty.

Figure 2.6. Head of a golden eagle. Courtesy Machi Log website.

Now let us revisit the *Ge* daggers with a ferrule. In the Yinxu period, there were four main types of *Ge* daggers:

1. with a plane and rectangular head
2. with a plane and carved head
3. with a plane and bird-patterned head
4. with a tube-style socket

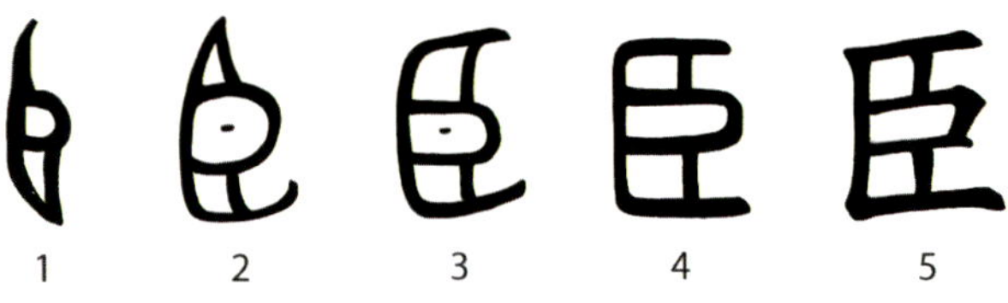

Figure 2.7. The transforming of the Chen 臣 fonts. Numbers 1 and 2: the inscription on the oracle bone; 3: the inscription on bronze, 4: the Xiao-zhuan小篆 font, 5: the Jie-shu 楷書 font. © Junko Uchida.

It is remarkable that the dominant type of *Ge* dagger is the third one, with a plane and bird-patterned head. To appreciate the significance of the bird-patterned dagger, we can consider who the dagger owners were. At the Yinxu site group, the bird-patterned daggers were excavated from the Xibeigang royal tombs and from the grave pits of lower-ranked individuals in lineage cemeteries such as Dasikong village 大司空村 and Xiaomintun 孝民屯 cemeteries, dating from Yinxu Phase I to Phase IV.

HPKM1001 is one of the large royal tombs in the Xibeigang royal cemetery, and I infer that it is the tomb of King Xiaoyi 小乙, based on the fact that the artifacts that escaped tomb robbing date from Yinxu Phase I.[13] The decoration of the *Ge* dagger from HPKM1001 (fig. 2.8) is inlaid with turquoise, and the bird clearly has a hooked beak and long, hairlike feathers with cornered eyes, representing a golden eagle. The entire body of the *Ge* (fig. 2.9, dagger 1) from the HPKM1550 royal tomb (Yinxu Phase II) is made of bronze, and the shape of the bird design is identical to that on the dagger from HPKM1001.[14]

Excavated in 2003–4 by the archaeological team of the Chinese Academy of Social Sciences, the Xiaomintun cemetery site covers an area of more than 60,000 square meters.[15] To date, 645 graves have been excavated. Investigations of the human bones unearthed from those graves have found that gender can be determined in 39 percent of the buried. In many of the graves of male occupants, a bronze *Ge* dagger decorated with a bird-patterned head was deposited (fig. 2.9, dagger 2–6).

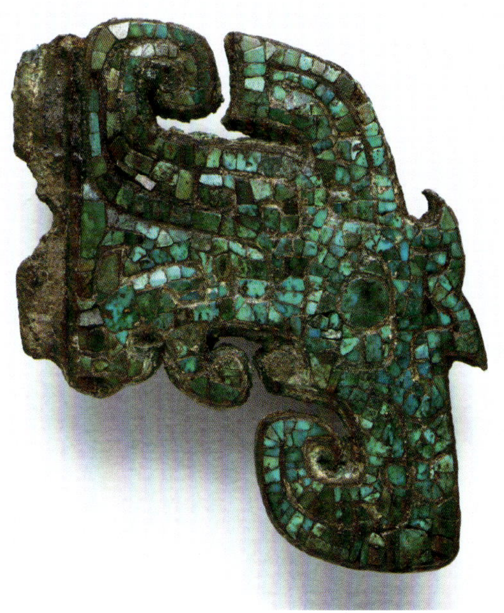

Figure 2.8. Bronze decoration of the *Ge* with inlaid turquoise, unearthed from HPKM1001 in Xibeigang royal cemetery, Anyang. Courtesy Institute of History and Philology, Academia Sinica.

According to Hayashi, the bird design frequently seen on the *Ge* could represent the golden eagle because of the long, hairlike feathers on the backs of their heads. Hayashi argued that bird decorations with the raptor head and long, hairlike feathers were created to protect the buried from evil.[16]

On many of the *Ge* daggers deposited with low-ranked males buried at the Xiaomintun cemetery, the depiction of this mighty bird of prey had undergone a stylistic change that some might describe as stylistic degeneration and deformation, to the point that the image was no longer recognizable as representing the raptor, as was so clear on the *Ge* daggers from the HPKM 1001 (see fig. 2.8) and HPKM1550 (see fig. 2.9, dagger 1) royal tombs. Overall, the *Ge* dagger with an eagle design represents the male member of that lineage living at Xiaomintun village, or a male member of the army stationed in Dayishang. Such a dagger could have been an essential item for men, regardless of its practical value. And, as mentioned earlier, the form of the inscribed character suggests that such daggers may originally have been fitted with a ferrule shaped like a bird's foot.

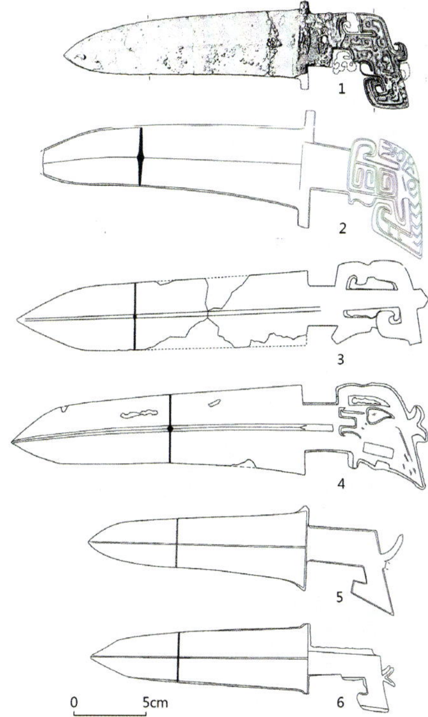

Figure 2.9. *Ge* dagger with a bird-patterned head from Anyang Yinxu site. Illustrations 2–6 are obviously simplified and not practical arms, unearthed from Xiaomintun cemetery. Image 1: Courtesy Institute of History and Philology, Academia Sinica; 2–6: From the Shehuikexueyuan kaoguyanjiusuo Anyang excavation team. From Yanjiusuo 中国社会科学院考古研究所編, Zhongguo Shehui Kexueyuan Kaogu, *Anyang Xiaomintun* 安阳孝民屯 [Late Shang burials, vol. IV] (Beijing: Wen-wu chu-ban-she, 2017).

The Bird and the Broom

Why and how was the broom related to the bird's foot? The old Japanese term *Ha-ha-ki* (羽はき) denotes a broom made from bird feathers. Figure 2.10 shows a broom used at a cocoonery (a site for raising silkworms) in the premodern period, now held as an ethnological object at Minokamo 美濃加茂 City Museum, Gifu prefecture, Japan. This broom is made from feathers that are bundled and attached to a short shaft. It was used to gather incubated worms at the initial stage of growth. The broom is also reminiscent of a small broom made from very soft and delicate bird feathers used for a Japanese tea ceremony,

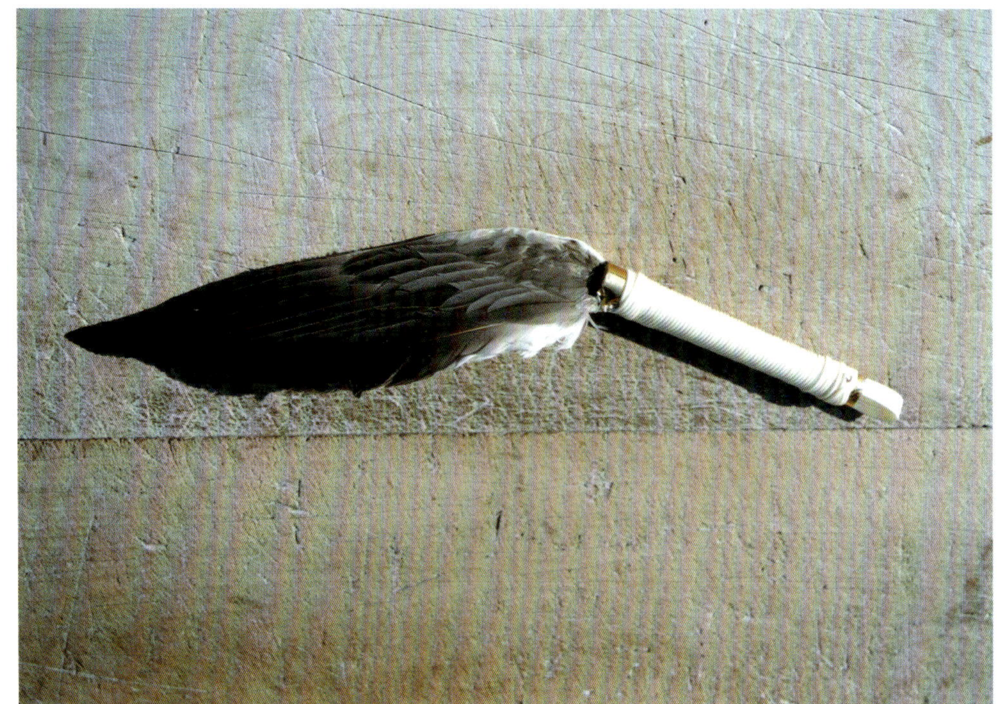

Figure 2.10. A broom made from bird feathers, used for gathering silkworms. Image courtesy of Minokamo City Museum, Gifu prefecture, Japan.

or a broom used for dusting in houses or cars. Brooms today are typically made of plants or plastic and other artificial materials. However, based on the etymology, we can infer that brooms in the premodern period were originally made from bird feathers. As to why the broom is fitted with a ferrule shaped like a bird's foot, it seems probable that the brush of the broom in China was also made of bird feathers and the entire broom was made to resemble a bird (fig. 2.11).

The examples of *Ge* and the broom, as their contexts show, seem to follow a gender-specific rule in that the bird/eagle-shaped broom (an example from the Fu Hao tomb) is a female possession, and the bird/eagle-shaped *Ge* dagger (an example from tomb 54 of the Huayuanzhuang cemetery) is a male possession. This rule also indicates that both men and women are faithful attendants to the kings, or to the Divine, who appeared in the shape of birds, as the above investigation demonstrates.

The broom, when used as an important female tool, is fitted with a shaft, and a bird-footed ferrule is attached to the shaft's tip. The feather brooms and *Ge* daggers, particularly those with the eagle design, are not daily-use objects but important instruments representing the gender and social status of their users, and the rack on the inscription

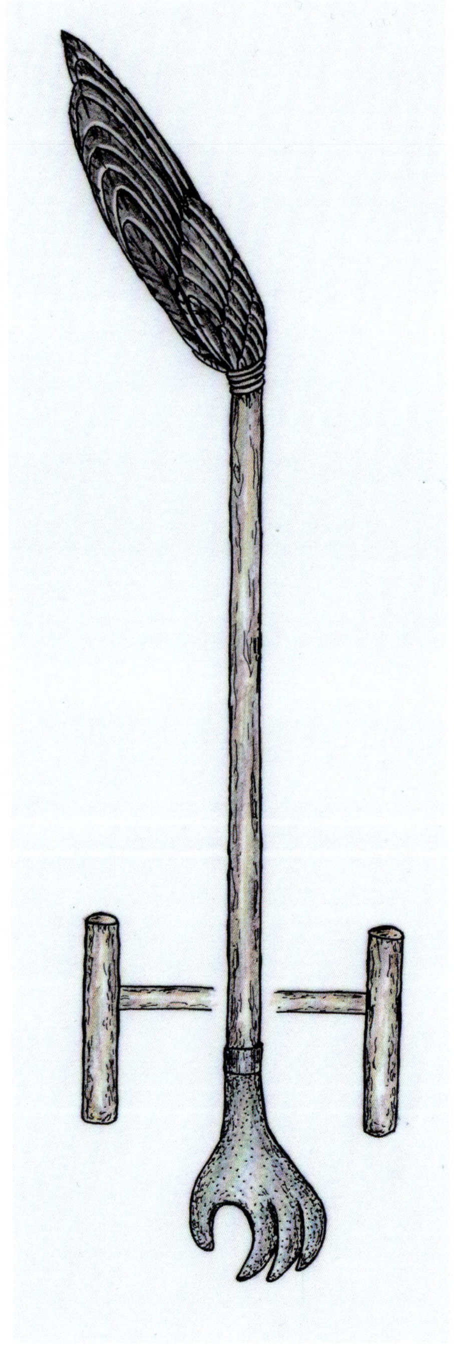

Figure 2.11. The restored image of the broom for high-class lady of Shang dynasty. © Junko Uchida and Weihui Zhu.

indicates the objects' importance and preciousness in that the broom attached to shafts would have leaned over to the rack, indicating the social identity/status of the owners.

The Relationship between the Broom and Women in the Classics

Women and brooms seem inextricably linked, and their relationship is apparent in the literature of later dynastic periods. We can refer to such literature to further enrich our understanding of the *Fu* character and broaden our appreciation of the gendered roles assumed by women. The following maxims are a few examples:

> 少康初作箕箒
> Shao Kang made a broom and a dustpan.[17]
>
> 從女持帚。灑掃也。
> Ladies should sweep and dust.[18]
>
> 一介嫡女願執箕箒，(以晐姓)于王宮
> A girl takes a broom and a dustpan to sweep the palace.[19]
>
> 婦人持箕箒為家事
> A lady should use a dustpan and a broom to take care of housecleaning.[20]

Texts throughout the Warring States period and later dictate that using a broom for household cleaning purposes is important work for women. However, there is evidence that the broom was also used for other, non-daily purposes. According to Shirakawa Shizuka 白川静, the broom held by a lady is not a common broom, but a sacred object used in conjunction with sacred liquor to purify the ancestral shrine.[21] This interpretation, however, is influenced by the above character in the *Shiben* (*Book of Origins*). In reference to the *Huainanzi* 淮南子 (The Writings of the Huainan Masters) of the Eastern Han dynasty, there is a commentary on the seemingly ordinary household object in *Taiping Yulan*太平御覽 (Imperial Reader), edited by Emperor Taizong 太宗 (939–997 CE; r. 976–997 CE) of the Song 宋 dynasty (960–1279).

> 周鼎不爨而不可賤，帚日用而不足貴。[22]
> Although the *Ding* tripod of the Zhou dynasty is no longer used as a cooker, it should not be considered worthless. The broom is used daily; however, this does not necessarily warrant reverence.

In some texts dated earlier than the *Huainanzi*, household brooms seem to be respected, which does not contradict my inference that the broom represented women.

Then how did the broom image evolve in subsequent dynasties? The following cases involving feather brooms offer more insight.

Case 1: Feather Fans Possessed by Waiting Maids in High Society

Japanese feather brooms are reminiscent of the feather fans depicted in paintings of the Ming 明 dynasty (1368–1644) (figs. 2.12, 2.13). The feather fan is held by a female attendant and used not only to create an airflow but also to fend off insects or prevent evil spirits from making physical contact with the empress.

Depictions of the feather fans held by attendants may even date back to the Warring States period: the curved picture on the bronze piece unearthed from Liuheqiao 六和橋 in Jiangsu province also shows there was a long shaft fan (probably made from feathers) held by an attendant beside the person of high class (fig. 2.14). The origin of the feather fans and feather brooms of later periods, even those from the Edo period (1603–1868) in Japan, can thus be traced back to the Shang dynasty feather broom.

Figure 2.12. A feather fan seen in this image of attendants beside an empress. The second girl on the far left has the fan made from white feathers. *Xiao kang-jing Huang-hou Zhang-shi shou-lu tu* 孝康敬皇后張氏授籙圖 © San Diego Museum of Art / Gift of Mr. and Mrs. John Jeffers / Bridgeman Images.

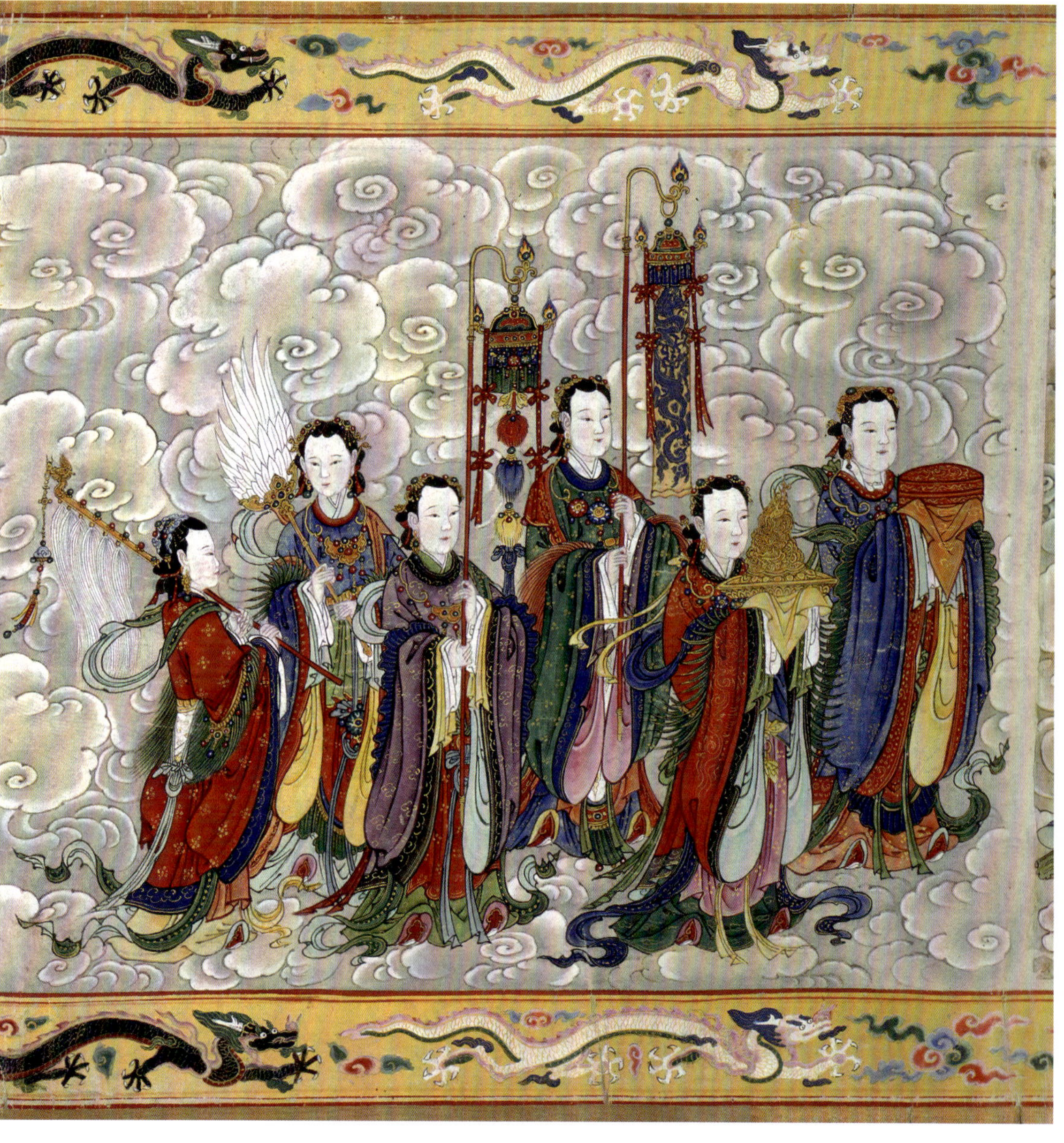

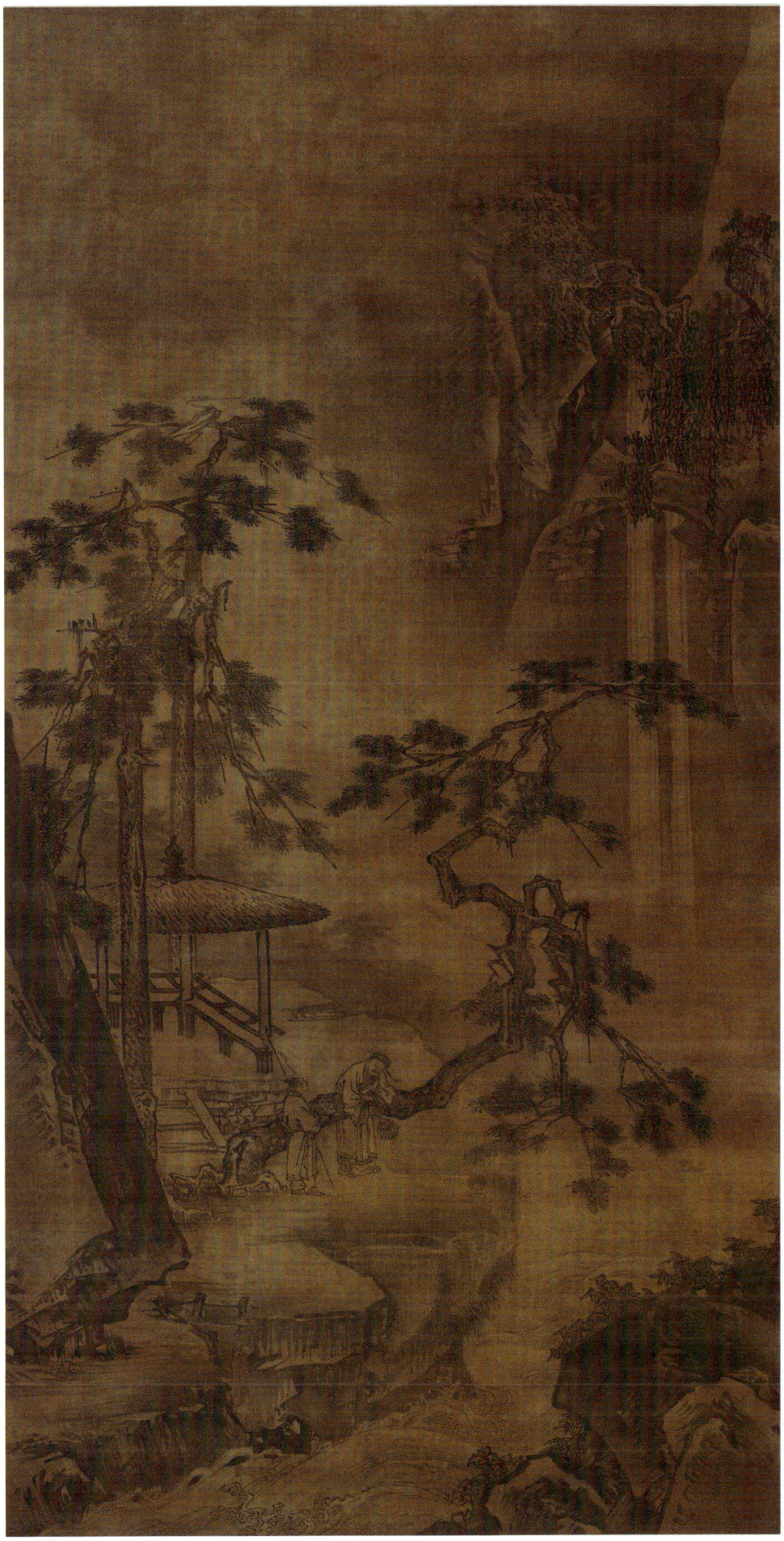

Figure 2.13. Dai Jin 戴進 *"Fu song guan pu"* 撫松觀瀑. A scholar, holding a feather fan in his hand, watches the waterfall while leaning on an old pine tree in the mountains. Although there is no artist's mark, the style is similar to that of Dai Jin or his disciples. Collection National Palace Museum, Taipei.

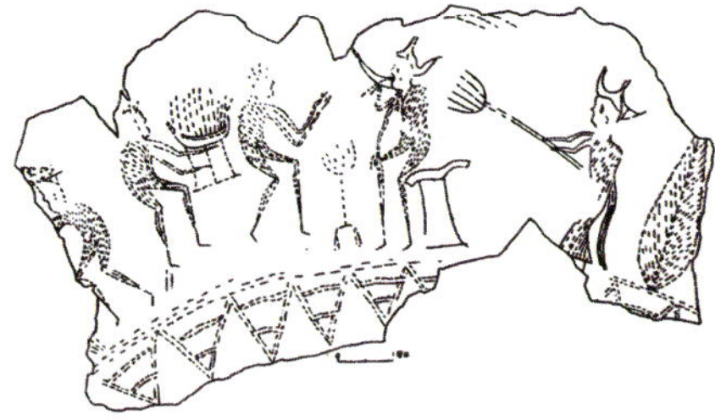

Figure 2.14. The curved picture on a bronze piece unearthed from Liuheqiao 六和橋, Jiang-su prefecture (Spring and Autumn period, 770–476 BCE). The figure sitting on the chair is a nobleman and another figure wearing a skirt holds a broom-like object.

Case 2: Feather Fans Possessed by Generals

Feather fans were used by military strategists such as Zhuge Liang (諸葛亮, 181–234 CE) of the Shu 蜀 Kingdom in the third century CE. Legend has it that the strategist's feather fan blew felicitous winds toward the army, dispelling evil spirits. Figure 2.15 is an illustration of a strategist fan illustrated with Emperor Sun Quan (孫權, 182–252; r. 229–252 CE) of the Wu 吳 kingdom in the Three Kingdoms period (三國時代, 220–280 CE).

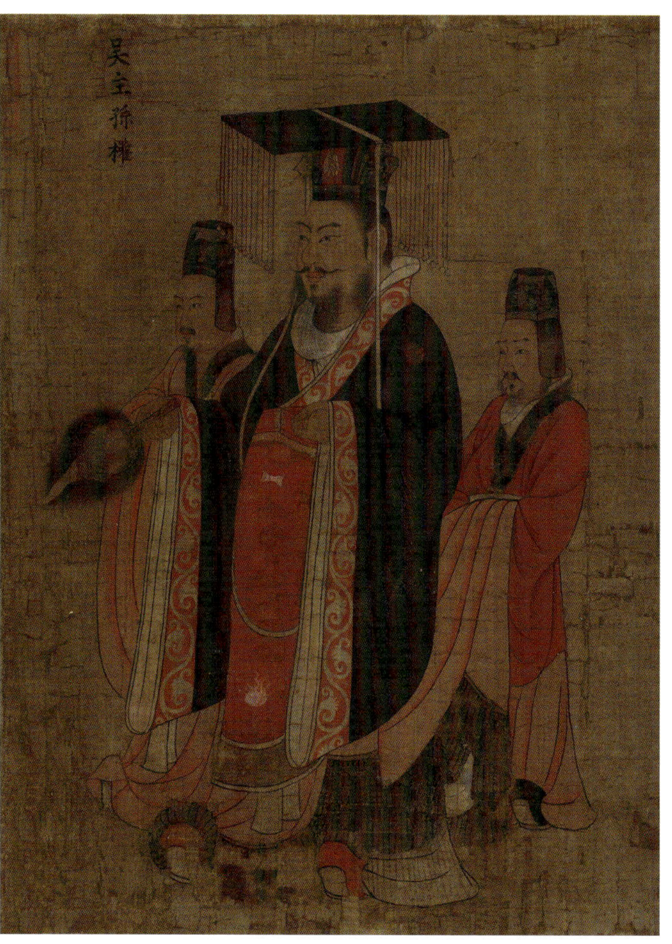

Figure 2.15. The painting of Emperor Sun Quan in Wu country. Sun Quan has a fan made from feathers—such a fan was used by strategists in ancient China. *The Thirteen Emperors* (detail), attributed to Yan Liben, c. 600–673. Ink and color on silk, Denman Waldo Ross Collection (31.643). Photograph © Museum of Fine Arts Boston, 2023.

Conclusion: Brooms and Women's Roles

Looking back at prehistoric times, humans were predominantly occupied by foraging for food and cooking, keeping themselves warm (shelter building and cloth making), and keeping themselves and their immediate environs clean. As society became increasingly complex and stratified, the gender-based division of labor was intensified and formalized. After the so-called urban revolution that witnessed the emergence of the mega urban center and the establishment of theocratic ruling systems, the gender-based division of labor became a formalized social order, represented by the symbolic material items used by ruling-class individuals.

The residents of Dayishang were almost completely reliant on the surrounding farming villages and the domains controlled by the ruling class for the supply of food and other vital resources for the sustenance of their inhabitants, and these areas were at times located quite far away. The fact that no trace of farming plots has been discovered inside the Anyang Yinxu site group, but instead a number of bronze-working, bone-working, and other sites of specialized production have been excavated, supports the supposition that Dayishang was indeed one of the first examples of such urbanized cities in the history of China. There is substantial evidence that specialized tasks such as divination, administration, soldiering, and bone- and metal-working were undertaken almost exclusively by men in Dayishang. Women were confined to activities relating to biological reproduction and caring for children, leading to their being increasingly relegated to domestic activities including childcare. This tendency would have been amplified by the increasing specialization of male labor such as the examples at Dayishang. Men became increasingly liberated from a range of subsistence activities that had been undertaken by both genders in pre-urbanized societies, and with child-rearing now mostly undertaken by women, the specialization of technology and its associated knowledge and skill sharing was increasingly undertaken exclusively by men. Within elite households, this trend led to the formation of an ideological social norm of men working outside the household, or in public settings, and women working inside the household, or in domestic settings. The establishment of these trends was significantly accelerated by urbanization.[23]

In this essay, I argued that the broom was originally styled to resemble a bird and was used by women to serve the king or the Divine. According to the description in the *Huainanzi*, the broom somehow fell from this sacred usage and became a common cleaning tool during the last years of the Warring States period.

As this process progressed, feather brooms became a uniquely symbolic possession of the aristocratic lady, who served as a royal retainer and protected the king from evil spirits. Subsequently, feather brooms became a symbol of women. Feather brooms later evolved into fans and were used by military strategists, as well as by aristocratic women. At the same time in Dayishang, the progression of urbanization appears to have increasingly confined women to domestic spheres, and the daily broom was used by common women as an ordinary household cleaning tool; the broom doubtless therefore came to be seen as a symbol of more common women.

The *Fu* inscription and the eagle-footed object unearthed from the Fu Hao tomb offer a glimpse into Shang-era women's social status. During the Shang dynasty, the female gender appears already to have tended to be fixed to the domestic spheres of the social world (although, as Fu Hao herself is recorded to have been, female elites were occasionally involved in such "manly" acts as military campaigns). That tendency continues in the twenty-first century, as we use the character *Fu* without noticing that it embodies the connection between the female gender and domesticity, which became symbolically captured in the form of the Chinese character so long ago. And the hurdles faced by women thousands of years ago to some extent continue to be experienced by women of today.

Notes

1. Li Chi 李濟, *Anyang* (Seattle: University of Washington Press, 1977), 79–82.

2. Yanjiusuo 中国社会科学院考古研究所编, *Zhongguo Shehui Kexueyuan Kaogu, Anyang Xiaomintun* 安阳孝民屯 [Late Shang burials, vol. IV] (Beijing: Wen-wu chu-ban-she, 2017), 1–3.

3. Some scholars speculate that Xibeigang HPKM1001 must be Wu Ding's tomb due to its temporal proximity to the Fu Hao burial goods discovered in the Xiaotun Palace zone, but I believe that Wu Ding's grave is tomb 1400, and 84AWBM260, which is situated directly in line with the southern ramp of HPKM1400, and in which the Simuwu 司母戊 (or Houmuwu后母戊) ding tripod was discovered. See S. Liang and Q. Gao梁思永、高去尋, *Houjiazhuang Di Er Ben, 1001 Hao Da Mu*侯家莊第一本 *1001*號大墓. (Taipei: Academia Sinica, 1962). The inscription "Mu (mother) Wu" is thought to be King Wu Ding's queen consort, Bi Wu妣戊, indicating that this is Queen Bi Wu's grave. See Koji Mizoguchi and Junko Uchida, "The Anyang Xibeigang Shang Royal Tombs Revisited: A Social Archaeological Approach," *Antiquity* 92, no. 363 (2018): 709–23, https://doi.org/10.15184/aqy.2018.19.

4. Minao Hiyashi 林巳奈夫, "In Chuki Ni Yurai Suru Kishin" 殷中期に由来する鬼神, *Touhou Gakuhou Kyoto*東方学報京都 1, no. 40 (1970): 1.

5. Luo Zhenyu 羅振玉also noted that the *H* shape should be a rack of a broom.

6. Xia is the name of the earliest dynasty referenced in the classics. Archaeologists now believe Erlitou culture predated that of the Shang dynasty. Therefore, it can be argued that Erlitou culture coincided with the Xia dynasty. However, it is currently unclear whether the Xia dynasty is legend or fact.

7. Yanjiusuo, *Zhongguo Shehui Kexueyuan Kaogu*, 27.

8. Although the shape of the front of the lid and beak are different, the shape of the body is very similar.

9. Minao Hayashi, "Shishin No Hitotsu Shuchou Ni Tuite" 四神の一、朱鳥について, *Shirin*史林 77, no. 6 (1994): 1–2.

10. See Xia Miao苗霞, "Yinxu Huayuanzhuang Dongdi 54haomu Chutu Qingtong Shouxingqi Yongtu Kao" 殷墟花园庄东地54号墓出土青铜手形器用途考, *Zhongguo Wenwu bao* 中国文物报, July 30, 2007; Yin-ling Xie谢银玲, "Huayuanzhuang Dongdi M54tongshou-Qi Kaoshi" 花园庄东地m54铜手形器考释, *Sandai Kaogu* 4 (2012): 290–304.

11. See Hayashi, "In Chuki Ni Yurai Suru Kishin," 12–17, 51–52; and "Shishin No Hitotsu Shuchou Ni Tuite四神の一、朱鳥について," *Shirin*史林 77, no. 6 (1994): 133–37.

12. Hayashi argued that there are two types of gods' eyes in Neolithic jade items in southern China: egg-shaped and sharp-cornered. Minao Hayashi, *Chugoku Kogyoku No Kenkyu* 中国古玉の研究 (Tokyo: Yoshikawa Koubunkan, 1991), 300–305.

13. Mizoguchi and Uchida, "Anyang Xibeigang Shang Royal Tombs Revisited," 4–11.

14. Liang and Gao, *Houjiazhuang Di Er Ben*, 319.

15. Yanjiusuo, *Zhongguo Shehui Kexueyuan Kaogu*, 7–11.

16. Hayashi, "Shishin No Hitotsu Shuchou Ni Tuite," 131–37.

17. Shao Kang was the sixth king of the Xia dynasty and is said to have been the first person to brew liquor. See *Shiben* [Book of origins], encyclopedia from the Spring and Autumn period, http://www.chinaknowledge.de/Literature/Historiography/shiben.html.

18. *Shuowen Jiezi* [Discussing writing and explaining characters], dictionary from Han dynasty. See http://www.chinaknowledge.de/Literature/Science/shuowenjiezi.html.

19. From *Guoyu* [Discourses of the states], collection of writings from Spring and Autumn period. See http://www.chinaknowledge.de/Literature/Historiography/guoyu.html.

20. "Eminent Females: Yang Qing qi Wangshi chuan," vol. 193 of the *Jiu Tangshu* [Old history of Tang], http://www.chinaknowledge.de/Literature/Historiography/jiutangshu.html.

21. Shizuka Shirakawa 白川静, *Ji-Tou*字統. (Tokyo: Hei-bon-sha, 1984), 543.

22. Emperor TaiZong 太宗 Taiping Yulan 太平御覽 (Imperial Reader) Department of crafts no.10 器物部十

23. Junko Uchida内田純子, "Chengshi-Hua Yu Xingbie-Hua Shehui—Yi Yinxu Wei Li" 城市化與性別化社會—以殷墟爲例, *Fuyanzongheng*婦研縱橫 1, no. 112 (2020): 10–21; Junko Uchida, "Gender Structure and Its Transformation in Pre-Qin China," *Journal of Japanese Archaeology* 10, no. 1 (2023): 3–34.

Bibliography

Hayashi, Minao 林巳奈夫. *Chugoku Kogyoku No Kenkyu* 中国古玉の研究. Tokyo: Yoshikawa Koubunkan, 1991.

———. "In Chuki Ni Yurai Suru Kishin" 殷中期に由来する鬼神. *Touhou Gakuhou Kyoto* 東方学報京都 1, no. 40 (1970): 1–70.

———. "Inshu Jidai Seidouki No Kenkyu" 殷周時代青銅器の研究(図版編). Tokyo: Yoshikawa Koubunkan, 1986.

———. "Shishin No Hitotsu Shuchou Ni Tuite" 四神の一、朱鳥について. *Shirin* 史林 77, no. 6 (1994): 125–44.

Imai, Kouki 今井晃樹. "Indai Seidou Buki No Hennen to Sono Seikaku" 殷代青銅武器の編年とその性格. *Koukogaku Zasshi* 85, no. 3 (2000): 59–82.

Li, Chi 李濟. *Anyang*. Seattle: University of Washington Press, 1977.

Liang, S., and Q. Gao 梁思永、高去尋. *Houjiazhuang Di Er Ben, 1001 Hao Da Mu* 侯家莊第一本 1001號大墓. Taipei: Academia Sinica, 1962.

———. *Houjiazhuang Di Er Ben, 1550 Hao Da Mu* 侯家莊第二本 1550號大墓. Taipei: Academia Sinica, 1976.

Luo, Zhenyu 羅振玉. *Sandai Jijin Wencun* 三代吉金文存. Beijing: Zhonghua Shuqu 中華書, 1934. Reprint, Shangwu: Bai-jue-qi 上虞百爵齋, 1983.

———. *Yinxu Shuqi Kaoshi* 殷虛書契考釋. N.p.: Yong-mu-yuan 永慕園, 1914.

Miao, Xia 苗霞. "Yinxu Huayuanzhuang Dongdi 54haomu Chutu Qingtong Shouxingqi Yongtu Kao" 殷墟花园庄东地54号墓出土青铜手形器用途考. *Zhongguo Wenwu bao* 中国文物报, July 30, 2007.

Mizoguchi, Koji, and Junko Uchida. "The Anyang Xibeigang Shang Royal Tombs Revisited: A Social Archaeological Approach." *Antiquity* 92, no. 363 (2018): 709–23. https://doi.org/10.15184/aqy.2018.19.

Shirakawa, Shizuka 白川静. *Ji-Tou* 字統. Tokyo: Hei-bon-sha, 1984.

Uchida, Junko 内田純子. "Chengshi-Hua Yu Xingbie-Hua Shehui—Yi Yinxu Wei Li" 城市化與性別化社會—以殷墟爲例. *Fuyanzongheng* 婦研縱橫 1, no. 112 (2020): 10–21.

———. "Gender Structure and Its Transformation in Pre-Qin China." *Journal of Japanese Archaeology*, 10, no. 1 (2023): 3–34.

Xie, Yinling 谢银玲. "Huayuanzhuang Dongdi M54tongshou-Qi Kaoshi" 花园庄东地m54铜手形器考释. In *Sandai Kaogu*, 290–304. Shanghai: Kexue chubanshe, 2012.

Yanjiusuo 中国社会科学院考古研究所编. *Anyang Yinxu Huayuanzhuang Dongdi Shangdai Muzang* 安阳殷墟花园庄东地商代墓葬. Beijing: Ke-xue chu-ban-she, 2007.

———. *Yinxu Fu-Hao Mu* 殷墟妇好墓. Beijing: Wen-wu chu-ban-she, 1980.

———. *Zhongguo Shehui Kexueyuan Kaogu, Anyang Xiaomintun* 安阳孝民屯 [Late Shang burials, vol. IV]. Beijing: Wen-wu chu-ban-she, 2017.

PART 2

Pioneers and Trailblazers

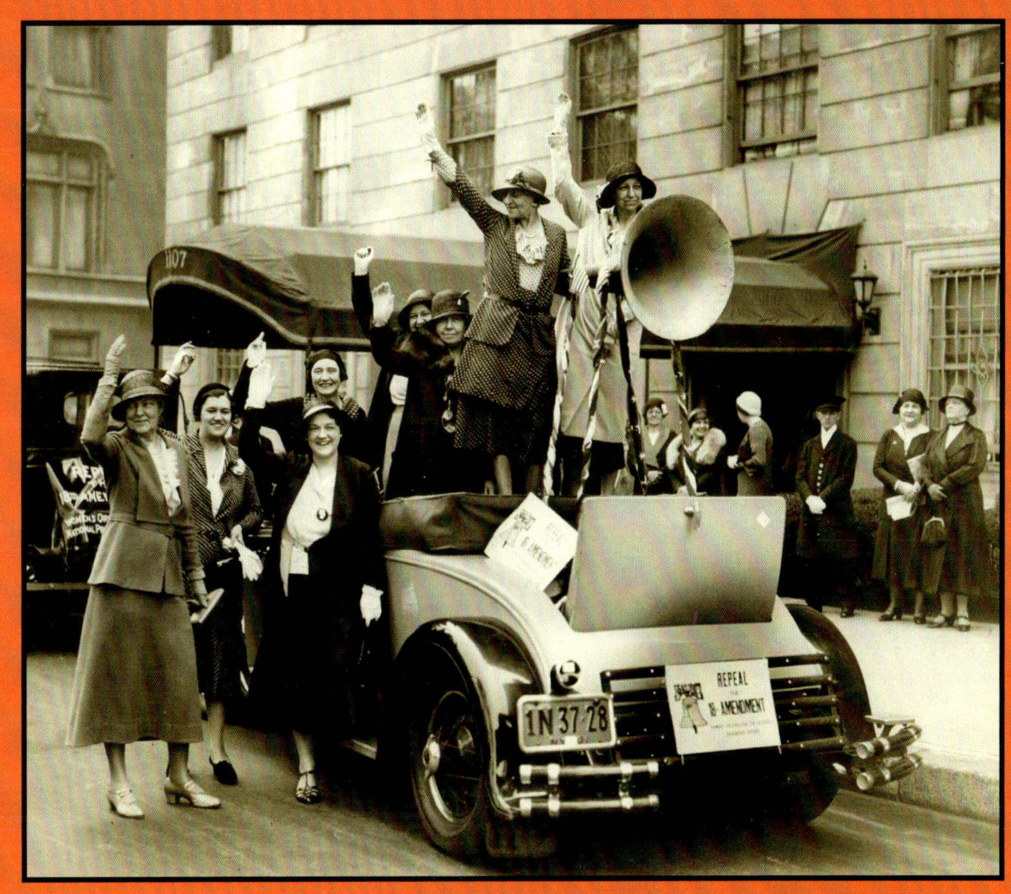

왕월 회빙연 전거일

대명녕종 녕간의황대부 츅각노신국 공정한의 조실계원이오 효

공경헌의 중현명도쳥셩후 예다셩 실여 즁이 원자 후 승의 나온

리 흘어 변녹호여 호학독셔 호며 인현호믈 구호여 도덕 셩힝이

학셰의 그치 아니 호더 큰 뜻을 구치 아니 향의 비린 뜻을 이스러

너르 태조황제 일등 호샤 갈 황의 경활 호나 심상 변쳐를 원치 아니

아니 호셔 부귀를 초치 못 보니 어 셩조 큰 황제 즉위 호샤 남션

을 구 호시미 큰 왕이 너 상을 깊 그 추천의 삼그 초쳐를 호촉 호샤

공쳥 금을 날의 셔로 비경 호시미 그의 덕 두 호되 엄그 궁의 스 근지 홍

라 변의 황쳐 덕이 취쥬의 독보 호더니 영종의 나라 더 황 그리 통 우문

시 연 동을 나 궁지 더 원 녀쳥 조황 대 남붕의 궁쳥의 게유 도 호샤 대 ᄌ

Scribing Their Alphabets

Women Calligraphers in the Joseon Dynasty

INSOO CHO

ALTHOUGH TRACES OF WOMEN are visible across various genres of Korean art,[1] in pictorial representation women are subject to men's gaze, and various objects related to women's daily life play a socially limited gender role as they are considered miscellaneous items rather than refined artworks. Female artists are invisible, and their artworks have been excluded from mainstream art history. Aligned with the resurgence of feminism in art history, this essay examines women's calligraphy in vernacular Korean and offers a corrective to its omission from the art historical canon.

During the Joseon dynasty (1392–1910) in Korea, calligraphy was a highly respected form of artistic expression due to the lofty position held by the scholar-official.[2] In Joseon society, with its ruling ideology of Confucianism, literacy was the most important determiner of status. A noteworthy characteristic of the Joseon dynasty's writing culture was the coexistence of Chinese characters (*hanja*) alongside the Korean alphabet (*hangeul*). The vernacular Korean script aligned with daily Korean speech and thus was embraced by common people, especially women. Most Korean women were excluded from studying Chinese classics; vernacular Korean script enabled them to express their thoughts and record their stories. Paradoxically, the wider vernacular Korean script reached, the more it was shunned by the male elite, who monopolized literary Chinese.

While literary Chinese writing was considered a male dominion, many letters in vernacular Korean from royal women to relatives have been preserved. This correspondence is remarkable not only for the secretive and candid content it holds but also for its elegant handwriting. Palace women also scribed in refined style many documents required for royal rituals. In addition, as vernacular novels enjoyed popularity among women, many works were copied out word for word by women. In their graceful exploration of

Facing: Madame Yi, *Wanwol hoemaengyeon*. See figure 3.17.

calligraphic possibilities, women calligraphers extended this indigenous writing system into a new realm of formal elegance.

Private letters and popular novels have long gone unnoticed in art history. As calligraphy in vernacular Korean was not regarded as a fine art, women calligraphers have not been included in the art history canon. From the beginning of the twentieth century, Korean women calligraphers have begun to receive attention, but their significance has not been properly examined. New understanding of women calligraphers' contribution to Korean art requires reassessment, asking questions such as: What is the difference between Korean women's calligraphy and calligraphy in literary Chinese? Does women's calligraphy have a different aesthetic quality to men's? What are the characteristics of the so-called palace style or *gungche*? Attempting to assert the importance of women's calligraphy in Korean art history, this essay provides a new perspective on the place of Korean women calligraphers in the Joseon kingdom.

The Place of Korean Women Artists in the Joseon Dynasty

At the beginning of the Joseon dynasty, Korea transformed into a Confucian society. In the newly developed patriarchal system, Korean women were marginalized: they were generally limited to careers in the home, fulfilling their primary obligation according to Confucian ethics. Most of the records of upper-class women were written by male writers, who described them as ideal wives, submissive spouses, and caregivers. Their artistic talent receives almost no mention.[3]

Geunyeok seohwa jing (Biographical Records of Korean Painters and Calligraphers), compiled in 1928 by Oh Sechang (1864–1953), contains 1,117 artists beginning in the Three Kingdoms period; only a few of these are female painters from the Joseon dynasty.[4] The book includes Sin Saimdang (申師任堂, 1504–1551), Heo Nanseolheon (許蘭雪軒, 1563–1589), Jang Gyehyang (張桂香, 1598–1680), and the courtesan Jukhyang (竹香, ac. nineteenth century). Besides Sin Saimdang and Jang Gyehyang, the only mentions of female calligraphers are anecdotes indicating that Lady Gang, a daughter of the literati painter Gang Huian (姜希顔, 1418–1464), and Seo Ik's (徐益, 1542–1587) concubine were good at calligraphy in literary Chinese. Compared to that in China, this number is too small.[5]

It is therefore difficult to find Korean women's calligraphy works, and in those that do exist, authenticity becomes problematic. Sin Saimdang was highly praised for her insect paintings, but recent studies have found that this evaluation was largely exaggerated and that most paintings attributed to her are unreliable in terms of authenticity (fig. 3.1).[6] She first gained a high degree of recognition as the mother of a famous man—the prominent Confucian thinker Yi Yi (李珥, 1536–1584)—and an exemplar of feminine virtue. As Yi Yi was the patriarch of the Old Doctrine faction, which seized political power in the late Joseon period, Sin Saimdang's promotion was politically motivated.

Figure 3.1. (*facing*) Sin Saimdang, *Rats, Butterflies and Watermelons*, first panel of eight-panel screen, 16th century, ink and pigment on paper, 33.2 × 28.5 cm. National Museum of Korea, Seoul.

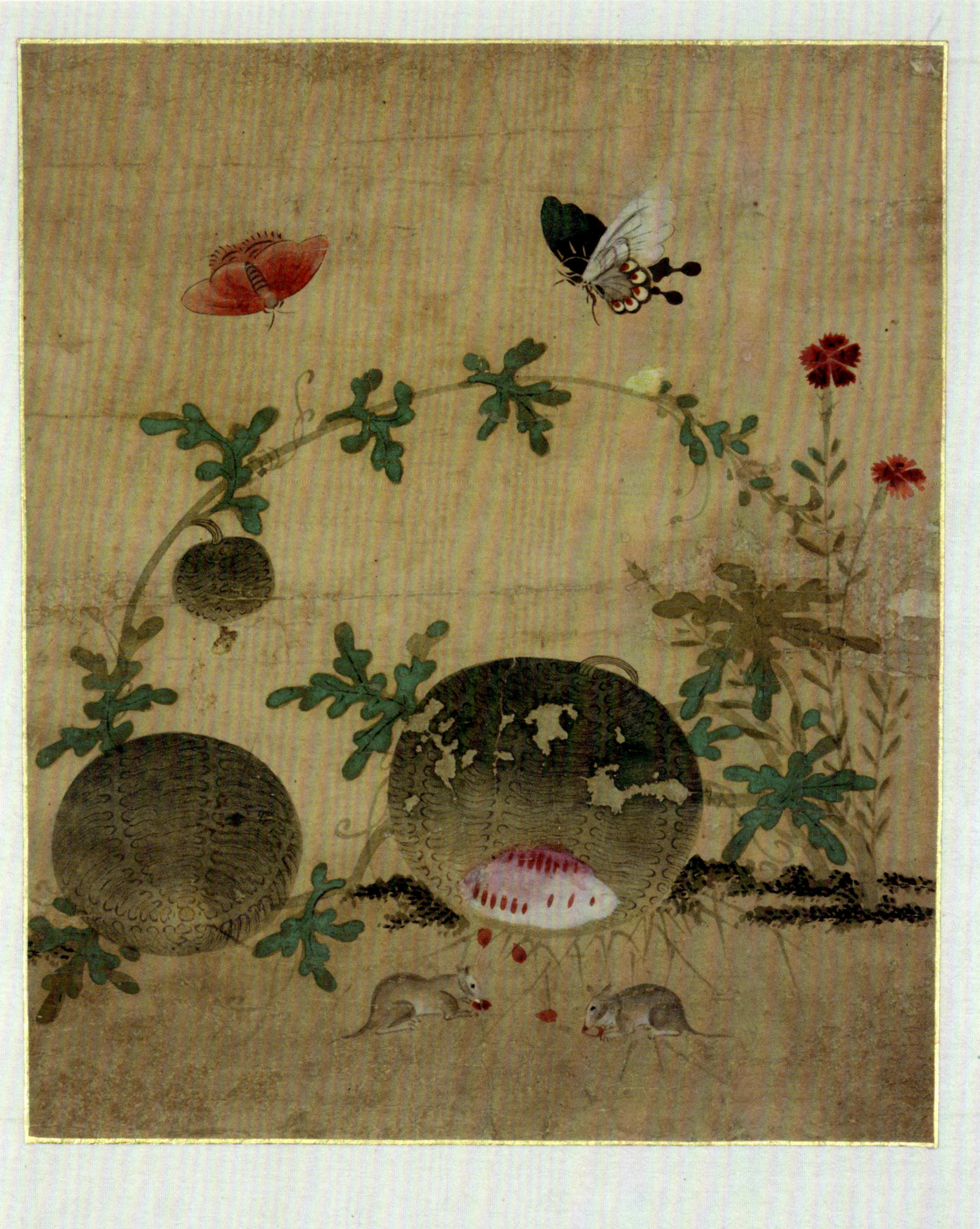

Although Sin Saimdang's outstanding artistic talent was not entirely fictional, it had already become difficult to determine her actual achievement by the late seventeenth century. Nevertheless, Yi Yi's followers continued to praise her paintings and calligraphies.

The situation is similar for Jang Gyehyang, who is often compared to Sin Saimdang.[7] She was good at calligraphy from the time she was a child, under the influence of her father, a famous calligrapher. An album attributed to her, *White Hair* (*Hakbalcheop*, 鶴髮帖), contains poetry she wrote in fluent cursive script (fig. 3.2). The scholar Sin Jwamo (申佐模, 1799–1877) visited the family house of Jang Gyehyang's descendants and viewed her works. He highly praised them, stating, "Dragon and snake seem to be jumping. I imagine that when the brush is applied to the paper, it looks like a rainstorm. The variety in writing surpasses Madame Wei Shuo [衛夫人, 272–349], and since Zhong You [鍾繇, 151–230] and Wang Xishi [王羲之, 303–361] have no one to match."[8] However, since the first record of the album appeared about a hundred years after she died, its authorship is uncertain.[9]

Jang Gyehyang's son wrote a biography of his mother in 1692, over a decade after her death. According to his record, Jang Gyehyang was good at poetry and calligraphy in her youth, but she stopped writing in her mid-teens because she considered it was not a woman's duty, so little of her works remained.[10] The biography does not refer to the *White Hair* album. Along with Sin Saimdang's case, Jang Gyehyang's situation indicates that works by female artists were difficult to preserve on their own merits. Instead, they were often (re)discovered according to the reputation of male descendants.

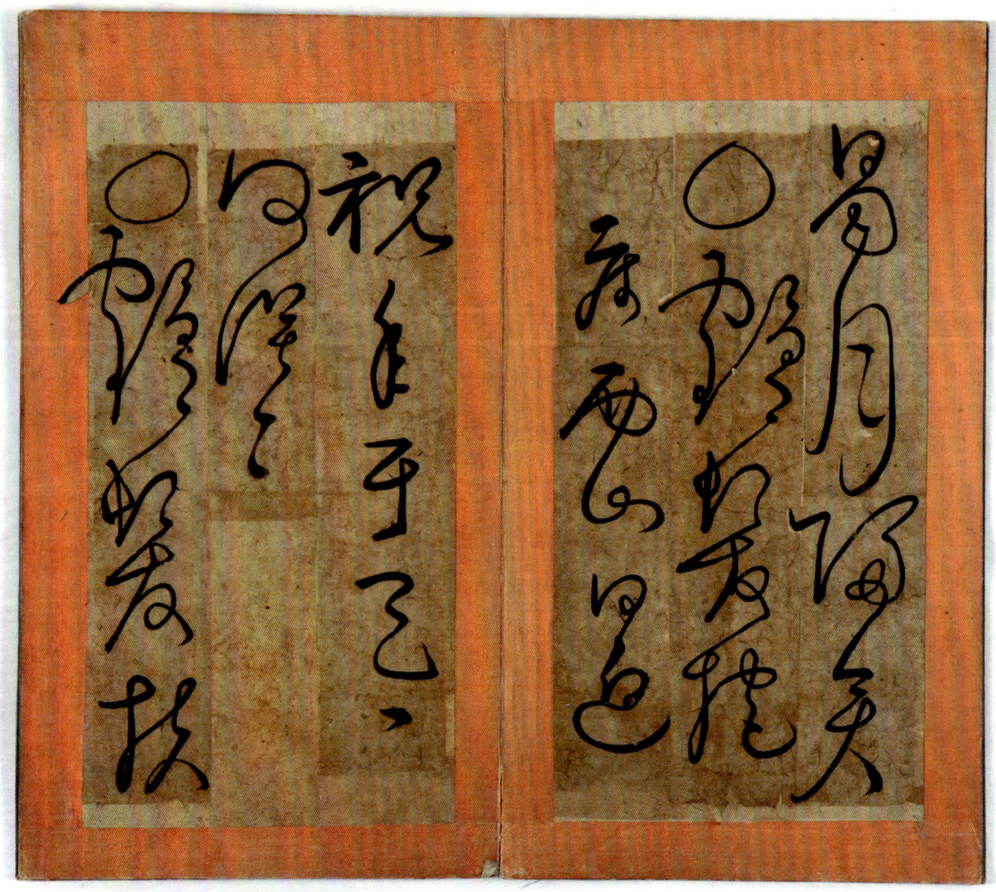

Figure 3.2. Jang Gyehyang, *White Hair*, six-leaf album, 17th century, ink on paper, 44 × 25.5 cm. Private collection, Andong.

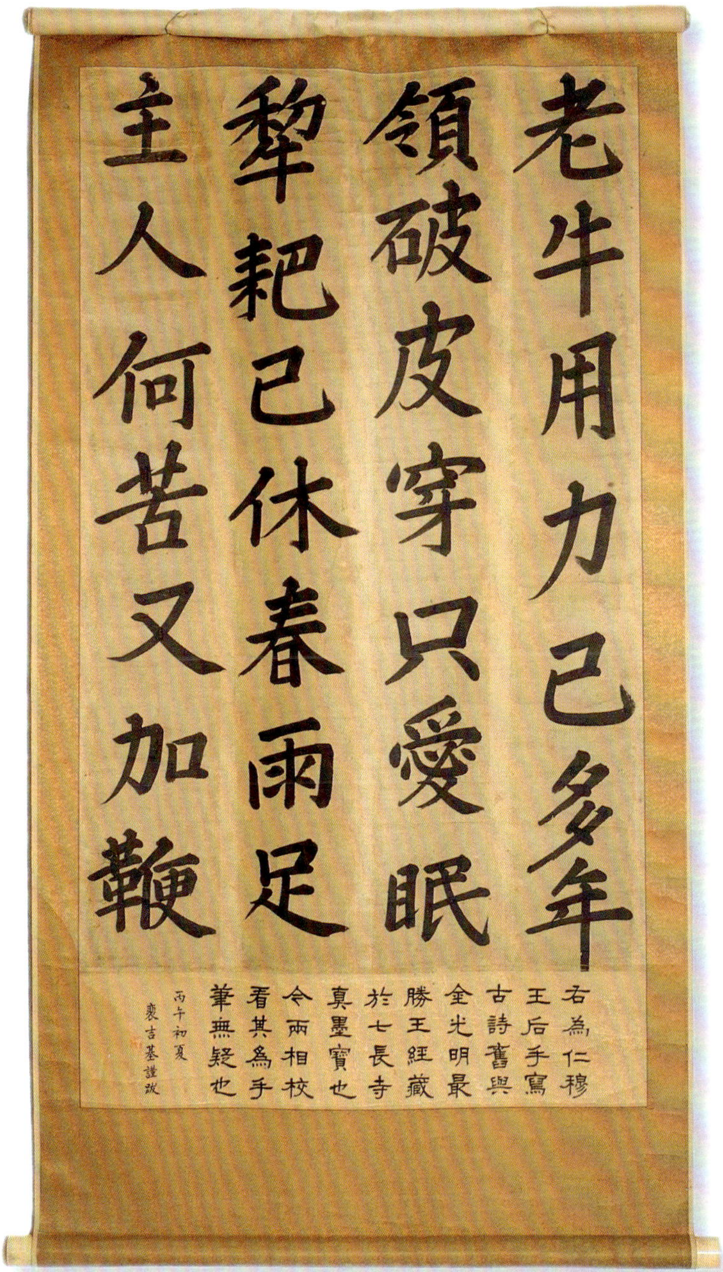

Figure 3.3. Queen Mother Inmok, *Pity the Cow*, 17th century, ink on paper, 105 × 67.3 cm. Chiljangsa Temple, Gyeonggi Province.

Royal women's calligraphy suffered a similar fate. King Seonjo (宣祖, r. 1567–1608), his wife, Queen Inmok (仁穆, 1584–1632), and their first daughter, Princess Jeongmyeong (貞明, 1603–1685), are known as representative calligraphers of the Joseon royal family by contemporary and later generations of art critics.[11] While King Seonjo's writing is regarded as having established a model for kings' calligraphy in the seventeenth century and later, the queen's and princess's writing became famous in connection with their personal misfortune. The next king, Gwanghae (光海君, r. 1608–1623), was a second son of King Seonjo, born of his secondary consort, and felt anxious about his authority. Eventually King Gwanghae killed the father of Queen Mother Inmok (his stepmother) and her son (his half-brother) for treason. The queen mother and Princess Jeongmyeong were placed under house arrest.[12] Queen Mother Inmok healed her heart and soothed her anxiety with calligraphy, leaving many writings. One of these is *Pity the Cow* (fig. 3.3).

A poem about having pity for an old cow, it analogously asked compassion for her miserable situation and thus indirectly criticized King Gwanghae. Confucian scholars disapproved of King Gwanghae's immoral tyranny and sympathized with Queen Mother Inmok. As a result, this work was regarded as a symbol of Confucian moral principle and was printed and distributed in woodblock prints.

It is believed that most of Princess Jeongmyeong's calligraphy works were written during her confinement in the West Palace from age fifteen to twenty. Although various records single out her calligraphic abilities, it is difficult to assess her achievement as a calligrapher because of the lack of authentic works. After King Gwanghae was dethroned by a coup in 1623, the princess was released from confinement and married into the Pungsan Hong family. After that, she considered literacy not to be part of a wife's duty and wrote all her letters in vernacular Korean; these were not preserved. Because of this, her calligraphy works are quite rare.

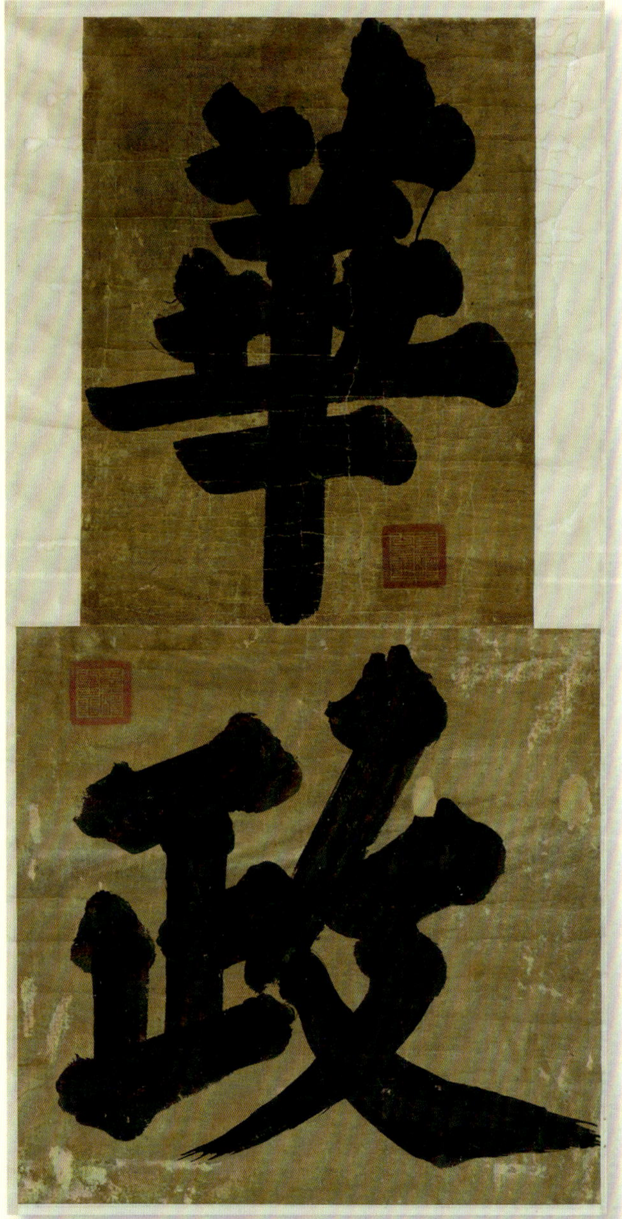

Figure 3.4. Princess Jeongmyeong, *Hwajeong*, 17th century. Ink on paper, 146 × 73.5 cm. Kansong Art Museum, Seoul.

Princess Jeongmyeong's famous work *Hwajeong* exhibits two large characters, over 70 centimeters tall (fig. 3.4).[13] *Hwajeong*, which means "illustrious" and "governance," originally belonged to a set of eight characters, two of which were inherited by her youngest son.[14] The son made copies of it in honor of his mother and distributed them widely after her death. Later, the work was seen by King Sukjong (肅宗, r. 1674–1720) and King Jeongjo (正祖, r. 1776–1800), who praised it for being strong like men's writing. Other critics also insisted that her writing was especially masculine. Thus, even a royal woman's calligraphy works were recognized only to the extent that the writer's feminine virtue was emphasized throughout, and their artistic value was not seriously considered. Moreover, all of these examples are written in Chinese characters; little is known about the writers' vernacular Korean calligraphy.

Women in Confucian Society

The rarity of Korean women calligraphers is closely linked to literary life in the Joseon dynasty. Joseon society advocated Confucianism and promoted civilian government. Learning classics was considered important for elite men. A degree of literacy, however, was beyond the reach of women. Conservative families protected their daughters from the distractions of literature and taught them little more than filial behavior and needle skills.

Indulging in reading and writing was not considered proper behavior for women because it was believed that learned women could get involved in politics. King Sejong (世宗, r. 1418–1450), who invented the vernacular Korean script, stated, "In China, women are able to read the text and participate in political affairs, but in Korea, there is no doubt that women did not participate in state affairs because women were illiterate."[15] In fact, in China, many upper-class women were educated and actively participated in politics.

Most Joseon women received no formal education. Daughters of scholar-official families were educated in reading and writing in their natal family, but this was limited to studying edited texts about women's social responsibilities, familial obligations, and proper conduct. These didactic texts gave women a kind of official characterization of obedient daughters, submissive wives, self-sacrificing mothers, and chaste widows. Since they were translated into vernacular Korean, these books were widely circulated and read by elite women.[16] Elite families often encouraged their daughters to copy these books.

Some girls who became literate had support and assistance from male family members.[17] For example, Kim Changhyup (金昌協, 1651–1708) was concerned about his daughter Kim Un (金雲, 1679–1700), saying, "My daughter's mind is calm and pure, and I think it would not hurt if she study." He allowed her to learn writing with her younger brother. However, even if he educated his daughter, this could not be public knowledge; rather, it had to be hidden. Kim Un's potential was limited by conventions designed to support the rigorously patriarchal social system of premodern Korea. She said, "If I was born as a man, I would like to build a house in the deep mountains, pile up hundreds and thousands of books, and grow old among them."[18]

Traditionally, a celebrated woman's virtue lay not in her skill in belles lettres but in her sacrifices for her family. Even when the Practical Learning School, which tried to reform orthodox Confucianism by pursuing practical studies, emerged in the late Joseon period, the negative opinion of women's education did not change. Yi Yik (李瀷, 1681–1763), regarded as a pioneer of Practical Learning, said, "It is a man's duty to read books. The wife must care about the items to be prepared in the morning and evening, summer and winter, in time, perform sacrifices, and greet guests. At what spare time can she read books?"[19] This statement reveals his prejudice against women based on the patriarchal kinship system.

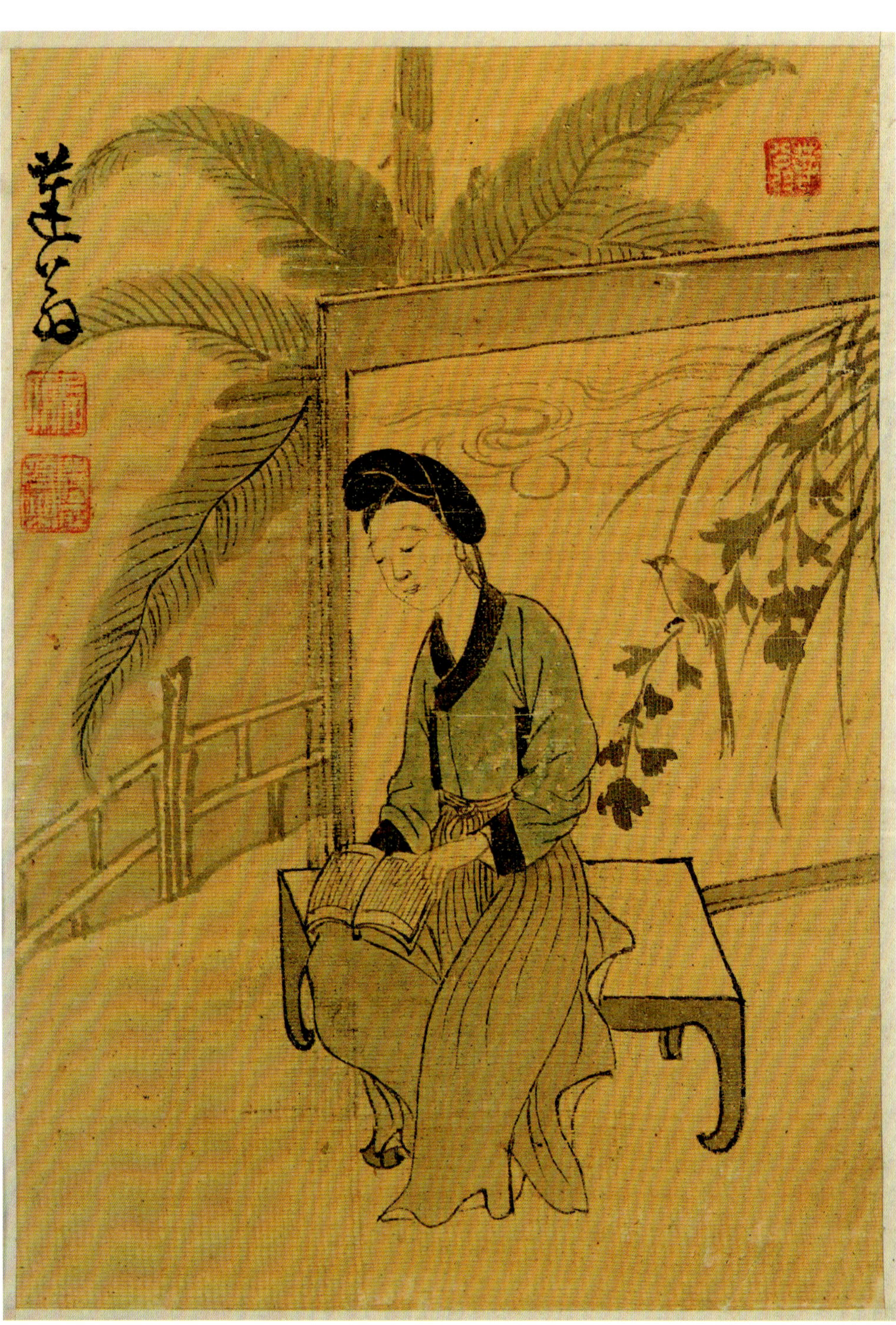

Figure 3.5. Yun Deokhui, *A Woman Reading a Book*, 18th century. Ink and pigment on silk, 20 × 14.3 cm. Seoul National University Museum, Seoul.

A Woman Reading a Book, by the literati painter Yun Deokhui (尹德熙, 1685–1776), is a rare example of this subject in illustrations (fig. 3.5). The painter was a son of Yun Duseo (尹斗緖, 1668–1715), who drew genre paintings from the point of view of Practical Learning School, so his painting also exhibits a realistic depiction of local Korean costume. By placing the woman inside a house, however, he indicated the subordination of women to men within the family and the exclusion of women from public life. In addition, the subject is still positioned within conservative Confucian gender ideology as she is reading a proper didactic book allowed only to women. Women's literacy was taboo, and women's voices could be transmitted only through oral and vernacular Korean writing.

Hangeul, a Korean alphabet

From ancient times, Korea had used Chinese characters for transcription. But the Korean language is completely different from Chinese, and it was inconvenient to use Chinese characters in daily life. Most common people were illiterate. To remedy this, King Sejong created a phonetic alphabet in 1443 and formally proclaimed it in 1446. This new indigenous script, commonly known as *hangeul*, was officially called *Correct Sounds to Instruct the People* (*Hunmin jeongeum* 訓民正音).[20] After the invention of vernacular script, the Korean written culture became diglossic. Most scholar-officials strongly opposed the use of vernacular Korean script, and literary Chinese was still used in most official documents. As male scholars in the ruling class continued to rely mainly on Chinese characters, writing in vernacular Korean did not contribute to their cultural capital.[21] However, the postscript to *Correct Sounds to Instruct the People* says, "A clever man can learn them in one morning, though a dull man may take ten days to study them."[22] This was not an exaggeration, and the use of vernacular Korean script quickly spread among women and common people; by the end of the nineteenth century, *hangeul* had become the script of these groups.[23]

Nevertheless, recent studies show that even in upper-class families, the teaching of vernacular Korean script was emphasized for domestic use.[24] Young elite males learned *hangeul* at home from female relatives. This was the same for the royal family. King Sukjong collected excerpts from *Elementary Learning* 小學 and *Classic of Filial Piety* 孝經 and translated them into vernacular Korean to enable a palace woman to teach the crown prince the texts.[25]

In *hangeul*, consonants and vowels are combined to form one character, and one character corresponds to one syllable. Traditionally, it is written in columns from top to bottom and from right to left. In this sense, vernacular Korean calligraphy is similar to Chinese calligraphy. Writing in vernacular Korean, however, tends to have less variety than writing in Chinese because of the smaller number of characters. Furthermore, each character is composed of fewer strokes than Chinese characters. Therefore, it is easy to write, but it is quite different from Chinese calligraphy in terms of artistic rendering.

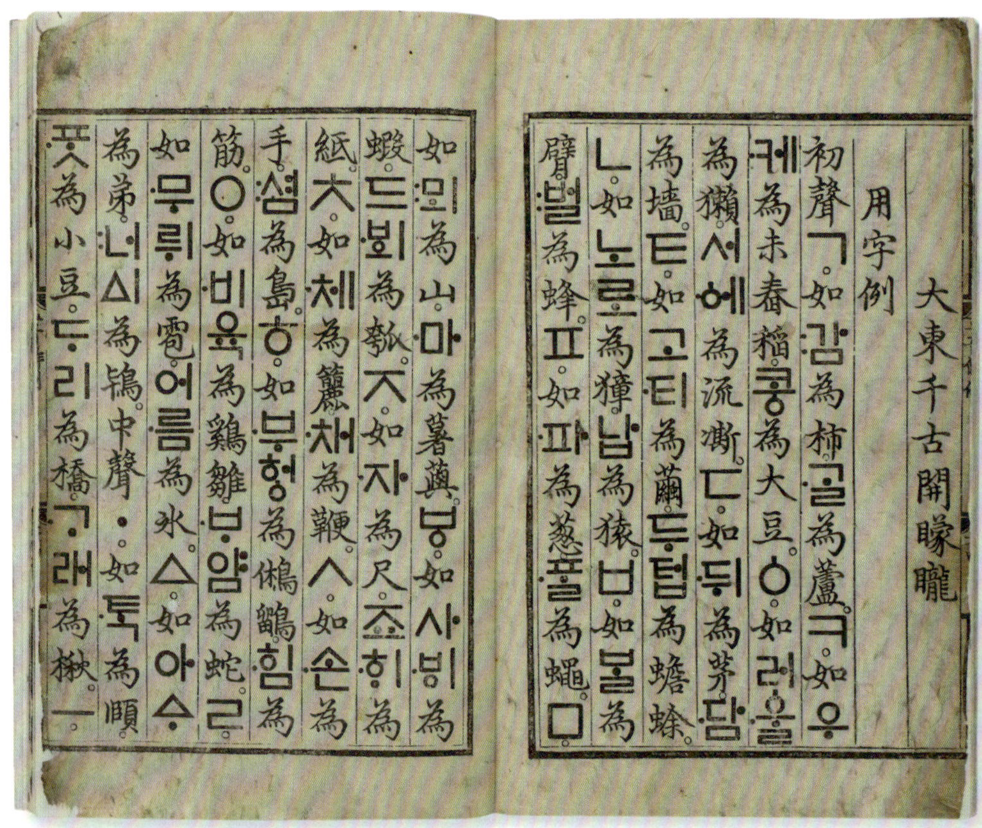

Figure 3.6. *Correct Sounds to Instruct the People*, 1446. Woodblock-printed book, ink on paper, 23.3 × 16.6 cm. Kansong Art Museum, Seoul.

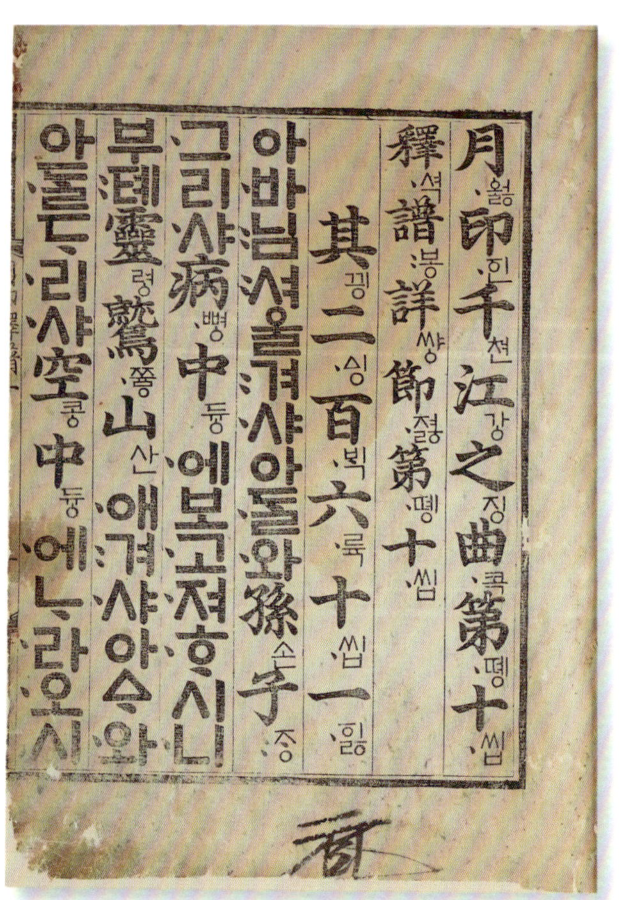

In *Correct Sounds to Instruct the People*, there is a detailed explanation of pronunciation but no description of writing. Only the forms of characters were said to follow the style of ancient Chinese seal scripts. The extant edition of *Correct Sounds to Instruct the People* is a woodblock-printed book; *hangeul* characters are visually expressed along with explanations in Chinese (fig. 3.6). The side-by-side juxtapositions of vernacular Korean and Chinese highlight the differences between the two scripts. *Hangeul* characters show lines of even thickness in their shape and maintain a geometrically balanced square form.

Vernacular Korean script includes geometric shapes such as ●, ○, and △ that are not found in Chinese characters. The early scripts are almost completely sans serif, with no protrusion. Without a sharp tip in the starting and closing strokes, it is hard to write with a soft brush. There is no angle or hook, which are distinctive characteristics of the Chinese calligraphy technique.

However, in *Worin Seokbo*, published a few years later, the *hangeul* style turns away from geometric shapes and toward a font that is easy to produce with a brush (fig. 3.7). The dot ●, which was originally composed separately from the vowel stroke, was changed to a comma shape or a short line attached to the long stroke. The brush marks appear in both the starting and the closing strokes, giving the impression of Chinese regular script.

Figure 3.7. *Worin Seokbo*, 1459. Woodblock-printed book, ink on paper, 32.5 × 22 cm. Dongguk University Library, Seoul.

Epistolary Korea

During the Joseon dynasty, letters were very important to literati elites, and letter writing was practiced in all communicative spaces, private and public. Confucian scholars often circulated important letters to one another, and it was fashionable to collect letters from famous people and compile them into an album. Letters exchanged between male elites were supposed to be written in literary Chinese.

Recent studies, however, show that vernacular Korean script was also widely used by men for personal correspondence with female relatives. Elite males wrote letters in vernacular Korean to women or children who did not understand literary Chinese. Their descendants valued the letters of their ancestors, including women, and these letters were passed down from generation to generation.[26]

Epistolary exchanges also became an accepted feature of social life among women of the elite class. Women who left their families upon marriage and lived with marital families maintained familial connections through letters written in vernacular Korean. These letters never achieved the public status of men's erudite literary Chinese writings. Elite men refused to apply the term "calligraphy" to women's handwriting in vernacular Korean.

Letters collected and preserved during a person's lifetime were often used to fill up space inside the coffin of the collector after their death.[27] A large number of vernacular Korean letters have also been found; for example, 189 pieces of letters were unearthed from the tomb of Madame Kim of Suncheon in 1977.[28] Of those, 107 were letters sent by Madame Gang of Sincheon (d. 1585), the mother of the deceased. Madame Gang was a prolific letter writer who poured her heart out to her daughter. When her husband took a concubine, Madame Gang erupted into a jealous tirade (fig. 3.8).[29] This shows that correspondence

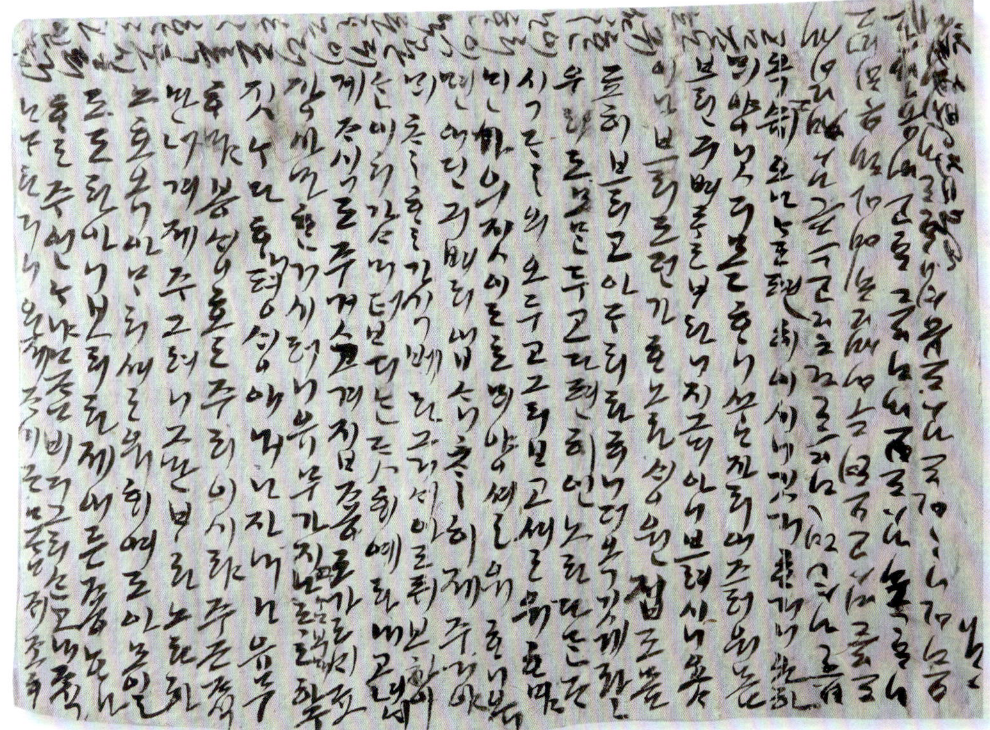

Figure 3.8. Madame Gang, *A Letter by Madame Gang of Sincheon to Her Daughter*, 16th century, ink on paper, 30 × 42 cm. Chungbuk National University Museum, Cheongju.

was active among upper-class women, who were not allowed to go outside freely. The proficient handwriting indicates that vernacular Korean writing was common among elite women. Quickly written characters are often linked to one another, giving an effect of gentle flow. The mother asked her daughter to burn the letter immediately after reading it, but the daughter kept it, and it was buried in the grave alongside her.

When her husband was ill, Wonyi's mother, whose given name is never mentioned, wove a pair of shoes for him—knitted together with her hair and a hemp band—and hoped that he would be cured. However, her husband died without ever wearing them. She wrote an elegy in vernacular Korean and put it into the coffin together with the shoes (figs. 3.9, 3.10).[30] At that time, she was pregnant, and her husband's death was consequently more tragic. Using vernacular Korean, she was able to express personal emotions clearly. The content of the letter is truly heartbreaking and reveals intimate aspects of the conjugal relationship between the young couple.

> Take me now with you because I cannot live after losing you and I want to follow your way. I cannot let go of my heart toward you in this world and my grief is endless. Where can I rest my heart toward you? How can I live with our children with this wretched heart? Read this letter and come to me in my dreams so that we may speak without restraint.[31]

Compared with works in literary Chinese, which tended to deal with serious issues in formal rhetoric, works in vernacular Korean were concerned with the ordinary and casual, with descriptions of everyday joys and sorrows. Vernacular Korean calligraphy was not bound by the strict rules of Chinese calligraphy, so people could write it in a more informal way. As a result, Korean calligraphy works display a great variety of brushwork, ranging from thin and delicate to graceful but more forceful. The practice of calligraphy among women engendered a kind of female social presence. Through letters, women were connected to the world beyond their home.

Vocabularies of art criticism on vernacular Korean calligraphy have not yet developed. At present, it is generally divided into "old style," which corresponds to seal and clerical scripts in Chinese calligraphy; "standard style," which corresponds to standard script; and "fluent style," which corresponds to running and cursive scripts.[32] The fluent style used for the letters was executed quickly by simplifying individual consonants and vowels and connecting characters. This style could be written freely, showing the personality and artistic skill of the author.

Letters by Royal Women

During the Joseon period, when a king was enthroned as a minor, the queen dowager served as regent until he reached maturity. Queen Jeonghui (貞熹, 1418–1483), the widow of King Sejo (世祖, r. 1455–1468), acted as regent for King Seongjong (成宗, r. 1469–1494) from 1469 to 1476, but she could not understand literary Chinese. To rule from "behind the curtain," the queen dowager sent out edicts written in vernacular Korean

Figure 3.9. Wonyi's mother, *A Letter by Wonyi's Mother to Her Husband*, 1586, ink on paper, 34 × 58.5 cm. Andong National University Museum, Andong.

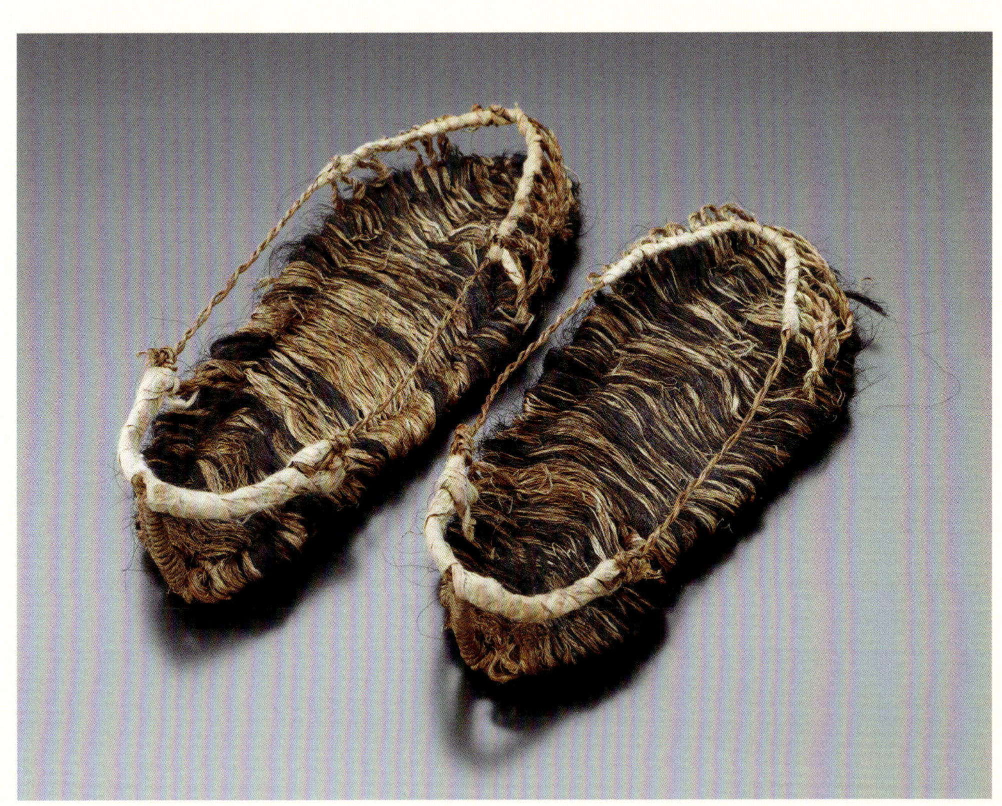

Figure 3.10. *A Pair of Shoes*, 16th century. Human hair and hemp, 23 × 9 cm. Andong National University Museum, Andong.

to high officials. Her original instructions in vernacular Korean were translated into literary Chinese and recorded in the *Sillok* (Veritable Records). The vernacular Korean documents were then discarded. Comments by the secretaries indirectly criticized the illiterate queen.[33] This does not mean that no queen could understand literary Chinese. Queen Munjeong (文定王后, 1501–1565), who served as a regent from 1545 to 1553 for her son King Myeongjong (明宗, r. 1545–1567), learned literary Chinese but ruled from behind the curtain using only vernacular Korean documents. No royal women have left their writings in Chinese, like some women in elite families. It is presumed that royal women were more often forced to use only vernacular Korean in the court.

One of the few ways that a queen could communicate with the outside world was letter exchange. A queen would often send vernacular Korean letters to her relatives outside of the palace.[34] When a princess married and left the palace, she would send greeting letters to the king or queen, and they would reply to her. The sending of greeting letters to elders became customary and a part of social etiquette. These letters are short and formulaic, and almost indistinguishable from one another; all were written in vernacular Korean.

Lady Hyegyeong (1735–1815), the mother of King Jeongjo, recalled, "Since I entered the palace at the age of ten, I exchanged letters with my family in the morning and evening. There were a lot of letters in my family house. But my father admonished not to store the letters from the palace and gathered all the letters to discard. So my handwriting does not remain in the house."[35] For the same reason, only a small portion of letters written by royal women to their relatives exist today.[36]

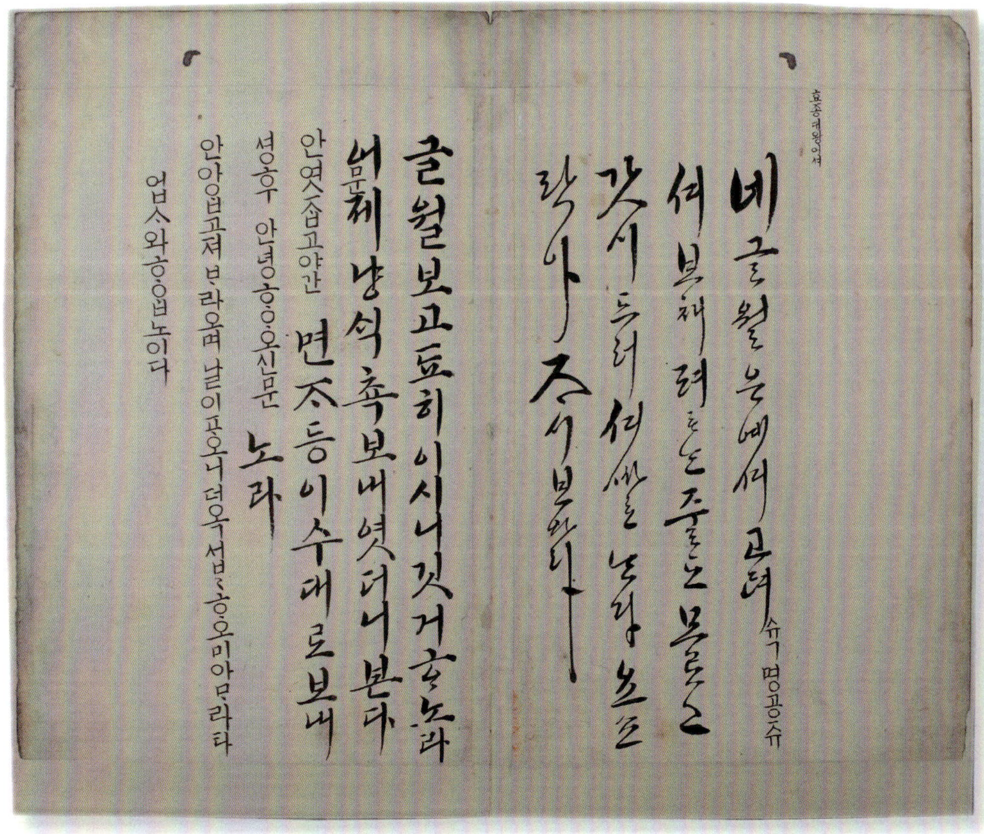

Figure 3.11. Princess Sungmyeong, *A Letter by Princess Sungmyeong to King Hyojong*, from *Sungmyeong sinhancheop*, 17th century, ink on paper, album 42.3 × 26.2 cm. Cheongju National Museum, Cheongju.

Sungmyeong sinhancheop is a collection of vernacular Korean letters received by Princess Sungmyeong (淑明, 1640–1699).[37] It is believed that a descendant of the princess preserved the letters as a remembrance of her ancestors and compiled them into an album, which demonstrates the filial reverence for the materiality of ancestral handwriting.

One of the letters contains a reply from King Hyojong (孝宗, r. 1649–1659), the princess's father (fig. 3.11). On the left, the princess's letter says, "I wonder if your majesty had a good night. As I haven't seen your majesty for a long time, I miss you so much." Using the same letter paper, the king wrote his reply on the right side: "Looking at the letter, you seem to be doing well. I sent two colored candles yesterday, have you seen them? I am also sending two cotton lamps." According to the etiquette of the time, the princess wrote in standard style but the king wrote in fluent style.[38]

A letter from Queen Insun (仁宣, 1618–1674), the princess's mother, in the same album shows the typical fluent style widely used in the palace (fig. 3.12). As the vowel " ㅣ " is slightly shifted to the right, the vertical lines are aligned. Placing these vertical strokes in similar positions makes them more legible and pleasing to the eye. Like the running and cursive scripts of Chinese calligraphy, the style represents the rhythm of writing with different stroke thicknesses and subtle ink tones. Two or three characters are also concatenated, and the final consonants " ㄹ " and " ㅁ " are written in a single stroke. When " ㅇ " is written as an initial sound, the starting part is pointed like a protrusion. In order to maximize the aesthetic features of *hangeul*, the queen utilized the soft brush and developed her own calligraphic beauty with fast and skillful strokes.

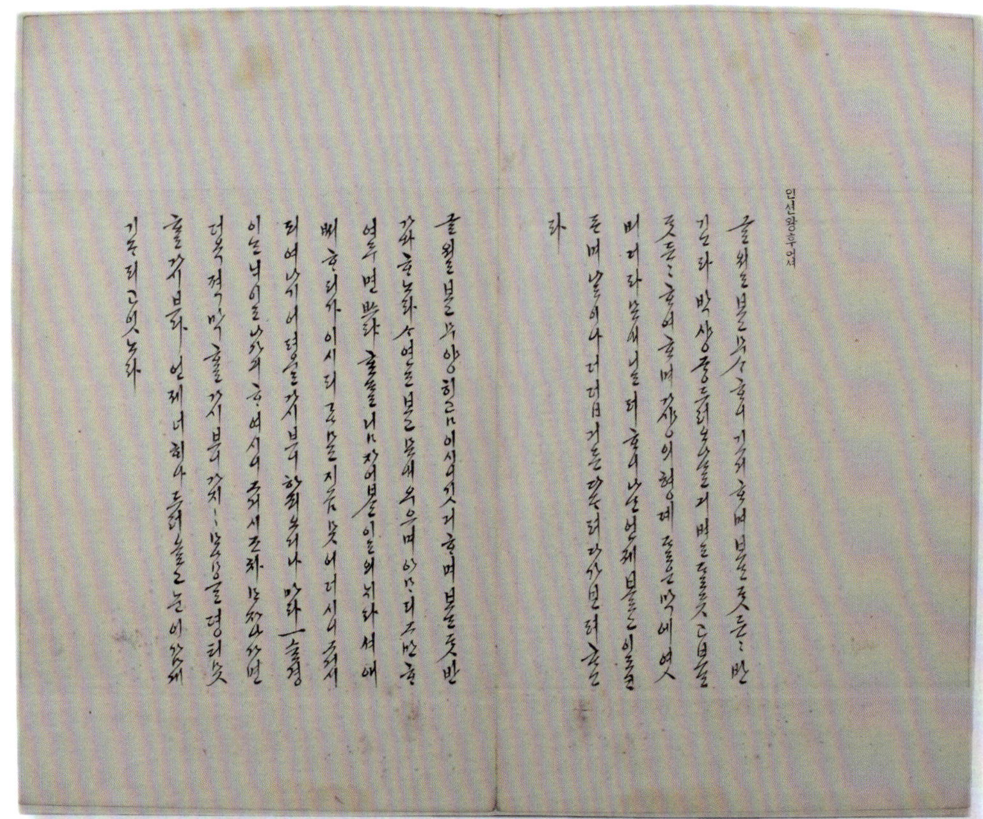

Figure 3.12. Queen Insun, *A Letter by Queen Insun to Her Daughter*, from *Sungmyeong sinhancheop*, 17th century, ink on paper, album 42.3 × 26.2 cm. Cheongju National Museum, Cheongju.

Queen Myeongseong (1851–1895), commonly known as Queen Min, the indomitable wife of King Gojong (高宗 r. 1863–1907), lived during a period of great political turbulence. Among her numerous vernacular Korean letters are 133 letters sent to her nephew Min Yeongso (閔泳韶, 1852–1917).[39] She used imported Chinese letter paper decorated with woodblock-printed patterns. One of her letters with cock and cockscomb motifs says that the king and crown prince are doing well (fig. 3.13). Written in a combination of standard and fluent styles, her calligraphy, with its overly curving strokes, is distinct and expressive. Individual strokes are joined by the brush, showing an ease and fluency of writing. The brush line itself tends to be thick rather than slender.

As we have seen, queens' and princesses' calligraphy have refined and elegant features. In the fifteenth century, Queen Sohye (昭惠, 1437–1504) compiled an etiquette book, *Instruction for Inner Quarters*, which emphasized good handwriting as a desirable female accomplishment.[40] Yi Deokmu (李德懋, 1741–1793), a renowned scholar of the Practical Learning School, wrote that in composing vernacular Korean letters, the handwriting should be orderly.[41] Considering good calligraphy as one of the female virtues, many male-authored commemorative texts for their female relatives praise women's ability to write vernacular Korean in a well-trained hand. The aesthetic dimensions of vernacular Korean calligraphy, however, were not emphasized even in the case of royal women.

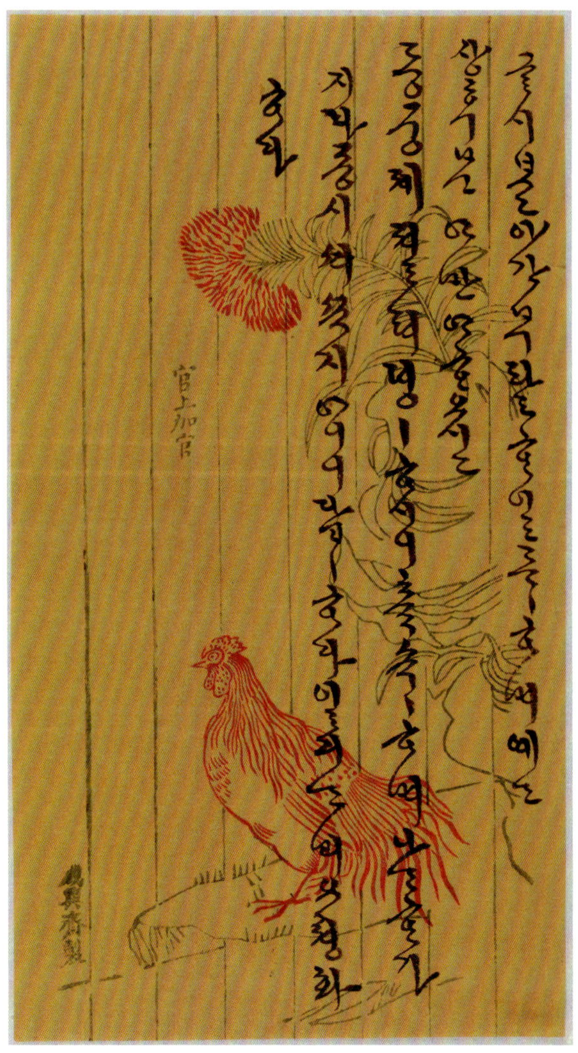

Figure 3.13. Queen Myeongseong, *A Letter by Queen Myeongseong to Her Nephew*, 19th century, ink on paper, 22.5 × 12.5 cm. National Palace Museum of Korea, Seoul.

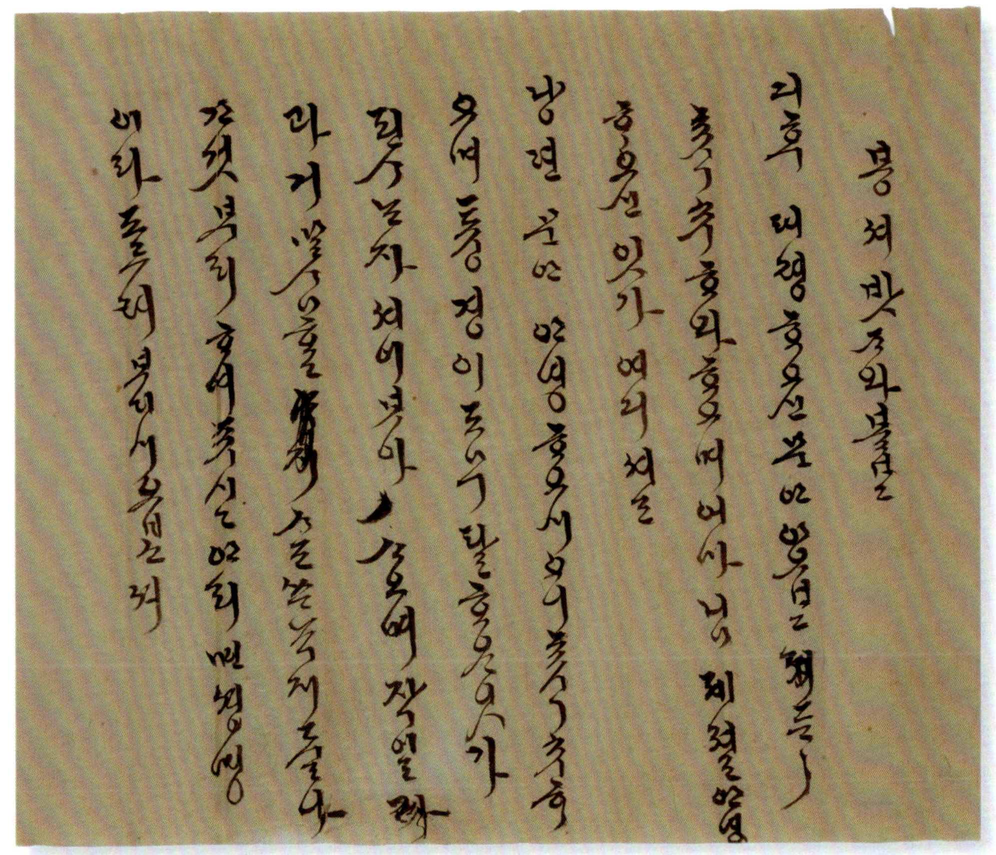

Figure 3.14. Anonymous, *A Letter from Queen Myeongseong to Her Mother*, 19th century, ink on paper, 25.7 × 28.3 cm. National Palace Museum of Korea, Seoul.

Invisible Hands: Palace Matron Calligraphers

Some of the letters sent by Queen Myeongseong were clearly written not by the queen herself but by palace women, as the handwriting is different (fig. 3.14). In the ghostwritten letters, the consistent size of the short characters, together with the angular shape at the top of the vertical strokes, makes a strong impression. Elegant thin lines connect characters as the writer moved from one to another without lifting the brush from the paper. It is a different style from the casual calligraphy style used by royal women.

Scholars believe that some of the palace women of the Joseon dynasty were in charge of writing the various vernacular Korean documents and letters of the superiors. The palace inner court was composed of various ranks of royal consorts, female officials, and female service personnel.[42] Among them, the palace matrons, or *sanggung* 尙宮, played a significant role in the royal court's operation. They served the queen and the concubine and had control over the lower palace women, who were engaged in trivial works.

Palace matrons were responsible for communicating the queen's wishes to other members of the palace, like a female equivalent of the royal secretary. Some palace matron calligraphers dominated the practice of ghostwriting for royal women and cultivated a certain style through repeated practice.[43]

Matron Scribe Yi is known as the most famous palace matron who specialized in vernacular Korean calligraphy, but there is no official record for her. Most modern scholarship relies mainly on what Yun Baekyeong (尹伯榮, 1888–1986), a descendant of Princess Deogon (德溫, 1822–1844) and famous calligrapher, recollected hearing from old palace matrons.[44] Matron Scribe Yi is believed to have served for Queen Mother Sinjeong (神貞, 1808–1890) before leaving the palace to marry; she then entered the palace again on the summons of the queen. Her reentry into the palace was exceptional, as palace women were not able to marry and were supposed to take a lifelong position in the palace.

In her calligraphy for the queen, Matron Yi's characters are connected by a clear line, and although they are of different sizes, they appear in harmony (fig. 3.15). Her style combines elegance and delicacy with confident, rounded forms. It is said that she contributed to developing the palace style of vernacular Korean calligraphy into a more refined style. However, there is no textual evidence that explicitly identifies Matron Yi as the queen's favorite scribe. Therefore, Matron Yi's association with those royal letters is not certain.

Many royal household registries, or *balgi* 件記 in vernacular Korean, are believed to have been written by palace matrons. These registries were usually a single document containing the names of various items used mainly in royal rituals. If the list was long, it became a handscroll, and colorful paper was used for auspicious occasions.[45] For example, a registry of dowries for Princess Deogon's wedding (fig. 3.16) exhibits an outstanding calligraphy style with even spacing of columns and a uniform line thickness. The ample space around each character keeps the list as clear and readable as possible.

Finally, I turn to the relationship between palace women and vernacular Korean novels. In the late Joseon period, as the use of vernacular Korean increased significantly, vernacular Korean novels circulated widely among elite families. While gentlemen were disagreeing about female literacy, women were busy reading vernacular novels. Yi Deokmu

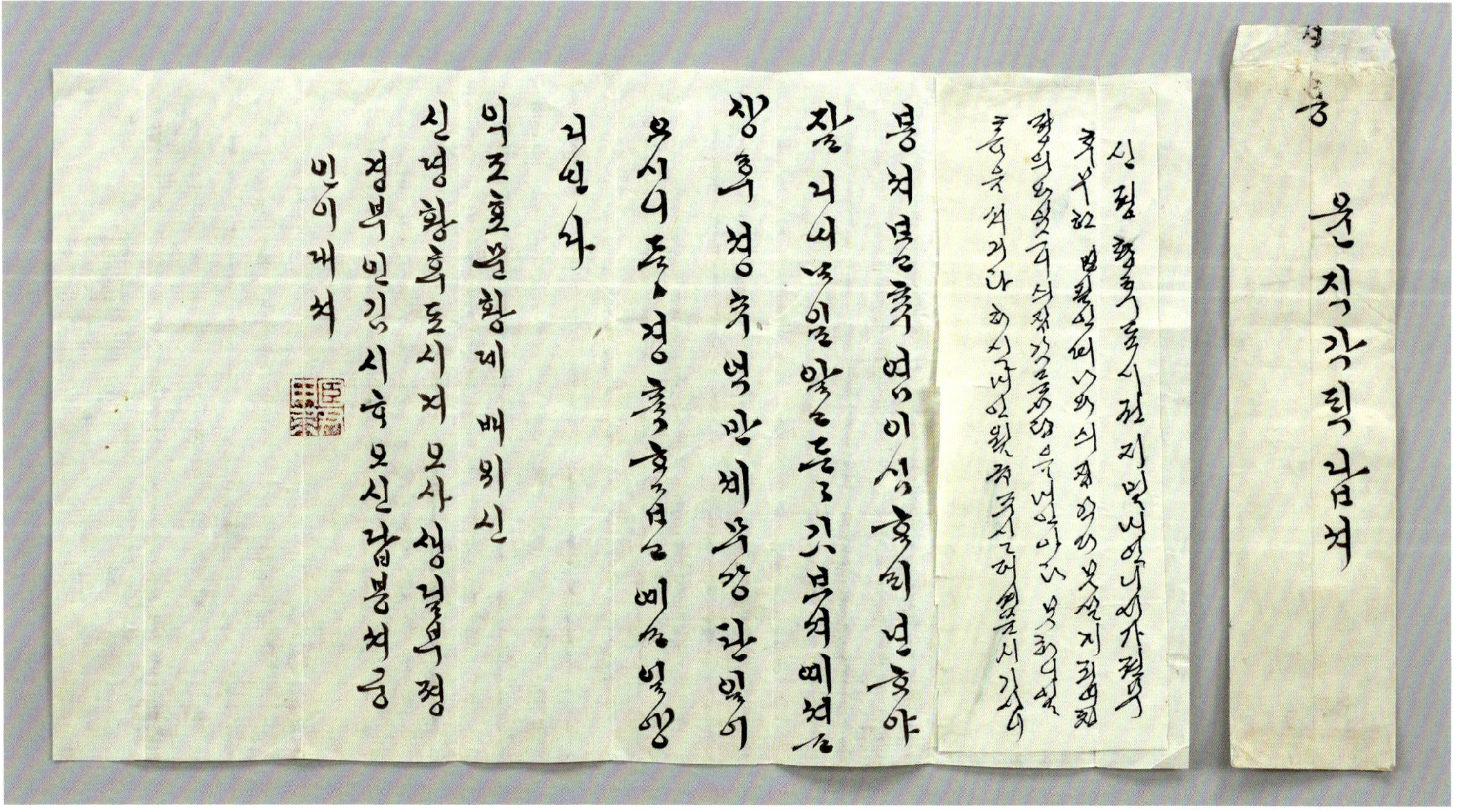

Figure 3.15. Matron Scribe Yi, *A Letter from Queen Mother Sinjeong to Madame Kim of Gwangsan*, 1874, ink on paper, measurements unknown. National Hangeul Museum, Seoul.

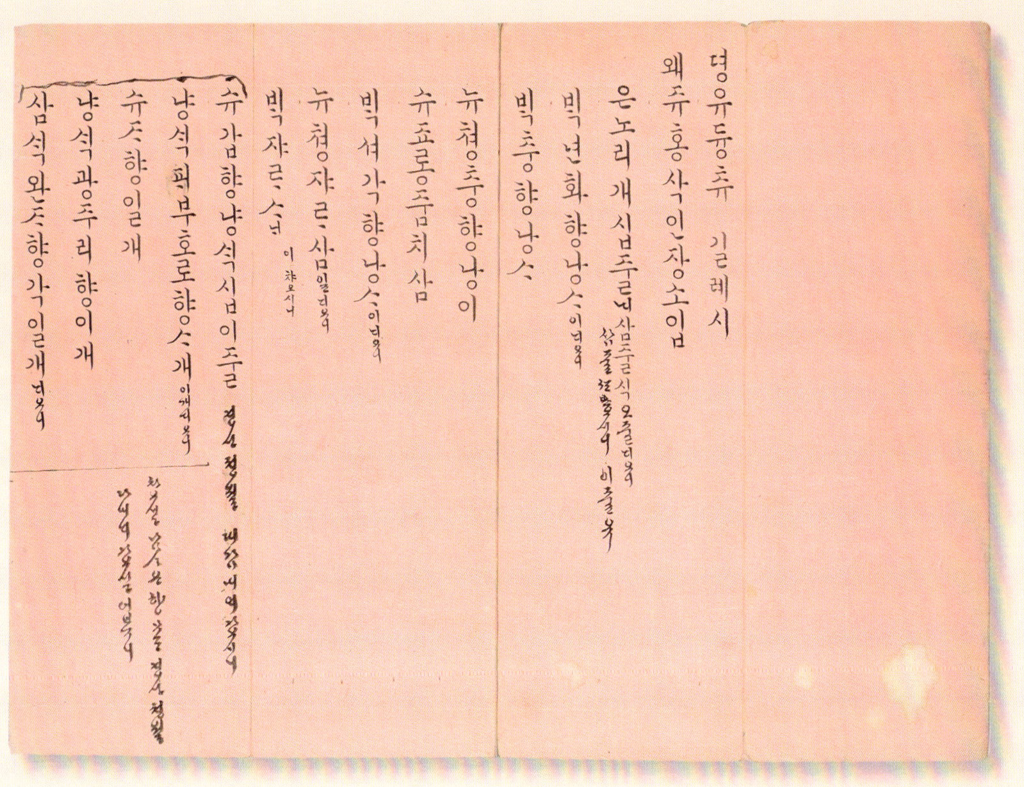

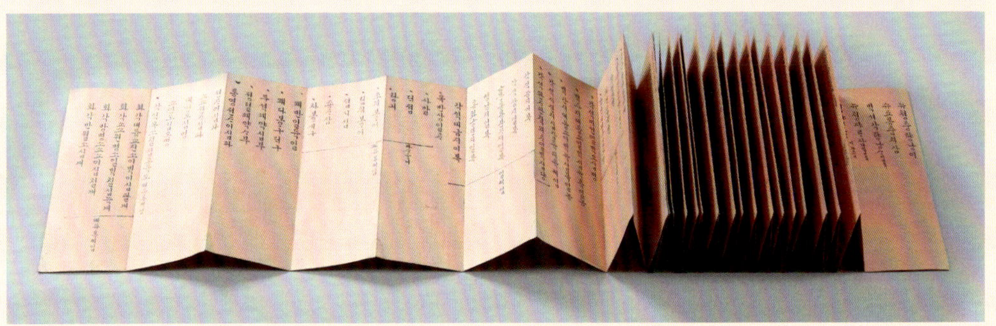

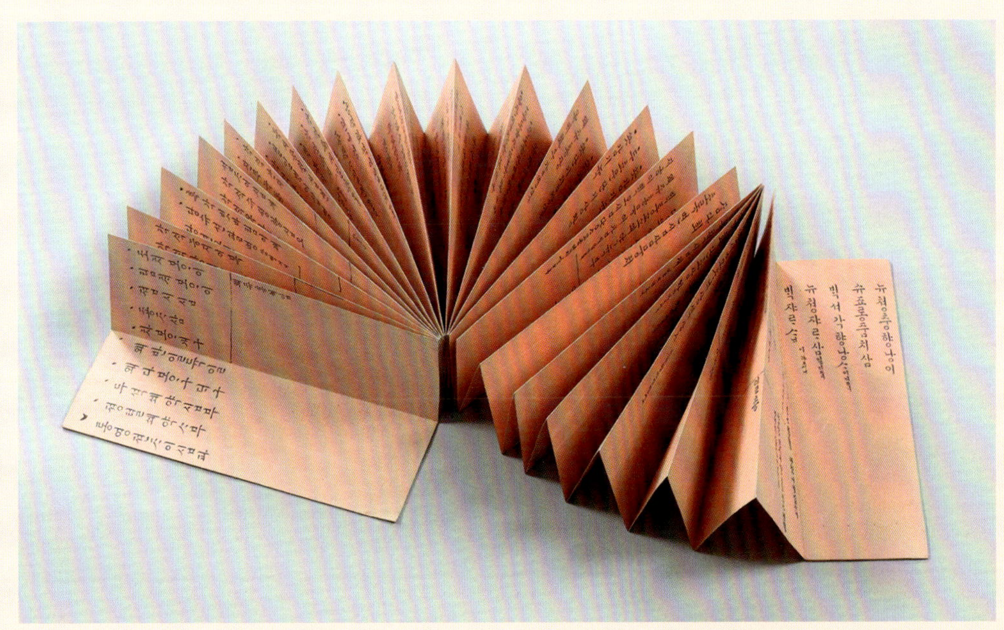

Figure 3.16. Anonymous, *List of Wedding Gifts Given by Queen Sunwon to Princess Deogon*, 1837, ink on paper, 32.8 × 541.5 cm. National Hangeul Museum, Seoul.

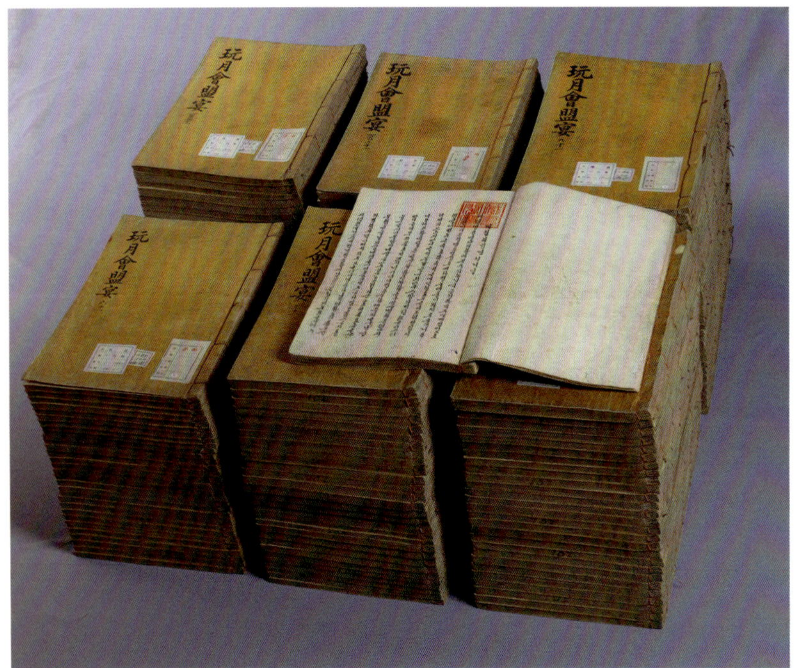

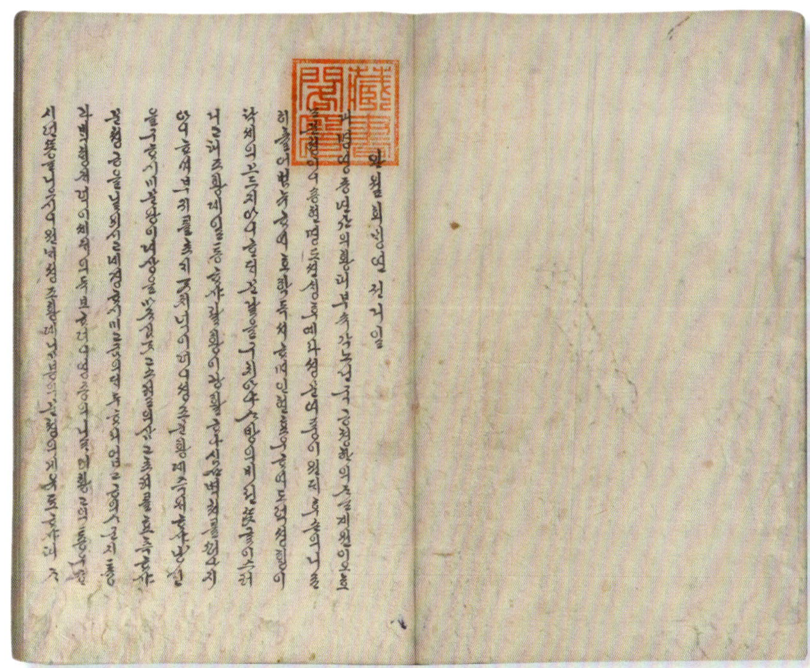

Figure 3.17. Madame Yi, *Wanwol hoemaengyeon*, 18th century. 180 volumes of hand-copied books, each 32.3 × 22 cm. Academy of Korean Studies, Seongnam.

complained that women often indulged in vernacular Korean novels and neglected household chores and duties.[46]

One of the distinctive features of Joseon print culture is the lack of commercial printing, which meant the practice of copying manuscripts by hand was very important.[47] Since there were no bookshops, many upper-class women borrowed novels from book rental establishments. Scholars believe that popular vernacular Korean novels from rental shops entered the palace, where the palace women copied them out again. For example, Nakseon Pavilion of the Changdeok Palace has thousands of vernacular Korean novels in storage. *Wanwol hoemaengyeon* (玩月會盟宴, A Promise of Marriage at the Banquet at Moon-Viewing Terrace) is known to have been written by Madame Yi (1694–1743) and was widely read and copied, even in the palace (fig. 3.17).[48]

Copying novels was important for upper-class women, who were able to decipher the vernacular Korean written in swift fluent style. The postscripts at the end of *Wanwol hoemaengyeon* indicate that elite women scribed the text in order to read the text carefully or to understand the content. The act of copying was also emotionally comforting.[49] The women often hoped that their handwriting would leave a trace by which they could be remembered by their descendants. For example, Madame Gwon of Andong copied a novel to help her grandson remember her through seeing the handwriting.[50]

Women's fine vernacular calligraphy works were highly praised by other women and considered as style guides. Descendants were able to identify who copied a work by looking at the handwriting. In the case of *Ogwon jaehap giyeon* (The Remarkable Reunion of Jade Mandarin Ducks), now in the collection of Gyujanggak Royal Library, female descendants recognized the copyists as Madame Jeong of Onyang, Madame Yun of Haepyeong, and Aunt Byeon, who had copied the book from 1786 to 1796.[51] With their copying practices, women collectively created the exquisite vernacular Korean calligraphy.

As mentioned earlier, the meaning of calligraphy in men's and women's lives diverged. Most elite men utilized calligraphy in literary Chinese as means of moral self-cultivation and aesthetic achievement that were highly praised by other elite men. In contrast, women added material significance to their calligraphy in vernacular Korean and formed a kind of bodily discipline with practical social value that was emphasized by Confucian principles.[52]

What Is *Gungche*?

Palace women developed a refined style of vernacular Korean calligraphy that today is referred to as *gungche* 宮體, or palace style.[53] In the Joseon dynasty, however, the term *gungche* is used to refer to the literature of the palace and is rarely mentioned as a style of calligraphy. The only instance occurs in the literary Chinese poem by Yi Ok (李鈺, 1760–1815):

> Since you learned the palace style calligraphy early on,
> You crown the round letter with a handsome sharp stroke.
> Your parents-in-law delight in your writing;
> "It is that of a female scholar-official!" they say.[54]

This is one of his poems describing women's life after marriage. It is uncertain whether the term *gungche* was widely used at the time. Many modern scholars thought that palace women and vernacular Korean calligraphy were closely related, and that *gungche* was developed in this context.[55] It was also believed that *gungche* spread outside the palace and became popularized among upper-class women, but there is no concrete evidence to prove this.[56] Choosing the term *gungche* for palace women's calligraphy and applying it retroactively to other premodern palace calligraphy has caused much confusion.

During the Joseon dynasty, when royal women attended court rituals, some documents in literary Chinese were translated into vernacular Korean for them to read. For female officials who participated in the ritual, detailed manuals and summarized procedures were also translated.[57] For example, both eulogy and lyrics were composed in literary Chinese by a scholar-official, but since palace women needed to read and sing for the queen in the royal inner quarters, vernacular Korean translations were also prepared. It has been thought that the majority of official documents in vernacular Korean were written by palace women, but recent studies indicate that many of these documents are the work of male scribes. An example is *Cheonuisogam* 闡義昭鑑, published in 1755 to demonstrate the legitimacy of King Yeongjo's (英祖 r. 1724–1776) succession to his elder brother, King Gyeongjong (景宗, r. 1720–1724), and to justify the punishment for traitors convicted of treason. When this book was translated into vernacular Korean for Elder Queen Mother Yinweon (仁元, 1687–1757), scribes were summoned from various offices; all of them were male officials.[58] JaHyun Kim Haboush has noted that the development and aestheticization of *gungche* calligraphy related to "the opening of an independent space for women in the visual scriptural culture."[59] However, recent research has questioned this view because many important books in vernacular Korean published by the court were scribed by male officials.[60]

Jagyeongjeon jinjak jeongnye uigwe 慈慶殿進爵整禮儀軌, published in 1827, records the royal banquet that Crown Prince Hyomyeong (孝明, 1809–1830) arranged for King Sunjo (純祖, r. 1800–1834) and Queen Sunwon (純元, 1789–1857). As a compilation of formal official documents, it includes meticulously detailed information. Besides the ten volumes in literary Chinese, the prince requested three additional volumes in vernacular Korean to be presented to the queen. While the original book in Chinese was printed with movable type, the Korean translation was handwritten (fig. 3.18). The original woodblock prints for the illustrations were reused for the Korean translation, but the

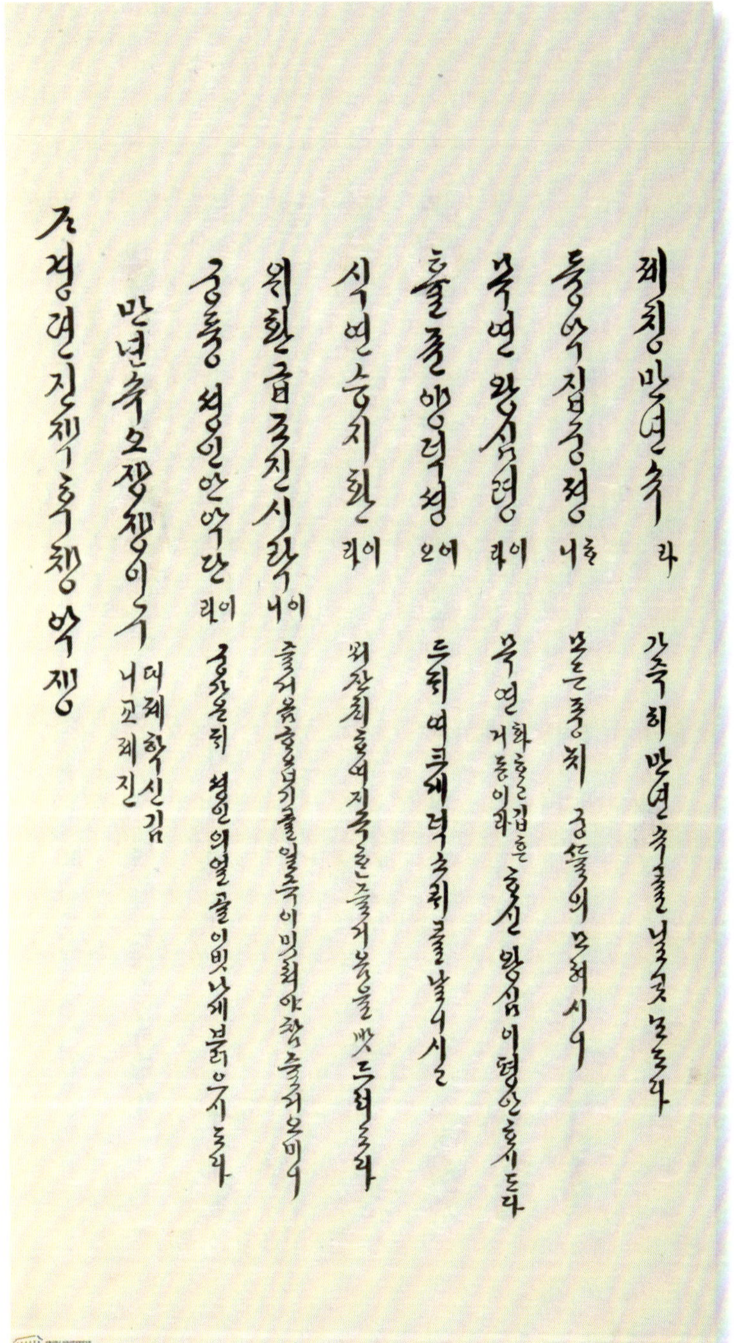

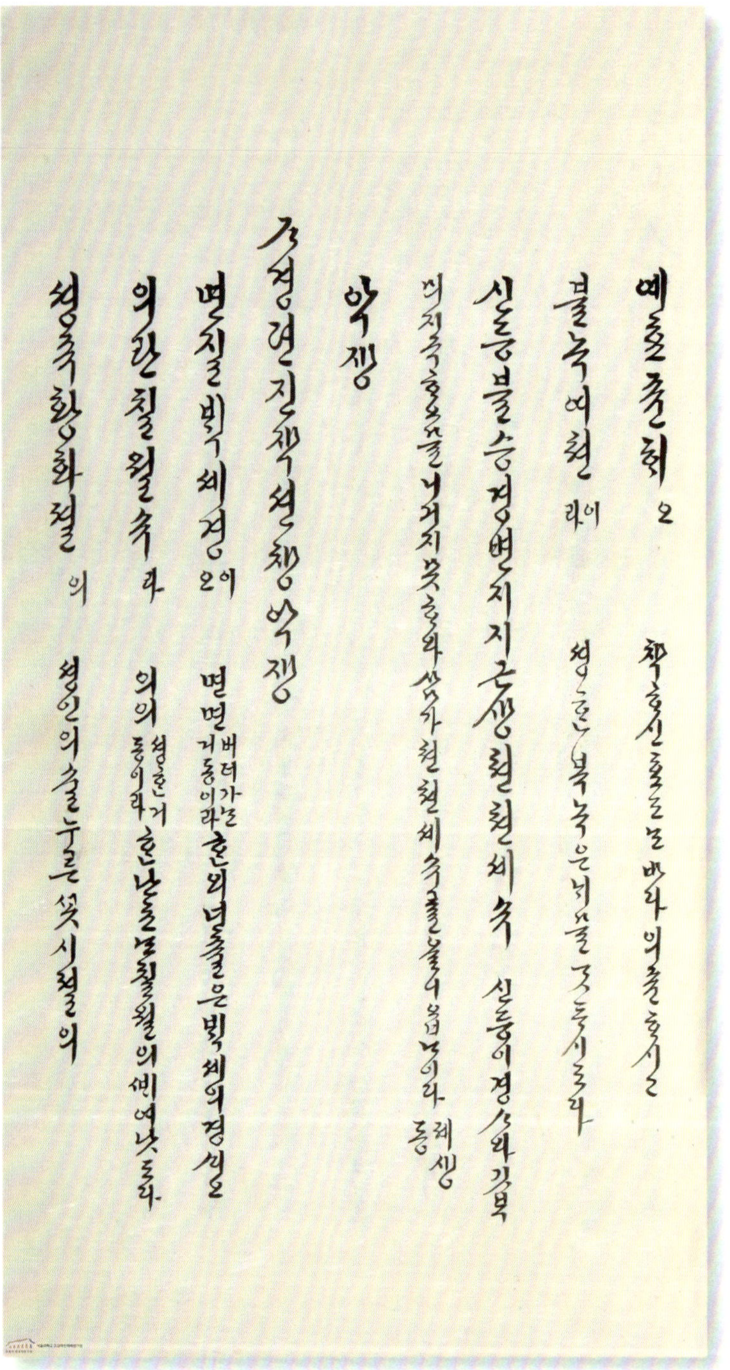

Figure 3.18. *Jagyeongjeon jinjak jeongnye uigwe*, 1827, 3 vols, ink on paper, 36.4 × 23.2 cm. Kyujanggak Institute for Korean Studies, Seoul.

captions were inscribed in vernacular Korean (fig. 3.19). The calligraphy exhibits skillful handwriting in so-called *gungche*. The flow of the writing down the columns is both firm and fluent, with forms almost touching one another but retaining their own integrity.

In the section of rewards given after the banquet, five court calligraphers including Baek Sanul 白師訥 are recorded; all are male officials.[61] If the vernacular Korean edition had been copied by palace women their names would have been recorded, because names of every participant are listed in great detail; for example, female nurses, dancers, and lower-level palace women with their titles and specific roles in the banquet are listed.

Figure 3.19. *Jagyeongjeon jinjak jeongnye uigwe*, 1827, 3 vols, ink on paper, 36.4 × 23.2 cm. Kyujanggak Institute for Korean Studies, Seoul.

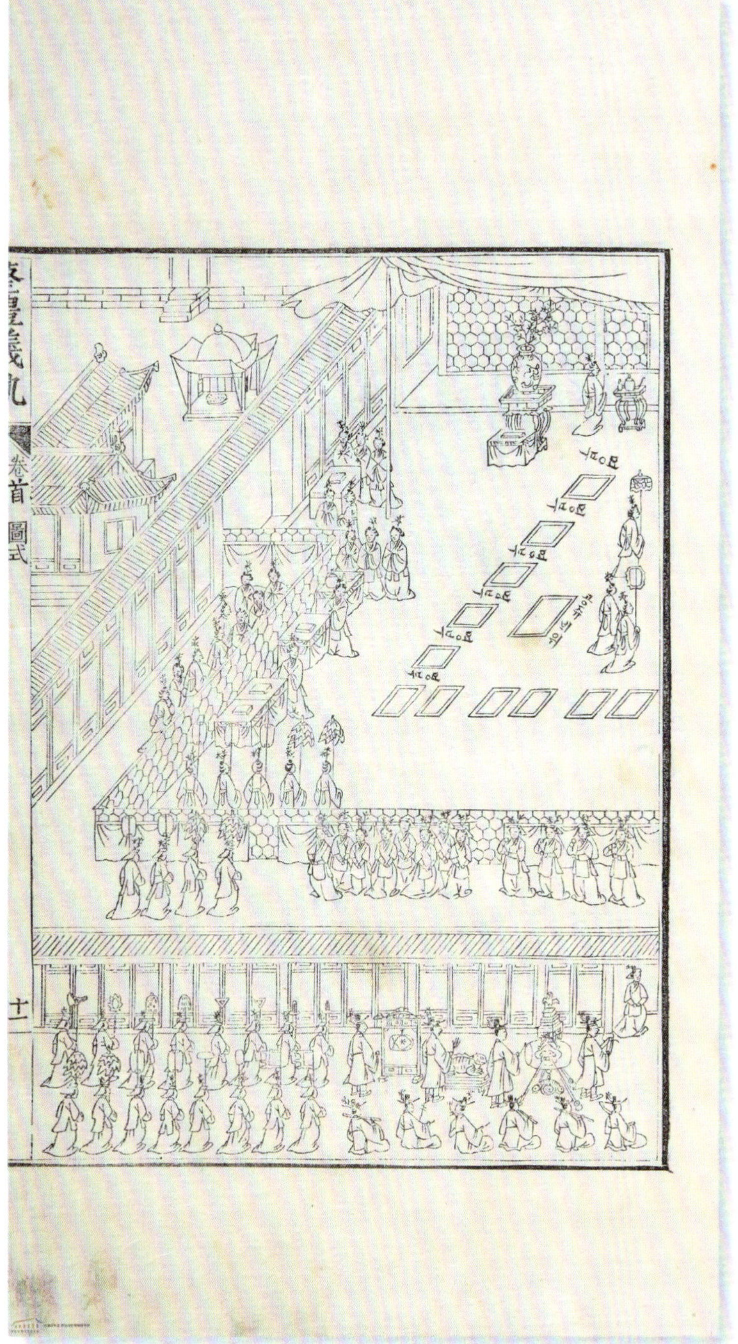

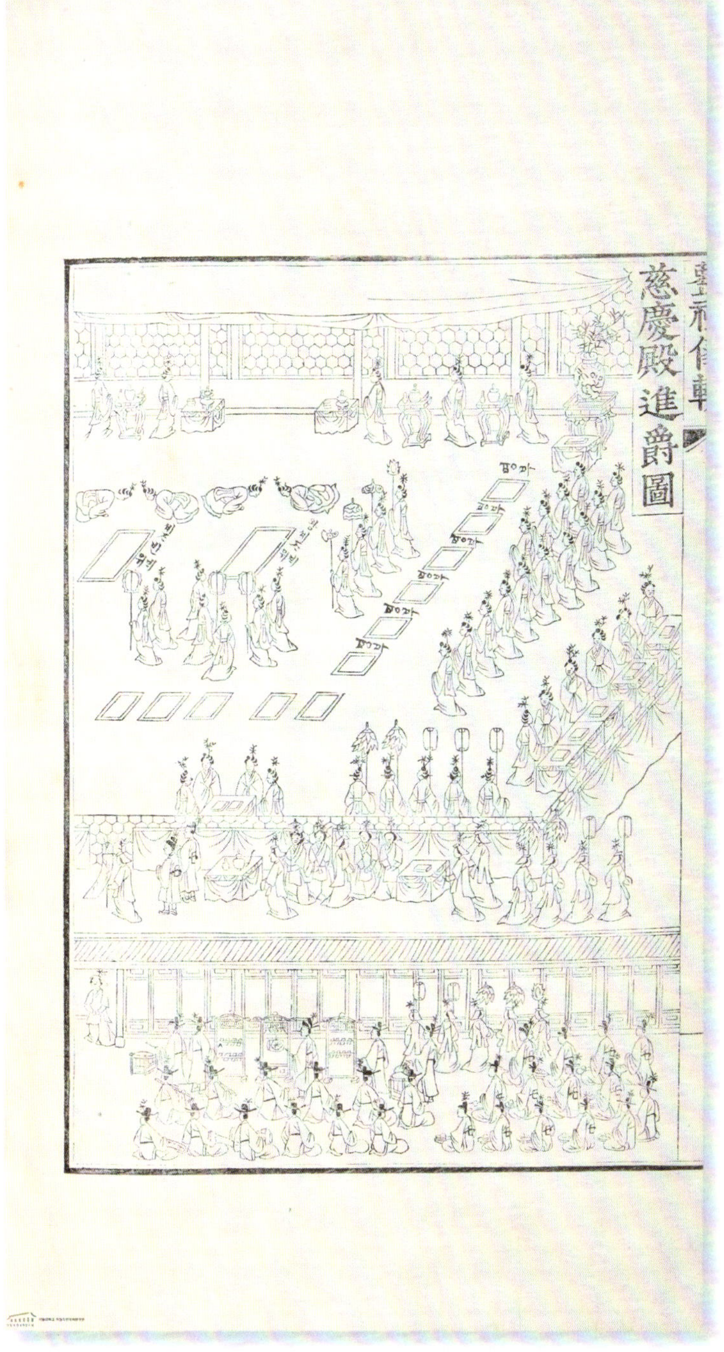

In another royal banquet record, compiled in 1828, the name of Baek Sanul appears again.[62] He was referred to as *Eonseo seosa* 諺書書寫, or scribe of vernacular Korean, which means he might have been good at both literary Chinese and vernacular Korean calligraphy. The title of *Eonseo seosa* continuously appears in later documents as these court calligraphers were responsible for scribing vernacular Korean. If the male court calligraphers rather than palace women were responsible for scribing the vernacular Korean versions of royal banquet records, we need to reassess claims that *gungche* constituted a women-only genre.

In 1848, Elder Queen Mother Sunwon would turn sixty years old and the queen mother would turn forty-one, according to the Korean method of calculating age (which includes the period of pregnancy and considers a child to be one year old at birth). A grand royal banquet was held for them, and an extant large screen illustrates the event in detail (fig. 3.20). At the first ceremony held in the inner quarter of the palace in Tongmyeong Hall, congratulatory eulogies written in vernacular Korean were delivered to both queens. The third and fourth panels of the screen depict the first banquet. The seat of honor is empty, though it indicates that the elder queen mother had been there celebrating her birthday.[63] While vernacular Korean writing was widely used in women's spaces, it was still often written by men. Palace women may well have been instrumental in the development of *gungche*, since they wrote letters and copied novels. However, existing scholarship promotes the idea that *gungche* was predominantly female despite insufficient evidence to support the claim and some evidence to the contrary.[64]

Most scholarship to date has posited that vernacular Korean calligraphy is related to women, and that the controversial concept *gungche* is also a unique style for palace women. This misinformed view has mainly relied on interviews with the surviving palace matrons in the 1960s and Yun Baekyeong's memoir, compiled in *Bongseo*. Her father, Yun Yonggu (尹用求, 1853–1939), was of the illustrious Hepyong Yun lineage and an adopted son of Prince Deogon. After passing the civil service examination he served in various offices, including those of head secretary of the royal secretariat, minister of rite, and minister of personnel. Recently, rare vernacular Korean documents stored in the house of the Yun family have been released in large quantities.[65] Among them is *Record of Jagyeong Hall*, which is skillfully written by Princess Deogon (figs. 3.21, 3.22). It was originally composed by her father, King Sunjo, in literary Chinese. She first transliterated the Chinese and then translated it into vernacular Korean. Her calligraphy has a refined style that she learned from her mother, Queen Sunwon. Later, Yun Yonggu followed this style and passed it on to her daughter Yun Baekyeong. The elegant *gungche* was passed down from generation to generation, through both men and women. It is inaccurate to understand *gungche* as an indication of the autonomy of female culture.

Figure 3.20. Anonymous, *Birthday Banquets for Elder Queen Mother Sunwon*, 1848. Eight-panel screen, ink and pigment on silk, each panel 136.1 × 47.6 cm. National Museum of Korea, Seoul.

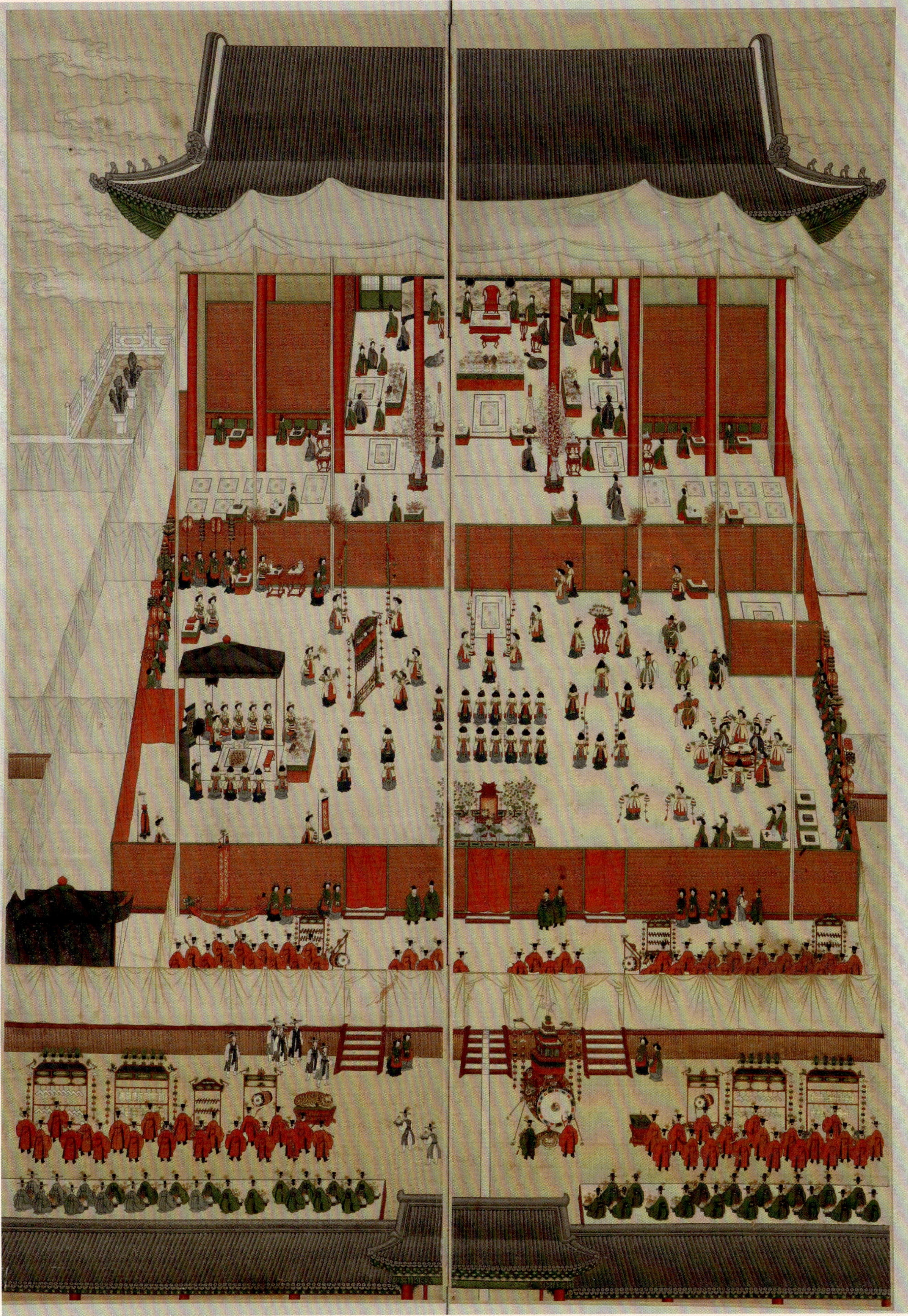

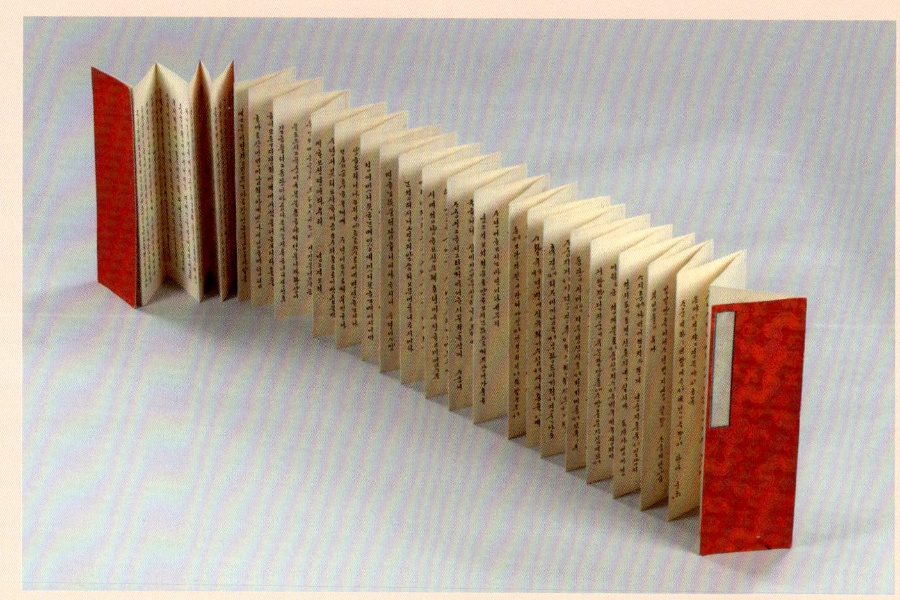

Figure 3.21. Princess Degon, *Record of Jagyeong Hall*, 19th century, ink on paper, 32 × 528 cm. National Hangeul Museum, Seoul.

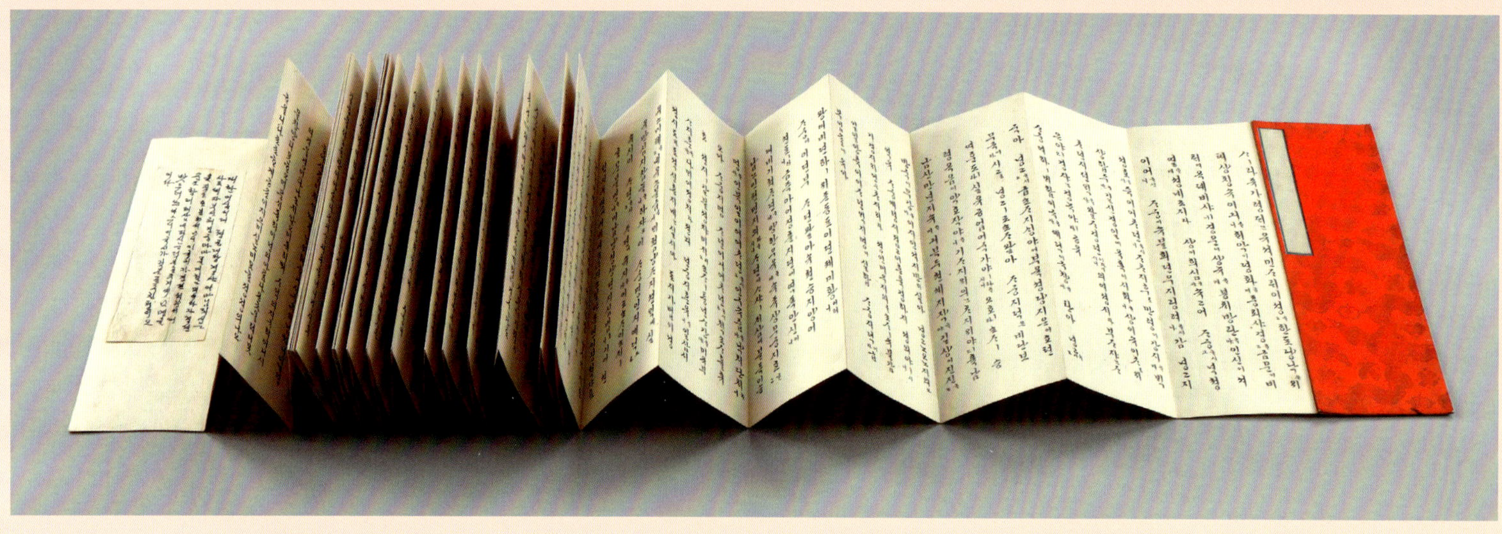

Figure 3.22. Princess Degon, *Record of Jagyeong Hall*, 19th century, ink on paper, 32 × 528 cm. National Hangeul Museum, Seoul.

Gender and Calligraphy in Korea

Scholarship has tended to view vernacular Korean and literary Chinese writing as dichotomous traditions divided by gender and class. The diglossic literary culture and its relations to gender were far too complex to be explained by a dichotomy—the one private, female, and local; the other public, male, and cosmopolitan. The relationship between vernacular Korean and literary Chinese was more complex than the simplistic notion that they were divided by gender. It is questionable whether men and women of the Joseon dynasty used different calligraphy styles according to their respective genders. Since vernacular Korean was also written by men, the differences between the calligraphy styles of men and women need clarifying.

Vernacular Korean letters sent by elite scholars to their female families demonstrate an individual style that often comes from their Chinese calligraphy.[66] Kim Jeonghui (金正喜, 1786–1856) is widely acknowledged to be the greatest calligrapher of the Joseon dynasty. When the political party with which his family was associated lost power, he was forced into exile on Jeju Island, off Korea's southern coast. His vernacular Korean letters to his wife, Madame Yi of Yean, in which he requests seasonal clothes and food precisely express his discomfort, longing, and suffering alone in a remote place. In a letter of 1841, his vernacular Korean calligraphy is composed of strong, willful strokes (fig. 3.23). As with his Chinese calligraphy style, he vertically compressed some characters and horizontally stretched others. By drawing many strokes diagonally and using "flying-white" or unevenly inked dry lines to connect each character, Kim Jeonghui applied the literary Chinese calligraphy technique of running script and provided a strong contrast between thick and thin strokes, lighter and heavier graphs, and stronger and weaker rhythms.

Figure 3.23. Kim Jeonghui, *A Letter by Kim Jeonghui to His Wife*, 1841, ink on paper, 22 × 41.6 cm. National Museum of Korea, Seoul.

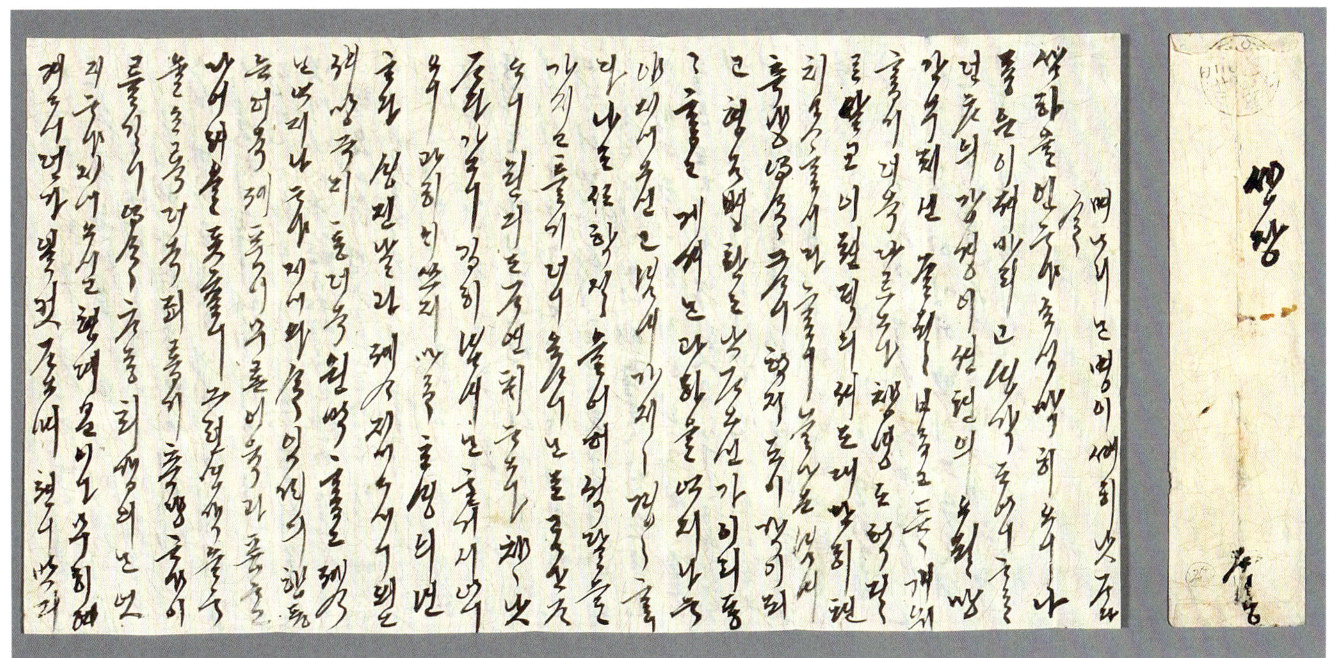

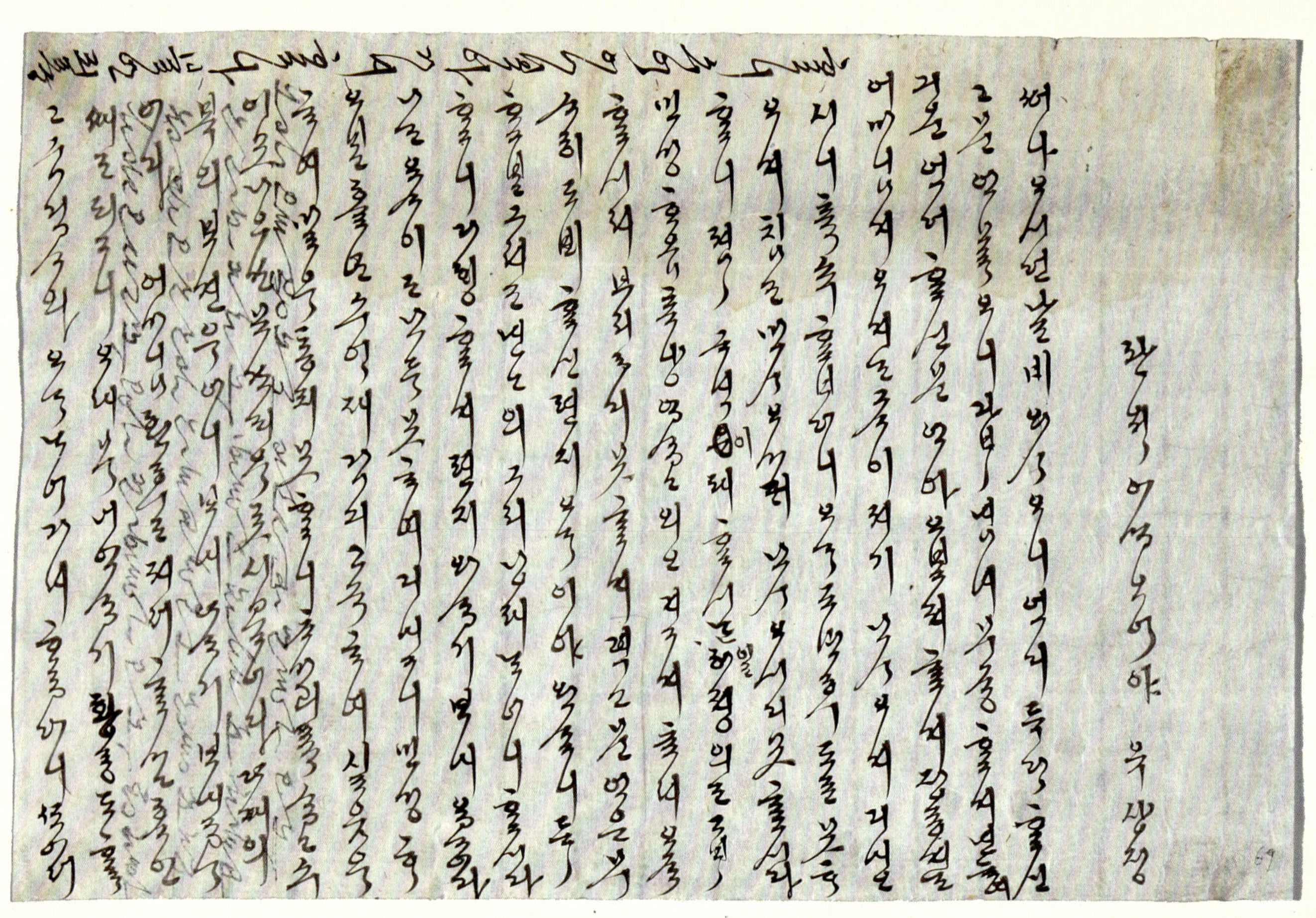

Figure 3.24. Madame Yu, *A Letter by Madame Yu to Her Husband*, ca. 1791, ink on paper, measurements unknown. National Museum of Korea, Seoul.

Comparing this with a letter from his mother, Madame Yu, to her husband in 1791, the reduced number of strokes and the simplified character shapes have a similar style (fig. 3.24).[67] Although each of the two letters reveal individuality, the difference is not one of gender. Should her calligraphy, with its preference for fleshy curves and circular motions, be considered feminine? This issue is further confused because both men and women shared a similar family style, indicating that any initial ties between style and gender were lost.

This seems to have been the same in the palace. We have already seen that the crown prince learned vernacular Korean. Around age eight, King Jeongjo penned a staggering volume of letters to an aunt, asking after her health (fig. 3.25).[68] He was still at an early stage of learning to write, so the brush strokes are somewhat clumsy. Characters are often quite different in size; they may be extremely tall or broad. However, a letter sent to Lady Min of Yeoheung in 1796, when King Jeongjo was forty-five years old, shows a much more fluent brushstroke (fig. 3.26).[69] Using thick strokes and fast movement, it is similar to King Jeongjo's calligraphy in literary Chinese. It shows his individual style but cannot be called masculine.

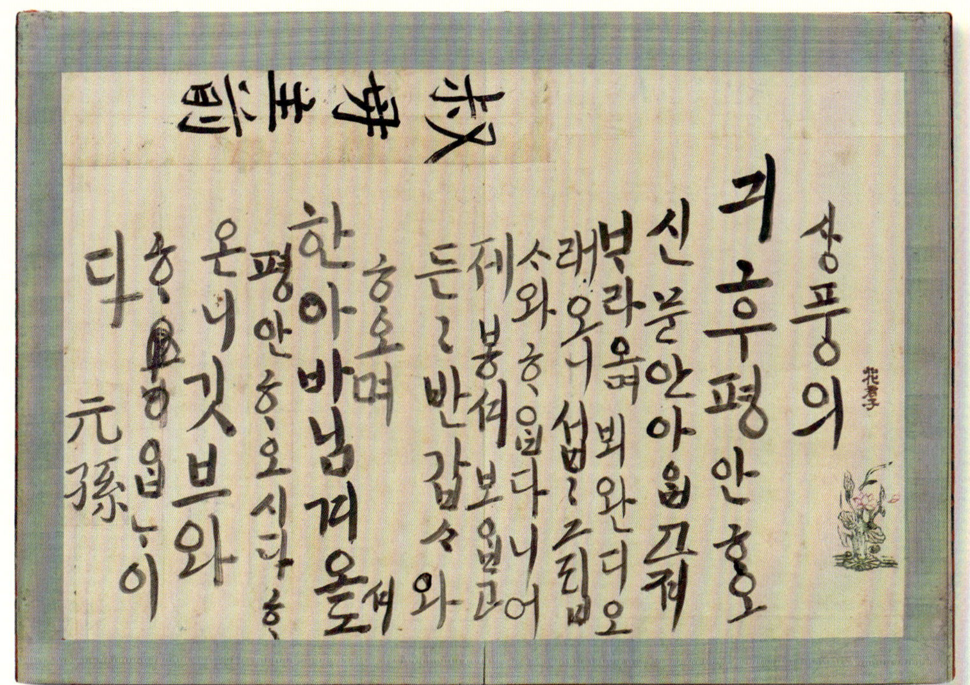

Figure 3.25. King Jeongjo, *A Letter by King Jeongjo to His Aunt*, from the album of King Jeongjo's letters, 18th century. Album 44.5 × 31.5 cm. National Hangeul Museum, Seoul.

Figure 3.26. King Jeongjo, *A Letter by King Jeongjo to Lady Min*, from the album of King Jeongjo's letters, 1796. Album 44.5 × 31.5 cm. National Hangeul Museum, Seoul.

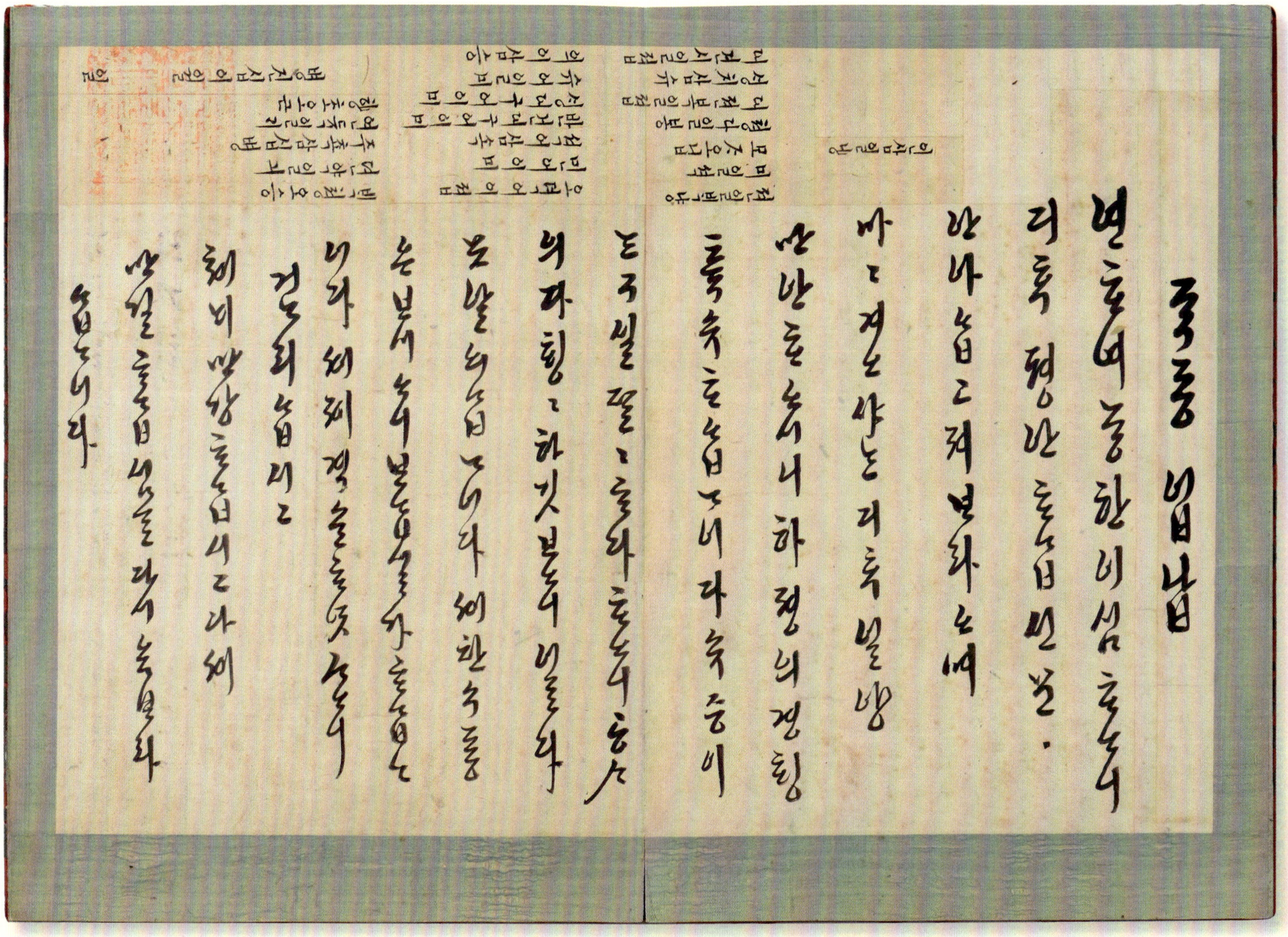

Attached to King Jeongjo's second letter was a list of gifts he sent, but this was not written by him. It may be the writing of the palace woman who assisted the king. Letters and other documents sent by the king to the queen were all in vernacular Korean, and since this was delivered by the palace woman, it is likely that there was a palace woman next to the king who was skillful in handwriting. We should also remember that the crown prince learned vernacular Korean from a palace woman. Another possibility is that the list is the writing of a male calligrapher. As mentioned earlier, among the official documents of the court, those in vernacular Korean were often written by court calligraphers or clerks. Some eunuchs were also good at writing in vernacular Korean.

The authorship of the list is difficult to judge in terms of gender. The important aspects are that the letters are written in fluent style and the list is in standard style, and that the different calligraphy styles were used for different functions. It is not a difference between men and women. There is no evidence that women wrote in calligraphy styles differing from those used by men. Thus, the calligraphy style of women is not distinct from that of their male counterparts.

In the Joseon court, it is difficult to identify distinctive calligraphy styles for men and women because vernacular Korean writing by the king, queen, palace women, eunuchs, and male scribes intersect and affect one another. This is different from literary Chinese calligraphy, which men practically monopolized.

Vernacular Korean calligraphy was centered on women and gained social and aesthetic recognition in women's practice. As Ksenia Chizhova has addressed, vernacular Korean had an intimate relationship with Confucian gender norms that linked bodily discipline, womanly work, and refined vernacular handwriting.[70] However, it cannot be said that women led the development of vernacular Korean calligraphy and *gungche* style. In terms of style, female engagement in the development of vernacular Korean calligraphy is not obvious.

The relation between vernacular Korean calligraphy and gender is complex, overlapping, and unstable; however, previous studies have tried to excavate an original femininity beneath layers of the patriarchal system. Many have perpetuated stereotypes such as the isolated, aestheticized category of "woman" and applied a limited formal analysis of the calligraphy style to explain the pragmatic or performative dimension of women's calligraphic practices. Gender in the domain of visual representation is rather labile.

The major concern of women calligraphers was not always to rebel against male tradition. Their calligraphy often adhered to the established script style even more strictly than the works of their male exemplars did. Traditional calligraphers usually operate within a closed system of forms, and repeated copying of former calligraphers' work is a crucial method for mastering techniques.[71] Joseon women calligraphers, whose literary talents were unsupported by Confucian society, may have had more reason to adhere to the conventions established by men.

Conclusion

In 1971, Linda Nochlin published an article titled "Why Have There Been No Great Women Artists?" and it has drawn feminist interventions in the histories of art. With this in mind, we can ask the question, "Why have there been no great women calligraphers in the Joseon dynasty?" In response, it can be said that Joseon Korea was a patriarchal society, so women were constrained by limited gender roles and could not properly produce calligraphy works. However, as we have seen above, it is difficult to find women calligraphers in literary Chinese, but many women actively wrote in vernacular Korean. Would the previous question be answered if we add Wonyi's mother, Princess Sungmyeong, Matron Scribe Yi, and nameless palace women to the list of great calligraphers and include their letters and documents in the corpus of calligraphy artworks? If that is the case, commoners and slaves who wrote in vernacular Korean during the Joseon dynasty should also be considered calligraphers, and it would be appropriate that the numerous handwritten *hangeul* novels became works of calligraphy. This is not a desirable solution.

The efforts to reinstate women calligraphers based on aesthetic and formalist criteria can rather distort the reality. In other words, attempts to incorporate vernacular Korean calligraphy by women into the existing calligraphy canon can further strengthen the history of calligraphy formulated from masculinist viewpoints. Moreover, a calligraphy history established on the premise of literary Chinese calligraphy cannot properly explain the distinctive characteristics of vernacular Korean calligraphy. Rather, it would be effective to go beyond calligraphy and deal with it with a new perspective of writing itself. This alternative approach is not to treat the writing as object but to consider writing as practice. It is similar to an attempt to replace art history with visual culture or material culture studies. Rather than asking whether vernacular Korean writings by Joseon women are calligraphy or not, we need to explore what kind of relationship these works had with the women who wrote them, and how they changed that relationship. When Korean women scribed *hangeul*, they could not posit their works as representative of their personality and an important means of self-expression. However, by using vernacular Korean, they could be the direct recorders of their daily lives.

Korean women played a significant role in reading, writing, and collecting vernacular Korean calligraphy, although they did not initiate the stylistic innovation. In the patriarchal society, male artists and their criticism monopolized artistic originality. As a result, female calligraphers and their works were not visible in the premodern Korean art world. If we shift our analytic focus from the formal element to the performative dimension and consider the physical ephemerality of writing and reading, we can imagine that women calligraphers in the Joseon dynasty scribed their alphabets and nurtured this domestic writing system.

Notes

1. Yi Song-mi, *Fragrance, Elegance, and Virtue: Korean Women in Traditional Arts and Humanities* (Seoul: Daewonsa, 2002).

2. Insoo Cho, "Writings in the Joseon Dynasty," in Stephen Little and Virginia Moon, eds., *Beyond Line: The Art of Korean Writing* (Los Angeles: Los Angeles County Museum of Art, 2019), 84–111.

3. Nothing developed in Korea like women's agency, which contributed to the rise of female visual culture in China. See Hui-shu Lee, *Empresses, Art, and Agency in Song Dynasty China* (Seattle: University of Washington Press, 2010).

4. On *Geunyeok seohwa jing* 槿域書畫徵, see Hong Sunpyo, "O Sech'ang's Compilation of *Kŭnyŏk sŏhwa sa* (History of Korean Painting and Calligraphy) and the Publication of *Kŭnyŏk sŏhwa ching* (Biographical Records of Korean Painters and Calligraphers)," *Archives of Asian Art* 63, no. 2 (2014): 155–63.

5. For Chinese women painters and calligraphers, see Marsha Weidner, ed., *Flowering in the Shadows: Women in the History of Chinese* (Honolulu: University of Hawaiʻi Press, 1990), and Zhou Xiaoru, 周小儒, Jiang Lingling, 蒋玲玲, *Zhongguo lldai nü shufa jia* 中国历代女书法家 (Jinan: Shandong huabao chuban she, 2012).

6. Yi Song-mi, "Sin Saimdang: The Foremost Woman Painter of the Chosŏn Dynasty," in Young-Key Kim-Renaud, ed., *Creative Women of Korea: The Fifteenth through the Twentieth Centuries* (New York: M. E. Sharpe, 2004), 58–77, and Burglind Jungmann, "Changing Notions of 'Feminine Spaces,' in Chosŏn-Dynasty Korea: The Forged Image of Sin Saimdang (1504–1551)," *Archives of Asian Art* 68, no. 1 (2018), 47–66.

7. Lee SoonGu, "The Exemplar Wife: The Life of Lady Chang of Andong in Historical Context," in Youngmin Kim and Michael J. Pettid, eds., *Women and Confucianism in Chosŏn Korea: New Perspectives* (Albany: State University of New York Press, 2011), 29–48.

8. Sin Jwamo, "Gyonam gihaeng" [Travel to Gyeongsang province] in *Daminjip* (1916); reprinted in *Hanguk munjip chonggan* 309 (Seoul: Minjongmunhwachujinhoe, 2003), 383. Unless otherwise noted, all translations are my own.

9. Jang Gyehyang's descendant Yi Upyo (李宇標, 1734–1793) explained that her father, Jang Heunghyo (張興孝, 1564–1633), kept one of her poems written on a sheet of paper and later gave it to her sons. Yuk Manjung (睦萬中, 1727–1810), "Issi jeonga bocheop seo" [Preface to a precious album preserved in the Yi family] in *Yeowa seonsaeng munjip* (undated); reprinted in *Hanguk munjip chonggan sok* 90 (Seoul: Hangukgojeonbeonyeogwon, 2009), 209.

10. Jang Gyehyang's son Yi Hyeonil (李玄逸, 1627–1704) wrote her biography. See *Jeongbuin andong jangssi silgi* [Biographical records of Lady Jang from Andong] (1904); Reprinted in *Gugyeok andong jangssi silgi* (Seoul: Gugyeogandongjangssisilgiganhaengso, 1999), 23–32.

11. All three were strongly influenced by Han Ho (韓濩, 1543–1605), the most famous calligrapher in the sixteenth century. Oh Sehyeon, "Hwajeong gwa Yuhap," *Seoulhagyeongu*, no. 70 (2018): 101–39.

12. JaHyun Kim Haboush, "The Vanished Women of Korea: The Anonymity of Texts and the Historicity of Subjects," in Anne Walthall, ed., *Servants of the Dynasty: Palace Women in World History* (Berkeley: University of California Press, 2008), 280–98.

13. The authenticity of this work has been debated. See Oh Sehyeon, "Hwajeong gwa Yuhap," 111n36.

14. This work was explained in detail in the inscription written by Nam Guman (南九萬, 1629–1711) at the request of Hong Manhoe (洪萬恢, 1643–1710), the youngest son of the princess, in 1701. Nam Guman, "Jeongmyeonggongju piljeok bal," [Inscription for Princess Jeongmyeong's calligraphy] in *Yakcheonjip* (1723); reprinted in *Hanguk munjip chonggan* 132 (Seoul: Minjongmunhwachujinhoe, 1994), 457.

15. *Sejong sillok* [Veritable records of King Sejong], vol. 79, 11/12 (1437), accessed on October 1, 2022, sillok.history.go.kr.

16. Gungmip gogung bangmulgwan et al., *Joseon ui yeoksa reul jikyeo on wangsil yeoseong* (Paju: Geulhangari, 2014), 61–62.

17. Kim Gyeongmi, *Ga wa yeoseong: Sippalsegi yeoseong saenghwal gwa munhwa* (Seoul: Yeoiyeon, 2012), 57–58.

18. Kim Gyeongmi, *Yim Yunjidang pyeongjeon* (Seoul: Hangyeorechulpan, 2019), 76–77.

19. Gang Myeonggwan, *Geurim euro ingneun Joseon yeoseong ui yeoksa* (Seoul: Hyumeoniseuteu, 2012), 141.

20. The term *hangeul* was coined in the 1920s. Before that, it had been called *eonmun*, or "vulgar writing."

21. Ksenia Chizhova, "Bodies of Texts: Women Calligraphers and the Elite Vernacular Culture of Late Chosŏn Korea (1392–1910)," *Journal of Asian Studies* 77, no. 1 (2018): 62.

22. Peter H. Lee and Wm. Theodore de Bary, eds., *Sources of Korean Tradition*, vol. 1, *From Early Times through the Sixteenth Century* (New York: Columbia University Press, 1997), 295.

23. Hwang Munhwan, *Joseonsidae ui hangeul pyeonji, Eongan* (Seoul: Yeongnak, 2015), 21–22.

24. Yun Jaeheung, "Joseon sidae yangban ga ui Hangeul gyoyuk ui yangsang," *Gyoyuksasangyeongu* 32, no. 1 (2018): 115–33.

25. *Sukjong sillok* [Veritable records of King Sukjong], vol. 23, 9/13 (1691), accessed on October 1, 2022, sillok.history.go.kr.

26. Ksenia Chizhova, "Vernacular Itineraries: Korean Letters from Family to National Archive," *Journal of Korean Studies* 24, no. 2 (2019): 351–55.

27. Sun Joo Kim, "Letters on Everyday Life," in JaHyun Kim Haboush, ed., *Epistolary Korea: Letters in the Communicative Space of the Chosôn, 1392–1910* (New York: Columbia University Press, 2009), 226–34; and Chizhova, "Vernacular Itineraries," 349–51.

28. JaHyun Kim Haboush, "The Sunch'on Kims: Vignettes of Family Life through Letters," in Haboush, ed., *Epistolary Korea*, 269–76.

29. Bak Jeongsuk, *Joseon ui Hangeul pyeonji* (Seoul: Daunsaem, 2017), 17–22.

30. Sun Joo Kim, "A Wife's Letter to Her Deceased Husband," in Haboush, ed., *Epistolary Korea*, 393–97. The eulogy was written to a deceased husband, Yi Ungtae (1556–1586), and buried alongside his body. It was excavated in 1998.

31. Quoted in Sun Joo Kim, "A Wife's Letter to Her Deceased Husband," 396.

32. These are *goche, jeongjache,* and *heullimche*. Jang Jihun, "Hangeul seoye ui mihak," *Seoyehagyeongu*, no. 34 (2019): 145–73.

33. JaHyun Kim Haboush, "Gender and Politics of Language in Chosŏn Korea," in Benjamin A. Elman, John B. Duncan, and Herman Ooms, eds., *Rethinking Confucianism: Past and Present in China, Japan, Korea, and Vietnam* (Los Angeles: University of California Press, 2002), 220–57.

34. Kim Yeonghui, "Joseon sidae Hangeul geulsseugi chegye ui baljeon gwa yeoseong," *Peminijeumyeongu* 17, no. 2 (2017): 149.

35. Hyegyeonggung Hongssi, *Hanjungnok*, trans. Jeong Byeongseol (Paju: Munhakdongne, 2010), 159.

36. There remain 289 letters from various queens. Han Soyun, "Joseon sidae wanghudeul ui eongan seoche teukjing yeongu," *Hanguksasanggwa munhwa*, no. 69 (2013): 404–24.

37. There are sixty-seven letters collected in the album. Gungmip cheongju bangmulgwan, *Joseon wangsil ui Hangeul pyeonji, Sungmyeong sinhancheop* (Cheongju: Gungmip cheongju bangmulgwan, 2011).

38. Baek Duhyeon, "Joseon sidae wangsil eongan ui munhwa jungcheungnon jeong yeongu," *Hangukangnonjip*, no. 59 (2015): 392–97.

39. Gungmip gogung bangmulgwan, *Myeongseong hwanghu hangeul pyeonji wa joseon wangsil ui sijeonji* (Seoul: Gungmip gogung bangmulgwan, 2010).

40. *Naehun*, "eonhaeng" (1475) 61a–63a in Kyujanggak Library collection, Seoul National University.

41. Yi Deokmu, "Sasojeol" [Small manners for scholars] in *Cheongjanggwan jeonseo* (1980); reprinted in *Hanguk munjip chonggan* 257 (Seoul: Minjongmunhwachujinhoe, 2000), 515.

42. Haboush, "Vanished Women of Korea," 282–84.

43. Kim Yongsuk, *Joseon jo gungjung pungsok yeongu* (Seoul: Iljisa, 1987), 54, 62–63. In China, imperial women's engagement with calligraphy became especially prevalent in the Song dynasty, and some imperial women served as ghostwriters to the emperor. Hui-shu Lee, *Empresses, Art, and Agency in Song Dynasty China*, 70–94.

44. Yun Baekyeong's comment on Matron Scribe Yi's letter (1974); reprinted in Jo Yongseon, ed., *Bongseo* (Seoul: Daunsaem, 1997), 21.

45. Kim Bongjwa, "Wangsil uirye reul wihan balgi ui jejak gwa teukseong," *Seojihagyeongu*, no. 65 (2016): 291–330.

46. Yi Deokmu, "Sasojeol," 515.

47. Ji-Eun Lee, "Literacy, Sosŏl, and Women in Book Culture in Late Chosŏn Korea," *East Asian Publishing and Society* 4, no. 1 (2014), 36–64.

48. Sim Gyeongho, "Nakseonjaebon soseol ui seonhaengbon e gwanhan ilgochal," *Jeongsinmunhwayeongu* 13, no. 1 (1990): 169–88.

49. Yi Jiyeong, "Hangeul pilsabon e natanan hangeul pilsa ui munhwa jeok maengnak," *Hangukgojeonyeoseongmunhagyeongu*, no. 17 (2008): 273–308.

50. Yi Wonju, "*Jamnok* gwa *Banjohwajeonga* e daehayeo," *Hangukangnonjip*, no. 7 (1980): 14.

51. Yi Jiyeong, "Hangeul pilsabon e natanan hangeul pilsa ui munhwa jeok maengnak," 273–308, and Chizhova, "Bodies of Texts," 67–76.

52. Chizhova, "Bodies of Texts," 67.

53. It is believed that *gungche* began to develop in the eighteenth century and reached its peak in the late nineteenth century. Yi Wanu, "Hangeul seoche ui geukseong," in *Sinpyeon hanguksa joseon sidae 35: joseon hugiui munhwa* (Gwacheon: Guksapyeonchanwiwonhoe, 1998), 494–96.

54. The translation is from Chizhova, "Bodies of Texts," 64.

55. Bak Jeongja et al., *Gungche iyagi* (Seoul: Daunsaem, 2001), 11–29.

56. Bak Jeongja et al., *Gungche iyagi*, 11–29.

57. Kim Bongjwa, "Sunjo dae jinjak uirye wa Hangeul girongmul ui jejak," *Jeongsinmunhwayeongu* 38, no. 3 (2015): 151–78.

58. These were the military official Song Gyubin (宋奎斌, 1696–1778) from the Eouigung Palace, the scribe Yi Yudam (李惟聃) from Jeyonggam, and the scribe Yu Segwan (柳世寬) from Hongmungwan. *Cheonuisogam chansucheong uigwe* (Seoul: Hangukgojeonbeonyeogwon, 2017): 144–45.

59. Haboush, "Vanished Women of Korea," 292.

60. Kim Bongjwa, "Wangsil Hangeul pilsabon ui jeonseung hyeonhwang gwa gachi," *Gugeosayeongu*, no. 20 (2015): 56.

61. *Jagyeongjeon jinjak jeongnye uigwe* in Kyujanggak Library collection, Seoul National University.

62. This time, the royal banquet was held to celebrate Queen Sunwon's fortieth birthday. *Muja jinjak uigwe*, vol. 2, chapter 37b in Kyujanggak Library collection, Seoul National University.

63. Hyonjeong Kim Han, "Beyond Birthday Banquets: Celebrations, Arts, and Politics of Queens in Nineteenth-Century Korea," in *In Grand Style: Celebrations in Korean Art during the Joseon Dynasty* (San Francisco: Asian Art Museum, 2013), 134–63.

64. Bak Jeongsuk, *Joseon ui Hangeul pyeonji*, 293–94.

65. National Hangeul Museum, *Gongjyu geulsi dyeogeusini* [Hangeul writings from three generations of the Princess Deogon family] (Seoul: National Hangeul Museum, 2019).

66. Bak Jeongsuk, "Joseon junggi Yeongnam jibang Hangeul pyeonji ui seoyemi gochal," *Hangukangnonjip*, no. 6 (2015): 153–96.

67. Bak Jeongsuk, *Joseon ui Hangeul pyeonji*, 49–53.

68. National Hangeul Museum, *Sojang jaryo chongseo* (Seoul: National Hangeul Museum, 2014), 26–27.

69. National Hangeul Museum, *Sojang jaryo chongseo*, 46–47.

70. Chizhova, "Bodies of Texts," 76.

71. Qianshen Bai, "Calligraphy," in Martin J. Powers and Katherine R. Tsiang, eds., *A Companion to Chinese Art* (West Sussex, UK: Wiley, 2016), 317–20.

Bibliography

Primary Sources

Cheonuisogam chansucheong uigwe. Seoul: Hangukgojeonbeonyeogwon, 2017.

Jagyeongjeon jinjak jeongnye uigwe. 1827. Kyujanggak Library collection, Seoul National University.

Jeongbuin andong jangssi silgi. 1904. Reprinted in *Gugyeok andong jangssi silgi.* Seoul: Gugyeogandongjangssisilgiganhaengso, 1999.

Muja jinjak uigwe. 1828. Kyujanggak Library collection, Seoul National University.

Naehun. 1475. Kyujanggak Library collection, Seoul National University.

Nam Guman. "Jeongmyeonggongju piljeok bal." In *Yakcheonjip.* 1723. Reprinted in *Hanguk munjip chonggan*, vol. 132. Seoul: Minjongmunhwachujinhoe, 1994.

Sejong sillok. Accessed via sillok.history.go.kr.

Sin Jwamo. "Gyonam gihaeng." In *Daminjip.* 1916. Reprinted in *Hanguk munjip chonggan*, vol. 309. Seoul: Minjongmunhwachujinhoe, 2003.

Sukjong sillok. Accessed via sillok.history.go.kr.

Yi Deokmu. "Sasojeol." In *Cheongjanggwan jeonseo.* 1980. Reprinted in *Hanguk munjip chonggan*, vol. 257. Seoul: Minjongmunhwachujinhoe, 2000.

Yuk Manjung. "Issi jeonga bocheop seo." In *Yeowa seonsaeng munjip.* Reprinted in *Hanguk munjip chonggan sok*, vol. 90. Seoul: Hangukgojeonbeonyeogwon, 2009.

Secondary Sources in Korean and Chinese

Baek Duhyeon. "Joseon sidae wangsil eongan ui munhwa jungcheungnon jeong yeongu." *Hangukangnonjip*, no. 59 (2015): 349–40.

Bak Jeongja, Sin jeonghui, Jo seongja, Jo juyeon, Ji namnye. *Gungche iyagi.* Seoul: Daunsaem, 2001.

Bak Jeongsuk. "Joseon junggi Yeongnam jibang Hangeul pyeonji ui seoyemi gochal." *Hangukangnonjip*, no. 6 (2015): 153–96.

———. *Joseon ui Hangeul pyeonji.* Seoul: Daunsaem, 2017.

Gang Myeonggwan. *Geurim euro ingneun Joseon yeoseong ui yeoksa.* Seoul: Hyumeoniseuteu, 2012.

Gungmip cheongju bangmulgwan. *Joseon wangsil ui Hangeul pyeonji, Sungmyeong sinhancheop.* Cheongju: Gungmip cheongju bangmulgwan, 2011.

Gungmip gogung bangmulgwan. *Myeongseong hwanghu hangeul pyeonji wa joseon wangsil ui sijeonji.* Seoul: Gungmip gogung bangmulgwan, 2010.

Han Soyun. "Joseon sidae wanghudeul ui eongan seoche teukjing yeongu." *Hanguksasanggwa munhwa*, no. 69 (2013): 404–24.

Hwang Munhwan. *Joseonsidae ui hangeul pyeonji, Eongan.* Seoul: Yeongnak, 2015.

Hyegyeonggung Hongssi. *Hanjungnok.* Paju: Munhakdongne, 2010.

Jang Jihun. "Hangeul seoye ui mihak." *Seoyehagyeongu* no. 34 (2019): 145–73.

Jo Yongseon, ed. *Bongseo.* Seoul: Daunsaem, 1997.

Kim Bongjwa. "Sunjo dae jinjak uirye wa Hangeul girongmul ui jejak." *Jeongsinmunhwayeongu* 38, no. 3 (2015): 151–78.
———. "Wangsil Hangeul pilsabon ui jeonseung hyeonhwang gwa gachi." *Gugeosayeongu*, no. 20 (2015): 39–64.
———. "Wangsil uirye reul wihan balgi ui jejak gwa teukseong." *Seojihagyeongu*, no. 65 (2016): 291–330.
Kim Gyeongmi. *Ga wa yeoseong: Sippalsegi yeoseong saenghwal gwa munhwa.* Seoul: Yeoiyeon, 2012.
———. *Yim Yunjidang pyeongjeon.* Seoul: Hangyeorechulpan, 2019.
Kim Yeonghui. "Joseon sidae Hangeul geulsseugi chegye ui baljeon gwa yeoseong." *Peminijeumyeongu* 17, no. 2 (2017): 127–55.
Kim Yongsuk. *Joseon jo gungjung pungsok yeongu.* Seoul: Iljisa, 1987.
National Hangeul Museum. *Gongjyu geulsi dyeogeusini.* Seoul: National Hangeul Museum, 2019.
———. *Sojang jaryo chongseo.* Seoul: National Hangeul Museum, 2014.
Oh Sehyeon. "Hwajeong gwa Yuhap." *Seoulhagyeongu*, no. 70 (2018): 101–39.
Sim Gyeongho. "Nakseonjaebon soseol ui seonhaengbon e gwanhan ilgochal." *Jeongsinmunhwayeongu* 13, no. 1 (1990): 169–88.
Sin Myeongho, Yi Minseon, Kim Jiyeong, Gwon Huisuk, Kim Jeonghui, Yi Minju, Jeong Eunim, Im Minhyeok. *Joseon ui yeoksa reul jikyeo on wangsil yeoseong.* Paju: Geulhangari, 2014.
Yi Jiyeong. "Hangeul pilsabon e natanan hangeul pilsa ui munhwa jeok maengnak." *Hangukgojeonyeoseongmunhagyeongu*, no. 17 (2008): 273–308.
Yi Wanu. "Hangeul seoche ui geukseong." In *Sinpyeon hanguksa joseon sidae 35: joseon hugiui munhwa*, 494–96. Gwacheon: Guksapyeonchanwiwonhoe, 1998.
Yi Wonju. "*Jamnok* gwa *Banjohwajeonga* e daehayeo." *Hangukangnonjip*, no. 7 (1980): 37–51.
Yun Jaeheung. "Joseon sidae yangban ga ui Hangeul gyoyuk ui yangsang." *Gyoyuksasangyeongu* 32, no. 1 (2018): 115–33.
Zhou, Xiaoru, and Jiang Lingling. *Zhongguo lldai nü shufa jia.* Jinan: Shandong huabao chuban she, 2012.

Secondary Sources in English

Bai, Qianshen. "Calligraphy." In *A Companion to Chinese Art*, edited by Martin J. Powers and Katherine R. Tsiang, 312–28. West Sussex, UK: Wiley, 2016.
Chizhova, Ksenia. "Bodies of Texts: Women Calligraphers and the Elite Vernacular Culture of Late Chosŏn Korea (1392–1910)." *Journal of Asian Studies* 77, no. 1 (2018): 59–81.
———. "Vernacular Itineraries: Korean Letters from Family to National Archive." *Journal of Korean Studies* 24, no. 2 (2019): 345–71.
Cho, Insoo. "Writings in the Joseon Dynasty." In *Beyond Line: The Art of Korean Writing*, edited by Stephen Little and Virginia Moon, 84–111. Los Angeles: Los Angeles County Museum of Art, 2019.
Haboush, JaHyun Kim, ed. *Epistolary Korea: Letters in the Communicative Space of the Chosôn, 1392–1910*. New York: Columbia University Press, 2009.
———. "Gender and Politics of Language in Chosŏn Korea." In *Rethinking Confucianism: Past and Present in China, Japan, Korea, and Vietnam*, edited by Benjamin A. Elman, John B. Duncan, and Herman Ooms, 220–57. Los Angeles: University of California Press, 2002.
———. "The Vanished Women of Korea: The Anonymity of Texts and the Historicity of Subjects." In *Servants of the Dynasty: Palace Women in World History*, edited by Anne Walthall, 280–98. Berkeley: University of California Press, 2008.

Han, Hyonjeong Kim. "Beyond Birthday Banquets: Celebrations, Arts, and Politics of Queens in Nineteenth-Century Korea." In *In Grand Style: Celebrations in Korean Art during the Joseon Dynasty*, 134–63. San Francisco: Asian Art Museum, 2013.

Hong Sunpyo. "O Sech'ang's Compilation of *Kŭnyŏk sŏhwa sa* (History of Korean Painting and Calligraphy) and the Publication of *Kŭnyŏk sŏhwa ching* (Biographical Records of Korean Painters and Calligraphers)." *Archives of Asian Art* 63, no. 2 (2014): 155–63.

Jungmann, Burglind. "Changing Notions of 'Feminine Spaces' in Chosŏn-Dynasty Korea: The Forged Image of Sin Saimdang (1504–1551)." *Archives of Asian Art* 68, no. 1 (2018): 47–66.

Lee, Hui-shu. *Empresses, Art, and Agency in Song Dynasty China.* Seattle: University of Washington Press, 2010.

Lee, Ji-Eun. "Literacy, Sosŏl, and Women in Book Culture in Late Chosŏn Korea." *East Asian Publishing and Society* 4, no. 1 (2014): 36–64.

Lee, Peter H., and Wm. Theodore de Bary, eds. *Sources of Korean Tradition*, vol. 1, *From Early Times through the Sixteenth Century.* New York: Columbia University Press, 1997.

Lee SoonGu. "The Exemplar Wife: The Life of Lady Chang of Andong in Historical Context." In *Women and Confucianism in Chosŏn Korea: New Perspectives*, edited by Youngmin Kim and Michael J. Pettid, 29–48. Albany: State University of New York Press, 2011.

Weidner, Marsha, ed. *Flowering in the Shadows: Women in the History of Chinese.* Honolulu: University of Hawai'i Press, 1990.

Yi Song-mi. *Fragrance, Elegance, and Virtue: Korean Women in Traditional Arts and Humanities.* Seoul: Daewonsa, 2002.

———. "Sin Saimdang: The Foremost Woman Painter of the Chosŏn Dynasty." In *Creative Women of Korea: The Fifteenth through the Twentieth Centuries*, edited by Young-Key Kim-Renaud, 58–77. New York: M. E. Sharpe, 2004.

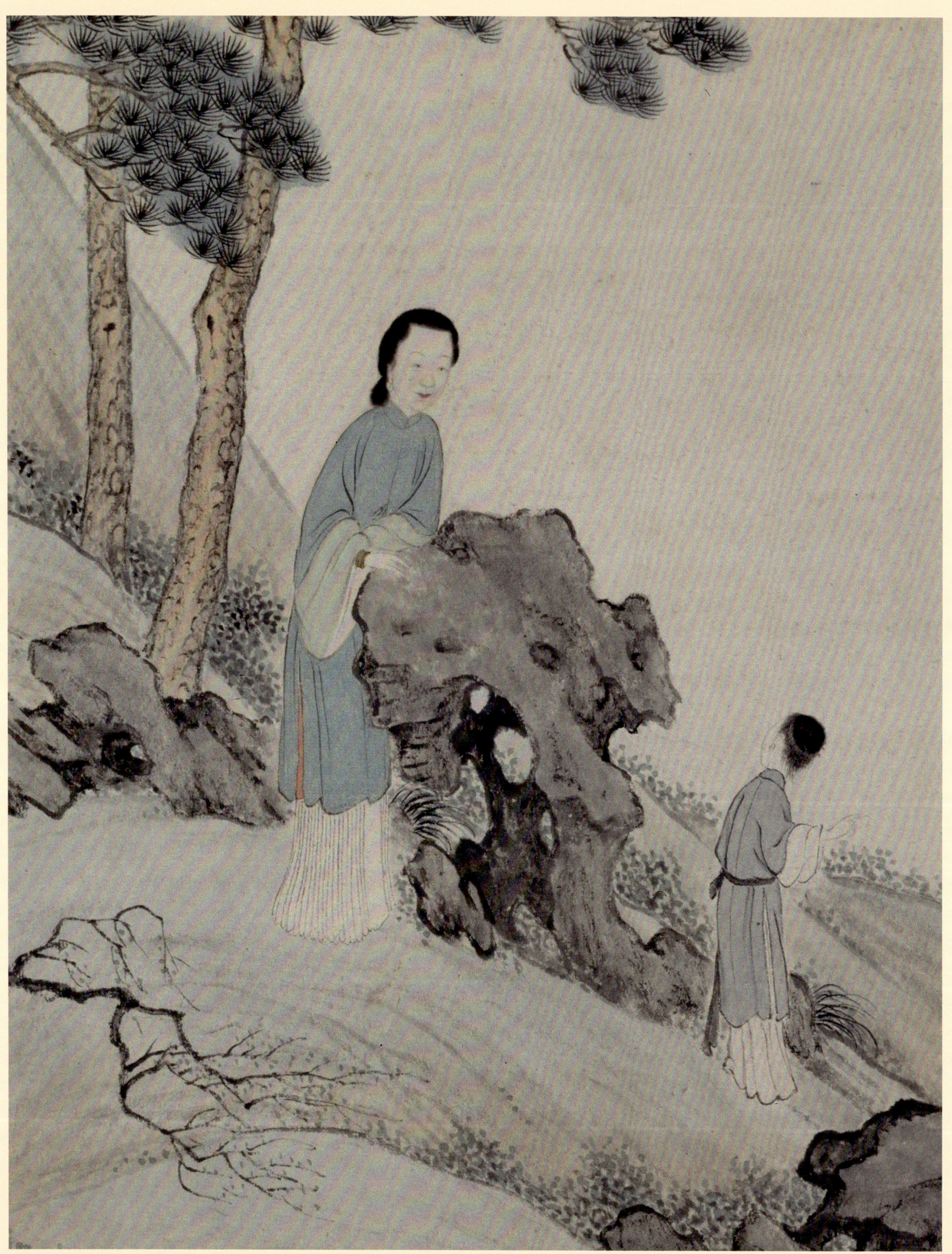

Promoting by Herself and Others

Luo Qilan (1756–after 1813) and Her Multiple Identities

Janet C. Chen

As a woman known for great talents and literary achievements, Luo Qilan 駱綺蘭 (1756–after 1813) led an unconventional life that began in the second half of the eighteenth century and continued into the early nineteenth century. Her portraits, which were often accompanied by inscriptions she requested from her male and female contemporaries, shaped her public identities. Some of them survive, and others are known through textual records. They show her in a variety of roles: a sightseeing poet in *Spring View at Pingshan* (*Pingshan chunwang tu* 平山春望圖) (fig. 4.1), a dutiful mother in *Tutoring My Daughter by the Autumn Lamp* (*qiudeng kenü tu* 秋燈課女圖), and a religious devotee in *Returning to the Way* (*guidao tu* 歸道圖).[1] Some pictures in *Eight Dreams* (*bameng tu* 八夢圖) (fig. 4.2) reflect her real life, while others show impossible identities for a woman in late imperial China, such as a government official and army general.[2] Why were these portraits made, and what do they show? Why did Luo request inscriptions for them, and what were the responses of these authors? How do the images and texts portray her, and how do they shape her identities? To address these questions, this paper begins by focusing on the touring poet depicted in *Spring View at Pingshan*; later it discusses Luo's other portraits and identities, primarily through examinations of an album and related Qing texts.

Luo Qilan: A Biography in Brief

Born into a family that had produced scholars for many generations and could trace its ancestral line back to the Tang poet Luo Binwang 駱賓王 (ca. 640–684), Luo Qilan received from her father an education in poetry from a young age.[3] She married a scholar named Gong Shizhi 龔世治 (fl. eighteenth century), with whom she shared a life with

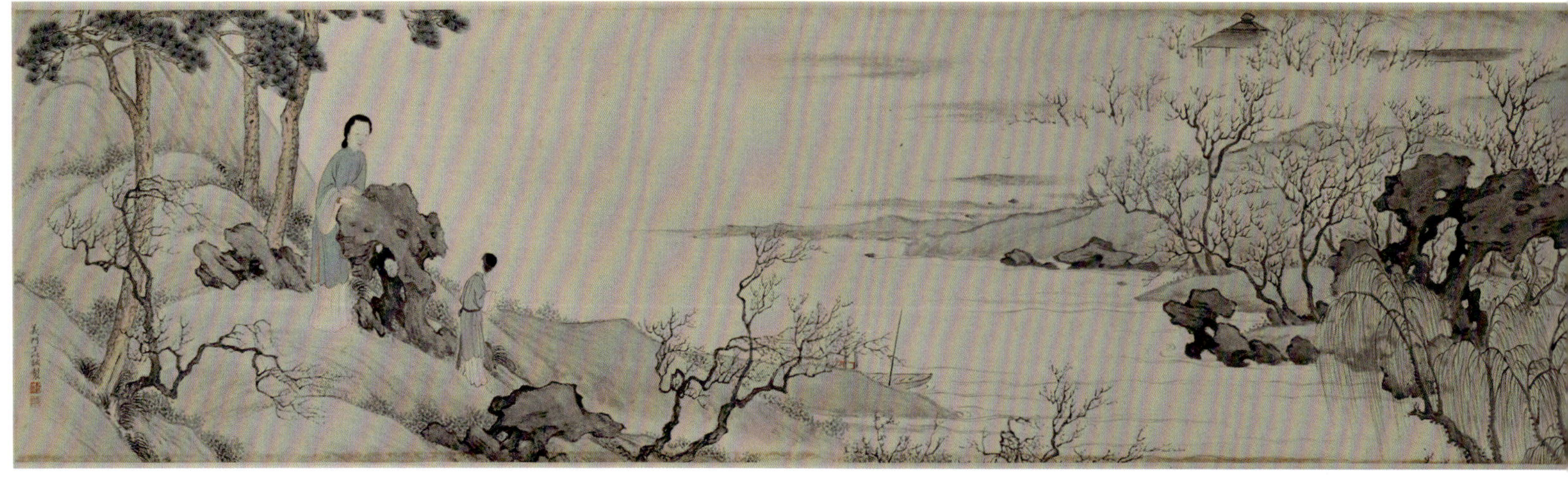

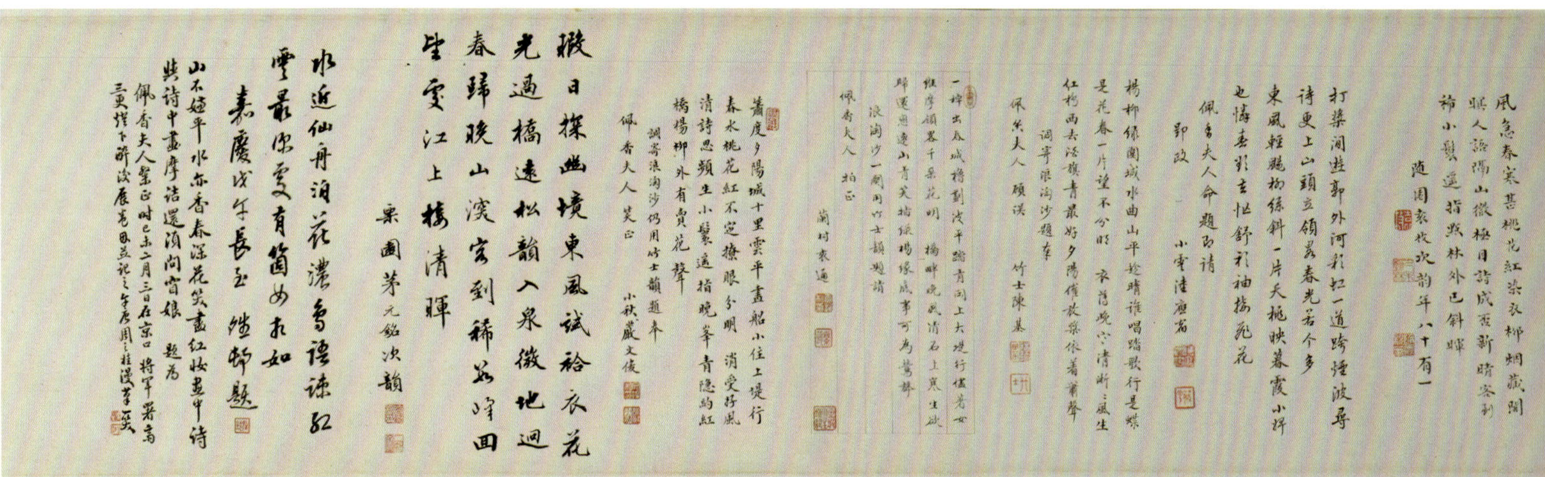

similar literary interests in Guangling 廣陵, or modern Yangzhou 揚州.[4] The couple's harmonious and fulfilling marital life was cut short, as Gong passed away when Luo was in her thirties.[5] She returned to her natal family, did not remarry, and raised an adopted daughter.[6] During her middle age, Luo enjoyed visiting scenic places and religious sites, associating with male and female intellectuals, and engaging in various literary and artistic activities. Later in life, she became a lay Buddhist practitioner.[7]

To Luo Qilan's contemporaries and later generations, she was an accomplished poet who wrote most of her extant poems after she became a widow.[8] She was a student of Yuan Mei 袁枚 (1716–97), Wang Wenzhi 王文治 (1730–1802), and Wang Chang 王昶 (1725–1806), and through their connections she developed relationships with many learned men and women.[9] During her widowhood, Luo had three volumes of collected writings published.[10] They not only represent her literary achievements as a poet and editor but also provide clues to her private and social lives. Luo was also known as a painter who mostly worked in the bird-and-flower genre, though the name of her teacher and the extent of her artistic education were not clearly recorded in texts. Painting provided a means for her to participate in the social customs of male literati, by giving her works as gifts or requesting inscriptions for them. Her paintings now survive in museums and private collections or are known through textual accounts.[11]

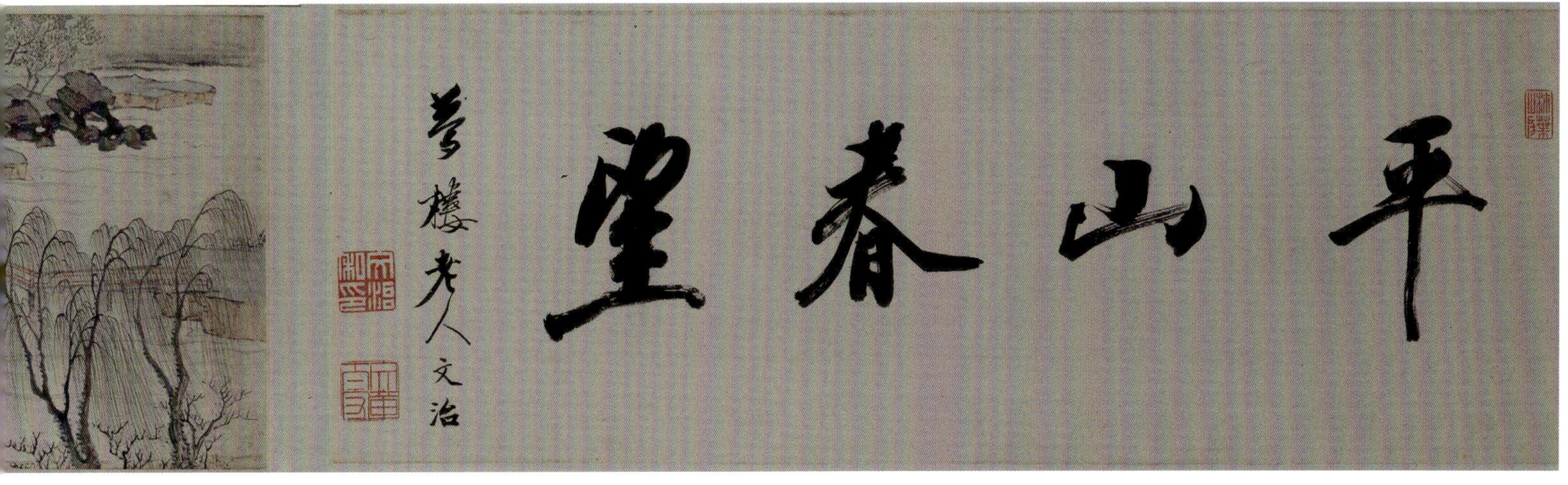

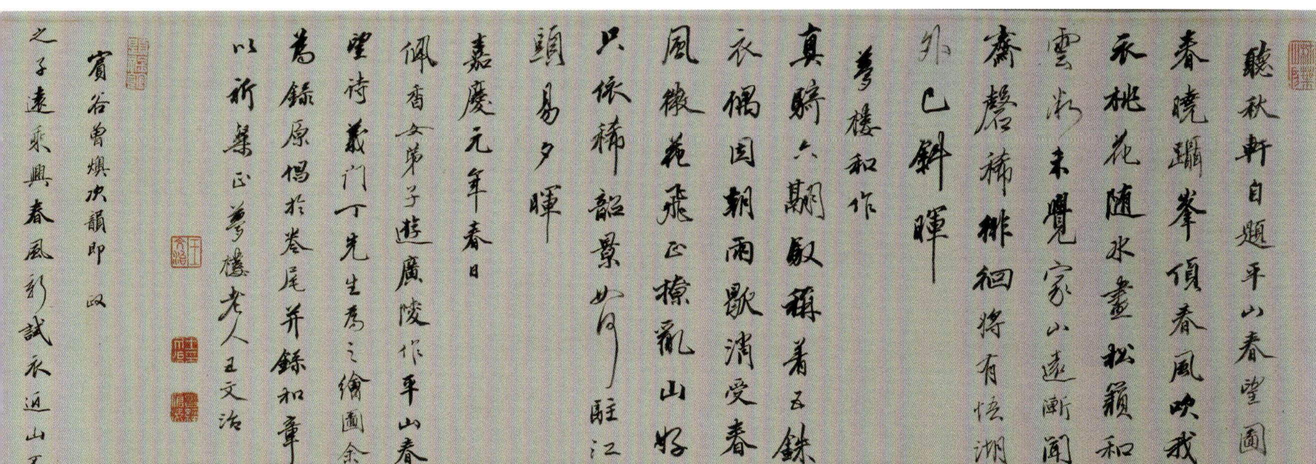

Figure 4.1. Ding Yicheng 丁以誠, *Spring View at Pingshan* (*Pingshan chunwang* 平山春望). Handscroll. Provided by the Palace Museum, Beijing.

Spring View at Pingshan

Entering the collection of the Palace Museum, Beijing, after 1949, *Spring View at Pingshan* portrays Luo Qilan as a touring poet who writes compositions in response to famous places.[12] The handscroll begins with the painting's title, *Pingshan chunwang tu*, written by Luo's teacher, Wang Wenzhi, who named the work after her poem, *Pingshan chunwang shi* 平山春望詩. Following the frontispiece is a picture depicting three land masses divided by water and mist. On the right, a bridge connects the first and second masses of land. Of the first, only a corner appears; the second is filled with porous rocks and trees with pink blossoms that identify the season as spring. Emerging from the mist, a pavilion stands in the background. Hills and pines occupy the third piece of land. Under a pine tree is Luo, wearing a blue dress and leaning against a rock. A few steps away from her is a young maidservant, who turns back toward Luo while pointing forward, as if she is suggesting that Luo might travel on a nearby boat to reach the land of blossoming trees. Following the painting are colophons by Luo's male contemporaries, including her literary teachers, Yuan Mei and Wang Wenzhi, and Yuan's acquaintances and relatives.

According to Wang Wenzhi's colophon, *Spring View at Pingshan* is a portrait of Luo Qilan, intended to represent her sightseeing of Guangling and to complement her poem on Pingshan Hall (*Pingshan tang* 平山堂). To the northwest beyond Guangling, or the Qing city of Yangzhou, was an area full of scenic places and historical sites, and many literati composed commemorations of their visits there. Pingshan, also known as Pingshan Hall, was one of these attractions.[13] Luo was likely attached to Yangzhou, where she lived with her sympathetic husband; therefore, she visited the city and its surroundings and wrote commemorative poems. Her composition, inspired by the scenery around Pingshan Hall, was singled out for *Spring View at Pingshan.* This hall was founded by and derived its fame from Ouyang Xiu 歐陽修 (1007–1072), a famous scholar and government official of the Northern Song dynasty (960–1124), who used the place for social and leisure activities. Later scholars often wrote of Pingshan Hall, most likely for its connection to the admired Ouyang Xiu. In these writings, the authors often referred either to the terms "Pingshan" or "Pingshan Hall."[14] Therefore, when male scholars read the title of Luo's poem, they would have recognized her participation in a popular literati pastime of leisurely touring and writing poetry in response to famous places.

In Luo Qilan's poem, she described what she observed, heard, and felt at the site. The spring scenery, the gentle breeze, and the sound of the Buddhist meal chime all combined to inspire poetic thoughts. Her poem reads:

Spring dawn tiptoes across the peaks;	春曉躡峰頂,
Spring wind sways my garment.	春風吹我衣.
The peach blossoms [blow about to] end in the water;	桃花隨水盡,
The sound of [wind in the] pines enters the clouds and grows faint.	松籟入雲微.
[I] do not sense that my hometown is far away;	未覺家山遠,
Gradually [I] hear the Buddhist meal chime in the distance.	漸聞齋磬稀.
Lingering, [I am] about to be awakened [by a flash of insight];	徘徊將有悟,
Beyond the lake already slanting are the rays of the evening sun.[15]	湖外已斜暉.

In fact, the poem recorded the religious aspect of Pingshan Hall. Even though the hall had a scholarly image, through its association with Ouyang Xiu and many literati of successive dynasties who wrote of the place and contributed to its renovations, one Qing account states that it had been incorporated into a monastery.[16] Luo's decision to include the sound of the Buddhist chime could also reflect her religious interests. As noted earlier, she became a lay Buddhist practitioner later in life.

In showing Luo Qilan outside her home and enjoying famous scenery, *Spring View at Pingshan* represents an unconventional aspect of her life after the death of her husband: roaming about the Jiangnan area to visit famous sites. Many of her trips were within modern southwestern Jiangsu 江蘇 province, and her destinations included attractions around the areas of modern Yangzhou 揚州, Nanjing 南京, Zhenjiang 鎮江, and her hometown, Jurong 句容. Occasionally, she went beyond these places, to Suzhou 蘇州 in southeastern Jiangsu, and to Hangzhou 杭州 in Zhejiang 浙江. Religious devotion, social activities, and sightseeing all led Luo away from her house. Like many male and some other female intellectuals, Luo's experiences of traveling and visiting famous sites inspired her poetry.[17]

The colophon writers for *Spring View at Pingshan* remarked on Luo's literary talent; their writings characterize her as an accomplished poet who roamed about, seeking inspiration from nature.

Who commissioned this handscroll is unknown, but Luo Qilan herself was certainly a possible candidate. The publication of Luo's collected writings, *Poems from the Tingqiu Studio* (*Tingqiuxuan shiji* 聽秋軒詩集), hints at her desire to make herself known as a writer. Having *Spring View at Pingshan* made and circulated among her contemporaries could also promote such an identity. However, as a widow who lacked the necessary social network for this scroll to reach her desired audience, assistance from male scholars was essential. Therefore, Wang Wenzhi and Yuan Mei, two of Luo's teachers who had social status and power, not only contributed their writings to the work but also likely motivated others to do the same on Luo's behalf.

Wang Wenzhi was another probable patron, as Wang did order or create paintings for his friends.[18] Wang's inspiration in creating *Spring View at Pingshan* would also explain why Pingshan Hall was selected as the subject over other Yangzhou attractions that Luo visited. To her male literati acquaintances and teachers, Luo's identity as a poet and her efforts to transmit their teachings were inspiring. In one text that documents Luo's poetic capabilities, Wang records that in a gathering of his students, she was the first to complete her composition.[19] In other words, her literary ability and quick wit surpassed that of her male contemporaries. Therefore, Pingshan Hall, a place related to Ouyang Xiu and many other scholars, was a more appropriate painting subject than sites that were famous but less associated with literati accomplishments.

Wang Wenzhi's colophon mentions Ding Yicheng 丁以誠 (active late eighteenth–early nineteenth century), a professional painter with some education, as the painter of *Spring View at Pingshan*. Ding's signature and seals in the lower left corner of the picture confirm this identification. Ding was able to write poetry and play the strategic game *weiqi* 圍棋 as well as paint figures and landscapes.[20] His capabilities in the pastimes of scholars likely facilitated his acceptance into literati circles, explaining his authorship of this painting. The colophon also indicates that Luo Qilan visited Pingshan Hall in the first year of the Jiaqing 嘉慶 reign (1796). The writing at the end of the scroll addresses Luo and mentions the *jiwei* 己未 year, and thus the inscription can be dated to 1799. Therefore, the creation and completion of this entire handscroll of painting and texts likely took place between 1796 and 1799, assuming the 1799 colophon was the last addition to the scroll.

Tutoring My Daughter by the Autumn Lamp

Another identity of Luo Qilan was that of a dutiful mother, promoted through *Tutoring My Daughter by the Autumn Lamp*. The whereabouts of the work is unknown; its existence is known through more than sixty inscriptions included in Luo's publications.[21] She personally requested some of these writings, sometimes through the assistance of her male mentors.[22] Of Luo's portraits, *Tutoring My Daughter* has the most recorded colophons, hinting at the frequent circulation of the work and her effort in making herself recognized as a dutiful mother.

The colophon writers responded to the pictorial content by praising Luo for taking up the responsibility of instructing her daughter, and thus the use of terms, such as "instructing the daughter" (*kenü* 課女), "female instructor" (*nüshi* 女師), and "female teacher" (*nüfu* 女傅), was common. Several mentioned the *wanxiong* 丸熊 medicinal pill, a reference that compared Luo with the mother of the Tang-dynasty (618–907) scholar Liu Zhongying 柳仲郢 (d. 864), who made the pill to provide her son energy to study.[23] Luo was active in a time when a woman's literary pursuits could have a negative impact on her reputation, as some still believed that "a woman without talent is virtuous" (*nüzi wucai bianshi de* 女子無才便是德) and that her "talent could hinder virtue" (*cai ke fangde* 才可妨德).[24] Therefore, the identity as a dutiful mother would have justified Luo's scholarly activities: the message was that these pastimes did not distract her from her womanly duties, and she put her knowledge to practical use, contributing to her family by providing an education for her daughter.

Reading the colophons for *Tutoring My Daughter by the Autumn Lamp*, a viewer would further perceive Luo Qilan as a talented and chaste woman. The authors complimented her literary achievements by likening her to earlier female poets: Bao Linghui 鮑令暉 (fifth century), a younger sister of the government official Bao Zhao 鮑照 (d. 466), who has several *shi* 詩 poems remain today; Zuo Fen 左芬 (second half of the third century), a younger sister of the poet Zuo Si 左思 (ca. 255–ca. 306) and a consort of Emperor Wu of Jin 晉武帝 (r. 265–90), who wrote both rhapsodies and *shi* poems; Xie Daoyun 謝道韞 (fl. mid–fourth century), a niece of the prominent statesman Xie An 謝安 (320–385) and the wife of the calligrapher Wang Ningzhi 王凝之, who is most famous for improvising a single poetic line on snowflakes during her youth.[25] These writers also mentioned Luo as a widow and praised her chastity by referring to the *bozhou* 柏舟 poem in the *Book of Poetry* (*Shijing* 詩經), which concerns a young widow's determination to not remarry.[26] In these ways, the colophon writers took part in constructing identities for Luo, elaborating them beyond the pictorial content of the painting.

The colophons also reveal various perspectives on women's education and attitudes toward those with literary talents. The writers differed from one another regarding the content of the instruction Luo provided to her daughter, and some thought she used poetry as her teaching material.[27] Others included the phrase "passing down classics" (*chuanjing* 傳經), a term reminding the reader of the "thirteen Confucian classics" (*Shisanjing* 十三經) that were standard for the education of boys.[28] "Family learning" (*jiaxue* 家學), or knowledge passed down within a family for generations, was another acceptable curriculum.[29] To these relatively open-minded literati, educational content did not have to be gender-specific, and women were capable of preserving and passing down family learning to the next generation.

A few writers presented a more conservative perspective, invoking the belief among some Qing scholars that women's artistic and literary talents could distract them from their female duties. One recommended Luo's daughter not to follow the footsteps of her

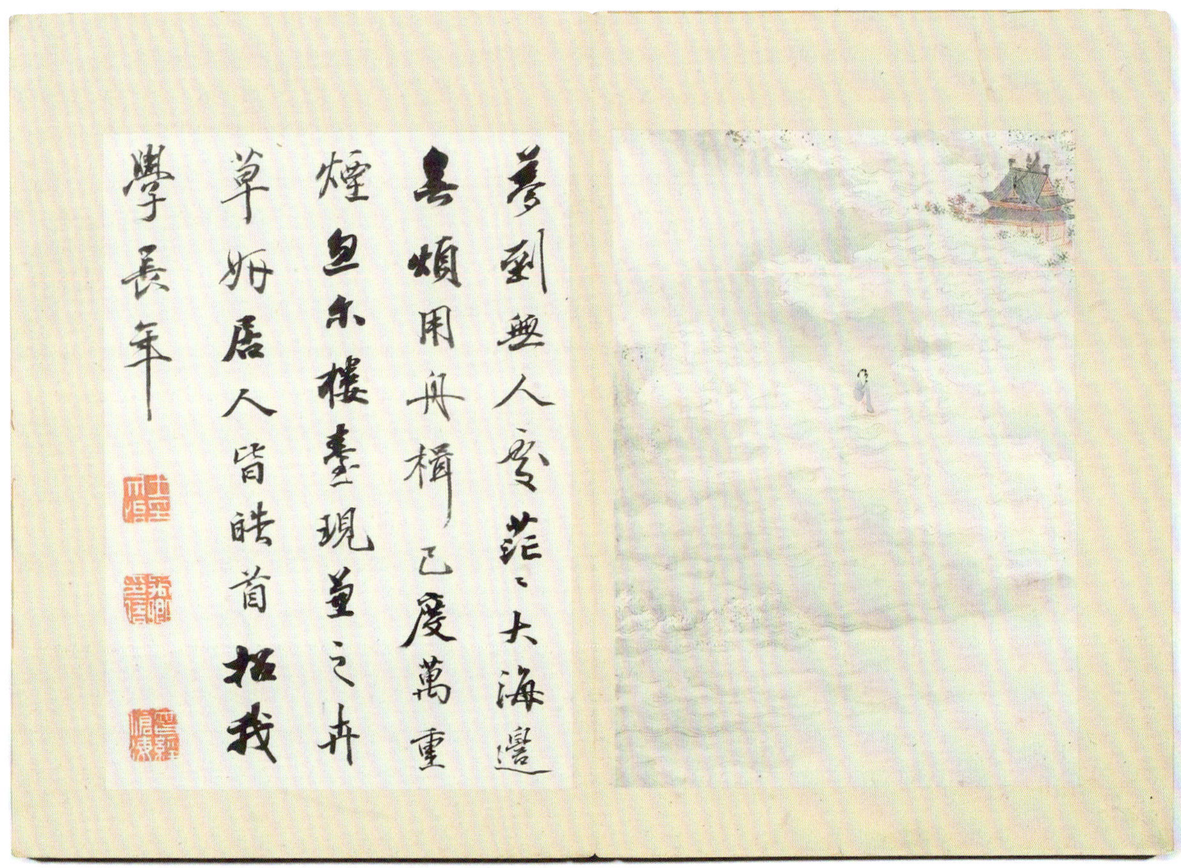

Figure 4.2. Pan Simu 潘思牧, *Record of Dreams from the Tingqiu Studio.* Album leaves. Image courtesy of Sotheby's.

mother, as talent and fame could be harmful to women.[30] One surmised that Luo taught the daughter a chapter from the "admonitions for women" (*nüzhen pian* 女箴篇), the didactic texts on ideal feminine behavior in a patriarchal society.[31] One thought the purpose of the daughter's education was to make sure that she would have a good disposition.[32] Such conservative views were likely the reason that motivated Luo to promote her identity, through the circulation of *Tutoring My Daughter by the Autumn Lamp*, as a mother responsible for the education of her child to justify her pursuits in literature.

Eight Dreams

In her pursuit of literary interests, Luo Qilan faced many limitations and criticism due to her gender. She addressed traditional gender roles in "Record of Dreams: Eight Poems" (*Jimengshi bashou* 紀夢詩八首), which were later illustrated in *Eight Dreams*.[33] An album titled *Record of Dreams from the Tingqiu Studio* contains eight paintings by Pan Simu 潘思牧 (1756–after 1843); the pictures on these facing leaves are paired with Luo's poems, transcribed by Wang Wenzhi. Pan was from the same family as Pan Gongshou 潘恭壽 (b. 1741), a painter and friend of Wang, and this connection possibly facilitated his authorship of the work.[34] Depicting her dreams, the paintings include small images of Luo, making them her portraits.

The poems and pictures portray Luo Qilan in various roles; while some hint at her real life, others portray her in positions she could only dream of occupying as a woman. In the second poem, Luo is a poet who writes compositions on the walls of her study and can memorize and recite the content of the scrolls in her collection. For this text, Pan Simu depicted Luo reading by a desk in front of shelves full of books in a room located at the rear of a residence (fig. 4.3). Near the gate of the property is a tree with red leaves to hint at autumn, the season recorded in Luo's poem. The text and picture are true, corresponding to Luo's art name (*hao* 號), Female Historian from Juqu (*Juqu nüshi* 句曲女史), and representing her interest in literature and public identity as a writer.

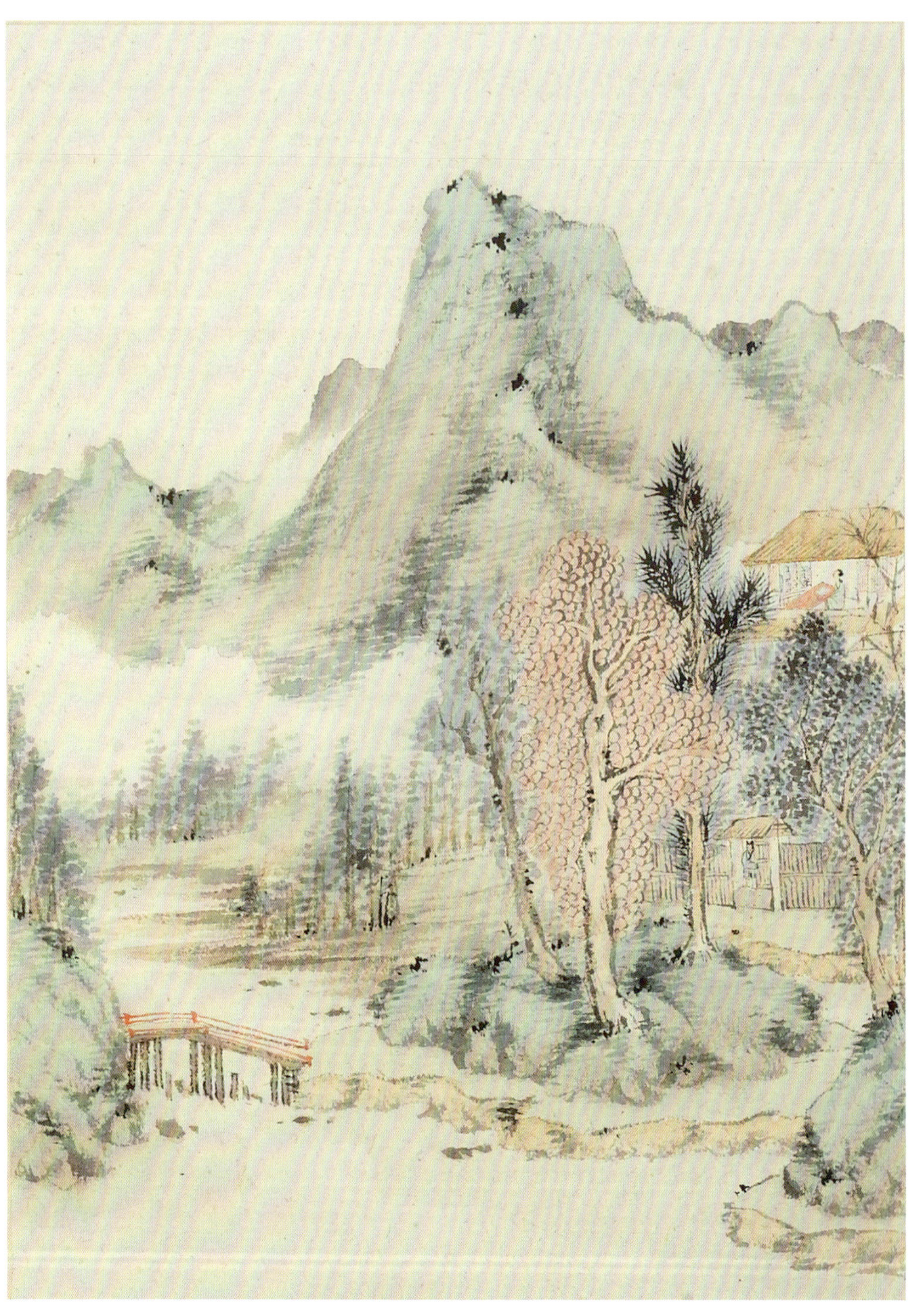

Figure 4.3. Pan Simu, *Record of Dreams from the Tingqiu Studio.* Album leaves. Image courtesy of Sotheby's.

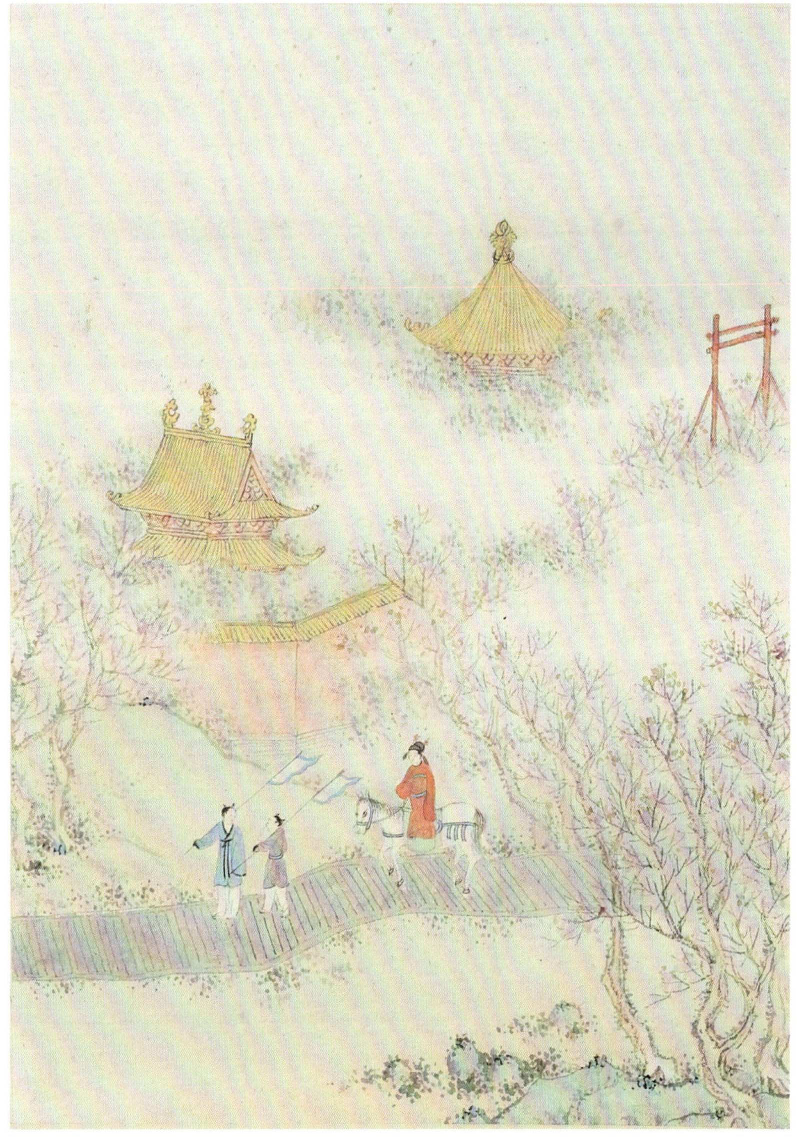

Figure 4.4. Pan Simu, *Record of Dreams from the Tingqiu Studio.* Album leaves. Image courtesy of Sotheby's.

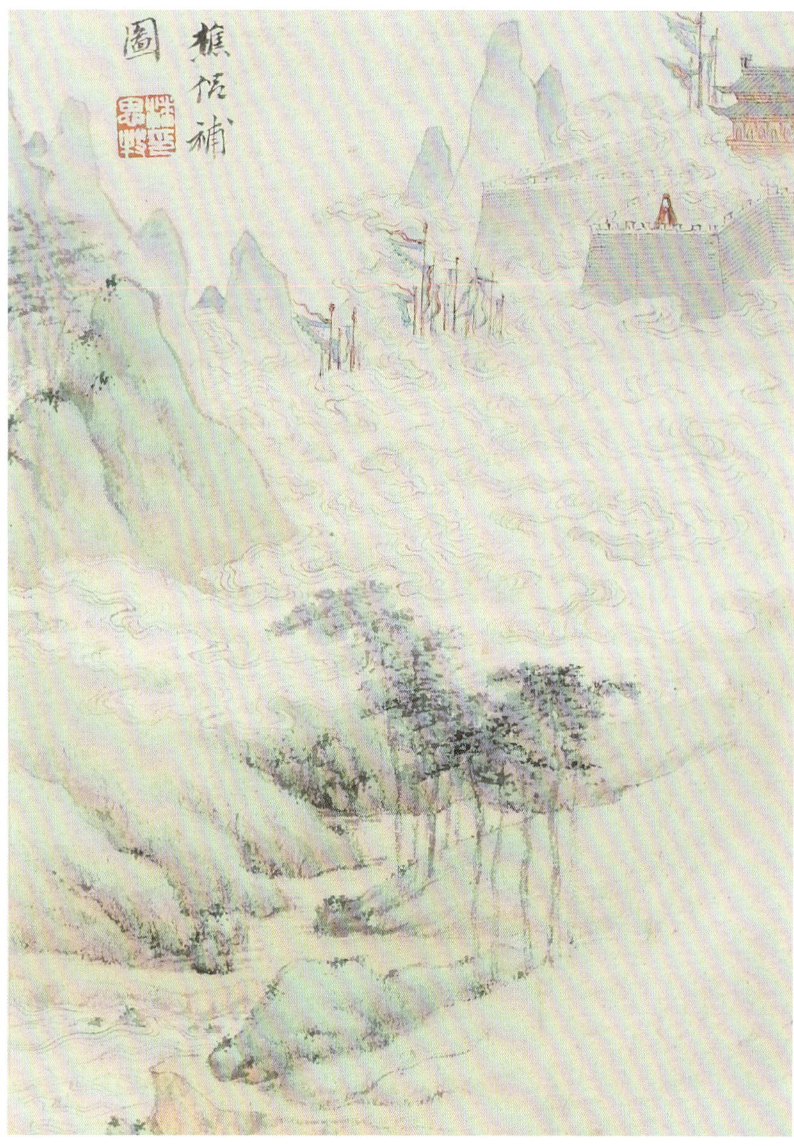

Figure 4.5. Pan Simu, *Record of Dreams from the Tingqiu Studio.* Album leaves. Image courtesy of Sotheby's.

Other poems, however, speak of unattainable ambitions for a woman at the time. In the third poem, Luo dreams of herself as a scholar who succeeds in the civil examination, which was open only to men. The paired painting shows her wearing the costume of a government official and riding on a white horse led by two attendants, suggesting the status she gained from passing the exams (fig. 4.4). In the seventh poem, she is a general in charge of an army at a border pass. In Pan's picture, she appears as a military leader reviewing her troops: she stands atop a fortress and overlooks an army, whose existence is suggested by flags partially hidden by clouds (fig. 4.5). As a woman, becoming a government official or military general was beyond Luo's reach, but her poems convey her ambitions and confidence that she could have obtained such positions if she had been born a man.

Four of the poems are about seeking spirituality and reclusion, two ways for Luo Qilan to deal with the criticism and social limitations she faced when exercising literary interests that some regarded as inappropriate for her gender. In these texts, terms from Buddhism and Daoism and descriptions of the dwelling of immortals hint at the writer's spiritual life. The first poem is one example that portrays Luo in the realm beyond the human world, as she is above layers of clouds and uses cranes as messengers. The mention of peach trees that take thousands of years to bear fruits suggests she is in the paradise of Queen Mother of West.[35] The paired picture depicts two buildings topped with yellow roof tiles and surrounded by swirling clouds (fig. 4.6). Standing in front of one, Luo is accompanied by four cranes that are traditionally regarded as vehicles of immortals. Like

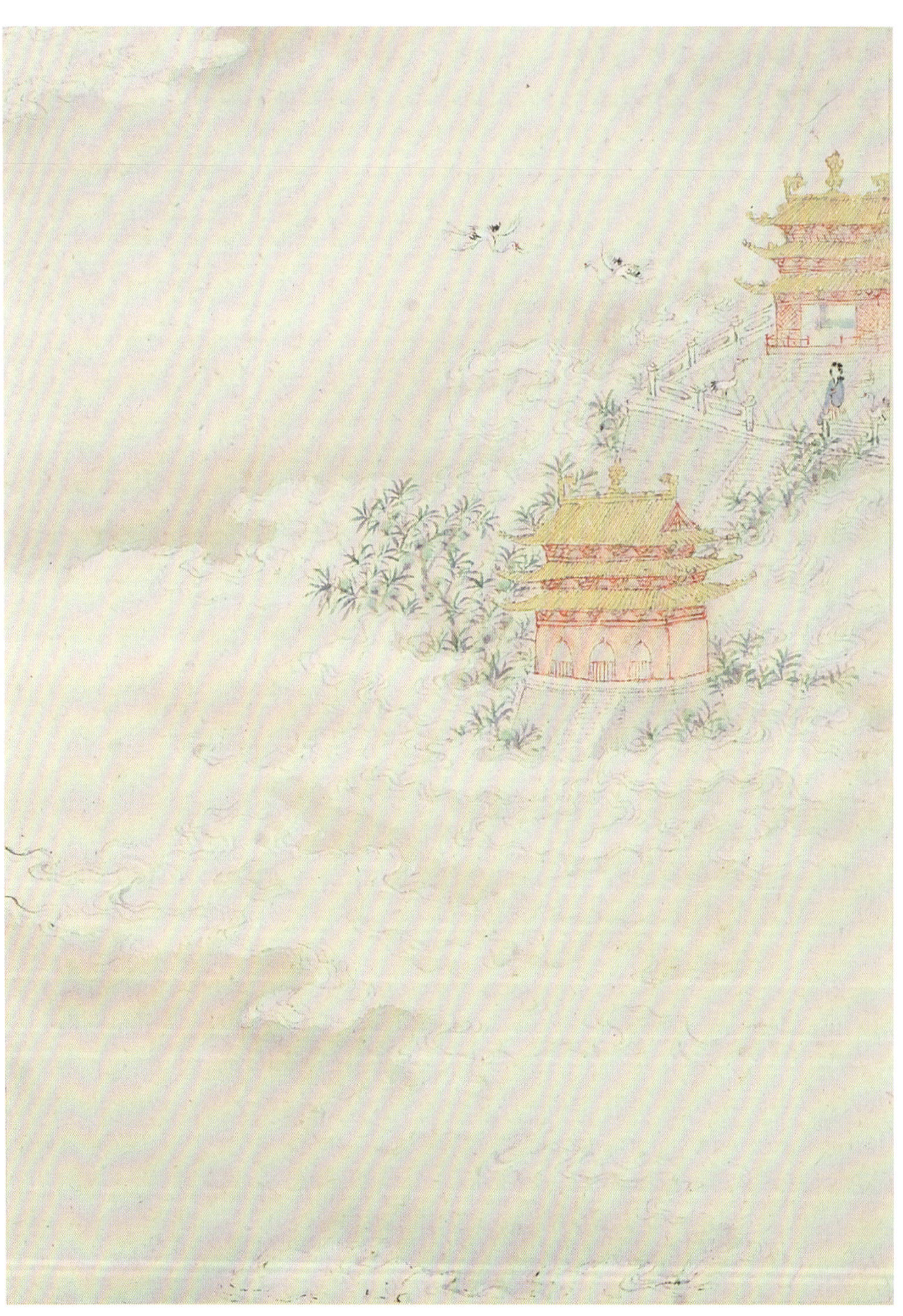

Figure 4.6. Pan Simu, *Record of Dreams from the Tingqiu Studio.* Album leaves. Image courtesy of Sotheby's.

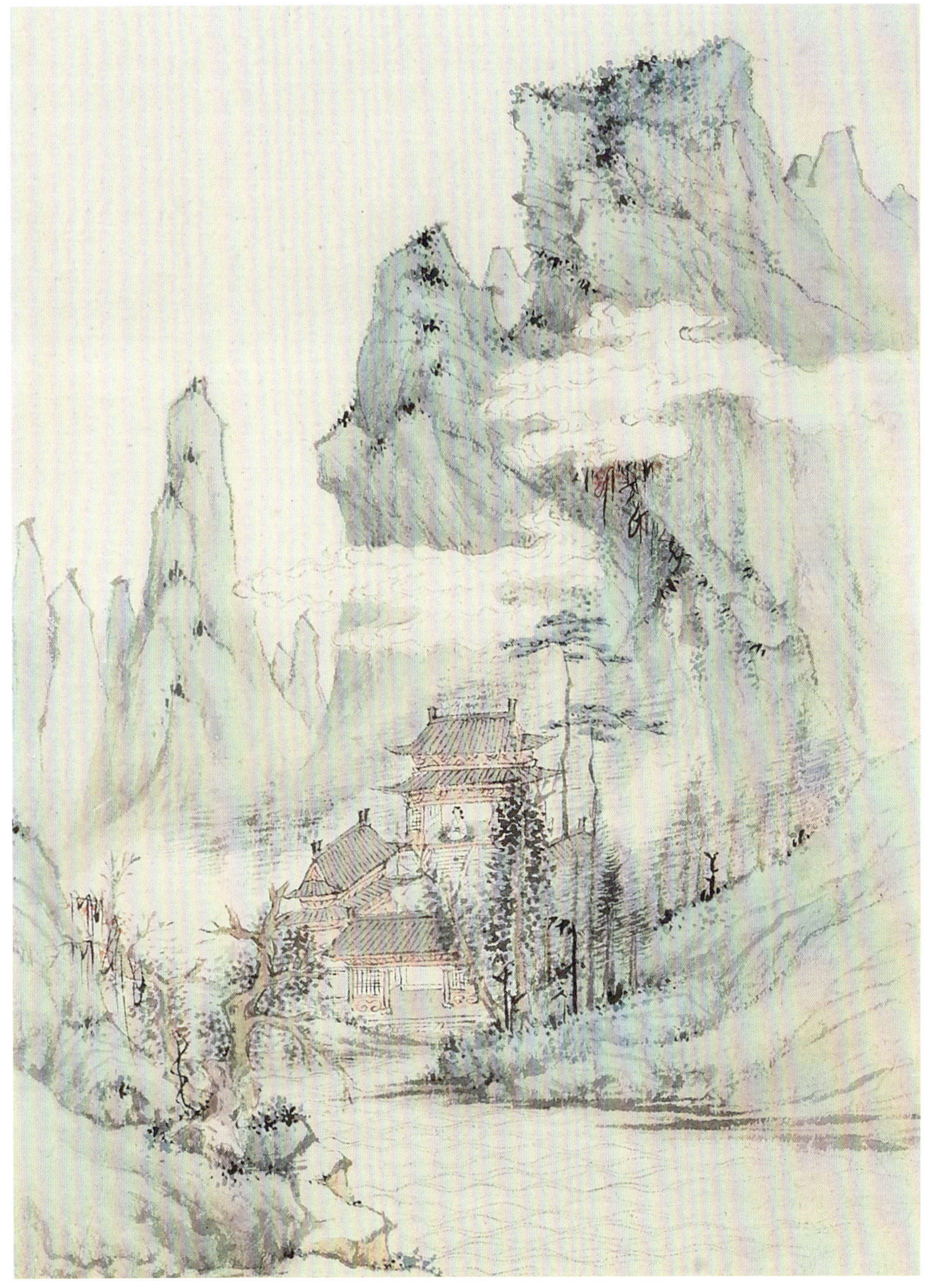

Figure 4.7. Pan Simu, *Record of Dreams from the Tingqiu Studio.* Album leaves. Image courtesy of Sotheby's.

many educated women of the Qing period, Luo became a devout Buddhist later in life.[36] She also visited famous Daoist sites, such as Mount Mao (Maoshan 茅山), indicating her interests in Daoism.[37] In the fourth dream poem, Luo arrives at a thatched hermitage deep in a forest, where she could practice meditative discipline. In the corresponding picture, hidden in a valley and surrounded by trees and water is a residence that consists of a courtyard enclosed with buildings on its four sides. Across from the entrance is the main hall, where Luo sits on a round mat on the floor and looks as if she is meditating (fig. 4.7). These texts and images thus reflect her life and religious interests and promote her identity as a reclusive, spiritually minded person.

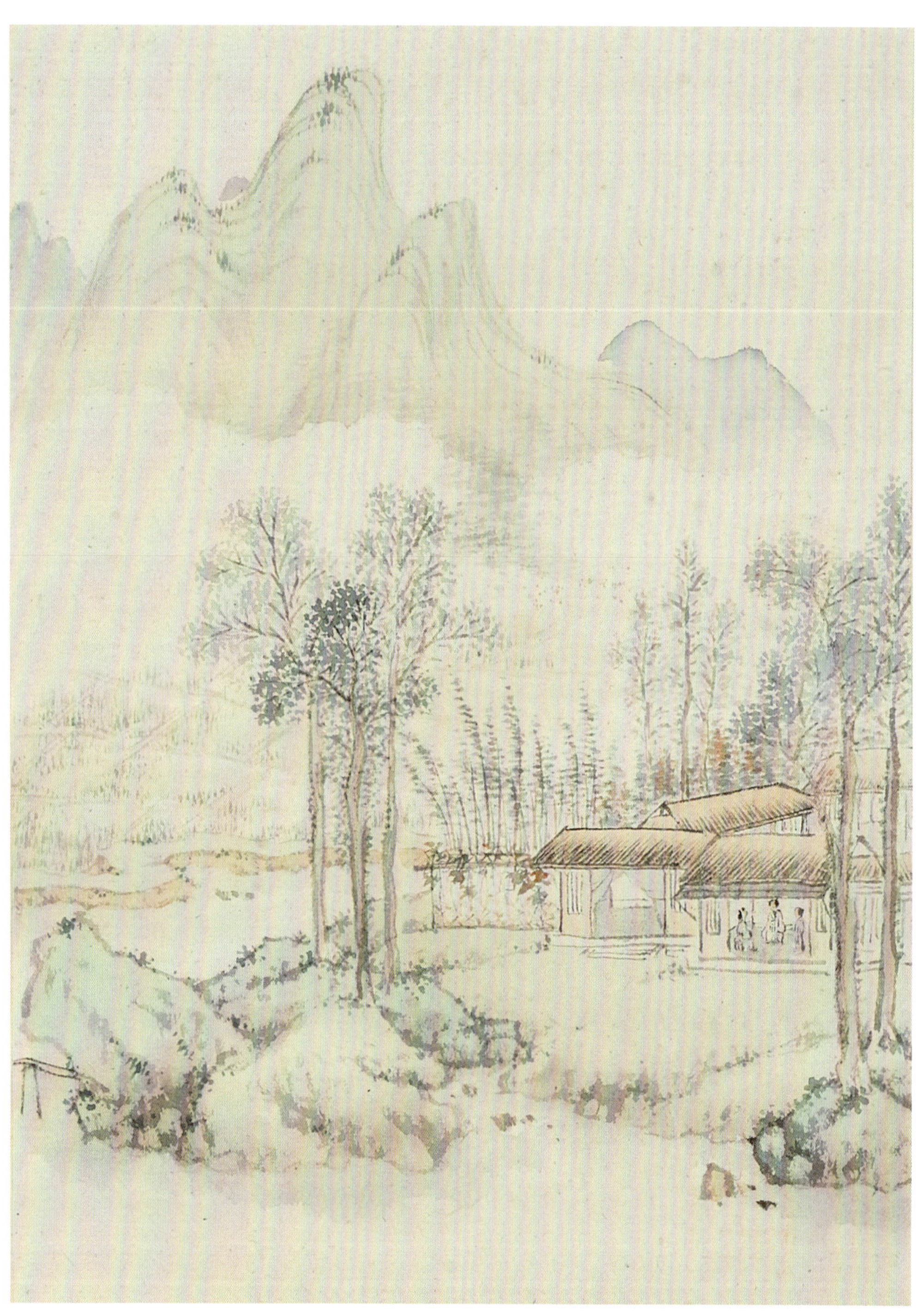

Figure 4.8. Pan Simu, *Record of Dreams from the Tingqiu Studio*. Album leaves. Image courtesy of Sotheby's.

Through literature, Luo Qilan could let her imagination roam and transform her ambitions and unfulfilled desires into words. However, she still had to face reality; at the end of the seventh poem, she wakes up and discovers that she is still a woman unable to realize her hopes.[38] Returning to her real life, Luo again had to confront criticism against her literary pursuits. She thus ended this series with a poem that refers to the traditional occupations of farming and making silk.[39] Pan Simu illustrated this poem by depicting Luo sitting in a rural residence adjacent to planted fields (fig. 4.8). From the traditional Chinese perspective, the phrase "men plow and women weave" (*nangeng nüzhi* 男耕女織) evoked an ideal society and designated the proper division of labor according to gender.[40] The text is thus Luo's declaration that she valued women's work; as with *Tutoring My Daughter by the Autumn Lamp*, she portrayed herself as a dutiful woman.

Returning to the Way

The religious side of Luo Qilan was further suggested in another portrait, *Returning to the Way*. Though the whereabouts of the work is unknown, it is recorded by Luo's writing and inscriptions she requested from her contemporaries. She wrote about the circumstance surrounding its creation, and the text hints at the picture being a self-portrait:

> I, since young, already desired to learn the Way, and [this desire] often [became] tangible in [my] dreams. [However,] worldly matters [have caused me to] idle my time away, and suddenly [I am] over forty. Today is the first day of the sixth moon in the first year of the Jiaqing reign (1796). [I] vow to renounce human affairs to concentrate in returning to the Way. [I] draw a picture to show my determination and tie it with poems.[41]
>
> 余少時即有學道之願, 往往形諸夢寐. 塵務蹉跎, 忽忽踰四十年矣. 今嘉慶元年六月朔日, 誓將屏棄人事, 悉心歸道. 寫圖見志并係以詩.

Following this statement are a series of four poems Luo composed for the portrait. She begins by lamenting the passing of spring and the emptiness in her heart, which urge her to embark on a spiritual quest. The second poem describes Luo seeking wisdom from Vimalakīrti, a lay Buddhist practitioner famous for eloquence, suggesting her turning toward Buddhism. As the text indicates, the hope this religion provides for the world of sufferings is like the lotus, a Buddhist symbol of rebirth, that blossoms in a burning house. Daoism offers another way out of the life she now considers meaningless, and thus she mentions the desire to arrive at Mount Penglai (Pengshan 蓬山), the dwelling of immortals, in the third poem. Luo ends the series by describing the freedom gained through her religious beliefs and through renouncing worldly concerns.

Despite Luo's effort to take on a religious persona, the literati who composed inscriptions for the picture addressed her identity as a poet and portrayed her as a female immortal to praise her literary abilities. Calling a poet an immortal was not without precedent, for the great Tang poet Li Bai 李白 (701–762) called himself and the Western Han scholar and official Dongfang Shuo 東方朔 an "exiled immortal" (*zhexian* 謫仙).[42] Relating Luo to beings beyond this world also politely compliments her physical appearance, as it is not uncommon in Chinese literature and popular imagination to depict female spirits or immortals as beauties. Such references then explain her unconventional life and excuse her from the norms of the Confucian patriarchy. Once again, the men in her social circle helped to construct her public identity, in this case as a poet on par with the immortals.

Conclusion

Portraits of Luo Qilan portray her as a dutiful woman who possesses great talent and a reclusive, religious temperament. The male and female intellectuals of her time affirmed and amplified these images through their inscriptions for the works, and they often addressed the pictorial depictions of Luo, her identities known to her contemporaries, and their ideas of who she really was. The large number of the colophons is also evidence of the circulation of the pictures, indicating how often the authors viewed these images and documenting their roles in promoting and constructing her identities. While representing the seemingly separate fractions of Luo's private life and unfulfilled ambitions, these materials are records of her social activities and unconventional lifestyle, justifications for her pursuit of literary interests, and documentations of the male support she received in the process.

Notes

1. *Spring View at Pingshan* is in the collection of Palace Museum, Beijing; the others are documented in Qing texts.

2. This album was sold through the Sotheby's auction house in New York on March 22, 2012.

3. Wang Wenzhi 王文治 mentions in his preface to Luo Qilan's poetry anthology that "generations [of the Luos] have [taken up] the profession of the Confucian scholar" 世業儒. Luo Qilan, *Tingqiuxuan shiji* 聽秋軒詩集, reprinted in *Qingdai shiwen ji huibian* 清代詩文集彙編, vol. 446 (Shanghai: Shanghai guji chubanshe, 2010), 763. Yuan Mei 袁枚 writes in his inscription for Luo Qilan's painting, *Tutoring My Daughter by the Autumn Lamp*, that "female historian Peixiang (Luo Qilan) is from Binwang's (Luo Binwang) clan" 佩香女史賓王族. Luo Qilan, *Tingqiuxuan zengyan* 聽秋軒贈言, in *Jiangnan nüxing bieji erbian* 江南女性別集二編, vol. 1, ed. Hu Xiaoming 胡晓明 and Peng Guozhong 彭国忠 (Hefei: Huangshan shushe, 2010), 724. Regarding Luo Qilan's education, see Luo Qilan, *Tingqiuxuan guizhong tongren ji* 聽秋軒閨中同人集, in *Jiangnan nüxing bieji erbian*, vol. 1, 695.

4. See Wang Wenzhi's preface to Luo Qilan's poetry anthology in Luo Qilan, *Tingqiuxuan shiji*, 763–64.

5. Lin Yu-chin 林妤秦, "Luo Qilan ji qi zuopin yanjiu 駱綺蘭及其作品研究" (master's thesis, Tunghai University, 2010), 38. According to Luo Qilan, she had no son of her own. Luo Qilan, *Tingqiuxuan shiji*, 803.

6. Xiao Mu 蕭穆 and Zhang Shaotang 張紹棠, *Xuzuan Jurong xianzhi* 續纂句容縣志, reprinted in *Zhongguo difangzhi jicheng Jiangsufu xianzhi ji* 中國地方志集成江蘇府縣志輯, vol. 35 (Nanjing: Jiangsu guji chubanshe, 1991), 359. For the gender of the child, see Luo Qilan, *Tingqiuxuan shiji*, 762.

7. Robyn Hamilton, "The Pursuit of Fame: Luo Qilan (1755–1813?) and the Debates about Women and Talent in Eighteenth-century Jiangnan," *Late Imperial China* 18, no. 1 (1997): 50.

8. Luo Qilan, *Tingqiuxuan shiji*, 764.

9. Luo Qilan, *Tingqiuxuan guizhong tongren ji*, 695.

10. These are: *Tingqiuxuan shiji* 聽秋軒詩集, *Tingqiuxuan zengyan* 聽秋軒贈言, and *Tingqiuxuan guizhong tongren ji* 聽秋軒閨中同人集.

11. For reproductions of Luo's paintings in the collection of Palace Museum, see Li Shi 李湜, *Ming Qing guige huihua yanjiu* 明清闺阁绘画研究 (Beijing: Zijincheng chubanshe, 2008), 205–7.

12. The accession number of this handscroll is: 新00145176. The *xin* 新 character indicates the museum registered the work after 1954. Therefore, it was not part of the imperial collection. Zheng Xinmiao 鄭欣淼, *Gugong yu gugong xue* 故宮與故宮學 (Taipei: Yuanliu chuban gongsi, 2011), 58.

13. Tobie Meyer-Fong devotes a chapter in her book on early-Qing Yangzhou to Pingshan Hall. Meyer-Fong, *Building Culture in Early Qing Yangzhou* (Stanford, CA: Stanford University, 2003), 128–64.

14. Examples can be found in Wang Yinggeng 汪應庚, *Pingshan lansheng zhi*平山攬勝志 (Yangzhou: Guangling shushe, 2004), 89, 92, and 122.

15. Unless otherwise noted, all translations are my own. The translation of this poem is based on Luo's composition in Luo Qilan, *Tingqiuxuan shiji*, 797. Variations in a few words can be seen in this printed text and Wang Wenzhi's transcription of Luo's poem in his colophon for the scroll.

16. Akedang'a 阿克當阿, *Yangzhoufu zhi* 揚州府志 (Taipei: Chengwen chubanshe, 1974), 2048.

17. The late Ming and Qing dynasties witnessed a growing number of women writing of their experiences on the road. Grace Fong studies these women and their writings in "Authoring Journeys: Women on the Road," in Grace S. Fong, *Herself an Author: Gender, Agency, and Writing in Late Imperial China* (Honolulu: University of Hawai'i Press, 2008), 85–120.

18. Wang Wenzhi, *Menglou shiji* 夢樓詩集, 23.3a.

19. Luo Qilan, *Tingqiuxuan zengyan*, 752.

20. For biographical information on Ding, see Wang Yun 汪鋆, *Yangzhou huayuan lu* 揚州畫苑錄, reprinted in *Qingdai difang renwu zhuanji congkan* 清代地方人物傳記叢刊, vol. 6 (Yangzhou: Guangling shushe, 2007), 409; Jiang Baoling 蔣寶齡, "Ding Hezhou zhuan chuanzhen xinling erjuan 丁鶴洲撰傳真心領二卷," in *Molin jinhua* 墨林今話 (Hefei: Huangshan shushe, 1992), 55.

21. Luo Qilan, *Tingqiuxuan zengyan*, 723–38, 773–76, and 781. The compositions by female writers are in *Tingqiuxuan guizhong tongren ji*, 697–99.

22. Luo Qilan, *Tingqiuxuan zengyan*, 784.

23. See inscriptions by Wang Youliang 王友亮 and Zhao Yi 趙翼 in Luo Qilan, *Tingqiuxuan zengyan*, 733 and 738. For the *wanxiong* pill, see Ouyang Xiu 歐陽修 and Song Qi宋祁, *Xin Tangshu* 新唐書 (Beijing: Zhonghua shuju, 1975), 5023.

24. For the saying, "a woman without talent is virtuous," see Clara Wing-chung Ho, "Nüzi wucai bianshi de shuode wenhua hanyi" 女子無才便是德說的文化涵義, in *Nüxing yu lishi: Zhongguo chuantong guannian xintan* 女性與歷史: 中國傳統觀念新探 (Hong Kong: Xianggang jiaoyu tushu gongsi, 1993), 89. For more on the idea that a woman's "talent could hinder virtue," see Clara Wing-chung Ho, "Zhongguo chuantong caideguan ji Qingdai qianqi nüxing caide lun" 中國傳統才德觀及清代前期女性才德論, in *De, cai, se, quan: lun Zhongguo gudai nüxing* 德, 才, 色, 權: 論 中國古代女性 (Taipei: Maitian chuban, 1998), 165–251.

25. See inscriptions by Zhu Delin 祝德麟, Xie Zhending 謝振定, and He Daosheng 何道生 in Luo Qilan, *Tingqiuxuan zengyan*, 726, 727, and 730. For information on Bao Linghui, Xie Daoyun, and Zuo Fen, see Wilt Idema and Beata Grant, *The Red Brush: Writing Women of Imperial China* (Cambridge, MA: Harvard University Asia Center, 2007), 43–52 and 136–44.

26. See inscriptions by Zhao Yi and Luo Jie 駱杰 in Luo Qilan, *Tingqiuxuan zengyan*, 737–38. For a translation of the *bozhou* poem, see John Minford and Joseph S. M. Lau, *Classical Chinese Literature: An Anthology of Translations*, vol. 1 (New York: Columbia University, 2000), 114–15.

27. See inscriptions by Yuan Mei and Xie Zhending in Luo Qilan, *Tingqiuxuan zengyan*, 724 and 726.

28. See inscriptions by Li Tingjin 李廷敬 and Yu Ji 余集 in Luo Qilan, 728.

29. See inscriptions by Li Chuanjie 李傳杰 and Wu Xinzhong 吳信中 in Luo Qilan, *Tingqiuxuan zengyan*, 775–76.

30. See inscription by Zhang Wentao 張問陶 in Luo Qilan, *Tingqiuxuan zengyan*, 732.

31. See inscription by Fang Ang 方昂 in Luo Qilan, 731.

32. See inscription by Zhou Houyuan 周厚轅 in Luo Qilan, 737.

33. Rachel Bartow Schram translates and studies these poems in chapter 3 of her thesis. Rachel Bartow Schram, "A Life in Dreams: The Dream Motif in the Poetry of Luo Qilan and Ming-Qing Women Writers" (master's thesis, University of California, Santa Barbara, 2012), 52–82. Idema and Grant provide translations of two poems in *Red Brush*, 616–17.

34. For Pan's biography, see Li Junzhi 李濬之, *Qinghuajia shishi* 清畫家詩史, reprinted in *Sanshisan zhong Qingdai renwu zhuanji ziliao huibian* 三十三種清代人物傳記資料彙編, vol. 40 (Jinan: Qilu shushe, 2009), 263, and Feng Jinbo 馮金伯, *Moxiangju huashi* 墨香居畫識, reprinted in *Sanshisan zhong Qingdai renwu zhuanji ziliao huibian*, vol. 43 (Jinan: Qilu shushe, 2009) 113–14.

35. For this fruit, see Stephen Little and Shawn Eichman, *Taoism and the Arts of China* (Berkeley: University of California Press, 2000), 159.

36. Susan Mann, *Precious Records: Women in China's Long Eighteenth Century* (Stanford, CA: Stanford University, 1997), 66.

37. Luo Qilan, *Tingqiuxuan shiji*, 780–81.

38. The last two lines of the poem are: "The sound of the bell hurries my waking, just as before, I am still wearing bow-shaped shoes." Schram, "Life in Dreams," 75. In China, women with bound feet wore these shoes.

39. For a translation of this poem, see Schram, "Life in Dreams," 80.

40. Susan Mann writes about women's work and proper labor division in chapter 6 of her *Precious Records*, 143–77.

41. This text and the following four poems are in Luo Qilan, *Tingqiuxuan shiji*, 798–99.

42. For Dongfang Shuo, see Li Bai, "Yuhuyin" 玉壺吟, in *Quan Tangshi* 全唐詩 (Shanghai: Shanghai guji chubanshe, 1986), 391. For Li Bai himself, see Li Bai, "Da Huzhou jiaye sima wen Bai shi heren" 荅湖州迦葉司馬問白是何人, in Peng Dingqiu, *Quan Tangshi*, 414.

Bibliography

Primary Sources

Akedang'a 阿克當阿 (fl. 1809–10). *Yangzhoufu zhi* 揚州府志. Taipei: Chengwen chubanshe, 1974.

Feng Jinbo 馮金伯 (fl. 18th century). *Moxiangju huashi* 墨香居畫識. Reprinted in *Sanshisan zhong Qingdai renwu zhuanji ziliao huibian* 三十三種清代人物傳記資料彙編, vol. 43. Jinan: Qilu shushe, 2009.

Jiang Baoling 蔣寶齡 (1781–1840). *Molin jinhua* 墨林今話. Hefei: Huangshan shushe, 1992.

Li Junzhi 李濬之 (b. 1868). *Qinghuajia shishi* 清畫家詩史. Reprinted in *Sanshisan zhong Qingdai renwu zhuanji ziliao huibian* 三十三種清代人物傳記資料彙編, vol. 40. Jinan: Qilu shushe, 2009.

Luo Qilan 駱綺蘭 (1756–after 1813). *Tingqiuxuan guizhong tongrenji* 聽秋軒閨中同人集. Transcribed in *Jiangnan nüxing bieji* 江南女性別集, *erbian shangce* 二編上冊, edited by Hu Xiaoming 胡晓明 and Peng Guozhong 彭国忠. Hefei: Huangshan shushe, 2010.

———. *Tingqiuxuan shiji* 聽秋軒詩集. Reprinted in *Qingdai shiwenji huibian* 清代詩文集彙編, vol. 446. Shanghai: Shanghai guji chubanshe, 2010.

———. *Tingqiuxuan zengyan* 聽秋軒贈言. Transcribed in *Jiangnan nüxing bieji* 江南女性別集, *erbian shangce* 二編上冊, edited by Hu Xiaoming 胡晓明 and Peng Guozhong 彭国忠. Hefei: Huangshan shushe, 2010.

Ouyang Xiu 歐陽修 (1007–1072) and Song Qi 宋祁 (998–1061). *Xin Tangshu* 新唐書. Beijing: Zhonghua shuju, 1975.

Peng Dingqiu 彭定求 (1645–1719). *Quan tangshi* 全唐詩. Shanghai: Shanghai guji chubanshe, 1986.

Wang Wenzhi 王文治 (1730–1802). *Menglou shiji* 夢樓詩集. 1795. University of Michigan Library.

Wang Yinggeng 汪應庚 (fl. 18th century). *Pingshan lansheng zhi* 平山攬勝志. Reprinted in *Pingshan lansheng zhi, Pingshantang tuzhi* 平山攬勝志, 平山堂圖志. Yangzhou: Guangling shushe, 2004.

Wang Yun 汪鋆 (b. 1816). *Yangzhou huayuan lu* 揚州畫苑錄. Reprinted in *Qingdai difang renwu zhuanji congkan* 清代地方人物傳記叢刊, vol. 6. Yangzhou: Guangling shushe, 2007.

Xiao Mu 蕭穆 (1835–1904) and Zhang Shaotang 張紹棠 (fl. 1901). *Xuzuan Jurong xianzhi* 續纂句容縣志. Reprinted in *Zhongguo difangzhi jicheng: Jiangsufu xianzhi ji* 中國地方志集 成: 江蘇府縣志輯, vol. 35. Nanjing: Jiangsu guji chubanshe: 1991.

Secondary Scholarship

Chen, Janet C. "Representing Talented Women in Eighteenth-Century Chinese Painting: *Thirteen Female Disciples Seeking Instruction at the Lake Pavilion.*" PhD diss., University of Kansas, 2016.

Fong, Grace. "Auto/biographical Subjects: Ming-Qing Women's Poetry Collections as Sources for Women's Life Histories." In *Overt and Covert Treasures: Essays on the Sources for Chinese Women's History*, edited by Clara Wing-chung Ho, 369–410. Hong Kong: Chinese University, 2012.

———. *Herself an Author: Gender, Agency, and Writing in Late Imperial China.* Honolulu: University of Hawai'i Press, 2008.

Hamilton, Robyn. "The Pursuit of Fame: Luo Qilan (1755–1813?) and the Debate about Women and Talent in Eighteenth-Century Jiangnan." *Late Imperial China* 18, no. 1 (June 1997): 39–71.

———. "The Unseen Hand: Contextualizing Luo Qilan and Her Anthologies." In *The Inner Quarters and Beyond: Women Writers from Ming through Qing*, edited by Grace Fong and Ellen Widmer, 112–16. Leiden, the Netherlands: Brill Academic, 2010.

Ho, Clara Wing-chung 劉詠聰. *Caide xiang hui: Zhongguo nüxing de zhixue yu kezi* 才德相輝: 中國女性的治學與課子. Hong Kong: Sanlian shudian, 2015.

———. *De, cai, se, quan: lun Zhongguo gudai nüxing* 德, 才, 色, 權: 論中國古代女性. Taipei: Maitian chuban, 1998.

———. *Nüxing yu lishi: Zhongguo chuantong guannian xintan* 女性與歷史: 中國傳統觀念新探. Hong Kong: Xianggang jiaoyu tushu gongsi, 1993.

Idema, Wilt, and Beata Grant. *The Red Brush: Writing Women of Imperial China.* Cambridge, MA: Harvard University Asia Center, 2004.

Ko, Dorothy. *Teachers of the Inner Chambers: Women and Culture in Seventeenth Century China.* Stanford, CA: Stanford University Press, 1994.

Lee, De-nin D. "More Than Mere Diversion: Painting and *Tihuashi* in the Life of Luo Qilan." *Archives of Asian Art* 67, no. 1 (April 2017): 61–82.

Lin, Yu-chin 林妤秦. "Luo Qilan ji qi zuo pin yan jiu 駱綺蘭及其作品研究." Master's thesis, Tunghai University, 2010.

Little, Stephen, and Shawn Eichman. *Taoism and the Arts of China.* Berkeley: University of California Press, 2000.

Mann, Susan. "'Fuxue' (Women's Learning) by Zhang Xuecheng (1738–1801): China's First History of Women's Culture." *Late Imperial China* 13, no. 1 (1992): 40–62.

———. *Precious Records: Women in China's Long Eighteenth Century.* Stanford, CA: Stanford University Press, 1997.

Meyer-Fong, Tobie. *Building Culture in Early Qing Yangzhou.* Stanford, CA: Stanford University Press, 2003.

Minford, John, and Joseph S. M. Lau. *Classical Chinese Literature: An Anthology of Translations.* New York: Columbia University, 2002.

Schram, Rachel Bartow. "A Life in Dreams: The Dream Motif in the Poetry of Luo Qilan and Ming-Qing Women Writers." Master's thesis, University of California at Santa Barbara, 2012.

Yang, Binbin. *Heroines of the Qing: Exemplary Women Tell Their Stories.* Seattle: University of Washington Press, 2016.

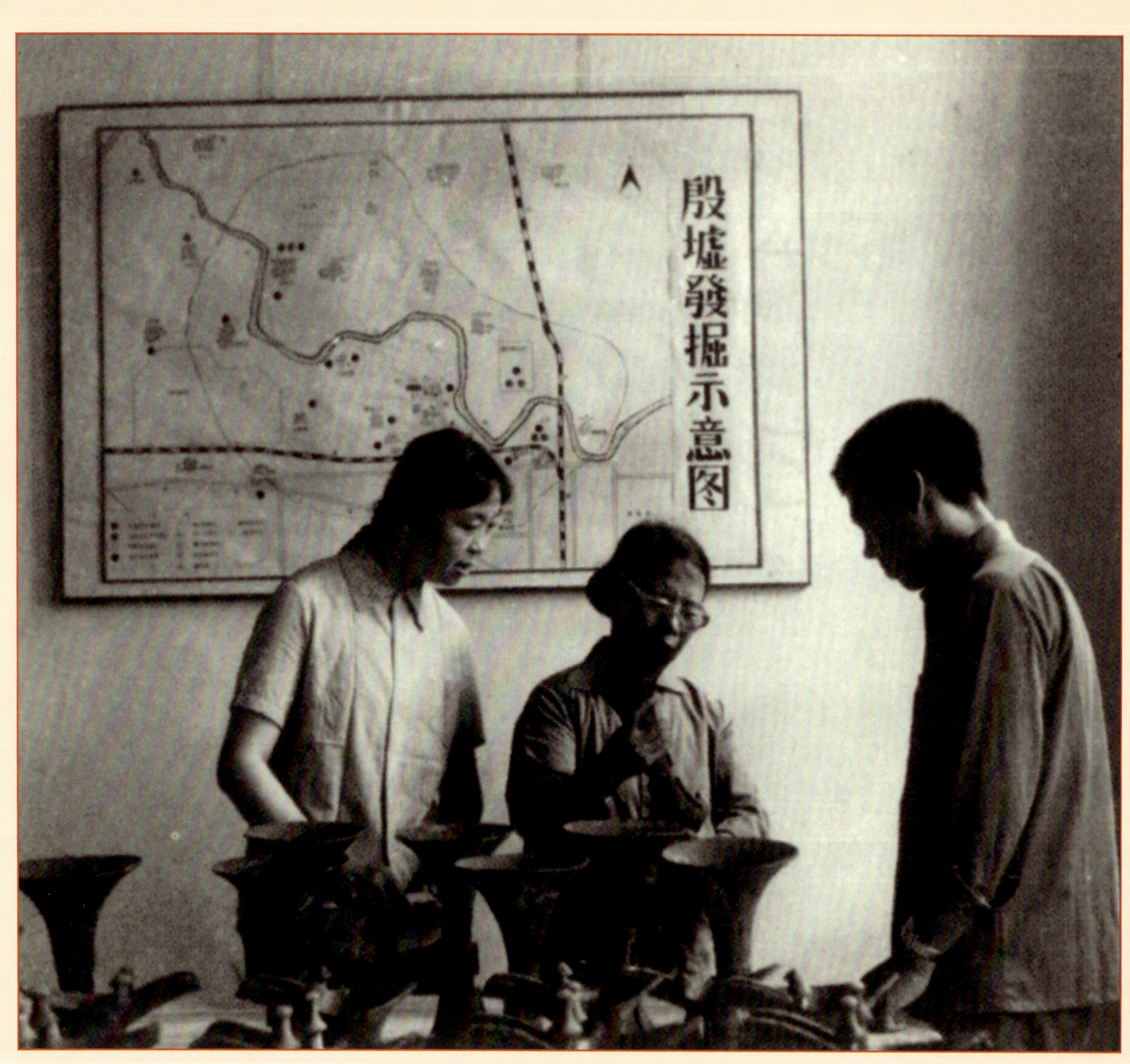
殷墟發掘示意图

5

China's "First" Female Archaeologists

Rong Yuan, Zhou Yingxue, Zeng Zhaoyu, and Zheng Zhenxiang

Shana J. Brown

Prologue: Woman Warriors

The winter of 1975–76 in China was cold in temperature, hot in politics. The country was still led by an infirm Mao Zedong, and was just emerging from the Cultural Revolution (1966–76), which virtually closed many economic and cultural institutions. Looking to the future, a younger generation of leaders began charting a path to revitalize the economy. From September to October of 1975, they met at a national conference and discussed ways to improve crop yields and jumpstart rural development. They agreed to implement a new campaign, called "In Agriculture, Learn from Dazhai," referencing the model village in China's northwest that since the 1950s underwent terracing and other forms of land transformation. The new campaign called for "mountains, rivers, farmlands, and roads to be tackled in a comprehensive way"—that is, roads built, rivers dammed, and mountains flattened for mechanized farming.[1]

News of the campaign was greeted with dismay by a small group of scholars a hundred miles away, in the small village of Xiaotun, northwest of the city of Anyang, Henan province. Archaeologists had resided in the village intermittently since 1928, supervising students and local laborers to unearth what lay beneath Xiaotun, namely Yinxu, the Ruins of Yin or the last capital city of the Shang dynasty (ca. 1600–1046 BCE). After millennia of obscurity, the city lay buried meters-deep below land farmed by Xiaotun residents, who subsisted by both agriculture and harvesting, as it were, archaeological artifacts pilfered from subterranean sites.[2] But foraging for artifacts ended after a 1930 law against private excavations and trade in antiquities under the Nationalist government, which controlled China from 1928 to 1949. After the Communist Party won control of the country in 1949

Figure 5.1. (*facing*) Zheng Zhenxiang (*center*) and other members of the Anyang archaeological team, c. 1976. From Hao Qian, *Out of China's Earth: Archaeological Discoveries in the People's Republic of China* (New York: H. N. Abrams; Beijing: China Pictorial, 1981), 12. Used with permission.

and established the People's Republic of China, responsibility for the area's preservation and systematic excavation was given to the PRC's new Institute of Archaeology.

In 1975, the onsite director of the Xiaotun research area was Zheng Zhenxiang 鄭振香 (b. 1929), a female scholar from the Institute of Archaeology (fig. 5.1). Work was not particularly active, a consequence of the general lack of support for academic endeavors during the Cultural Revolution, and even political attacks on members of the Chinese archaeological and historical community. Still, Zheng and her colleagues were concerned the new campaign threatened fields northwest of the village that were in the important Palace-Temple Complex of the ancient city. In November of 1975, hoping to justify stricter preservation, Zheng rounded up a few laborers and began digging. Within a few days, the team discovered a layer of rammed earth, evidence of a Shang building site. This was enough to persuade sympathetic village leaders to postpone field leveling in the area. Proper excavation began in the spring of 1976, leading to the identification of a cluster of some ten tombs (fig. 5.2). In mid-May a truly momentous discovery occurred, namely of an un-looted tomb that yielded substantial quantities of grave goods—ultimately almost 2,000 items, including over 700 pieces of jade, almost 500 bronze items including weapons and tools, thousands of cowrie shells, and hundreds of inscribed oracle bones, divination implements used by Shang rulers to ask dynastic ancestors to predict the outcome of important events. "The tomb itself is not too large," the team reported in 1977, "but it is intact. In the abundance and refinement of its burial objects, this is the most complete set of materials recovered from any Shang Dynasty tomb."[3] Over half the bronze vessels recovered were inscribed with the name of the tomb's owner: Fu Hao 婦好 or Lady Hao (d. c. 1200 BCE), a Shang queen.

It was the first time that archaeologists were able to date an Anyang tomb conclusively, and uniquely identify its inhabitant. Even more momentously, the inhabitant was a woman, and a woman of exceptional political skill and military prowess. Fu Hao served as a military commander for her husband, Shang King Wu Ding 武丁 (c. 1250–1192 BCE), leading successful campaigns against rival states. Materials recovered from her tomb included over forty bronze weapons—many showing signs of use—including a 20-pound axe, as well as ornate decorative weapons made with jade blades and turquoise-inlaid hafts. Bronzes dedicated by other Shang generals and clan leaders were found along with gifts from rival kingdoms and Fu Hao's natal family, a powerful lineage. Her tomb included ritual vessels used to conduct sacrifices in honor of female ancestors, as well as the skeletons of human servants, including at least two children, and six sacrificial dogs, one buried directly below her body. She also owned numerous pieces of jewelry and adornment, including twenty-eight hairpins made of jade.[4]

Even before the discovery of her tomb, Fu Hao was known within the archaeological community. In the summer of 1936, during the last Anyang excavation season before World War II, a cache of inscribed oracle bones was discovered that included hundreds of divination questions posed by Wu Ding about Fu Hao, one of his favorite wives: whether her military expeditions would meet with success; whether her pregnancy and delivery would proceed well; whether she would recover from illness. She died tragically

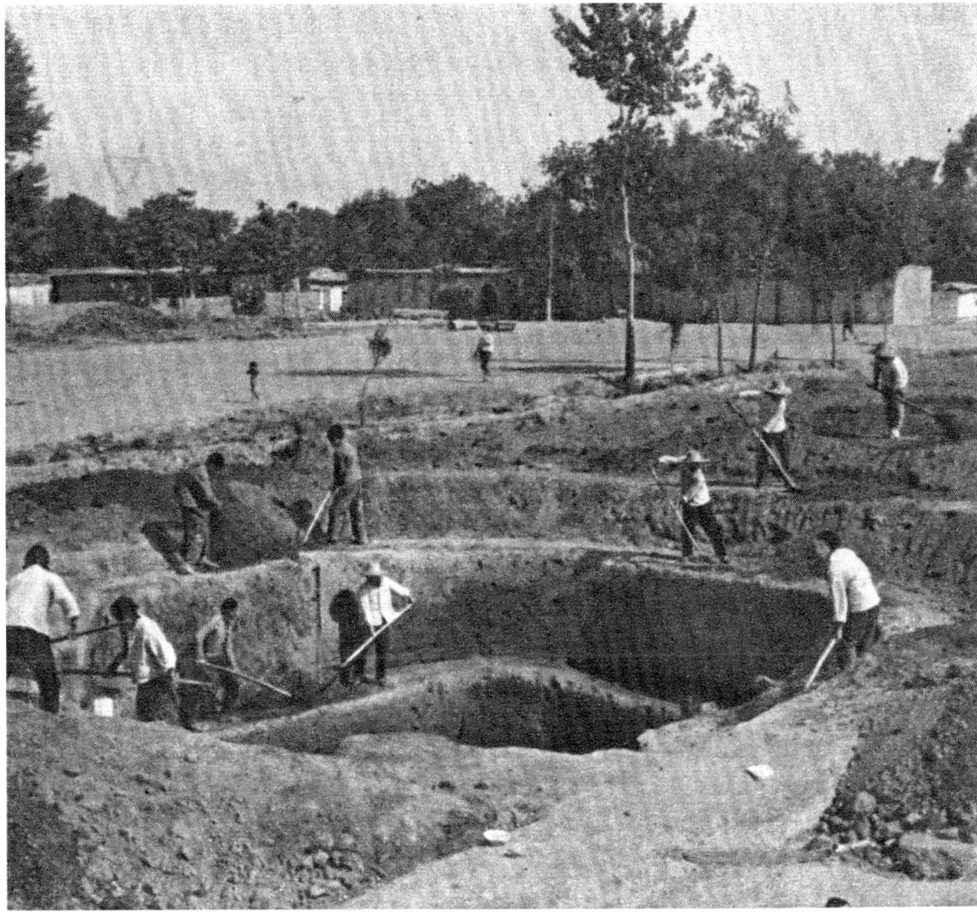

Figure 5.2. Workers excavating Fu Hao's tomb. *Yinxu Fuhao mu* (Beijing: Wenwu chubanshe, 1980). Used with permission.

young after wounds received in a hunting expedition. After she died, Wu Ding continued to inquire about her well-being in the afterlife.[5]

Zheng Zhenxiang knew about Fu Hao from oracle bone inscriptions, and recalled that the first sight of her name on an artifact from the tomb brought feelings of "tremendous shock and joy."[6] Indeed, the discovery of Fu Hao's tomb, and by a female archaeologist, caused enormous excitement in China and internationally. Fu Hao was hailed as a Chinese shieldmaiden, while Zheng Zhenxiang became an academic heroine, dubbed "China's First Female Archaeologist" by the Xinhua News Agency.[7] Articles pointed to the symmetry that "Fu Hao, the princess who was doted on by Wu Ding and the first verifiable female general, was brought into daylight by the first female archaeologist of New China."[8]

While there is no disputing Zheng's tremendous contributions, these jubilant reports had the inadvertent effect of obscuring other Chinese women who had previously made significant contributions as archaeologists, historians, folklore specialists, and paleographers, tightly interwoven and prestigious academic fields in twentieth-century China. Trailblazers included Rong Yuan 容媛 (1899–1996), a folklore specialist who became an academic journal editor and expert on ancient inscriptions; Zhou Yingxue 周英學 (b. 1911), the first woman on the Anyang archaeological team; and Zeng Zhaoyu 曾昭燏 (1909–1964), archaeologist and director of the Nanjing Museum. This essay seeks to understand better the "shock and joy" of the Fu Hao moment in Chinese archaeological studies by tracing its prehistory, so to speak, in the earlier contributions of women and women's studies to Chinese archaeology.

The growth of archaeology as a field in China was improved both by the presence of women as scholars and by research questions regarding women and gender in history. And yet women in archaeology and related fields in the first half of the twentieth century, in China as elsewhere, faced significant barriers to participation, from a lack of educational opportunities to unwelcoming professional climates. They also entered a field where the topic of women's history was often neglected. This essay seeks to center the question of women in twentieth-century Chinese archaeology in two respects. Who were the women in the field, and what were their contributions? And how did the study of women and gender become important to Chinese prehistory?

Rong Yuan: From Folklore to Marxist Historiography

Prior to the midcentury—if not later as well—women globally were a tiny minority within academic fields like archaeology, folklore studies, and history. The absence of women was consequential. In twentieth-century China, history was a prestigious and highly public-facing discipline. Debates over China's diplomatic, economic, and social condition drew evidence from history, as social thinkers looked for clues as to why some nations surged ahead while others lost influence, unity, and prosperity. For many intellectuals of the era, historical research, including studies of ancient texts and artifacts (in China, archaeology is often taught within history departments), were a way to celebrate and preserve China's strengths while seeking cures for its modern disadvantages. Discovering ancient artifacts, (re)writing national history, and examining the origins of the Chinese state and even the Chinese race, as understood at the time, were national priorities.

But with structural barriers blocking the participation of all but a few women, the history of China was written almost exclusively by, and largely about, men. Indeed, women were virtually absent from modern historical fields for many decades worldwide. One reason was the lack of educational opportunities.[9] In China, even elite female children were typically given far fewer academic resources than male children. Women might be tutored at home, joining their brothers in private lessons, but this opportunity typically ended when brothers were old enough to attend school outside the home.[10] Some women did become scholars and even creative writers, as evidenced by the boom in anthologies of women's poetry starting in the seventeenth century. But most women, even those of means, were primarily taught household management, decorative arts, and moral training. Those who received formal education were encouraged to use their skills to facilitate the education of their children.[11]

On the positive side, without conventional schooling, women developed self-taught and frequently trans-methodological approaches, transmuting the difficulties of their educational paths into a source of scholarly distinction. Rong Yuan was this kind of self-taught polymath, a "living dictionary" according to a colleague, who for several decades was a leading figure among specialists in Chinese folklore, history, and artifact studies.[12] She came from a family of political reformers, scholars, and artists in Dongguan, southeast of Guangzhou (or Canton). Her grandfathers passed the highest level of the imperial civil service examinations and were prominent educators at modern (all-male) academies in the late nineteenth century; indeed, they were friends, and later betrothed their two children. Rong Yuan's maternal grandparents even considered (but ultimately rejected) the idea of keeping their daughter's feet natural or unbound, an example of distinctly progressive thinking.[13] They did, however, educate their daughter, a pattern which continued into Rong Yuan's generation.

Rong Yuan's father died young in 1908. Following this tragedy, her family moved to bring her brothers close to good schools, while depending for financial support on her maternal uncle Deng Erya 鄧爾雅 (1884–1954). This was perhaps the first educational boost that Rong Yuan received. Deng Erya was a well-known calligrapher, seal-carver, and poet, later a leading figure in the Lingnan art movement of the early twentieth century. He took under his wing his nephews, Rong Geng 容庚 (1894–1983), a paleographer who wrote important works on bronze artifact inscriptions and Han dynasty funerary texts; and Rong Zhaozu 容肇祖 (1897–1994), historian and folklore specialist, who wrote well-regarded works on China's ethnic minorities. Although probably not to the extent of her brothers, Rong Yuan may also have been trained by her uncle in authenticating and interpreting ancient inscriptions, an opportunity to learn the basics of research on historical texts afforded few women.

When they reached an age for formal schooling, the Rong sons were sent to modern academies in Canton. Rong Yuan had no such opportunity. Indeed, in 1916 only some 8,000 women were enrolled in secondary schools throughout China (by comparison, in Japan, a much smaller country, ten times that number of female students went to school).[14] But Chinese feminists, whose support was crucial to the 1911 Republican revolution, were working to establish a range of women's educational and vocational institutions.[15] In 1919, a wave of activism began amid national protests against the pro-Japan Treaty of Versailles. Chinese women joined the international suffrage movement and advocated for women's educational, civil, and social equality. In 1920, Cai Yuanpei 蔡元培 (1868–1940), head of Beijing University (Beida) and later director of the Academia Sinica research institution, declared his university coeducational, setting off a national trend. In 1925, feminists succeeded in establishing a women's college in Canton, directed by He Xiangning 何香凝 (1878–1972), Hong Kong–born socialist, feminist, painter, and poet who organized the city's first Women's Day march in 1924. Rong Yuan enrolled at the women's college, gaining access to formal education for the first time at age twenty-six.[16]

Moving to Canton, she was also able to access directly one of the most important intellectual trends of the period, namely the folklore studies movement (generally seen in the West as a branch of anthropology, but in China then closely connected to historical research). Scholars who later became prominent in archaeological and historical research were central to the field, including Dong Zuobin 董作宾 (1895–1963), who helped establish the pioneering Folklore Studies Society in Beijing and became a foremost expert on oracle bone inscriptions; and famous historian Gu Jiegang 顧頡剛 (1893–1980), later at Beijing University.[17] The movement was politically progressive, connected to the New Culture Movement, which encouraged intellectuals to "go to the people" and fight for social equality. Folklore specialists hoped to create an egalitarian national literary tradition, based on rural and working-class cultural artifacts. To this end, they collected and interpreted the customs, music, mythology, and religious practices of the lower classes, including women.[18]

Indeed, in contrast to many other academic disciplines at the time, folklore studies in China and the West prominently included women as scholars, and also studied women's culture.[19] Albeit with some gender bias, Chinese folklorists studied the cultural practices, legends, and social structures in which women were crucial mythic figures, fieldwork informants, or both. They documented women's work responsibilities, clothing, and marital customs, and promoted the importance of female perspectives and experiences to politics and society. [20] The folklorist Liu Jing'an 劉經庵 (active 1920s–30s), for example, published *Folksongs and Women* (*Geyao yu funü*《歌謠與婦女》), focusing on social situations (betrothal, marriage, dealings with in-laws and other family members) that were of special importance to women. Not only were women important as the subjects of folklore, but also as their creators and contributors: "Women have created half of popular literature, and women's problems constitute half of folkstudies," he wrote.[21] In his own collection of folksongs, Gu Jiegang relied on his grandmother as an informant, and also focused to a large extent on songs by and about women. Together with academic scholarship, women's popular magazines also explored folklore. *Women's Weekly* (Funü zhoukan 婦女週刊) and *The Ladies Journal* (Funü zazhi 婦女雜誌) published folksongs and other vernacular literature, while specialist magazines like *Folk Monthly* published an issue on the "Tiger's Grandma" genre, similar to Little Red Riding Hood.[22]

Women scholars made important, if sometimes uncredited contributions to the field. One of the first published collections of Beijing folksongs was authored by a pseudonymous female scholar Xueru nüshi 雪如女士; Gu Jiegang complimented her for "drumming up the courage" to conduct fieldwork in Beijing amid warlord violence, and for keeping "the songs of the masses from disappearing."[23] Chen Qiufan 陳秋帆 (1909–1982) was fluent in Japanese, having studied abroad in Japan, and published translations of Japanese folktales including tales of vengeful female spirits.[24] As a middle school student in Hangzhou, the teenage Zhu Yuke 朱玉珂 (1902–1969) was chosen as the vice chairperson of the revolutionary student federation; later she married folklore specialist and future Beida faculty member Jiang Shaoyuan 江紹原 (1898–1983). Inspired by a Shanghai magazine article on German marriage customs, she began ethnographic fieldwork in her home county and documented practices related to pregnancy, childbirth, and marriage, which she generously shared with her husband for use in his research. He later commented that it was difficult to disentangle his own work from Zhu Yuke's contributions.[25]

In 1926, the Beijing academic community fell into turmoil amid rising warlord violence. Many scholars moved south to Canton, then under the relatively stable control of the Nationalist party. The Nationalists had established National Canton University (later renamed Zhongshan University in honor of Sun Yat-sen), whose explicit purpose was to use academic research to promote cultural and social development. Among those exiting the capital and finding shelter in Canton were folklore specialists Dong Zuobin and Gu Jiegang. Other progressive intellectuals arrived from abroad, like Fu Sinian 傅斯年 (1896–1950), returned from London and Berlin, and Liang Siyong 梁思永 (1904–1954), son of reformer and journalist Liang Qichao, who had done graduate work in archaeology at Harvard. They brought their expertise to an experimental new research organization, the Institute of History and Philology 語言歷史研究所, part of the Academia Sinica. Fu Sinian became its first director, with Liang Siyong later serving as deputy director of its Institute of Archaeology.[26]

In addition to other research, the institute developed a significant program in folklore studies. Scholars conducted fieldwork to preserve local vernacular songs and poetry, collected inscribed artifacts and historical documents, and displayed objects in galleries on campus. Gu Jiegang taught a class on the method of studying legends, and Liang Siyong assisted by drafting a work plan for the institute, which included a "systematic survey of the folklore of Guangdong and Guangxi," collecting ethnographic data and training folklore investigators.[27]

Although she was formally enrolled (and teaching) in the women's college, Rong Yuan audited courses at Zhongshan, where her brother Rong Zhaozu was faculty and also active in the folklore movement.[28] In 1927, she joined Gu Jiegang to conduct fieldwork in her hometown of Dongguan, visiting the City God temple and creating a detailed map of the temple complex and its idols. Rong Yuan was asked by her brother to provide an explanatory text. "I have never learned anything about things having to do with folk religion, how can I understand its complexities?" she wrote. "To be an obliging younger sister, as well as to create a reference of what I have learned, my explanation follows. This has been done hurriedly, and doubtless there are mistakes, I hope my esteemed readers may provide criticisms!"[29] Thus very humbly, but confidently (the essay was eighteen pages long) did Rong Yuan begin her career as a folklore specialist. But her deferential exterior hid a core of feminist activism; at this time she was a member of the Dongguan branch of the Nationalist Party Women's Liberation Association and, along with her sister Rong Xian 容嫻, helped establish a women's vocational school.[30]

Over the next few years, Rong Yuan took an increasingly important role in the folk studies movement. For *Folklore* she wrote numerous essays on Dongguan, including religious practices, folk music, burial practices, and new year's customs. She wrote a series of articles on the use of areca palm fronds and betel nuts as symbolic items in wedding ceremonies, arguing that their use in Dongguan was evidence of the influence of Southeast Asian culture. And she collected and published unique local character riddles (the riddle allows you to guess a character).[31]

In 1929 she accompanied Gu Jiegang and several academics and their wives on an excursion to the temple of the Goddess of Fertility or Niangniang Miao 娘娘廟 on Mount Miaofeng in northwestern Beijing, where an annual festival was celebrated each spring (fig. 5.3). During the early twentieth century thousands of pilgrims trekked up the mountain to worship the goddess each year. Piety required pilgrims to make their journey as arduous as possible, for example by deliberately backtracking the walk to make it longer, or climbing the mountain on all fours. Once at the top of the mountain, gifts of money and other valuables to the goddess were hoped to bring favor to pilgrims, often childless women. Itinerant drama troupes also made the pilgrimage and performed in front of the goddess's temple, asking for good fortune for the upcoming year as they made their rounds of performances in rural communities[32] (fig. 5.4).

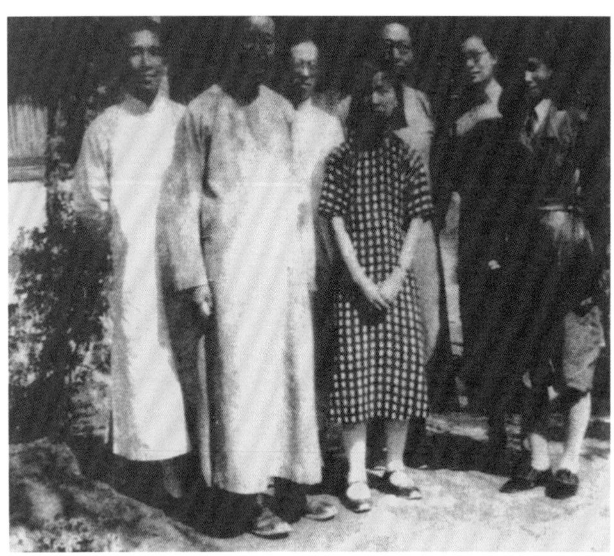

Figure 5.3. Rong Yuan and her colleagues at Yenching University, May 1933. *From left to right*: Rong Geng, Gu Jiegang, Rong Yuan. From Huang Hefang, *Wudai shuxiang zhuan* (Guangzhou: Huanan ligong daxue chubanshe, 2006), 145.

Gu Jiegang, Rong Geng, Rong Zhaozu, and other folklorists had visited Miaofeng and other Beijing temples four years earlier, and wrote path-breaking articles on their customs. On her visit Rong Yuan sought to make the trek on foot, joining the pilgrims like a true participant-observer, but relented after being reminded that her canvas shoes would be unlikely to last the twenty-mile journey. Her male companions urged her to speak to the female participants, but instead she focused on compiling information about stone stelae[33] (fig. 5.5). Her research, then and later, blurred historical studies and ethnography, with ancient customs in the historical literature interpreted like folklore. This approach, to systematically study historical texts as evidence of China's social and cultural traditions, alongside the inclusion of what we might consider material and archaeological evidence, was not perfect—later archaeologists criticized it for producing studies that could be biased toward traditional assumptions—but it was highly influential at the time. Rong Yuan was not the only scholar pursuing this methodology, but she became one of the most prominent, helping to energize a new wave of historical and archaeological scholarship that became dominant in Chinese intellectual circles in the 1930s.

One example of Rong Yuan's innovative scholarship was a catalog of Chinese scholarly works on the study of inscribed bronzes and stelae, with an introduction by her brother Rong Geng, which she published with the Academia Sinica in 1930; as evidence of its impact and importance, a revised edition was printed with the Shanghai Commercial Press in 1936, and a new expanded edition again in 1955. The catalog listed and described over a thousand works of traditional Chinese antiquarian scholarship—the forerunner to modern Chinese historical and archaeological studies—and was well reviewed by leading scholars of ancient inscriptions.[34] Her brother started compiling the bibliography, but Rong Yuan was ultimately given credit for the project, and took responsibility for defending its contents when critiqued by other scholars.[35] The work was considered innovative for its focus on artifact types as well as genres of antiquarian scholarship, and created an important resource for other scholars who approached historical studies as she did, using traditional textual sources to help interpret the latest scientific and archaeological evidence.[36]

Rong Yuan's influence grew when she went to work for the *Harvard-Yenching Journal*, published at Yenching University, where her brother Rong Geng was faculty.[37] Yenching was one of the most well-financed and liberal Christian higher educational institutions in China, with an international Sino-American faculty based on a bucolic campus in a northwestern suburb of the city (now the site of Beijing University). Among the faculty were many eminent Chinese scholars—perhaps drawn by higher-than-average salaries—including Gu Jiegang.[38] In the fall of 1931, Rong Yuan became staff at the Harvard-Yenching Institute and was made an editor of its journal; Rong Geng and Gu Jiegang both served as editor in chief. One of the foremost academic publications of its period, the journal has been praised for its "timely, complete, and objective" coverage of the academic community, one of the few journals of its stature during that era to publish reviews of Marxist historiography, risky at that time due to censorship and even political attacks by the Nationalist government on intellectuals who were viewed as sympathetic to communism.[39]

Rong Yuan was responsible for the scholarly news column, which included reviews of recent publications as well as bulletins on museum exhibitions and scholarly conferences. She wrote reports on the archaeological digs at Anyang that began in 1928 under the direction of the Institute of History and Philology, whose founding she had seen at Zhongshan a few years before.[40] She also reviewed hundreds of recent books and articles on history, etymology, archaeology, numismatics, and folklore. She even reviewed her brother Rong Zhaozu's work on Ming dynasty intellectual history, criticizing him for not including enough political and economic context.[41] She reviewed one of the first pieces of Marxist scholarship to deal with Shang dynasty history, *The Bronze Age* by Guo Moruo 郭沫若 (1892–1978). She recommended that readers devote serious attention to Guo's scholarship, complementing his "splendid achievements and original interpretations."[42] And she complemented the work of the Marxist (and ethnically Uyghur) historian Jian Bozan 翦伯贊 (1898–1968, later professor of history and vice-president at Beijing University), for using recently excavated oracle bone inscriptions and other stone age materials to "smash through conventional barriers" of previous historical studies.[43] It was perhaps in this era that she developed a reputation among her colleagues for seriousness and candor.[44]

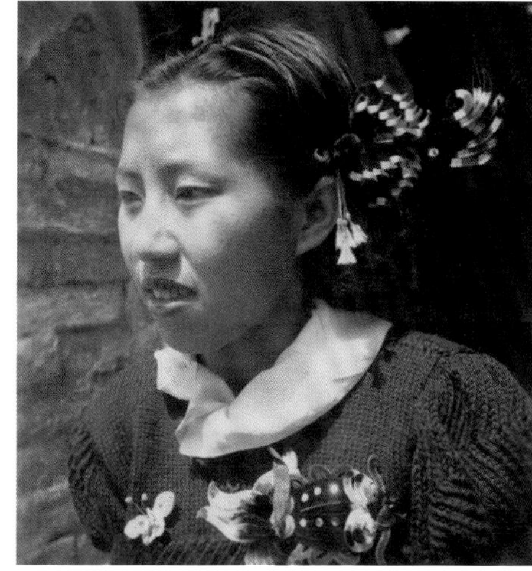

Figure 5.4. Pilgrim wearing souvenirs on Mount Miaofeng. Hedda Morrison Collection, circa 1933–1946. © President and Fellows of Harvard College.

After the Japanese invasion of Beijing in 1937, many scholars fled coastal cities for the wartime capital of Chongqing or other remote cities in the Southwest. By 1941, Japan and the United States were at war. Yenching's president and many faculty were sent to an internment camp in Shandong province. By 1942, refugees in Chongqing established a wartime Yenching University as well as an office of the Harvard-Yenching Institute.[45] Demonstrating considerable personal courage, in the summer of 1943 Rong Yuan traveled to Sichuan where she taught in the Chinese and history departments and worked in the library, while continuing to write for the journal.[46]

After the end of the war, Rong Yuan returned to Beijing. Yenching University was absorbed in 1952 into Beida (which moved to Yenching's suburban campus). Her brother Rong Geng was sent to Canton to teach at Zhongshan, but Rong Yuan continued to work for the Beida History Department. Over the next decade, she was given responsibility for cataloguing rubbings of stelae and epigraphic materials collected by Gu Jiegang,

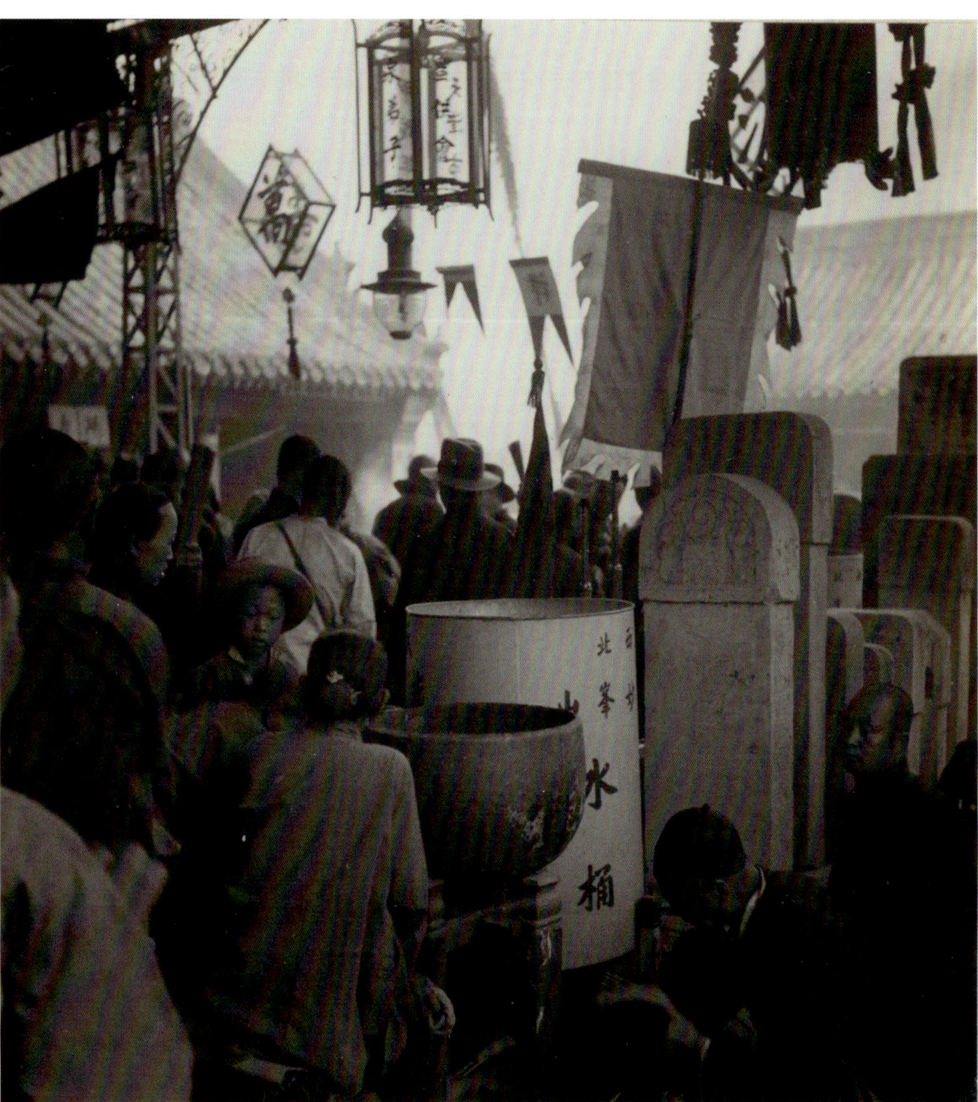

Figure 5.5. Pilgrims visiting a Miaofeng Mountain temple, which has stone stelae of the kind that Rong Yuan was interested in studying. Hedda Morrison Collection, circa 1933–1946. © President and Fellows of Harvard College.

Rong Geng, and other scholars. Her work to identify, systematically organize, and conserve thousands of epigraphic materials created the basis of the still-significant Beida collection. In the words of Hu Haifan, a scholar in the inscriptions department of the Beida library, Rong Yuan "went from a clerical secretary who had only a middle school education, to a highly respected scholar, an expert known for mastery and accomplishment in the fields of inscriptions, archaeology, archives, and cataloging."[47] She retired in the early 1960s, living with her sister in Beijing and continuing her research until her death in 1996. Her magnum opus, a collection of prefaces and colophons on Qin- and Han-dynasty stone inscriptions, was published by Beida in 2009.

Zhou Yingxue: The Girl at the Dig

In the 1930s, the academic spotlight in China shifted from folklore to archaeology, a booming field internationally. Foreign archaeologists in China were unearthing exciting finds, like the Dunhuang Buddhist texts located by Paul Pelliot (1878–1945) and Aurel Stein (1862–1943), and *Homo erectus pekinesis* (or "Peking Man") discovered by Swedish geologist Johan Gunnar Andersson (1874–1960). In London, an academic program in Chinese art and archaeology was inaugurated in 1930, with Perceval Yetts (1878–1957) its chair, a position funded by Chinese payments to settle the Boxer Indemnity.[48] Giving a lecture to introduce the department—the Crown Prince and Princess of Sweden attended, as did the Chinese ambassador—Yetts spoke of the importance of archaeology as establishing an innovative (and incidentally, then largely foreign-led) approach to understanding Chinese culture and history, one that would provide "a clue to the enigma of Chinese origins," believed by some scholars to lie outside of China proper, based on evidence like the fact that archaic Chinese script included a way to write elephant, an animal not then endemic to China.[49] Meanwhile, among Chinese scholars, much of the work on ancient history was being done by classically trained historians, who collected artifacts via antiques markets and private relationships with other scholars rather than scientific excavations.

Aiming to define a field that was distinct from both foreign and traditional Chinese approaches, a new generation of scholars embraced archaeology. In 1928, folklore specialist Dong Zuobin persuaded Fu Sinian that the Institute of History and Philology should open an archaeology department and sponsor excavations in Xiaotun, at that time primarily known as the site of the discovery of the oracle bones. The first expedition turned up only a few artifacts. By 1930, with support of the new Nationalist government and leadership by Harvard-trained anthropologist Li Ji 李濟 (1896–1979), digging resumed and continued for fifteen seasons, until June 1936.[50] The first major scientific excavations directed by Chinese scholars, the project eventually uncovered thousands of oracle bones, bronze vessels, pottery, and other materials that helped establish the historical existence of the Shang dynasty and the longevity of Chinese civilization, as well as the essential accuracy of much traditional Chinese historical scholarship.

Female scholars were no doubt eager to enter this exciting field, but few of them did at first, for at least two reasons. First, compared to folklore studies, archaeology had a greater emphasis on formal training. Although the teaching of archaeology worldwide was only taking shape in the 1920s, expectations grew that practitioners should train in the discipline at the university level, which for Chinese scholars at that time meant going abroad.[51] This was expensive and difficult, and furthermore, women were unwelcome at many overseas universities. They could not emulate Li Ji and Liang Siyong in studying at Harvard, for example, since Harvard restricted women from the anthropology department.[52]

In addition to educational roadblocks, women who wished to get involved in archaeology faced barriers due to gendered expectations about fieldwork.[53] Folklore materials—songs, stories, customs—could be collected where women lived, had personal networks, and were surrounded by other women, as in well-visited sites like temples. Female scholars were also valued as participant-observers with unique abilities to access folksongs and customs. In contrast, the open-air exertions of archaeological excavations, often taking place in remote and rural communities, were assumed to be more naturally suited to men. Women were also viewed as distractions or hindrances to male social styles.[54] Indeed, internationally, the field was described as having a macho culture.[55] Limited in their opportunities to conduct fieldwork, women did conservation work, linguistic studies, analysis of plant and animal remains, etcetera, but these subfields were often deemed less professionally or scientifically significant than the onsite recovery of cultural materials.[56]

Yet there *were* women at the Anyang digs, even in the 1930s. Commemorative group photos include one young woman, spectacled, with bobbed and crimped hair, in some photos dressed in fashionable knee-length dresses, in others wearing the long gown of the scholar.[57] The woman was later identified by her niece as Zhou Yingxue, who is mentioned without being gendered in Li Ji's account of the excavations. But for this information, we may never have realized that some of the most important work of the early years at Anyang was done with the contributions of a female scholar (fig. 5.6).[58]

Born into a family of Henan scholar officials, not too far from Xiaotun, at the time of the first Anyang excavations Zhou Yingxue was a student in Beijing. In the spring of 1931, when she was twenty, Zhou participated in the fourth expedition, joining leader Dong Zuobin, who at thirty-six was the oldest member of the team; Liang Siyong; and Wu Jinding 吳金鼎 (1901–1948), who had already discovered another archaeological site. Over the course of a momentous season, the team established that strata of pounded

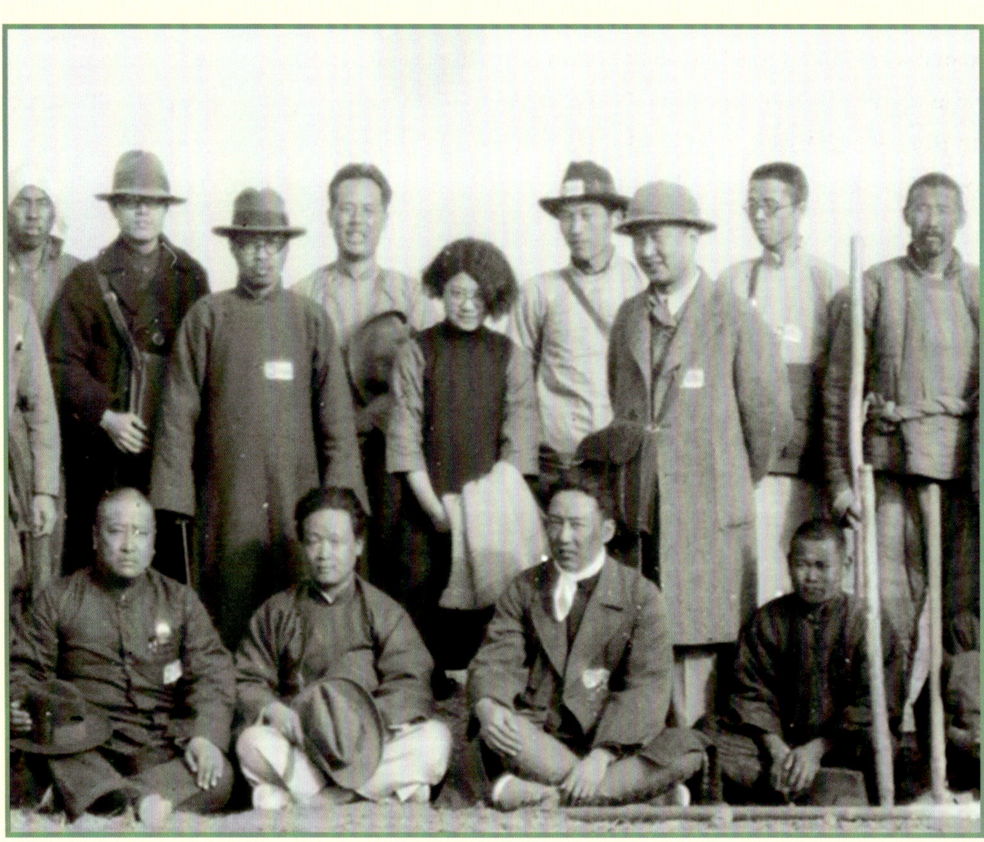

Figure 5.6. Zhou Yingxue and excavation team at Anyang, 1931. Sitting on the ground and to her right is Dong Zuobin; behind her left shoulder is Liang Siyong. From the collections of the Institute of History and Philology at the Academia Sinica, Republic of China.

earth, rather than representing ancient flood deposits from the Huan River as previously assumed, were indications of Shang architectural structures—an insight that later allowed Zheng Zhenxiang to discover Fu Hao's tomb. Subsequent excavation teams focused on "intensive study of the various stages of development of the 'pounded earth methods,' since it was evident that mastery of this technique was the basic training for civil engineers of the Yin-Shang period," according to Li Ji.[59] The fourth expedition also discovered quantities of black pottery, later identified by Liang Siyong as belonging to Longshan culture, which preceded the Shang in the Xiaotun region. In the spring of 1932, Zhou Yingxue returned for the sixth season at Anyang, together with Wu Jinding and others. This team also found the intact foundations of a rammed earth building. This further assisted in reconstructing the principles of Shang architecture, facilitating the later discovery and preservation of Shang royal tombs including the tomb of Fu Hao.

Zhou Yingxue left archaeology around 1933; spurning an arranged marriage, she became involved in left-wing drama circles, married a member of the theater and film community, and had two children.[60] But she was not the only woman at Anyang. Li Fuman 李福曼 (b. 1908) was there to accompany her husband Liang Siyong. A graduate of the education department at Yenching University, Li became pregnant while living at Xiaotun.[61] Later she worked for the Archaeological Institute of the Chinese Academy of Social Sciences, where her husband served as deputy director. Another woman likely there was Wu Jinding's wife, Wang Jiechen 王介忱, who later studied archaeology in London with her husband. In addition to these three women, there may have been other female family members among the archaeological team whose contributions were unrecorded. As in previous decades of Chinese intellectual life, the wives, daughters, and sisters of male intellectuals were often uncredited assistants and collaborators.[62] In any case, despite the contributions of Zhou Yingxue and other women at Anyang, it was left to the next generation of female scholars to fully embrace, and be accorded, the status of archaeologist.

Zeng Zhaoyu: The Importance of Museums

On December 28, 1937, a twenty-eight-year-old woman went to a theater in Berlin to see a performance of *La Boutique fantasque* (also known as *The Magic Toyshop*), a French ballet that was a popular Christmas production. The performance took place in the Deutsches Opernhaus, then under the control of Joseph Goebbels and the Reich Ministry of Public Enlightenment and Propaganda. An elegant theater with soaring ceilings and crystal chandeliers, seating over two thousand audience members, the Deutsches Opernhaus was a star in the Nazi theater firmament. The young woman, Zeng Zhaoyu, was impressed; the music and dancing were excellent, and the set design was far superior to a production she saw the previous year in London.[63] Zeng's host that night was Carl Brittner (1883–1958), director of the conservation laboratory in the Museumsinsel and Zeng's mentor while she lived in Berlin, one of some 1,600 Chinese

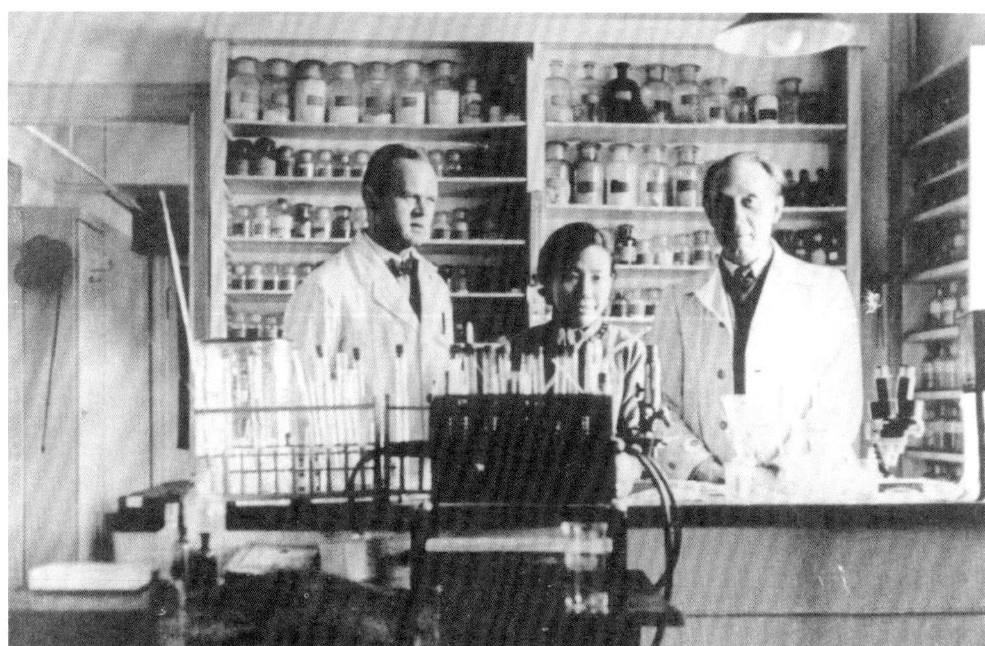

Figure 5.7. Zeng Zhaoyu (*center*) with Carl Brittner (*right*) at the Museumsinsel laboratory, Berlin. Wikimedia Commons.

students in Germany, then a close national ally[64] (fig. 5.7). But the evening occurred at a time of great personal sorrow for Zeng; the city of Nanjing, where she went to university, had fallen to Japanese invasion, and she was desperate for news of family and friends. Nonetheless, she was determined to make the most of her study tour in Germany. This dedication paid off, as she became not only a well-known archaeologist, but ultimately director of the Nanjing Museum.

Zeng Zhaoyu was born into a family of even higher scholar-official status than Rong Yuan, and luckily a family that also prioritized education for women. Her great-grandfather was the younger brother of Zeng Guofan 曾國藩 (1811–1872), the Qing dynasty general who defeated the Taiping Rebellion. She was born in a home built on the grounds of Zeng Guofan's rural estate in Hunan. Her mother was the daughter of late-Qing official Chen Baozhen 陳寶箴 (1831–1900), who rose to the position of governor of Hunan province but was dismissed from office in 1898 due to reformist sympathies. On her mother's side Zeng was a cousin of Chen Yinke 陳寅恪 (1890–1969), famed historian and specialist in Chinese ethnic minority studies, who also studied in London and Berlin.

This distinguished lineage may have accelerated Zeng's professional success while also making her more vulnerable to political trends. In January of 1956, she was appointed to the Chinese People's Political Consultative Conference, the primary legislative body in the PRC, and along with other female delegates was invited to dine with Mao Zedong. A history buff and Hunan native, Mao admired the victorious Qing general who was her great-uncle, and later mentioned the archaeologist in some remarks as "a descendent of Zeng Guofan."[65] In 1958, Zeng wrote to *People's Daily*, the leading PRC media outlet, to express condolences to Mao, whose oldest son Anying died eight years earlier in the Korean War.[66] She may have been prompted by political motives. In 1957, her older brother Zeng Zhaolun 曾昭掄 (1899–1967), a chemist and faculty member at Beida and vice-minister for education, was attacked during the Anti-Rightist Campaign, imprisoned, and demoted to Wuhan University. Zeng may have been trying to help her brother, or herself, or both, with a public declaration of sympathy for Mao.

Like Rong Yuan, Zeng's early schooling was at home, but as a member of the next generation she benefitted from educational opportunities available for women after the May Fourth Movement. At fourteen she attended a girl's school in Changsha directed by a female cousin, Zeng Baosun 曾寶蓀 (1893–1978), the first Chinese women to study abroad, who earned a bachelor of science degree from the University of London before studying at both Oxford and Cambridge. Zeng Baosun impressed on her cousin not only her love of learning and her daring to go overseas, but also her advice that marriage meant limiting her talent to serve one person (a husband), while the single life would leave her free to help many people. Later a Russian expert asked Zeng Zhaoyu why she never married, and she responded, "I'm already married—to the museum."[67]

Zeng's family viewed her as a genius who was destined for an academic life.[68] At nineteen she was admitted to National Central University and entered the foreign languages department. Living in the new national capital of Nanjing in the early 1930s exposed her to some of the most famous intellectuals and ideas of the era, like museology. Cai Yuanpei, director of the Academia Sinica, was eager to build a national museum, in emulation of similar institutions around the world. In 1933 he was able to establish a government office to manage the process, aided by Fu Sinian and Li Ji. Antiquities discovered at archaeological sites, including Anyang, were deposited at the nascent museum. During this period Zeng grew close to Nanjing native Hu Xiaoshi 胡小石 (1888–1962), a legendary bibliophile and scholar of Chinese literature, history, and calligraphy. She also became friends with another talented female protégé of Hu Xiaoshi, You Shou 游壽 (1906–1994), a calligrapher and specialist in Chinese literature, history, and oracle bone and bronze inscriptions, who later had a distinguished career of her own as a museum specialist and academic.[69] Indeed, within archaeology and historical studies, museum work has continued to be a relatively welcoming path for female scholars.[70]

A few years after completing her undergraduate degree, Zeng self-funded her graduate education in London, becoming the first Chinese woman to study archaeology abroad. She joined a small community of Chinese archaeologists in London, then a growing center internationally for archaeological training. She went to the Courtauld Institute of Art at the University of London, joined by Xia Nai 夏鼐 (1910–1985) and Wu Jinding, who was there with his wife, Wang Jiechen. With encouragement from Fu Sinian and Li Ji, they all studied with Perceval Yetts—an arrangement that was evidently highly dissatisfactory. As Zeng Zhaoyu wrote to Fu Sinian, "we have very little to learn here," since Yetts offered no training in prehistoric archaeology. There was also a concern that British Sinologists took advantage of Chinese students to bolster their own credentials. Fortunately Zeng was able to learn fieldwork when she joined excavations directed by another University of London faculty member, archaeologist Mortimer Wheeler (1890–1976), whose wife, Tessa Verney Wheeler (1893–1936), was herself a pioneering female archaeologist. When Li Ji visited the UK for four months in early 1937, Zeng and her classmates accompanied him to lectures and research trips.[71] Later that year she finished her MA with distinction, writing a thesis on "The Evolution of Bronze Scripts in the Zhou Period," examined by Yetts and L. C. Hopkins, another prominent Sinologist who had been one of the earliest scholars of oracle bones.[72]

She was led to Germany by her desire for more specialized training. The German archaeological system was then highly state-sponsored, given extensive funding for excavations and accorded great significance within the Nazi propaganda machine.[73] The museum system was also highly political. Since the era of German unification in the mid-nineteenth century, museum work had expanded to support narratives of German cultural and political identity, racial homogeneity, and imperial glory.[74] In this era of heightened state investment, Germany was the place internationally to be trained in museum work. Zeng interned at the Staatliches Museum für Vor und Frühgeschichte in Berlin, and took part in a German excavation at Schleswig; she also spent two months in Munich. She spent her free time in Berlin surveying the city's museums, among them the Museumsinsel Pergamonmuseum and Altes Museum, the Museum für Naturkunde and Völkerkunde, the Zoologisches Museum, and a dozen others showcasing German architecture, porcelain, handicrafts, and history.

After half a year in Germany, Zeng returned to London for not quite another year, lecturing at the university.[75] She may very well have stayed and completed a PhD (as did Wu Jinding), but she was preoccupied with China's suffering under Japanese occupation, and felt anguish over her inability to help from abroad. No matter how many public lectures she attended, or how many books she read on the crisis—like Edgar Snow's sympathetic account of the communists, *Red Star over China* (1937), which she read in Germany—Zeng believed her purpose lay in returning to help her family and her country.[76] She skipped graduation festivities, reasoning it was selfish to celebrate personal accomplishments in safety while her compatriots were shedding blood to resist Japanese invasion.[77] In September 1939, she set off across Europe to Marseilles and boarded a boat for Saigon, joining other returning students like the anthropologist Fei Xiaotong 費孝通 (1910–2005) on the journey home.

A month later the expats landed in Vietnam. Zeng boarded a train for China and began an arduous trek to reunite with her family. Her mother had fled her hometown for the south, and they were only reunited by a classified ad in a newspaper.[78] Eventually she moved to Sichuan, where thousands of Chinese academics gathered in the picturesque town of Lizhuang to teach, conduct research, and write. Many members of the national archaeological community were there, including Li Ji, Wu Jinding, Wang Jiechen, and Liang Siyong.[79]

While in the Southwest, Zeng participated in several archaeological expeditions. In 1939, she traveled with Wu Jinding and Wang Jiechen to the Dali region, long a site of ethnographic fieldwork. The three "sea turtles" (returning expats) spent seven months in the mountains surveying famous peaks, collecting folklore, and excavating stone-age sites. Notably, their published report listed the three of them as coauthors, two of them female: Wu Jinding, Zeng Zhaoyu, and Wang Jiechen, in that order.[80] Later she traveled with Li Ji to study a Han-dynasty hanging tomb in Sichuan (fig. 5.8). But Zeng's close

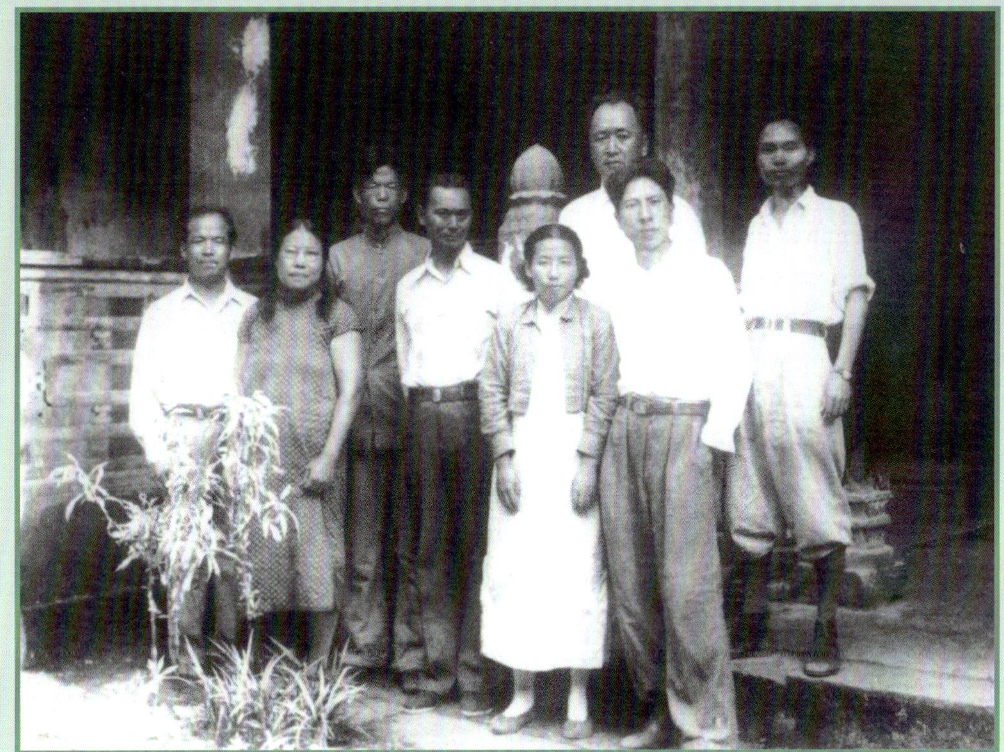

Figure 5.8. Zeng Zhaoyu and fellow archaeologists at Lizhuang, 1941. *Front row, from left to right*: Wu Jinding, Wang Jiechen, Zeng Zhaoyu, Xia Nai. Li Ji stands behind Zeng Zhaoyu and Xia Nai. Wikimedia Commons.

collaboration with Li Ji, a dozen years her senior and married, resulted in significant gossip. Fu Sinian mentioned in his diary the "strange business [i.e., romance] between Li and Zeng." From this distance it is hard to know the truth of the rumors; were they platonic colleagues, did they have a consensual relationship, was she pressured into an affair? During the Cultural Revolution, she was also accused of having an improper relationship with a young protégé at the Nanjing Museum, which the protégé denied and characterized as the kind of personal attack common in that period.[81] To be unmarried may have conveyed some professional advantage to women, allowing them to be perceived as independent scholars, yet it also carried a heavy risk of gossip.

Some of Zeng's most important work was a continuation of her interest in museums and their national value, a crucial part of her overseas training. While in Europe she began an essay on museum organization and methods, which she later revised with Li Ji into a pamphlet called *Museums* (*Bowuguan*). Zeng was confident that China could build institutions to support scientific study, patriotism, national unification, and a consciousness of China's splendid history.[82] When the war ended in 1945, she moved to Nanjing to work as the general manager of the new National Museum (after 1949, when the capital reverted to Beijing, the Nanjing Museum), during a highly politicized era when the Nationalist government was struggling to maintain control of China as well as its antiquities—indeed, much of the museum's collection was taken to Taiwan. In 1955, she was named head of the museum, surely one of the most prestigious positions held by a woman in the Chinese cultural and academic world during that period and one of the only museums of its size worldwide led by a woman. She gave speeches stressing the importance of museum work to build socialist culture, to protect the nation's history, and to increase educational opportunities for the masses.[83] She joined campaigns calling for the return of art and antiquities from Taiwan.[84] Under her leadership, exhibits included natural science topics like human evolution and Neolithic cultures, as well as fine artworks from China's imperial dynasties.[85]

Unfortunately, a high professional position could not insulate her from the worsening political climate, and like many intellectuals she was subjected to various episodes of ideological training. In 1963, a major campaign began: the Socialist Education Movement or "four cleanups" (*siqing yundong* 四清運動) that eventually targeted millions of people. Zeng became clinically depressed and anxious. She was hospitalized and, upon release, asked to be driven to a temple in Nanjing, where she committed suicide by jumping from its pagoda. She was fifty-five years old. Her subordinates at the museum remembered her modesty, kindness, and concern for their well-being.[86] She remains highly admired, and is often accorded the compliment of being described as "China's first female archaeologist."

Matriarchy in Chinese Archaeology

Starting in the 1920s and reaching a crescendo in the 1950s–60s, Chinese intellectual life was significantly influenced by Marxist theories of social, cultural, and historical development. One example is the theory of the matriarchal period of social development. The strict adherence of Chinese archaeologists to Marxist developmental paradigms like matriarchy has been criticized for a number of reasons, including rigid application, not to mention distance from actual feminist concerns.[87] However, some scholars view the matriarchy debates as diverse and productive, encouraging the historical community to assess archaeological findings more creatively as well as to foreground questions of gender.[88] Perhaps not since the women-centered folklore studies movement were so many scholars engaged in historical research about women.

The theory of the matriarchal stage of human social development emerged in European anthropological literature in the nineteenth century, part of a wave of scholarship periodizing human history. These theories influenced Friedrich Engels (1820–1895), whose *The Origin of the Family, Private Property and the State* (1884) argued that social structure characterized by descent through the female line, i.e., matrilineal society, occurred just prior to the patriarchal stage, which was characterized by private wealth and class formation. Nineteenth-century anthropologists and historians believed that matriarchal societies still survived in precapitalist societies around the world. Up for debate was the question of whether matrilineal societies also enjoyed non-patriarchal social structures, namely whether in addition to descent through the female line, women also had robust political, economic, and social power.

Leftist scholars in China engaged with Marxist theories of matrilineal and matriarchal societies at least from the 1930s onward. Disposed at that time—as were many historians around the world—to view history as the unfolding of empirically demonstrable stages in human development, historians were increasingly attuned to issues of gender in social development. In his 1930 *Research on Ancient Chinese History*, Guo Moruo examined notable women in history, like concubines to legendary kings, to better understand marriage customs and kinship relations.[89] Other social thinkers looked to the textual tradition for evidence of pre-patriarchal, female-dominant social formations. Fei Xiaotong's 1933 BA thesis from Yenching University, for example, focused on an unusual custom, found in scattered counties, for the groom to escort his bride personally to their wedding. Noting that this custom was present in ancient texts as well as modern practice, Fei argued that it was a surviving vestige of a matrilocal social system.[90] In 1935, Ren Darong 任達榮, who went on to write many works on women's history, published "Textual Proof of China's Ancient Matrilineal Society" in *Eastern Miscellanae*, one of the foremost journals of the era. He emphasized passages like this one, in the *Shijun* 恃君 or "Relying on Rulers" chapter of *Master Lü's Spring and Autumn Annals* (*Lüshi Chunqiu* 呂氏春秋): "Of old, in high antiquity, there was no ruler. The masses lived and dwelled in groups. They knew their mothers but not their fathers. They did not distinguish between relatives, elders, younger brother, husband and wife, or male and female."[91] Examples of matrilineal descent and maternal authority were discovered in etymological dictionaries, historical annals, philosophical texts, and inscribed artifacts. While the evidence overall was not archaeological, the argument was clear: prehistoric society knew of alternatives to patriarchy.

After 1949, Marxist developmental paradigms became orthodoxy, and archaeologists engaged significantly with the idea of matrilineal or matriarchal society. Chinese archaeologists interpreted prehistoric societies in light of gender roles and social organization, and compared them to contemporary ethnic minority groups, arguing that ancient societies in China were indeed matriarchal, with women active in farming, handicrafts, and warfare. A 1961 archaeology textbook, published to mark the first decade of the field in the PRC, stated in the introduction that Neolithic cultures could be divided into eras of matriarchal and patriarchal society.[92] The question of China's matrilineal or matriarchal social past remained a lively topic of research in subsequent decades, with issues related to marriage structure and the role of women receiving significant scholarly attention.

This research began to slow in the late 1970s. The reopening of Chinese academia to Western scholarship reduced interest in matriarchy and matrilineal social development, as well as the topic of women and gender in archaeology more generally.[93] Another factor was political. Mao's wife, Jiang Qing 江青 (1914–1991), referred to theories of matriarchal society to promote radical feminism, and may have claimed something like "primitive society was matrilineal, before it became patrilineal. In the future, when the socialist society has arrived, this will be reversed. Men will yield, and women will be the managers." After Mao's death, she was attacked as one of the architects of the Cultural Revolution and was blamed for its extremism. Archaeologists charged that she misapplied theories of matriarchal society as part of her plot to "usurp the leadership of the party and seize power."[94] In 1984, when a new edition of the same archaeology textbook was issued, the introduction no longer referenced matriarchal society.

Yet the concept of matriarchy remained important in studies of women's history. *Ancient Chinese Women and Marriage* (1988) by Zheng Huisheng 鄭慧生 discussed the Xiwangmu or "Queen Mother of the West," the progenitor of "the last matrilineal community," ruled by women. The community was thought to have survived to the Western Zhou period, overlapping with the era of Fu Hao.[95] Du Fangqin's *The Evolution of the Concept of Women* (1988) cited Engels's theory of matriarchy to explain China's social development. According to Du, archaeology confirmed that in the age of the Three Sovereigns, the legendary time when mythical sovereigns invented writing, farming, and other civilizational practices, "the female sex was revered."[96]

Chinese archaeology has remained active in global research to examine the role of women in prehistoric societies including research on female icons or goddess figures in Neolithic societies, which have been found in Europe and China.[97] In 2010, Nanjing University held a conference on feminist archaeology and women's history in ancient to early modern China, with papers on Fu Hao and other Shang female generals, gender divisions of labor, goddess religions, foot binding, and other topics.[98] Much of this scholarship has developed in conversation with Western feminist archaeology. But the era of research related to matriarchy no doubt also remains influential. Although no longer the dominant paradigm, this theory created a space for Chinese scholars to engage with questions of women in ancient history, and remains important today.

Zheng Zhenxiang and Female Archaeologists in Socialist China

Thanks to the achievements of generations of women campaigners, the institution-building of the Nationalist regime, as well as the focus of the new Communist state on women's rights, more women were able to obtain formal education after 1949 than at any time in China's history. Education was also free at that time, removing another frequent obstacle to the participation of women. In addition, history and archaeology underwent a renaissance, with questions of early Chinese historical development widely debated in academic journals.[99] Starting in 1952, the Beida History Department advertised an archaeology program, the first in the country.[100] The Institute of Archaeology (whose collections had been taken to Taiwan) partnered with Beida to begin an ambitious program to train field archaeologists, including women.[101] Hundreds of young people were recruited for training programs, with teachers including Zeng Zhaoyu, Xia Nai, Liang Siyong, and Guo Moruo. In combination, these factors had the impact of significantly increasing the participation of women in archaeology. Indeed, in the post-1949 era, some 161 women joined the field.[102] However, in numerical terms they were only 10 percent of the discipline, and structural inequalities persisted, including stressful negotiations of women's dual commitments to home and career, or the second shift problem.

Zheng Zhenxiang was part of Beida archaeology program's first class. Over the four seasons the training program continued, it launched the careers of several prominent women archaeologists, among them Zheng Xiaomei 鄭笑梅 (1931–2014), a researcher at the Shandong Museum who was well known for her work on the Neolithic Dawenkou culture; Ye Xiaoyan 葉小燕 (b. 1933), later of the Institute of Archaeology and a specialist on China's northwest; Li Dejin 李德金 (b. 1934), who trained with Zheng Zhenxiang at Anyang and became a specialist in Chinese ceramics; and Fan Jinshi 樊錦詩 (b. 1938), who became a Dunhuang specialist. Indeed, some 80 percent of women archaeologists in China after 1949 were trained at Beida, mostly at the undergraduate level.[103]

Zheng Zhenxiang completed her studies at Beida just as Anyang was established as a conservation area for archaeological work. The Institute of Archaeology established a permanent workstation at Anyang, with two excavation seasons planned each year, spring and fall, but Zheng had to lobby for a fieldwork assignment.[104] By 1962 she was leading small teams of Beida students and laborers at the Anyang station. Then came the Cultural Revolution, during which time archaeological teams continued to travel to Anyang, but excavation work came to a halt. While the human cost of this period was enormous (among those persecuted were Jian Bozan and other Beida historians), from a conservation standpoint the slowdown may not have been entirely disadvantageous; some archaeologists believe the careful examination of materials excavated previously made it easier to understand the momentous discoveries of the 1970s and later.[105]

Zheng Zhenxiang, Ye Xiaoyan, and other successful women in the field were responsible for tremendous scholarly achievements. Yet many women who entered academic studies—most likely anywhere in the world—reported feeling pushed to the back of the field, or made to do "archaeological housework."[106] Zheng Zhenxiang, even after her momentous discovery of Fu Hao, was still asked if archaeology was suitable for women.[107] In addition, women with families faced complex challenges, including managing personal commitments during fieldwork. Ye Xiaoyan mentioned in interviews the stress of raising children at rural excavation sites, far from grandparents and other support networks.[108] Zheng Zhenxiang was fortunate to have met her husband, fellow archaeologist Chen Zhida 陳誌達, at the Anyang excavations in the late 1950s, so they both understood the profession and its demands. They took turns living in Beijing, where their daughter stayed, and Anyang. Although equitable in terms of family responsibilities, the time spent apart was not easy; on one occasion Zheng's daughter hid her train ticket back to Anyang to prevent her from leaving.[109] Perhaps in recognition of the difficulty of being both a scholar and a parent, the media still refers to female scholars having "married" their field sites, and lauds scholars like Fan Jinshi, who was separated from her husband for some two decades while she worked in Dunhuang and he taught at Wuhan University.[110] Some scholars are fortunate to enjoy egalitarian partnerships where both people share tasks evenly, but data indicates that the time demands of domestic chores for professional women remains a significant disparity in the experiences of men and women in China, as in many other nations.[111]

Meanwhile, the work of feminist scholarship in archaeology as well as history and related fields is ongoing, as scholars grapple with gender bias in the interpretation of evidence, uses of gender categories in scholarship, and equity issues in the practice of our fields. Fu Hao remains a potent icon for feminists, for whom the Shang princess proves that "it is a Chinese tradition for women to lead troops and fight battles."[112] The number of women in the field of archaeology is still far lower than male counterparts, and women are more likely to be engaged in administrative tasks rather than fieldwork.[113] However, if efforts toward inclusion and support continue, hopefully women scholars may someday no longer be viewed as exceptional due primarily to gender, or overshadow each other in recognition as the media seeks to anoint one symbolic female figure. Public praise will not be directed to a token (and apocryphal) "first" female archaeologist, but rather there will be acknowledgment that women have been leaders in Chinese historical, archaeological, and anthropological research for over a century.

Notes

1. Jijun Zhao and Jan Woudstra, "'In Agriculture, Learn from Dazhai': Mao Zedong's Revolutionary Model Village and the Battle against Nature," *Landscape Research* 32, no. 2 (2007): 21–22. Unless otherwise noted, all translations are my own.

2. Shana J. Brown, *Pastimes: From Art and Antiquarianism to Modern Chinese Historiography* (Honolulu: University of Hawai'i Press, 2011), 88–92.

3. Anyang Archaeological Team, "Anyang Yinxu wu hao mu de fajue" 安陽殷墟五號墓的發掘 [Excavation of tomb no. 5 at Yin-hsü in Anyang], *Kaogu xuebao* 考古學報 2 (1977): 57.

4. Zheng Zhenxiang 鄭振香, "Jiyi Yinxu Fu Hao mu" 記憶殷墟婦好墓 [Memories of the Yinxu tomb of Fu Hao], *Dazhong kaogu* 大眾考古 4 (2014): 19–20; Zheng Zhenxiang 鄭振香, "Yinxu fajue liushi nian gaishu" 殷墟發掘六十年概述 [Sixty years of excavations at Yinxu], *Kaogu* 考古 10 (1988): 929–30; Ying Wang, "Rank and Power among Court Ladies at Anyang," in *Gender and Chinese Archaeology*, ed. Katheryn M. Linduff and Yan Sun (Walnut Creek, CA: Altamira Press, 2004), 102–3.

5. Guo Peng 郭鵬, "Zhi 'zi' zhi shou, yu 'zi' xie lao—Fu Hao mu yu Zheng Zhenxiang" 執'子'之手，與'子'偕老—婦好墓與鄭振香 [Grasp a seed in your hand, grow old with the seed: The tomb of Fu Hao and Zheng Zhenxiang], *Qunyan* 羣言 6 (2016): 36–7.

6. Xu Jin 徐津, "Zheng Zhenxiang: Nüren ye yao wu suo weiju" 鄭振香：女人也要無所畏懼 [Zheng Zhenxiang: Women also want to be fearless], *Peking University News*, July 6, 2007, https://news.pku.edu.cn/bdrw/137-115503.htm.

7. "Profile: China's First Female Archaeologist," *Xinhua News Agency*, August 31, 1999. Zhao Wei writes, "Born at a time when society was dominated by men and women stayed in the home, Fu Hao led military campaigns to protect her kingdom and is hailed as China's first female general. . . . In a remarkable coincidence, Zheng Zhenxiang, the archaeologist who directed the excavation of Fu Hao's tomb, is the first female archaeologist in China. Zheng spent 36 years in Yinxu and witnessed its archaeological development." Zhao Wei, "The Queen Who Rode to War," *Beijing Review*, April 7, 2016, http://www.bjreview.com/Lifestyle/201605/t20160527_800058022.html.

8. Liu Yaming 劉雅鳴 and Gui Juan 桂娟, "Hui kan bainian Yinxu" 回看百年殷墟 [Looking back at a century of Yinxu], *Liaowang xinwen zhoukan* 瞭望新聞周刊 21 (2001): 45.

9. See Virginia Woolf's essay entitled "On Not Knowing Greek" (1925), a wry performance of outsider status. Women in the UK were not admitted to elite private schools where systematic instruction in Greek and Latin typically began at age five or six. Woolf only read Greek because she had been tutored privately at home.

10. This practice is described in Susan Mann, *The Talented Women of the Zhang Family* (Berkeley: University of California Press, 2007), 62–68.

11. Lu Yanzhen, *Zhongguo jindai nüzi jiaoyu shi(1895–1945)* 中國近代女子教育史 *(1895–1945)* [History of modern women's education in China, 1895–1945] (Taipei: Wenshizhe chubanshe,

1989), 1–7; Nanxiu Qian, *Politics, Poetics, and Gender in Late Qing China: Xue Shaohui and the Era of Reform* (Stanford, CA: Stanford University Press, 2015), 123–25. Writing in the early twentieth century, Ida Lewis noted that before modern education, "while [Chinese] women were illiterate they were not uneducated. The responsibilities of the home were heavy and called for many kinds of skill." Ida Belle Lewis, *The Education of Girls in China* (New York: Teachers College, Columbia University, 1919), 10.

12. Huang Hefang 黄河方, *Wudai shuxiang zhuan: Yimen liangjia Rong Geng jiazu* 五代書香傳 一門兩大家 容庚家族 [Biography of five generations of intellectuals: One house, two great families, Rong Geng's extended family] (Guangzhou: Huanan ligong daxue chubanshe, 2006), 141.

13. Huang Hefang, *Wudai shuxiang zhuan,* 137.

14. Timothy Weston, *The Power of Position: Beijing University, Intellectuals, and Chinese Political Culture, 1898–1929* (Berkeley: University of California Press, 2004), 197; Koyama Shizuko, *Ryōsai Kenbo: The Educational Ideal of "Good Wife, Wise Mother" in Modern Japan* (Leiden, the Netherlands, and Boston: Brill, 2012), 78.

15. Louise Edwards, *Gender, Politics, and Democracy: Women's Suffrage in China* (Stanford, CA: Stanford University Press, 2008), 77–79.

16. Faculty included Deng Yingchao 邓颖超 (1904–1992), later chair of the People's Political Consultative Conference and wife of Premier Zhou Enlai. Jia Meixian 賈梅仙, "Rong Yuan zhuanlüe" 容媛傳略 [Biographical sketch of Rong Yuan], in *Rong Geng Rong Zhaozu xueji* 容庚容肇祖學記 [Studies on Rong Geng and Rong Zhaozu], ed. Dongguang shi zhengxie (Guangzhou: Guangdong renmin chubanshe, 2004), 423.

17. Wei-pang Chao, "Modern Chinese Folklore Investigation. Part II. The National Sun Yat-Sen University," *Folklore Studies* 2 (1943): 79–81.

18. Flora Shao, "'Seeing Her Through a Bamboo Curtain': Envisaging a National Literature through Chinese Folk Songs," *Twentieth-Century China* 41, no. 3 (October 2016): 260–62.

19. Several famous women intellectuals were trained via the folklore movement in the West, among them Zora Neale Hurston (1891–1960) who studied folklore and anthropology at Columbia with Franz Boas (1858–1942); other female Boas students included anthropologist Margaret Mead (1901–1978) and Yankton Dakota folklorist Ella Deloria (1889–1971). The folklore studies community in China was influenced by British folklorist Charlotte Sophia Burne (1850–1923), the first woman president of the British Folklore Society. See Liu, "Translingual Folklore and Folklorics in China," in *A Companion to Folklore*, ed. Regina F. Bendix and Galit Hasan-Rokemj (Chichester, UK: Blackwell, 2012) 198–99. In the United States, however, sexism minimized the contributions of women in leadership; president of the American Folklore Society from 1924 to 1926, Louise Pound (1872–1958), was described by fellow folklorists as "a mother bitch figure with whom it was dangerous for [male scholars] to tangle." See Rosan A. Jordan and F. A. De Caro, "Women and the Study of Folklore," *Signs* 11, no. 3 (Spring 1986): 501.

20. Chang Hui 常惠, "Women weishenme yao yanjiu geyao" 我們為什麼要研究歌謠 [Why we study folksongs], *Geyao* 歌謠 1, no. 2 (1922): 1–2. Regulations for collecting folksongs at Beijing University referred specifically to the appropriateness of collecting the songs of "vagrant girls or unhappy women," suggesting that these were prevalent. For example, in some cases folklore specialists had to apply their own gender assumptions regarding oral literature, namely how to interpret the spoken pronoun "ta" (he / she / it). See Shao, "Seeing Her Through a Bamboo Curtain," 275–76. Haiyan Lee also notes (male) folklorists often "depicted women in particular as prepolitical, subaltern subjects who spoke poetic truth from their bleeding hearts." Haiyan Lee, "Tears That Crumbled the Great Wall: The Archaeology of Feeling in the May Fourth Folklore Movement," *Journal of Asian Studies* 64, no. 1 (February 2005), 59–60.

21. Liu Jing'an 劉經庵, *Geyao yu funü* 歌謠與婦女 [Folksongs and women] (Shanghai: Shanghai shudian chubanshe, 1992), 6.

22. Jie Gao, *Saving the Nation through Culture: The Folklore Movement in Republican China* (Vancouver: University of British Columbia Press, 2019), 74, 90, 96, 99, 180. Ge Henggang 葛恆剛, "Beida geyao zhengzi yundong de huigu yu fansi" 北大歌謠徵集運動的回顧與反思 [Review and reflection of the Beida folksong collection movement], *Nanjing shida xuebao* 南京師大學報 1 (January 2017): 137. After the establishment of the People's Republic in 1949, folklore remained influential on popular culture, for example the 1960 film *Liu Sanjie*, based on a legendary medieval female singer from the Zhuang ethnic minority. Liu, "Translingual Folklore," 205–6.

23. Gu Jiegang 顧頡剛, "Xueru nüshi Beiping geyao zhuangji xu ling" 雪如女士北平歌謠撞集序鈴 [Short preface to the *Collection of Beijing Folksongs* by female scholar Xueru], in *Gu Jiegang quanji. Gu Jiegang minsu lunwen ji juan 1.* 顧頡剛全集 14. 顧頡剛民俗論文集 卷1 [Collected works of Gu Jiegang, vol. 14, Gu Jiegang writings on folk studies vol. 1] (Beijing: Zhonghua shuju, 2016), 374.

24. Dong Xiaoping 董曉萍, "Guojia, lishi, minsu: nüxing xuezhe de minsu yichan" 國家·历史·民俗：女性學者的民俗學遺產 [Nation, history, folklore: The legacy of female scholars in folklore studies], *Xibei minsu yanjiu* 西北民俗研究 3 (2018): 123.

25. Wang Wenbao 王文寶, "Woguo minsu yundong zhong de nü minsu xuezhe" 我國民俗學運動中的女民俗學者 [Female folklore scholars in the Chinese folklore movement], *Minsu yanjiu* 民俗研究 2 (1992): 95. Another example of a female folklorist is the poet Xu Fang 徐芳 (1921–2008), who became active in folksong studies in Beijing while a student at Beida in the mid-1930s. She is pictured in the front row of the attendee photo of the Folksong Studies conference in 1935 at Beida, along with three other female participants whose names are not identified. See Wang Wenbao 王文寶, *Zhongguo minsuxue shi* 中國民俗學史 (Chengdu: Bashu shushe, 1995), xxv.

26. Chao, "Modern Chinese Folklore Investigation," 79–88, 80–81.

27. Shi Aidong 施愛東, "Minsuxue shi yimen guoxue—Zhongshan Daxue minsuxue yundong de gongzuo jihua yu zaoqi minsu xuezhe due xueke de renshi" 民俗學是一門國學—中山大學民俗學運動的工作計劃與早期民俗學者的學科的認識 [Folk studies is a kind of national study: The work plans of the folklore studies group at Zhongshan University and the understanding of the field by early folklore scholars], *Minsu yanjiu* 民俗研究 2, no. 132 (2017): 5–6. Chao, "Modern Chinese Folklore Investigation," 79–88, 82–83. Even Deng Erya participated in folklore studies, publishing a short article on the Dongguan Earth God shrine in *Folklore*.

28. Jia Meixian, "Rong Yuan zhuanlüe," 423. At least one faculty member at the women's college, Yang Chengzhi楊成誌 (1902–1991), was a folklore specialist and taught for the institute; he traveled to the mountainous Southwest to study ethnic minorities. See Chao, "Modern Chinese Folklore Investigation," 82, 86.

29. Rong Yuan 容媛, "Dongguan Cheng Huang miao tushuo東莞城隍廟圖說 [Explanatory map of the Cheng Huang temple in Dongguan]," *Minsu* 民俗 nos. 41/42 (1929): 31.

30. Weston, *Power*, 197–99; Huang Hefang, *Wudai shuxiang zhuan*, 141–42. Rong Xian was the first female student to attend Dongguan Middle School.

31. Collecting riddles, tongue twisters, and jokes was a significant activity in the folklore movement; see Gao, *Saving the Nation*, 122.

32. Susan Naquin, "The Peking Pilgrimage to Miao-feng Shan: Religious Organizations and Sacred Sites," in *Pilgrims and Sacred Sites in China*, ed. Susan Naquin and Chün-fang Yü (Berkeley: University of California Press, 1992), 343–45.

33. Rong Yuan 容媛, "You Miaofeng shan riji" 游妙峰山日記 [Diary of a journey to Mt. Miaofeng], *Minsu* 民俗 nos. 69/70 (1929): 108–19.

34. Jia Meixian, "Rong Yuan zhuanlüe," 427–28.

35. Rong Yuan 容媛, "Kaogutu shiwen zhi zuozhe" 考古圖釋文之作者 [The author of the *Kaogutu shiwen*], *Kaogu* 考古 5 (1936), 141.

36. Shen Chang 申暢, *Zhongguo mulu xuejia cidian*中國目錄學家辭典 [Dictionary of Chinese bibliographers], (Zhengzhou: Henan renmin chubanshe, 1988), 422.

37. Philip West, *Yenching University and Sino-Western Relations, 1916–1952*, Harvard East Asian Series 85 (Cambridge, MA: Harvard University Press, 1976), 187–93.

38. West, *Yenching University*, 34, 191–93. For Rong Geng's financial situation at Yenching, see Yi Xinnong 易新农 and Xia Hexun 夏和顺, *Rong Geng zhuan*容庚传 [Biography of Rong Geng], (Guangdong: Huacheng chubanshe, 2010), 43.

39. Zhang Yue 張越, "'Shuping' zhong de xueshu piping—Yenching xuebao 'shuping' lanmu de tese" "書評" 中的學術批評— 《燕京學報》 "書評" 欄目栏目的特色 [The critical scholarship of the book review: Characteristics of the book review column in *Yenching Journal*], *Langfang shifan xueyuan xuebao* 廊坊師範學院學報 6 (2008): 45. 47. Shuhua Fan, "'Cultural Engineering': The Harvard-Yenching Institute and Chinese Humanities, 1924–1951" (PhD diss., University of North Carolina at Chapel Hill, 2007), 108–9, ProQuest (3267818).

40. Rong Yuan 容媛, "Yinxu fajue zhi zhongyao jishu yu xun" 殷墟發掘之重要記述余遜 [Additional account of important excavations at Yinxu], *Yanjing xuebao* 燕京學報 8 (1930): 190–91.

41. Rong Yuan 容媛, "Review of Rong Zhaozu" 容肇祖, *Mingdai sixiang shi*明代思想史 [History of Ming dynasty thought], *Yanjing xuebao* 燕京學報 31 (1946): 201–2.

42. Rong Yuan 容媛, "Review of Guo Moruo" 郭沫若, *Qingtong shidai*青銅時代 [The bronze age], *Yanjing xuebao* 燕京學報 32 (1947): 233.

43. Rong Yuan 容媛, "Review of Jian Bozan" 翦伯贊, *Shiqian shi Yin Zhou shi* 史前史殷周史 [Prehistoric history: Yin and Zhou history], *Yanjing xuebao* 燕京學報 31 (1946): 198–201. Not all her works were critical; for example, she also wrote a 7,000-character essay on the scholarship of the late-Qing historian and paleographer Li Wentian 李文田 (1834–1895), who helped pioneer the collection and study of temple stelae inscriptions.

44. Hu Haifan 胡海帆, "Rong Yuan dui jinshixue de gongxian" 容媛對金石學的貢獻 [Rong Yuan's contributions to epigraphy], in *Lingnan shuxue yanjiu (lunwen ji)* 嶺南書學研究論文集 [Research on Lingnan calligraphy (essay volume)], ed. Lin Yajie 林亚杰 and Zhu Wanzhang 朱万章 (Guangzhou: Guangdong renmin chubanshe, 2004), 400.

45. Fan, *Cultural Engineering*, 118–20.

46. Jia Meixian, "Rong Yuan zhuanlüe," 423.

47. Hu Haifan, "Rong Yuan dui jinshixue de gongxian," 400.

48. Zhao Hui, "Field Archaeology Training at Peking University," in *Concepts of the Past to Practical Strategies: The Teaching of Archaeological Field Techniques*, ed. Peter Ucko, Qin Ling, and Jane Hubert (London: Saffron, 2007), 54.

49. "Archaeology in China: Racial and Cultural Origins of Chinese Unsolved," *North China Daily News*, December 22, 1930, 19.

50. Zhang Liangren, "The Chinese School of Archaeology," *Antiquity* 87, no. 337 (2013): 896; Guolong Lai, "Imperialism, Nationalism, and Regionalism in Yinxu," in *Unmasking Ideology in Imperial and Colonial Archaeology: Vocabulary, Symbols, and Legacy*, ed. Bonnie Effros and Guolong Lai (Los Angeles: Cotsen Institute of Archaeology Press, University of California, Los Angeles, 2018), 98.

51. Lydia C. Carr, *Tessa Verney Wheeler: Women and Archaeology before World War Two* (Oxford: Oxford University Press, 2012), 147.

52. Wang Tao and Peter Ucko, "Early Archaeological Fieldwork Practice and Syllabuses in China and England," in *Concepts of the Past to Practical Strategies*, 50. Into the 1960s and 1970s the Harvard Department of Anthropology (where archaeology was housed) was considered inhospitable to female students. Carr, *Women and Archaeology*, 12; and David L. Browman and Stephen Williams, *Anthropology at Harvard: A Biographical History, 1790–1940* (Cambridge, MA: Peabody Museum Press, 2013), 401–2.

53. He Yun'ao 賀雲翱, "Yidai fenghua, liangwei nüxi—nü kaoguxue jia Zeng Zhaoyu he You Shou xiansheng lizan" 一代風華两位女傑—女考古學家曾昭燏和游壽先生禮讚 [A magnificent generation, two women of distinction: Praise for female archaeologists Zeng Zhaoyu and teacher You

Shou], in *Nüxing kaogu yu nüxing yichan* 女性考古與女性遺產 [Feminist archaeology and the heritage of women], ed. He Yun'ao 賀雲翱 (Nanjing: Nanjing daxue chubanshe, 2011), 215.

54. Carr, *Women and Archaeology*, 8; Kelley Hays-Gilpin, "Feminist Scholarship in Archaeology," *Annals of the American Academy of Political and Social Science* 571, no. 1 (2000): 92.

55. J. N. Woodall and P. J. Perricon, "The Archeologist as Cowboy: The Consequence of Professional Stereotype," *Journal of Field Archaeology* (Boston) 8, no. 4 (1981): 506–7. Several male archaeologists portrayed themselves as swashbuckling colonial adventurers, among them Harvard professor Langdon Warner (1881–1955), notorious for having removed significant antiquities from China under loose local supervision, later considered one of the inspirations for Steven Spielberg's character Indiana Jones. For a description of Warner's view of his expeditions and his self-described treatment as a "sun god" by local residents, see Justin M. Jacobs, "Langdon Warner at Dunhuang: What Really Happened?" *Silk Road* 11 (2013): 4.

56. Zhang Meifang 章梅芳 and Meng Xin 孟欣, "Zhongguo nü kaoguxue jia qunti de xingcheng fazhan yu zhiye zhuangkuang" 新中國女考考古學家群體的形成發展與職業狀況 [The formation and development and professional situation of the community of female archaeologists in New China], *Zhongguo wenwu* 中國文物 2 (2014): 35–36.

57. Liang Baiyou 梁柏有, *Siwen yongzai: wo de fu qin kao gu xue jia Liang Siyong* 思文永在：我的父親考古學家梁思永 [Thinking and language are eternal: My father, archaeologist Liang Siyong] (Beijing: Gugong chubanshe, 2016), 71; photographs of Zhou Yingxue are on 71–73.

58. He Wenjing 何文竟 and Wu Ling 吳玲, "Zhou Yingxue: Woguo zui zao de nü kaogu gongzuozhe" 周英學: 我國最早的女考古工作者 [Zhou Yingxue: China's earliest female archaeology worker], *Dazhong kaogu* 大眾考古 9 (2017): 34.

59. Li Chi [Li Ji] 李濟, *Anyang* (Seattle: University of Washington Press, 1977), 70–73.

60. He Wenjing, "Zhou Yingxue," 35–36.

61. Dai Jun 岱峻, "Liang Siyong: Wei jungong de kaoguxue zhongzhen" 梁思永: 未竣工的考古學重鎮 [Liang Siyong: Hub of uncompleted archaeology], *Mingren zhuanji* 名人傳記 10 (2013): 63–64.

62. Lyce Jankowski, *Les Amis des monnaies: La sociabilité savante des collectionneurs et numismates chinois de la fin des Qing* (Paris: Hemispheres, 2019), 139–40.

63. Zeng Zhaoyu曾昭燏, *Zeng Zhaoyu wenji. Riji shuxin juan* 曾昭燏文集. 日記書信卷. [Collected works of Zeng Zhaoyu: Diary and letters volume] (Nanjing: Nanjing bowuyuan, 2013), 7. The 1937–38 opera season can be viewed at https://www.usmbooks.com/nazi_opera_program_1.html.

64. William C. Kirby, *Germany and Republican China* (Stanford, CA: Stanford University Press, 1984), 154.

65. Yue Nan 岳南, "Gaocai duanming ren shei cun" 高才短命人誰忖 [A great talent dies young, who would guess], in *Nandu beigui* 3: libie 南渡北歸3: 離別 [Crossing the south, returning north, vol. 3: Leaving on a journey] (Changsha: Hunan wenyi chubanshe, 2013), 286–87.

66. Zeng Zhaoyu 曾昭燏, "Shi wo wanfeng gandong" 使我萬分感動 [I feel completely moved], *Renmin ribao* 人民日報 8 (November 2, 1958): 8.

67. Zeng Zhaoyu 曾昭燏, *Zeng Zhaoyu wenji. Kaogu juan*曾昭燏文集.考古卷. [Collected works of Zeng Zhaoyu: Archaeology volume] (Nanjing: Nanjing bowuyuan, 2009), 1.

68. Yue Nan 岳南, "San zhi xin shengdai 'hai gui" 三只新生代海龜 [Three "returning turtles" of the new age], in *Nandu beigui: nandu* 南渡北歸: 南渡 [Crossing the south, returning north, vol. 1: Crossing the south] (Changsha: Hunan wenyi chubanshe, 2011), 332.

69. Li Youning 李又寧, "Zeng Zhaoyu (1909–1964)—Woguo zui jiechu de nüxing kaoguxue jia ji bowuguan xue jia" 曾昭燏 *(1909–1964)* 我國最傑出的女性考古學家及博物館學家 [Zeng Zhaoyu (1909–1964): China's most prominent female archaeologist and museumologist], *Jindai Zhongguo funü shi yanjiu* 近代中國婦女史研究 1 (1993), 38–39.

70. Zhang Meifang, "Xin Zhongguo nü kaoguxue jia," 37.

71. Yue Nan, "San zhi xin shengdai 'hai gui,'" 335.

72. Wang Tao, "Early Archaeological Fieldwork Practice," 55–57.

73. Brent Maner, *Germany's Ancient Pasts: Archaeology and Historical Interpretation since 1700* (Chicago: University of Chicago Press, 2018), 262–71. While in retrospect it is unsettling that Zeng Zhaoyu, or any other foreign student, should have traveled to Germany during the Nazi period, this perspective was anachronistic given that the Chinese government was allied with Germany. Furthermore, throughout the 1930s British intellectuals continued to visit and study in Germany, even after significant persecution of Jews, the disabled, and other groups had begun (and were reported in the British press). Future French Resistance fighter Samuel Beckett, for example, self-financed a study tour of Berlin in 1936–37. In any case, Zeng Zhaoyu left Berlin before Kristallnacht (November 9–10, 1938), widely considered a turning point in the international public understanding of Nazism as dedicated to active genocidal annihilation of Jews and other groups.

74. Chinese scholars in the anthropology and archaeology community, notably Li Ji, were also interested in identifying and defining a historically distinct Han Chinese racial group. See Frank Dikötter, *The Discourse of Race in Modern China* (Oxford: Oxford University Press, 2015), 84–85.

75. Wang Tao, "Early Archaeological Fieldwork," 55–57.

76. Zeng Zhaoyu, *Riji shuxin juan*, 10.

77. Yue Nan, "San zhi xin shengdai 'hai gui,'" 337.

78. Yue Nan, 340.

79. Other archaeologists relocated to the Communist-controlled territories in the Northwest, including He Zhenghuang 何正璜 (1914–1994), who along with her husband, Wang Ziyun 王子雲 (1897–1990), participated in the 1940 expedition to collect art and artifacts in the Northwest, and spent much of the war living in Dunhuang, where they studied and helped preserve the famous Buddhist cave temples.

80. See Wu Jinding 吴金鼎, Zeng Zhaoyu 曾昭燏, and Wang Jiechen 王介忱, *Yunnan Cang'erjing kaogu baogao* 云南苍洱境考古报告 [Archaeological report of Cang'erjing, Yunnan] (N.p.: Zhongyang bowuyuan, 1942).

81. Yue Nan, "San zhi xin shengdai 'hai gui,'" 319–20 n. 34. She was also said to have had a romantic attachment with Xia Nai in London.

82. Zeng Zhaoyu 曾昭燏, "Bowuguan" 博物館 [Museums] (1943), reprinted in *Zeng Zhaoyu wenji* 曾昭燏文集 [Collected works of Zeng Zhaoyu] (Beijing: Wenwu chubanshe, 1999), 248–49.

83. Zeng Zhaoyu 曾昭燏, "Guanyu wenhua gongzuo de liang dian yijian" 關於文化工作的兩點意見 [Speech on two views of cultural work], *Renmin ribao* 人民日報 4 (March 12, 1957): 4.

84. See editorials in *People's Daily*, April 8, 1959, and February 2, 1960.

85. Yang Xuemei 楊雪梅, "Shenmeyang de zhanlan shi hao zhanlan" 什麼樣的展覽是好展覽 [What kind of exhibit is a good exhibit], *Renmin ribao* 人民日報 8 (May 30, 2020): 8.

86. Li Youning, "Zeng Zhaoyu," 44.

87. Critics of the matriarchy thesis ranged from William Skinner, who accused Chinese anthropologists of not having made any progress since the theory's nineteenth-century adherents, to Judith Stacey, who notes that debates over matriarchy had little practical application. See William Skinner, "The New Sociology in China," *Far Eastern Quarterly* (August 1951): 365–71, and Judith Stacey, "China's Socialist Revolution, Peasant Families, and the Uses of the Past," *Theory and Society* 9, no. 2 (March 1980): 269–81.

88. Gideon Shelach, "Marxist and Post-Marxist Paradigms for the Neolithic," in *Gender and Chinese Archaeology*, ed. Katheryn M. Linduff and Yan Sun (Lanham, MD: Altamira Press, 2004), 14–16.

89. Cao Fangfang 曹芳芳, "Xingbie kaogu yanjiu zongshu—yi Zhongguo kaoguxue wei zhongxin" 性別考古學研究綜述—以中國考古學為中心 [Summary of research on gender archaeology: Centered on Chinese archaeology], *Nanfang wenwu* 南方文物 (2013): 114.

90. Fei Xiaotong 費孝通, "Qinying hunsu zhi yanjiu" 親迎婚俗之研究 [Research on the qinying marriage custom], in *Fei Xiaotong wenji, di yi juan, 1914–1937* 費孝通文集第1卷 *1924–1937* [Collected works of Fei Xiaotong, vol. 1, 1924–1937] (Beijing: Qunyan chubanshe, 1999), 187.

91. Ren Darong 任達榮, "Guanyu Zhongguo gudai muxi shehui de kaozheng" 關於中國古代母系社會的考證 [Textual verification of China's ancient matrilineal society], *Dongfang zazhi* 東方雜誌 32, no. 1 (1935): 72. Translation adapted from James D. Sellmann, *Timing and Rulership in Master Lü's Spring and Autumn Annals (Lüshi Chunqiu)*, SUNY Series in Chinese Philosophy and Culture (Albany: State University of New York Press, 2002), 87.

92. Zhongguo kexueyuan kaogu yanjiusuo 中國科學院考古研究所, *Xin Zhongguo de kaogu shouhuo* 新中國的考古收穫 [Results of the archaeology of New China] (Beijing: Wenwu chubanshe, 1961), 1, 12.

93. Shelach, "Marxist and Post-Marxist Paradigms," 12.

94. Cai Fengshu 蔡鳳書, "Pi Jiang Qing suowei de 'muxi shehui'" 批江青所謂的'母系社會' [Critique of Jiang Qing's so-called matrilineal society], *Wen shi zhe* 文史哲 1 (1977): 60.

95. Zheng Huisheng 鄭慧生, *Shanggu Huxia funü yu hunyin*上古華夏婦女与婚姻 [Ancient Chinese women and marriage] (Zhengzhou: Henan renmin chubanshe, 1988), 63–66.

96. Du Fangqin 杜芳琴, *Nüxing guannian de yanbian*女性觀念的衍變 [The evolution of the concept of women] (Zhengzhou: Henan renmin chubanshe, 1988), 2. For an excellent overview of the development of this area of scholarship, see Liu Wenming, "The Rise of a 'New Women's History' in Mainland China," *Chinese Studies in History* 45, no. 4 (2012): 71–89.

97. Jiao Tianlong, "Gender Studies in Chinese Neolithic Archaeology," in *Gender and the Archaeology of Death*, ed. Bettina Arnold and Nancy L. Wicker (Lanham, MD: Altamira Press, 2001), 57–60.

98. See the conference volume edited by He Yun'ao, 2011.

99. Zheng Zhenxiang 鄭振香, "Nan wang de daxue shenghuo" 難忘的大學生活 [Unforgettable university life], in *Na shi women zheng jianqing: Beijing daxue lishi xi xiyou huiyilu* 那时我們正年輕: 北京大學歷史系系友回憶錄 [At that time we were really young: Alumni recollections of the Beijing University history department], ed. Wang Chunmei 王春梅 and Wang Meixiu 王美秀 (Beijing: Xiandai jiaoyu chubanshe, 2007), 2–3.

100. Zheng Zhenxiang, "Nan wang de daxue shenghuo," 1.

101. Meng Xin 孟欣 and Zhang Meifang 章梅芳, "Nü kaoguxue jia de xueshu zhi lu—Ye Xiaoyan yanjiuyuan fangtan lu" 女考古學家的學術之路—葉小燕研究員訪談錄 [The scholarly path of a female archaeologist: Interview with researcher Ye Xiaoyan], *Guangxi minzu daxue xuebao (ziran kexue ban)* 18, no. 4 (December 2012): 1–2.

102. Zhang Meifang, "Xin Zhongguo nü kaoguxue jia," 35–36.

103. Zhang Meifang, "Xin Zhongguo nü kaoguxue jia," 38.

104. Zheng Zhenxiang, "Yinxu fajue liushi nian gaishu," 931.

105. Wang Sida 王思達, "Zheng Zhenxiang: huanxing Fu Hao de nü kaoguxue jia" 鄭振香: '喚醒' 婦好的女考古學家 [Zheng Zhenxiang: The female archaeologist who awakened Fu Hao], *Hebei xinwenwang*, March 10, 2016, http://www.kaogu.cn/cn/gonggongkaogu/2016/0310/53242.html. On the Cultural Revolution and the Beida history department, see Robin Munro, "Settling Accounts with the Cultural Revolution at Beijing University, 1977–78," *China Quarterly* 82 (June 1980), esp. 329–30.

106. Zhang Meifang, "Xin Zhongguo nü kaoguxue jia," 35.

107. Wang Min 王敏, "Zheng Zhenxiang: Fu Hao kaogu chumo Shangdai" 鄭振香 婦好考古觸摸商代 [Zheng Zhenxiang: The archaeology of Fu Hao connects us with the Shang dynasty], *Xinhua hangkong* 新華航空 6 (2008): 100.

108. Zhang Meifang, "Nü kaoguxue jia de xueshu zhi lu," 4.

109. Xu Jin, "Zheng Zhenxiang."

110. Wu Zhifei 吴志菲, "'Jia gei' Dunhuang de nüren Fan Jinshi: ba yanjiu yu baohu shiku dangcheng zhongsheng shiye" '嫁給'敦煌的女人樊錦詩:把研究與保護石窟當成終生事業 [The 'married to Dunhuang' woman Fan Jinshi: Research and conservation of the stone grottoes is her lifelong career], *Hebei ribao* 河北日报, April 4, 2014, http://www.wenming.cn/wmzh_pd/rw/rwdt/201404/t20140405_1852246_2.shtml.

111. Wang Qi 王琦, Ji Wenwen 纪雯雯, Sun Zhenglin 孙政琳, Ma Lihong 马立红, "Nüxing 'di er lunban' xianxiang zhen de cunzai ma? Jiyu nüxing jiaoyu, zhiye he shouru tezheng de shizheng yanjiu" 女性"第二輪班" 現象真的存在嗎?—基於女性教育、職業和收入特徵的實證研究 [Does the women's "second shift" really exist? Empirical evidence from women's education, professions, and salaries], *Zhongguo laogong guanxi xueyuan xuebao* 中國勞工關係學院學報 33, no. 1 (2019): 9.

112. Lu Xinning 盧新寧 and Zhu Huaxin 祝華新, "Dongfang nüxing ruhe rongru xiandai shehui—shoudu bufen nüxing jiexi nüxing wenhua" 東方女性如何融入現代社會—首都部分女性解析女性文化 [How Asian women assimilated into modern society: Beijing women analyze women's culture], *Renmin ribao* 人民日報, April 17, 1995, 11.

113. Zhang Meifang, "Xin Zhongguo nü kaoguxue jia," 39–40.

Bibliography

Anyang Archaeological Team. "Anyang Yinxu wu hao mu de fajue" 安陽殷墟五號墓的發掘 [Excavation of tomb no. 5 at Yin-hsü in Anyang]. *Kaogu xuebao* 考古學報 2 (1977): 57–134.

Browman, David L., and Stephen Williams. *Anthropology at Harvard: A Biographical History, 1790–1940*. Cambridge, MA: Peabody Museum Press, 2013.

Brown, Shana J. *Pastimes: From Art and Antiquarianism to Modern Chinese Historiography*. Honolulu: University of Hawai'i Press, 2011.

Cai Fengshu 蔡鳳書. "Pi Jiang Qing suowei de 'muxi shehui'" 批江青所謂的'母系社會' [Critique of Jiang Qing's so-called matrilineal society]. *Wen shi zhe* 文史哲 1 (1977): 59–60, 66.

Cao Fangfang 曹芳芳. "Xingbie kaogu yanjiu zongshu—yi Zhongguo kaoguxue wei zhongxin" 性別考古學研究綜述—以中國考古學為中心 [Summary of research on gender archaeology: Centered on Chinese archaeology]. *Nanfang wenwu* 南方文物 (2013): 113–18.

Carr, Lydia C. *Tessa Verney Wheeler: Women and Archaeology before World War Two*. Oxford: Oxford University Press, 2012.

Chang Hui 常惠. "Women weishenme yao yanjiu geyao" 我們為什麼要研究歌謠 [Why we study folksongs]. *Geyao* 歌謠 1, no. 2 (1922): 1–2.

Chao, Wei-pang. "Modern Chinese Folklore Investigation. Part II. The National Sun Yat-Sen University." *Folklore Studies* 2 (1943): 79–88.

Dai Jun 岱峻. "Liang Siyong: Wei jungong de kaoguxue zhongzhen" 梁思永：未竣工的考古學重鎮 [Liang Siyong: Hub of uncompleted archaeology]. *Mingren zhuanji* 名人傳記 10 (2013): 62–69.

Dikötter, Frank. *The Discourse of Race in Modern China*. Oxford: Oxford University Press, 2015.

Dong Xiaoping 董曉萍. "Guojia, lishi, minsu: nüxing xuezhe de minsu yichan" 國家·历史·民俗：女性學者的民俗學遺產 [Nation, history, folklore: The legacy of female scholars in folklore studies]. *Xibei minsu yanjiu* 西北民俗研究 3 (2018): 114–29.

Du Fangqin 杜芳琴. *Nüxing guannian de yanbian* 女性觀念的衍變 [The evolution of the concept of women]. Zhengzhou: Henan renmin chubanshe, 1988.

Edwards, Louise. *Gender, Politics, and Democracy: Women's Suffrage in China*. Stanford, CA: Stanford University Press, 2008.

Fan, Shuhua. "'Cultural Engineering': The Harvard-Yenching Institute and Chinese Humanities, 1924–1951." PhD diss., University of North Carolina at Chapel Hill, 2007. ProQuest (3267818).

Fei Xiaotong 費孝通. "Qinying hunsu zhi yanjiu" 親迎婚俗之研究 [Research on the qinying marriage custom]. In *Fei Xiaotong wenji, di yi juan, 1914–1937* 費孝通文集第1卷 1924–1937 [Collected works of Fei Xiaotong, vol. 1, 1924–1937], 157–212. Beijing: Qunyan chubanshe, 1999.

Gao, Jie. *Saving the Nation through Culture: The Folklore Movement in Republican China.* Vancouver: University of British Columbia Press, 2019.

Ge Henggang 葛恆剛. "Beida geyao zhengzi yundong de huigu yu fansi" 北大歌謠徵集運動的回顧與反思 [Review and reflection of the Beida folksong collection movement]. *Nanjing shida xuebao* 南京師大學報 1 (January 2017): 136–43.

Gu Jiegang 顧頡剛. "Xueru nüshi Beiping geyao zhuangji xu ling" 雪如女士北平歌謠撞集序鈴 [Short preface to the *Collection of Beijing Folksongs* by female scholar Xueru]. In *Gu Jiegang quanji. Gu Jiegang minsu lunwen ji juan 1.* 顧頡剛全集 14. 顧頡剛民俗論文集 卷1 [Collected works of Gu Jiegang, vol. 14, Gu Jiegang writings on folk studies vol. 1], 373–76. Beijing: Zhonghua shuju, 2016.

Guo Peng 郭鵬. "Zhi 'zi' zhi shou, yu 'zi' xie lao—Fu Hao mu yu Zheng Zhenxiang" 執'子'之手，與'子'偕老—婦好墓與鄭振香 [Grasp a seed in your hand, grow old with the seed: The tomb of Fu Hao and Zheng Zhenxiang]. *Qunyan* 羣言 6 (2016): 36–39.

Hays-Gilpin, Kelley. "Feminist Scholarship in Archaeology." *Annals of the American Academy of Political and Social Science* 571, no. 1 (2000): 89–106.

He Wenjing 何文竞, and Wu Ling 吳玲. "Zhou Yinxue: Woguo zui zao de nü kaogu gongzuozhe" 周英學：我國最早的女考古工作者 [Zhou Yingxue: China's earliest female archaeology worker]. *Dazhong kaogu*大眾考古 9 (2017): 34–36.

He Yun'ao 賀雲翱. "Yidai fenghua, liangwei nüxi—nü kaoguxue jia Zeng Zhaoyu he You Shou xiansheng lizan" 一代風華两位女傑—女考古學家曾昭燏和游壽先生禮讚 [A magnificent generation, two women of distinction: Praise for female archaeologists Zeng Zhaoyu and teacher You Shou]. In *Nüxing kaogu yu nüxing yichan* 女性考古與女性遺產 [Feminist archaeology and the heritage of women], edited by He Yun'ao 賀雲翱, 214–21. Nanjing: Nanjing daxue chubanshe, 2011.

Hu Haifan 胡海帆. "Rong Yuan dui jinshixue de gongxian" 容媛對金石學的貢獻 [Rong Yuan's contributions to epigraphy]. In *Lingnan shuxue yanjiu (lunwen ji)* 嶺南書學研究論文集 [Research on Lingnan calligraphy (essay volume)], edited by Lin Yajie 林亚杰 and Zhu Wanzhang 朱万章, 400–11. Guangzhou: Guangdong renmin chubanshe, 2004.

Huang Hefang 黄河方. *Wudai shuxiang zhuan: Yimen liangjia Rong Geng jiazu* 五代書香傳 一門兩大家 容庚家族 [Biography of five generations of intellectuals: One house, two great families, Rong Geng's extended family]. Guangzhou: Huanan ligong daxue chubanshe, 2006.

Jacobs, Justin M. "Langdon Warner at Dunhuang: What Really Happened?" *Silk Road* 11 (2013): 1–11.

Jankowski, Lyce. *Les Amis des monnaies: La sociabilité savante des collectionneurs et numismates chinois de la fin des Qing.* Paris: Hemispheres, 2019.

Jia Meixian 賈梅仙. "Rong Yuan zhuanlüe" 容媛傳略 [Biographical sketch of Rong Yuan]. In *Rong Geng Rong Zhaozu xueji* 容庚容肇祖學記 [Studies on Rong Geng and Rong Zhaozu], edited by Dongguang shi zhengxie, 423–30. Guangzhou: Guangdong renmin chubanshe, 2004.

Jiao Tianlong. "Gender Studies in Chinese Neolithic Archaeology." In *Gender and the Archaeology of Death*, edited by Bettina Arnold and Nancy L. Wicker, 51–62. Lanham, MD: Altamira Press, 2001.

Jordan, Rosan A., and F. A. De Caro. "Women and the Study of Folklore." *Signs* 11, no. 3 (Spring 1986): 500–518.

Kirby, William C. *Germany and Republican China.* Stanford, CA: Stanford University Press, 1984.

Lai, Guolong. "Imperialism, Nationalism, and Regionalism in Yinxu." In *Unmasking Ideology in Imperial and Colonial Archaeology: Vocabulary, Symbols, and Legacy*, edited by Bonnie Effros and Guolong Lai, 83–120. Los Angeles: Cotsen Institute of Archaeology Press, University of California, Los Angeles, 2018.

Lee, Haiyan. "Tears That Crumbled the Great Wall: The Archaeology of Feeling in the May Fourth Folklore Movement." *Journal of Asian Studies* 64, no. 1 (February 2005): 35–65.

Lewis, Ida Belle. *The Education of Girls in China*. New York: Teachers College, Columbia University, 1919.

Li Chi [Li Ji] 李濟. *Anyang*. Seattle: University of Washington Press, 1977.

Li Youning 李又寧. "Zeng Zhaoyu (1909–1964): Woguo zui jiechu de nüxing kaoguxue jia ji bowuguan xue jia" 曾昭燏 (1909–1964) 我國最傑出的女性考古學家及博物館學家 [Zeng Zhaoyu (1909–1964): China's most prominent female archaeologist and museologist]. *Jindai Zhongguo funü shi yanjiu* 近代中國婦女史研究 1 (1993): 35–48.

Liang Baiyou 梁柏有. *Siwen yongzai: wo de fu qin kao gu xue jia Liang Siyong* 思文永在 : 我的父親考古學家梁思永 [Thinking and language are eternal: My father, archaeologist Liang Siyong]. Beijing: Gugong chubanshe, 2016.

Linduff, Katheryn M., and Yan Sun, eds. *Gender and Chinese Archaeology*. Lanham, MD: Altamira Press, 2004.

Liu Jing'an 劉經庵. *Geyao yu funü* 歌謠與婦女 [Folksongs and women]. Shanghai: Shangwu yinshuguan, 1927. Reprinted by Shanghai shudian chubanshe, 1992.

Liu, Lydia H. "Translingual Folklore and Folklorics in China." In *A Companion to Folklore*, edited by Regina F. Bendix and Galit Hasan-Rokemj, 190–210. Chichester, UK: Blackwell, 2012.

Liu Yaming 劉雅鳴, and Gui Juan 桂娟. "Hui kan bainian Yinxu" 回看百年殷墟 [Looking back at a century of Yinxu]. *Liaowang xinwen zhoukan* 瞭望新聞周刊 21 (2001): 44–46.

Lu Xinning 盧新寧, and Zhu Huaxin 祝華新. "Dongfang nüxing ruhe rongru xiandai shehui—shoudu bufen nüxing jiexi nüxing wenhua" 東方女性如何融入現代社會—首都部分女性解析女性文化 [How Asian women assimilated into modern society: Beijing women analyze women's culture]. *Renmin ribao* 人民日報, April 17, 1995, 11.

Lu Yanzhen 盧燕貞. *Zhongguo jindai nüzi jiaoyu shi* (1895–1945) 中國近代女子教育史 (1895–1945) [History of modern women's education in China, 1895–1945]. Taipei: Wenshizhe chubanshe, 1989.

Maner, Brent. *Germany's Ancient Pasts: Archaeology and Historical Interpretation since 1700*. Chicago: University of Chicago Press, 2018.

Mann, Susan. *The Talented Women of the Zhang Family*. Berkeley: University of California Press, 2007.

Meng Xin 孟欣, and Zhang Meifang 章梅芳. "Nü kaoguxue jia de xueshu zhi lu—Ye Xiaoyan yanjiuyuan fangtan lu" 女考古學家的學術之路—葉小燕研究員訪談錄 [The scholarly path of a female archaeologist: Interview with researcher Ye Xiaoyan]. *Guangxi minzu daxue xuebao (ziran kexue ban)* 18, no. 4 (December 2012): 1–6.

Munro, Robin. "Settling Accounts with the Cultural Revolution at Beijing University, 1977–78." *China Quarterly* 82 (June 1980): 308–33.

Naquin, Susan. "The Peking Pilgrimage to Miao-feng Shan: Religious Organizations and Sacred Sites." In *Pilgrims and Sacred Sites in China*, edited by Susan Naquin and Chün-fang Yü, 333–77. Berkeley: University of California Press, 1992.

Qian, Nanxiu. *Politics, Poetics, and Gender in Late Qing China: Xue Shaohui and the Era of Reform*. Stanford, CA: Stanford University Press, 2015.

Ren Darong 任達榮. "Guanyu Zhongguo gudai muxi shehui de kaozheng" 關於中國古代母系社會的考證 [Textual verification of China's ancient matrilineal society]. *Dongfang zazhi* 東方雜誌 32, no. 1 (1935): 71–76.

Rong Yuan 容媛. "Dongguan Cheng Huang miao tushuo" 東莞城隍廟圖說 [Explanatory map of the Cheng Huang temple in Dongguan]. *Minsu* 民俗 nos. 41/42 (1929): 31–49.

———. "Kaogutu shiwen zhi zuozhe" 考古圖釋文之作者 [The author of the *Kaogutu shiwen*]. *Kaogu* 考古 5 (1936): 141–42.

———. "Review of Guo Moruo" 郭沫若, *Qingtong shidai* 青銅時代 [The bronze age]. *Yanjing xuebao* 燕京學報 32 (1947): 233–38.

———. "Review of Jian Bozan" 翦伯贊, *Shiqian shi Yin Zhou shi* 史前史殷周史 [Prehistoric history: Yin and Zhou history]. *Yanjing xuebao* 燕京學報 31 (1946): 198–201.

———. "Review of Rong Zhaozu" 容肇祖, *Mingdai sixiang shi* 明代思想史 [History of Ming dynasty thought]. *Yanjing xuebao* 燕京學報 31 (1946): 201–2.

———. "Yinxu fajue zhi zhongyao jishu yu xun" 殷墟發掘之重要記述余遜 [Additional account of important excavations at Yinxu]. *Yanjing xuebao* 燕京學報 8 (1930): 190–91.

———. "You Miaofeng shan riji" 游妙峰山日記 [Diary of a journey to Mt. Miaofeng]. *Minsu* 民俗 nos. 69/70 (1929): 108–19.

Sellmann, James D. *Timing and Rulership in Master Lü's Spring and Autumn Annals (Lüshi Chunqiu)*. SUNY Series in Chinese Philosophy and Culture. Albany: State University of New York Press, 2002.

Shao, Flora. "'Seeing Her Through a Bamboo Curtain': Envisaging a National Literature through Chinese Folk Songs." *Twentieth-Century China* 41, no. 3 (October 2016): 258–79.

Shelach, Gideon. "Marxist and Post-Marxist Paradigms for the Neolithic." In *Gender and Chinese Archaeology*, edited by Katheryn M. Linduff and Yan Sun, 11–27. Lanham, MD: Altamira Press, 2004.

Shen Chang 申暢, ed. *Zhongguo mulu xuejia cidian* 中國目錄學家辭典 [Dictionary of Chinese bibliographers]. Zhengzhou: Henan renmin chubanshe, 1988.

Shi Aidong 施愛東. "Minsuxue shi yimen guoxue—Zhongshan Daxue minsuxue yundong de gongzuo jihua yu zaoqi minsu xuezhe due xueke de renshi" 民俗學是一門國學—中山大學民俗學運動的工作計劃與早期民俗學者的學科的認識 [Folk studies is a kind of national study: The work plans of the folklore studies group at Zhongshan University and the understanding of the field by early folklore scholars]. *Minsu yanjiu* 民俗研究 2, no. 132 (2017): 5–16.

Shizuko, Koyama. *Ryōsai Kenbo: The Educational Ideal of "Good Wife, Wise Mother" in Modern Japan.* Leiden, the Netherlands, and Boston: Brill, 2012.

Skinner, William. "The New Sociology in China." *Far Eastern Quarterly* (August 1951): 365–71.

Stacey, Judith. "China's Socialist Revolution, Peasant Families, and the Uses of the Past." *Theory and Society* 9, no. 2 (March 1980): 269–81.

Ucko, Peter, Qin Ling, and Jane Hubert, eds. *From Concepts of the Past to Practical Strategies: The Teaching of Archaeological Field Techniques*. London: Saffron, 2007.

Wang Min 王敏. "Zheng Zhenxiang: Fu Hao kaogu chumo Shangdai" 鄭振香 婦好考古觸摸商代 [Zheng Zhenxiang: The archaeology of Fu Hao connects us with the Shang dynasty]. *Xinhua hangkong* 新華航空 6 (2008): 96–100.

Wang Qi 王琦, Ji Wenwen 纪雯雯, Sun Zhenglin 孙政琳, Ma Lihong 马立红. "Nüxing 'di er lunban' xianxiang zhen de cunzai ma? Jiyu nüxing jiaoyu, zhiye he shouru tezheng de shizheng yanjiu" 女性"第二輪班" 現象真的存在嗎?—基於女性教育、職業和收入特徵的實證研究 [Does the women's "second shift" really exist? Empirical evidence from women's education, professions, and salaries]. *Zhongguo laogong guanxi xueyuan xuebao* 中國勞工關係學院學報 33, no. 1 (2019): 8–18.

Wang Wenbao 王文寶. "Woguo minsuxue yundong zhong de nü minsu xuezhe" 我國民俗學運動中的女民俗學者 [Female folklore scholars in the Chinese folklore movement]. *Minsu yanjiu* 民俗研究 2 (1992): 94–96.

———. *Zhongguo minsuxue shi* 中國民俗學史. Chengdu: Bashu shushe, 1995.

Wang, Ying. "Rank and Power among Court Ladies at Anyang." In *Gender and Chinese Archaeology*, edited by Katheryn M. Linduff and Yan Sun, 95–114. Lanham, MD: Altamira Press, 2004.

West, Philip. *Yenching University and Sino-Western Relations, 1916–1952*. Harvard East Asian Series 85. Cambridge, MA: Harvard University Press, 1976.

Weston, Timothy. *The Power of Position: Beijing University, Intellectuals, and Chinese Political Culture, 1898–1929*. Berkeley: University of California Press, 2004.

Woodall, J. N., and P. J. Perricon, "The Archeologist as Cowboy: The Consequence of Professional Stereotype." *Journal of Field Archaeology* 8, no. 4 (1981): 506–9.

Wu Jinding 吴金鼎, Zeng Zhaoyu 曾昭燏, and Wang Jiechen 王介忱. *Yunnan Cang'erjing kaogu baogao* 云南苍洱境考古报告 [Archaeological report of Cang'erjing, Yunnan]. N.p.: Zhongyang bowuyuan, 1942.

Yi Xinnong 易新农, and Xia Hexun 夏和顺. *Rong Geng zhuan* 容庚传 [Biography of Rong Geng]. Guangdong: Huacheng chubanshe, 2010.

Yue Nan 岳南. "Gaocai duanming ren shei cun" 高才短命人誰忖 [A great talent dies young, who would guess]. In *Nandu beigui 3: libie* 南渡北歸3: 離別 [Crossing the south, returning north, vol. 3: Leaving on a journey], 271–323. Changsha: Hunan wenyi chubanshe, 2013.

———. "San zhi xin shengdai 'hai gui'" 三只新生代海龜 [Three "returning turtles" of the new age]. In *Nandu beigui: nandu* 南渡北歸: 南渡 [Crossing the south, returning north: Crossing the south], 322–48. Changsha: Hunan wenyi chubanshe, 2011.

Zeng Zhaoyu 曾昭燏. "Bowuguan" 博物館 [Museums] (1943). In *Zeng Zhaoyu wenji* 曾昭燏文集 [Collected works of Zeng Zhaoyu], 245–81. Beijing: Wenwu chubanshe, 1999.

———. "Guanyu wenhua gongzuo de liang dian yijian" 關於文化工作的兩點意見 [Speech on two views of cultural work]. *Renmin ribao* 人民日報, March 12, 1957, 4.

———. "Shi wo wanfen gandong" 使我萬分感動 [I feel completely moved]. *Renmin ribao* 人民日報 November 2, 1958, 8.

———. *Zeng Zhaoyu wenji. Kaogu juan* 曾昭燏文集.考古卷 [Collected works of Zeng Zhaoyu: Archaeology volume]. Nanjing: Nanjing bowuyuan, 2009.

———. *Zeng Zhaoyu wenji. Riji shuxin juan* 曾昭燏文集. 日記書信卷 [Collected works of Zeng Zhaoyu: Diary and letters volume]. Nanjing: Nanjing bowuyuan, 2013.

Zhang Liangren. "The Chinese School of Archaeology." *Antiquity* 87, no. 337 (2013): 896–904.

Zhang Yue 張越. "'Shuping' zhong de xueshu piping—Yenching xuebao 'shuping' lanmu de tese" "書評"中的學術批評—《燕京學報》"書評"欄目栏目的特色 [The critical scholarship of the book review: Characteristics of the book review column in *Yenching Journal*]. *Langfang shifan xueyuan xuebao* 廊坊師範學院學報 6 (2008): 45–49.

Zhao, Jijun, and Jan Woudstra. "'In Agriculture, Learn from Dazhai': Mao Zedong's Revolutionary Model Village and the Battle against Nature." *Landscape Research* 32, no. 2 (2007): 171–205.

Zheng Huisheng 鄭慧生. *Shanggu Huaxia funü yu hunyin* 上古華夏婦女与婚姻 [Ancient Chinese women and marriage]. Zhengzhou: Henan renmin chubanshe, 1988.

Zheng Zhenxiang 鄭振香. "Jiyi Yinxu Fu Hao mu" 記憶殷墟婦好墓 [Memories of the Yinxu tomb of Fu Hao]. *Dazhong kaogu* 大眾考古 4 (2014): 19–23.

———. "Nan wang de daxue shenghuo" 難忘的大學生活 [Unforgettable university life]. In *Na shi women zheng jianqing: Beijing daxue lishi xi xiyou huiyilu* 那时我們正年輕: 北京大學歷史系系友回憶錄 [At that time we were really young: Alumni recollections of the Beijing University history department], edited by Wang Chunmei 王春梅 and Wang Meixiu 王美秀, 1–6. Beijing: Xiandai jiaoyu chubanshe, 2007.

———. "Yinxu fajue liushi nian gaishu" 殷墟發掘六十年概述 [Sixty years of excavations at Yinxu]. *Kaogu* 考古 10 (1988): 929–41.

———. "Yinxu Fu Hao mu yu Shangdai li zhi" 殷墟婦好墓與殷商禮制 [Fu Hao's tomb in the ruins of Yin and the Shang dynasty ritual system]. In *Wanghou, muqin, nüjiang: jinian Yinxu Fu Hao mu kaogu fajue sishi zhounian* 王后·母親·女將: 紀念殷墟婦好墓考古發掘四十周年 [Queen, mother, woman general: Commemorating the fortieth anniversary of the excavation of the Yinxu tomb of Fu Hao], edited by Wang Weibai 王巍白 and Tian Kai 田凱, 10–17. Beijing: Kexue chubanshe, 2015.

Zhongguo kexueyuan kaogu yanjiusuo 中國科學院考古研究所. *Xin Zhongguo de kaogu shouhuo* 新中國的考古收穫 [Results of the archaeology of New China]. Beijing: Wenwu chubanshe, 1961.

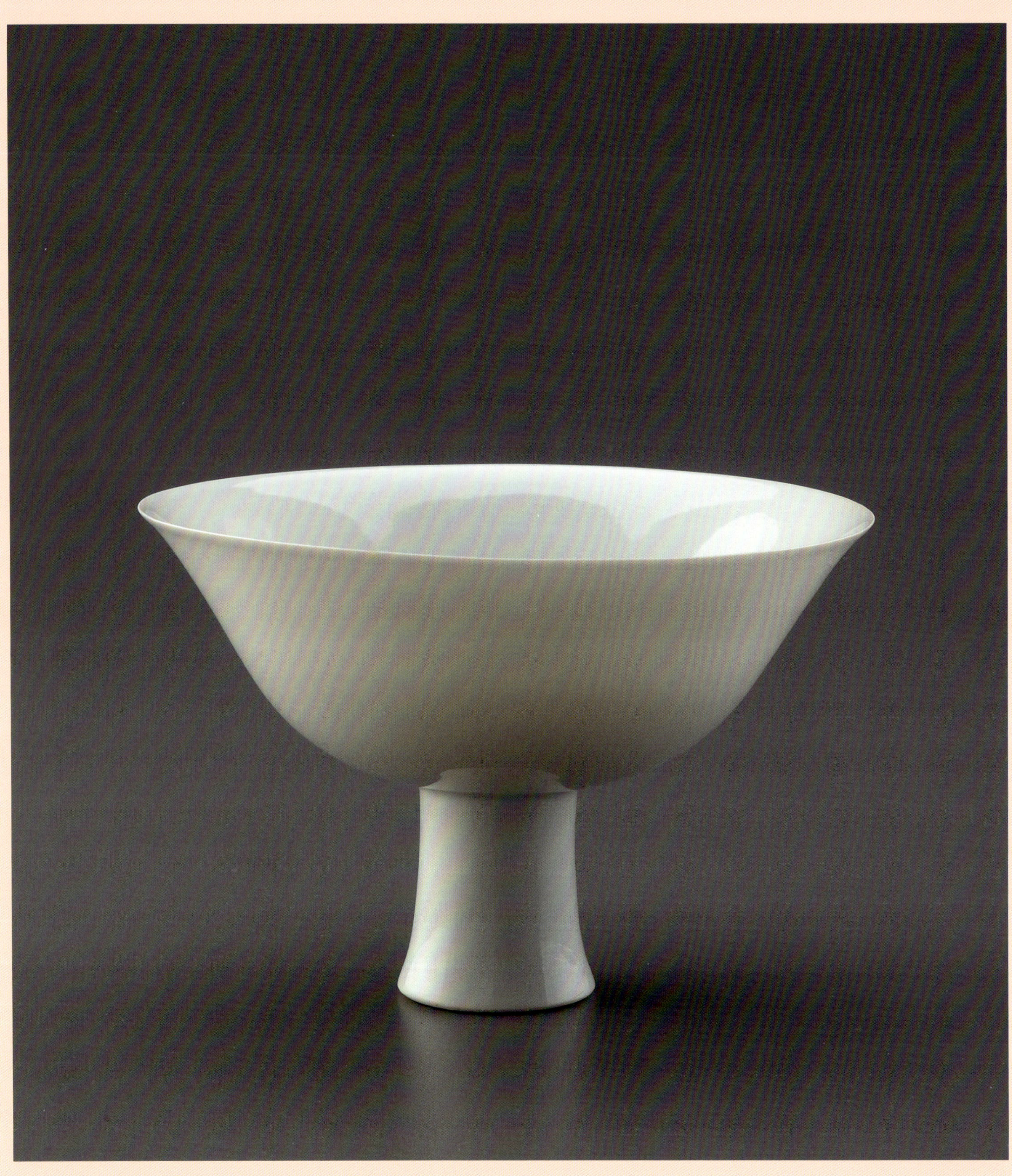

Private Passion, Public Benefit

Brenda Zara Seligman and the Seligman Collection of Chinese Art

Nick Pearce

Women collectors, in any field, have too often been dismissed as mere consumers, as decorators of their homes, or as appendages to the collecting activities of their husbands.[1] Those women who have managed to transcend these attitudes, such as Isabella Stewart Gardner or Peggy Guggenheim, are outweighed by many more who have either been overlooked or whose worth has been undervalued. In the field of the collecting of Chinese art, particularly during the period of intense activity between the world wars, the picture is even starker. In America there is Kate Sturges Buckingham (1858–1937), whose collection of Chinese ritual bronzes, jades, ceramics, and other materials formed the foundation of the Art Institute of Chicago's East Asian art holdings, and, equally significant, Bettie Fleischmann Holmes (Mrs. Christian Holmes, 1871–1941), who formed a fine Chinese collection, which included ceramics, jades, and bronzes, and all collected it seems following her husband's death in 1920.[2] She was a major lender to both the 1929 *Chinesische Kunst* exhibition in Berlin and to the *International Exhibition of Chinese Art* at the Royal Academy in 1935–36, but after her death in 1940, the collection was dispersed in a number of auction sales. Holmes as collector will be returned to later in this chapter. In Britain, two women collectors of Chinese art of the interwar period stand out in importance: Alice Mariquita Sedgwick (1883–1967), who was benefactor to many museums in the UK, and Brenda Zara Seligman (1883–1965), whose collecting activities are explored in detail in this chapter.[3]

During their collecting careers, both Alice Sedgwick and Brenda Seligman were known by their husband's names, Mrs. Walter Sedgwick and Mrs. C. G. Seligman respectively, even though Walter Sedgwick had no interest in collecting Chinese art, and Charles

Facing: Stem cup, porcelain with white glaze. See figure 6.16.

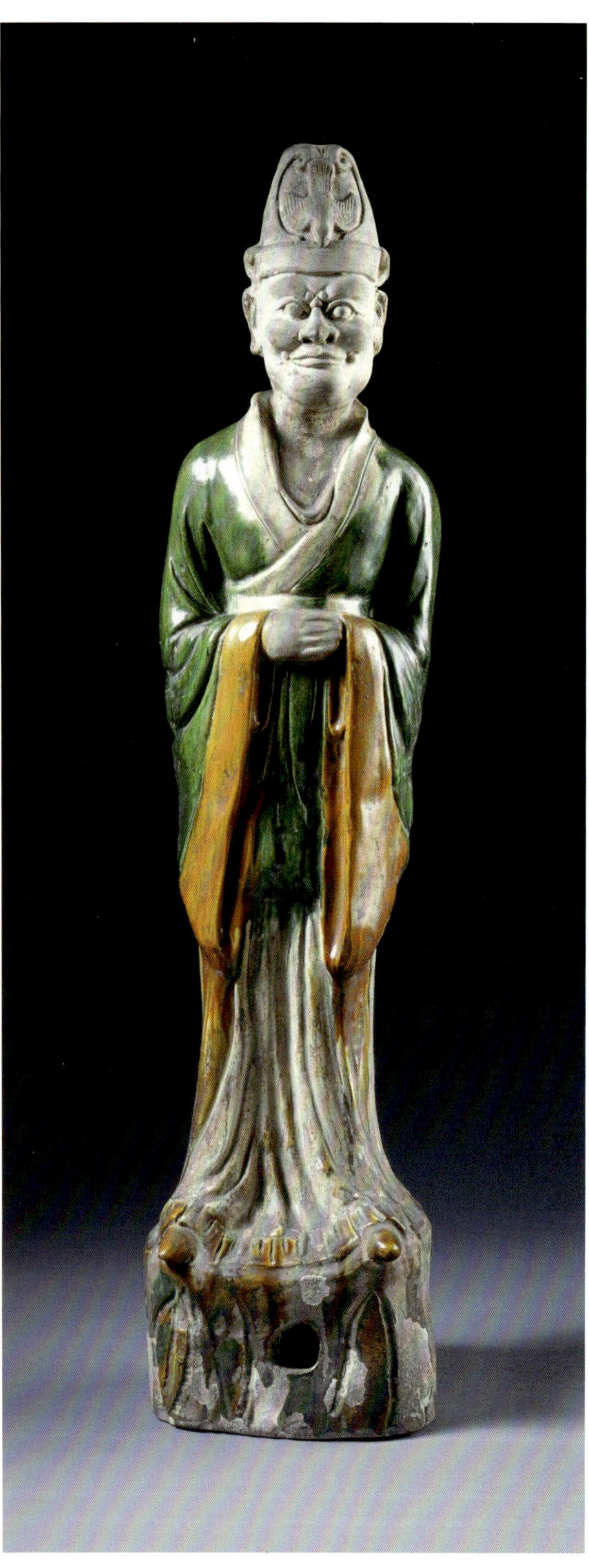

Figure 6.1. Figure of an official. Earthenware covered with a lead *sancai* glaze. Tang dynasty, 8th century. © The Victoria & Albert Museum (FE.160–1974).

Seligman, although a fellow collector, died twenty-five years in advance of Brenda, who continued to collect, reshape, and manage the legacy of the collection. The conventions of address of the period should not obscure the fact that women collectors were prominent players in their own right. Membership of the Oriental Ceramic Society (OCS), formed by a coterie of male tastemakers in London in 1921, widened its membership from the mid-1930s and included both Alice Sedgwick and Brenda Seligman who were active in its management and administration, Brenda becoming a member in her own right by the mid-1940s and later a member of the OCS Council.[4] As has been noted elsewhere, by 1947, when the list of 245 British and overseas members of the OCS was first published in the *Transactions* journal of the society, it included thirty-nine women.[5] Nevertheless, for many years Brenda's contribution to building the Seligman Collection of Oriental Art was somewhat overshadowed by that of her husband and this extended into her professional life, where, as an untrained anthropologist she began as "Seligman's general assistant and bottle-washer," and even in later years when she had carved out her own reputation (notably in the area of kinship and social organization), she "looked on her own anthropological research as ancillary to her husband's."[6] However, unlike her anthropological work and perhaps the ethnological material that she also collected with her husband, where, it has been noted, their individual contributions are difficult to unpick, her life as a collector of Chinese art arguably offers a clearer picture.[7] Not only did she refine the collection qualitatively and aesthetically following Charles's death, but she also demonstrated skilled stewardship in transitioning it into public ownership as a bequest.[8] If we are to take C. S. Myers's remarks literally in his obituary of Charles Seligman, it was Brenda who encouraged her husband to collect Chinese art "as an aesthetic hobby," even if Myers gives little recognition of her own agency.[9] The collection as refined and bequeathed to the nation by Brenda finally consisted of some 500 ceramics, jades, and bronzes, from the Neolithic to the early Ming period (and including a small group of Korean, Thai, and Vietnamese wares), more than half of which were ceramics (fig. 6.1).[10]

Beginnings

Brenda Zara Seligman, née Salaman, was born in Kensington, London, on June 26, 1883, the youngest of fourteen children to Sarah and Myer Salaman (fig. 6.2).[11] Myer Salaman (1836–1896), headed up I. Salaman and Company, a highly successful Anglo-Jewish ostrich feather trading business operating out of offices in Falcon Square in London. The company had been created by Myer's father, Isaac, in 1816, but Myer had transformed a one-man operation into "the largest wholesale ostrich feather business in the world, with depots in Cape Town, Port Elizabeth and Durban . . . in addition to offices and warehouses in London, Paris, New York and Buenos Aires."[12] It flourished during a brief period between the 1880s and the First World War, when the ostrich feather was the fashion for women's hats and boas in the major cities of Europe and North America.[13] As well as the feather business, Myer with his brother, Nathan, also invested in property in the City of London, this diversification most probably cushioning the company from the ostrich feather crash in 1914 and allowing Brenda and her siblings to enjoy a comfortable legacy.[14] Brenda was first educated at home and then at Roedean, from where she entered Bedford College, University of London, as a premedical biology student. Her studies were never completed. She met Charles Gabriel Seligman (1873–1940), a medical colleague of her brother, Redcliffe, and they were married on July 4, 1905 (fig. 6.3). "Sligs" (as Charles Seligman was affectionately known) was the son of a wealthy London wine merchant, Hermann Seligmann (1836–1889) and his wife, Olivia Mendes da Costa (1843–1890), and trained in medicine at St. Thomas' Hospital in London.[15] At the time of his marriage he was a research pathologist, but was already taking an active interest in ethnology, having joined the Cambridge anthropological expedition to the Torres Straits in 1898, on which he received his first anthropological training under Alfred Cort Haddon (1855–1940) and William Halse Rivers (1864–1922). In 1904 he joined an expedition to Papua New Guinea, led by Major William Cooke Daniels (1870–1918), the research from which was published in 1910. The same year he was appointed to a lectureship in ethnology at the London School of Economics (LSE) and in 1913, a chair, before war intervened and he was commissioned into the Royal Army Medical Corps. After the war he returned to the LSE, eventually retiring in 1934.

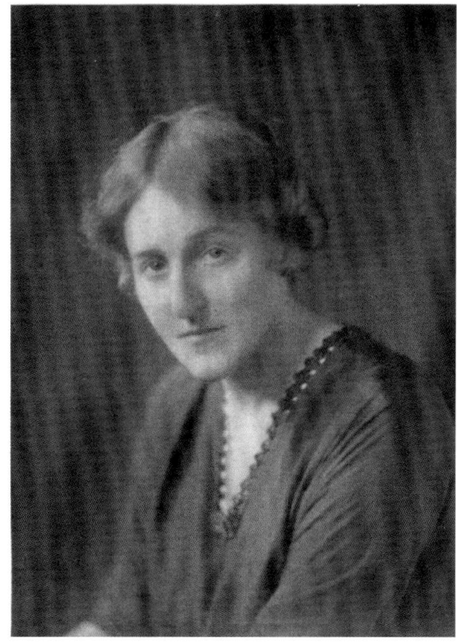

Figure 6.2. Portrait of Brenda Zara Seligman as a young woman. Reproduced in *Man*, January 1961.

Professionally, Brenda began to engage with Charles's work at the outset of their marriage, initially with editing his New Guinea research results, which then stimulated her further interest. She joined him in anthropological fieldwork in Ceylon in 1907 and then in three expeditions to Sudan in 1909–10, 1911–12, and 1921–22.[16] Her contribution to the emerging discipline of anthropology has been attributed to work on kinship and social organisation, as "a supplement" to Charles's research, but as Meyer Fortes goes on to admit, "it would take a microscopic investigation to tell apart their respective contributions to *The Veddas*, the book in which they reported the results of the expedition (1911)."[17] In her later years, her pioneering work would be recognized by her presidency of the Association of Social Anthropologists (1959), the award of the Royal Anthropological Institute's first Patron's Medal (1963), and a *Festschrift* in her honor (*Studies in Kinship and Marriage*), which was presented to her on her eightieth birthday.[18] According to Charles Seligman's obituary in *Transactions of the Oriental Ceramic Society* and repeated by others, their collecting of Chinese art also began on the date of their marriage in 1905, when they were gifted a Ming-period beaker vase.[19] The information is thin, but this seems to have marked the beginning of active collecting on the part of both Charles and Brenda, which would, within a few years, take them beyond the conventions of the familiar to that of an avant-garde taste in Chinese art collecting that was fueled by the newly discovered archaeological material emerging from Chinese tomb sites and the many private Chinese collections being broken up in the wake of the 1911 Chinese revolution (fig. 6.4).

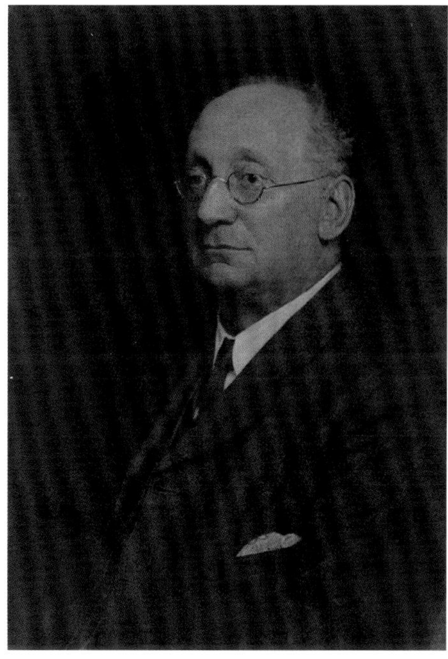

Figure 6.3. Charles Gabriel Seligman, by Walter Stoneman. Bromide print, 1933. © National Portrait Gallery, London (NPG x185208).

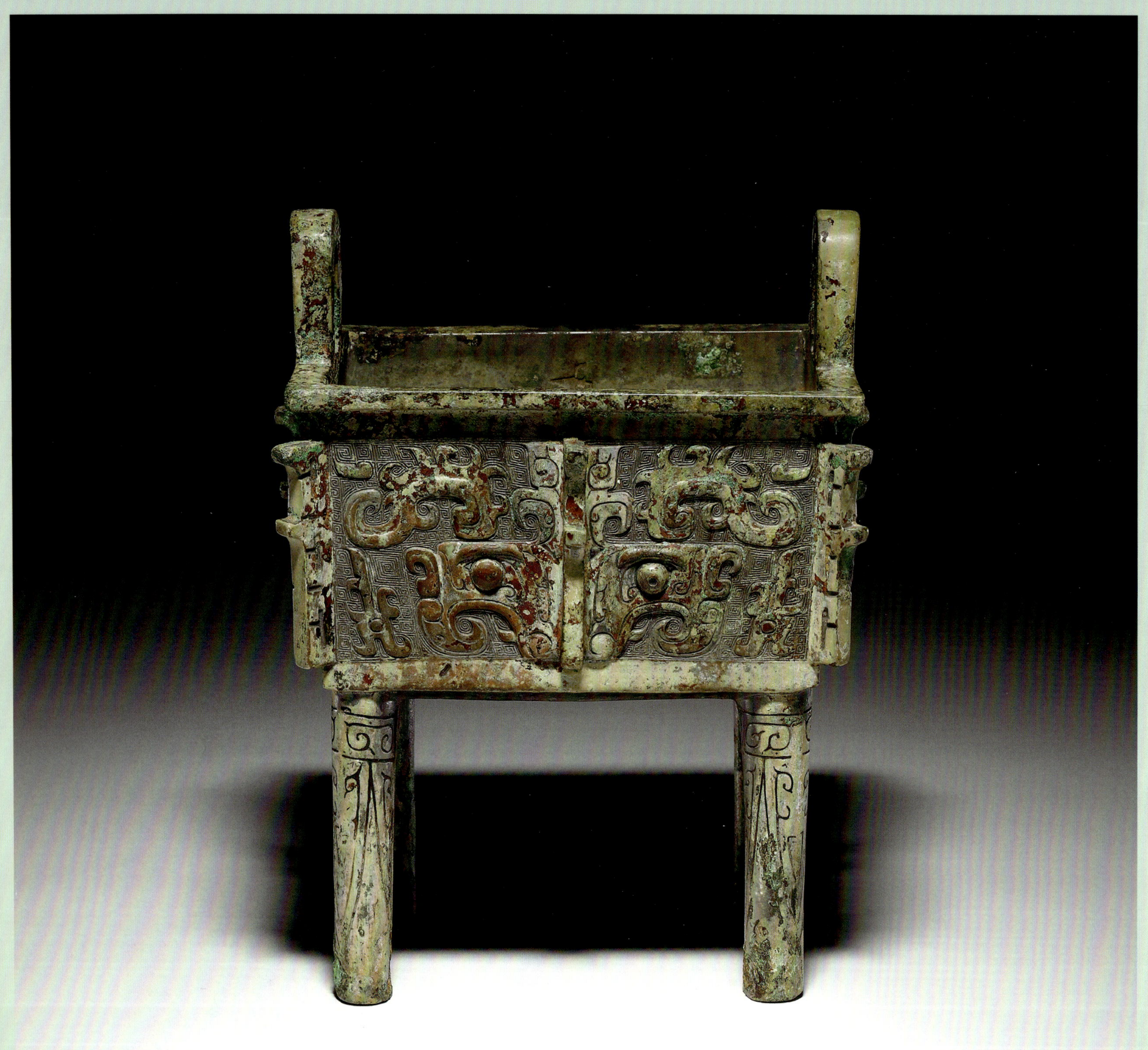

Figure 6.4. Fang ding ritual vessel. Cast bronze, Western Zhou dynasty (1250–771 BCE). © The Trustees of the British Museum (1973,0726.3).

The Seligmans' joint collecting activities in the Chinese art field before World War I are captured in two sources that help place not only the material that they now began to acquire, but also their origin. Brenda kept detailed journals of their visits abroad and in her journal for 1909, when they were in Paris en route to Sudan, she details some of the "early Chinese stuff" they were acquiring at this early date. They included Tang, Song, and Ming figures and bowls, many of them the result of "Early Ming and Sung [Song] graves . . . being dug up and fairly looted."[20] Nicky Levell remarks on the clandestine way in which this activity is recorded by Brenda as if this was "an illegal enterprise," but this degree of caution on the part of collectors was not unusual at the time.[21]

Just prior to their Paris visit the Seligmans were visited in London by Charles Trick Currelly (1876–1957), the director of the then-nascent Royal Ontario Museum, who was on a buying trip (fig. 6.5). In his autobiography, *I Brought the Ages Home,* Currelly describes his friendship with the couple and the secrecy surrounding the source of the early Chinese material coming onto the market.[22] Currelly had heard of a new shipment arriving at an unknown dealer in London but found that both museum curators and collectors were reluctant to share this information. It was through the agency of Charles Seligman that Currelly at last gained entrée to the mysterious dealer. "One evening," wrote Currelly, "Seligman said, 'I would like to take you tomorrow to see some wonderful Chinese things that have recently arrived in London. I didn't say anything about it until I knew whether you would be received or not; if you went on your own you would probably not be admitted.'"[23] Currelly went on to describe his visit to a large warehouse in the City of London situated on several floors. The warehouse, which turned out to be S. M. Franck, had received its shipment directly from China, where its representatives were being supplied by "a certain man keenly interested in Chinese art."[24]

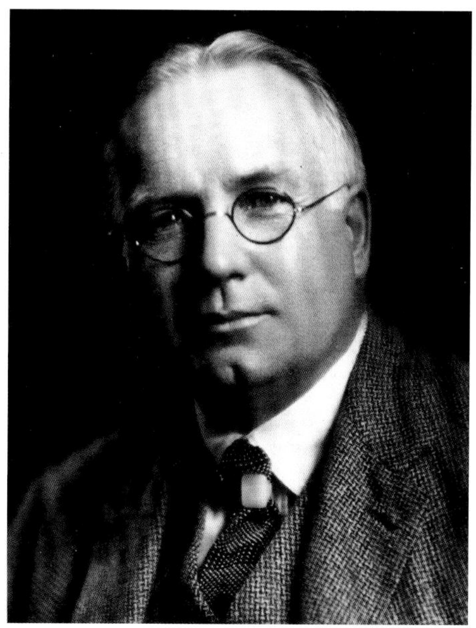

Figure 6.5. Charles Trick Currelly (1876–1957). University of Toronto Archives (2004–30–7MS).

S. M. Franck was a wholesale dealer situated, at the time of Currelly's visit, at 25 Camomile Street, off Bishopsgate and near the London docks.[25] Established by Solomon Mark Franck (1849–1922) in the 1880s, its position as an importer of a range of new material, at the time little known and understood, directly from China seems to have been the result of the company being taken over around 1909 by Franck's former manager, Julius Spier (1848–1923). Although information on S. M. Franck is sparse it was significant internationally as a wholesale supplier to private collectors, museum institutions, and high-street dealers throughout the 1910s, 1920s, and 1930s, including the British Museum, Victoria & Albert Museum, the Royal Ontario Museum, and collectors such as Charles and Brenda Seligman and their friends, George Eumorfopoulos (1863–1939) and Oscar Raphael (1874–1941). One of Franck's suppliers in China described by Currelly above as "this certain man" was the Irish-Canadian fur trader George Crofts (1874–1925), who had been operating his business out of Tianjin since 1896 and was now beginning to buy up Chinese antiquities as they became available through his local contacts (fig. 6.6).[26] Crofts would go on to supply the Royal Ontario Museum directly, but the quality of the material he was sourcing overall is indicative of what was available to the Seligmans even at this relatively early date in their collecting history through outlets such as S. M. Franck and the major Bond Street dealers.

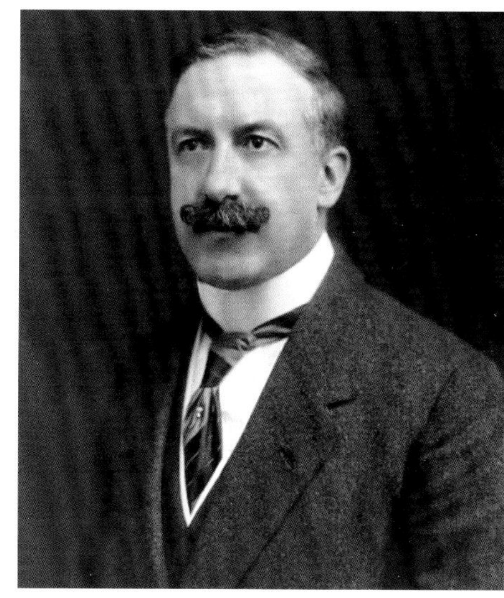

Figure 6.6. George Crofts (1874–1925). Far Eastern Library of the Royal Ontario Museum.

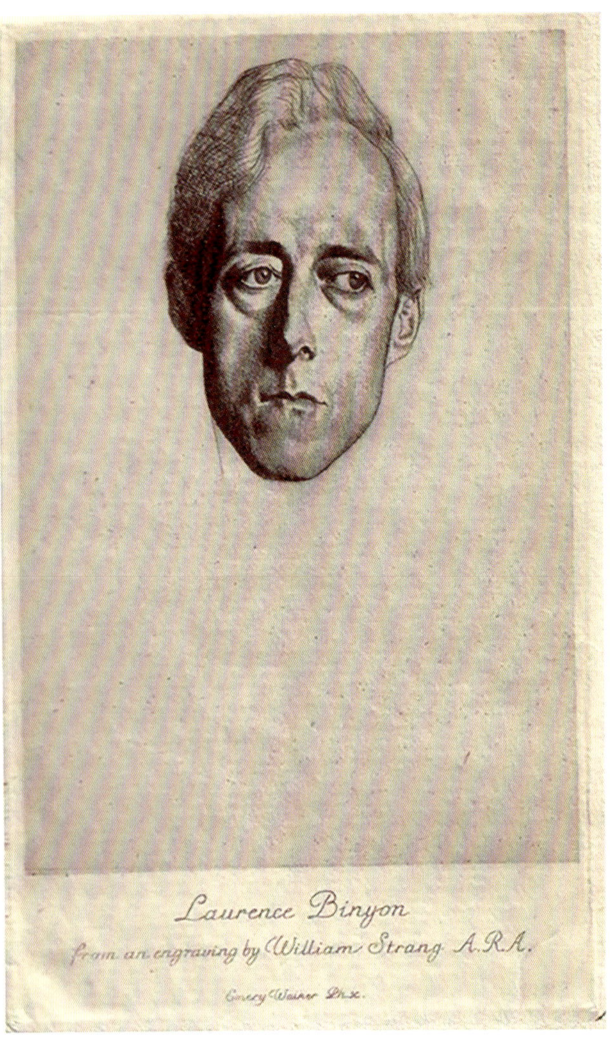

Figure 6.7. Laurence Binyon from an engraving by William Strang, on the cover of *The Four Years: War Poems Collected and Newly Augmented* (1919). Photo by the author.

Formation

At this period and into the 1920s, it is difficult to separate out what Nicky Levell describes as Brenda's "marital and professional partnership" with her husband, in which she modestly subordinated herself, and the formation of the Chinese art collection.[27] However, returning to her journals and in particular her journals recording the Seligmans' visit to Japan, Korea, and China in 1929 to 1930, these provide a clearer picture of her involvement in collecting, her knowledge of the subject, and her confidence among other—predominantly male—collectors and specialists. As will be discussed later, her shaping and management of the collection following Charles's death in 1940 became significant, but during her husband's lifetime these journals provide a rare insight into her thoughts and ideas about the art and culture she was experiencing and with a clarity that is absent in Charles's notes of the visit.[28]

Charles and Brenda Seligman's trip to the Far East likely owed its genesis to Laurence Binyon's (1869–1943) invitation from colleagues at Tokyo University to come to Japan and give a series of lectures on British art. At the time Binyon was assistant keeper in the Department of Prints and Drawings at the British Museum, which included responsibility for its collections of Eastern prints and paintings (fig. 6.7).[29] He had never visited either China or Japan and his endeavors to do so were continually frustrated by the British Treasury, which declined the expense. Through the invitation from Tokyo, Binyon was granted leave and his travel expenses were met by collector and British Museum benefactor Oscar Raphael.[30] Charles and Brenda Seligman joined Binyon and his wife, Cicely, Oscar Raphael, and Ronald Lockhart (R. L.) Hobson (1872–1941), then keeper of the Department of Ceramics and Ethnography at the British Museum, and they sailed on the first leg of the journey on the *Empress of Scotland* to Canada on August 10, 1929.[31] Brenda captured the embarkation in her journal with a direct brevity: "The Binyons, Oscar Raphael and Hobson all turned up and we shared a table."[32] While in Canada the Seligmans went to visit Currelly at the new Royal Ontario Museum, which Brenda declared "a stupendous achievement."[33] Traveling overland, they sailed to Yokohama from Vancouver on the *Empress of France* and on arrival were met by George Sansom (1883–1965), the historian of Japan, but then a diplomat at the British Embassy in Tokyo. They then went quickly on to Kobe, then a boat to Busan in Korea and a train to Seoul, where they arrived on September 15. They were enroute to Beijing, but in Seoul as well as museum visiting they went to a number of curio shops "where we have bought a very good Korean celadon bowl, mended, and a small Tang bronze."[34] Arriving at Mukden on September 21, another buying trip secured "a white porcelain Tang bowl."[35] The party arrived in Beijing on September 23 and checked into the exclusive Le Grand Hôtel de Pékin.

While in Beijing, they were hosted by such luminaries as Ding Wenjiang (1887–1936), founder of China's National Geological Survey; Li Ji (1896–1979), archaeologist then leading the Academia Sinica excavations at the Shang capital of Anyang, and geologist Weng Wenhao (1889–1971), who was working with Davidson Black (1884–1934) on the analysis of fossils found at Zhoukoudian, southwest of Beijing, and about to discover the skull that would be named Peking Man. They toured the sites of the city and following a visit to the Temple of Heaven, Brenda noticed "a fine blue and white bowl. Going back I spotted it again and stopped. It is a genuine Ming bowl, Mohammedan blue, bashed and mended with iron rivets. The man knew it was Ming and refused 3 dollars asked 24 (I expect he would take 12). The trouble is it is large and much mended, else it would have been worth it."[36] Later that day when being shown some of the porcelains in the Forbidden City, she noticed that "amongst the blue and white I saw the fellow to my bowl in the market. Obviously broken pieces from the Palace find their way into the poorest quarters, that accounts for the relative commonness of good pieces in the poorest stalls, all mended with large iron rivets. Pieces of such good quality are not to be seen in the ordinary dealer's shops."[37]

Showing her the porcelains in the former Imperial collection was John Calvin Ferguson (1866–1945), a onetime Methodist missionary who in 1897 had become head of Nanyang Public School, and then from 1902 occupied various posts in the administration of the Chinese Qing government (fig. 6.8). He later became foreign advisor to the newly formed Republic of China until his retirement in 1928, and during all this time he operated as a dealer and collector of Chinese art.[38] At the time of the Seligmans' visit he was a member of the "Committee of Reference," reviewing the collections in the newly formed Palace Museum, the only foreigner to join an illustrious team of Chinese scholars.[39] As Lara Netting has observed, "Ferguson's position on the committees of reference both reflected and gave stimulus to his connections with Peking scholars and collectors in the late 1920s and early 1930s."[40] At the center of the City's social and intellectual scene, Ferguson used his contacts with official circles to open doors and to source objects that might be for sale. His most visible client was Charles Lang Freer (1854–1919). The visit of the Hobson-Binyon-Raphael group was noted in a letter Ferguson wrote to his daughter, although neither Charles nor Brenda are mentioned specifically and there is no indication that they bought objects from him during their visit.[41] To judge from the comments noted above, Brenda seems not to have been overawed by Ferguson, but, on the contrary, took some relish in her own connoisseurial observations.

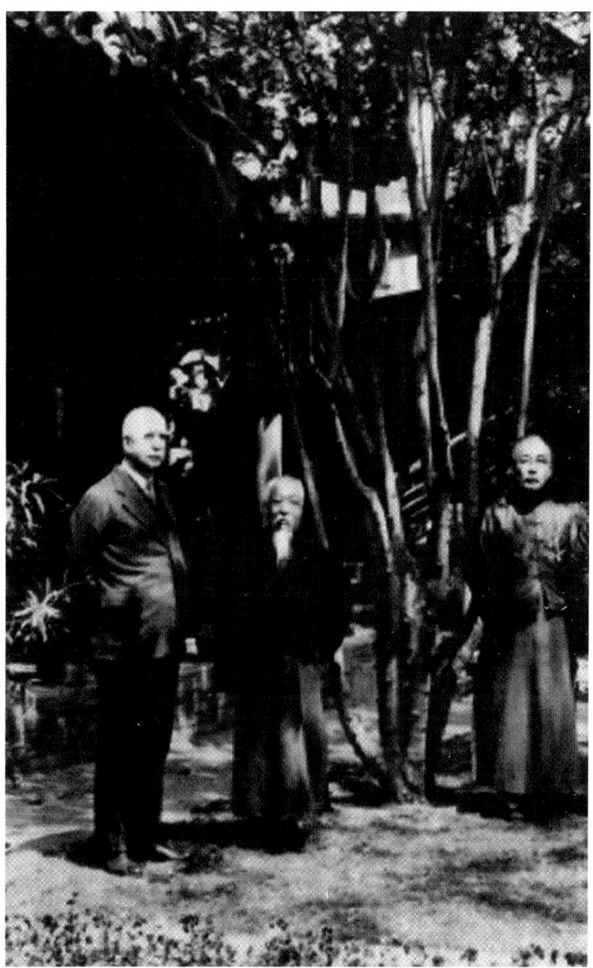

Figure 6.8. John C. Ferguson (*left*) with Guo Baochang (*far right*), in the garden of Ferguson's Beijing home, April 1937. The John Calvin Ferguson Papers, Freer Gallery of Art and Arthur M. Sackler Gallery Archives. Donated by Peter Ferguson, 1999. Photographer: Chu Sin, FSA.A1993 box 15, folder 3.

Brenda's visits to dealers and collectors are documented in some detail in her journal. On September 28 she wrote: "Shopping. Saw Mr. Okawa (Yamanaka's man) in shops. Then to Mrs Calhoun who had two dealers to meet us—really good paintings—we bought some and very fine tapestry. Buddhist figure we bought." [42] Mrs. Calhoun was Lucy Monroe Calhoun (1865–1950), sister of the poet and editor Harriet Monroe and widow of William J. Calhoun, American minister to China between 1909 and 1913 (fig. 6.9).[43] Widowed in 1916, she returned to Beijing in 1921 and became known as "Aunt Lucy," acting as a counterpoint to Ferguson, hosting parties for the expatriate community and visitors.[44] During her time as the minister's wife, she hosted Charles Lang Freer when he visited Beijing, collected for the Art Institute of Chicago (most particularly Chinese dress), and during her time in the city wrote about her experiences of collecting.[45] Brenda also met another expatriate, this time British, the erstwhile mining engineer "Captain" William Frederick Collins (1882–1956), who, residing in Beijing and working for various

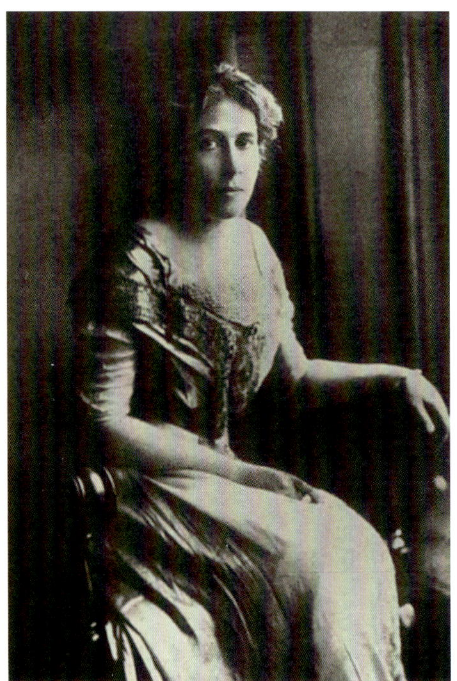

Figure 6.9. Lucy Monroe Calhoun, c. 1911. Photo: C. E. Lemunyon. Reproduced in Harriet Monroe, *A Poet's Life: Seventy Years in a Changing World* (New York: Macmillan, 1938), facing page 93.

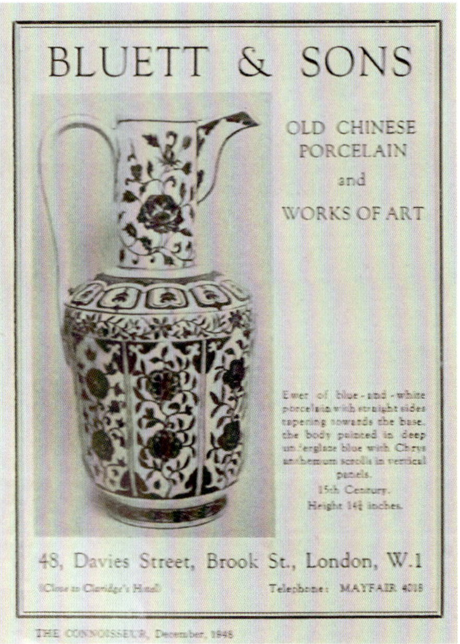

Figure 6.10. Xuande-period (1425–35) ewer sold by Brenda Seligman through Bluett & Sons. *The Connoisseur*, December 1948, viii.

mining concessions since 1906, had built up a network of Chinese dealers through whom he acted as an agent for a number of major London dealers including the Bluetts and John Sparks.[46] He seems also to have been a ready guide to visitors around the city, including the explorer and naturalist Roy Chapman Andrews and art historian Osvald Sirén, which included collecting expeditions.[47] Brenda noted in her journal for October 2, 1929: "Lunched with Collins . . . Very good Chinese food. Collins is shepherding R & H [Raphael and Hobson], he is really a dealer! He says he will look out for a Tang horse for us."[48] Later during the visit, "Collins took us to two shops in the Liu Li Chang. We bought a blue green and yellow Tang plate that S had longed for for years."[49]

She and Charles also met some significant Chinese collectors and dealers in Beijing, including Guo Baochang (1879–1942), a dealer who had been for the briefest of periods director of the imperial porcelain factory at Jingdezhen, which had been reestablished by Yuan Shikai when the latter created a constitutional monarchy in 1915 (see fig. 6.8).[50] Guo specialized in supplying foreigners with porcelains and worked closely with Ferguson.[51] In 1925, he was appointed to the new Palace Museum and would be heavily involved in the future International Exhibition of Chinese Art that would take place in London in 1935–36. Brenda was well informed about Guo's interesting past and delighted to see "a few perfect pieces, Chun-yao [Junyao], etc, and the famous piece of purple Ting [Ding]."[52] On October 5, she went "to the dealer Wu Lai Hsi [Wu Laixi]." She continued, "He specialises in Ming and has a fine collection of yellow which he does not intend to sell. We bought 5 pieces from him at reasonable prices." Wu Laixi (1881–1951) was an overseas Chinese citizen from Singapore who had studied medicine at Cambridge and had settled in Beijing in 1915.[53] He was a collector as well as dealer with a passion for ceramics, although he also collected paintings and his name has been associated with the so-called David Vases, even though this has been disputed. The quality of the items seen by Brenda and purchased by her that day was such that years later the Seligmans purchased a Xuande (1425–35) period ewer (through Yamanaka) from the Wu Laixi sale at Sotheby's in 1937 (fig. 6.10), although this would be a piece she would sell again ten years later.[54]

Laurence and Cicely Binyon had already left Beijing for Tokyo at the end of September and they were now joined by the Seligmans, who took part in the celebrations honoring Binyon.[55] During the month in Tokyo and Kobe, the Beijing purchases were shipped off home and more shopping was undertaken as well as visits to collections: Baron Fujita Heitaro (1869–1940) and Baron Kawasaki Shōjō (1837–1912), who created the first art museum in Japan, but whose collection was sold in 1936. On December 9, 1929, the group arrived in Shanghai and Brenda records her and Charles's visit to Hangzhou, arranged she writes through the Academia Sinica then in the process of excavating the Shang dynasty site near Anyang under the directorship of Li Ji, by whom the Seligmans had been received in Beijing. In Shanghai, they recommenced their buying activities. In the "Jade Bazaar or 'Thieves Market,'" Brenda "bought quite a nice jade hairpin and some oddment, Sligs mirrors."[56] On December 21 they "dined with the Sowerbys. Their house is delightful. One of the few houses we have seen where Chinese furniture and decoration are used well and the house made comfortable too."[57] Arthur de Carle Sowerby (1885–1954) was from a missionary family and a long-standing resident of Shanghai whose life encompassed exploration, natural history, writing, and art collecting and was founder and editor of the *China Journal* (fig. 6.11).[58] We also know that they saw Chinese paintings at E. A. Strehlneek's (b. 1871), a dealer whose collection had been published in 1914, and who had presumably built another one, which, according to Brenda, was exhibited in Japan. She also most probably visited John Sparks's Shanghai shop at 103 Jiao Tong Road, as she mentions Sparks's manager, Frederick James Abbott, visiting the hotel at which they were staying and taking Charles "curio Hunting."[59] Their visit to Japan, Korea, and China ended in Hong Kong and Guangzhou, before they embarked for Sumatra, beginning their homeward journey.

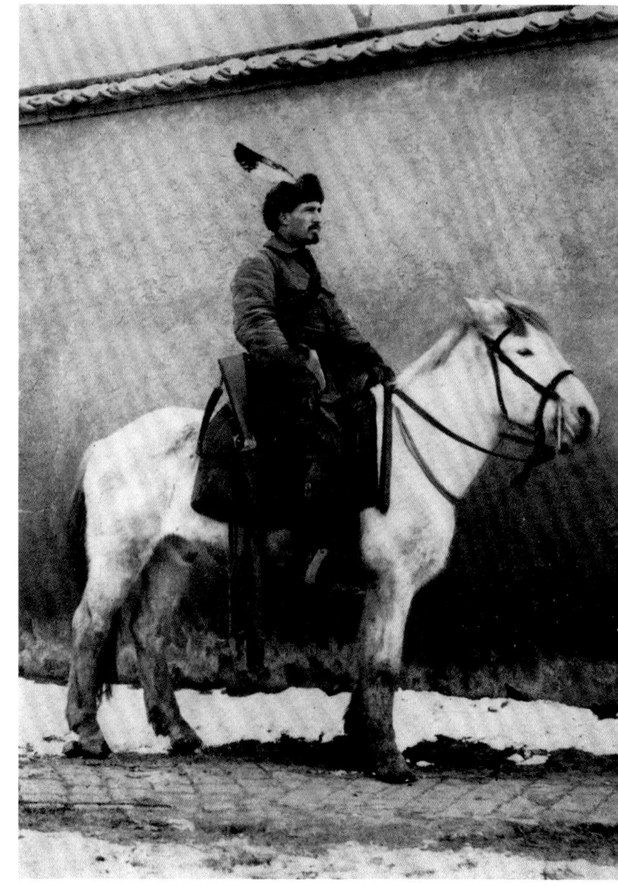

Figure 6.11. Arthur de Carle Sowerby on his return from the Shensi Relief Expedition in 1912. Reproduced in R. R. Sowerby, *Sowerby of China* (Kendal: Titus Wilson & Son Ltd, 1956), frontispiece.

Brenda Seligman's journals provide an interesting insight into the community of dealers, scholars, and government officials with whom she and Charles were interacting during their visit, most of whose names are familiar to those researching this period in the collecting of Chinese art. They also provide a window into Brenda's views on collecting. This will be explored further on when discussing the Seligman Collection and its shaping after Charles's death, but here a word should be said about the Karlbeck Syndicate (1930–34), of which at least Charles Seligman was a member.[60]

Orvar Karlbeck (1880–1967) was a Swedish engineer who, working in China for the Tientsin-Pukow Railway Company responsible for building the line between Beijing and Shanghai, first encountered ancient Chinese artifacts as the result of tomb disturbances during railway excavation. Political instability forced him to leave China in 1927, but he returned to China in September 1928, collecting for the Museum of Far Eastern Antiquities in Stockholm. He formed the Karlbeck Syndicate in 1930 and mounted three collecting expeditions between 1930 and 1934 on behalf of its seventeen institutional and private members. Charles was a member, but, as Valérie Jurgens has argued, there is little to indicate that Brenda was also a client and suggests that Charles Seligman made a clear differentiation between archaeology and art, a distinction that was perhaps not shared by his wife (fig. 6.12).[61]

Those who have studied Charles Seligman's anthropological work and reflected on aspects of his collecting have discussed his interest in diffusionist theories current at the time.[62] Diffusionism proposed that cultural innovations were developed once and then spread through wider borrowing or migration. Civilizations or cultures were therefore linked with developments occurring from one dominant source and then spreading outward.[63] Fed by a complex mix of disillusionment with industrial progress, nationalism, and theories around race and the biological inferiority of certain peoples when compared with Europeans, diffusionism influenced both emerging fields of anthropology and archaeology. In relation to China, diffusionist theories can be traced back to the Jesuit polymath Athanasius Kircher (1602–1680), who had first discussed similar ideas in his *Prodromus coptus sive aegypticus* (Coptic or Egyptian Forerunner) of 1636, and in which he explored

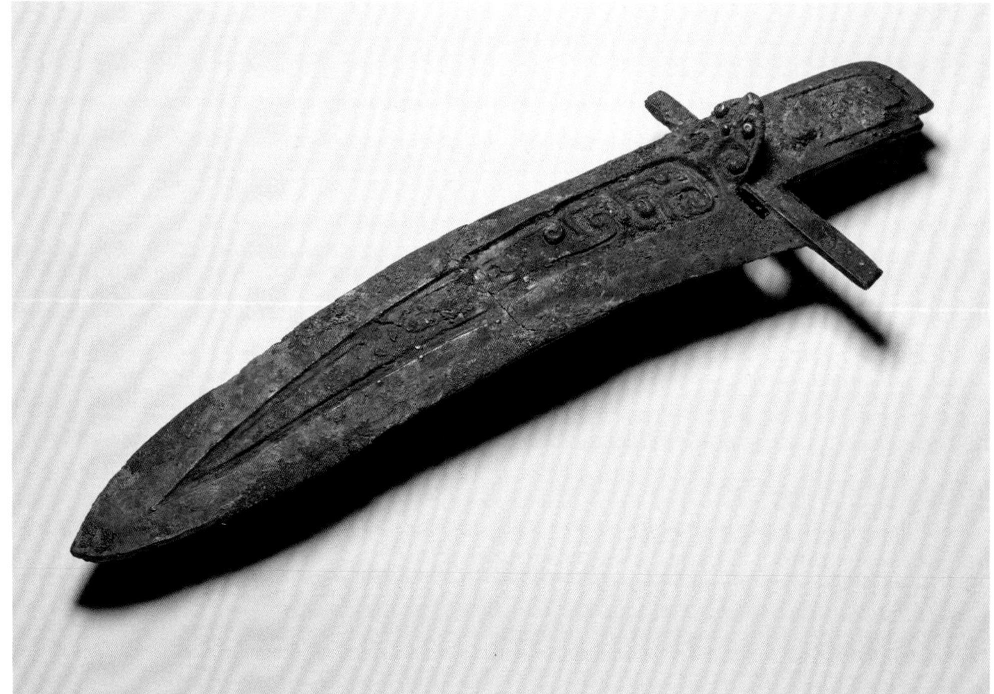

Figure 6.12. Bronze dagger-axe, *ge*, bronze, Western Zhou dynasty (1050–771 BCE). Collected by Orvar Karlbeck for Charles Seligman in 1932 and donated to the British Museum by Brenda Seligman in 1940. © The Trustees of the British Museum (1940,1214.287).

the relationship of Chinese script to Egyptian hieroglyphs. This stemmed from an important part of the Renaissance hermetic tradition that placed a primacy on ancient Greek and Egyptian culture. These ideas on the origins of the Chinese language and its culture persisted into the nineteenth and early twentieth centuries across a range of fields, including through the work of philologist Albert Etienne Terrien de Lacouperie (1845–1894), art historian Ludwig Bachhofer (1894–1976), and Johan Gunnar Andersson (1874–1960). It was Andersson, working with the China Geological Survey, who uncovered the first evidence of a Chinese Neolithic culture at Yangshao village, situated along the Yellow River valley in Henan province in 1921. He went on to become founding director of the Museum of Far Eastern Antiquities in Stockholm, for which Karlbeck was first collecting. While Andersson's discoveries were welcomed by Chinese archaeologists of the Academia Sinica such as Li Ji, his diffusionist ideas were less positively received.[64]

There is a clear relationship between the objects Charles Seligman collected and his interest in diffusionism. As Valérie Jurgens has noted, it was through the application of the comparative method to China's archaeological objects that enabled them to be visually connected with other past cultures, allowing a tentative chronology to be formed based on typology and stylistic development.[65] From the evidence of Charles Seligman's publications and the surviving Seligman papers relating to the Karlbeck Syndicate, he used collected material, particularly Tang tomb figures, glass, glazed beads, and early bronze mirrors and weaponry in his research.[66] Jurgens claims, convincingly, that there was a clear division in the collection: "Objects of ethnological interest are separated from the aesthetic. Especially the selection process for this division was influenced by Seligman."[67] Tellingly, she goes on: "This was also considered by Brenda when she segregated this particular collection from the larger whole after her husband's death"[68] (fig. 6.13).

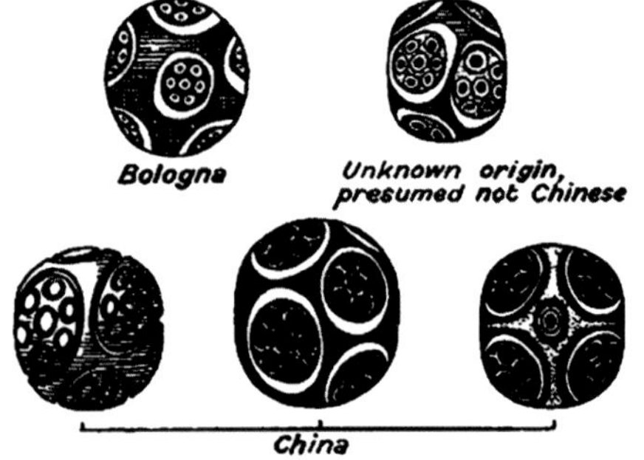

Figure 6.13. Drawing by Charles Seligman of Chinese beads in his collection. Reproduced in his article "The Roman Orient and the Far East," *Antiquity* 11 (1937): 21.

Legacy

Following Charles Seligman's death on September 19, 1940, Brenda quickly initiated a reordering of the Chinese collection; according to Howard Hansford, only retaining "the more important pieces and those groups which appeal to her most for aesthetic reasons."[69] John Ayers also referred to her particular interest in Song dynasty glazed wares, writing that "visitors to Mrs. Seligman's house will perhaps recall most vividly the rare display of celadon which illuminates her drawing-room, or the contrasting beauties of her *ch'ing-pai* [*qingbai*] and *Tz'u-chou* [*cizhou*]: in virtually every class, however, there are pieces of unusual distinction."[70] While she augmented the Song wares, she also reduced pieces of a later period, while retaining some fine Ming blue-and-white porcelains of the fifteenth and sixteenth centuries.[71] Indeed, Brenda's intention to reshape the collection was clearly articulated in an article by one of the major dealers from whom she bought and sold, Edgar Bluett, where he wrote: "With a view to maintaining the highest possible standard in the several sections both in respect of quality and artistic merit a number of items and one whole section have been elımınated. The result is the collection we see today, a collection comprising pottery from Neolithic days onward, bronzes and jades from the earliest days of China's history, porcelain of several types from the T'ang to the Sung period, including several superb examples of *Chekiang* celadon, *Ting yao*, *Chün yao* and *pai ch'ing* [*sic*]—extending into the *Ming* only in order to admit the splendid blue-and-white porcelain of the XIVth and XVth-century potters"[72] (fig. 6.14).

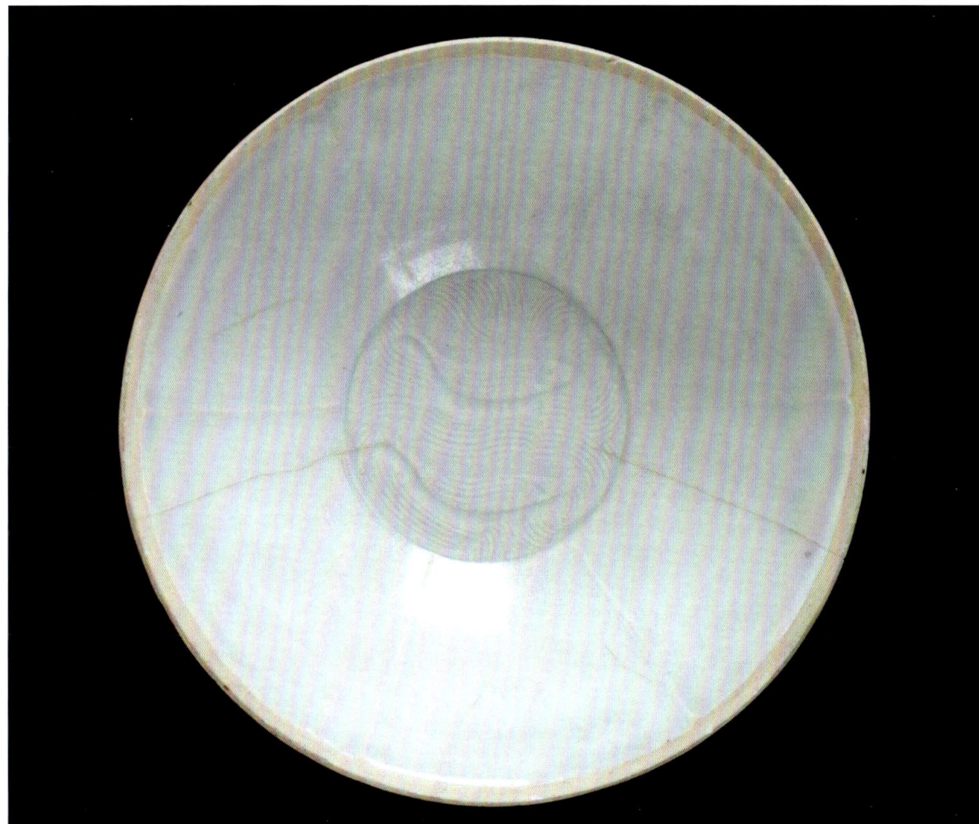

Figure 6.14. Bowl, porcelain with *qingbai* glaze. Southern Song dynasty (12th–13th century). © The Victoria & Albert Museum (FE.192–1974).

This re-shaping process started at the end of 1940 when she gave the collection of glass beads, some early bronze articles, a Ming period cloisonné box and cover, and a Korean vase to the British Museum in her husband's memory (fig. 6.15).[73] A few years later she initiated a series of sales of further Chinese material at Sotheby's in 1945 and 1947, in preparation for her move from her house at Toot Baldon in Oxfordshire to 22 Ilchester Place in London.[74] One piece that left the collection around this time was an early fifteenth-century stem cup, loaned to the 1948 OCS *Monochrome Porcelain of the Ming and Manchu Dynasties* exhibition and now in the Smithsonian's National Museum of Asian Art (fig. 6.16).[75] With her husband she had participated in loaning objects to key exhibitions, most particularly the 1935–36 International Exhibition of Chinese Art at the Royal Academy in London, and after his death she continued to lend, particularly to OCS exhibitions and in 1951 was elected to the society's council.[76]

While Brenda's purpose in reshaping the collection was to better reflect her own taste and priorities (she would also progress her earlier interest in Chinese painting), there was also a monetary consideration that might be pertinent to her decision to part with objects. This was the financial deficit that the Royal Anthropological Institute was facing in the mid-1950s. Brenda supported the establishment of an endowment fund, to be

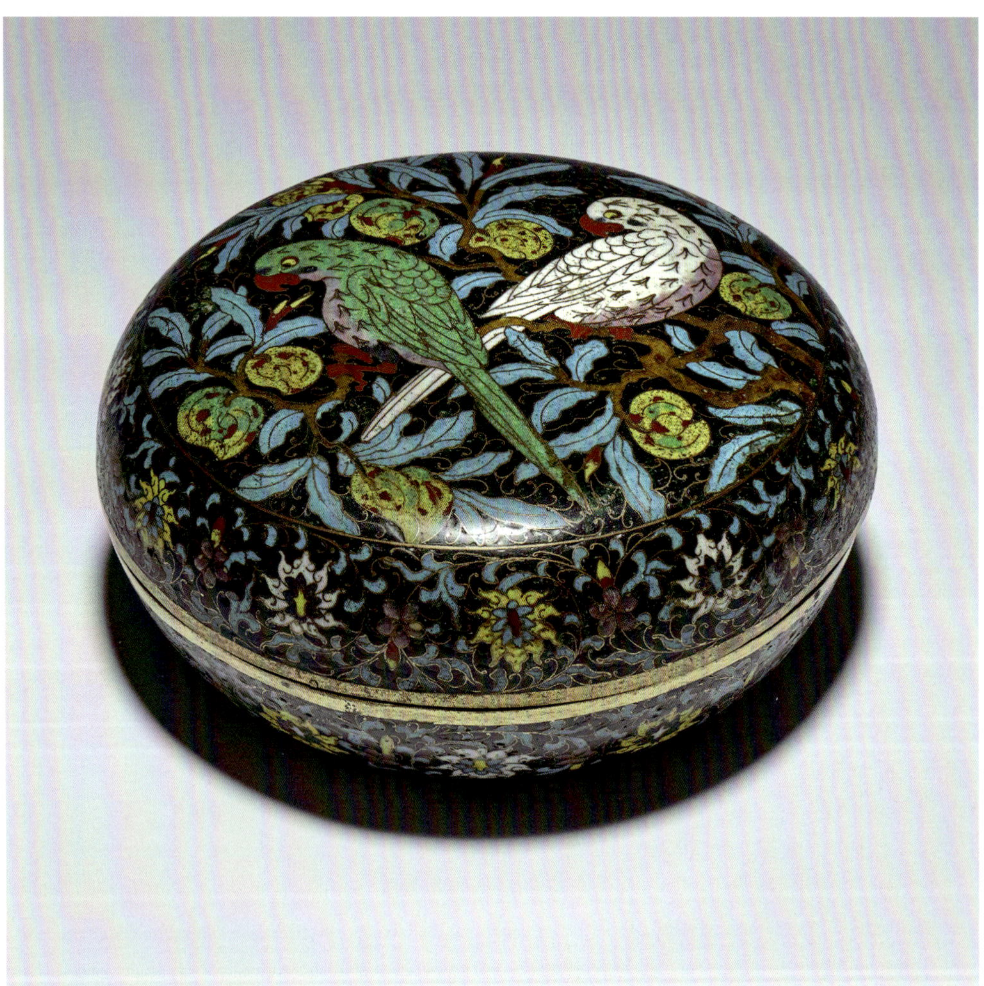

Figure 6.15. Box and cover, copper with cloisonné decoration. Ming dynasty, 15th century. Donated by Brenda Seligman to the British Museum in 1940. © The Trustees of the British Museum (1940,1214.314).

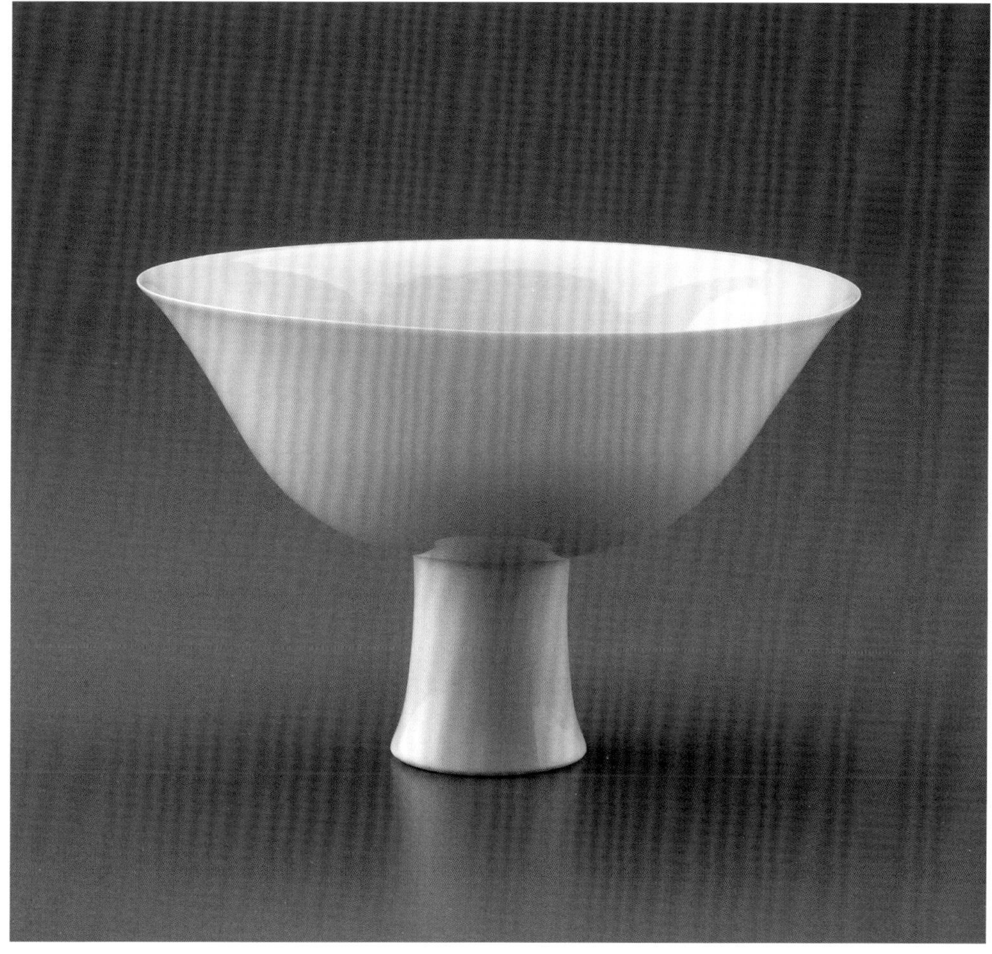

Figure 6.16. Stem cup, porcelain with white glaze. Ming dynasty, Yongle period (1403–24). Formerly in the Seligman Collection. Freer Gallery of Art, Smithsonian Institution, Washington, DC: Purchase—Charles Lang Freer Endowment, F1998.7.

named the C. G. Seligman Endowment Fund, to which she would contribute at least half, the remaining half to be raised through match funding. The object she sold to raise the capital was the ivory mask from Benin, which Charles had obtained at a 1909 Sotheby's sale of the collection of Sir Ralph Moor (1860–1909), a participant in the 1897 British punitive expedition to Benin, along with its pendant mask that he had sold to the British Museum in 1910.[77] It seems that she had tried to sell the mask in 1948 when negotiations were opened with the then-new National Museum of Nigeria in Lagos, which came to nothing.[78] The sum asked in 1948 was £1,000, but by 1957, when the sale of the mask became somewhat more urgent, the figure had risen to £20,000. The buyer was Nelson A. Rockefeller, who loaned it to the Museum of Primitive Art, New York, to whom it was gifted in 1972 and then transferred to the Metropolitan Museum of Art in 1978 (fig. 6.17).[79] This is not the place to detail the story of this object, but having achieved such a large sum for the ivory, this might have allowed Brenda to satisfy her commitment to the institute and her husband's memory and proceed with the gift of the Chinese collection to the nation.

In her will, drawn up in 1963, she instructed that the collection be held in trust by the Arts Council of Great Britain "for a period of 21 years, or such lesser period as trustees decide, for the advancement of, and the study and appreciation of, Chinese art, and for

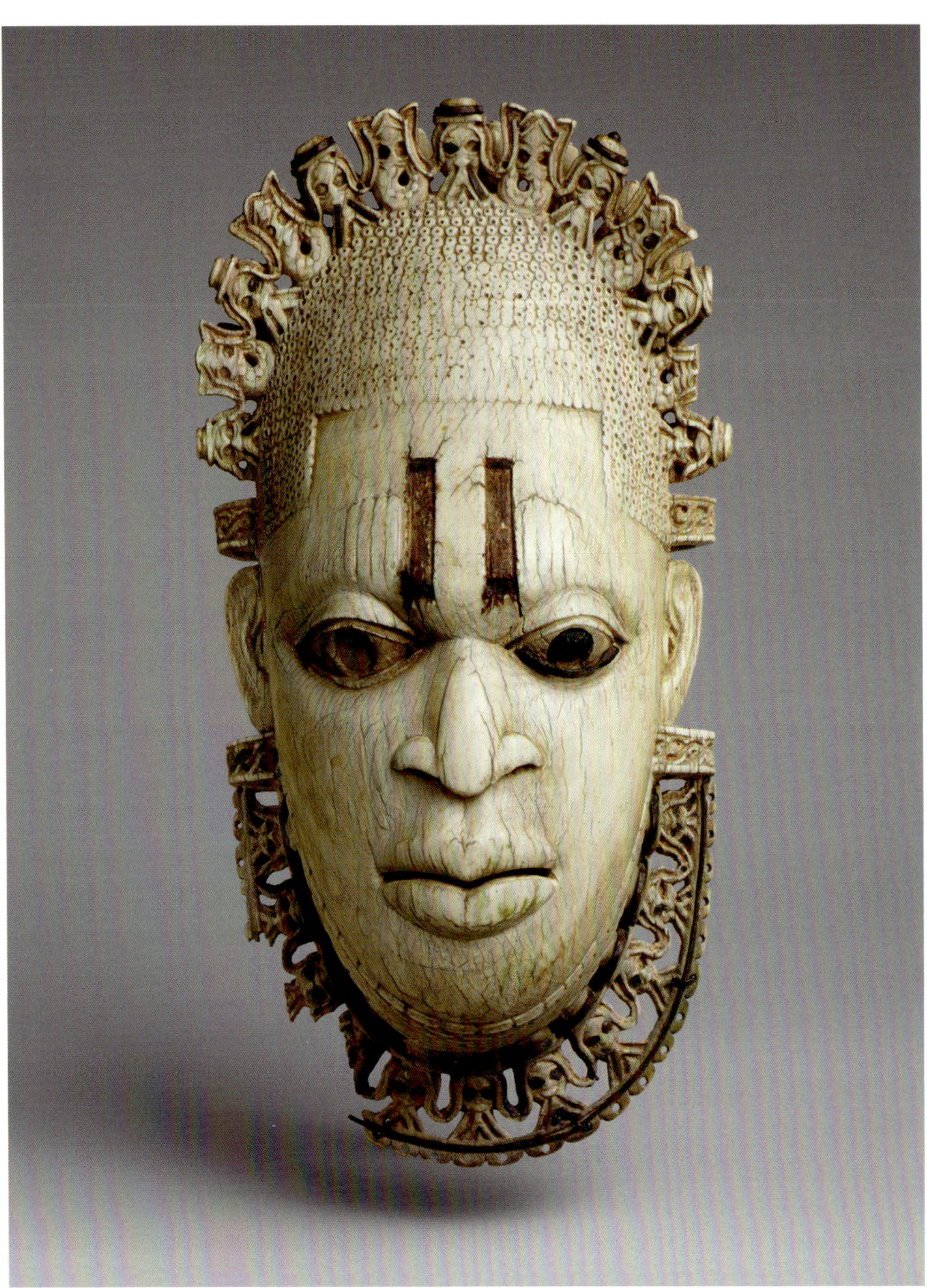

Figure 6.17. Queen mother pendant mask: Iyoba. Ivory, Benin, 16th century. Formerly owned by Charles and Brenda Seligman. The Michael C. Rockefeller Memorial Collection, Gift of Nelson A. Rockefeller, 1972. Courtesy of the Metropolitan Museum of Art, New York (1978.412.323).

exhibition purposes, and then to the British Museum."[80] While under the trust of the Arts Council the collection was to be toured in whole or part to museums around the UK, and although the will allowed for twenty-one years, the tour was completed in less than ten, with the British Museum receiving the majority of the objects and selected items going to the Victoria & Albert Museum in 1973.[81] Brenda's collection of paintings was not included, and instead her executors were instructed to apply to the treasury to have these items exempted from duty as "articles of national artistic importance" and offered for sale to the British Museum, Victoria & Albert Museum, the Ashmolean, the

Bristol Museum & Arts Gallery, the Scottish National Gallery, and the Durham Art Gallery, in descending order of importance.[82] Her Epstein bronze *The Seraph* and painting of Jerusalem by David Bomberg were gifted to the Tel Aviv Museum of Art in Israel.

Commentators have remarked on the fact that neither Charles nor Brenda Seligman achieved a legacy that promoted either of them as collectors, or the collection as a coherent whole.[83] It is suggested that the absorption of the Seligman Collection of Oriental Art into the larger holdings of two national museums, and in the case of Brenda's Chinese paintings an even wider dispersal, has resulted in a loss of profile; that while the fact or source of the bequest may survive in institutional records, the public headline does not. However, this presupposes that a discrete identifiable collection was sought in the first place—that Brenda envisaged what Anne Higonnet has defined as signs of a collector's personal identity or the collection meaning "at once the activity of accumulating and the totality of the objects assembled."[84] While the published catalogues form a body of evidence of the Seligman Collection and (again to reference Higonnet), with a clear nod to curatorial practice, there is little in their accompanying text that unduly promotes the collector(s). Brenda Seligman seems always to have foregrounded the material over the collector and her gift of the collection to two encyclopedic national museums—the amalgam of thousands of gifts, bequests, and purchases—would seem to confirm this. Although absorbed somewhat, the Seligman Collection still shares in the "immortality" of museums, as Susan Pearce terms it, in the sense that "collections received within them share this immortality."[85] Furthermore, the personal taste of the individual is confirmed where objects by their entry into a national museum are deemed "intrinsically desirable . . . to which a high cultural value is attached."[86]

Brenda's approach to legacy seems eminently pragmatic. She had neither the resources to form a discrete collection museum, nor, it may be argued, did she have time on her side. To quote Higonnet again, "By the 1950s, the establishment of new professional hierarchies in museums threatened the credibility of all collection museums, even the best of them. . . . Collection museums had gone out of fashion."[87] Seen in this light, Brenda's skillful stewardship should be recognized as no mean achievement when compared with another woman collector of an equally important collection of Chinese art, Bettie Fleischmann Holmes (Mrs. Christian Holmes), mentioned at the beginning of this chapter. While the Seligman Collection retained most of its integrity through its bequest, Bettie Holmes's collection by contrast, although remarkable, was broken up and sold at a series of sales after her death.[88] In many ways Bettie's life and collecting mirrored that of Brenda's. Born into a successful Jewish American business family in 1871, her father was Charles Louis Fleischmann (1835–97), founder of the Fleischmann Yeast Company of Cincinnati, who revolutionized the production, promotion, and distribution of compressed yeast in America.[89] In 1892, she married Danish émigré Dr. Christian Rasmus Holmes (1858–1920), an eye, ear, nose, and throat specialist, who—with Fleischmann money—founded the Cincinnati General Hospital and the University of Cincinnati College of Medicine. After Christian's death, Bettie established the Christian R. Holmes Memorial Hospital and the Christian R. Holmes Foundation. Her philanthropy was significant and extended to supporting the New York Philharmonic, the Metropolitan Opera Guild, and the Cincinnati Symphony Orchestra, and she campaigned vigorously against Prohibition and in support of the repeal of the Eighteenth Amendment (the 1919 Volstead Act), which was achieved in 1933 (fig. 6.18).

Unlike Brenda, Bettie's collecting of Chinese art seems to have begun after her husband's death in 1920 and included the widest possible range of Chinese art: ceramics, sculpture, painting, silver, jade, and bronzes. In particular, the quality of her collection, most notably the early bronzes, was recognized during her lifetime by the loans she made to the major international exhibitions of Chinese art in Berlin (1929) and London (1935–36), and after her death when those who acquired pieces from her collection made clear their sadness at its dispersal, while also recognizing the opportunity it offered.[90] In 1945, Alan Priest noted that "Mrs. Holmes had one of the great collections of Chinese bronzes of our time" going on to lament that "it is a sad thing to have it dispersed," noting "but it is a satisfaction to see much of it entering museum collections."[91] The Metropolitan Museum of Art, New York, acquired six pieces from the 1942 sale (fig. 6.19). In anticipation of the first sale in 1942, the Tonying Company's New York branch published selected bronzes from the collection with a text by its manager, C.F. Yau, most of which entered major museum collections, including the Asian Art Museum, San Francisco, the Smithsonian's National Museum of Asian Art, as well as the Metropolitan Museum of Art.[92]

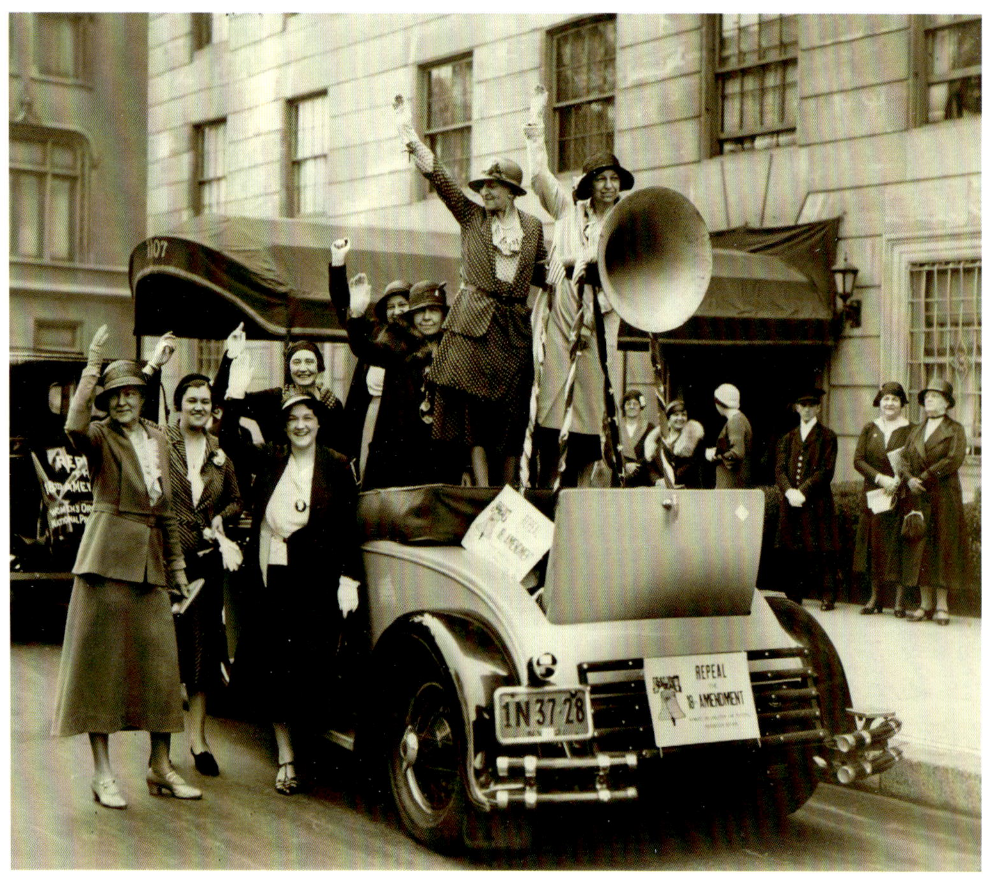

Figure 6.18. Bettie Fleischmann Holmes (*second from the right*) on a motorcade through New York with other members of the Women's Organization for National Prohibition Reform, May 1931. Photographer unknown, May 1931, Museum of the City of New York, gift of Mrs. William B. Remington, 56.71.123.

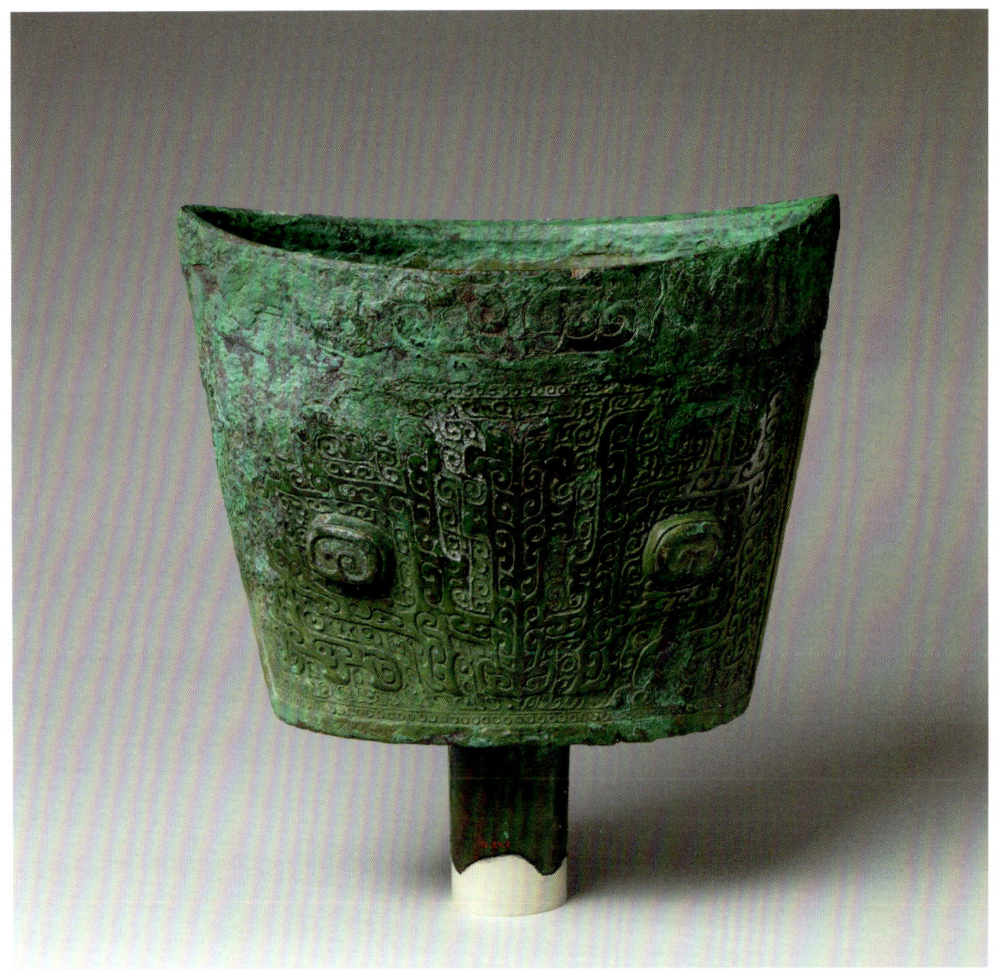

Figure 6.19. Bell, bronze, Shang dynasty (1500–1246 BCE). Formerly in the Bettie Fleischmann Holmes Collection, now in the Metropolitan Museum of Art, New York (43.24.2a,b).

Despite the construction in 1929 of the Chimneys, an Elizabethan-style mansion situated at Sands Point, Lewis, in Long Island, New York, the perfect backdrop to her collection, Bettie did not attempt to secure its legacy in any way, or create a collection museum. Instead it became the vehicle for the Holmes Foundation that proceeded to sell the collection off over the next two decades, eclipsing the collector for the most part and obscuring her achievement in forming one of the great Chinese collections in America. We know next to nothing about how she acquired her objects, from whom, how she built her knowledge, or even what motivated her. While much of this information remains obscure with regard to Brenda Seligman and, unlike her husband, she never published her thoughts or ideas on the subject, we can at least reconstruct some of this from her diaries, her actions, and what others have written about her. The collection that she helped build and actively re-formed before having it catalogued and secured as a bequest for the "advancement of the study and appreciation of Chinese art," remains as a lasting testament.[93] As Meyer Fortes wrote of her in his obituary: "In keeping up, during her 25 years of widowhood, the splendid collections of Chinese and Far Eastern art begun by her husband and herself, she satisfied both her perennial joy in things of beauty and her passion for knowledge"[94] (fig. 6.20).

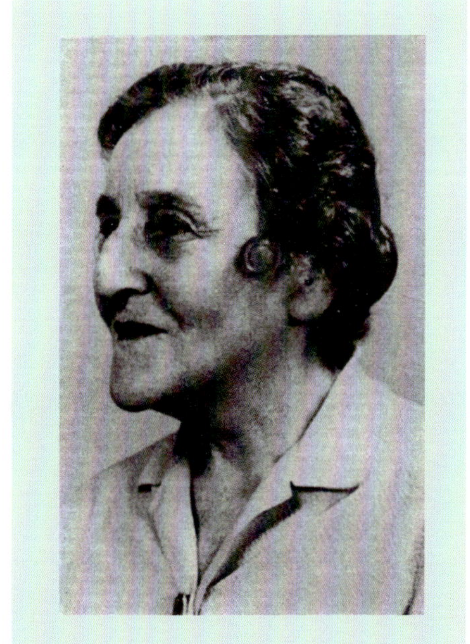

Figure 6.20. Brenda Zara Seligman taken not long before her death. Reproduced in *Man*, November–December 1965, 179.

Notes

1. This is explored in some detail in Susan M. Pearce, "Feminine Endings," in *On Collecting: An Investigation into Collecting in the European Tradition* (Oxford: Routledge, 1995), 206–10.

2. For Holmes's biography, see "Holmes, Mrs. Christian," last modified February 29, 2016, https://asia.si.edu/wp-content/uploads/2020/08/Holmes-Mrs-Christian.pdf; and for Kate Sturges Buckingham, see "Case 2: Katie Sturges Buckingham," Art Institute of Chicago, accessed September 9, 2022, https://archive.artic.edu/ryerson/making-history/2.

3. For brief details of Alice Sedgwick's life, see "Obituary," in *Transactions of the Oriental Ceramic Society* 37 (1967–69), xviii. The British Museum, the Victoria & Albert Museum, the Bristol Museum & Art Gallery, and the Fitzwilliam Museum, Cambridge, all benefited from her generosity.

4. "Mrs. Seligman" is listed as a member in her own right in the *Transactions of the Oriental Ceramic Society* 1, no. 20 (1944–45): 57.

5. Craig Clunas, *The Barlow Collection of Chinese Ceramics, Bronzes and Jades: An Introduction* (Sussex: University of Sussex, 1997), 8n2.

6. Meyer Fortes, "Brenda Zara Seligman, 1882–1965: A Memoir," *Man* 65 (November–December 1965): 177–81, 178, 180.

7. Frances Larson, "Charles Gabriel Seligman and Brenda Zara Seligman," *The Relational Museum Project*, Pitt Rivers Museum, 2002–6, accessed June 13, 2019, http://history.prm.ox.ac.uk/collector_seligman.html. The Seligmans collected objects from Egypt, Sri Lanka, Algeria, Sudan, Australia, and Papua New Guinea, five thousand of which were given to the Pitt Rivers Museum in Oxford.

8. This chapter will diverge somewhat from Nicky Levell's approach, which looked at the Seligman Collection as a "conjugal activity," at least up until the death of Charles Seligman in 1940, and hopefully offer some contrasting and complementary insights into Brenda's own tastes and ideas. See Nicky Levell, "Scholars and Connoisseurs, Knowledge and Taste: The Seligman Collection of Chinese Art," in *Collectors: Expressions of Self and Other*, ed. Anthony Shelton (London and Coimbra: The Horniman Museum and Museu Antroplógico de Universidade de Coimbra, 2001), 73–89.

9. C. S. Myers, "Charles Gabriel Seligman, 1873–1940," *Obituary Notices of Fellows of the Royal Society* 3, no. 10 (December 1941), 626–46, 636.

10. The collection as bequeathed was published in two volumes: S. Howard Hansford, *The Seligman Collection of Oriental Art, Vol. I: Chinese, Central Asian and Luristan Bronzes and Chinese Jades and Sculptures* (London: The Arts Council of Great Britain, Lund Humphries, 1957) and John Ayers, *The Seligman Collection of Oriental Art, Vol. II: Chinese and Korean Pottery and Porcelain* (London: The Arts Council of Great Britain and Lund Humphries, 1964). For an overview of the collection when first displayed at the Arts Council Gallery between May 7 and June 7, 1966, see Harry M. Garner, "Chinese Works of Art from the Seligman Collection," *Apollo* 83, no. 51 (May 1, 1966): 351–57.

11. F. J. West, "Charles Gabriel Seligman (1873–1940)," *Oxford Dictionary of National Biography*, 2012, accessed June 12, 2019, https://www.oxforddnb.com. For further biographical information, see also Marilyn Bailey Ogilvie and Joy Dorothy Harvey, *The Biographical Dictionary of Women in Science*, 2 vols. (New York and London: Routledge, 2000), 1:1174; Basil Gray, *Transactions of the Oriental Ceramic Society* 35 (1963–64): xxvi.

12. Sarah Abrevaya Stein, *Plumes: Ostrich Feathers, Jews, and a Lost World of Global Commerce* (New Haven, CT: Yale University Press, 2008), 54. The quotation is taken from the Redcliffe Nathan Salaman Papers, "Boyhood and Family Background," held at the University Library Cambridge (RNS 8171/27, 11).

13. For details of the Salaman business, see Stein, *Plumes*, chapter 2, especially 76–83.

14. Stein, *Plumes*, 78.

15. The following brief details of Charles Seligman's career are taken from Myers, "Charles Gabriel Seligman." He dropped the double *n* from his name at the outbreak of World War I.

16. Fortes, "Brenda Zara Seligman," 177–78.

17. Fortes, 178.

18. Fortes, 180. *Studies in Kinship and Marriage: Dedicated to Brenda Zara Seligman in Her Eightieth Birthday*, ed. Isaac Schapera (London: Royal Anthropological Institute of Great Britain & Ireland, 1963).

19. "Professor C.G. Seligman," *Transactions of the Oriental Ceramic Society* 18 (1940–41): 15. The reference is also made by John Ayers in the preface to *The Seligman Collection of Oriental Art*, 1:viii.

20. Brenda Seligman, Egyptian Journal, 1909, Charles and Brenda Seligman Papers, Seligman 1/4/3, London School of Economics Library, 2.

21. Levell, "Scholars and Connoisseurs," 76.

22. Charles T. Currelly, *I Brought the Ages Home* (Toronto: Ryerson Press, 1956).

23. Currelly, *I Brought the Ages Home*, 181.

24. Currelly, 181.

25. For more information on S. M. Franck, see Nick Pearce, "CARP-ON: Further Thoughts on Chinese Art Provenance Research," in *Collectors, Collections and Collecting the Arts of China: Histories and Challenges*, eds. Jason Steuber and Guolong Lai (Gainesville: University Press of Florida, 2014), 295–312.

26. See Dennis Duffy, "Triangulating the ROM," *Journal of Canadian Studies* 40, no. 1 (Winter 2006): 157–81. See also Chen Shen, "Past, Present and Future of Collecting Chinese Antiquities in the Royal Ontario Museum: Objectives and Challenges," in Steuber and Lai, eds., *Collectors, Collections and Collecting*, 245–64.

27. Levell, "Scholars and Connoisseurs," 81.

28. Brenda's journals are written in a lively style and with a detail absent in Charles's own journal, which is largely written as a series of notes.

29. For a comprehensive biography of Laurence Binyon, see John Hatcher, *Laurence Binyon: Poet, Scholar of East and West* (Oxford: Oxford University Press, 1995).

30. Hatcher, *Laurence Binyon*, 244 and 244n4.

31. Hatcher, 244.

32. Brenda Seligman, Journal of Japan, Korea and China, 1929. The Seligman Papers, Seligman 5/2, London School of Economics Library.

33. Seligman, Journal of Japan, Korea and China, 1929, 6.

34. Seligman, 25.

35. Seligman, 28.

36. Seligman, 30.

37. Seligman, 31–32.

38. For a comprehensive survey of Ferguson's life and work, see Lara Jaishree Netting, *A Perpetual Fire: John C. Ferguson and His Quest for Chinese Art and Culture* (Hong Kong: Hong Kong University Press, 2013). See also Thomas Lawton, "A Time of Transition: John C. Ferguson (1866–1945)," in *A Time of Transition: Two Collectors of Chinese Art, The Franklin D. Murphy Lectures XII* (Lawrence: Spencer Museum of Art, University of Kansas, 1991), 65–104.

39. Netting, *Perpetual Fire*, 122–23.

40. Netting, 123.

41. Netting, 156. Ferguson to his daughter Florence, October 3, 1929, in the Ferguson Family Papers.

42. Seligman, Journal of Japan, Korea and China, 1929, 36.

43. Elinor Pearlstein, "Color, Life, and Moment," *Art Institute of Chicago Museum Studies* 26, no. 2 (2000): 80–93 and 106–12.

44. The title was referred to by Beijing resident George N. Kates and quoted by Karl E. Meyer and Shareen Blair Brysac in *The China Collectors: America's Century-Long Hunt for Asian Art Treasures* (New York: Palgrave Macmillan, 2015), 241.

45. Lucy Calhoun, "The Streets of Peking," *New York Times*, November 26, 1922, 5 and 12.

46. Nick Pearce, "'I shall set at once about the work': Some Agents in China," in *Art Markets, Agents and Collectors: Collecting Strategies in Modern Europe and the United States, 1550–1950*, eds. Susan Bracken and Adriana Turpin (London: Bloomsbury, 2021), 241–51, 247–48. For Collins's agent work for the Bluetts, see Dominic Jellinek, "Bluett Essay," and biographical entry on "Captain Collins," both on Chinese Art Research into Provenance (CARP), accessed July 10, 2019, https://carp.arts.gla.ac.uk. Collins's title of "Captain" probably originated from his commanding the 115th company of the Chinese Labour Corps during World War I.

47. Pearce, "'I shall set at once about the Work.'" For reference to Sirén, see Minna Törmä, *Enchanted by Lohans: Osvald Sirén's Journey into Chinese Art* (Hong Kong: Hong Kong University Press, 2013), 114–15.

48. Seligman, Journal of Japan, Korea and China, 1929, 36.

49. Seligman, 46.

50. Ellen Huang, *China's China: Jingdezhen Porcelain and the Production of Art in the Nineteenth Century* (doctoral thesis, University of California, San Diego, 2008), chapter 1. See also Netting, *Perpetual Fire*, 117–18. Guo was responsible for the production of Hongxian porcelain during this brief period.

51. Netting, 117–18.

52. Seligman, Journal of Japan, Korea and China, 1929, 58. Purple Ting (Ding) is a rare aubergine-brown rather than the usual ivory-white glaze. At the time Brenda was writing it was still elusive for most collectors. Writing in 1925, OCS member F. N. Schiller described the search for specimens as "A Quest" (*Transactions of the Oriental Ceramic Society*, 1925–26, 15–20) and A. L. Hetherington was still grappling with the subject a few years later ("Purple Ting," *Transactions of the Oriental Ceramic Society* (1928–30): 28–33).

53. Adam T. Kessler, *Song Blue and White Porcelain on the Silk Road* (Leiden, the Netherlands: Brill, 2012), 219n25. See also Wen Yuan-ning's Intimate Portrait of "Mr. Wu Lai-Hsi," in *Zhongguo pinglun zhoubao* (The China Critic), VII, no. 36 (September 6, 1934), 384. Wen Yuanning, "Mr. Wu Lai-Hsi," in Christopher Rea, ed., *Imperfect Understanding, Intimate Portraits of Chinese Celebrities by Wen Yuan-ning and others* (Amherst, NY: Cambria Press, 2018), 75–76.

54. See Dominic Jellinek and Roy Davids, *Provenance: Collectors, Dealers and Scholars in the Field of Chinese Ceramics in Britain and America* (Oxford: Roy Davids, 2011), 395–96 and P1.148, 397. The Wu Laixi Collection was sold at Sotheby's London on May 26, 1937.

55. Hatcher, *Laurence Binyon*, 246. Brenda notes in her journal that they lunched with Baron Dan Takuma, head of the Mitsui company (*zaibatsu*), who was part of the committee hosting and financing Binyon's visit to Japan: "Binyon was an immense success." She also notes that Hobson and Raphael were also joined by Sir Percival David (1892–1964). As well as being in Japan to celebrate Binyon's visit, he was probably there because he was funding the excavation of Seobongchong, a tomb site of the Silla Kingdom in Korea, then under Japanese control.

56. Brenda Seligman, Journal of Japan, Korea and China, 1930. The Seligman Papers, Seligman 6/2, London School of Economics Library, 5.

57. Seligman, Journal of Japan, Korea and China, 1930, 6.

58. R. R. Sowerby, *Sowerby of China* (Kendal, UK: Titus Wilson and Son, 1956). See also Keith Stevens, "Naturalist, Author, Artist, Explorer and Editor and an Almost Forgotten President: Arthur de Carle Sowerby, 1885–1954, President of the North China Branch of the Royal Asiatic Society, 1935–1940," *Journal of the Royal Asiatic Society Hong Kong Branch* 38 (1998): 121–36.

59. E. A. Strehlneek, *Zhonghua minhua* [Chinese pictorial art] (Shanghai: Commercial Press), 1914. Seligman, Journal of Japan, Korea and China, 1930, 7. For some details on Strehlneek, see

Lindsay Shen, *Knowledge Is Pleasure: Florence Ayscough in Shanghai* (Hong Kong: Hong Kong University Press, 2012), 54–56. For more on John Sparks, see Pearce, "CARP-ON," 301–7.

60. For a comprehensive history of the syndicate, see Valérie A. M. Jurgens, *The Karlbeck Syndicate 1930–1934: Collecting and Scholarship on Chinese Art in Sweden and Britain* (Saarbrücken, Germany: LAP Lambert Academic Publishing, 2012), and Valérie A. M. Jurgens, "Ovar Karlbeck and the Karlbeck Syndicate (1928–1934)," *Transactions of the Oriental Ceramic Society* 70 (2005–6): 35–38.

61. Jurgens, *Karlbeck Syndicate*, 321.

62. Jurgens, 319–52.

63. For a definition and brief history of diffusionism, see Bruce G. Trigger, *A History of Archaeological Thought*, 2nd ed. (Cambridge: Cambridge University Press, 2006), 217–23.

64. For a detailed account of Andersson and the context of his work in China, see Magnus Fiskesjö and Chen Xincan, *China before China*, Museum of Far Eastern Antiquities Monograph Series, no. 15 (Stockholm: Östasiatiska Museet, 2004).

65. Jurgens, *Karlbeck Syndicate*, 45.

66. Seligman's publications in this area include: "Bird Chariots and Socketed Celts in Europe and China," *Journal of the Royal Anthropological Institute of Great Britain and Ireland* 50 (January–June 1920): 153–58; "Further Note on Bird Chariots in Europe and China," *Journal of the Royal Anthropological Institute of Great Britain and Ireland* 58 (January–June 1928), 247–54; "The Roman Orient and the Far East," *Antiquity* 11, no. 41 (March 1937), 5–30; (with H. Beck), "Far Eastern Glass: Some Western Origins," *Bulletin of the Museum of Far Eastern Antiquities* 10 (1938): 1–64; "Early Chinese Glass," *Transactions of the Oriental Ceramic Society* 18 (1940–41): 19–26. The Karlbeck Syndicate papers relating to Charles Seligman are retained by the Asia department at the V&A in London.

67. Jurgens, *Karlbeck Syndicate*, 349. See also Levell, "Scholars and Connoisseurs," 77–78.

68. Jurgens, 349.

69. Hansford, *Seligman Collection*, vol. 1, preface, ix. This emphasis on raising the aesthetic quality of the collection was reiterated by Basil Gray in her obituary: *Transactions of the Oriental Ceramic Society* 35, xxvi.

70. Ayers, *Seligman Collection*, vol. II, preface, viii.

71. Ayers, viii.

72. E. E. Bluett, "Chinese Works of Art in English Collections: A Selection from the Seligman Collection," *Apollo* 66 (October 1957): 69–74. Charles and Brenda were clients of the Bluetts from the 1920s, with Brenda transferring the account into her name in 1940. She remained a client until 1961. See Jellinek and David, *Provenance*, 396.

73. William Watson and Soame Jenyns, "The Seligman Gift," *British Museum Quarterly* 15 (1941–1950): 95–103.

74. Sotheby & Co., *Catalogue of Fine Chinese Pottery and Porcelain, Jades and Bronzes, Comprising the Property of Mrs. C.G. Seligman and the Property of the Late Mrs. Robert Benson*, May 2, 1945; *Catalogue of Fine Chinese Pottery and Porcelain . . . Early Jade Carvings and Bronzes, the Property of E. L. Paget . . . Mrs. Seligman . . . Mrs. A. Loria . . . the Rt. Hon. Earl Castle Stewart . . . R. H. Hewins . . . Gaspard O. Farrer (Decd) . . . Mrs. Hackenbroch and . . . the Rt. Hon. Lord Audley*, January 23, 1947.

75. Oriental Ceramic Society, *Illustrated Catalogue of an Exhibition of Monochrome Porcelain of the Ming and Manchu Dynasties*, October 27 to December 18, 1948, exhibit 97.

76. Frances Wood, "Towards a New History of the Oriental Ceramic Society: Narrative and Chronology," *Transactions of the Oriental Ceramic Society* 76 (2011–12): 95–116, 111. The Seligmans loaned fourteen items to the 1935–36 exhibition.

77. The mask is museum number Af1910,0513.1. See https://www.britishmuseum.org/collection/object/E_Af1910-0513-1, accessed July 12, 2019.

78. Felicity Bodenstein, "Notes for a Long-Term Approach to the Price History of Brass and Ivory Objects Taken from the Kingdom of Benin in 1897," in *Acquiring Cultures: Histories of World Art on Western Markets*, eds. Bénédicte Savoy, Charlotte Guichard, and Christine Howald (Berlin and Boston: de Gruyter, 2018), 267–88, 284.

79. Bodenstein, "Notes for a Long-Term Approach," 283–84. See https://www.metmuseum.org/art/collection/search/318622, accessed July 12, 2019. Progress of the sale can be followed in letters held by the Royal Anthropological Institute in London: RAI Archives: Appeals A154, Correspondence and papers, 1947, accessed July 12, 2019, https://www.therai.org.uk.

80. "Latest Wills," *Times*, July 6, 1965, 14.

81. Basil Gray, "Mrs. Brenda Seligman," *Times*, January 8, 1965, 13. See also Ayers, *Seligman Collection*, vol. II, vii. Rose Kerr also quotes Robert Charleston, a former keeper of the ceramics department at the Victoria & Albert Museum, who credits John Ayers with helping Brenda Seligman over many years while maintaining the museum's interest. Rose Kerr, *Song Dynasty Ceramics* (London: V&A Publications, 2004), 19–20.

82. "Latest Wills," 14.

83. Levell, "Scholars and Connoisseurs," 84.

84. Anne Higonnet, *A Museum of One's Own: Private Collecting, Public Gift* (Pittsburgh and New York: Periscope Publishing, 2009), xiii.

85. Pearce, *On Collecting*, 249.

86. Pearce, 249.

87. Higonnet, *Museum of One's Own*, xv.

88. These were: Parke-Bernet Galleries, *Art Collection of the Late Mrs Christian Holmes: Chinese Ceramics & Jades, Persian Pottery, Egyptian Antiquities*, April 15–18, 1942; Parke-Bernet Galleries, New York, *English & French Furniture, Rugs, Table China, Silver, Glass, Linens & Laces Removed from "The Chimneys," Sands Point, Port Washington, Long Island, Residence of the Late Mrs. Christian R. Holmes, Property of Holmes Foundation*, September 26–30, 1944; Parke-Bernet Galleries, New York, *Important Chinese Art: Early Dynastic Bronzes, Silver and Gold, Chinese Jade, Coral and Other Semi-Precious Mineral Carvings, Early Dynastic Pottery, Porcelain, Tomb Jades, Single-Color and Decorated Porcelains, Japanese and Chinese Ivories, Chinese, Siamese, and Indian Sculptures, Chinese Furniture, Paintings, Lamps and Decorative Arts Collected by Late Bettie F. Holmes (Mrs. Christian Holmes), Sold by the Order of the Holmes Foundation*, November 14–15, 1963.

89. Details of the Fleischmann family and company can be found in P. Christiaan Klieger, *Images of America: The Fleischmann Yeast Family* (San Francisco: Arcadia Publishing, 2004). Bettie Fleischmann's biographical details that follow are taken from chapter 5, 45–52.

90. She lent a bronze *gui* and two pieces of Tang silver to the Berlin *Chinesische Kunst* exhibition (loans 14, 425, and 436) and twenty-two pieces of bronze, gilt bronze, silver, jade, and ceramics to the International Exhibition of Chinese Art in London (loans 123, 135, 139, 188, 212, 229, 233, 234, 300, 310, 358, 378, 394, 395, 535, 571, 655, 667, 786, 805, 2307, and 2453).

91. Alan Priest, "Chinese Bronzes," *Metropolitan Museum of Art Bulletin* 4, no. 4 (December 1945), 106–12, 106.

92. *Selected Ancient Chinese Bronzes from the Collection of Mrs. Christian R. Holmes* (New York: Orientalia, privately printed, n.d.).

93. Ayers, *Seligman Collection*, vol. 2, foreword, vii.

94. Meyer Fortes, "Brenda Zara Seligman," 177.

Bibliography

Ayers, John. *The Seligman Collection of Oriental Art*, vol. 2, *Chinese and Korean Pottery and Porcelain*. London: Arts Council of Great Britain and Lund Humphries, 1964.

Bluett, E. E. "Chinese Works of Art in English Collections: A Selection from the Seligman Collection." *Apollo*, no. 66 (October 1, 1957): 69–74.

Bodenstein, Felicity. "Notes for a Long-Term Approach to the Price History of Brass and Ivory Objects Taken from the Kingdom of Benin in 1897." In *Acquiring Cultures: Histories of World Art on Western Markets*, edited by Bénédicte Savoy, Charlotte Guichard, and Christine Howald, 267–88. Berlin and Boston: de Gruyter, 2018.

Clunas, Craig. *The Barlow Collection of Chinese Ceramics, Bronzes and Jades: An Introduction*. Sussex, UK: University of Sussex, 1997.

Currelly, Charles T. *I Brought the Ages Home*. Toronto: Ryerson Press, 1956.

Duffy, Dennis. "Triangulating the ROM." *Journal of Canadian Studies*, 40, no. 1 (Winter 2006): 157–81.

Fiskesjö, Magnus, and Xincan Chen. *China before China*. Museum of Far Eastern Antiquities Monograph Series 15. Stockholm: Östasiatiska Museet, 2004.

Fortes, Meyer. "Brenda Zara Seligman, 1882–1965: A Memoir." *Man*, no. 65 (November–December 1965): 177–81.

Garner, Harry M. "Chinese Works of Art from the Seligman Collection." *Apollo* 83, no. 51 (May 1, 1966): 351–57.

Gessellschaft für Ostasiatische Kunst und der Preussischen Akademie der Künste, Berlin. *Ausstellung Chinesischer Kunst*. Berlin: Würfel Verlag Berlin, 1929.

Gray, Basil. "Obituary, Brenda Seligman." *Transactions of the Oriental Ceramic Society*, no. 35 (1963–64): xxvi.

Hansford, Howard. *The Seligman Collection of Oriental Art*, vol. 2, *Chinese, Central Asian and Luristan Bronzes and Chinese Jades and Sculptures*. London: Arts Council of Great Britain, Lund Humphries, 1957.

Hatcher, John. *Laurence Binyon: Poet, Scholar of East and West*. Oxford: Oxford University Press, 1995.

Higgonet, Anne. *A Museum of One's Own: Private Collecting, Public Gift*. Pittsburgh and New York: Periscope, 2009.

Jellinek, Dominic, and Roy Davids. *Provenance: Collectors, Dealers and Scholars in the Field of Chinese Ceramics in Britain and America*. Oxford: Roy Davids, 2011.

Jurgens, Valérie A. M. *The Karlbeck Syndicate 1930–1934: Collecting and Scholarship on Chinese Art in Sweden and Britain*. Saarbrücken, Germany: LAP Lambert Academic Publishing, 2012.

———. "Ovar Karlbeck and the Karlbeck Syndicate (1928–1934)." *Transactions of the Oriental Ceramic Society*, no. 70 (2005–6): 35–38.

Kerr, Rose. *Song Dynasty Ceramics*. London: V&A Publications, 2004.

Kessler, Adam T. *Song Blue and White Porcelain on the Silk Road*. Leiden, the Netherlands: Brill, 2012.

Klieger, P. Christiaan. *Images of America: The Fleischmann Yeast Family*. San Francisco: Arcadia, 2004.

Lawton, Thomas. "A Time of Transition: John C. Ferguson (1866–1945)." In *A Time of Transition: Two Collectors of Chinese Art, The Franklin D. Murphy Lectures XII*, 65–104. Lawrence: Spencer Museum of Art, University of Kansas, 1991.

Levell, Nicky. "Scholars and Connoisseurs, Knowledge and Taste: The Seligman Collection of Chinese Art." In *Collectors: Expressions of Self and Other*, edited by Anthony Shelton, 73–89.

London: Horniman Museum; Coimbra, Portugal: Museu Antroplógico de Universidade de Coimbra, 2001.

Meyer, Karl E., and Shareen Blair Brysac. *The China Collectors: America's Century-Long Hunt for Asian Art Treasures.* New York: Palgrave Macmillan, 2015.

Myers, C. S. "Charles Gabriel Seligman, 1873–1940." *Obituary Notices of Fellows of the Royal Society* 3, no. 10 (December 1941): 626–46.

Netting, Lara Jaishree. *A Perpetual Fire: John C. Ferguson and His Quest for Chinese Art and Culture.* Hong Kong: Hong Kong University Press, 2013.

Ogilvie, Marilyn Bailey, and Joy Dorothy Harvey. *The Biographical Dictionary of Women in Science*, 2 vols. New York and London: Routledge, 2000.

Oriental Ceramic Society. *Illustrated Catalogue of an Exhibition of Monochrome Porcelain of the Ming and Manchu Dynasties, October 27 to December 18, 1948.* London: Oriental Ceramic Society, 1948.

Parke-Bernet Galleries. *Art Collection of the Late Mrs. Christian Holmes: Chinese Ceramics & Jades, Persian Pottery, Egyptian Antiquities.* New York: Parke-Bernet Galleries, 1942.

———. *English & French Furniture, Rugs, Table China, Silver, Glass, Linens & Laces Removed from "The Chimneys," Sands Point, Port Washington, Long Island, Residence of the Late Mrs. Christian R. Holmes, Property of Holmes Foundation.* New York: Parke-Bernet Galleries, 1944.

———. *Important Chinese Art: Early Dynastic Bronzes, Silver and Gold, Chinese Jade, Coral and Other Semi-Precious Mineral Carvings, Early Dynastic Pottery, Porcelain, Tomb Jades, Single-Color and Decorated Porcelains, Japanese and Chinese Ivories, Chinese, Siamese, and Indian Sculptures, Chinese Furniture, Paintings, Lamps and Decorative Arts Collected by Late Bettie F. Holmes (Mrs. Christian Holmes), Sold by the Order of the Holmes Foundation.* New York: Parke-Bernet Galleries, 1963.

Pearce, Nick. "'I shall set at once about the work': Some Agents in China." In *Art Markets, Agents and Collectors: Collecting Strategies in Europe and the United States, 1550–1950*, edited by Susan Bracken and Adriana Turpin, 241–51. London: Bloomsbury, 2021.

Pearce, Susan M. *On Collecting: An Investigation into Collecting in the European Tradition.* Oxford: Routledge, 1995.

Pearlstein, Eleanor. "Color, Life, and Moment." *Art Institute of Chicago Museum Studies* 26, no. 2 (2000): 80–93, 106–112.

Priest, Alan. "Chinese Bronzes." *Metropolitan Museum of Art Bulletin*, n.s. 4, no. 4 (December 1945): 106–12.

Royal Academy of Arts. *International Exhibition of Chinese Art, Catalogue and Illustrated Supplement.* London: Royal Academy of Arts, 1935.

Schapera, I., ed. *Studies in Kinship and Marriage: Dedicated to Brenda Zara Seligman in Her Eightieth Birthday.* London: Royal Anthropological Institute of Great Britain and Ireland, 1963.

Selected Ancient Chinese Bronzes from the Collection of Mrs. Christian R. Holmes. New York: Orientalia, privately printed, n.d.

Seligman, C. G. "Bird Chariots and Socketed Celts in Europe and China." *Journal of the Royal Anthropological Institute of Great Britain and Ireland*, no. 50 (January–June 1920): 153–58.

———. "Further Note on Bird Chariots in Europe and China." *Journal of the Royal Anthropological Institute of Great Britain and Ireland*, no. 58 (January–June 1928): 247–54.

———. "The Roman Orient and the Far East." *Antiquity* 11, no. 41 (March 1937): 5–30.

Seligman, C. G., with H. Beck. "Early Chinese Glass." *Transactions of the Oriental Ceramic Society*, no. 18 (1940–41): 19–26.

———. "Far Eastern Glass: Some Western Origins." *Bulletin of the Museum of Far Eastern Antiquities*, no. 10 (1938): 1–64.

Shen, Lindsay. *Knowledge Is Pleasure: Florence Ayscough in Shanghai.* Hong Kong: Hong Kong University Press, 2012.

Sotheby & Co. *Catalogue of Fine Chinese Pottery and Porcelain … Early Jade Carvings and Bronzes, the Property of E.L. Paget … Mrs. Seligman … Mrs. A. Loria … the Rt. Hon. Earl Castle Stewart …*

R.H. Hewins . . . Gaspard O. Farrer (decd) . . . Mrs. Hackenbroch and . . . the Rt. Hon. Lord Audley. London: Sotheby & Co., January 23, 1947.

———. *Catalogue of Fine Chinese Pottery and Porcelain, Jades and Bronzes, Comprising the Property of Mrs. C. G. Seligman and the Property of the Late Mrs. Robert Benson.* London: Sotheby & Co., May 2, 1945.

Sowerby, R. R. *Sowerby of China.* Kendal, UK: Titus Wilson and Son, 1956.

Stein, Sarah Abrevaya. *Plumes: Ostrich Feathers, Jews, and a Lost World of Global Commerce.* New Haven, CT, and London: Yale University Press, 2008.

Steuber, Jason, and Guolong Lai, eds. *Collectors, Collections and Collecting the Arts of China: Histories and Challenges.* Gainesville: University Press of Florida, 2014.

Stevens, Keith. "Naturalist, Author, Artist, Explorer and Editor and an Almost Forgotten President: Arthur de Carle Sowerby, 1885–1954, President of the North China Branch of the Royal Asiatic Society, 1935–1940." *Journal of the Royal Asiatic Society Hong Kong Branch*, no. 38 (1998): 121–36.

Strehlneek, E. A. *Chinese Pictorial Art (Zhonghua minhua).* Shanghai: Commercial Press, 1914.

Törmä, Minna. *Enchanted by Lohans: Osvald Sirén's Journey into Chinese Art.* Hong Kong: Hong Kong University Press, 2013.

Transactions of the Oriental Ceramic Society, no. 5 (1925–26); no. 8 (1928–30); no. 18 (1940–41); no. 20 (1944–45); no. 37 (1967–69).

Trigger, Bruce G. *A History of Archaeological Thought.* 2nd ed. Cambridge, UK: Cambridge University Press, 2006.

Watson, William, and Soame Jenyns. "The Seligman Gift." *British Museum Quarterly*, no. 15 (1941–50): 95–103.

Wen Yuanning. "Mr. Wu Lai-Hsi." In *Imperfect Understanding, Intimate Portraits of Chinese Celebrities by Wen Yuan-ning and Others*, edited by Christopher Rea, 75–76. Amherst, NY: Cambria Press, 2018.

Wood, Frances. "Towards a New History of the Oriental Ceramic Society: Narrative and Chronology." *Transactions of the Oriental Ceramic Society*, no. 76 (2011–12): 95–116.

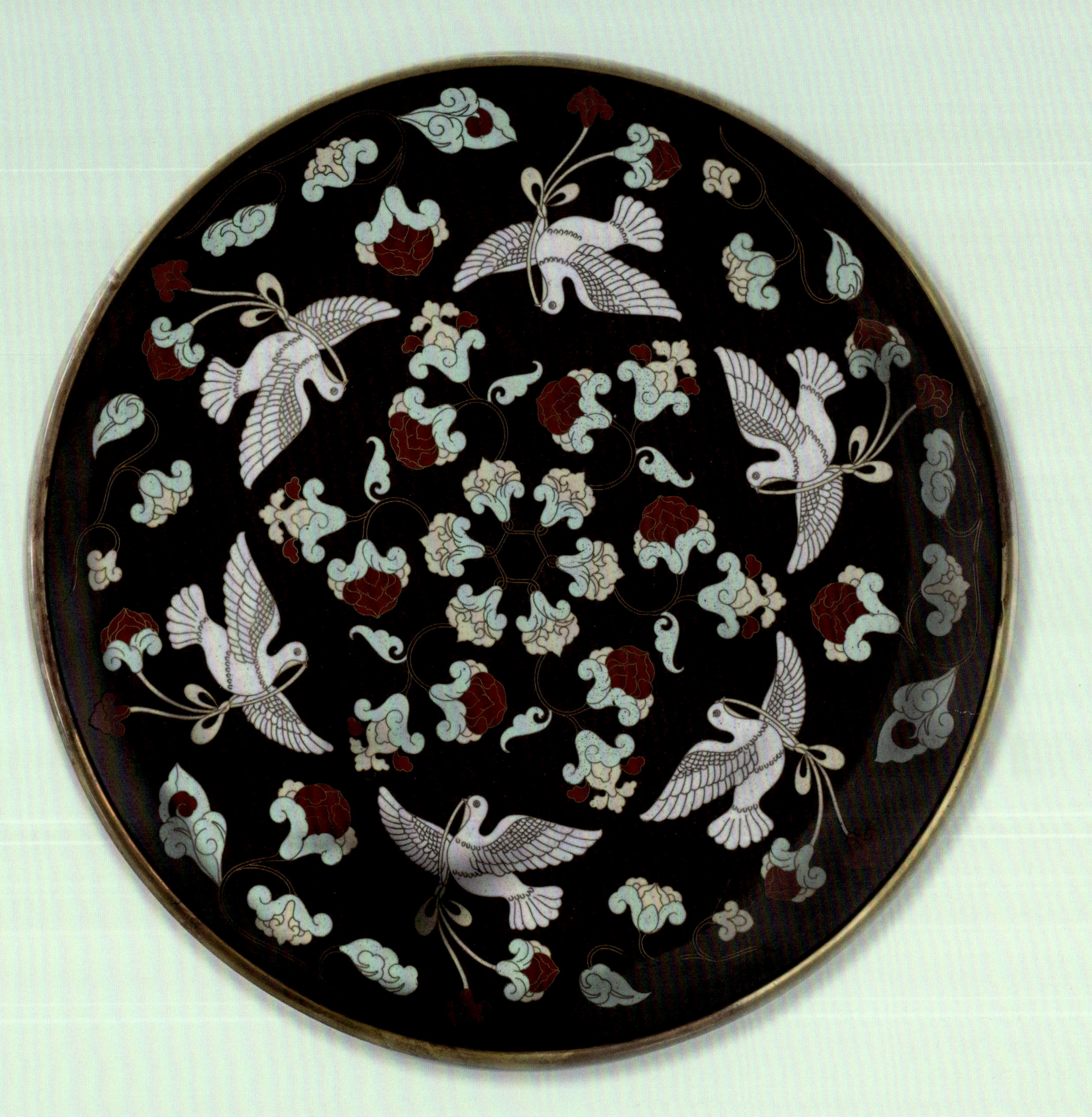

7

Building Modern China

In the Vision of Lin Huiyin (1904–1955)

Wei-Cheng Lin

Stop the blood's galloping flow.
It doesn't need to be lax,
or turn into tears.
Just take a few more turns and go upstream.
No matter how confusing it has become before your eyes,
all it needs is to rid the logic of architecture.
Let the desperately needed conclusion be slowly reached,
delayed in time—
Postpone the rational judgment—
So, the emotion will again have some hope.
—"Postpone," Lin Huiyin, May 4, 1947

Lin Huiyin 林徽因 (also spelled Lin Whei-yin, a.k.a. Phyllis Lin, 1904–1955) was the only woman among the first-generation Chinese architects who returned to China after receiving education overseas during the 1920s.[1] Widely recognized as the "first female architect" in China, her achievement, however, seems forever overshadowed by her husband and career partner, Liang Sicheng 梁思成 (Liang Ssu-cheng, 1901–1972), an architect and leading scholar who spearheaded the research of Chinese architectural history as a modern discipline.[2] Most of Lin's writings on architecture, with only a few exceptions, were coauthored with Liang. The close partnership between the architect couple was to such an extent that it is challenging to assess Lin's work without framing it in conjunction with Liang's career and his prolific scholarship as an architectural historian.

Facing: Plate with pigeons and floral patterns. See figure 7.13.

A close friend and biographer of the couple, Wilma Fairbank (1909–2002), notes the mode of collaboration between them since their time in graduate school as follows:

> During these student years [in the US], the characteristic differences in their ways of working asserted themselves. Whei [i.e., Huiyin], full of creative ideas, would start to draft a plan or elevation. . . . As the deadline approached . . . Sicheng would step in and reduce the frenzied product to a clear finished presentation in his precise and elegant draftsmanship. This kind of collaboration, in which each contributed to the architectural work of the other according to his or her own special gifts, persisted throughout their professional life together.[3]

Liang and Lin were both tremendously gifted, but between them, it appears, Lin was the one who was more creative and inspirational. While Liang is most remembered as a pioneer in modern architecture and founder of a modern discipline, Lin is praised as his indispensable helper. Lin's career was furthermore plagued and eventually truncated by a chronic lung disease that ended her life in 1955 at the age of fifty-one, leaving much promising future work undone. Over her tomb, designed by Liang, the tombstone was inscribed, "Tomb of Architect Lin Huiyin" (Jianzhushi Lin Huiyin mu 建筑师林徽因墓) (fig. 7.1). Indeed, Lin was the first Chinese woman to have been identified as an architect;[4] yet she was never offered an opportunity to show off her achievement separate from her husband's. The epitaph "architect" on her tombstone thus prompts the question as to how one should adequately write it into her legacy.[5]

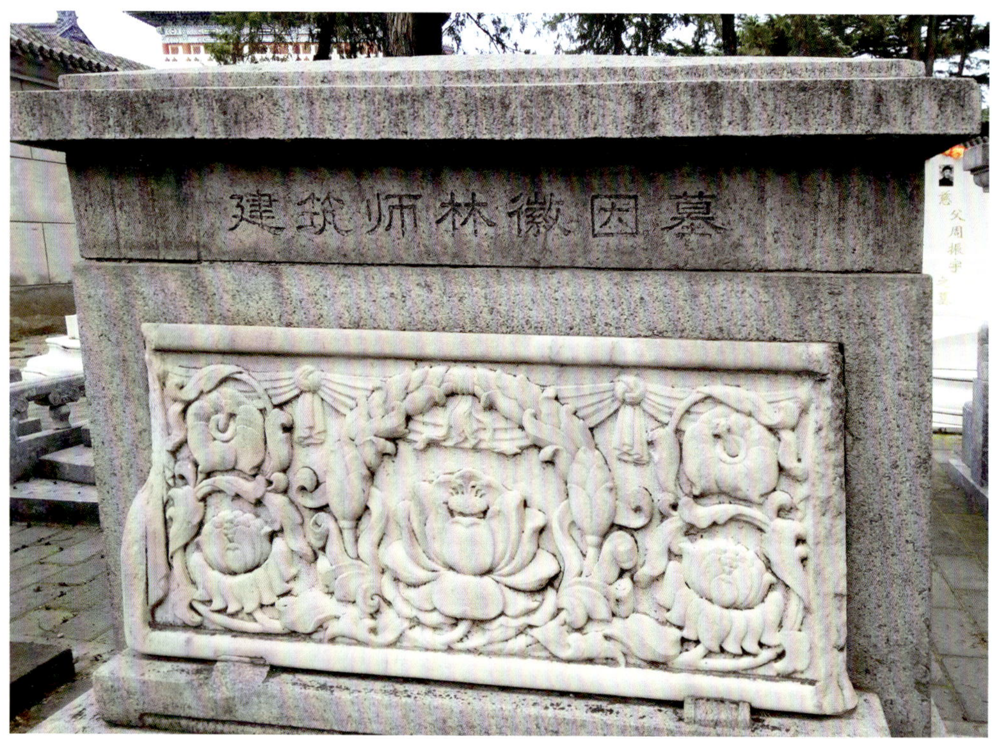

Figure 7.1. Tombstone of Lin Huiyin, designed by Liang Sicheng, 1955. Babaoshan Revolutionary Cemetery, near Beijing. Photograph by author.

Some scholars have tried to answer the question by arguing that Lin must have played a more significant role in Liang's career as an architect and scholar. Citing several people close to the couple, including Lin and Liang's son, Liang Congjie 梁从诫 (1932–2010), those scholars are convinced that Lin was indeed the chief contributor behind what passed as Liang's work.[6] This argument is also echoed in Lin's uncompromising pursuit of an architectural career as an independent woman. The modernist stance in both her work and gender identity, to many, was associated with the spirits and inspirations of the May Fourth Movement during the 1920s.[7] Young intellectuals then perceived modernity that prioritized democracy, rationality, and science as a rupture of Chinese history and a path forward with no return to the tradition.[8] It is therefore fair to portray Lin as representative of the new blood of the society, regardless of the gender, that spurred critical and independent thinking about China's past, present, and future. As such, it begs clarifications for Lin's inability to claim her own standing in the field. In particular, in the passages quoted in the epigraph from a poem, entitled "Postpone" ("Zhanhuan" 展缓), Lin brushed aside the "logic of architecture" and advocated for the use of emotion, rather than rationality, as hope for the future appeared all the more surprising. In fact, published on May 4, 1947, the poem no longer bore the same youthful vigor and rationality of the 1920s that weaponized China in making its transition into the modern era. Written in the dawn of the People's Republic of China (PRC), founded in 1949, the sentiment of the poem instead seems to suggest a somewhat different perception and vision of modern China. The question thus also arises as to how the shift of the political climate would have any bearing on the ways in which Lin's gender identity factored into her work and vision.

To frontload my argument, Lin's career, to a great extent, reveals how early twentieth-century modernism subsumed gender issues, unintentionally leaving the male/female divide unquestioned. While Lin was in the position to define herself as a female architect in the male-dominated field of architecture in the first decades of China's modern period, she struggled to assert her subjective self, separate from her husband. As will be demonstrated through her own writings, Lin as the modernist was expected to think and write about China's building tradition in ways that informed her husband's modernist approach (which contributes to the remarkable similarity between their scholarships), and her gender identity was only fostered in her work when she suspended the "logic of architecture" later in her career when Chinese modernism had all but disappeared. It is thus instrumental for our purpose to observe how her identity and vision of modern China as the first Chinese female architect transformed over time. As Lin's career was fastened to the broader ambition of her generation to build modern China, her vision provides us a unique point of access to the modern construct of China's architectural history.

Chinese Modern Woman Lin Huiyin

Born into privilege, Lin had a unique experience as a Chinese woman of her time. She was the favorite child of her father, Lin Changmin 林长民 (1876–1924), a scholar and influential diplomat. Huiyin attended a girl's school established by British missionaries in China, before entering St. Mary's Collegiate School in London in 1920 at the age of sixteen. In Europe, she met famous scholars and intellectuals, learned about poetry, and most importantly, became fascinated with architecture when traveling across Europe with her father. Returning to China, Huiyin was enthusiastic about her newly discovered interest and persuaded her future husband Liang Sicheng to pursue architecture as a profession. In 1924, Lin and Liang embarked on a journey to the United States for an opportunity to study architecture, a field still relatively unknown in China. They both entered the University of Pennsylvania later that year. Sicheng was successfully accepted into the architectural program, while Huiyin chose, involuntarily, to enroll in the School of Fine Arts after realizing that the School of Architecture did not admit female students. Still, Lin managed to acquire knowledge and valuable training in architecture by taking a part-time assistantship on the architectural design staff, and again a part-time instructorship to teach architectural design in 1926–27.[9]

After graduation in 1927, they were both employed as the assistant to Paul P. Cret (1876–1945), professor at the University of Pennsylvania and then a leading architect in the Beaux-Arts tradition of architecture, until they decided to return to China later in the year. In 1928, then a married couple, Lin and Liang began their professional career at the Northeastern University (Dongbei daxue 东北大学) in Shenyang (a.k.a. Mukden). Liang was appointed the chair of the Department of Architectural Engineering, and Lin, a professor of architecture. The architect couple also took on their first architectural commissions then.[10] In 1932, Japanese troops made inroads in their invasion of Manchuria, forcing the university to close. The couple had already been relocated to Beijing one year earlier, in 1931.

The trajectory of Lin's upbringing both in family and education was nothing but extraordinary in her time. At a young age, she had the luxury of experiencing the outside world when China was still struggling to reorient itself to the new global order and modernity. Lin's family background and education enabled her to decide where she wanted to go and who she wanted to be in life, concurrently taking responsibility for her self-fulfillment. To a great extent, Lin exemplified the burgeoning individualism of the 1920s, or the May Fourth Movement, responding to the call for a new definition of womanhood in China's modern era.[11] When Nobel laureate Rabindranath Tagore (1861–1941) came to China and gave a lecture at the Peking University during his two-week visit in 1924, Lin served as his interpreter. Apparently charmed by the young lady and very fond of her company, Tagore penned a poem to describe Lin:

> The blue of the sky fell in love with the green of the earth.
> The breeze between them sighs, "Alas!"[12]

Youthful and beautiful, indeed, Lin was seen as the fresh air in modern China unbound and unfettered by the cultural and societal expectations of her gender engrained in old China.

The Modernist Lin Huiyin

However, Lin, like Liang, was not an anti-traditionalist. It has been well documented that the intellectual profile of both Lin and Liang was shaped by Liang's father, Liang Qichao 梁启超 (1873–1929), a prominent politician and thinker in the early Republican period. Described as "the mind of modern China,"[13] the elder Liang openly called for a fuller, but not blind, acceptance of Western learning and cultural ideology, claiming that Chinese cultural and intellectual traditions had both lost the battle in their position and validity in the modern, global context. By the early 1920s, however, he was disillusioned with Western culture after witnessing the ravages of World War I. Instead, Liang believed it was extremely important for China to resurrect its traditions by resuscitating the longstanding ideals with pragmatism. The mandate of the new nation, to him, was to quickly recognize the new global order and historicism while revamping the native culture as the critical foundation, a stance also shared by the young couple.[14]

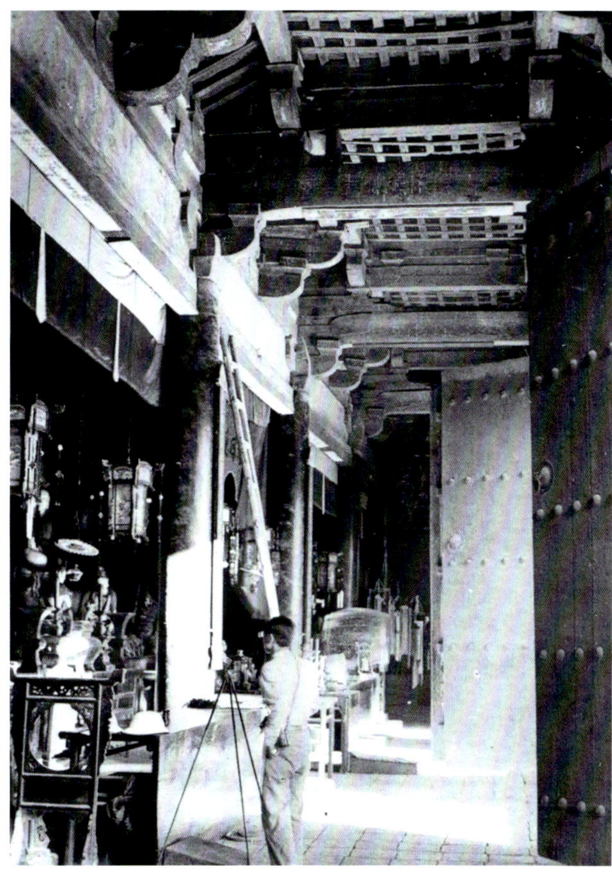

Figure 7.2. Liang Sicheng conducting fieldwork at the main Buddha Hall of Foguang Monastery, Mount Wutai, Shanxi, 1937. From Liang Ssu-Cheng, *Tuxiang Zhongguo jianzhushi* (A Pictorial History of Chinese Architecture), edited by Wilma Fairbank and translated by Liang Congjie, included in *Liang Sicheng quanji* (Complete Collection of Liang Sicheng) (Beijing: Zhongguo gongye chubanshe, 2001), vol. 8, fig. 24d.

Perfectly bilingual, Lin and Liang discovered their cultural heritage while being away from their native land. Lin, a frequent visitor to the art museum, found herself often awed by the Chinese art collection at the Penn Museum. When looking at two tricolor ceramic horses from the Tang dynasty, she felt "a sudden rediscovery of a China that has been lost."[15] Yet this rediscovery did not alienate her as much as urge her to appreciate her native culture anew. Sicheng also experienced a similar appreciation in 1925 when his father mailed him a reprint of a newly discovered book, *Yingzao fashi* 营造法式 (Building Standards), an official building treatise compiled during the Northern Song dynasty (960–1279) and promulgated in 1103.[16] In his accompanying letter, the elder Liang noted: "A thousand years ago to have a masterpiece like this . . . what a glory to the culture of our past!"[17] Then learning about the history of Western architecture at the University of Pennsylvania, Liang was impressed and intrigued by the book's existence but completely baffled by its abstruse content that is, in fact, an essential part of the building tradition of his own cultural heritage. Although Liang could not fully comprehend the treatise until much later, the bicultural approach to the history of Chinese architecture cultivated during their time in the United States was key to their understanding and writing of Chinese architectural history throughout their careers.

After moving to Beijing in 1931, Lin and Liang joined the Institute for Research in Chinese Architecture (Zhongguo Yingzao Xueshe 中国营造学社; the Institute hereafter), established in 1929 by Zhu Qiqian 朱启钤 (1872–1964), a retired official and erudite of architecture in the early Republican period. From 1931 until 1947, Lin and Liang, along with other colleagues of the Institute, undertook extensive fieldwork in a series of research trips throughout the country to survey and photograph surviving ancient structures (figs. 7.2 and 7.3), interrupted only by the Sino-Japanese War.[18] The undertaking

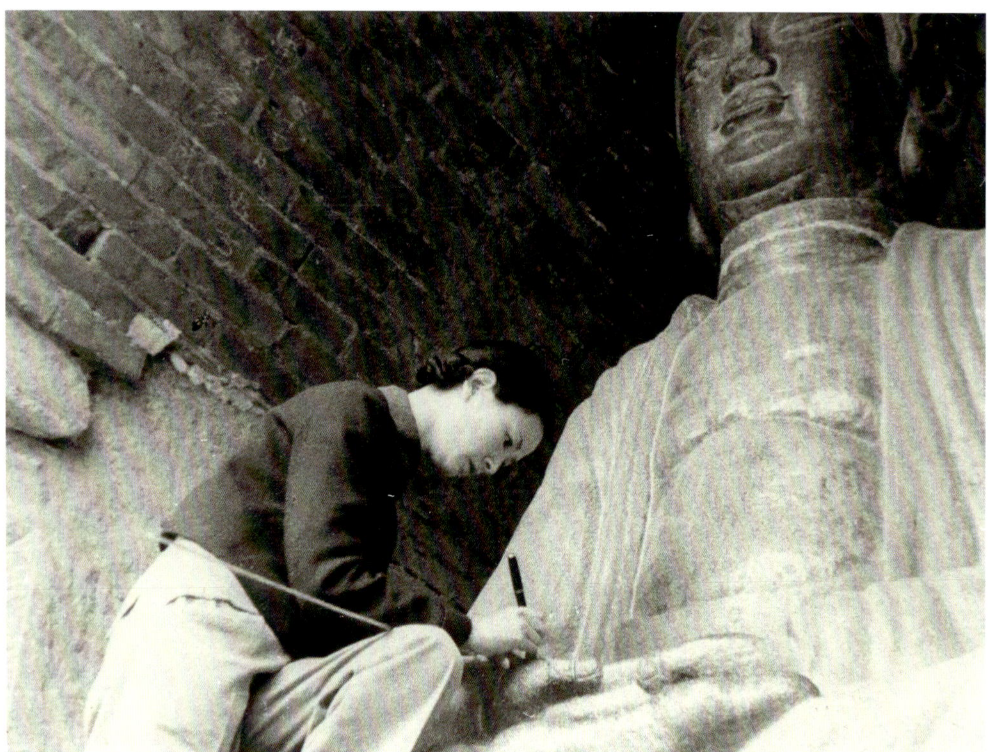

Figure 7.3. Lin Huiyin working at a local temple outside Xi'an, Shaanxi, 1936. From Qinghua daxue jianzhu xueyuan, *Jianzhushi Lin Huiyin* (The Architect, Lin Huiyin) (Beijing: Qinghua daxue chubanshe, 2004), 167. Photograph by permission of School of Architecture, Tsinghua University.

was unprecedented, in particular its empirical research based on the on-site investigation as a critical method to intellectualize the building tradition and bring the knowledge of it into modern China. The firsthand investigation of the extant historical buildings also greatly facilitated Lin and Liang's study and understanding of the Northern Song building treatise. In addition, Liang made an effort to consult master craftsmen then in charge of maintaining the palatial buildings at the former Forbidden City (reappropriated into the National Palace Museum in 1925).[19] While *Building Standards* remained obscure, in 1934, Liang published his annotations of the official building treatise of the Qing dynasty (1644–1911), entitled *Qing gongbu gongcheng zuofa* 清工部工程做法, or *Building Methods [Issued by] the Department of Work of the Qing Dynasty*, with diagrams that illustrate the basic forms and principles of Qing palatial architecture.[20]

Through fieldwork and research, Liang was convinced that the timber-frame structure was the most essential part of China's building history (figs. 7.4 and 7.5). The fieldwork led by Liang was planned to comb all historical sites for surviving wooden structures that could help reconstruct the history of timber-frame structures—how they originated, evolved, and developed over time. Lin and Liang's early career was preoccupied primarily with writing such a history. However, it was Lin, rather than Liang, who first elucidated clearly the timber-frame structure in terms of its basic components and features and explored its historical significance in a theoretical framework through her writings.

Her article, "On Some Characteristics of Chinese Architecture," published in 1932, was the first such writing.[21] Briefly, in the article Lin proposes to observe Chinese timber-frame structures in a tripartite construction, consisting of the foundation, post-and-lintel

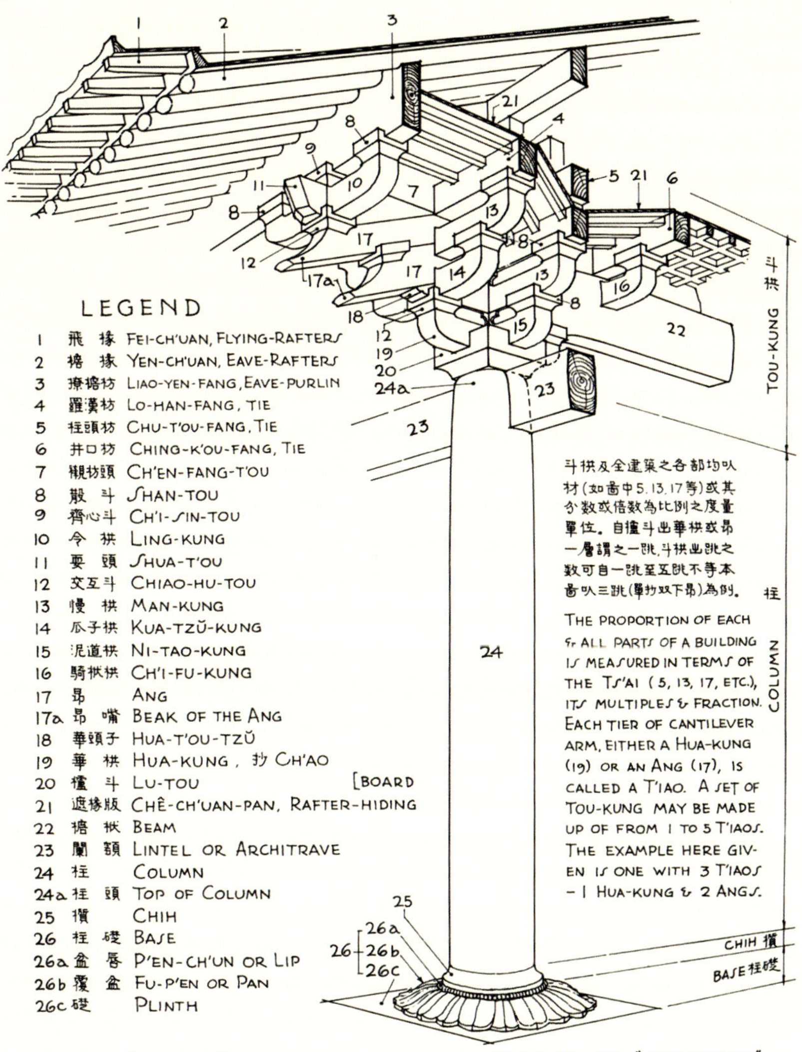

Figure 7.4. A diagram showing the bracketing system that connects the roof truss and the column. From Liang Ssu-Cheng (Liang Sicheng), *Tuxiang Zhongguo jianzhushi*, fig. 2.

Figure 7.5. Principal parts of a Chinese timber-frame building. From Liang Ssu-Cheng (Liang Sicheng), *Tuxiang Zhongguo jianzhushi*, fig. 1.

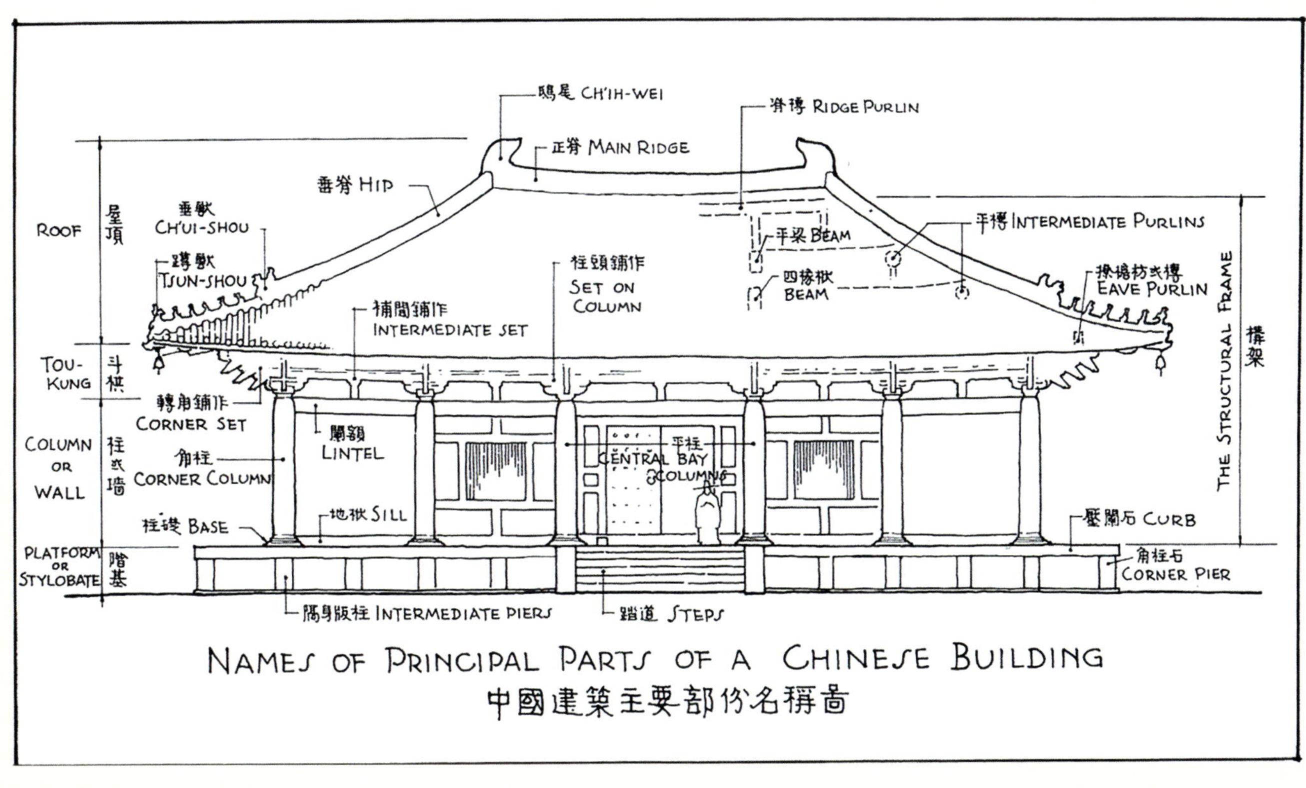

structure, and roof. The foundation elevates a building on a solid base that separates it from the moisture-laden ground while providing its architecture with a monumental presentation. The post-and-lintel "framing system" (*jiagou zhi* 架构制) builds the "skeleton," so to speak, to support the entire structure, thus freeing all the partition walls from bearing weight. Finally, the roof truss comprising the main ridge pole and sloping sides caps the structure to complete the entire framework. The degree of complexity with which a timber-frame structure was built varied from period to period, but the principles that underline the structure remained unchanged. The timber frame was straightforward, structurally sound, and could stand as long as its material permitted. Its form was decided not by a predetermined shape but by the ways in which the structure was built to meet its function. The structural clarity and rationality observed in the timber-frame tradition, Lin argued, are not dissimilar to the principles that govern modern structures built in concrete and steel. They are both characterized by a skeletal structure and non-bearing walls, enabling the building master/architect to design the exterior and allocate the interior space flexibly.

"On Some Characteristics of Chinese Architecture" was the first theoretical essay ever written about China's building tradition. Most significantly, it was written in the analytical terms and vocabulary adopted from the West. In 1926, still uncertain about how traditional Chinese architecture was compared with its Western counterpart, Lin stated:

> During my travels [through Europe in 1920] I dreamed for the first time of studying architecture. The splendor of the classics of the modern west inspired me, filled me with desire to carry some back to my country. We need the theories of sound construction which enable [our] buildings to stand for centuries.[22]

In 1932, Lin was very certain about the merits of China's building tradition vis-à-vis those of Western architecture. As explained in the article, she characterizes a good timber-frame building with three fundamental qualities: utility (*shiyong* 适用), firmness (*jiangu* 坚固), and beauty (*meiguan* 美观).[23] These three qualities match almost verbatim the three elements of a good building proposed by Roman architect Vitruvius (c. 80–70 BCE—after 15 CE), namely *firmitas*, *utilitas*, and *venustas*.[24] More explicitly than Vitruvius, however, Lin posited that the beauty of architecture has resulted from the building's structural integrity (i.e., firmness) meeting its functional needs (utility), which was fully materialized in traditional Chinese architecture. She reiterated the similar idea again in the "introduction" written for Liang's 1934 annotated transcription of the Qing official building treatise: "The beauty in architecture could not exist without the rational, functional, and practical structure."[25] The structure, additionally, should be designed to reflect its architectonic functionality; building materials should be applied following their particular capacities; and excessive ornamentation should be strictly avoided. All of these are the "prerequisites" for achieving "architectural beauty" (*jianzhu mei* 建筑美).[26]

This comparative, or bicultural, approach that recontextualizes China's timber-frame architecture thus re-historicizes its tradition in the historical narrative of the newly restructured global world. In this light, Lin and Liang's endeavor in both fieldwork and writing was itself a project of Chinese modernism in their efforts to transform not only the study of Chinese architectural history into a modern discipline but also historical architecture into an art, an expression, and a cultural heritage that could still be relevant in the present and appreciated anew. This art, as Lin argues, could be comprehended through the terms of Greco-Roman architecture, but concurrently comparable with the then ultramodern steel-and-concrete architecture in its building principles and tenets. However, one would be hard-pressed to claim that Lin owns the sole authorship of these field-defining writings without giving due credit to Liang. In fact, neither Lin's nor Liang's writings reveal any intent to distinguish one from the other. It seems, as suggested by some, that only when one recognizes Lin's modernist stance could one begin to appreciate the contribution of her rational structuralist approach, perhaps more than Liang's, to the building of the theoretical foundation of the new modern discipline.[27] Lin appears to have identified herself with the kind of modernist portrayed in her architectural writings.

A photo (fig. 7.6) taken in 1936, shows Lin and Liang sitting on the roof of the Hall of Prayers for Good Harvest (Qinian dian 祈年殿) at the Temple of Heaven (Tiantan 天坛) in Beijing, then renamed Beiping 北平. During 1935–36, historical structures in Beiping underwent extensive restorations, commissioned by the central government then in Nanjing.[28] Liang, serving on the committee that supervised the restoration, visited several of the buildings under restoration with his wife, as seen in the photo. The Hall of Prayers for Good Harvest was the building where the emperor performed state religious rites dedicated to heaven regularly.[29] The ritual building until modern times thus witnessed the succession of emperors enacting the role of the empire's patriarch in the dedicatory rite. On that day when the photo was taken, Lin, as she recalled years later, felt great pride in being "the first woman ever to stand on top of the Temple of Heaven."[30] Wearing a *qipao*, a type of feminine body-hugging dress popular in modern China, Lin in the photo unapologetically showed off her femininity and, more importantly, her identity as a modern woman by mounting atop the solemn building within the massive imperial complex laden with symbolic meanings of China's patriarchal society and cultural past. Her stance transgressed both symbolically and physically the spatial boundary of her gender in traditional society. Yet simultaneously it also suggests illustriously that, more than her husband, Lin embodied the ideology of China's early modernism—as a female architect.

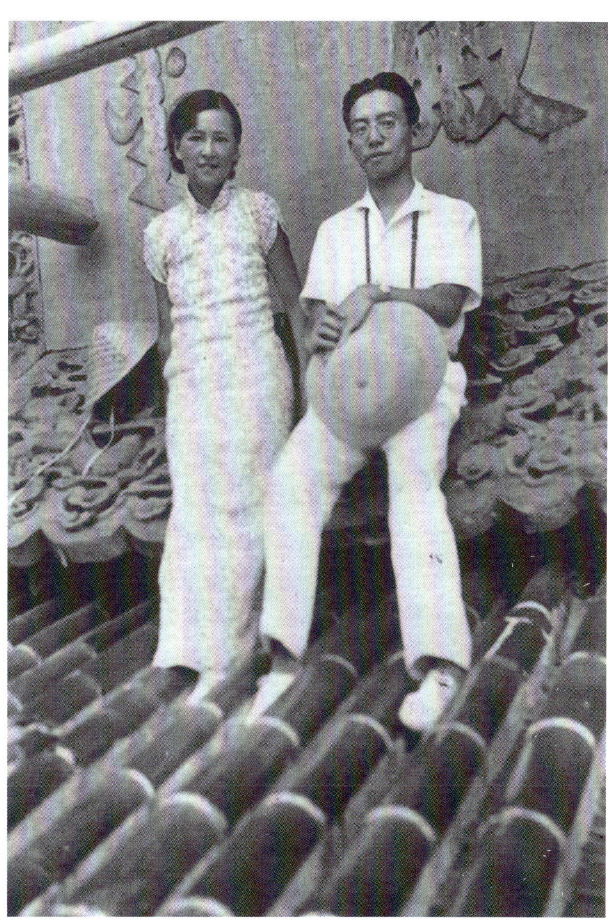

Figure 7.6. Lin Huiyin and Liang Sicheng on the roof of the Hall of Prayers for Good Harvest (Qinian dian) at the Temple of Heaven (Tiantan) in Beijing. From Qinghua daxue jianzhu xueyuan, *Jianzhushi Lin Huiyin*, 164. Photograph by permission of School of Architecture, Tsinghua University.

The Female Writer Lin Huiyin

The restoration of the Hall of Prayers for Good Harvest was part of the "Plan for Restoring Cultural Relics in the Former Capital" (*Jiudu wenwu zhengli jihua* 旧都文物整理计划), devised by the Nanjing government to transform the cultural past of the imperial capital into the indivisible "cultural relics" (*wenwu* 文物) of modern China.[31] As the country's premier modern architects and historians, Lin and Liang's involvement in the project was expected. However, standing on top of the imperial building and captured in the photograph, one wonders what exactly went through the couple's mind when facing the ancient, and now defunct, capital city that required a great deal of effort to bring it into the modern era. Or were they thinking about the same thing?

One may never be able to find out the answer; nonetheless, Lin left some clues that arouse speculation. While working as a professional architect and scholar, Lin also developed a second career as a writer. By the early 1930s, she was already known for her creative writings in prose, poetry, and drama. Interestingly, in her literary work, one can sense some sentiments toward architecture quite different from what one may expect from the modernist Lin Huiyin. In 1935, for instance, Lin published a poem, "On the Gate Tower" ("Chenglou shang" 城楼上), in which she evokes the ambiance of ancient architecture through juxtaposed scenes of an old city viewed from the vantage point on a gate tower. Its final verses read:

> Who's being talkative again?
> You prefer this city wall,
> the ancient tombs, the solemn dirges,
> wildflowers blooming amid tall grasses.
> Fine, I won't speak any more
> of the past. Think only of us on the gate tower,
> today . . .
> White doves,
> (Surely you know they are white doves)
> flying before us.[32]

The solemn dirges that could be heard on the gate tower eulogize the ancient tombs and walls, evoking the poetic sense of the past architecture, which continues to linger in the present. This poem was written one year before Lin's heroic ascendance onto the imperial building in 1936. At that moment captured in the photo, could it be possible that Lin called to mind the sensorial and provocative image that arose from the poem? This is an unanswerable question, of course, but it seems plausible to suggest two different visions of China's historical architecture in Lin's writings. On the one hand, as a modernist, Lin envisioned Beijing, the former imperial capital, with its historical buildings restored and architectural beauty preserved; on the other hand, Lin as a female writer seems more interested in exploring the ambiance, memories, and history that could still be seen, heard, or experienced in its ancient monuments.

Indeed, alongside her modernist rationality, Lin also took a much more perceptual and experiential approach toward the history of Chinese architecture. In 1932, she penned an article entitled "Miscellaneous Records of Architecture in Beiping's Suburbs," published in the *Journal of the Institute for Research in Chinese Architecture*.[33] To begin, she reminds readers that historical buildings like those that could still be seen around Beijing are not simply structures; some are part of historical sites, and some others, traces of oblivious memories. The "aura" (*yi* 意) of each building is necessarily tied to its "lives" through time. On the point of "aura," Lin further explains: "Whether it is a soaring ancient city tower or dilapidated palatial building foundation, the soul [of its architecture] is always recounting, or even eulogizing, unnoticeably, time's untrustworthy rise and fall. . . . The aura it imparts is 'poetic' and 'picturesque' . . . [but] there's still something in it that transpires beyond poetry and picture . . . [for which we could call the aura of architecture] 'architecturesque' [*jianzhu yi* 建筑意]."[34]

The idea of "architecturesque" seems diametrically opposite from that of "beauty of architecture" (*jianzhu mei*) elucidated in Lin's theorization of China's classical architecture. While the former takes ambiance as the essential quality of historical architecture that should be preserved as is, the latter is embedded in the architectonic rationality. To be sure, approaching architecture from the perspective of architecturesque was no less modernist since it also involved reconfiguring the building form and its cultural referent in a modern context. Yet as Lin was lauded as the first scholar to theorize China's traditional architecture through the lens of structural rationalism by her colleagues—including her husband—in the primarily male-dominated field, this exploration of poetic and picturesque qualities of China's building tradition in her other writings seems to indicate her ambivalent relation with the traces of China's architectural past and, I should argue, a sanctioned recuperation of her gender-specific viewpoint.

After joining the Institute in 1931, Lin Huiyin participated in most of the Institute's architectural expeditions, many of which were taken in difficult circumstances or required traveling for hundreds of miles to locate the gems of historical architecture. For her, being able to roam freely across the country, no different from her male colleagues, was itself a remarkable feat as a woman. In addition to reporting the investigation in situ, Lin, for example, wrote about local people and kids flocking to see them using gadgets to photograph, measure, and document old structures and building details to such a point that it became difficult for them to work.[35] Lin and her colleagues, nonetheless, took satisfaction in confirming to local folks the historical value of the old structures that they and their ancestors had treasured for generations.

More than her male colleagues, Lin was conscientious about the urban/rural, modern /traditional, and scholar/peasant divides in the construct of their modernist stance. In 1934, while conducting fieldwork through Shanxi province with Liang and other colleagues of the Institute, Lin wrote an essay entitled "Outside the Window" (Chuangzi yiwai 窗子以外), in which she contemplates the modernist gaze by using a window that divides inside and outside as an analogy.[36] Addressing an imaginary modern urban scholar, she wrote, "You are still seated inside a window, whether a train's, a car's, or an inn's, as well as an invisible window constructed out of habit which encloses you." In a self-reflexive manner, she continued: "Yes, many fashionable scholars often proudly put on the air of an 'investigator' wearing a pair of scientific glasses. They occasionally stop by a strange place to observe; nevertheless, the invisible window still exists."[37] The pair of scientific glasses might help them see the building tradition anew, but they may never comprehend things outside the window, regardless of how many different ways they tried, as Lin remarked at the end of the essay.

After their research expedition in Shanxi, Lin and Liang published the fieldwork report to bring to light several historical structures that survived in the region. The report focused on the structural analysis, documenting the buildings they investigated objectively.[38] Concurrently, Lin also published a separate essay about the journey of the fieldwork in a contrasting tenor:

> In the past ten days everything we have seen is a picture, and everyday an ancient tale to be sung and recited. . . . In order to visit those ancient sites, we have walked a lot and are moved by the rise and decline of the past and the present. Reading inscriptions on the stelae buried in wild grass or coming across a bodhisattva's hands or smile amid a brick pile—all of these stimulate uncommon feelings.[39]

This is neither a self-orientalization nor a learned nostalgia of the bygone past. Rather, it was a perception of history from a different perspective: Lin's own attempt to negate the window. The result was an alternative narrative, or vision, of China's building history by subverting the priority of objectivity to craft a unique position in order to locate the agency of architecture otherwise left unexplored, or dismissed, in the modernist (male-dominated) discourse of Chinese architectural history.

Unlike in these "other" writings, Lin never had an equal opportunity to assert herself with a particular female vision and subjectivity in her partnership with Liang. In 1936, she wrote in a letter to Wilma Fairbank that she had made every effort to help her husband's work and research in her way, "though no one would ever believe its truth."[40] And this was at the brink of the outbreak of the Sino-Japanese War, which would last until 1945.

Wartime China until 1949

The war interrupted all fieldwork of the Institute and forced it to relocate to southwest China, first to Kunming, the capital city of Yunnan province, and two years later to a rural village, Lizhuang, in the Sichuan province, where the Institute became affiliated with the Academia Sinica (Zhongyan Yanjiuyuan 中央研究院), the nation's central research institute. In a letter dated 1942, to Fu Sinian 傅斯年 (1896–1950),[41] a renowned scholar and close friend, Lin wrote:

> I feel I've wasted thirty years of [my career], which is like a bounced check full of empty promises. I waited for my children to grow up, so I could work in full strength

> for a few years. Now the war forced us to stay in this miserable place where the daily living was reduced nearly to poverty, and I, again, wasted another five years that could've been great. Recently, I have suffered from my illness; the level of my physical and intellectual energy was poor. My scholarly work can only suffer, too.[42]

Lin's pneumonia flared up once again, and the living conditions further exacerbated it, taking a heavy toll on her body. In retrospect, however, the prolonged wartime exile was decisive in Lin's career. In leaving cultural and metropolitan centers such as Beijing or Nanjing, the sense of displacement reoriented the research of the Institute.[43] With China slackening its grip on modernism, the reorientation also steered Liang's research away from the history of imperial/official architecture built mainly in China's central plain. Liang turned to the architectural species in China's peripheral regions, including those of ethnic minorities. Despite the hardship, Lin was finally able to breathe some fresh air, seeing aspirations outside the "window." She noted how "the sun steals in curious angles into one's aching sense of awareness of quiet and beauty"[44] even under the desperate circumstance. Lin became enchanted by the beauty of the vernacular and residential architecture. She further developed her interest in the art of architectural decoration, based on those motifs and patterns in extant building structures and Buddhist caves found in her past fieldwork. None of these had hitherto received any serious scholarly attention as legitimate research topics; yet Lin's exploration of those materials during this period and subsequent scholarship shaped by her unique sensibility would later become one of her most important contributions to the history of Chinese architecture.

After the end of World War II in 1945, the civil wars between the nationalist and communist regimes continued the political turmoil. Modernism could no longer hold the reins of the shifting cultural ideology from prewar to postwar China. In the new political climate and cultural context, Lin and Liang's family returned to Beijing in 1946. Before the end of the year, Liang Sicheng was invited to give several lectures in the United States and also be the Chinese representative on the International Design Board in charge of building the UN's headquarters in New York.[45] Lin was entrusted with founding the first architectural department at Tsinghua University. While it appeared that Lin and Liang had resumed their scholarly lives after returning to Beijing, Lin seems to have a different mindset. There was no longer an impulse to build a modern China as during the 1930s; rather, she called for a more moderate pace, "so, the emotion will again have some hope," as she wrote in the 1947 poem, "Postpone," quoted at the outset of the essay. Indeed, a change of pace became necessary during the advent of the founding of the PRC in 1949.

During the war, many of the projects devised by the central government in Nanjing to renovate the former capital were halted. As soon as the war was over, the municipal city government of Beijing (then Beiping) went back to the drawing table and sketched new plans in order to continue the prewar endeavor, which aimed at transforming the city into a modern capital of China's historical heritage. The endeavor, however, was met with much criticism that considered continuing to capitalize on Beijing's cultural past as wasteful and unpractical, since one could never resurrect the outdated tradition.[46] In

1948, likely as a reaction to the debate about Beijing's future, Lin wrote a poem, "The Twilight of the Ancient City":

> I saw the gazes of the ancient city bathed in rays of the setting sun.
> One gate-tower gazes at another one.
> They pay no attention to the glazed roofs of palatial buildings between them.
> The hustle and bustle of ten streets are below them.
> Pedestrians like ants can be seen numerously.
>
> I saw the gazes of the ancient city bathed in the twilight of the setting sun.
> Crows caw while flying in a circle.
> Dilapidated gardens and ancient cypress trees still tenaciously persevere but in exhaustion.[47]

In this ancient city, there are no poetic images of "ancient tombs" and "solemn dirges" depicted vividly in Lin's "On the Gate Tower," written in 1935. Instead, "dilapidated gardens" and "ancient cypress trees" now signaled the twilight of the city.

In December 1948, about one month before the People's Liberation Army (PLA) sieged Beijing, an official approached Liang Sicheng, requesting a list of historical buildings and cultural artifacts that should be protected from armed conflicts. He later recalled: "I had no idea of what the Communist Party was all about, but on that day, I fell in love with it instantly."[48] Like her husband, Lin felt emotional about this impending regime change that might give some hope to the ancient imperial city.

Her Vision: After 1949

After the founding of a new China in 1949, the highly regarded architect and scholar couple were frequently consulted by the leaders of the Communist Party. They were invited to serve on many national committees and requested to design, most notably, the national emblem, a monument dedicated to the People's Heroes, and a new urban plan for Beijing, now designated as the capital. While Lin and Liang shared some ambitions with the Party leaders, they also quickly realized that their modernist approach to architecture would need to adjust to the Party's proletarian worldview and socialist ideology. Standing on the rostrum of Tiananmen, Liang was told, Chairman Mao once looked at the city and said, in the future, "we'll see a forest of chimneys from here!"[49] Rather than being restored as a modernized historical city as Lin and Liang had worked hard to achieve before, Beijing was to be rebuilt into the political center and industrial base of the nation.

Working to modernize and thus preserve China's building tradition throughout his career, Liang tried every means he could to challenge Mao's vision of Beijing. It is well documented that in 1950 Liang Sicheng, teamed with Chen Zanxiang (Chen Chan-siang, a.k.a. Charles Chen, 1916–2001), a British-trained expert in urban design, submitted a proposal that strongly disapproved of the overuse and industrialization of the historical Beijing.[50] Instead, they proposed a new administrative center to be built in the western suburb to preserve the ancient city; it was famously known as the "Liang-Chen Plan" (fig. 7.7).[51] The two experts argued that to revive Beijing as a historical city, it needed "decentralization, clear zoning, balancing between development and preservation, and conservation of the imperial city on its north-south axis" that has dictated the cityscape of the imperial capital for hundreds of years.[52] In the end, however, the Party still chose to build the new administrative and political center in the heart of the old imperial city while reconfiguring the rest of the city such that it could increase the efficiency in terms of mobilizing labor and industrial production.

The setback of the "Liang-Chen Plan" was more than a disappointment to Liang. He was further criticized as guilty of attempting to "museumize" or "fossilize" Beijing, rather than conceiving its future progressively, an accusation that would later haunt Liang repeatedly until his death during the Cultural Revolution in 1972. Lin was in unison with her husband in blueprinting a future Beijing after 1949; yet they could do nothing but hopelessly witness the destruction of old Beijing's city walls and gate towers

Figure 7.7. The location of the new administrative center to the west of Beijing, proposed in the "Liang-Chen Plan," 1950. From Liang Sicheng and Chen Zhanxiang, "Guanyu zhongyang renmin zhengfu xingzheng zhongxinqu weizhi de jianyi" (Suggestion for the Location of the People's Central Government), in Liang, *Liang Sicheng quanji*, vol. 5, fig. 1.

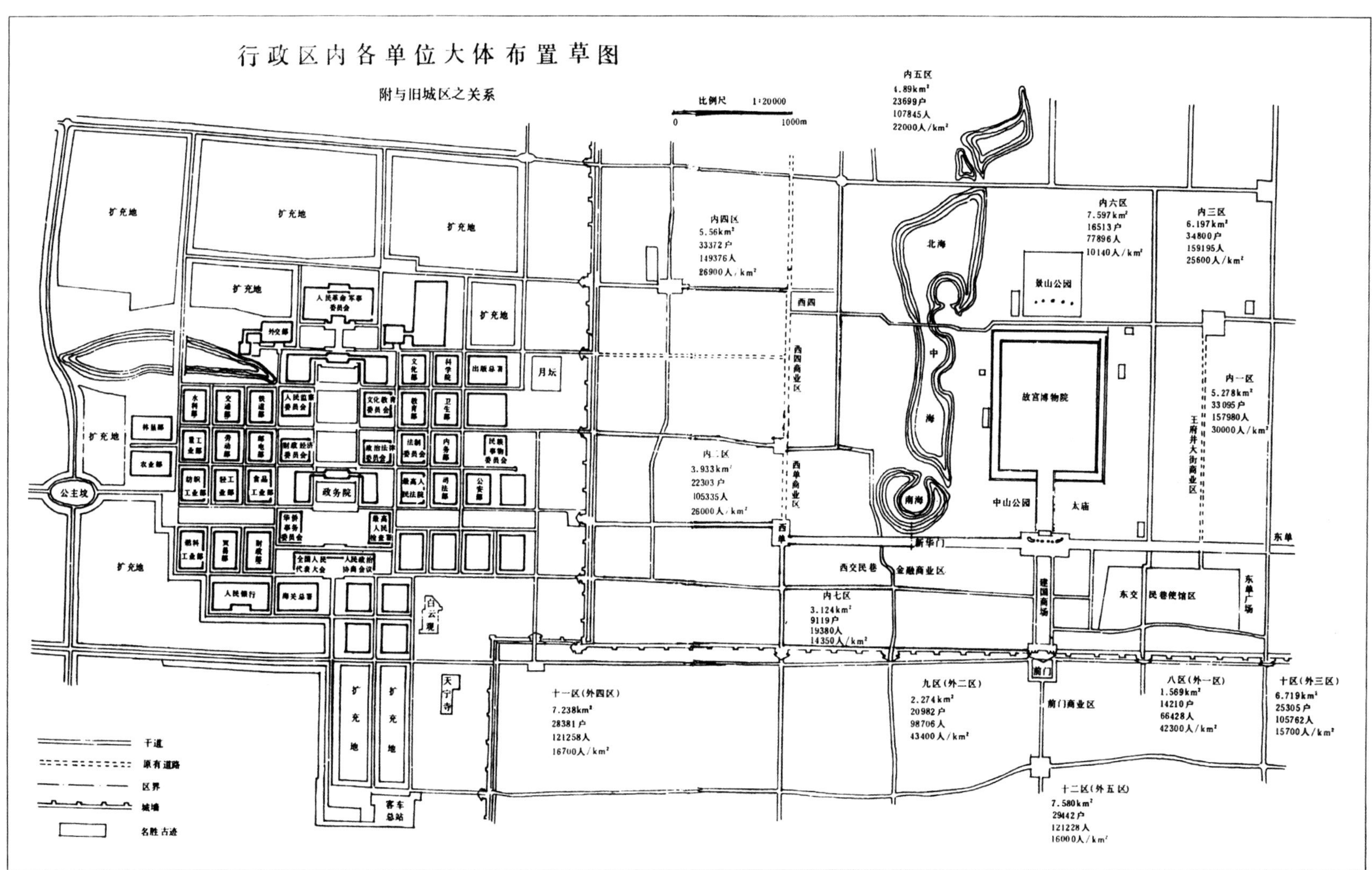

that determined the fate of old Beijing. Lin and Liang were both forced to compromise with the Party's policies in their approach to China's modern architecture under the new political climate. In an article published by the couple in 1951, they wrote: "Beijing, the capital of People's China, is an extremely old city, but also an extremely young city. . . . Today, Beijing is a new capital basking *in the dawn light* vigorously welcoming Socialism."[53] The broader political reality dictated both Lin's and Liang's deliberations of China's architecture, as well as their professional and scholarly productions. However, different from Liang, who continued to conceive China's future architecture in terms of modernist language and structural framework, Lin had a different vision.[54]

In an unpublished manuscript, entitled "A Draft of the Preliminary Research on Border Decorative Patterns in Dunhuang [Caves]," Lin explores the significance of what is otherwise a relatively insignificant aspect in the history of Chinese architecture.[55] The decorative patterns carved or painted on the structural components that border non-bearing walls or interior spaces, though not as critical as the skeletal framework in scaffolding a building structure, Lin argues, reveal to us much more substantively how the art of Chinese architecture developed. China's timber-frame structure is notorious for its persistence throughout history without major changes.[56] In comparison, architectural decoration (*jianzhu zhuangshi* 建筑装饰) designed by local craftsmen shows stylistic shifts and changes with genuine creativity in accordance with regional practices in different periods (fig. 7.8). Unfortunately, Lin could not complete the manuscript before her passing in 1954, leaving much of the result of her research unwritten. The incomplete manuscript, published for the first time by Tsinghua University in 2004, suffices to suggest at least two implications. First, it expands the parameter of Chinese architectural

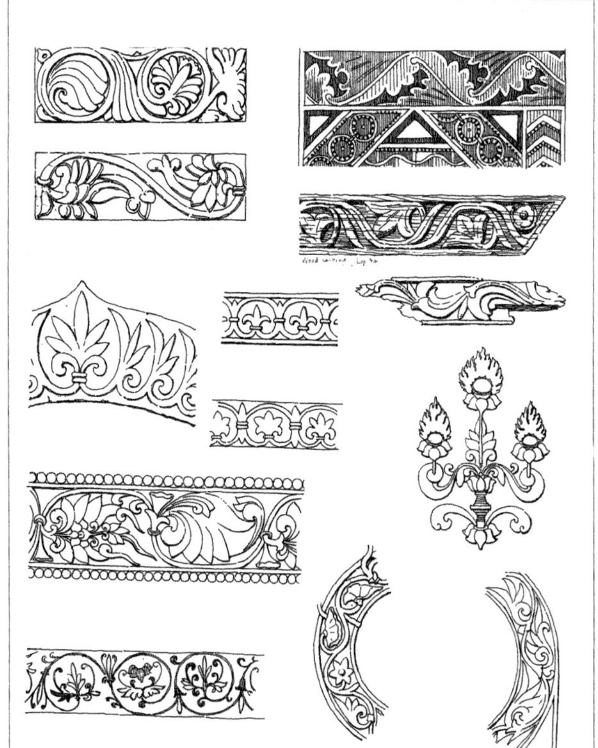

Figure 7.8. Illustration included in Lin Huiyin's article, "A Draft of the Preliminary Research on Border Decorative Patterns in Dunhuang [Caves]." From Qinghua daxue jianzhu xueyuan, *Jianzhushi Lin Huiyin*, 23. Photograph by permission of School of Architecture, Tsinghua University.

history and the scope of its research. Although the manuscript did not address architectural history per se, it places architecture in a network of artistic creations interconnected through the application of decorative patterns. Architecture, in this regard, could not be constricted by the "modernist" approach that took the timber-frame structure as its primary focus of inquiry and treated architecture as an abstract, architectonic, and formalist art. Second, it has been argued that the history of Chinese architecture written by Liang Sicheng—based chiefly on high-ranking buildings and filtered through his research on official building treatises—was ostensibly orthodox and elitist.[57] In contrast, in her manuscript, Lin was interested in all other aspects of a building, including coloration, pigments, labor division, process of production, and craftsmanship, thus conceiving architecture from the ground up in a humanistic perspective. In other words, if Liang's persistent commitment to studying the timber-frame structure could be considered elitist and orthodox in nature, Lin's dedication to non-structural decoration may be understood as feminist and alternative.

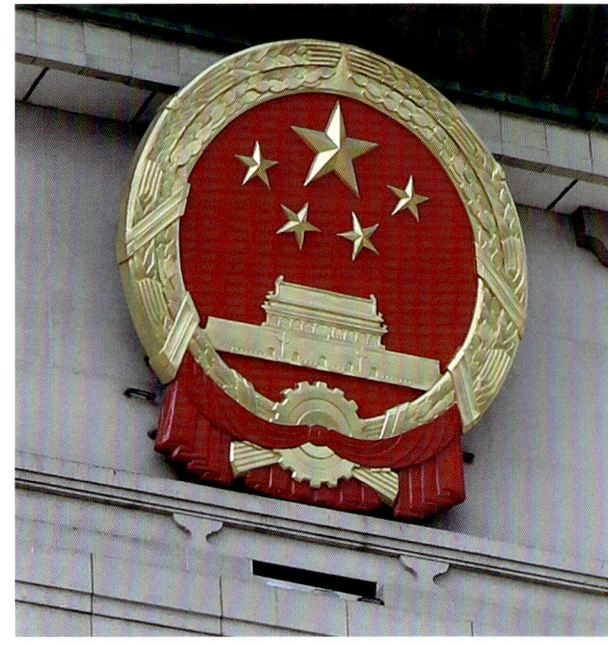

Figure 7.9. PRC's national emblem, final design by Lin Huiyin, 1950. Photograph by author.

This divergence between Lin and Liang, in fact, could be dated back to the early years of their careers. In their field research during the 1930s, Lin and Liang often came across "subjects of artistic and ethnological interest" in rural areas. While he was more eager to locate historical buildings, she "being also a writer and lover of dramatic art, more often than I, let her attention stray and enthusiastically insisted on some subjects for the camera at any cost," Liang later recalled.[58] In 1933, colleagues of the Institute reached Datong, the historical city in northern Shanxi, on a research trip. Liang and Liu Dunzhen (1897–1968), another key member of the Institute, surveyed two major Buddhist temples of the Liao dynasty (916–1125) among the largest wooden structures still extant in China. From there, Liang made a side trip to visit for the first time the Pagoda of Fogong Temple located in a remote town, Yingxian, ninety kilometers south of Datong. Built in 1056, the pagoda reaches a total height of 67.31 meters, and survives as the tallest wooden structure in the world; and its sophisticated timber frame testifies to an unparalleled level of architectural achievement in the history of China.[59] Lin, however, bypassed all these opportunities to "discover" gems in China's building history; instead, she chose to visit the Yungang Buddhist cave site outside Datong constructed during the fifth and sixth centuries. At Yungang, she sketched and photographed architectural details and decorative patterns as references for the wooden architecture of the same period that was no longer standing.[60] These trivial and perhaps less significant materials that might have then been considered distractions to Liang and his male colleagues nonetheless became important firsthand sources and inspirations in the last few years of Lin's career.

In the PRC, Lin was best known for her contribution to the design of the national emblem and the Monument to the People's Heroes (Renmin yingxiong jinianbei 人民英雄纪念碑).[61] For the former (fig. 7.9), it was Lin's idea to use the wreath that contains sheaves of wheat and rice tied with a cog, symbolizing proletarian workers and farmers, to encircle a relief of the Tiananmen Gate and stars that represent the four social classes surrounding the Communist Party. For the latter (fig. 7.10), Lin and Liang were responsible for its design, consisting of a Chinese architectural roof placed atop an enormous traditional Chinse stele (*bei* 碑), which then sits on a double plinth and two terraces.[62]

Lin, additionally, was in charge of designing the monument's decorative scheme, including the molding carved with floral patterns in bas-relief (fig. 7.11), inspired by patterns of architectural decoration from her recent research. Similar applications of decorative patterns could also be seen in the artifacts made of cloisonné coated with enamel—a traditional craft technique known as *jingtaolan* 景泰蓝—promoted earnestly by Lin (fig. 7.12).[63] She also advocated for this style of design by adopting patterns and pictorial motifs that decorate cave ceilings at the Mogao cave site near Dunhuang, Gansu, one of the most important Buddhist sites in medieval China (fig. 7.13).[64] None of these design projects are strictly "architecture" as defined in the research carried out by Lin and Liang in their early careers; yet, it could be argued that it is precisely beyond what was expected from Lin as a female architect that we begin to observe her unique contribution to broadening the field of Chinese architecture in modern China.

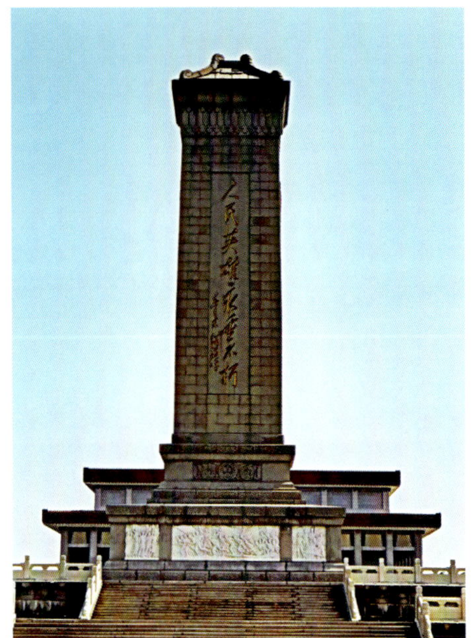

Figure 7.10. Monument to the People's Heroes, designed by Liang Sicheng and Lin Huiyin, Tiananmen Square, Beijing, 1952–58. Photograph by author.

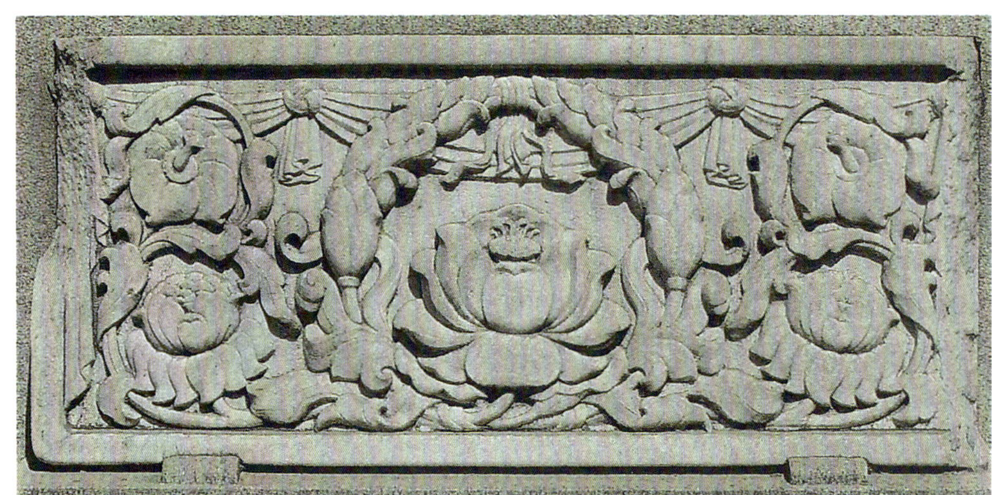

Figure 7.11. Decorative molding carved with floral patterns in bas-relief, designed by Lin Huiyin, for Monument to the People's Heroes, 1952. From Qinghua daxue jianzhu xueyuan, *Jianzhushi Lin Huiyin*, 13. Photograph by permission of School of Architecture, Tsinghua University.

Conclusion

It is true that Lin Huiyin's architectural career peaked in the early years of communist China. She was involved in advising Beijing's urban planning, designing the national monuments, founding the first architectural program, and writing Chinese architectural history. Her career took a turn when China's early modernism was interrupted and halted by the war, and it seems that as the modernist context in which architecture in China was established as a modern profession and discipline discontinued, Lin's interior reality of emotional, psychological, and gender-specific experience with architecture was revealed. As she wrote in 1947, only by forgetting the "logic of architecture" and postponing "rational judgment" could the emotion again have some hope in her pursuit of the profession as both an architect and a woman. It is thus only appropriate that on her tombstone (see fig. 7.1), under the epitaph is the decorative molding carved with the floral patterns that Lin designed for the Monument to the People's Heroes, which speaks aloud her subjective self and definition of her career.

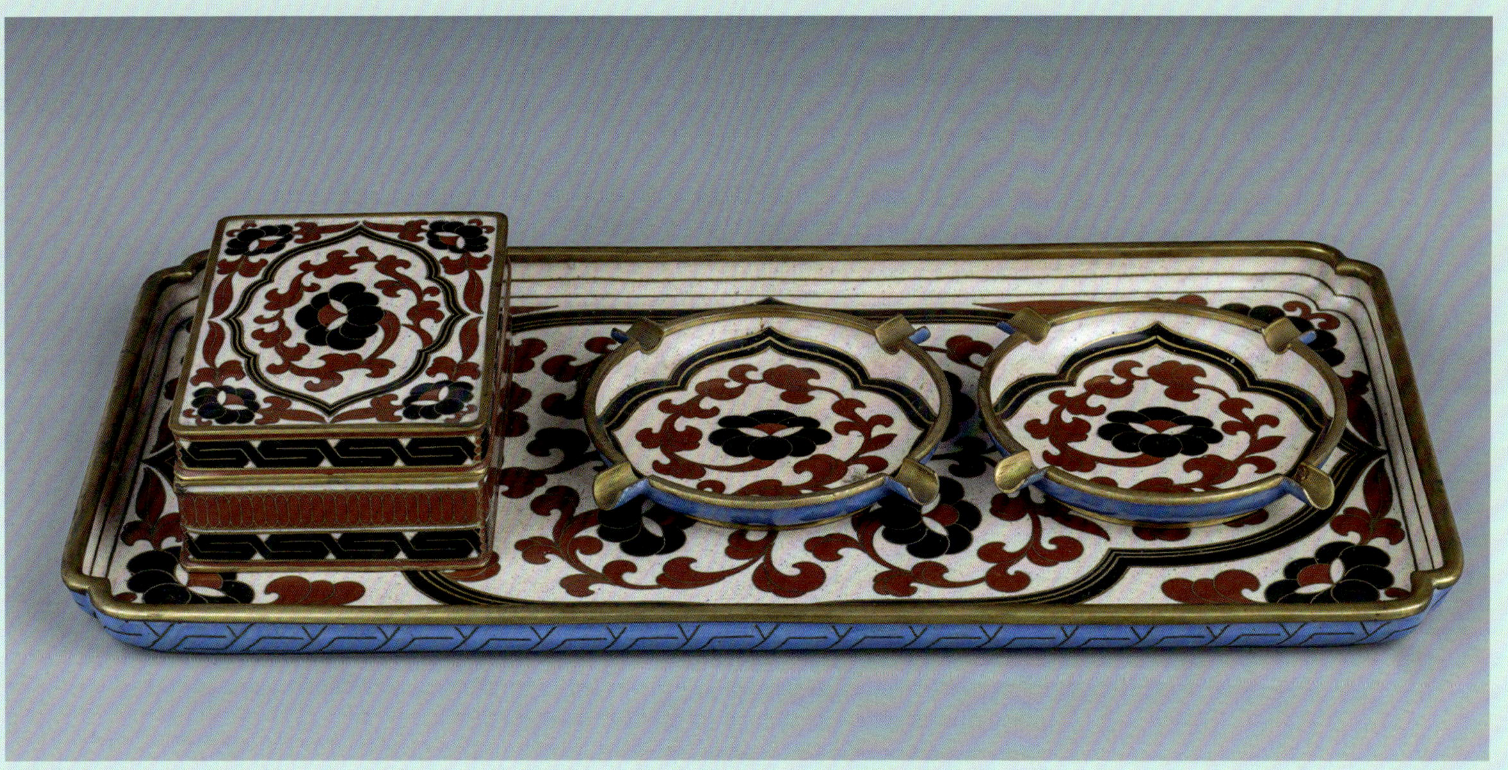

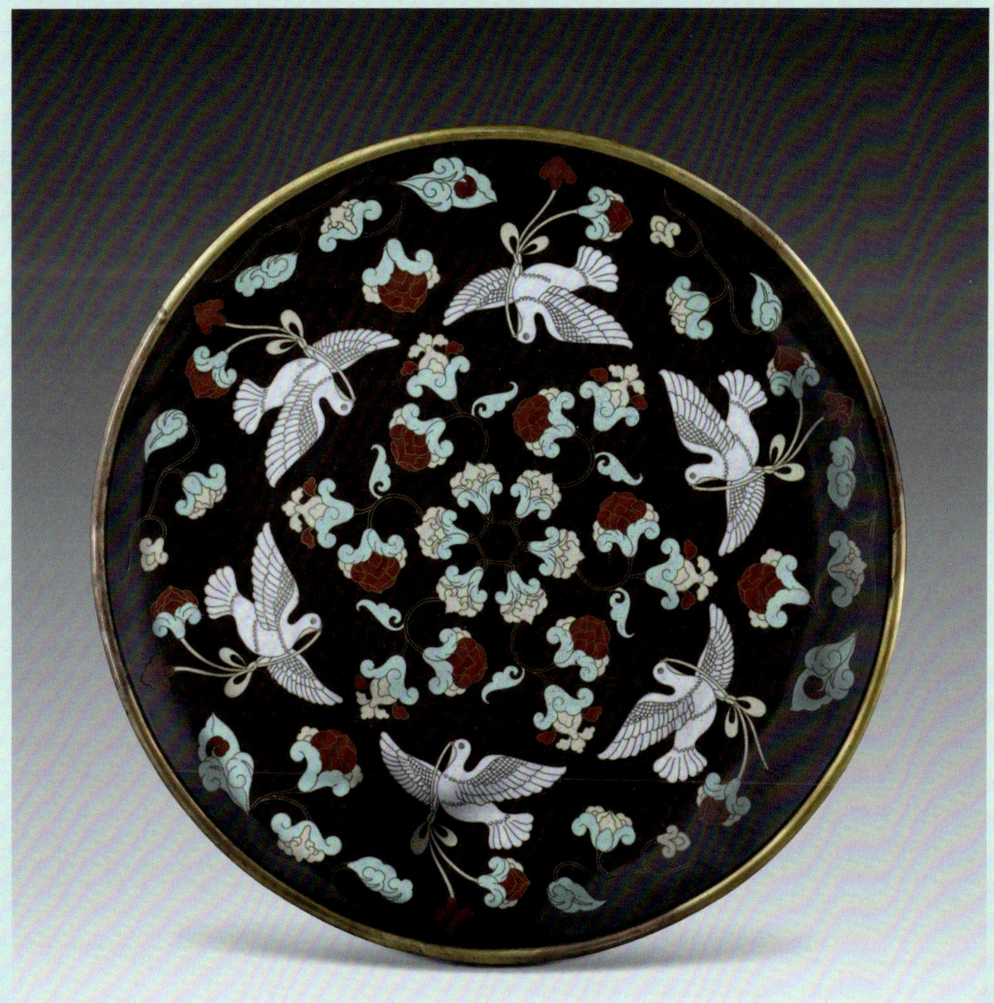

Figure 7.12. A set of Chinese cloisonné enamelware (*jingtailan*) with floral patterns, designed by Lin Huiyin, 1952. From Qinghua daxue jianzhu xueyuan, *Jianzhushi Lin Huiyin*, 31. Photograph by permission of Tsinghua University Art Museum.

Figure 7.13. Plate with pigeons and floral patterns, Chinese cloisonné enamelware (*jingtailan*), designed by Chang Shana under the direction of Lin Huiyin, 1953. Photograph by permission of Tsinghua University Art Museum.

Notes

1. Epigraph is from the poem "Postpone" (Zhanhuan 展缓) by Lin Huiyin, first published in *Ta Kung Pao* (*Dagong bao* 大公报, formerly *L'Impartial*), May 4, 1947; reprinted in Chen Xueyong, ed., *Lin Huiyin wencun: shige, xiaoshuo, xiju* [Writing collection of Lin Huiyin: Poetry, fiction, and drama] (Chengdu: Sichuan wenyi chubanshe, 2005), 68.

2. The best reference of the couple's lives and careers is still Wilma Fairbank, *Liang and Lin: Partners in Exploring China's Architectural Past* (Philadelphia: University of Pennsylvania Press, 1994). Most of the biographical information of Lin and Liang discussed in this essay, if not otherwise noted, is based on Fairbank's account. About the "first-generation" Chinese architects trained overseas, see Nancy S. Steinhardt, "East Asia: Architectural History across War Zones and Political Boundaries," *Studies in the History of Art* 35 (1990): 177–89.

3. Fairbank, *Lin and Liang*, 25.

4. The comprehensive *Who's Who in Modern Chinese Architecture* includes four female architects active before 1955 when Lin Huiyin died. Of the four, Lin was the oldest and began her career as an architect the earliest. The other three female architects are Yu Junxiang 于均祥 (1907–?), Zhang Yuquan 张玉泉 (1912–2004), and Li Ying 李莹 (1924–?). Female architects have certainly contributed just as much to the field of architecture as their male counterparts. In the first half of the twentieth century, however, it is not an exaggeration to assert that male architects and scholars dominated the field of architecture and its historical research. See Lai Delin, ed., *Jindai Zhejiang lu: Zhongguo jindai zhongyao jianzhushi, jianzhu shiwusuo minglu* [Who's who in modern architecture: Records of important architects and architectural offices in modern China) (Beijing: Zhongguo shuidian shuili chubanshe, 2006).

5. A publication dedicated to Lin Huiyin was published by the Qinghua University in 2004 in commemoration of the one-hundred-year anniversary of Lin's birth. It includes several essays that celebrate Lin's legacy as an architect. See Qinghua daxue jianzhu xueyuan, ed., *Jianzhushi Lin Huiyin* [Architect Lin Huiyin] (Beijing: Qinghua daxue chubanshe, 2004). Separately, a useful article that aims to reevaluate Lin's achievements and contributions is Zhao Chen, "Zuowei Zhongguo jianzhu xueshu xianxingzhe de Lin Huiyin" [Lin Huiyin as a pioneer of Chinese architecture], *Jianzhu shi* 21 (2005): 1–12.

6. See, for instance, Harold Kalman, "'Chinese Spirit in Modern Strength': Liang Sicheng, Lin Huiyin, and Early Modernist Architecture in China," *Journal of the Royal Asiatic Society Hong Kong Branch* 58 (2018): 156; Xiao Qian, "Yidai cainü Lin Huiyin" [The talented lady of a generation, Lin Huiyin], *Dushu* 10 (Oct 1984): 115–16.

7. This refers to the May Fourth Movement, an anti-imperialist movement that started from student demonstrations in Beijing on May 4, 1919. The demonstrations sparked nationwide protests and subsequent requests for political and cultural reforms from the Chinese government by rejecting traditional values and adopting Western ideas of science and democracy.

8. See the section on Lin Huiyin in Shu-Mei Shih, *The Lure of the Modern: Writing Modernism in Semicolonial China 1917–1937* (Berkeley: University of California Press, 2001), 204–15.

9. See Tony Atkin, "Chinese Architecture Students at the University of Pennsylvania in the 1920s," in Jeffrey W. Cody, Nancy S. Steinhardt, and Tony Atkin, eds., *Chinese Architecture and the Beaux-Arts* (Honolulu: University of Hawai'i Press, 2011), 45–72; Fairbank, *Liang and Lin*, 23–30.

10. Together with three other architects also trained in the United States, Chen Zhi (1902–2002), Tong Jun (1900–83), and Cai Fangyin (1901–63), Liang formed an architectural practice called Liang, Chen, Tong, and Cai Partnership Co. Lin, then a new mother, was an informal partner. For their architectural projects commissioned during this early period of their careers, see Kalman, "'Chinese Spirit in Modern Strength.'"

11. See the introduction by Michelle Yeh in *Anthology of Modern Chinese Poetry*, ed. Michelle Yeh (New Haven, CT: Yale University Press, 1993), xlvi.

12. Tagore's meeting with Huiyin and different English translations of the poem are discussed in *Tagore and China*, ed. Tan Chung et al. (Thousand Oaks, CA.: SAGE Publications, 2011), 99.

13. This is the phrase coined by Joseph R. Levenson in his *Liang Ch'i-ch'ao and the Mind of Modern China* (Cambridge, MA: Harvard University Press, 1953).

14. A useful discussion on Liang Qichao can be found in Shih, *Lure of the Modern*, chapter 6.

15. Lin Shan, *Lin Huiyin zhuan* [Biography of Lin Huiyin] (Taipei: Shijie shuju, 1993), 68–69. Unless otherwise noted, all translations are my own.

16. For the influence of the Northern Song building manual on Liang's history writing, see Li Shiqiao, "Writing a Modern Chinese Architectural History: Liang Sicheng and Liang Qichao," *Journal of Architectural Education* 56, no. 1 (2002): 34–55. For the building manual, see Else Glahn, "On the Transmission of the *Ying-Tsao Fa-Shih*," *T'oung Pao* 61, no. 4–5 (1974): 232–65, and Qinghua Guo, "*Yingzao Fashi:* Twelfth-Century Chinese Building Manual," *Architectural History* 41 (1998): 1–13.

17. Fairbank, *Liang and Lin*, 29.

18. The Institute was funded by the war indemnity money paid through the US government to support Chinese studies. The Institute also published *Zhongguo yingzao xueshe huikan*, or *Bulletin of the Society for Research of Chinese Architecture*, and most reports of the fieldwork led by Liang were first published in the bulletin. See Lin Zhu, *Zhongguo yingzao xueshe shilue* [A history of the Institute for Research in Chinese architecture] (Tianjin: Baihua wenyi chubanshe, 2008).

19. Fairbank, *Liang and Lin*, 52.

20. See Liang Sicheng, *Qingshi yingzao zeli* [Qing-style building regulations], compiled in 1932, first edition published in 1934; reprinted in *Liang Sicheng quanji* [Complete collection of Liang Sicheng] (Beijing: Zhongguo gongye chubanshe, 2001), 6:1–120.

21. Lin Huiyin, "Lun Zhongguo jianzhu zhi jige tezheng," *Zhongguo yingzao xueshe huikan* 3, no 1 (March 1932): 163–79.

22. Quoted in Fairbank, *Liang and Lin*, 27.

23. Lin, "Lun Zhongguo jianzhu zhi jige tezheng," 164–65.

24. A discussion of Lin's borrowing of the three qualities from Vitruvius can be found in Li Jun, "Gudian zhuyi, jiegou lixing zhuyi yu shixing de luoji: Lin Huiyin, Liang Sicheng zaoqi jianzhu sheji yu sixiang de zai jiantao" [Classicism, structural rationalism, and the poetic logic: A reevaluation of the early architectural work and thoughts of Lin Huiyin and Liang Sicheng], *Zhongguo jianzhu shilun huikan* 5 (2012): 407–11.

25. Lin Huiyin, "Introduction," in Liang, *Qingshi yingzao zeli*, 6:18.

26. Lin Huiyin, "Introduction," 6:18.

27. On this point, see Lai Delin, "Liang Sicheng, Lin Huiyin Zhongguo jianzhushi xiezuo biaozheng" [On Liang Sicheng and Lin Huiyin's writings of Chinese architectural history], in Lai Delin, *Zhongguo jindai jianzhushi yanjiu* (Beijing: Qinghua daxue chubanshe, 2007), 313–30.

28. About the citywide restoration of historical buildings in the 1930s, see my article, Wei-Cheng Lin, "Collectable Artifacts: The Former Capital (Beiping) of the 1930s in Photographs," in *Photography and East Asian Art*, ed. Wu Hung and Chelsea Foxwell (Chicago: Center for the Art of East Asia, University of Chicago), 299–326.

29. For a quick reference to the Temple of Heaven in the context of the state religion during late imperial China, see Susan Naquin, *Peking: Temples and City Life, 1400–1900* (Berkeley: University of California Press, 2000), 324–31.

30. See Wu Liangyong, "Lin Huiyin de zuihou shinian zhuiyi" [Remembering Lin Huiyin's last ten years], in *Jianzhushi Lin Huiyin*, ed. Qinghua daxue jianzhu xueyuan, 110–16.

31. See Lin, "Collectable Artifacts," 309–10.

32. Lin Huiyin, "Chenglou shang," first published in *Ta Kung Pao,* November 8, 1935, reprinted in Chen, ed., *Lin Huiyin wencun,* 28. Translation after Weijie Song, "The Aesthetic versus the Political: Lin Huiyin and Modern Beijing," *Chinese Literature: Essays, Articles, Reviews* 36 (December 2014): 68. Song's article provides a good analysis of Lin's literary production in relation to modern Beijing.

33. Lin Huiyin, "Pingjiao jianzhu zalu," *Zhongguo yingzao xueshe huikan* 3, no. 4 (November 1932): 98–110.

34. Lin Huiyin, "Pingjiao jianzhu zalu," 99. The English translation of the phrase *jianzhu yi* as "architecturesque" was proposed by Wu Liangyong; see Zhao Chen, "*'Limian' de wuhui: jianzhu, lilun, lishi* [The misunderstanding of "elevation": Architecture, theory, and history] (Beijing: Sanlian shudian, 2007), 53.

35. See Lin Huiyin, "Shanxi tongxin" [Letter from Shanxi], first published in *Ta Kung Pao,* August 25, 1934; reprinted in Chen, ed., *Lin Huiyin wencun,* 21–22.

36. Lin Huiyin, "Chuangzi yiwai," first published in *Ta Kung Pao,* September 5, 1934; reprinted in Chen, ed., *Lin Huiyin wencun,* 23–28. A useful discussion of the essay is Wang Ping's "Chuangzi neiwai" [Inside and outside of the window], *Wenyi zhengming* 5 (2011): 108–12.

37. The translation is after Song, "The Aesthetic versus the Political," 78.

38. See Lin Huiyin and Liang Sicheng, "Jin Fen gu jianzhu yucha jilue" [Records about the preliminary survey of historical buildings in the Jin and Fen regions], *Zhongguo yingzao xueshe huikan* 5, no. 3 (March 1935), 12–67.

39. Lin, "Shanxi tongxin"; translation after Song, "The Aesthetic versus the Political," 84.

40. Fairbank, *Liang and Lin,* 92.

41. Fu Sinian, a renowned scholar and one of the leaders of the May Fourth Movement, was director of the Institute of History and Philology at the Academia Sinica and later chancellor of the Peking University.

42. See Chen, ed., *Lin Huiyin wencun,* 97.

43. Qian Yi, "Liang Sicheng yu Lin Huiyin kangzhan qijian zai Kunming de jianzhu huodong [Liang Sicheng's and Lin Huiyin's architectural activities in Kunming during the anti-Japanese war]," *Jianzhushi xuekan,* no. 2 (2021): 104–16.

44. Fairbank, *Liang and Lin,* 112.

45. The honors Liang received immediately after the war are well documented. See Fairbank, 148–54.

46. Zhu Ziqing 朱自清 (1898–1948), a well-known and influential poet and essayist, lashed out forcefully with criticism; see Zhu's "Wenwu, jiushu, maobi" [Cultural relics, old books, and pen-brushes], first published in *Ta Kung Pao,* March 31, 1948.

47. Lin Huiyin, "Gucheng huanghun," first published in *Yishibao* [Yishi daily], August 2, 1948, reprinted in Chen, ed., *Lin Huiyin wencun,* 75.

48. Fairbank, *Liang and Lin,* 169.

49. Quoted in Wang Jun, *Chengji* [Records of the city] (Beijing: Sanlian shudian, 2003), 67. Also see Jianying Zha, *China Pop: How Soap Operas, Tabloids, and Bestsellers Are Transforming a Culture* (New York: The New Press, 1996), 63.

50. For a detailed discussion of the plan, see Wang, *Chengji,* 73–96.

51. The plan, entitled *Guanyu zhongyang renmin zhengfu xingzheng zhongxinqu weizhi de jianyi* [Suggestion for the location of the PRC's central government], is reprinted in *Liang Sicheng quanji,* 5:60–81.

52. See the discussion in Jianfei Zhu, *Architecture of Modern China: A Historical Critique* (London and New York: Routledge, 2009), 81.

53. Liang Sicheng and Lin Huiyin, "Beijing: dushi jihua de wubi jiezuo" [Beijing: Unparalleled masterpiece of urban planning], first published in *Xin guancha,* April 1951, reprinted in *Liang Sicheng quanji,* 5:101 (my italics).

54. I discuss Liang's adjustments to the political reality during the 1950s in Wei-Cheng Lin, "Structural, Visual, or Iconic: Transmutations of Wooden Brackets in Modern China," *Frontiers of History in China* 10, no. 2 (2015): 323–65. See also K. Sizheng Fan, "A Classicist Architecture for Utopia: The Soviet Contacts," in Cody, Steinhardt, and Atkin, eds., *Chinese Architecture and the Beaux-Arts*, 91–126.

55. Lin Huiyin, "Dunhuang bianshi chubu yanjiu gao," unfinished manuscript, collected in Qinghua daxue jianzhu xueyuan, ed., *Jianzhushi Lin Huiyin*, 14–25.

56. A point succinctly discussed in the introduction to Nancy S. Steinhardt, *Chinese Architecture: A History* (Princeton: Princeton University Press, 2019), 1–7.

57. See Nancy S. Steinhardt, "The Tang Architectural Icon and the Politics of Chinese Architecture History," *Art Bulletin* 86, no. 2 (2004): 228–54.

58. See Fairbank, *Liang and Lin*, 66.

59. The Institute never published an investigation report on the Pagoda of Fogong Temple, but it was briefly discussed in Liang's *A Pictorial History of Chinese Architecture* (Cambridge, MA: MIT Press, 1984), 68–71. About this pagoda, see Nancy S. Steinhardt, *Liao Architecture* (Honolulu: University of Hawai'i Press, 1997), 103–21.

60. Fairbank, *Liang and Lin*, 67–72. Lin, coauthored with Liang and Liu Dunzhen, later published their investigation at Yungang in the article, "Yungang shiku zhong suo biaoxian de Beiwei jianzhu" [Northern Wei architecture as represented in Yungang caves], *Zhongguo yingzao xueshe huikan* 4, no. 3–4 (June 1934): 169–217.

61. For Lin's role in both designs, see Gao Jun and Zhu Mian, "Lin Huiyin zai guohui he renmin yingxiong jinianbei sheji zhong dui minzu xingshi de tansuo yu zhuiqiu" [Lin's exploration and pursuit of a Chinese style in her designs of the national emblem and Monument to the People's Heroes], *Dangdai Zhongguoshi yanjiu* 16, no. 1 (Jan. 2009): 58–62.

62. The design of the monument was summarized in Liang Sicheng, "Renmin yingxiong jinianbei sheji de jingguo" [The design process of the Monument to the People's Heroes], reprinted in *Liang Sicheng quanji*, 5:462–64. See also Zhu, *Architecture of Modern China*, 79–81.

63. See Lin Huiyin, "Qinghua daxue jianzhu xueyuan Jingtailan xin tuyang sheji gongzuo yinian zongjie" [Annual report on the design of new patterns for Jingtailan by the School of Architecture in Tsinghua University], originally published in *Guangming ribao* [Guangming daily], August 13, 1951; reprinted in Qinghua daxue jianzhu xueyuan, *Jianzhushi Lin Huiyin*, 26–31.

64. See Lin Huiyin, "Heping liwu" [Token of peace], first published in *Xin guancha* (October 1952), reprinted in Qinghua daxue jianzhu xueyuan, *Jianzhushi Lin Huiyin*, 32–34.

Bibliography

Cody, Jeffrey W., Nancy S. Steinhardt, and Tony Atkins, eds. *Chinese Architecture and the Beaux-Arts.* Honolulu: University of Hawai'i Press, 2011.

Fairbank, Wilma. *Liang and Lin: Partners in Exploring China's Architectural Past.* Philadelphia: University of Pennsylvania Press, 1994.

Gao Jun and Zhu Mian. "Lin Huiyin zai guohui he renmin yingxiong jinianbei sheji zhong dui minzu xingshi de tansuo yu zhuiqiu" [Lin's exploration and pursuit of a Chinese style in her designs of the national emblem and Monument to the People's Heroes]. *Dangdai Zhongguoshi yanjiu* 16, no. 1 (January 2009): 58–62.

Glahn, Else. "On the Transmission of the *Ying-Tsao Fa-Shih*." *T'oung Pao* 61, nos. 4–5 (1974): 232–65.

Guo, Qinghua. "*Yingzao Fashi*: Twelfth-Century Chinese Building Manual." *Architectural History* 41 (1998): 1–13.

Kalman, Harold. "'Chinese Spirit in Modern Strength': Liang Sicheng, Lin Huiyin, and Early Modernist Architecture in China." *Journal of the Royal Asiatic Society Hong Kong Branch* 58 (2018): 154–88.

Lai Delin. "Liang Sicheng, Lin Huiyin Zhongguo jianzhushi xiezuo biaozheng" [On Liang Sicheng and Lin Huiyin's writings of Chinese architectural history]. In *Zhongguo jindai jianzhushi yanjiu*, 313–30. Beijing: Qinghua daxue chubanshe, 2007.

Levenson, Joseph R. *Liang Ch'i-ch'ao and the Mind of Modern China.* Cambridge, MA: Harvard University Press, 1953.

Li Jun. "Gudian zhuyi, jiegou lixing zhuyi yu shixing de luoji: Lin Huiyin, Liang Sicheng zaoqi jianzhu sheji yu sixiang de zai jiantao" [Classicism, structural rationalism, and the poetic logic: A reevaluation of the early architectural work and thoughts of Lin Huiyin and Liang Sicheng]. *Zhongguo jianzhu shilun huikan* 5 (2012): 383–427.

Li Shiqiao. "Writing a Modern Chinese Architectural History: Liang Sicheng and Liang Qichao." *Journal of Architectural Education* 56, no. 1 (2002): 34–55.

Liang Sicheng. *Liang Sicheng quanji* [Complete collection of Liang Sicheng]. 8 vols. Beijing: Zhongguo gongye chubanshe, 2001.

———. *A Pictorial History of Chinese Architecture.* Cambridge, MA: MIT Press, 1984.

Lin Huiyin. *Lin Huiyin wencun: sanwen, shuxin, pinglun, fanyi* [Writing collection of Lin Huiyin: Prose, letters, critiques, and translations]. Edited by Chen Xueyong. Chengdu: Sichuan wenyi chubanshe, 2005.

———. *Lin Huiyin wencun: shige, xiaoshuo, xiju* [Writing collection of Lin Huiyin: Poetry, fiction, and drama]. Edited by Chen Xueyong. Chengdu: Sichuan wenyi chubanshe, 2005.

———. "Lun Zhongguo jianzhu zhi jige tezheng" [On some characteristics of Chinese architecture]. *Zhongguo yingzao xueshe huikan* 3, no. 1 (March 1932): 163–79.

Lin Huiyin and Liang Sicheng. "Jin Fen gu jianzhu yucha jilue" [Records about the preliminary survey of historical buildings in the Jin and Fen regions]. *Zhongguo yingzao xueshe huikan* 5, no. 3 (March 1935): 12–67.

Lin Huiyin, Liang Sicheng, and Liu Dunzhen. "Pingjiao jianzhu zalu." *Zhongguo yingzao xueshe huikan* 3, no. 4 (November 1932): 98–110.

———. "Yungang shiku zhong suo biaoxian de Beiwei jianzhu" [Northern Wei architecture as represented in Yungang caves]. *Zhongguo yingzao xueshe huikan* 4, nos. 3–4 (June 1934): 169–217.

Lin Shan. *Lin Huiyin zhuan* [Biography of Lin Huiyin]. Taipei: Shijie shuju, 1993.

Lin, Wei-Cheng. "Collectable Artifacts: The Former Capital (Beiping) of the 1930s in Photographs." In *Photography and East Asian Art*, edited by Wu Hung and Chelsea Foxwell, 299–326. Chicago: Center for the Art of East Asia, University of Chicago, 2021.

———. "Structural, Visual, or Iconic: Transmutations of Wooden Brackets in Modern China." *Frontiers of History in China* 10, no. 2 (2015): 323–65.

Lin Zhu. *Zhongguo yingzao xueshe shilue* [A history of the Institute for Research in Chinese architecture]. Tianjin: Baihua wenyi chubanshe, 2008.

Naquin, Susan. *Peking: Temples and City Life, 1400–1900.* Berkeley: University of California Press, 2000.

Qinghua daxue jianzhu xueyuan, ed. *Jianzhushi Lin Huiyin* [Architect Lin Huiyin]. Beijing: Qinghua daxue chubanshe, 2004.

Shih, Shu-Mei. *The Lure of the Modern: Writing Modernism in Semicolonial China 1917–1937.* Berkeley: University of California Press, 2001.

Song, Weijie. "The Aesthetic versus the Political: Lin Huiyin and Modern Beijing." *Chinese Literature: Essays, Articles, Reviews* 36 (December 2014): 61–94.

Steinhardt, Nancy S. *Chinese Architecture: A History.* Princeton, NJ: Princeton University Press, 2019.

———. "East Asia: Architectural History across War Zones and Political Boundaries." *Studies in the History of Art* 35 (1990): 177–89.

———. *Liao Architecture.* Honolulu: University of Hawai'i Press, 1997.

———. "The Tang Architectural Icon and the Politics of Chinese Architecture History." *Art Bulletin* 86, no. 2 (2004): 228–54.

Tan Chung, Amiya Dev, Wang Bangwei, and Wei Liming. *Tagore and China*. Thousand Oaks, CA: SAGE Publications, 2011.

Wang Jun. *Chengji* [Records of the city]. Beijing: Sanlian shudian, 2003.

Wang Ping. "Chuangzi neiwai" [Inside and outside of the window]. *Wenyi zhengming* 5 (2011): 108–12.

Xiao Qian. "Yidai cainü Lin Huiyin" [The talented lady of a generation, Lin Huiyin]. *Dushu* 10 (October 1984): 113–21.

Yeh, Michelle. *Anthology of Modern Chinese Poetry.* New Haven, CT: Yale University Press, 1993.

Zha, Jianying. *China Pop: How Soap Operas, Tabloids and Bestsellers Are Transforming a Culture.* New York: New Press, 1996.

Zhao Chen. *"Limian" de wuhui: jianzhu, lilun, lishi* [The misunderstanding of "elevation": architecture, theory, and history]. Beijing: Sanlian shudian, 2007.

———. "Zuowei Zhongguo jianzhu xueshu xianxingzhe de Lin Huiyin" [Lin Huiyin as a pioneer of Chinese architecture]. *Jianzhu shi* 21 (2005): 1–12.

Zhu, Jianfei. *Architecture of Modern China: A Historical Critique.* London and New York: Routledge, 2009.

Zhu Ziqing. "Wenwu, jiushu, maobi" [Cultural relics, old books, and pen-brushes]. *Ta Kung Pao,* March 31, 1948, n.p.

PART 3

Modern and Contemporary Makers

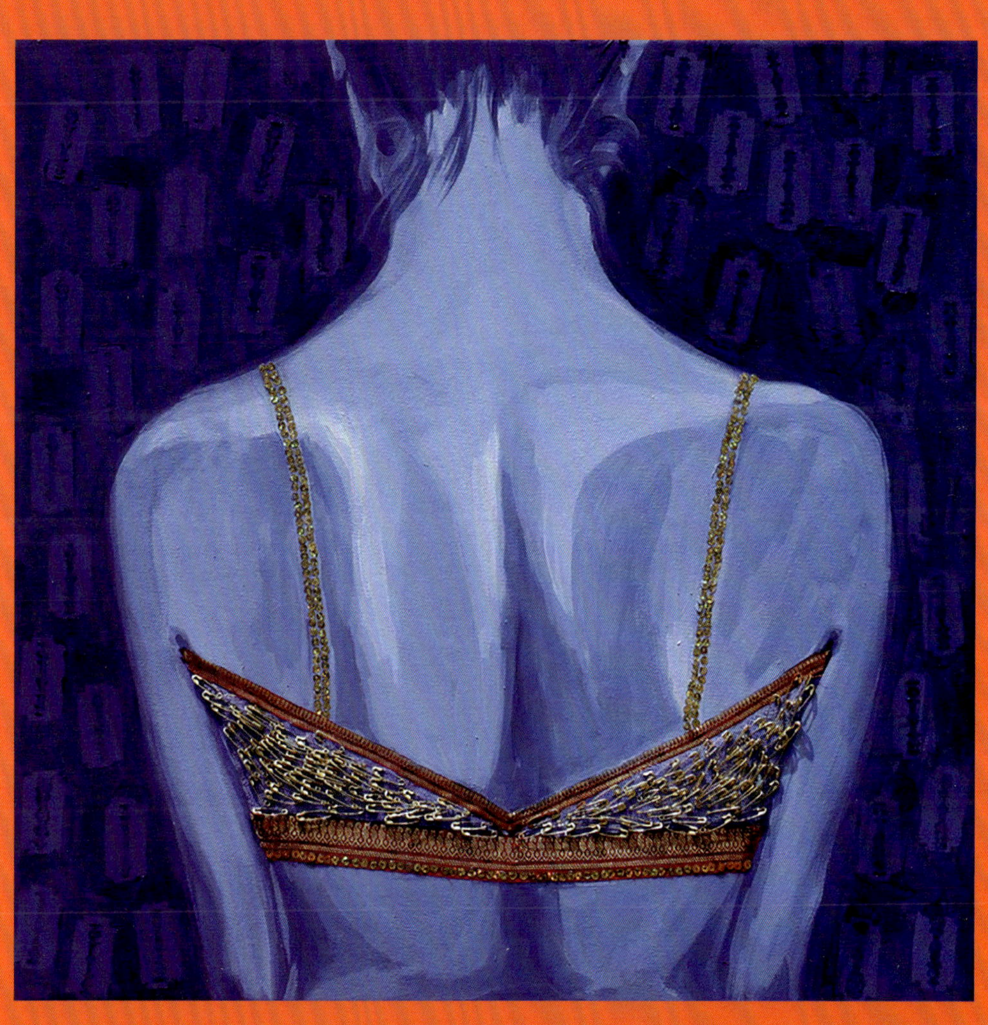

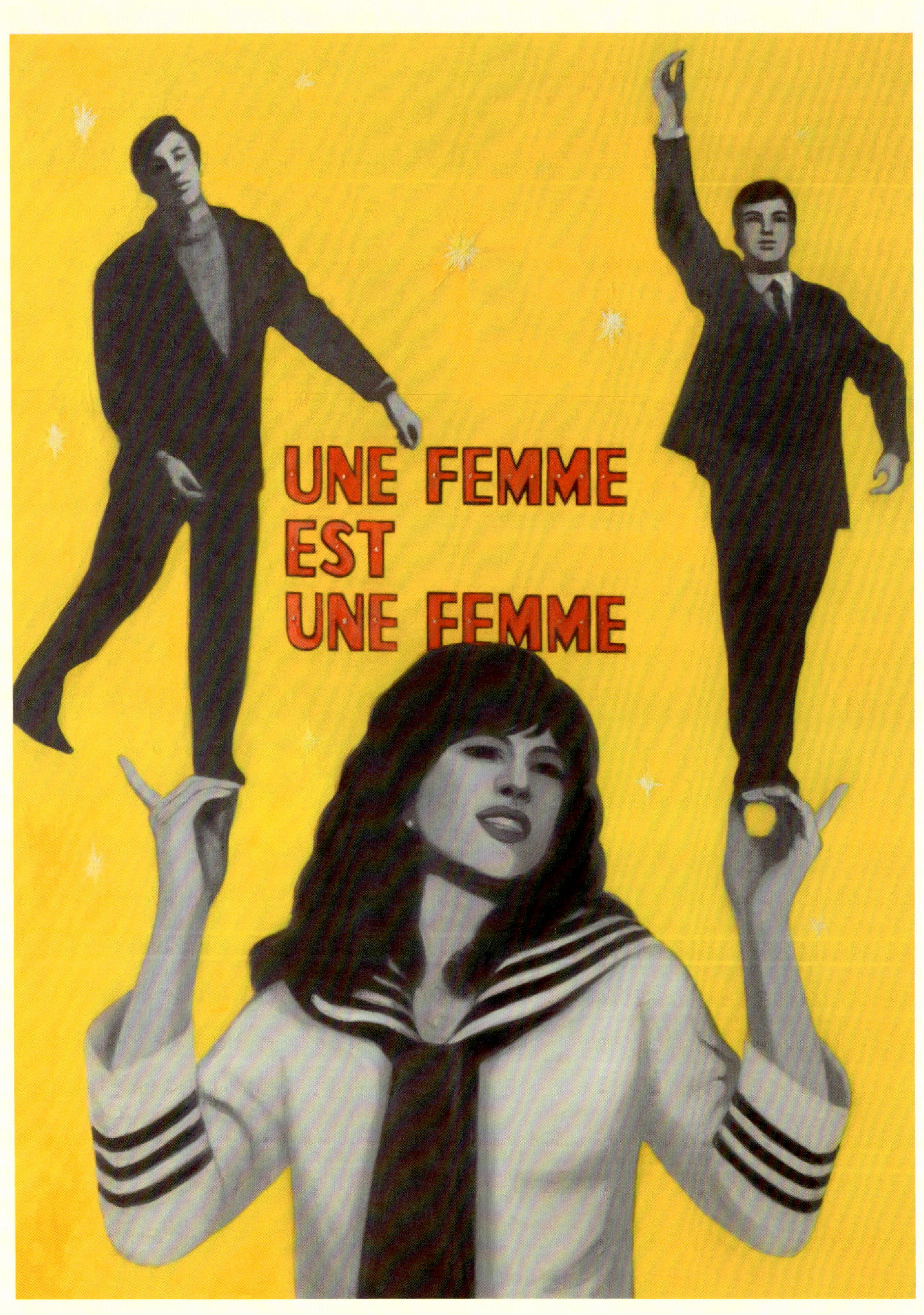
UNE FEMME
EST
UNE FEMME

8

Exploring a Moment of 超少女 (*Chōshōjo*)

Japan's Economic Bubble, Saison Culture, and New Women's Art, 1986–1996

MIDORI YAMAMURA

IN AUGUST 1986, the influential art journal, *Bijutsu Techō* (*BT*), published an all-female-artists edition, titled *Bijutsu no Chōshōjo tachi* (*Super Girls of Art*); it was an atypical volume, because, despite Japan's postwar democratization policies that offered women artists equal access to art education, female artists continued to suffer from obstinate gender-based discrimination. However, "during the time of the economic bubble (1986–91), women artists suddenly rose to prominence," as the editor of *Chōshōjo* (Super Girls), Yutaka Mikami, remembers today. And curiously, he believes it was due in part to the "accelerated consumerism targeted at young women."[1]

The time was when Seibu Department Stores emerged as Japan's foremost purveyor of contemporary art. Headed by the self-proclaimed communist Seiji Tsutsumi (a.k.a. Takashi Tsujii, 1927–2013), the Seibu (later Saison) Group politicized consumerism by establishing a lifestyle industry. Tsutsumi viewed the new social conformity that had been induced by information and the politics of corporate capitalism as a prime case of what Herbert Marcuse called in 1964 a "technocracy."[2] In this brave new information society where the collective consciousness could easily absorb an individual's opinion, Tsutsumi's ultimate goal was to create an "autonomous consumer" who could also make individual judgments as a "constituent."[3] To pursue this political goal, culture became important, as "one of the human beings' imaginative and creative activities, which as a whole constructs human life."[4] Women were situated in the center of his commercial plot, which ultimately instilled a new confidence in female artists. The introduction of the Equal Employment Opportunity Law in 1985 also helped to put women artists on more equal footing with men.

Facing: Mio Shirai, *A Woman Is a Woman.* See figure 8.14.

And yet, while women artists were gaining momentum,[5] the art world's old guard kept harassing them. "Women get married and discontinue art-making," was how a distinguished professor at Tokyo University of the Arts (TUA) explained his policy of not taking female advisees in 1989.[6] With the exception of Women's University of Art and Design (Joshibi), in the 1980s, full-time teaching positions in art schools were mostly reserved for men. That gender inequality has little changed since. In February 2018, a group of frustrated Tama Art University sculpture department students sent an open letter to school officials reporting harassment and demanding gender balance in the faculty.[7]

Notwithstanding their social disadvantage, Kazuko Matsuoka oddly noted, the *Super Girls* generation diverged from their female predecessors, "who wanted to acquire their identity using masculine logic and structure."[8] Many women of this new generation began incorporating their inherent experience in art. Such gender-based expression prominent among the "young female artists," according to a progressive critic, Yoshiaki Tono, was "some of the most marked trends in contemporary art in the 1980s Japan."[9] *Super Girls* reflected this crucial moment when women artists began exploring ideas outside the patriarchal purview.

But scholarly attention has been veering away from this noteworthy moment. A possible reason is the outright neglect of the *BT* volume, *Super Girls,* for its focus on female artists under thirty years old and calling them "girls"; not all thirty-nine artists featured in the journal continued their careers. Still, the mid-1980s saw momentum for female artists. This essay centers on women artists of the 1980s and the 1990s in Japan, who were establishing a new field outside patriarchal values and logics. They include Masayo Koizumi, Mayumi Terada, and Mika Yoshizawa, all featured in *Super Girls.* I will then expand the scope to include the slightly later generation, Rei Naito and Mio Shirai, whose works were equally significant and became influential to the new generation of female artists. Since *Super Girls* excluded *nihonga* (modern Japanese painting) and photography, I have added Hiroko Ohno and Yurie Nagashima from the respective fields to give a fuller picture of the Japanese art scene of this time. Most of the artists established their practice in dialogue with the previous generation. However, their unique social encounters resulted in different worldviews, which the cohort of artists embraced and reflected in their inherent expressions.

Saison Culture and *On'na no Jidai* (Women's Epoch)

For artists working in the 1980s in Japan, it was almost impossible to remain untouched by Saison culture. Starting in 1971 as a small operation, the Seibu Group grew in the 1980s into a revolutionary retail and distribution conglomerate, offering a range of businesses such as hotels, financial institutions, and property developers, thereby creating the lifestyle industry. The group's first president, Seiji Tsutsumi, was an acclaimed poet, novelist, and unlikely businessman. He was a steadfast communist, establishing a labor union in the company that he inherited. The culture was Seibu's "image core."[10] In 1973,

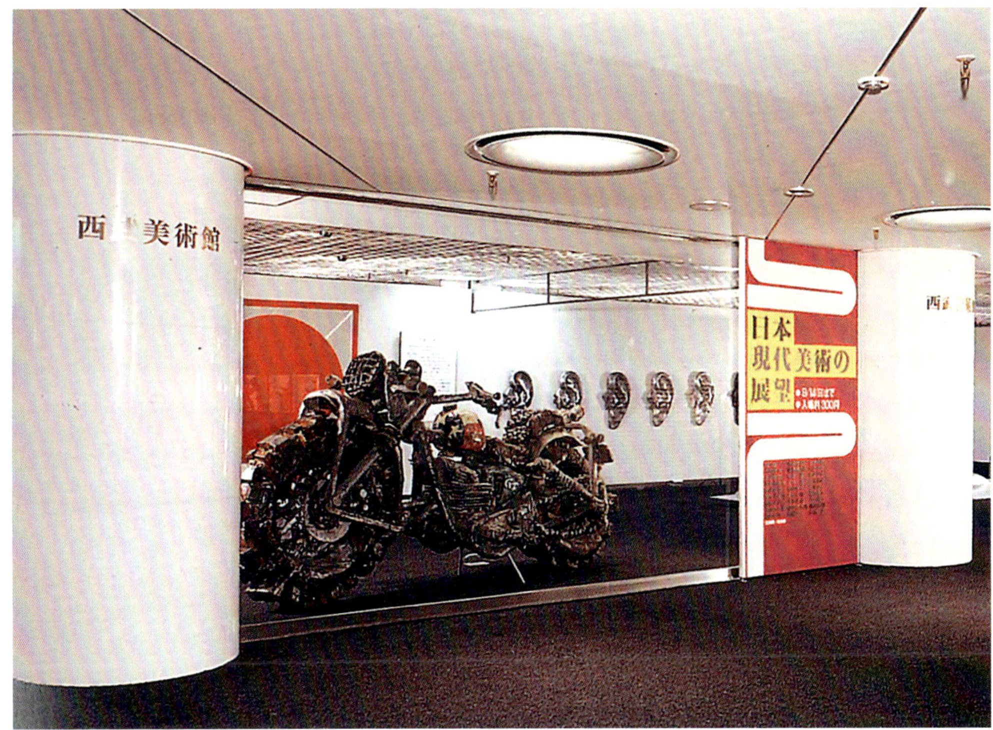

Figure 8.1. Seibu Museum of Art, *A View of Japanese Contemporary Art*, September 1975. Courtesy of Sezon Museum of Art, Nagano, Japan.

Tsutsumi established the Cultural Affairs Department in his company, intending to make an economically autonomous division and calling it a "cultural industry," so that culture could have a power of its own, independent of its bourgeois patrons. At the same time, he believed that "culture can become business, but art cannot."[11] Such a paradoxical creed resulted in an unprofitable operation, once the economic bubble burst in 1991.

Still, between 1975 and the mid-1990s, the Saison Group was the impetus behind Japanese contemporary art. In September 1975, Tsutsumi unveiled a mammoth cultural zone in its flagship store, Ikebukuro Seibu. Situated on the top (twelfth) floor, the Seibu Museum of Art (later called the Sezon Museum of Modern Art) embodied the spirit of the time.[12] At a time when Japanese museums rarely featured the nation's contemporary artists, its opening exhibition—*A View of Japanese Contemporary Art* (fig. 8.1)—featured works by twenty-seven Japanese artists (including one woman), mostly born after 1930. Adjacent to the museum was ART VIVANT,[13] Asia's biggest art-book store that sold imported titles. People were welcome to browse the latest publications and rare books from the United States and Europe.

The eleventh floor and part of the tenth floor comprised the Seibu Book Center (later Libro), which became responsible for introducing books on *nyū aka* (new academism) by such authors as Gilles Deleuze, Félix Guattari, and Michel Foucault. The tenth floor, Disc Port (later WAVE), sold records by contemporary composers rarely heard in Japan, such as Steve Reich and John Cage.[14] Customers could listen to music right there in the store. For almost every artist coming of age in the 1980s and early 1990s in Japan, Saison's cultural zone and its nationwide franchise quickly made it a singular influence base. This was a time when the art curricula in Tokyo focused on the fundamentals of painting and sculpture, while artists nationwide were seeking the latest information on art and culture. Sachigusa Yasuda (b. 1968), who entered TUA in 1989, recalls being eager to learn about contemporary art, and moving near Ikebukuro to take advantage of Seibu's cultural zone.[15]

The retail empire began as Tsutsumi's response to growing up under Japan's militaristic totalitarian regime, which resulted in his peculiar brand of consumerism. His initial motivation for selling a rich selection of imported goods was to liberate Japanese consumers from the thriftiness that the wartime military government had forced upon the people.[16] During Japan's period of remarkable economic growth, Tsutsumi viewed the new social conformity that had been induced by information and the politics of corporate capitalism as a prime case of what Herbert Marcuse called in 1964 a "technocracy."[17] In this brave new information society where the collective consciousness could easily absorb an individual's opinion, Tsutsumi's ultimate goal was to create an "autonomous consumer" who could also make individual judgments as a "constituent."[18] To pursue this political goal, to reiterate, culture became important, because culture "is one of the human beings' imaginative and creative activities, which as a whole constructs human life."[19]

Seibu's cultural zone played a definitive role in nurturing Japan's contemporary artists. While preparing for art school, Yoshiaki Kaihatsu (b. 1966) remembers that his instructor at Tachikawa Supplementary Art School, Takashi Murakami (b. 1962), instructed students to visit Seibu Libro and buy at least two of their favorite art books.[20] Akira Nagae, who worked at ART VIVANT, recalls his frequent encounters with the young New Painting hopeful, Shinro Ohtake, at the shop. "It is safe to call our generation 'the Seibu Museum generation,'" commented *nihonga* artist Hiroko Ohno (b. 1956) on Saison culture.[21]

In 1979, Seibu Department Stores launched an advertising campaign calling the forthcoming decade the "On'na no jidai (Woman's epoch)."[22] Its sister company, PARCO, encouraged women in 1974 with their catchy copy, "On'na tachiyo, taishi wo idake!" ("Women, be ambitious!"). These ad campaigns were visible everywhere: on trains, throughout the city, and on television. And they situated women's creativity at the core of their cultural campaign.[23]

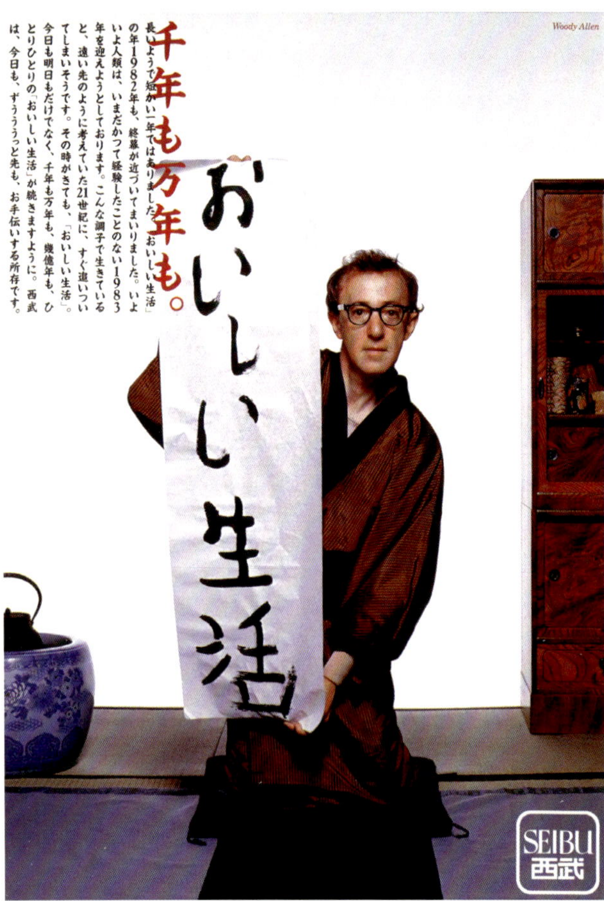

Figure 8.2. Katsumi Asaba, *Oishii seikatsu* (1982). Courtesy of Katsumi Asaba Design Studio.

Hiroko Ohno and the *Nihonga* New Wave

Ohno represents Aratana Nihonga (*Nihonga* New Wave), a group of young *nihonga* painters who were hesitant to establish themselves within the traditional apprenticeship system that governs the discipline. This new generation included Rieko Hidaka, Hiroshi Senju, and Takashi Murakami, among other painters, who eschewed conventional salon-style art competition and established themselves through gallery shows.[24] Ohno explains today that it was not a self-conscious movement,[25] but a curatorial distinction. Still, this new generation of *nihonga* artists were rediscovering traditional art materials, just as average Japanese citizens were reassessing their cultural heritage.

The nation's moment of reawakening to tradition is best captured in Seibu's 1982 epoch-making ad campaign, *Oishii seikatsu* (Delicious Life). Starring Woody Allen, its poster (fig. 8.2) featured the American filmmaker in a plain winter kimono, seated in a humble Japanese setting, writing out the commercial slogan in the manner of a new year's resolution. By incorporating an old-fashioned cupboard and brazier in the background, the art director, Katsumi Asaba, reminded consumers of "the wonderful things that [traditionally] existed in Japan," as another one of Seibu's inner-circle members, Kazuko Koike, explained it.[26] During this time, the average Japanese person finally had some surplus money and time to rethink and reinvent their lifestyle beyond the pastiche of the West, as did artists.

Explaining her work today, Ohno echoes Koike's call that she did not want to create a "pastiche of American art using Western media." She thus chose to paint with *nihonga* pigments but never thought of "repeating the age-old tradition," trying to find a new significance in the *nihonga* pigments. What distinguished Ohno from other *nihonga* New Wave painters was her subject matter. While others focused on nature or abstraction, Ohno painted urban dwellings without delineating their inhabitants. *Dispatch from Seneca* (1985–present) (fig. 8.3), for example, captured a large rectangular silver table, a circular rug, and a chair. Akin to how the novelist Haruki Murakami describes protagonists indirectly through their taste for music, beer, and clothing without revealing their features, Ohno suggests protagonists by the objects he or she owns.

Here, that person may be an architect, hinted by a foregrounded shadowy chair called Geo Ponti 699 Superleggera. Its light, sophisticated body and thin legs echo those of the silver table in the room's center. A rolled-up map on the table also hints at its owner's

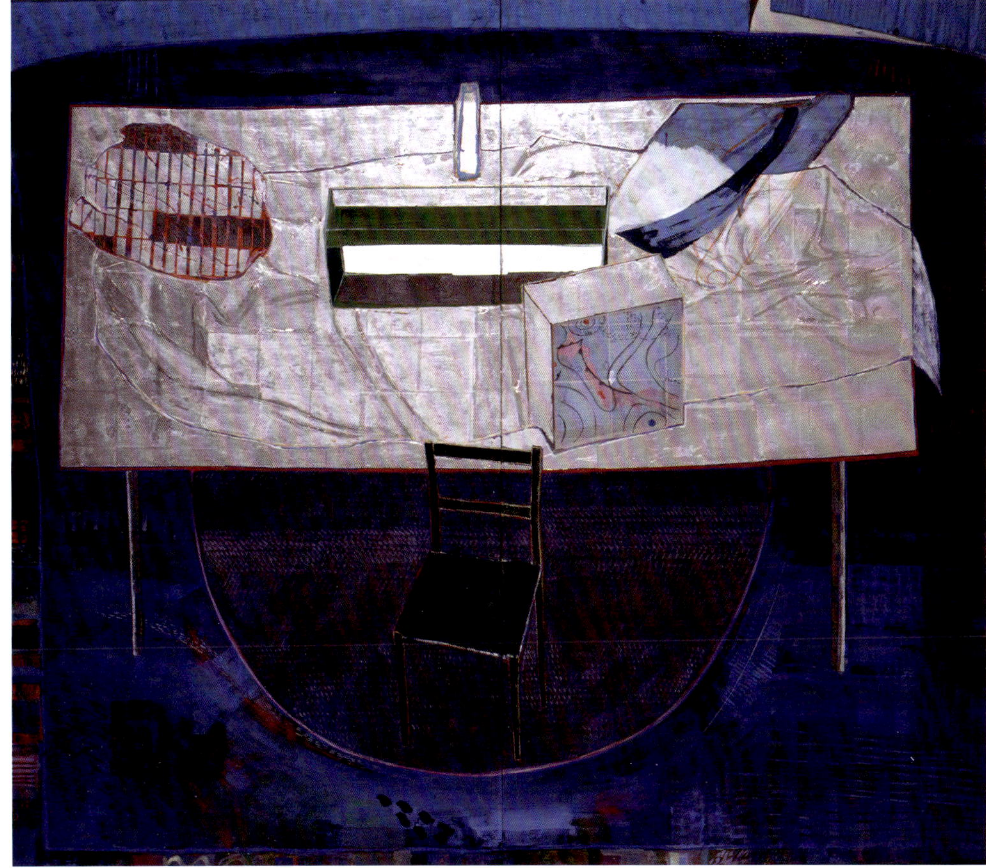

Figure 8.3. Hiroko Ohno, *Dispatch from Seneca* (1985–present). Mineral pigment and silver leaf on rice paper mounted on wood panel, 195 × 220 cm. Collection of Hiratsuka Museum of Art. Courtesy of the artist.

profession. Spread across the table is a large swatch of organdy; its transparency and the dominant colors of the interior, blue and silver, relay a cool atmosphere, suggesting urban solitude. The artificiality of urban life is further emphasized by eliminating all signs of nature—the vase is empty and the fish tank uninhabited. A shirt and a small television randomly placed on the table recall the fancy boutique displays of popular fashion brands like Comme des Garçons or Yoji Yamamoto, who often played videos of their seasonal collections on a closed-circuit loop.

Although Ohno was not part of *Super Girls*, the volume's contributor, Ryoichi Enomoto, explains that such a collection of objects represents the *Super Girls* generation, who "most probably starts reading [popular lifestyle] magazines like *anan* or *Popeye*." They typically "comprehend the world through merchandise." For them, "the structure of the world equates with commercial products."[27] For Ohno, flaunting her collection of objects was a valuable way of relaying her identity. And her eye for good design made Ohno the epitome of Tsutsumi's concept of an "autonomous consumer."

Aside from her object collection, Ohno was reconfiguring *nihonga*. Today she explains that her use of mineral pigments was key to this exploration. In *Dispatch from Seneca*, scrutiny of the subject matter reveals the five essential elements: "earth," in a map of Japan on the television; "water," in the fish tank; "sky," on the rolled-up map; "fire," under the grid pattern of the shirt; and "wind," in the movement of the organdy swatch. She further wanted the semicircle below the table to represent "the moon or other celestial body,"[28] and conceived *nihonga*'s mineral pigments as the elements that constitute the universe.

Like Ohno, the thirty-nine "remarkably active young woman artists" featured in *Super Girls* incorporated their experience of contemporary life and material culture into their artworks.[29] Prominent among them was the use of commonplace objects, such as fabric, beads, and clothing. But according to Matsuoka, unlike Marcel Duchamp, who negated the conventional idea of "art" with his readymades, *Super Girls* artists' use of everyday objects was "Epicureanism."[30]

Mayumi Terada

Matsuoka explained that Epicureanism refers to the artists "reversing" readymades by invalidating their "'utilitarian' aspect . . . making them unusable and playing with them."[31] Their affirmative embrace of commonplace objects is akin to how Lawrence Alloway described the neo-Dada tendency in 1960.[32] In Japan, Jasper Johns's first retrospective exhibition was held at the Seibu Museum of Art in 1978, which had a great impact on artists. An artist featured in *Super Girls*, Mayumi Terada (b. 1958), suggested her work's connection with neo-Dada, by calling her work *Mr. Johns* (1986). Without the first name, Terada's title is purposely ambiguous. However, she explains today, her deliberate allusion to Jasper Johns—her favorite artist—was for the work's "semiotic nature."[33] Like Johns's *Painted Bronze* (1960), Terada recreated a woman's futuristic walk-in closet with clothes and accessories made of transparent plastic, with an aim to generate new meanings (fig. 8.4).

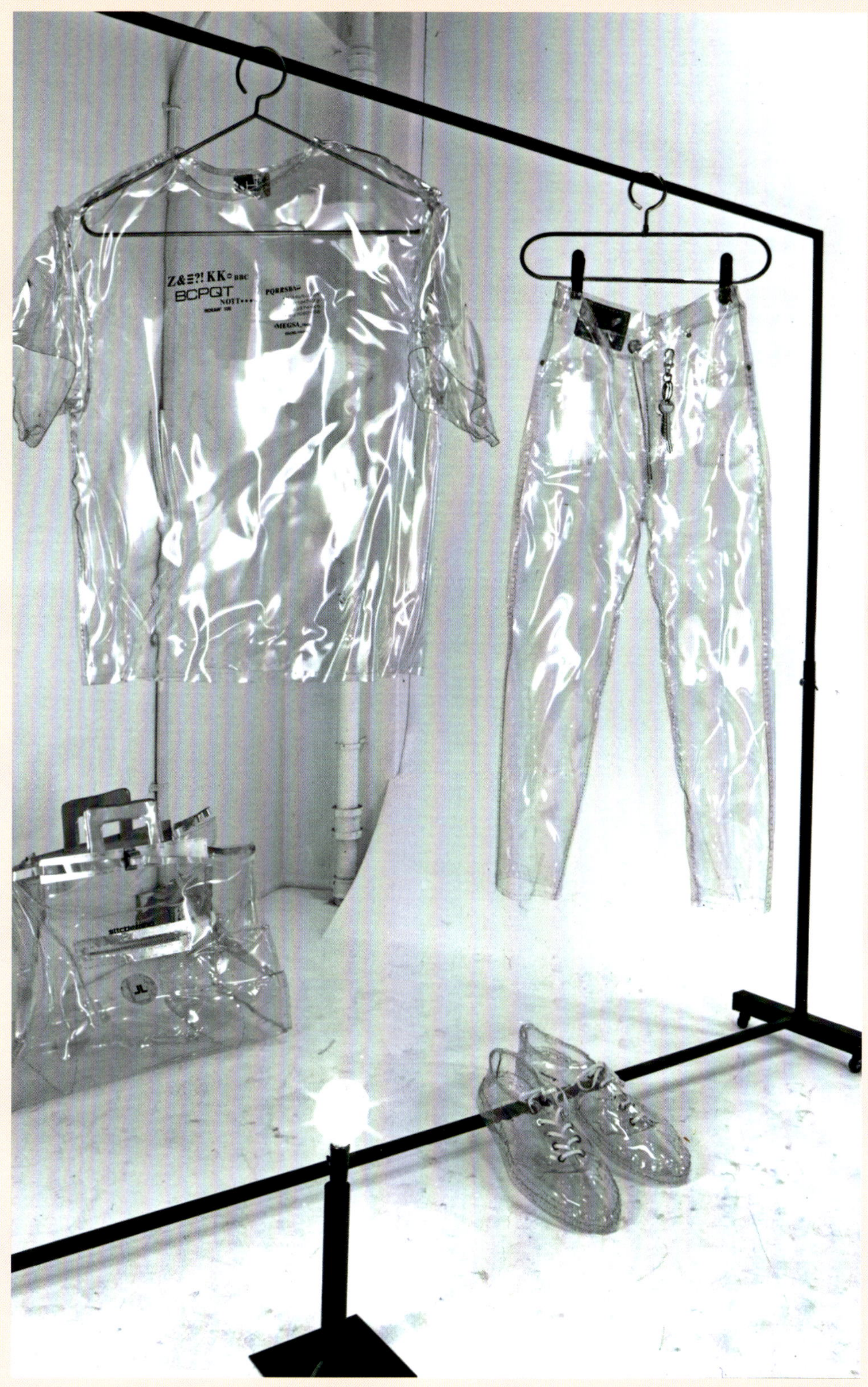

Figure 8.4. Mayumi Terada, *Mr. Johns* (1986). Clear rigid vinyl sheet, clear nylon thread, iron, brass, stainless steel, light bulb. Variable sizes. Collection of the Nerima Art Museum, Tokyo. Courtesy of the artist.

Gender played the essential factor in her embrace of commonplace objects. Like Yayoi Kusama before her, Terada sewed her wardrobe, which at first glance might seem like a feminine endeavor. But she explains how assembling the plastic sheets required drilling the holes and lacing together parts with fishing gut.[34] She also welded the iron furniture. Such physically demanding work betrays our stereotypical idea of what women can do, and consequently challenges our conventional values.

Mr. Johns further betrays female stereotypes by mocking the sales floor of a department store. Here, Terada made trendy merchandise her "object of desire." According to Freud, for a child to develop heterosexual desires, the "Oedipus complex must collapse"—for boys via castration anxiety and girls via penis envy.[35] But Terada's desire is addressed to a fancy bag, a pair of shoes, and women's clothing; with her penchant for merchandise, she breaks from the governing principle of patriarchy. Seibu's lifestyle industry was an impetus behind her interest in material culture. Terada, like many other artists of her generation, recalls submitting her work to Seibu-sponsored art competitions; Saison culture was a driving force behind Japanese art in the 1980s. It opened up the art world for further participation by women artists like Terada.

Mr. Johns was more than its subject matter for Terada; it was her effort to develop a new domain of "photographic sculpture."[36] She studied art at University of Tsukuba's Graduate School, learning from former Jikken Kobo (Experimental Workshop) artists Katsuhiro Yamaguchi and Kiyoshi Otsuji, and former member of Group I, Tatsuo Kawaguchi. Tsukuba encouraged experimental art that utilized technology and the department was tolerant of female students. The Experimental Workshop not only had a female member, but also its leader, Shuzo Takiguchi, was famous for curating women artists at

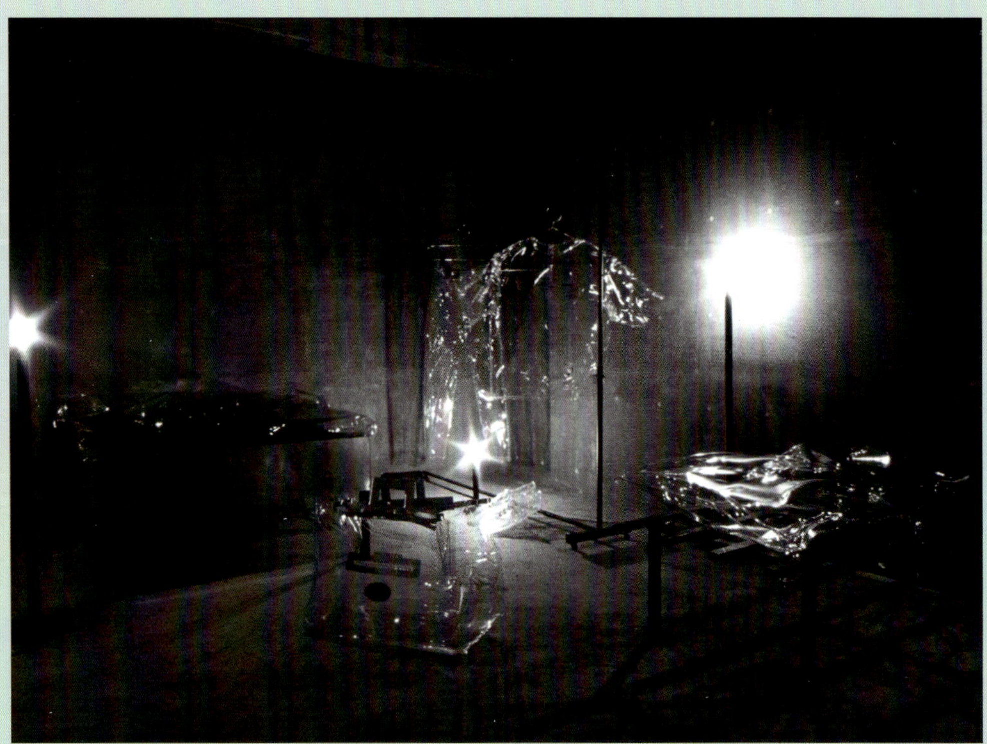

Figure 8.5. Mayumi Terada, *Mr. Johns* (1986). Clear rigid vinyl sheet, clear nylon thread, Iron, brass, stainless steel, light bulb. Variable sizes. Collection of the Nerima Art Museum, Tokyo. Courtesy of the artist.

Takemiya Gallery, including the young Kusama and Toshiko Okanoue. Combining sculpture and photography, Terada wanted to open a new field that amalgamated art and technology.

In the installation view of *Mr. Johns* (fig. 8.5), the deliberately darkened space, lit by three strong lights, Terada's plastic clothes reflected the light illuminating the crumpled surfaces of the dresses and a large handbag, converting her sculptures into pure light. The weightlessness of her photographic sculpture and the use of industrial materials are the two elements that critics writing in the 1980s often associated with women's art.[37] These aspects were especially prominent in the work of another artist featured in *Super Girls*, Mika Yoshizawa.

Mika Yoshizawa

Representing Japan at the Bienal de São Paulo in 1985 and participating in documenta 8 in 1987, Mika Yoshizawa (b. 1959) is one of the most significant artists to emerge in the late 1980s. She entered the oil painting department of Tama Art University (TAU) in 1978, the school famous for Mono-ha, which translates to the "School of Things." Although Mono-ha is categorized as sculpture today, the mainstay of the movement—Nobuo Sekine, Katsuro Yoshida, Shingo Honda, Katsuhiko Narita, Susumu Koshimizu, and Kishio Suga—had all graduated from the painting department of TAU between 1968 and 1969. The cohort of artists thought painting had reached an impasse and focused instead on exploring unprocessed materials (*mono*) and their psychological effects on the viewers' direct encounter with materials.[38] During her school years, Yoshizawa recalls, most students saw painting as dead and experimented by grappling with earth, stone, wood, iron, and glass in the manner of Mono-ha, or by exploring the globally prominent practice of conceptual art.[39] Notwithstanding all objections against painting, Yoshizawa reembraced the medium, seeking to create art different from that of the immediate postwar generation.

A crucial aspect of Yoshizawa's art is a logical development out of Mono-ha into a new painterly practice. In the 1990s, the curator Yoko Hayashi, for example, commented that Yoshizawa's "paintings have a depth and maturity."[40] However, today, Yoshizawa's work is categorized as New Wave, which refers to the postmodern pluralism in Japan. In a way, this distinction obscured her contributions to the field of painting. More problematically, greater attention was paid to Yoshizawa's persona than her art, which meant female artists were not taken as seriously as they should be and seen merely as curiosities. A volume like *Super Girls*, featuring only young women and calling them "girls," in Yoshizawa's opinion, was there to "entertain middle-aged men."

Yoshizawa's late 1980s popularity can be deduced from a billboard installed across the Harajuku station platform—the epicenter of Japan's fashion world—featuring Yoshizawa with her artworks.[41] While her reputation helped popularize contemporary art, the fact of her being a young woman put her art on a path different from her male counterparts—the cohort categorized as "New Painting."

Epitomized by Tadanori Yokoo (b. 1936), Shinro Ohtake (b. 1955), and Katsuhiko Hibino (b. 1958), New Painting is an all-male category. But New Painting itself was not initially a critically established field, Mikami remembers today, it was only a "temporary term."[42] Art editors in the 1980s initially called the new figurative tendency "New Image Painting" or "Neo-Expressionism," after US Neo-Expressionism.[43] When the historicization of 1980s Japanese art began with a comprehensive chronology, *The 20th Century Art in Japan* (2014), followed by two survey exhibitions in 2018, the art journalist Makoto Murata explained both the New Painting and the New Wave movement from this time as "the revival of colors, decorativeness, and narrative tendency"; all of these elements became part of the plurality that characterized postmodernism.[44] Considering the fine line between New Painting and New Wave, Murata distinguished New Painting artists as being subjects of mass media who shunned rental galleries for newly emerging curated art spaces.[45]

Yoshizawa not only meets both criteria, but she and Yokoo were also part of the Bienal de São Paulo in 1985. Its commissioner, Yoshiaki Tono, was known to champion the neo-Dada movement in Japan. Although Yoshizawa was not working under that aegis, her use of discarded industrial materials might have attracted Tono's attention. Neo-Dada artists like Rauschenberg had impacted another New Painting artist—Shinro Ohtake. In principle, she could pass as a New Painting artist.

Furthermore, out of all the artists exhibiting in 1982, Yoshizawa's work comes closest to that of the star of New Painting, Katsuhiko Hibino, whose artwork incorporated subcultural elements. In 1982, the same year Yoshizawa's artwork captured Tono's attention with her BFA exhibition (fig. 8.6),[46] Hibino won the Japan Graphic Award from Seibu's sister company, PARCO. In reaction to the professionalism of Mono-ha, Yoshizawa chose to paint on "humble objects," such as a vacuum cleaner, cupboard, and gas heater (fig. 8.7). Embracing boys' favorite subjects—like airplanes (fig. 8.8), a baseball mitt, and a brand-new pair of sneakers—Hibino painted on cardboard. Through playfulness and humble materials, Hibino's work exuded the naïve creativity of young boys. Today, the artist/writer Hideki Nakazawa designates Hibino's art as "hetauma [deftly unskilled],"[47] emphasizing Hibino's calculated unskillfulness by adding *uma* (deftness) to *heta* (unskilled). No one would address Hibino as a *zukō shonen*.

Zukō is an abbreviation for *zugakōsaku*, the term used to address an elementary school art class, and *shōnen* means "boy." In the catalog of the 2018 survey exhibition, *New Wave: Japanese Contemporary Art of the 1980s*, curators dismissed Yoshizawa as a "zukō shōjo,"[48] an "elementary school girl creating art." Although both Hibino and Yoshizawa explored subculture, their artworks demonstrate an equally natural desire to create. She was identified with elementary school while Hibino was not; these discrepancies in perception indicate how internalized biases lead to gender stereotyping in art. Looking back at the *Super Girls* phenomenon, "calling a thirty-year-old woman a 'girl,'" Yoshizawa spoke of her media coverage as "the editors treating women as children." But she converted such biases against her gender into motivations to transform her art.

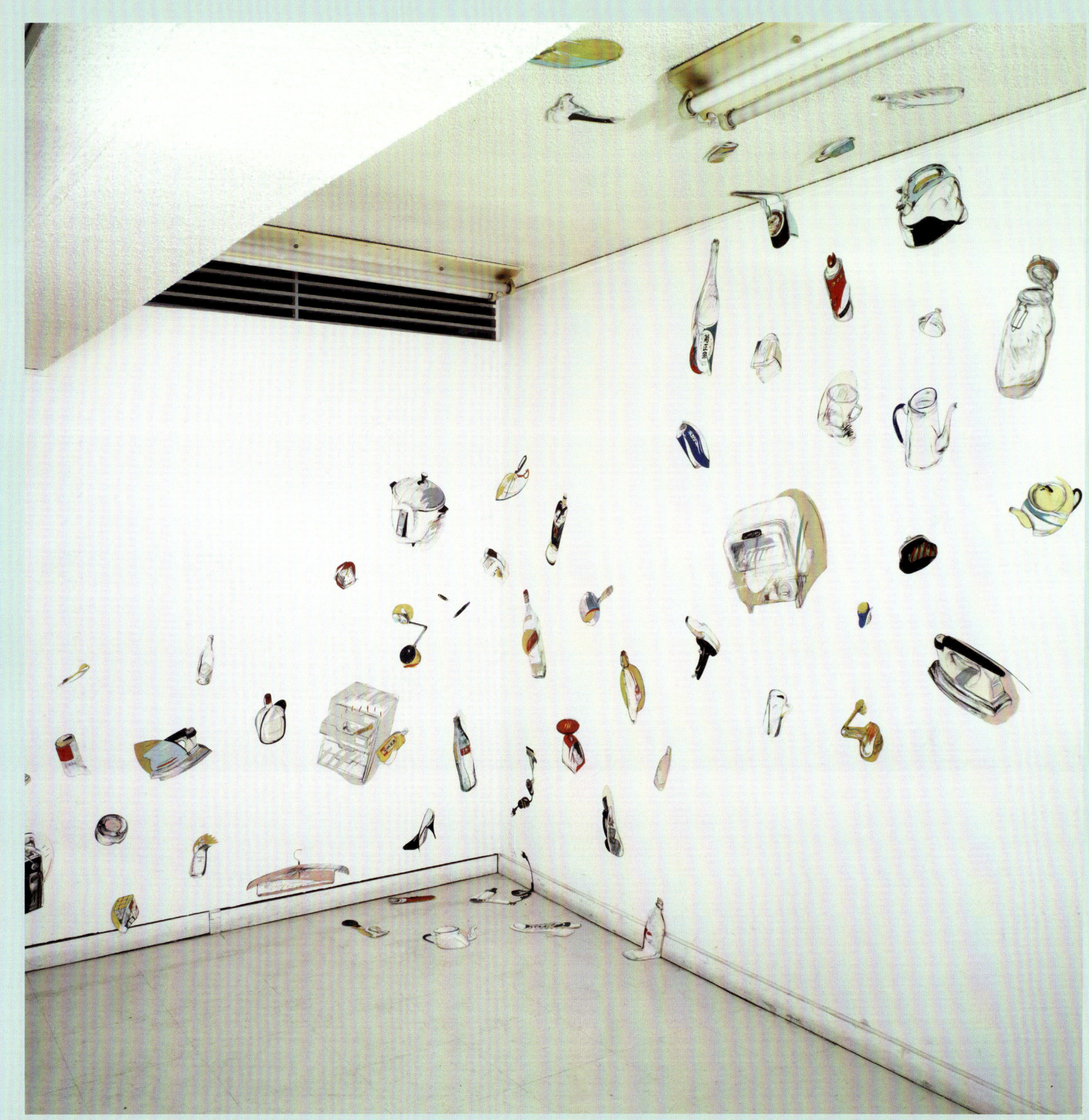

Figure 8.6. Mika Yoshizawa, *Untitled* (1982). Acrylic on paper, variable sizes. Photo by Mika Yoshizawa. Courtesy of the artist.

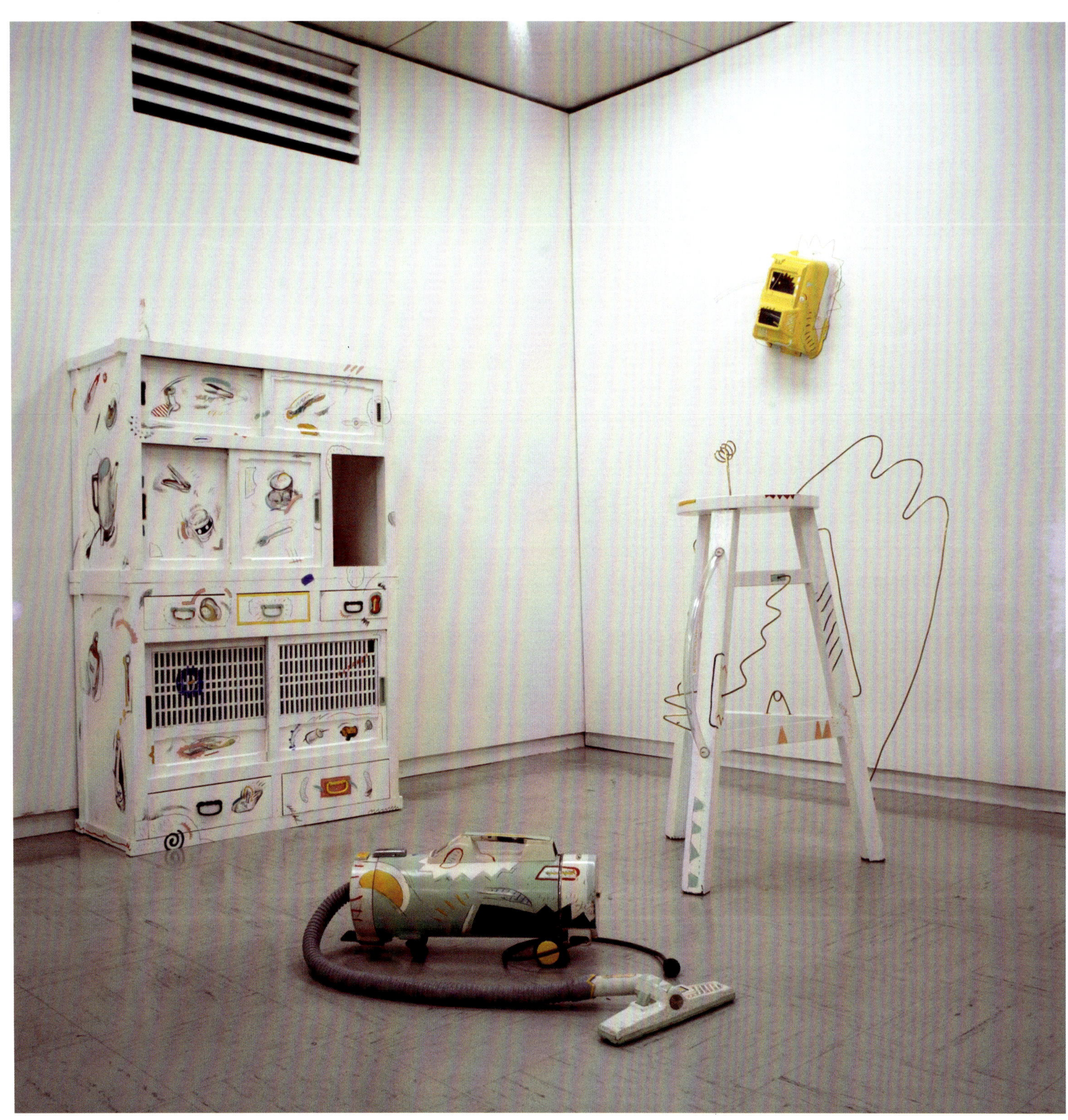

Figure 8.7. Mika Yoshizawa, *Cupboard, Stool, SOUJIKI (vacuum cleaner), Kiroino (Yellow one)* (1982). Each item: acrylic paint, colored pencil, etcetera. Photo by Shigeo Anzaï. © Estate of Shigeo Anzaï, courtesy of the artist and Zeit-Foto.

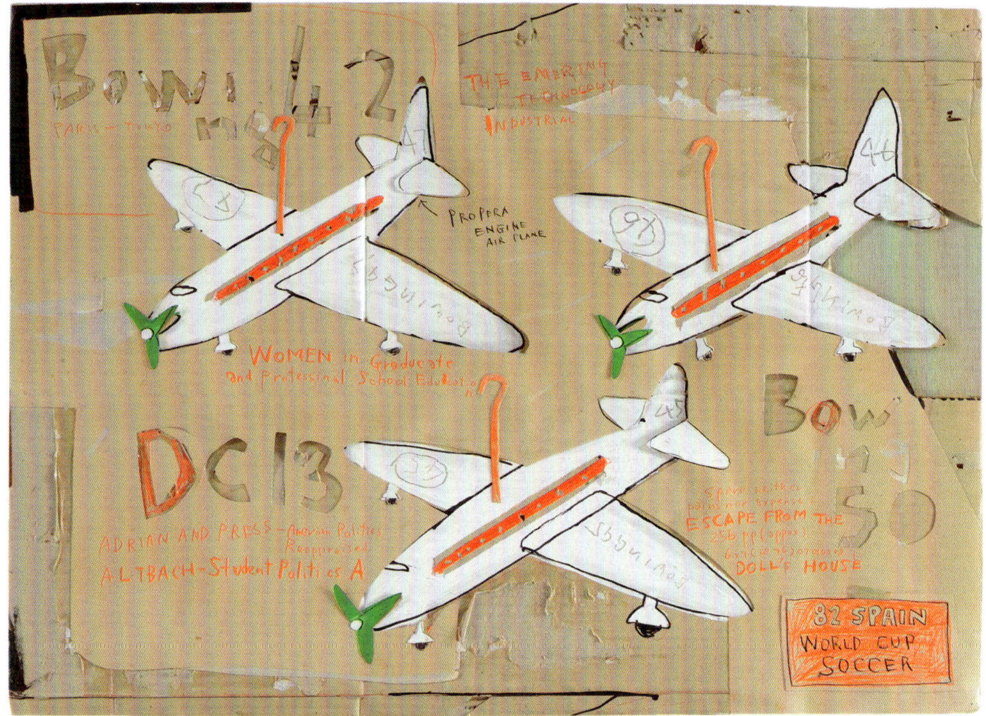

Figure 8.8. Katsuhiko Hibino, *PRESENT AIRPLANE* (1982). Cardboard, paper, acrylic color pencil, ink, 72.8 × 103 cm. Collection of The Museum of Fine Arts, Gifu.

After Yoshizawa's initial encounter with Tono, he included her works in *Today's Artists* (1982), the Third Hara Annual (1983), and the Bienal de São Paulo—all gateways to the art world in Japan. When Yoshizawa introduced a group of works painted on caramel wrappers and confectionery boxes at the Hara Annual, she received a heavily gender-based critique. The appraisal led her to "consciously remove womanly color" from her artwork and she began developing abstraction. The decision was not against her will, however. "While nobody saw value in a good painting," recalled Yoshizawa, she was grappling with the issues of the painting itself by defying the conventional four-edged canvas and seeking untraditional paints and supports that would help substantiate her fluid brushwork. For Hibino and Yokoo—who both focused on graphic design rather than the inherent formal issues of painting—the subject matter was essential to their practice. For Yoshizawa, embracing commonplace objects was a way to experiment with the works' supports. Regarding feminism, although she was aware of the "feminist art movement," she "wanted to be free of such a concern." Her remark confirms that her interests were more formal than societal.[49] But the media rejected "anything serious," Yoshizawa said in the author's conversation with her, and only "published nonsensical comments."

Although Yoshizawa's name is missing from the latest chronology,[50] she participated in *Art in Japan Since 1969: Mono-ha and Post Mono-ha* at the Seibu Museum of Art in 1987. She was an important bridge between the 1970s "stoic" movement and the 1980s plurality of expression. Her conscious development out of Mono-ha is evident in her series from the mid-1980s, in which she began capturing the zeitgeist through materials and style. In these works, she consciously distanced herself from Mono-ha. Works by "the previous generation," she explained, "retained the vestiges of the war," whereas her generation had grown up with "plastic products, and shopping at the supermarket," and watching MTV. Since things were "changing through consumer society," the new generation "eagerly accepted the culture of the mass-information and consumer society." This "fusion of . . . high art and sub-culture," according to Tono, was "some of the most marked trends in contemporary art in Japan of the 1980s."[51]

Yoshizawa's new series incorporated sensations from everyday life into abstract paintings. The shallow surface structure symbolically represented plastic culture. She recalls admiring Willem de Kooning's fluid brushwork at the Seibu Museum of Art. To achieve a similar effect, Yoshizawa continued experimenting with supports by introducing polypropylene, vinyl, ABS resin, and even vinyl chloride, which raised some conservation concerns among professionals. What mattered for her was the rigid surface achieved, so that the ink remained on it for a long time and enabled her smooth brushwork. By erasing and repainting the forms, similar to the way de Kooning worked on his painting, Yoshizawa deliberately left traces of erasure and imparted a sense of weightlessness with her abstraction (fig. 8.9). Her surface structure acutely captured the atmosphere of the last leg of Japan's economic bubble without reference to figural images.

Yoshizawa's paintings that evoke lightness, such as *Ni-24* (1991), seem to have inspired the subsequent generation—Neo-pop artists. Comparing *Ni-24* with Takashi Murakami's famed "superflat" character, Mr. Dob, we see that although Murakami employed a recognizable image adopted from a Disney animation, Dob's floating formation and Yoshizawa's levitating form have much in common—namely, regarding their shapes, placement, and the imparted weightless atmosphere. In 1991, when Yoshizawa painted *Ni-24*, Murakami was still completing his PhD in *nihonga* at TUA, surveying contemporary artists. His art collection exhibited at Kaikaikiki Gallery in 2017 was, in a way, testimony that Murakami was familiar with some of the best works to emerge from the late 1980s Japanese contemporary art scene. Although Yoshizawa's art is not part of his collection, it is almost certain that he was aware of her painting and its surface structure.[52]

As discussed above, gender put Yoshizawa's work on a "track to modify painting,"[53] which separated her from the New Painting artists, whose emphasis was on the subject matter. By contrast, her focus became the formal quality of the painting. Yoshizawa is a painter's painter. Although formalism has little to do with identity, she candidly accepted her gender by admitting her physical limits, so she used "light materials." It enabled her to maneuver her artwork alone. Without "confronting being a woman," Tono observed, "women are now distancing themselves from the range of men's vision."[54] The Saison group and its associates supported Yoshizawa after her graduation. Not only did Seibu's contemporary art gallery become her business partner, but also Koike hosted Yoshizawa's one-woman show at Sagacho Exhibit Space in 1987.

In the 1990s, Yoshizawa became the first female professor of the oil painting department at TAU. In contrast, the school's sculpture department was taught predominantly

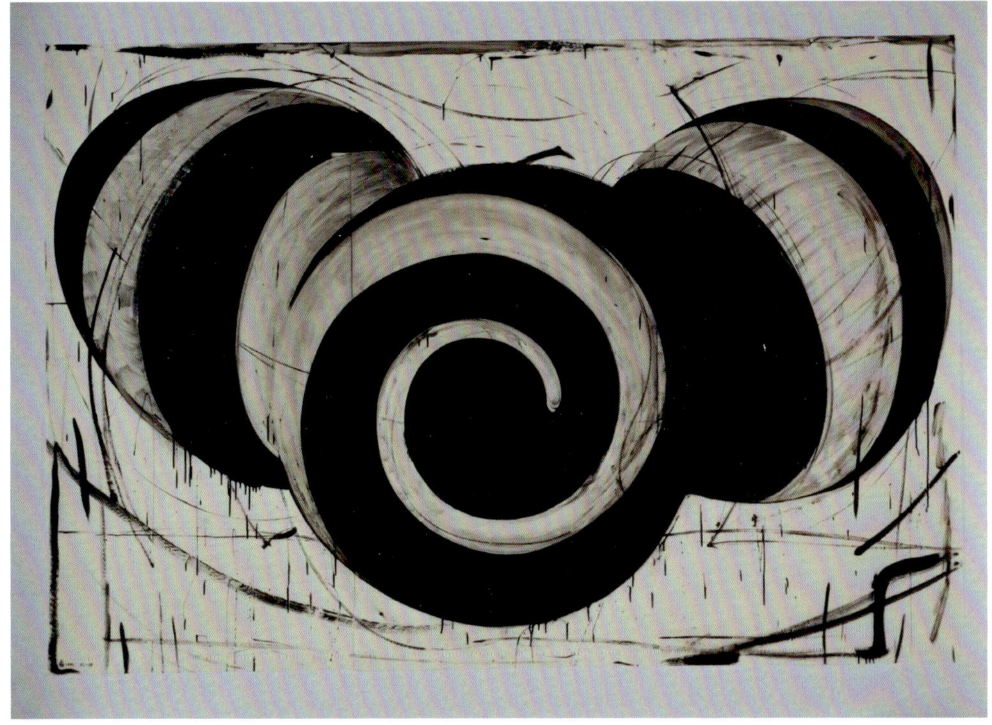

Figure 8.9. Mika Yoshizawa, *Ni-24* (1991). 140 × 200 cm. Industrial Ink on ABS resin, Courtesy of the artist.

by males that led to the 2018 students' protest against school authority. The ratio of men to women teaching in Yoshizawa's department has reached 5:4. Yoshizawa is far more than just a *zukō shōjo*. She was the key figure who resuscitated painting after the Mono-ha artists turned away from painterly practice. She reflected the sensation of everyday life in her work, created a new type of painting, and frankly accepted her gender in her practice. Yoshizawa's contributions to Japanese contemporary art at various levels need to be reassessed.

Masayo Koizumi

Making her three-month-old son a part of her live-in installation, Masayo Koizumi (b. 1959) stunned visitors at Utsubo Gallery with *Infant* (1985) (fig. 8.10). Over two overlapping red and black carpets, Koizumi sewed small golden spheres, each placed on a hand-sewn square cushion. At the center of this galaxy lay the artist's infant son. The work's key colors—red and black—accentuated the baby's cottony hair and ruddy tones of his cherubic limbs. Despite the calculated color coordination, the baby stood out because he was a product of the artist's biological function, representing what feminist art historian Anne Higonnet addresses as the "natural, primitive, even animal" feminine.[55]

While the female gallery visitors tended to adore the baby, men expressed apparent repulsion, asking the artist, if "this could be called art."[56] As the artist breastfed during the course of a week-long exhibition—no different from how she would care for her son at home—*Infant* further emphasized women's biological function. The work's apparent theme was maternity—an unusual topic in Japan—though, historically, it was the subject for such female artist predecessors as Sonia Delaunay-Terk and Paula Modersohn-Becker. Both began their respective careers in conjunction with significant twentieth-century art movements, Cubism and German Expressionism, yet their art diverged during pregnancy. Delaunay-Terk made a baby quilt based on geometric patterns. Modersohn-Becker rendered her pregnant body as self-portraiture.

Art that dealt with birth was rare,[57] because under patriarchy, the "cycle of birth has traditionally looked ugly," as Higonnet explains.[58] Gazing at Modersohn-Becker's pregnant self-portraits, her husband even commented that she was "attracted to ugly subjects."[59] At TUA, professors often remarked that pregnancy prevents women from pursuing their art. Consequently, out of seven women who had enrolled in the graduate school at TUA in the early 1990s, only one had children.[60]

Koizumi explains that she made *Infant* as a holdover from the postwar vanguard practice. Like Terada and Yoshizawa, whose works were established in dialogue with the immediate postwar generation, Koizumi attended the fine arts department of Osaka University of Arts. The faculties included former Gutai artists, whose famed motto was "Do what no one has done before!"[61] A year after graduating, Koizumi showed an artwork made from human excretions in a group show. The scatological work was a means to liberate herself from any self-consciousness. After this particular work, she could dispel all vanity and create what she truly wanted.[62] Her economic autonomy was also a catalyst for her creative freedom. Thinking of her future, Koizumi started a private art school in her second year of university, which became a successful business. Only with psychological and financial autonomy could Koizumi create her *Infant*.

Although Koizumi doesn't speak explicitly about feminism, gender played a central role in *Infant*, with which she challenged preconceived notions of pregnancy and maternity. She points out that the male and female roles in pregnancy are profoundly different; women undergo a psychological and biological transformation. Koizumi tried to capture these changes based on her experience, and challenged age-old thinking about pregnancy and motherhood. *Infant* is one of the ten series of works that dealt with the topic. Some artworks were collaboratively made with her then-husband, Yasuhiro Ozaki. Later, in 1994, she cooperated with a contemporary haiku poetess Kimiko Nakanaga and published this series as a book entitled *Annunciation*.[63]

According to Koizumi, *Annunciation* was about "capturing a process of becoming a mother then returning to a woman again."[64] Page by page, the book captures the subtleties of women's feelings during and after their pregnancy. The first few images focus on her interior body. The third image shifts to birth; a giant white sphere penetrates a sea of red with dim incandescence. Then comes *My Baby's Cry*. In this work, Koizumi embodied a new mother's tremendous joy at hearing her baby's first cry with red cylinders sewn from cloth, literally filling the hallways of Fujita Vante Museum, where Koizumi had her first museum exhibition. The book ends with *Infant*,[65] suggesting that the work captured the moment of returning from motherhood to womanhood.

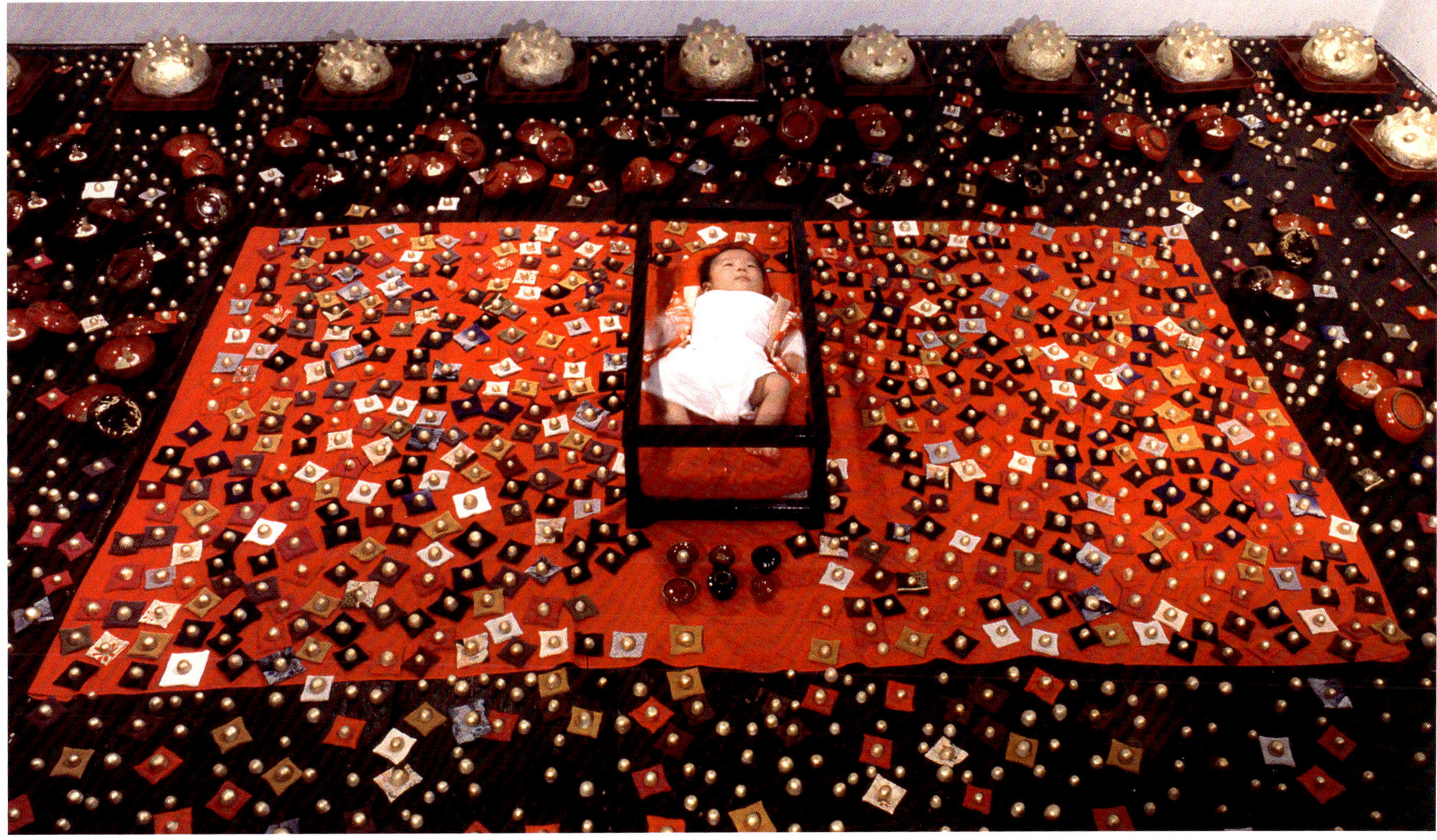

Figure 8.10. Masayo Koizumi, *Infant* (1985). Mixed media with a three-month-old child, gold leaf, clothes, lacquered dinnerware, etcetera, variable sizes. Courtesy of the artist.

Such images of "what [it] feels like to be pregnant, give birth, or protect and feed a tiny infant"—in other words, women's subjective view of pregnancy, according to Higonnet—were virtually nonexistent until Modersohn-Becker's self-portraits. This lack owed mostly to the legacy of discrimination based on gender. Although a child is created jointly by a man and woman, the social expectations for a woman in Japan are to be a good mother and a good wife. For women artists to be socially active, they had to be discreet about their pregnancy; it thus became an uncommon subject. Koizumi remembers the "shock" that visitors expressed on seeing her work, as if they "saw something they did not want to see."[66]

The adverse reaction may have been due to the biological bond of the mother and son. It is because in "the civilizing process," feminist theorist Janet Wolff has noted that the body is "increasingly patrolled, the range of acceptable behavior increasingly carefully and narrowly defined."[67] In a patriarchal society, women's biological body—subject to processes of eating, excreting, menstruation, sex, pregnancy, aging, and illness—is often regarded as a "grotesque body."[68] Once the collective feminist art movement took place in the 1970s in places like New York, women tried to liberate themselves from the "narrowly defined" civilized body that fulfills the patriarchal gaze. If considered more fully, Koizumi's artwork challenged Japanese society to accept biological women's bodies, making the world more habitable for women because women's physical function is different from men. In this respect, her work can be seen as a feminist art.

With *Infant*, Koizumi also tried to save the matriarchal lines of her first husband's family home in Awaji Island. "When women get married [in Japan], they lose their family name, and women's bloodlines become obscure." But one day, Koizumi found the remnants of tailored kimonos in a tea box in the attic of her in-laws' two-hundred-year-old family house. Koizumi used swatches for hand-sewn cushions in her installation to represent a line of women who had married into the family. By incorporating these fabrics, Koizumi aimed to make that genealogy of women tangible. The design and the colors of the hems relay each woman's identity within her restricted life. With scrutiny, viewers could recognize that the family's female blood line's modest assertion continued in her son.[69]

From the silk swatches' gorgeous appearance, viewers might imagine that these women led lavish lives as brides, and later, mother of the heirs of an established landowning family. However, what awaited them was women's unchanging role. When Koizumi married her former husband and lived with his family, their expectation was for her to be a good wife. She cooked three meals a day, cleaned the house, and attended mothers' association meetings while teaching six hundred students at her private art school. She only had time for her art at night, and she still needed to take care of her newborn. In this respect, *Infant* was a continuation of her daily routine in the gallery.

Not all of the artists featured in *Super Girls* continued making art. Women needed to abort art-making because they lost control over their time once they got married. In Koizumi's case, her hectic schedule ultimately seems to have taken its toll on her health. In 2004, she was diagnosed with cancer. Due to her chemotherapy-induced hormone disorder, Koizumi started experiencing deep depression. Her mood impacted her creative output. She recalled that "horrifying colors and forms" emerged from her imagination. Her artwork reflected her "unstable psychological condition," which resulted in her creative hiatus. Until then, she had viewed art-making as her life's purpose; she thought that a "person who can no longer create has no value." When Koizumi decided to stop making art, she felt like "the earth crumbled, I had nothing that supported my body. I was filled with awful anxiety."[70]

Unlike previously discussed artists, Koizumi eschewed fancy consumer items for found objects.[71] In *Infant*, she used the elevated trays and lidded lacquer bowls uncovered from her family storage. These objects are typically used in Japan for special banquets—like those at birth events, weddings, or funerals; they remind people of important events in their life. Integrating the symbolism of found objects is far from the consumerism Seibu promoted. But with the arrival of the "Women's Epoch," spectators were changing. Koizumi remembers she was in the limelight more so than her artist husband.[72] Her brief success is testimony to Saison culture's influence, as the Japanese art world started to open up for women artists.

"Just Be a Woman," Kazuko Koike and Sagacho Exhibit Space

Few people in the United States have heard of Kazuko Koike (b. 1936), but most US city dwellers are familiar with the Muji brand. When Seibu began developing what would become their most successful business venture in 1979, Koike was one of its concept makers. Against the grain of the growing middle-class taste for foreign brands, Muji's original Japanese title, Mujirushi Ryohin (no brand with good quality), was the ultimate test "for consumers to be capable of selecting goods beyond the name brand."[73] It was part of the group's political mission to nurture autonomous individuals capable of making their judgments as constituents.

In this light, Koike is the model consumer Seibu envisioned. Her self-awareness manifests in her impeccable clothing selection—complete with jewelry, scarf, and perfume, articulating her personality. Her personality defines her lifestyle and work. In the 1970s, Koike's vigorous creativity and critical acumen coincided with Japan's accelerated economic growth and cultural energy, resulting in unique curatorial projects. The first exhibition she curated was a show of contemporary clothing entitled *Gendai ifuku no genryūten* (Source of Contemporary Clothing Exhibition) (1975), at the National Museum of Modern Art, Kyoto. It was a rare example of a clothing show receiving international recognition.[74] That same year, the Seibu Museum of Art (SMA) opened with Koike as an associate curator.

Koike has her roots in social realist theater, and her ideas about art accord with some of SMA's best-known exhibitions, such as *Art and Revolution* (1982), which featured works by Russian Constructivists and Productivists from 1910 to 1932. Koike, like the Russian artists before her, curated shows, such as *Issey Miyake in Museums* (1977) and *Mackintosh Design* (1979), which brought art and life together. As a feminist, she introduced some important female artists to the Japanese audience, including Frida Kahlo (1989). Since public museums were not ready to show contemporary artists, in 1983, Koike rented the third floor of the Shokuryō (Grocery) building in Kōtō Ward, Tokyo, which became Sagacho Exhibit Space, the "fixed-point observatory of contemporary art."[75]

Koike, like Tsutsumi, did not believe in commodifying art, so the space was nonprofit. There, she showed both Japanese and international contemporary artists. They included Mika Yoshizawa, Shinro Ohtake, Hiroshi Sugimoto, and Yasumasa Morimura, along with Niki de Saint Phalle and Tracey Emin. She also curated a cross-discipline exhibition featuring the trio of Rei Kawakubo (fashion), Takashi Sugimoto (interior design), and Tadao Ando (architecture).

Rei Naito

In September 1991, Sagacho was the talk of the town. From newspapers to fashion and art magazines, diverse media competed in writing about Rei Naito's (b. 1961) singular work, *une place sur la Terre (One place on the Earth)* (1991). Inside Sagacho's darkened spacious gallery emerged an architecturally scaled, 15-by-5.5-meter ellipse with the height of 2.6 meters, covered with white flannel. The tentlike structure emitted an organic glow from the inside (fig. 8.11). Since the artist conditioned the viewing experience by allowing only one person in the artwork for ten minutes, there was a long queue to view this work. Based on Sagacho's open hours (11 a.m.–6 p.m.), and the fact that the artist entered the installation once every hour for ten minutes to make adjustments, only thirty-five people could view the artwork each day, yet almost one hundred lined up every day to see this work; more than half the visitors waited in vain.[76]

What attracted people was the rarity of experience. Before entering the light-enveloped space, people were asked to remove their shoes. By doing so, the visitors literally could feel this work with their skin. Upon entering the ellipse (fig. 8.12), the audience encountered a sight that they had never seen before. As the work's title suggests, the only place of its kind on Earth. The space was meant to induce an emotional swell in viewers through an encounter with the feeling of exaltation, which the artist described as a "blessing."[77] Naito successfully realized her vision by creating the sight lit with the gentle light from fourteen small naked lightbulbs. The light gave warmth to the installation and imparted a subtle gradation to the two inverted U-shaped overlapping dark and light beige segments.

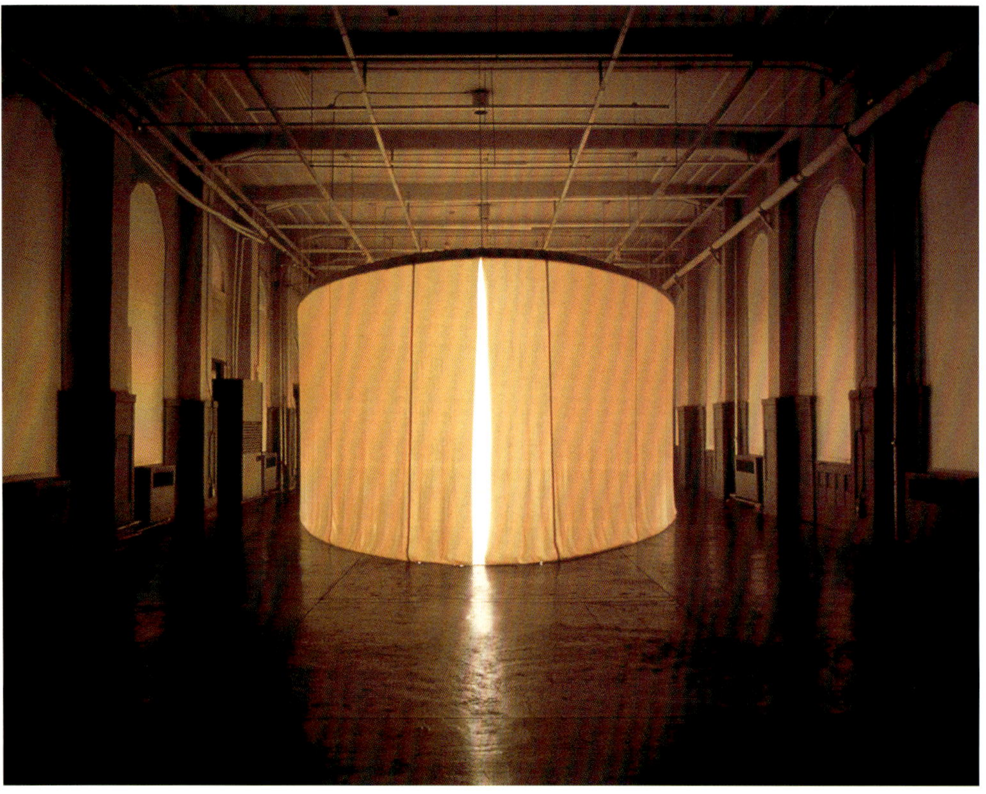

Figure 8.11. Rei Naito, *une place sur la Terre* (1991). Sagacho Exhibit Space, Tokyo. Photo by Naoya Hatakeyama. Courtesy of Taka Ishii Gallery and Naoya Hatakeyama.

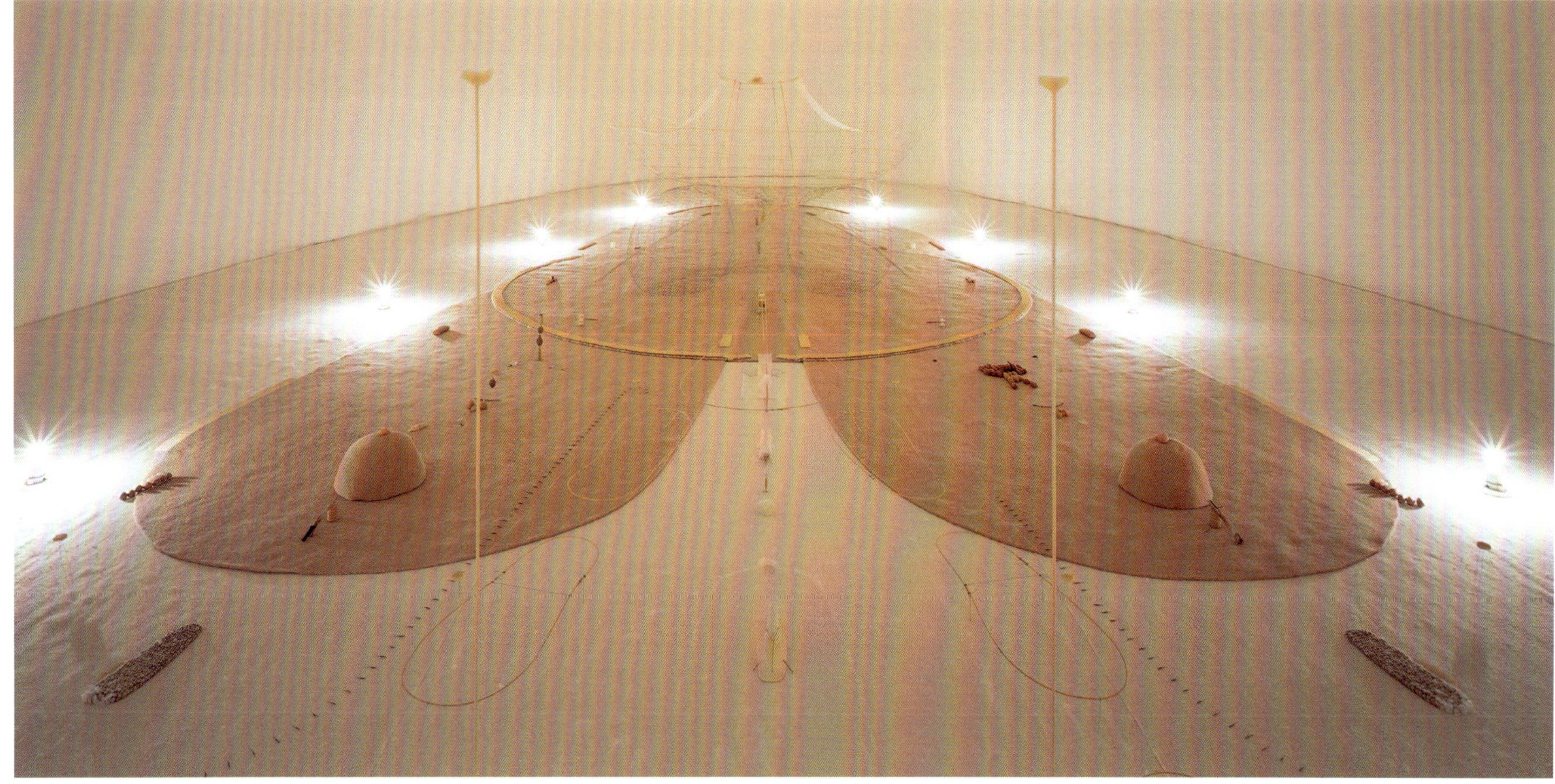

Figure 8.12. Rei Naito, *une place sur la Terre* (1991); interior view. Sagacho Exhibit Space, Tokyo. Photo by Naoya Hatakeyama. Courtesy of Taka Ishii Gallery and Naoya Hatakeyama.

Light occupies a peculiar space in Naito's work. The artist instructed that all the artificial lights be turned off in the museum at her 2018 solo exhibition held at Art Tower Mito. Inside the darkened gallery lit by natural light, the artworks became more visible only when onlookers' five senses were fully alert. In *Being Given* (2001), housed in Kinza, part of an Art House Project on Naoshima Island in the Seto Inland Sea, the light entered through a slight opening between the earth floor (*doma*) and the bottom of the architecture's elevated walls, making the intricate objects of the installation visible in silhouette. For *One place on the Earth,* in the "salient and softly tactile space," the "infinitesimally small and delicate objects" emerge in the light from the light bulbs reflected on the flannel and filling the whole space. Because these objects are delicate, each detail can only be perceived with careful observation. "Inside" the artwork, the artist intended that "the viewers can spend time in any ways they wanted."[78] The viewers are allowed to be in proximity with the objects. From the details that appeared, onlookers became aware of the objects' lively existence. The artist explained this moment as: "the space that starts breathing . . . emerges as filled with good feeling," which was the moment of blessing.[79]

Inside the tent, the viewers first encountered the vertically lined objects that combined the thin bamboo sticks with a cocoon-like shape, creating a procession in the center of the two arms of the inverted U, which continued toward the rear. Some were found objects like seashells, seeds, bars of soap, and pieces of driftwood, all of which added a poetic tone to this work. Other items, like a sewn breast-like sculpture, had a substantial presence. The intricate work developed out of two years of planning and struggle in solitude. Naito invited each viewer to face this work alone, as she had done each day during its creation. The distance between the work and an onlooker naturally became intimate as one needed to approach the objects for a detailed view (fig. 8.13).

The above factors, especially the conditions of each viewing, gave every onlooker an extraordinary encounter with this work. The work's subject matter was "motherhood." The inverted U-shapes can be seen as a woman's upper and lower body. However, it was not the result of conscious planning. Sagacho's structure came out of a series of drawings that Naito repeatedly created during a concentrated period in 1990, in order to grasp the image of her installation.[80] The artist explains her choice as follows: "Without being aware, I started sensing a woman's body." In the beginning, Naito was reluctant to embrace it because in "contemporary society, being a woman is a liability." Nonetheless,

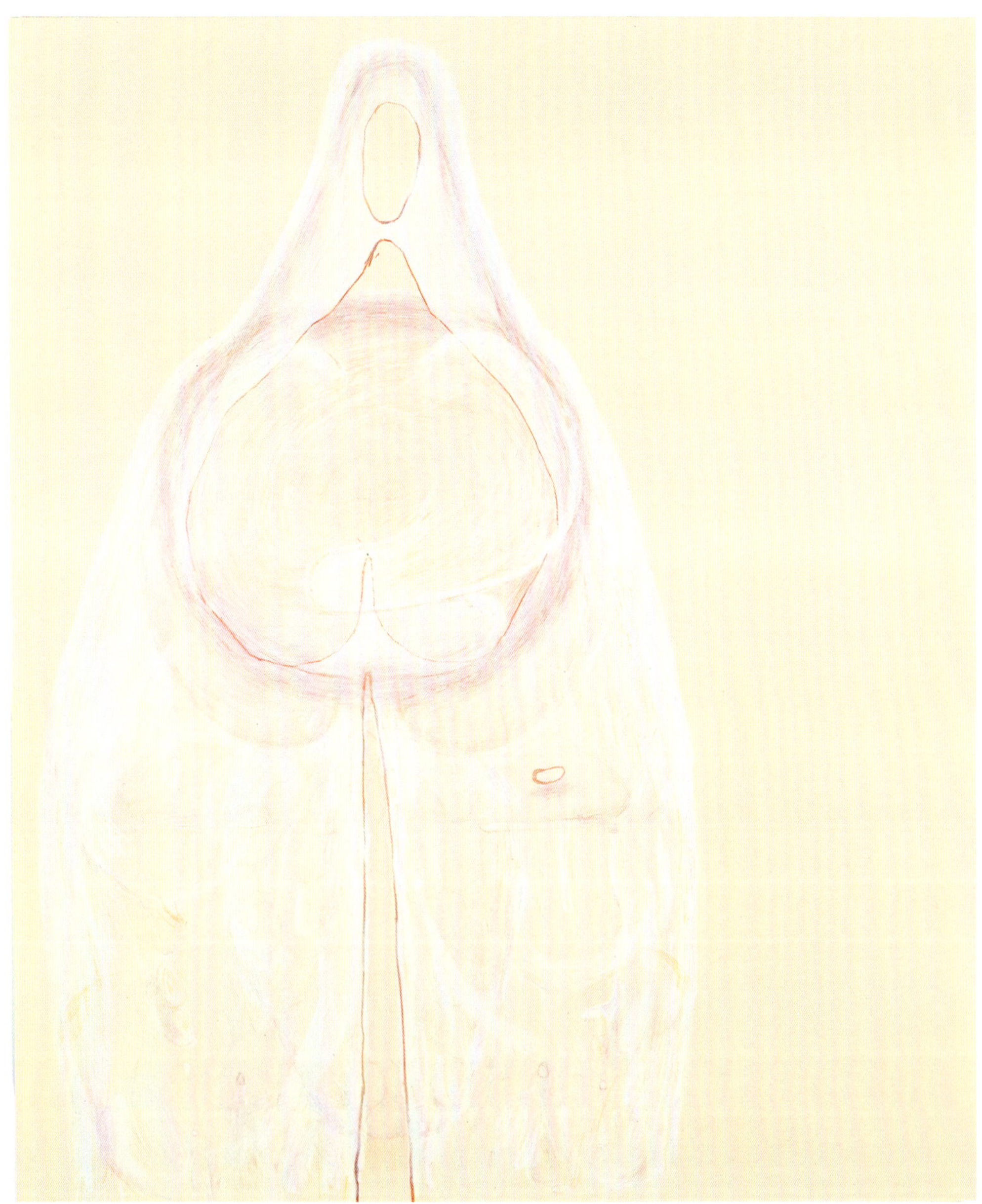

Figure 8.13. Rei Naito, *une place sur la Terre* (1990). Pencil and oil pastel on paper, 45.5 × 37 cm. Collection of the National Museum of Art, Osaka. Courtesy of Taka Ishii Gallery and Naoya Hatakeyama.

she "wanted to feel the joy of being a woman." From such a genuine attitude, "femininity came out strongly in this work."[81] That femininity, according to the cultural anthropologist Shin'ichi Nakazawa, is an "Ur-space (primal space)."[82] It is a pre-Oedipal space before a child starts speaking and forming a relationship with its mother. It is the space that exists before meaning "unites with the structure of language."[83] As I see it, this is the space where the new meaning emerges, opening up countless possibilities. With her artwork, Naito shifted the significance of female corporeality from a liability to a "blessing."[84]

Mio Shirai

If we suppose that women's art establishes starkly different values, then we need a different set of principles to understand it, which requires that we fundamentally change our worldview from patriarchal to matriarchal. And such change happens slowly. In 1996, Koike co-curated *Sosie*, a contemporary art exhibition that dealt with the one-hundred-plus-year stigma against fashion models. The mid-nineteenth century models for the haute couture houses were called "sosies" (doubles). These women bore similarities with the couturier's clients, and functioned as live mannequins. As women's social position improved over the course of the twentieth century, with the suffrage act and feminism, models became both muse and idol—like the famed British supermodel Naomi Campbell. They came to possess a definite sense of themselves. Featuring eight female artists from five different countries, *Sosie* focused on shifting women's position in their respective societies—from the object of the male gaze to her subject.[85]

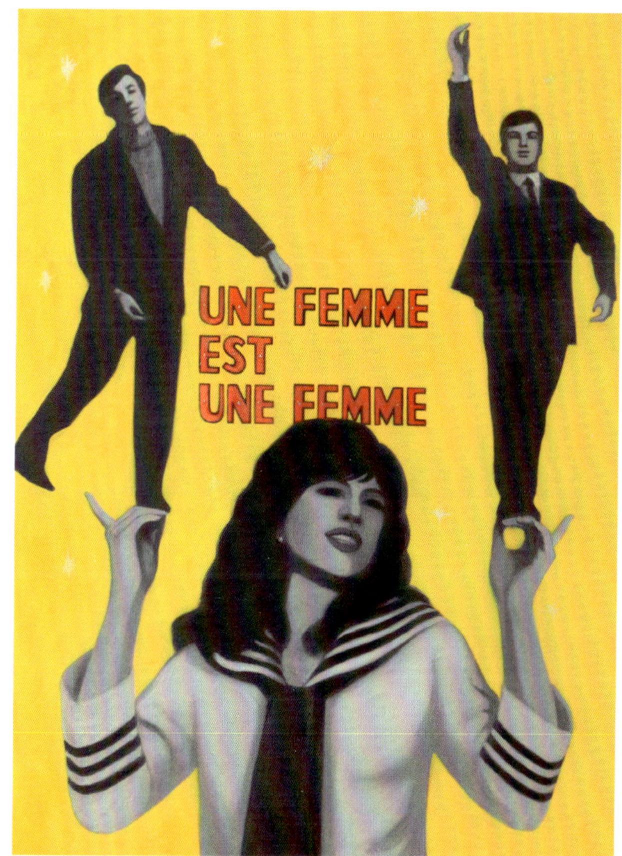

Figure 8.14. Mio Shirai, *A Woman Is a Woman* (1996/2015). Oil on canvas, 155 × 114 cm. Courtesy of the artist.

One participating artist, Mio Shirai (b. 1962), observed that these artists were quite distinctive from the previous generation in that they "strategically reflected women's social positioning in their works."[86] Shirai's own contribution was an evocative image: *Une Femme Est Une Femme* (*A Woman Is a Woman*, 1996/2015) (fig. 8.14); a duplicate of Jean-Luc Godard's still image of the eponymous film (1961). Through this image, Shirai posed a profound question: "What is a woman?"

Shirai studied with a Mono-ha artist, Koji Enokura, at TUA. Her often intentionally elusive, mid-1990s oeuvre occasionally replaced Mono-ha's focus on material reality with the reality of information society by appropriated images. Through this information plate, *A Woman Is a Woman* invites people to scrutinize the idea of womanhood.

In the appropriated title, the first "woman" comes without a definition, converting the word "woman" into an empty sign that waits for viewers to fill it with meaning. The image part of this work renders a protagonist of Godard's film, Angela. She is a striptease artist, who weighs two men—trivialized by their scale—on her fingers. In the film, Angela is a woman who wants to have a child. She tries to persuade her boyfriend, Emile, but when he disagrees, she asks his friend Alfred to father her child. A decade before the collective feminist movement of the 1970s, Angela demonstrated her independent will and power over women's reproductive rights, overturning the Freudian idea of women being sexually passive. The image of Angela certainly helps audiences to yield the significance of woman to fill the first sign, which becomes the signifier of the second "woman" based on the film, confirming the emergence of a new woman.

Like Angela, Shirai marked various turning points for women artists. In 1989, she became the first female assistant of the oil painting department at TUA. With the globalization of art, she was selected by foreign curators and invited to show in Europe and the United States. For the first time, her impressive exhibition record set an example for the women students at TUA. Through her efforts to change people's opinions about women, and release females from age-old thinking, Shirai's work is definitively feminist. At TUA, turning her credo into action, Shirai protected many female students from the insensitive criticisms and neglect of male instructors. Consequently, during her tenure at the university, a remarkably original and talented cohort of female artists, such as Naoyo Fukuda, Akiko Ikeuchi, Yasuko Toyoshima, and Sachigusa Yasuda, emerged from the program.

Coda: Yurie Nagashima and a Matrixial Gaze

The Great Hanshin-Awaji earthquake and the Tokyo subway sarin attack in 1995 significantly compounded the effects of the economic crash four years earlier, and Saison's cultural industry quickly dwindled, replaced by conservatism. Within this milieu emerged the "girly photo" movement. A group of female photographers in their late teens and early twenties, Yurie Nagashima (b. 1973), HIROMIX (b. 1976, née Hiromi Toshikawa), and Mika Ninagawa (b. 1972), were suddenly in the limelight of the photographic world. After Nagashima won the PARCO Prize at the URBANART2, HIROMIX and Ninagawa successively won the prestigious photo award in 1995 and 1996,[87] the term "On'nanoko Shashin" ("girly photo") emerged. Editing the girly photo anthology in 2010, the photo critic Kōtarō Iizawa characterized their work based on what he defined as the "female principle," which means: intimate photography of objects that exist within a "radius of five meters"; the use of an inexpensive, lightweight, easy to operate, compact camera; and taking some form of self-portraiture, including nudity. Being young women means "premature," or "unskilled," and their photographs are contingent snapshots filled with flashes of sensation.[88]

Nagashima, who may be considered part of the last Saison generation, found Iizawa's gender-biased critique disagreeable. She decided to defend her work by studying feminism. College classes on feminism being rare in Japan, Nagashima went to the United States, and ultimately published a book entitled *From Their On'nanoko-Shashin to Our Girly Photo*.[89] By transforming women from the object of photography into the subject, she refuted male critics' writings by pointing out how they dismiss women's work as "intuitive," "light," "impulsive," "ignorant," and technically "immature," without carefully examining their work.[90]

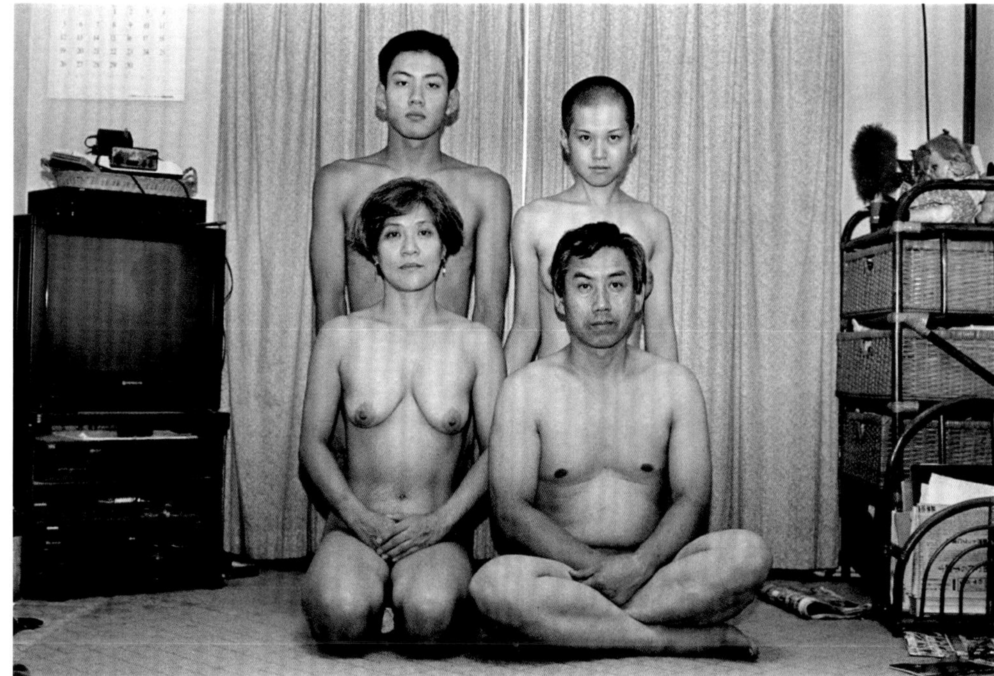

Figure 8.15. Yurie Nagashima, *Self-Portrait (Family #26)*, from the series *Self-Portrait* (1993). Gelatin silver print, 387 × 580 mm. Collection of Tokyo Photographic Art Museum. Courtesy of the artist and Maho Kubota Gallery.

Nagashima makes a convincing point. Take, for example, her PARCO Prize image, *Self-Portrait (Family #26)*, 1993 (fig. 8.15): A well-composed image is far from an intuitive snapshot. An image like this required deliberate preparation, starting with relaying her ideas and asking her family members to remove their clothes. In fact, the work was two years in the making after Nagashima developed a distaste for the way people perceived the unaltered nude photobook of a barely eighteen-year-old actress, Rie Miyazawa. The actress happened to be the same age as Nagashima.

"The response to the book was only concerned with sex," wrote Nagashima, "not the situation its subject was put in. It left me with a great deal of suspicion that society only sees women as sexual objects."[91] The incident made her think about humanizing nude photography. One day, she stumbled on the idea of taking a family portrait in the nude. A black-and-white print captures four people, all nude, organized in two rows. They sit closely in the center of a small apartment room. The room's size echoes the intimacy of this family. Perhaps out of moral concerns, the parents shielded their children's upper bodies by sitting in the front row. Despite their concerns, no erotic atmosphere can be detected in this picture. The humility of this family nude photograph recalls the bodies one encounters at the public bathhouse. Since Eros is removed, the attention is directed toward each sitter's character.

Although stripped to the buff, the father still sits with dignity, while the mother's undyed hair and firm body suggest she is a hardworking housewife. Nagashima's brother occupies the left side of the back row looking nervous, while the artist poses next to him. She seems to be the most relaxed of the four. Her shaved head conveys her nonconformist spirit—she is an admirer of the underground feminist punk movement Riot grrrl.[92]

Trying to be a woman beyond the predetermined standard ideal, her work emerged as a reaction to the patriarchal conservatism of Japan. Still, gender is pivotal in her practice, through which she invented a new way of representing nudes.

Likewise, the works discussed in this essay neither fall under the "masculine logic and structure," to reiterate Matsuoka's analysis, nor put on a masquerade of "womanliness to avert anxiety and the retribution feared from men."[93] What comes closest to these artworks is the notion of "pre-Oedipal space," to borrow from Nakazawa's description. During the pre-Oedipal period of psychosexual development, the mother dominates. From Koizumi's effort to uncover the lost maternal bloodline, Naito's female corporality in emergence, Shirai's reconceptualization of woman, and Nagashima's attempt to un-objectify naked female bodies, women artists of the 1980s and the 1990s in Japan were establishing a new field outside patriarchal values and logic. Energized by the politicized consumer culture that engendered a strong sense of self in women artists, during Japan's economic bubble artists such as Ohno, Terada, and Yoshizawa demonstrated a positive embrace of commodity and created brand-new art. Given that patriarchal values already undermine our worldviews, for the fair understanding of women's art, we must dispose of stereotypical ideals, return to the pre-Oedipal state, and interpret women's work through a matrixial gaze. Only then can we acquire new worldviews and meanings.

Acknowledgments

I would like to thank the artists Akiko Ikeuchi, Masayo Koizumi, Yurie Nagashima, Hiroko Ohno, Rei Naito, Mio Shirai, Mayumi Terada, Sachigusa Yasuda, and Mika Yoshizawa for sharing their experiences and views with me. I also thank Tanzina Ahmed, Kastumi Asaba, Eric Berlin, Lesley Broder, Ivana Espinet, Luis H. Francia, Susan Gamble, Mona Hadler, Kagari Hashimoto, Chikako Ikegami, Taka Ishii Gallery, Masao Katayama, Hideki Kikkawa, Kazuko Koike, Maho Kubota, Yutaka Mikami, Ristu Ozawa, Sara Rutkowski, Emily Schnee, Sezon Museum of Modern Art, Akira Shibutami, Jun Shioya, Akie Terai, and Michael Wenyon for supporting this research. The CUNY Graduate Center Rewald Seminar helped me shape this text. Last but not least, I thank Anna C. Chave, who taught me feminist scholarship. This research project was partially funded by the ACLS/Mellon Foundation Community College Faculty Fellowship (2020–23).

Notes

1. Yutaka Mikami, conversation with author, Tokyo, August 20, 2019. In Mikami's opinion, consumerism resulted in the publication of an "increasing number of women's magazines assigning more pages to arts and culture." This in turn gave rise to female art writers, many of whom introduced works by women artists. Newly established female gallerists, such as Hitomi Kobayashi, Toyoko Tsukamoto, and Kazuko Koike, also helped female artists to prevail. However, almost all the artists I interviewed in Japan acknowledged the impact of Saison culture. Unless indicated, all translations from Japanese to English are by the author.

2. Herbert Marcuse, *One-Dimensional Man: Studies in the Ideology of Advanced Industrial Society* (Boston: Beacon Press, 1964). When asked about his commitment to New Left ideas in 2008, Tsutsumi nodded and explained that the "base" of the zeitgeist can be interpreted as the New Left term for "shutsugeki kyoten" [a base for carrying out a sortie]. Akira Nagae, *Sezon bunka wa nani wo yumemita* [What Saison culture dreamt of] (Tokyo: Asahi shin'bun shuppan, 2010), 244–5.

3. Seiji Tsutsumi, interviewed by Akira Nagae, *Sezon bunka wa*, 258.

4. Kinokuni, cited in Nagae, 169.

5. Art critic Yoshiaki Tono was an impetus behind this. The exhibition he curated with his students, *Tama Vivant '84 Capricious Surface* (1984), was an all-women exhibition. As the commissioner of the Bienal de São Paulo in 1985, he selected two female and two male artists for the exhibition.

6. Sachigusa Yasuda, in conversation with author, Yasuda Studio, New York, May 18, 2019. Yasuda is uncertain whether the remark came from Koji Kinutani or Teruo Onuma; however, all of the professors and their assistants were male and everyone similarly discriminated against female students. Similar remarks came from other former TUA students, such as Mio Shirai and Akiko Ikeuchi.

7. "News Headline: Interested Tama Art University Sculpture Department Students Submitted the University an Open Letter Reporting Harassment, etc.," *BT*, February 23, 2018, https://bijutsutecho.com/magazine/news/headline/12328.

8. Ryoichi Eonomoto and Kazuko Matsuoka, "Featured Article, Art [World's] Super Girls," *BT*, no. 566 (August 1986): 19, 46. *BT* began digital publishing in 2017.

9. Yoshiaki Tono, "Introduction: From Avant-Garde Pioneer to New Women Artists," *Bienal de São Paulo* (Tokyo: Japan Foundation, 1985), 5.

10. "Image core" is how Ken'ichi Kinokuni, manager of Seibu's cultural affairs department, described the company's approach to culture. Nagae, *Sezon bunka wa*, 173.

11. Nagae, 246.

12. Seiji Tsutsumi, "Jidai seishin no konkyochi to shite" [As a base for spirits of the times], in *Nihon gendai bijutsu no tenbō* [A view of Japanese contemporary art], exh. cat. (Tokyo: Seibu Museum of Art, 1975), n.p.

13. Capitalization follows the store logo.

14. Seibu Department Stores frequently changed their floor layout. This section is based on how Akira Nagae, a former employee of New Art Seibu (ART VIVANT being its shop), remembered things around 1981. Nagae, *Sezon bunka wa*, 12, 145, 229.

15. Almost all of the artists I interviewed who were born around 1960 mentioned the influence of Saison culture. Yasuda, May 18, 2019.

16. Nagae, *Sezon bunka wa*, 257–8.

17. Herbert Marcuse, *One-Dimensional Man: Studies in the Ideology of Advanced Industrial Society* (Boston: Beacon Press, 1964); Nagae, *Sezon bunka wa*, 244–5.

18. Seiji Tsutsumi, interviewed by Akira Nagae, *Sezon bunka wa*, 258.

19. Kinokuni, cited in Nagae, 169.

20. Yoshiaki Kaihatsu in conversation with author, July 6, 2015.

21. Hiroko Ohno, email message to author, December 26, 2016. Ohno was the recipient of the first Kawabata Ryushi Award in 1986.

22. A television commercial of this campaign is available at https://www.youtube.com/ watch?v=BgYvUDQBcm8, accessed January 15, 2020.

23. *Nihonga* artist Takako Azamia's younger brother worked at Seibu Group. The observation is his. Takako Azami, email message to author, August 28, 2019.

24. Kawakami Gallery in Ginza often curated group shows of young *nihonga* painters. Takashi Murakami was one of the artists included in these shows. Hiroko Ohno, email message to author, January 20, 2020.

25. Hiroko Ohno, email message to author, May 31, 2020.

26. Akira Nagae, "Mujirushi Ryohin: Koike Kazuko to Atte Omotta Koto" [Muji: What I thought when I met Kazuko Koike], in *Sezon bunka wa*, 133.

27. Eonomoto and Matsuoka, "Art [World's] Super Girls," 51.

28. Hiroko Ohno, email message to author, January 3, 2020.

29. Eonomoto and Matsuoka, "Art [World's] Super Girls," 19.

30. Eonomoto and Matsuoka, 46–47.

31. Eonomoto and Matsuoka, 46–47.

32. Lawrence Alloway, "Junk Culture as a Tradition," *New Forms—New Media I*, exh. cat. (New York: Martha Jackson Gallery, 1960), n.p. Orthography as in original.

33. Mayumi Terada, email message to author, November 2, 2020.

34. Mayumi Terada, phone interview by author, February 2, 2020. Unless otherwise indicated, all quotes from Terada in this section come from this conversation.

35. Sigmund Freud, "The Dissolution of the Oedipus Complex," in *The Freud Reader*, ed. Peter Gay (New York; London: W.W. Norton & Company, 1989), 662.

36. This is Terada's term.

37. Yoshiaki Tono, *Bienal de São Paulo*, 6.

38. Toshiaki Minemura, "What Was 'Mono-ha?" August 15, 1986, https:// www.kamakura.gallery /mono-ha/minemura-en.html.

39. Mika Yoshizawa, conversation with author, Tokyo, The National Art Center, Tokyo, January 20, 2020. Unless otherwise indicated, all quotes from Yoshizawa in this section come from this conversation.

40. Yoko Hayashi, "Mika Yoshizawa," *Art in Japan Today, 1985–1995*, exh. cat. (Tokyo: Museum of Contemporary Art, 1995), 144.

41. Yutaka Mikami, in-person response to author's presentation on Japanese contemporary art. Tokyo, Tokyo National Institute for Cultural Properties, April 25, 2017.

42. Yutaka Mikami, email message to author, May 11, 2020.

43. Yutaka Mikami, in conversation with author, Meguro, Tokyo, January 31, 2020.

44. Makoto Murata, "The 1980s: From the Rise of Post Mono-ha to the Burst of Bubble Economy," in *The 20th Century Art in Japan* (Tokyo: Heibon-sha, 2014), 386–88. The two recent exhibitions are *Starting Points: Japanese Art of the '80s*, exh. cat. (Tokyo: My Book Service, 2018) and *New Wave: Japanese Contemporary Art of the 1980s*, exh. cat. (Osaka: The National Art Museum of Osaka, 2018).

45. Murata, "1980s," 388–89.

46. The image is a reinstallation of her BFA exhibition at Komai Gallery in 1982.

47. Hideki Nakazawa, speaking at a pre-event for Trans Arts Tokyo, July 29, 2015, Tokyo, 3331 Arts Chiyoda.

48. *New Wave*, 120.

49. Her later works are grounded in more social themes using figurative images, such as trophies, sculls, snakes, and spiders, among other things, symbolizing psychological effects of the figures, with descriptive titles.

50. Murata, "1980s," 386–87.

51. Tono, "Introduction," 5.

52. *What Is the Relationship Between Ceramics and Contemporary Art? Considering the Context of Ceramics in the Lineage of Contemporary Art*, Kaikai Kiki Gallery, August 3–30, 2017.

53. Yoshizawa, email message to author, April 16, 2020.

54. Tono, *Bienal de São Paulo*, 5.

55. Higonnet's observation about pregnant women. Anne Higonnet, "Making Babies, Painting Bodies: Women, Art, and Paula Modersohn-Becker's Productivity," *Woman's Art Journal* 30, no. 2 (Fall/Winter 2009): 15.

56. Masayo Koizumi, email message to author, January 18, 2020.

57. So far, there is only one academic book on pregnant female images. See Sandra Matthews and Laura Wexler, *Pregnant Pictures* (London and New York: Routledge, 2000).

58. Higonnet, "Making Babies," 15.

59. Higonnet, 15.

60. Sachigusa Yasuda, email reply to author's question, June 2, 2020.

61. Jirō Yoshihara, "10 Years of Gutai Group: Part One," *Bijutsu janaru* 9 (1958): 6–7.

62. Masayo Koizumi, phone conversation with author, February 1, 2020. Unless otherwise indicated, all quotes from Koizumi in this section come from this conversation.

63. Masayo Koizumi and Kimiko Nakagawa, *Annunciation* (Osaka: Village Press, 1994).

64. Masayo Koizumi, email message to author, January 17, 2020.

65. Masayo Koizumi, email message to author, January 17, 2020.

66. Masayo Koizumi, email message to author, January 18, 2020.

67. Janet Wolff, "Reinstating Corporeality: Feminism and Body Politics," in *Feminine Sentences: Essays on Women and Culture* (Berkeley: University of California Press, 1990), 124.

68. Wolff, "Reinstating Corporeality," 128.

69. Masayo Koizumi, email message to author, January 18, 2020.

70. Masayo Koizumi, email message to author, January 24, 2020.

71. Masayo Koizumi, email message to author, January 26, 2020.

72. Masayo Koizumi, email message to author, January 17, 2020.

73. Nagae, *Sezon bunka wa*, 136.

74. Koike was invited to give a talk at the East-West Center at the University of Hawai'i.

75. Gunma Modern Art Museum's subtheme for the Sagacho Archive exhibition. September–November 2020.

76. Yoshiko Ikoma, "Rei Naito," *Ryûkôtsûshin*, no. 339 (December 1991): 157.

77. Rei Naito, cited in "Art Front Interview," unidentified biweekly magazine, August 29–September 9, 1991, clippings, Sagacho Archives.

78. "One Can Openly Appreciate Being Alive at This Place: Rei Naito, One Place on the Earth," *anan*, no. 4 (October 1991), clippings, Sagacho Archives.

79. "One Can Openly Appreciate Being Alive at This Place," n.p.

80. Unidentified magazine, clippings, Sagacho Archives.

81. "Art Front Interview."

82. Shin'ichi Nakazawa, "Where Do Children Come From?" in *Rei Naito: One Place on the Earth* (Tokyo: Sagacho Exhibit Space, 1991), n.p.

83. Nakazawa, "Where Do Children Come From?" n.p.

84. "Art Front Interview."

85. The invitation card for the show only mentions seven artists from four countries, but a Dutch artist seems to have been a last-minute addition. In one of the exhibition reports, a writer who visited Sagacho mentions eight artists from five countries, so I took this account as the fact about this exhibition.

86. Mio Shirai, email message to author, June 21, 2020.

87. The awards are the New Cosmos of Photography Excellence Award for HIROMIX in 1995 and the Grand Prize at Shashin Hitotsubo Ten for Ninagawa in 1996.

88. Aiko Kato, "The Reasons for Photographer Yurie Nagashima began Speaking in Words," *Huffington Post*, March 10, 2020, https://www.huffingtonpost.jp/entry/story_jp_5e5cf1e6c5b601022113ffb2.

89. Yurie Nagashima, *"Bokura" no "on'nanoko shashin" kara watashitachi no gari photo* [From "our" (subject male) "girls' photography" to our (subject female) girly photo] (Tokyo: Daifuku Shoorin, 2020). In Japanese, "girly photo" is distinguished by using its Japanese form for the male subject and English for the female subject, so the translation followed Nagashima's use of both Japanese and English terms.

90. Yuzuru Murakami, "Book Review," March 3, 2020, https://imaonline.jp/articles/bookreview/20200303yurie-nagashima/?fbclid=IwAR1aiy-MxaScn7AujHPTsM2S1ykoxbTA5ApZSexXmLKqOnBP1yfADujqbAY#page-1.

91. Momo Nonaka, "The Personal Is Political, Public, Private, Poetic—The Confusion and Exploration of Nagashima Yurie," trans. Dan Abbe, in *Nagashima Yurie and a Pinch of Irony with a Hint of Love* (Tokyo: Tokyo Photographic Art Museum, 2017), 193n3.

92. Emiko Inoue, unpublished book review, "From Their On'nanoko-Shashin to Our Girly Photo," for *CAA Review*.

93. This is an observation made by the female psychoanalyst Joan Riviere, "Womanliness as a Masquerade," in *Formations of Fantasy*, ed. Victor Burgin et al. (New York: Methuen, 1986), 35.

Bibliography

Archival Materials

File section, "Rei Naito." Sagacho Archives.

File section, "Sosie." Sagacho Archives.

Published Sources

Alloway, Lawrence. "Junk Culture as a Tradition." In *New Forms—New Media I*, n.p. New York: Martha Jackson Gallery, 1960. Exhibition catalog.

Chiba Shigeo. *Japanese Art, Yet to Be Born*. Tokyo: Shobunsha, 2006.

Dissonances. Aichi: Toyota City Museum, 2008.

Eonomoto Ryoichi and Kazuko Matsuoka. "Art [World's] Super Girls." *BT Magazine*, no. 566 (August 1986): 46–51, 58–59.

Favell, Adrian. *Before and After Superflat*. Hong Kong: Blue Kingfisher Ltd., 2011.

Freud, Sigmund. *The Freud Reader*. Edited by Peter Gay. New York and London: W. W. Norton, 1989.

Hayashi Yoko. "Mika Yoshizawa." In *Art in Japan Today, 1985–1995*, 144. Tokyo: Museum of Contemporary Art, 1995. Exhibition catalog.

Higonnet, Anne. "Making Babies, Painting Bodies: Women, Art, and Paula Modersohn-Becker's Productivity." *Woman's Art Journal* 30, no. 2 (Fall/Winter 2009): 15–21.

Iizawa Kōtarō. *On'nanoko shashin no jidai.* Tokyo: NTT-shuppan, 2010.

Ikoma Yoshiko. "Rei Naito." *Ryûkôtsûshin*, no. 339 (December 1991): 157.

Jirō Yoshihara, "10 Years of Gutai Group: Part One," *Bijutsu janaru* 9 (1958): 6–7.

Katayama Masao. *Sezon bunka no chosen.* Tokyo: Shosekikobo Hayama, 2016.

Koizumi Masayo and Nakanaga Kimiko. *Annunciation.* Osaka: Village Press, 1994.

Kunimoto, Namiko. *The Stakes of Exposure: Anxious Bodies in Postwar Japanese Art.* Minneapolis and London: University of Minnesota Press, 2017.

Marcuse, Herbert. "Art as a Form of Reality." In *On the Future of Art.* New York: Viking, 1970.

———. *One-Dimensional Man: Studies in the Ideology of Advanced Industrial Society.* Boston: Beacon Press, 1964.

Matthews, Sandra, and Laura Wexler. *Pregnant Pictures.* London and New York: Routledge, 2000.

Murata Makoto. "The 1980s: From the Rise of Post Mono-ha to the Burst of Bubble Economy." In *The 20th Century Art in Japan.* Tokyo: Heibon-sha, 2014.

Nagae Akira. *Sezon bunka wa nani wo yumemita* [What Saison culture dreamed of]. Tokyo: Asahi shin'bun shuppan, 2010.

Nagashima Yurie. *"Bokura" no "on'nanoko shashin" kara watashitachi no gari photo* [From their on'nanoko-shashin to our "girly photo"]. Tokyo: Daifuku Shorin, 2020.

Nakajima, Izumi. *Anti-Action: Postwar Japanese Art and Women Artists.* Tokyo: Brücke, 2019.

Nakazawa Shin'ichi. "Where Do Children Come From?" In *Rei Naito: Une place sur la Terre*, n.p. Tokyo: Sagacho Exhibit Space, 1991. Exhibition catalog.

New Wave: Japanese Contemporary Art of the 1980s. Osaka: National Art Museum of Osaka, 2018. Exhibition catalog.

Nonaka Momo. "The Personal Is Political, Public, Private, Poetic—The Confusion and Exploration of Nagashima Yurie." Translated by Dan Abbe. In *Nagashima Yurie and a Pinch of Irony with a Hint of Love*, 188–202. Tokyo: Tokyo Photographic Art Museum, 2017. Exhibition catalog.

Riviere, Joan. "Womanliness as a Masquerade." In *Formations of Fantasy*, edited by Victor Burgin, James Donald, and Cora Kaplan, 35–44. London and New York: Methuen, 1986.

Sawaragi Noi. *Nihon·Gendai·Bijutsu.* Tokyo: Shincho-sha, 1998.

Shirai Mio. *Mio Shirai Works 1987–2016.* Tokyo: Mio Shirai, 2016.

Starting Points: Japanese Art of the '80s. Tokyo: My Book Service, 2018. Exhibition catalog.

Tono Yoshiaki. "Introduction: From Avant-Garde Pioneer to New Women Artists." In *Bienal de São Paulo*, 5–7. Tokyo: Japan Foundation, 1985. Exhibition catalog.

Tsujii Takashi. *Houko no kisetsu no nakade.* Tokyo: Chuo koron-sha, 2009.

———. *Waga kioku, waga kiroku.* Tokyo: Chuo koron-sha, 2015.

Tsutsumi Seiji. "Jidai seishin no konkyochi to shite" [As a base for spirits of the times]. In *Nihon gendai bijutsu no tenbō* [A view of Japanese contemporary art], n.p. Tokyo: Seibu Museum of Art, 1975. Exhibition catalog.

Volk, Alicia. "Art and Women's Liberation in Nearly Democratic Japan, with a Focus on Migishi Setsuko and Akamatsu Toshiko." *US-Japan Women's Journal* 57 (2020): 21–56.

Wolff, Janet. "Reinstating Corporeality: Feminism and Body Politics." In *Feminine Sentences: Essays on Women and Culture*, 120–41. Berkeley and Los Angeles: University of California Press, 1990.

Yoshitake, Mika, ed. *Parergon: Japanese Art of the 1980s and 1990s.* Los Angeles, New York, and Tokyo: Blum & Poe, 2020.

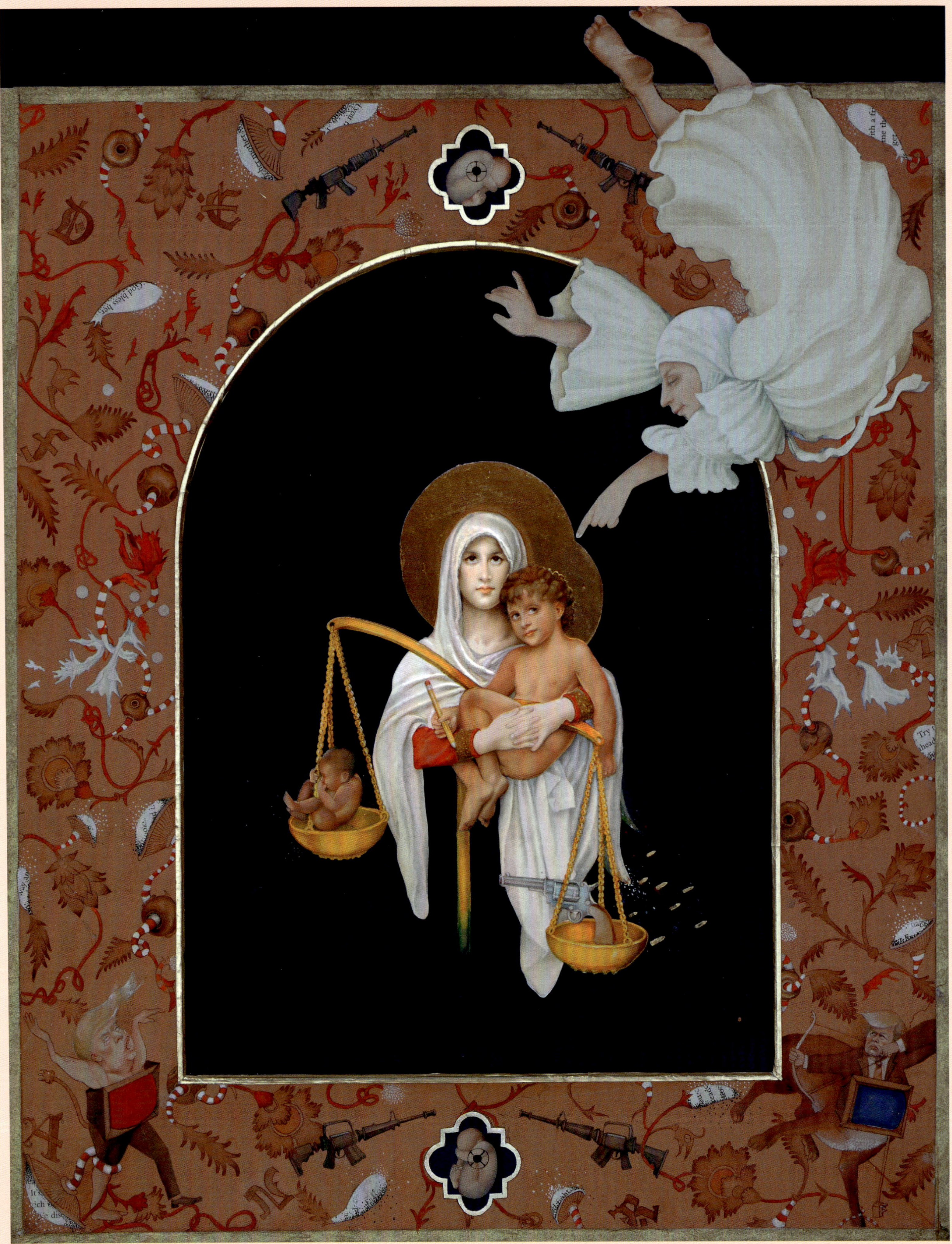

The Decorative, the Feminine, the Disruptive

Neo-Miniatures and the Satirical Paintings of Saira Wasim

Saleema Waraich

The purported "miniature" schools of painting that are associated with the courts of South Asia and Persia have been at the center of debates involving patronage, tradition, Hindu-Muslim relations, artistry as opposed to craft, precolonial heritage, exoticism, and gendered roles, among many other key issues. Many of these debates emerged out of Western hegemonic discourses, beginning during the colonial period and continuing to the present in Western academia and art markets. This essay argues that while such discourse contributed to the denigration and dismissal of local South Asian artistic practices, it also has informed and activated its reinvention as neo-miniature painting in Pakistan in the late twentieth and early twenty-first centuries, a transformation striking for its move from a virtually exclusive male practice to one that is now dominated by female artists.

This essay begins by questioning the term "miniature" that was and is used to refer to a vast body of Persianate and South Asian paintings, even though equivalent terms were never employed to refer to such bodies of material in the regions where they were produced. The term is in fact European, and in relation to painting, would come to refer to a distinct European practice of portraiture that was projected onto and would influence local South Asian artists beginning in the late eighteenth century. In the process, European attitudes toward their own miniature portrait painting traditions merged with European ideas regarding femininity, Orientalist constructions of the "East," and European rhetoric that sought to separate ideals involving art from notions of craft and tradition. This resulted in the ideologically motivated devaluation of South Asian artistic practices as decorative craft, or souvenir, as well as fictive evidence for their unchanging, static, and thus non-intelligent cultures.

The next part of the paper explores the ways in which the artistic techniques and styles associated with illustrated manuscripts and *muraqqas* (albums consisting of collections of paintings and calligraphy) have been transformed from their imperial past, with male artists producing works for elite male patrons, to a contemporary art form in Pakistan in which female neo-miniaturists are at the forefront. I aim to show how this transformation was initially informed by Victorian-era ideas of acceptable female pastimes and activated by the role of women as nurturers of "tradition" during the struggle for independence and the emergence of the newly independent nation-state. Such ideological constructions eventually enabled the neo-miniature genre to be utilized to give voice and agency to female artists, with their work prominently exhibited at international biennials, museums, and galleries.

The final component of the paper focuses on the works of Saira Wasim, a contemporary neo-miniaturist known for her satirical sociopolitical critiques, a form of visual criticism that has been generally associated with men. Not only does the content of Wasim's works defy gendered assumptions, but also her use of satire and employment of caricature to criticize, among others, Pakistani and American public figures and their politics, actively resists attempts to romanticize and exoticize the neo-miniature genre. Focusing on Wasim's engagement with two types of print culture—the political cartoon and the fashion magazine—this essay concludes by addressing the ways in which her work participates in various acts of subversion: of Mughal courtly patronage, of Western hegemonic canons, practices, and ideologies, and of the divide between high art and popular culture.[1]

From Imperial Manuscripts to Decorative Miniatures

The artistic practices associated with the illustrated manuscripts and collections of paintings bound in albums produced for various Indo-Persian courts in the medieval and early modern eras were originally the province of male artists,[2] passed down through patrilineal transmission. In the imperial and royal ateliers, where such artistic production was collaborative, an assembly of male artists created painted folios in service of rulers and other elite, predominantly male patrons. These paintings included idealized representations of important events from patrons' lives, aggrandizing portraits (fig. 9.1), and illustrations for canonical literary works, which were bound in lavish manuscripts or collected as a series of paintings in an album (*muraqqa*). Although artists associated with Indo-Persian courts did not receive the individual distinction granted to renowned artists of Renaissance Europe—relatively few names of the miniaturists are known to us—this difference did not diminish their significance to a given patron.

Figure 9.1. *Emperor Jahangir Triumphing over Poverty*, attributed to Abu'l Hasan, Mughal empire, circa 1620–25. Opaque watercolor, gold, and ink on paper. Image: 9 ⅜ × 6 in. (23.81 × 15.24 cm); sheet: 14 ½ × 9 ¹¹⁄₁₆ in. (36.83 × 24.61 cm). From the Nasli and Alice Heeramaneck Collection, Museum Associates Purchase (M.75.4.28), Los Angeles County Museum of Art.

Considerable confusion exists around the popular but problematic usage of the term "miniature" to refer to Persianate and South Asian painting. Although widely used to refer to this body of visual material, the story of how a European term came to be misapplied to Indo-Persianate painting is not as well known. Understanding Indo-Persianate

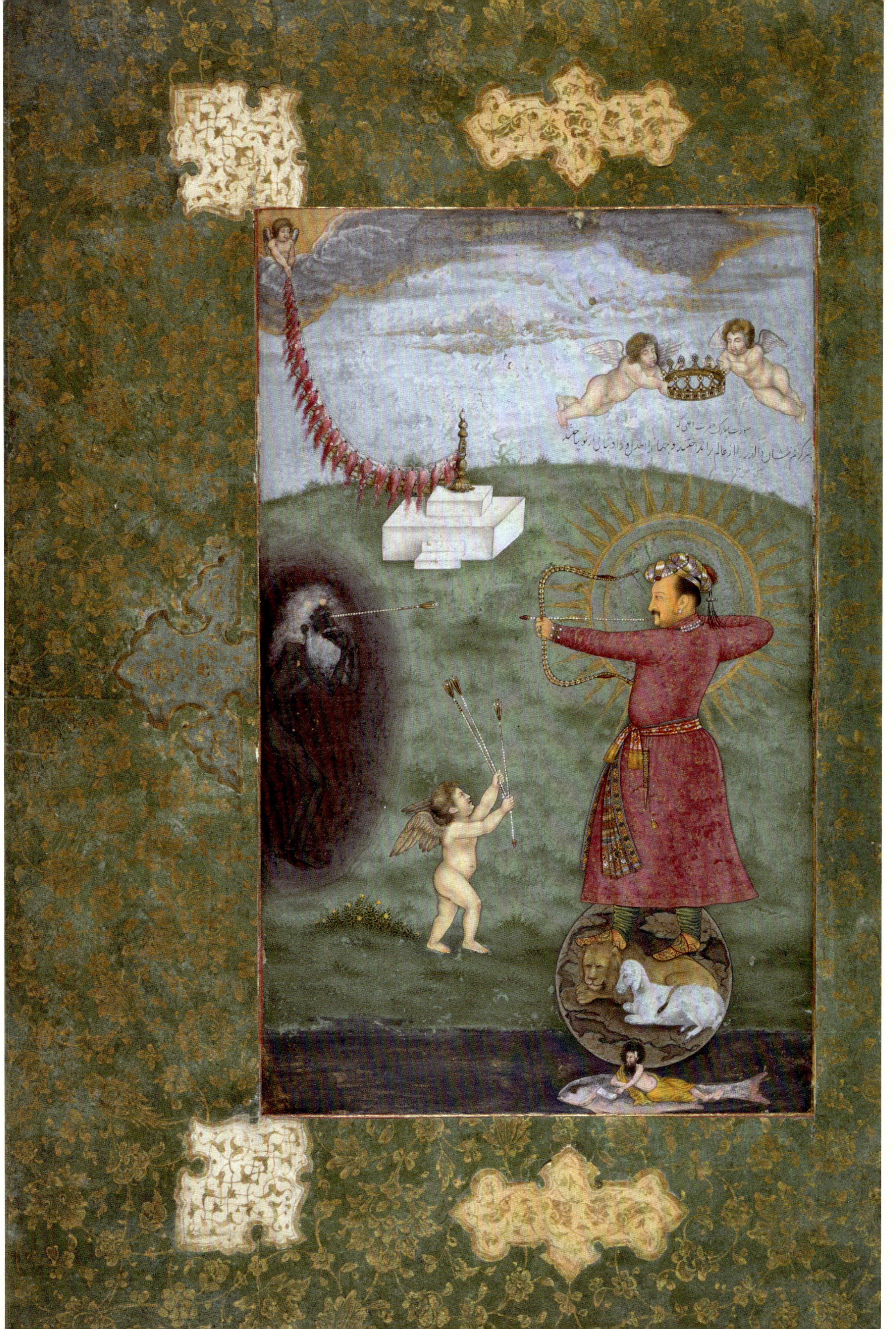
صورت مبارک حضرت اعلی که

painting must first and foremost decouple the historic Indo-Persian practice from the later Western appellation, as no analogous or equivalent term was used in various related Indo-Persian contexts. In actuality, the term originated in Europe, where it referred to European medieval manuscripts; originally it did not refer to size but instead to color, specifically the red—made from cinnabar or red lead—used for titles, large initial capital letters, and decorative drawings that in Latin were called *minium*. The correlate Latin verb, *miniare*, means "to color with minium" and eventually the association of *miniare* with illustrative drawings resulted in the broadening of the term so that it meant "to decorate a manuscript." The noun form, *miniatura*, referred to the addition of illustrations to a manuscript. Since the paintings were small, the same word, *miniatura*, would also come to refer to small paintings, particularly portraits—emerging out of and distinct from the illuminated manuscript tradition in the early 1500s—and eventually anything small.[3] This word and its meanings would be integrated into English—as "miniature"—in the late sixteenth century. The expanding scope of the term coincided with the availability of miniature portraits among the European elite in the seventeenth century, reaching its height of popularity among the British in the eighteenth century. Admired for "the virtuoso ability of the *craftspeople* who made miniatures,"[4] these portraits were small, portable, and enabled intimate encounters between the depicted sitter and the beholder. Miniature portrait painting was considered "an established genteel pastime," rather than a full-time profession, and until the 1760s professional training was not required.[5]

When British colonialists utilized the term "miniature" to refer to a diverse and complex body of Indo-Persian paintings, their (mis)appellation not only neglected to engage with this material on its own terms but also brought with it attitudes and biases informed by modernist, colonial, patriarchal discourses: that in the "East," paintings were never "liberated" from the book; that these decorative and ornamental illustrations were devoid of internal meanings and had no meaning or significance beyond illustrating and decorating the text; and that the smaller scale of the folio-size, richly detailed paintings was seen as comparably diminutive in value when compared to the large oil paintings on canvas that populated the salons of Europe. As seen in comparison to the European practice of miniature portrait painting, a lesser art itself, it was associated with amateurs and considered to be an appropriate pastime for women. As such, bias toward miniature painting was interwoven with Victorian constructions of gender as well as prejudices toward "others," those South Asian artists imagined to have stagnated in a timeless, traditional (craft-based) past. Such constructs contrasted with ideas about modernity, progress, and art, of which European powers claimed themselves to be the exclusive proprietors and harbingers.[6]

Alongside the ideological maneuvers that shaped perspectives on Indo-Persian painting, the introduction of European miniature portraiture in South Asia in the late eighteenth century influenced the practice of local artists, who needed to find new ways of securing an income now that they could not rely on court patronage.[7] This period saw the arrival of painting portraits of Mughal and Sikh rulers, images of Mughal beauties (imagined as rulers' wives and consorts; fig. 9.2), British visitors, and Mughal monuments. In a South Asian context, the term "miniature" as a genre of painting applied best to these small painted ivories that appear in the nineteenth century to fulfill Western demands. Like their European counterparts, these painted images were either framed and displayed or encased with precious metals and gems and worn as pins, earrings, necklaces, bracelets, and rings, reinforcing the idea of miniature as ornament and decoration.

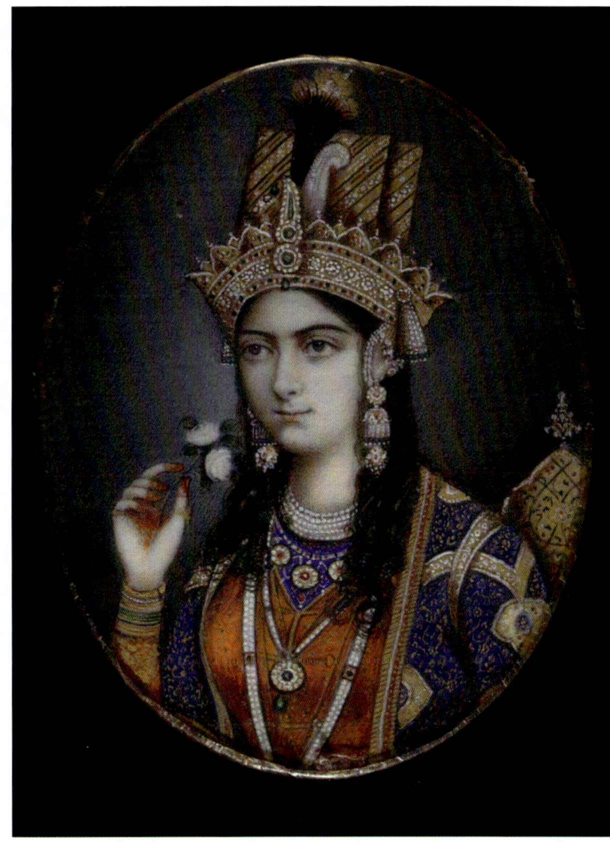

Figure 9.2. An imaginary miniature portrait of Arjumand Banu Begum (Mumtaz Mahal), favorite wife of Shah Jahan Delhi, ca. 1820. Painted in watercolor on ivory. Length: 6.5 cm, width: 5 cm. IM.277–1913, Victoria and Albert Museum.

One must remain mindful of the adjectives used to describe the "miniature" practice as it applies to Indo-Persian painting, then and now. In his critique of the historiography of Persianate painting, David Roxburgh notes that words like "beautiful," "romantic," "fantastic," and "exquisite" helped solidify the link between Persianate painting and the realm of decoration, highlighting "the painting's power to distract us or to transport our minds, effectively deferring us from pursuing other questions about pictures."[8] In "Micrographia," Roxburgh cites from B. W. Robinson's commentary from 1965 on Persian painting and drawing in order to draw attention to the repercussions of emphasizing its beauty as well as illustrative and decorative attributes: "Indeed, it would be foolish, when looking at Persian painting or drawing, to ask the sort of question that springs to mind when we contemplate Western pictorial art: 'What is the artist's message for us?' The Persian artist's message is simple and invariable: 'This is the most beautiful and effective illustration I can make to this story; I hope you will like it.'"[9]

Having asserted the beautiful, illustrative content of Persian painting, Robinson asks the Western viewer to view "these elaborate yet uncomplicated works with the simple eyes of children . . . delighting in their beauty of line and richness of color, and enjoying the strange stories they tell. Their beauties are all on the surface; no spiritual message or Freudian symbolism lurks beneath their exquisite forms and colors."[10] Thus, according to Robinson, Persianate painting is devoid of internal meaning, its function and value limited to that of beautifully decorating a manuscript and its ability to transport a Western viewer to times and places far away. Yet, as Roxburgh shows us, there exists extraordinary complexity and depth in Persianate painting, illuminating its own structures of meaning.[11]

Such attitudes about the surface simplicity of miniatures persist, and they have influenced the ways in which Western viewers approach contemporary neo-miniature painting. As an example of how earlier discourses continue to place limits on Western viewers' ability to engage with related bodies of visual material, consider Robinson's quote next to that from a review of the exhibition *The American Effect* at the Whitney Museum of American Art in 2003. In the reviewer's description of one of Saira Wasim's paintings, *Friendship After 11 September 2* (2003), the author writes:

> [It] offers convincing *craftsmanship*—the artist reinterprets Raphael's "School of Athens" as a Mughalesque miniature—but she is hampered by a lack of thematic subtlety. A drawing of George W. Bush in the guise of a victorious Roman emperor, flanked by Pakistan's president, Pervez Musharraf (with Napoleon and

> sundry imperialists nearby), leaves nothing to the imagination. The complicity of our government in the tragedies of developing nations, including Ms. Wasim's native Pakistan, demands an accounting, but her work is as relentlessly "on-message" as a Pentagon news briefing, if more compelling and tongue in cheek.[12]

As my later discussion of Wasim's work will demonstrate, her work engages with multiple subversions that extend beyond the perceived immediacy of the subject matter that are not captured in the reviewer's critique. Rather, this reviewer's comments are cited to support a trend observed by Debbie Lisle regarding the criticism of works of art by non-American artists in exhibition reviews of *The American Effect*. Lisle notes that "art using traditional or 'native' formats to critique US hegemony" is praised for "its 'convincing craftsmanship' . . . [however] art using a 'native' format does not quite count as art, but is a quaint and charming effort."[13] The way in which Shteyngart frames Wasim's work is a result of the inherited Western discourse and language (e.g., the use of the term "craftsmanship" and *his* surface level reading of the painting), by which he's been conditioned to perceive it. What is necessitated now is an interrogation of the lens through which Indo-Persian paintings and their contemporary incarnation, neo-miniatures, were derided by colonialist, Orientalist ideologies. First and foremost, one must contextualize and challenge narratives of modernity and art as reflected against their imagined foil, tradition and craft.

De/Re-Constructing Narratives of Modernity and Tradition: Reconstituting "Miniature" Painting

The patronage of opulent illustrated manuscripts and bound collections of paintings declined in the late eighteenth and early nineteenth centuries as local polities waned in power and Western influence took hold in the region. The British, who succeeded the Mughals as rulers of South Asia, introduced a set of values that privileged Western conceptions of fine art over applied art and relegated indigenous artistic production to the lower position of applied art, craft, and/or souvenir. The now identifiable "miniature" painting came to be seen as an exotic curiosity, and local artists produced images for the European trading companies and stereotypical scenes of legendary people and places to sell as tourist memorabilia; especially popular were images of monuments, Mughal and Sikh rulers, and women associated with the Mughal court. Virginia Whiles, in her landmark book on reinventing miniature painting, comments that painters from royal ateliers lost their courtly prestige and were reclassified as artisans, "craftsmen," or "artist designers," whose roles included producing local crafts for international trade and memorabilia for British officers and tourists, and serving as interior decorators.[14] Such efforts were furthered by Orientalists—albeit for different reasons—who were committed to reviving indigenous traditions within new art schools in response to the detrimental effects of colonial policies, in part by encouraging the offspring of artisans to pursue their family's inherited "craft." One of four such art and craft schools (schools of industrial art) established in British India in the last quarter of the nineteenth century was the Mayo School of Industrial Art in Lahore, founded in 1872, which would eventually become the National College of Arts (NCA) about a decade after independence from British rule in 1947.[15]

With the name change, the NCA remodeled itself as a modern art college based on the European Bauhaus model and, in reaction to its colonial legacy, distanced itself from its "craft-school" curriculum that was viewed as inimical to a modernist agenda.[16] The NCA turned toward instruction in modern Western artistic practices, especially avant-garde abstract styles. Pakistani artists drew on the language of Western abstract modern art as a means of upending colonial academic styles and claiming for themselves practices associated with modernity, otherwise deemed exclusively Western products. At this time, miniature painting courses continued to be offered at the NCA, but the tradition was treated as a historical remnant, not as a practice that had relevance for modern artistic production. As Anna Molka Ahmed observed, "the literary figures were the 'artists' and the painters were the 'craftsmen' at par with the shoe-maker and the tailor."[17] Such attitudes toward miniature painting began to shift when Zahoor ul-Akhlaq, an NCA graduate studying in London in the 1960s, encountered Mughal paintings at the Victoria and Albert Museum and drew on their subjects, themes, and styles for his modern large-scale abstract paintings. When he returned to the NCA in the 1970s, Akhlaq urged students to explore the potential of miniatures for their own work. In 1982, he encouraged Bashir Ahmed, a student of one of the last master "miniaturists" in Pakistan, to establish a specialized field in miniature painting within the fine art department at the NCA, alongside the established fields of modern painting and sculpture.[18] At this moment, the NCA elevated miniature painting to an area of specialization largely because of its historic and regional relevance; as such, it reflects postcolonial efforts to restore local artistic practices damaged by colonial discourses as a response to the anxieties of "a postcolonial society embroiled in debates about identity, tradition and future 'routes.'"[19] Yet, so deeply ingrained was the perceived dichotomy between modernity and tradition, that when the miniature practice was integrated into the curriculum in the 1980s, as a means of reviving pride in what was still considered craft albeit one associated with elite forms of artistic practice, it was met with reluctance and disdain.[20] As the NCA reasserted the importance of miniature painting as a regional and historical practice, it reaffirmed the practice as traditional, distinct from mainstream contemporary art. Thus, the revival of miniatures involved learning a variety of traditional techniques, such as preparing hand-made paper *(wasli)*, making brushes (which initially involved catching a squirrel and pulling out hairs from its tail), grinding pigments, using mussel shell palettes, and adopting the appropriate posture. Since these were seen as craft techniques, and because copying; repetitive, meticulous exercises; hours of labor; and the observance of ritual were necessary for the development of the technique and mastering associated skills,[21] they were derided as "anti-intellectual"; miniature painting in relationship to Westernized contemporary art was considered "low versus high art, illustration versus fine art, skill versus critique, tradition versus the avant-garde."[22] Such ideas were further fueled by the fact that the NCA program included rigorous copying of *photos* of Persian, Mughal, Rajput, and Pahari paintings—regional courtly painting styles that form the basis of neo-miniature training—since vast numbers of the originals were now part of collections in the West. Thus, efforts to reclaim and revalue the miniature tradition from internalized colonial discourses and the rhetoric of Westernized modernity proved a challenging and complicated project. The devaluing of tradition that resulted from the discourse of Western colonialism and modernity involved changing mind-sets and mentalities. As contemporary artist Shahzia Sikander observed, "[miniature painting] supposedly represented our heritage, yet we reacted to it with suspicion and ridicule."[23] Such attitudes were mirrored in and reinforced by popular media and the circulation of commodities such as calendars, cushion covers, and advertisements in marketplaces, where reproductions of Mughal paintings circulated as kitsch and as "low, cheap" objects.[24] As Duccio K. Marignoli and Enrico Mascelloni poignantly express, the "things that double as both 'knick knacks' and reminders of our deepest cultural inheritance" speak to "the historical chasm *amongst* us (and even within us)," a moving comment on the continued effects of colonial discourses.[25]

Although the incipient revival of miniatures must be considered within the context of the highly Westernized teaching methods in Lahore at the time, it is significant that this process was still inflected by the living legacy of colonial biases toward the practice. Intriguingly, the insistence on technique, skill, and rigor possessed "its own mystique, with an undertone of sitting in judgment on the apparent laxity of the discipline in contemporary [Western] art procedures."[26] Indeed, as it emerges and develops into a full-fledged contemporary artistic "attitude" in the last decade of the twentieth century and the first two decades of the twenty-first, the neo-miniature school rejects modernist and postmodern critiques that shun notions of skill, talent, and beauty as antithetical to intellectual creativity and their collective efforts aim to destabilize ideological bifurcations between modernity and tradition, art and craft, as well as "West" and "East."[27] The international success of neo-miniature art meant that "the miniature department, once the least popular department in the fine arts faculty, has now become the most popular."[28]

Decoration, Detail, and the "East": Miniature Painting and the Feminine

The majority of neo-miniaturists are women, a phenomenon that emerges out of the marginal status of a perceived "decorative" art form and to the history and relationship between women and the arts in Pakistan. By 2010, 80 percent of contemporary neo-miniaturists were women.[29] The gendered development of this practice is significant, especially when one considers that ateliers were not only made up of male artists but, according to Whiles, "the women, mothers and daughters, were there to 'service' the male artists—fathers, brothers, and sons—by pounding pigments and plants, both for creative and culinary production. Not only were they . . . banned from patriarchal transmission, but also this subsidising service is totally absent from all art-historical accounts. Women were invisible."[30]

Yet, today, most of the well-known international neo-miniaturists are women. This, I propose, is not simply a story of female empowerment but it also relates to how Victorian attitudes toward decoration and appropriate artistic pastimes for women (both demeaning) and their perseverance in women's convent schools in Pakistan mesh with the history of women's roles in the arts in Pakistan. As they would merge together, these shifts enabled the transfiguration/translation of a male-dominated practice to a female-dominated practice.

It is important to consider the ways in which Western attention to the decoration, detail, and illustrative function of Indo-Persian painting mirrored and intersected with what were considered desirable "feminine" qualities and pursuits in Europe. Modernist denunciations of the decorative declare it to be "mere decoration and characterized as superficial, meaningless and lacking in intellectual rigour."[31] In the late eighteenth and nineteenth centuries, the association of women with decoration was tied to ideologies that identified women with the private, domestic sphere—as sites of conspicuous consumption, along with women's bodies—whereas men were connected with public spaces.[32] As such, the decorative is linked to fashion, beauty, and ornamental detail.[33] As Naomi Schor observes, detail is "bounded on one side by the ornamental, with its traditional connotations of effeminacy and decadence, and on the other, by the everyday, whose 'prosiness' is rooted in the domestic sphere of social life presided over by women."[34] These two qualities—the ornamental and the everyday—merged in activities such as needlework, line drawing, watercolors, pastel, and miniature painting, which embodied "innately feminine . . . qualities of delicacy, meticulous execution and preciosity" and were commended to women as appropriate and laudable pastimes since the execution of small minute detail cultivated and demonstrated "the female virtues of patience, diligence and perseverance."[35] The entry "Amateur Artists" in the *Concise Dictionary of Women Artists* makes special mention of miniature painting: "a highly popular medium for amateur women artists, with its costly materials and minutely detailed finish, was not only seen as jewel-like in its execution and scale, but was frequently framed by gems and metalwork and functioned as jewelry for the adornment of the female body."[36] Perhaps nowhere is the link between decoration, ornament, and miniature painting made more explicit. While knowledge of drawing, as well as music and needlework, were designated as desirable "feminine" accomplishments, and part of the established educational curriculum of middle- and upper-class women, illustration also provided women with a viable career choice. Illustration could be practiced at home and therefore not impede upon her "'real' role as wife and mother . . . since illustration wasn't 'real' art, it was suitable for 'mere' women."[37] Yet as Elliot and Heiland comment, although such activities were intended to facilitate patriarchal formulations of femininity, these "feminine" activities and institutions also held subversive potential. That is, within these marginal spheres, women were able to advance their education, improve their skills, and potentially support themselves.[38]

Many of these Victorian beliefs and practices were transposed to British South Asia, and disseminated through women's educational curriculum, journals, and pamphlets. Moreover, a British colonial education for women was imposed by the British in the all-women English medium of convent schools.[39] We see such ideological constructs pertaining to acceptable female pursuits at play in the establishment of the first fine arts department at Punjab University in the early years of Pakistan's independence. As related by Anna Molka Ahmed, the first appointee to the fine arts department, the vice-chancellor of the university, Mian Akhtar Hussain, declared: "Women's emancipation means that women are beginning to take up subjects like chemistry and physics, and we don't want to clutter up those classes with them. It's a waste of space and time since they'll get married anyway. The Department of Fine Arts will admit only female students!"[40] As suggested by the vice-chancellor's statement, the arts were an acceptable, noncompetitive, nonthreatening female pursuit that would not conflict with women's marital futures. Rather, an art education "would 'enhance the natural proclivities of women,' making them better 'home decorators,' and nurture the finer sensibilities expected of mothers, wives, and daughters."[41]

In the same way that female students were trained to become "artistic," but not "artists,"[42] female teachers filled colleges and universities as art instructors, coinciding with their roles as nurturers and guardians of tradition, but for a few exceptions women were absent as professional artists, while male artists exploring avant-garde "international" styles were positioned as trailblazers.[43] Nevertheless, in the 1980s, during the military dictatorship of General Zia ul-Haq, what had been considered a safe educational endeavor for middle-class Pakistani women was mobilized into a vehicle for expression and protest in the public domain.[44] Like their male counterparts, these female artists (e.g., Zubeida Agha, Salima Hashmi, Lala Rukh) engaged with international modernist styles but in the next decade, within the nexus of tradition, identity, and gender, the miniature practice emerged as a preferred medium for the following generations of women artists.[45] While accommodating British colonial constructs of feminine practice, simultaneously recast in service of the nation and household (i.e., the woman as guardian of traditions and the domestic sphere), female neo-miniaturists can be seen as destabilizing both models.

For women to dominate what was previously an elite male practice, larger ways of thinking about and seeing Indo-Persian painting needed to occur that must be traced to the thick of the colonial era. The fact that it had been devalued and marginalized by colonial discourses meant it was up for grabs so to speak, and there is no denying that the neo-miniature impetus derived from a resistance to a Western model of abstract, conceptual art that dominated at NCA. In addition, however, Indo-Persian paintings' attention to detail merged with Western discourses that associated this body of paintings with illustrative and decorative qualities and altered the ways in which local South Asian audiences perceived it as well. This is not to simply say that it was now perceived as an acceptable female preoccupation but rather that, as feminine and marginal, it was a disruptive and empowering space. Neo-miniaturists not only subvert colonial discourses that had led to the deprecation and stigmatization of "miniature" painting, but they also subvert tradition itself in order to justify neo-miniaturist painting as a contemporary art form worthy of Western and international recognition. These artists also subvert Western expectations of Muslim Pakistani women, although each artist does so in her own way. As prominent Pakistani artist, art historian, and curator Salima Hashmi eloquently writes, these paintings "speak of longings, rebellions, and subversion,"[46] upturning what was constructed as an emulative, decorative vestige of the past into an active, "fiercely independent" mode of resistance.[47]

It is worth considering how and why so many women are drawn to miniature painting as well as how it is perceived by women themselves in order to underscore the relationship between Victorian colonial ideations of the feminine and their extension as well as transformation in time. In regard to the former, one possible explanation is that young women from families with certain means attend convent schools, which as mentioned previously continues to impart a British colonial informed education. Their curriculum includes the domestic arts, including previously described feminine pursuits, for example embroidery. It is possible that their convent education influenced their attraction toward this genre, at the same instilling an awareness of the arbitrariness of ascribed gender roles and attitudes since they are well aware that this was historically a male practice. Moreover, several female artists themselves have referred to the subordinate and/or feminine nature of the practice. Shahzia Sikander refers to the "submissive nature" and its ritualistic, meditative qualities. Salima Hashmi elucidates on the radically distinct physical environment of the miniature studio where "students sit sedately cross-legged on the floor on mats or cushions; their backs to the walls, they bend over the diminutive waslis, making delicate slow marks, holding their limbs close to their bodies."[48] To Hashmi this environment brings to mind a Victorian embroidery circle or sewing school.[49] Consider this in tandem with an experience recounted by Aisha Khalid when she was at the Royal Academy of Visual Art in Amsterdam: during an open studio visit, a European student found her seated on the floor, bent over a miniature, and thought Khalid was in the midst of a performance-art piece—acting out the role of an "oppressed maker of women's work."[50] Thus, it can be argued that what was previously a male practice is now viewed—through an altered lens—as feminine, enabling women, now lauded as trailblazers for contemporary Pakistani art, to enter and inhabit a space from which they were previously excluded.

A key moment in the transformation of the miniature practice occurred in 1987, when Nahid Fakhruddin, a final-year miniature student at the NCA, presented a series of four paintings depicting traditional domestic games played by women. The shift in her work from male to female subjects and from an imperial context to a domestic one was significant.[51] It is Sikander's 1991 thesis project, *The Scroll*, however, which is recognized as "the real breakthrough" that commenced a career that would bring international attention to the neo-miniature practice.[52] As Murtaza Vali commented in 2007, "the contemporary miniature has become the dominant face of present-day Pakistani art abroad, in part due to the international success of individual artists such as New York–based Shahzia Sikander."[53]

It is noteworthy that the painting recognized as the pivot from tradition to modernity for miniature painting and an inspiration for its revival was a meter-long depiction of a female, autobiographical, domestic scene. Not only did Sikander enlarge the then popularly assumed size and format of the folio page—hers being more akin to the large panoramic scrolls of cities painted by "miniaturists" in the nineteenth century but instead directly referencing *patua* scrolls—she shifts attention from an elite male subject to herself (a woman) and from a court scene to a domestic interior (her home). Moreover, Sikander was intrigued by the possibilities of exploring "the interiority of space" as inspired by Safavid painting and examining domestic labor (including class divisions within). Sikander's choice to explore the possibilities of depicting a domestic space (her home) also reflected the times, an era that was "defined by the looming Hudood ordinances and [as a result] as a young, single woman, one could not freely roam around the city."[54] *The Scroll* upended deeply embedded if misinformed assumptions about the "miniature" paintings, "setting the groundwork for the miniature as a contested space."[55] One wonders if a nondomestic, non-feminine subject would have had the same effect, if it in fact it could only have been "domestic" and "feminine" to have elicited such a stir. This recalls Toril Moi's commentary on Julia Kristeva's work on marginality, subversion, and dissidence: "Since women are defined as marginal by patriarchy, their struggle can be theorized in the same way as any other struggle against a centralized power structure."[56] Thus, it was because miniature painting became marginalized through colonial and patriarchal discourses, because it was constructed and disregarded as feminine, that it held such potential to construct a revolutionary, subversive space, one that would engage with multiple ideological and hegemonic subversions.

Before proceeding to a discussion of Saira Wasim's work, it must be said that the visibility and success of the neo-miniature school has not been without its detractors and is a subject that fuels passionate debates. Critics of neo-miniature painting take issue with the popularity of the practice abroad, because they believe it panders to Western desires for authentic or exotic art. Its success, they argue, derives from fulfilling expectations of what an "other" art should be. Although Western desires, made manifest by the fact that it is still the West that governs the international art market, may play a role in the visibility of neo-miniatures globally, this does not take away from the fact that the practice emerged as an act of resistance to Western hegemony. After all, forgoing one's heritage is in essence also to acquiesce to Western discourses. Many neo-miniaturists, for their part, are invested in reclaiming a local visual language and practice but are aware that they must engage with and challenge Western audience expectations that are informed and internalized by deeply embedded colonial ideologies. Perhaps embracing local visual languages cannot be separated from fulfilling Western audience expectations in international markets but nevertheless, generally speaking, neo-miniaturists who exhibit internationally each have their own ways of resisting the romanticization and exoticization of their practice. Moreover, once allowed "in," it is an opportunity to resist, to criticize from the inside the very Western discourses that may have enabled its entrance.

Between Painting and Print Cultures: Satire, Parody, and the Decorative in the Art of Saira Wasim

The works of Saira Wasim, a prominent neo-miniaturist presently based in Massachusetts, provide rich, provocative material for discussing strategies of resistance. Wasim is well known for her embrace of political and social satire, a genre generally associated with men historically in the West. She thus stands out as a distinctive figure among neo-miniaturists and destabilizes gendered expectations in terms of wider satiric expression. By connecting her meticulous, time-consuming painting practice (Wasim reports that a given painting may take her up to four months to complete) with different types of print media (specifically sociopolitical satire and fashion magazines)—her work challenges the preciousness of the "miniature" painting while blurring the division between high art and popular culture. Interestingly, her use of satire and attention to detail led to an invitation to produce a series of Mughal painting–influenced neo-miniatures for a fashion story featured in the fifth anniversary of *Vogue India* in 2012. Although in seeming contrast to her politically inflected work, the fashion layout, which needed to fulfill the broad contours of *Vogue*'s commission, nevertheless participates in ongoing debates about the relationship between art, commerce, fashion, heritage, and East-West relations. In this way the *Vogue* paintings communicate a sociopolitical point of view, decentering the Western canon of beauty and power relations in the fashion industry.

In Wasim's artist statement, she writes that her neo-miniatures "explore social and political issues that divide the modern world."[57] Throughout her career, she has engaged frequently with themes involving corruption, both religious and political, and her paintings often feature inept, duplicitous figures—politicians, soldiers, mullahs—embodying sullied ideals.[58] Wasim's satirical caricatures of world leaders including South Asian, Middle Eastern, European, and US politicians charge the West of the very behaviors that the West has (for at least a couple hundred years), accused the "East" of. There are no heroes here, only clowns and puppets. Nor does she exhibit nostalgia for the past; rather, the Mughal imperial past is as guilty of political propaganda as the US neo-imperial present.[59] Her paintings parody the past and present, the "East" and "West." Comical and irreverent of the past and critical of the present, her paintings are pleas "for social justice, respect, and tolerance through the use of caricature and satire."[60] Prior to coming to United States, Wasim focused most of her work on critiquing Pakistani politics and social issues as well as the hypocrisy and fallout of the post-9/11 US-Pakistan alliance. Although no stranger to forms of persecution as a member of the Ahmadiyya sect in

Pakistan (as the Ahmadiyya are not recognized as part of the Muslim *ummah* by the Pakistan government), Wasim was suddenly identified and referred to as a Muslim artist after relocating to the United States. This was a welcome shift for Wasim on a personal level, even though the shift came with new forms of persecution:

> The post 9/11 climate of fear, scrutiny, and surveillance of Muslims in the West shape[s] my current work. . . . This is an era of cross-cultural misunderstandings; misperceptions created by the Western media that are mostly hostile to Muslim societies and Islam. Much of this misperception is attributable to the Western media, which often presents a distorted version of reality and only one side of the global debate. My new works unmask the injustices and hypocrisy of both the Eastern and the Western worlds. . . . Although they provide comic relief, they are critical of ignorance and prejudice, manipulation of governments and religious heads.[61]

Such concerns inspired Wasim's response to the Danish cartoon controversy in 2005, when a Danish newspaper published offensive images of the Prophet Muhammad in the painting *Ignorance Is Bliss* (2006) (fig. 9.3). Distressed by the misinformed, incendiary Western representations of the Prophet Muhammad and of Muslims broadly as well as by the violent responses by groups of aggrieved Muslims that run counter to the precepts

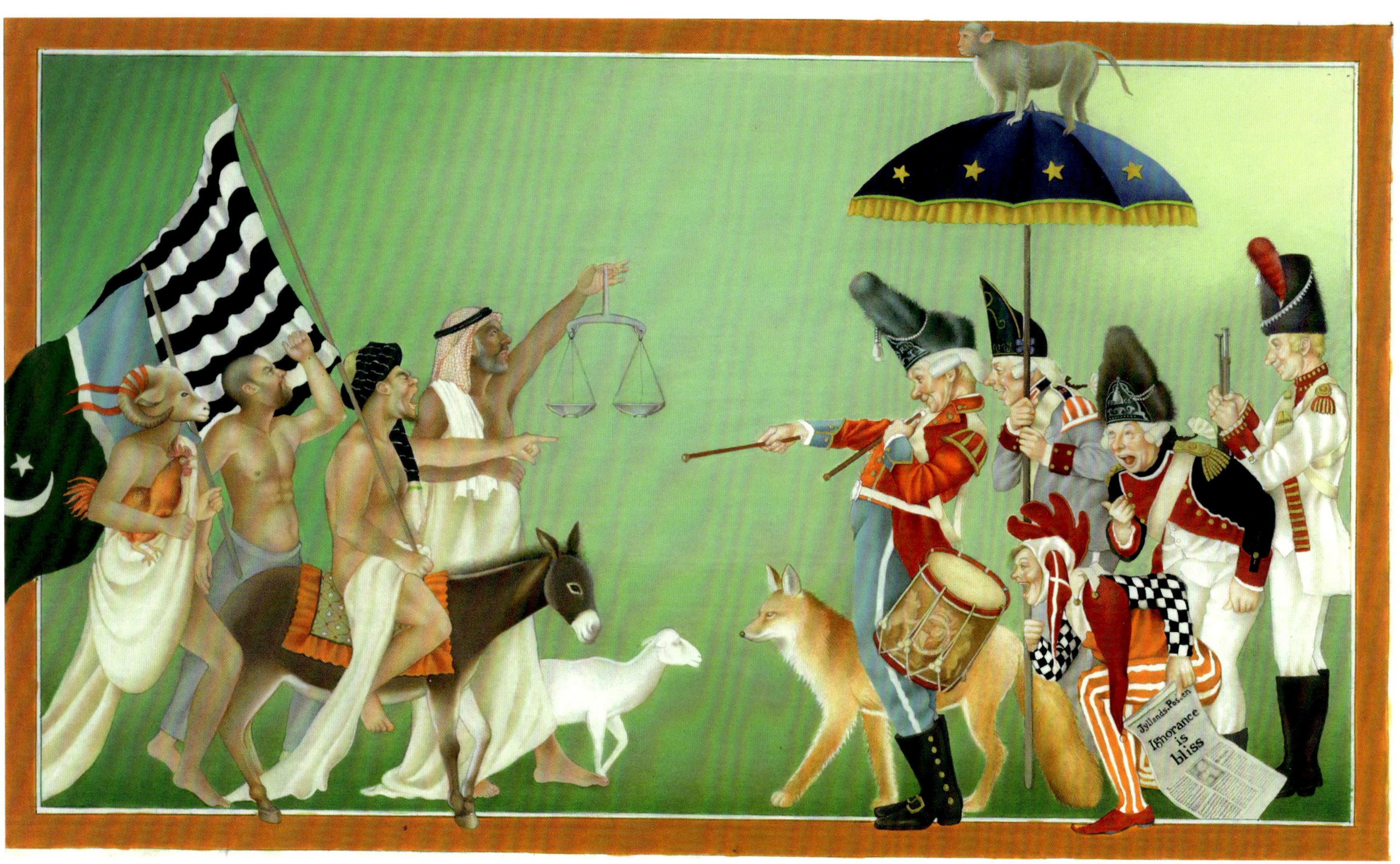

Figure 9.3. Saira Wasim, *Ignorance Is Bliss* (2006). Gouache and gold on wasli, 21.1 × 36.1 cm. Image courtesy of the artist.

of Islam, Wasim maintains that Western hegemonic structures and militant forms of extremism "both share intolerance towards other cultures and a disregard for diversity, both seek to impose their version of the world on others."[62] By alluding to *Yankee Doodle Dandy* (1937), the satiric mural painting by iconic American illustrator Norman Rockwell, Wasim uses pastiche and conflation to collapse history, in order for the viewer to reflect upon the ways in which Western colonial history is embedded in the present and continues to influence current events. "Yankee Doodle," after all, is a pejorative term used by the British to refer to the American colonists, but eventually reclaimed and embraced by the colonists. Even if the British colonialists laugh at Yankee Doodle, he rides on unperturbed, confident that the tides will turn and ultimately the joke will be on them. By contrast, the figures being ridiculed in *Ignorance Is Bliss* respond with anger and fury because of the long and deeply embedded history of Western oppression and provocation, that there are no signs of restitution nor justice, and because they remain subjugated, marginalized communities as a result of global imbalances of power. Pastiche and conflation combine to invoke a history of European colonization, America's neo-imperialism, and global inequities that ask people to pause and reflect, to consider a specific crisis through a longer and wider historical and geopolitical lens.

The range of Wasim's references is far-reaching: she is inspired by Mughal court scenes and allegorical portraits, Renaissance art, neoclassical French painters (especially Jacques-Louis David and Ingres), theater, circuses, and Bollywood sets.[63] Her references to imperial allegorical Mughal portraiture, in particular under Emperor Jahangir, interact with satiric imagery disseminated through print media in the West. Her paintings, to the culturally informed viewer, may thus recall images of the allegorical portraits of the Mughal emperor Jahangir and/or the political satires of William Hogarth (1697–1764) and James Gillray ("the father of political cartoon," 1756–1815). Her satiric paintings refer to and engage with mass-mediated print culture; by linking her paintings with sociopolitical satire, Wasim couples her intensely time-consuming and laborious practice with a genre (satire) associated with an ephemeral medium (print). Her paintings, like most sociopolitical satire, refer to contemporary political figures and events. A 2001 exhibition of James Gillray's satirical prints at Tate Britain in London addresses the perceived immediacy and ephemeral characteristics of this body of material: "Satire has often been seen as the disposable art of an urban, commercialized culture, one of the plethora of consumer goods which are continually outdated and replaced by new offerings. Graphic satire usually deals with fleeting events, so that its value as art, whether of the cartoons in our daily papers or 18th century caricatures, appears to last no longer than the topicality of its subject matter."[64]

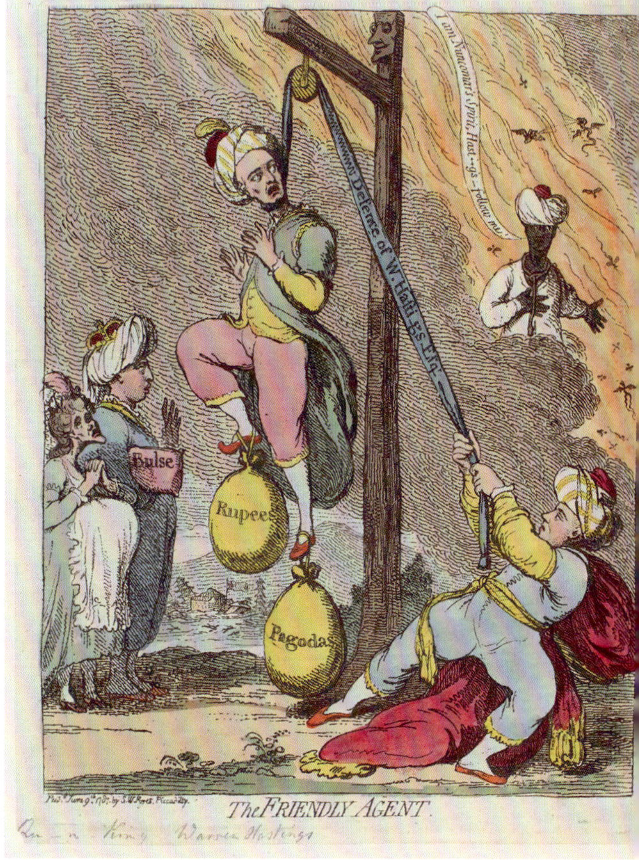

Figure 9.4. James Gillray, *The Friendly Agent* (Charlotte of Mecklenburg-Strelitz; King George III; Warren Hastings; John Scott-Waring), published by Samuel William Fores, June 9, 1787. Hand-colored etching, 8 ¾ in. × 6 ⅞ in. (22.3 cm × 17.5 cm) plate size; 9 ⅛ in. × 7 ⅜ in. (23.3 cm × 18.7 cm) paper size. NPG D12364, National Portrait Gallery, London.

Similar to the goal of the Tate exhibition, which sought to underscore the tension between such a view of satirical political cartoons and the prolonged examination necessitated by Gillray's detailed work (please see fig. 9.4 for an example),[65] a similar tension exists in Wasim's work. This tension takes shape in a review of Wasim's painting of the Asia Society exhibition on Asian American art, *One Way or Another* (2006), which draws attention to Wasim's interest in "sheer physical perfection" and then comments that "her best images are exquisite political cartoons."[66] Such comments, which appear fairly regularly in regard to Wasim's work, juxtapose the time-consuming precision of the technique and details that fill Wasim's paintings with reference to (printed) satirical cartoons. This response suggests that Wasim's work is not only making jabs at political figures and events, but it also doesn't seem to take itself or the perceived preciousness associated with the technique (too often connected with craft) too seriously. She thereby actively resists the tendency to fetishize an "ethnic" or "other" tradition, a pitfall that numerous non-Western artists exhibiting in the West feel trapped by. Moreover, the juxtaposition of meticulous paintings with caricatures of absurd topical subject matter—whether of current leaders or events—resists the tendency to cast traditional practices into a timeless, ahistoric space. In these ways, she destabilizes the artificial boundaries that divide high and popular culture as they fold into debates of the ideological divide between art and craft, a divide that all neo-miniaturists continue to confront. Despite the currentness of her topics, it's important to note that Wasim's paintings critique larger, broader processes and institutions; as she comments about her satirical caricatures of former president Musharraf, "it's less a statement about Musharraf [i.e., a particular political figure] than it is about the political structure of Pakistan, which seems to be trapped in this carousel-like repetition of history."[67]

This approach, commenting on the longer, larger hegemonic processes behind today's headlines, applies to her paintings involving Western leaders and events. For example, *OIL on Canvas (Operating Iraqi Liberation)* (2006) (fig. 9.5) underscores the preeminent role so-called black gold has in driving modern-day politics, not—as the title of the painting simultaneously references—ideals of liberty. Her representation of the Bush administration's invasion of Iraq as a circus highlights the absurd, ludicrous, self-serving behaviors of Western societies that have long tried to hide behind Western constructions of modernity and tandem constructs of liberty and democracy. As Anna Sloan writes about Wasim's work, she shows us "a 20th century democracy more akin to the autocratic rule of pre-modern empires than we often presume," and in doing so she reminds us that ideas of progress are constructed and ideological, not noble truths that the West lives by.[68]

Wasim drives the point of the profound hypocrisy embedded within the United States commitment to "liberty and justice for all" (to her adopted) "home" in a painting, titled *The Silent Plea* (2018) (fig. 9.6). As a "migrant Muslim woman artist in [the] USA and mother of three school-going kids," Wasim identifies with every mother's concern to keep schools safe. Citing the 1,300 children who die each year from gun-related injuries in the United States, violence that has been met by ongoing fierce resistance to gun control, Wasim comments on the irony of "a country most inimical towards others is actually under threat by its own citizens." *The Silent Plea* is based on the painting *The Madonna of the Roses* (1903) by French artist William-Adolphe Bouguereau (1825–1905). In Wasim's rendering, Madonna and child (who holds a pencil, signifying a school-going child) hold the scales of justice; Wasim asks us to consider why, in the United States, the right to bear arms is worth more than innocent human lives.[69] If this "right" is tied to the idea of protection, then why are so many innocent children allowed to be murdered? The inhumanity and absurdity of privileging the right to bear arms over the lives of innocent children negates the very precept upon which this "right" is predicated. Since those people who actively resist gun control are popularly associated with the Christian right, this image might strike a discordant chord among gun supporters, asking them to consider how their religious beliefs are in conflict with their political ones. Drawing on the richly detailed, visually dense margins of Persianate painting (including Mughal painting), the gravely rendered central image is contrasted with a deceptively ornate border, filled with ornate stylized foliage, guns, snippets of printed text, two infants marked with a bullseye, as well as two hybrid Trump creatures who are part human, part animal, part television, with the one in the lower right corner seemingly taking aim at the one in the lower left corner.

While a satirical mode characterizes most of Wasim's work, she has transformed her training in miniature painting in surprising directions. I turn now to a unique series of paintings that she was commissioned to produce for *Vogue India*'s fifth anniversary issue in 2012. A ten-page fashion story,[70] consisting of seven paintings (full-page images, with three spread out over two pages), this fashion shoot features a Mughal princess

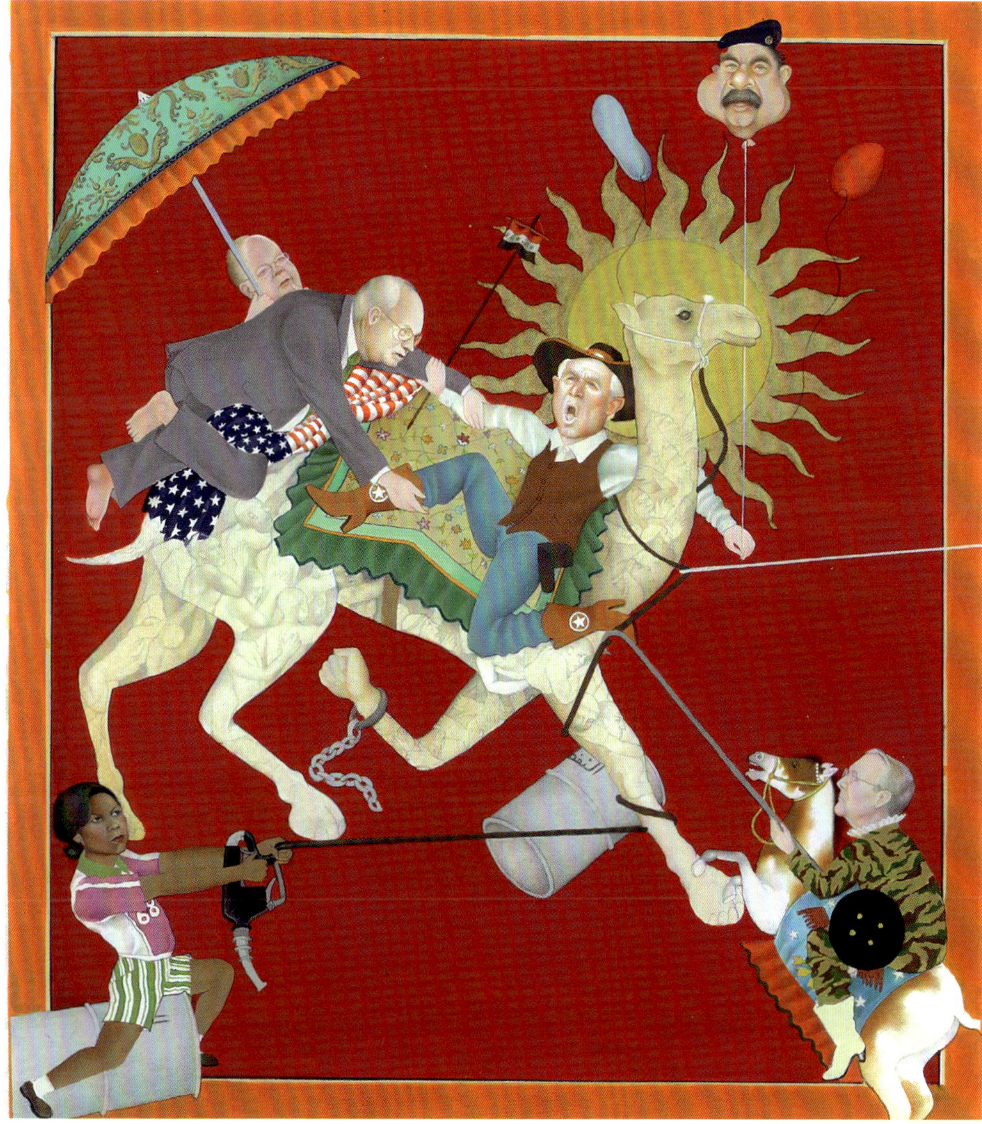

Figure 9.5. Saira Wasim, *OIL on Canvas (Operation Iraqi Liberation)* (2006). Gouache and gold on wasli, 25 × 22.1 cm. Image courtesy of the artist.

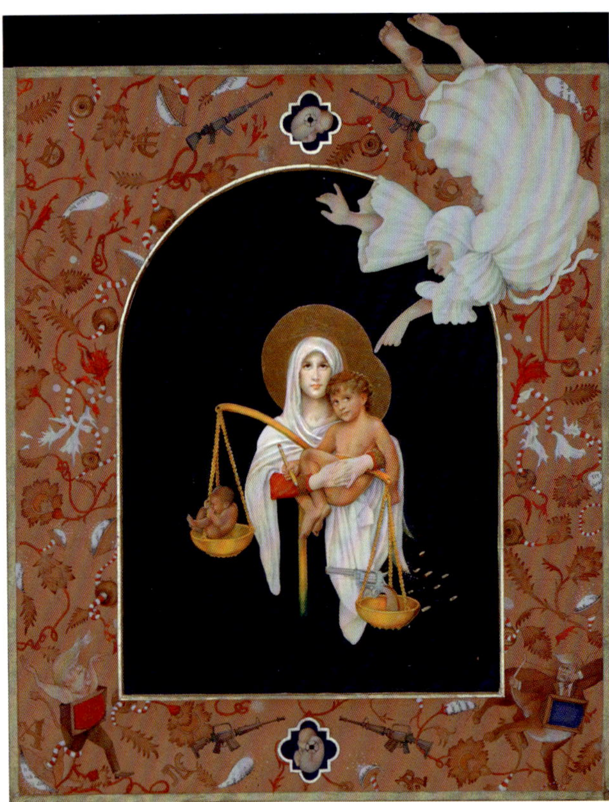

Figure 9.6. Saira Wasim, *Silent Plea* (2018). Paper cutouts, ink, gold leaf, and gouache on wasli, 28.5 × 26 × 2 in. (72.39 × 66.04 × 5.08 cm). Image courtesy of the artist.

reimagined as a modern-day "it girl."[71] Please see figures 9.7 through 9.13 for images of the original paintings, along with the text that accompanied the printed version of the "fashion shoot." Titled "The Princess Diaries," this fashion spread for the Indian edition of an international fashion magazine marks various "returns": a return—in print form—of paintings' function as part of a manuscript or album (now magazine), and a return to the feminine of "miniature" painting by utilizing a Mughal miniature style to feature women's fashion and gendered luxury consumption. Representing a distinctive approach to a fashion shoot, these paintings were conceived and commissioned as a series of images that would circulate in a print magazine, again blurring the line between fine art and popular visual culture. Although markedly different from her larger body of work,[72] these paintings also grapple with forms of Western hegemony here exerted through modernist discourses on fashion and canons of Western beauty.

It is worth noting that *Vogue India* commissioned a neo-miniaturist of Pakistani descent living in the United States for this series, since in India this style of painting is still associated with interior decoration and souvenirs. As Louis Werner points out in his essay on reinventing miniature painting, "in India today, in contrast to the approach at NCA, miniature painting is taught almost purely as a copyist art for the tourist trade. Only in Pakistan does one find radical innovators."[73] It's also indicative of *Vogue India*'s efforts to maintain a broad South Asian lens, featuring people, trends, etcetera from other South Asian countries. After reviewing the works of a number of neo-miniaturists, the magazine chose Wasim for her playful engagement with the practice, her virtuoso detailed renderings, and her specific approach to contemporizing the miniature tradition.

"The Princess Diaries" was envisioned as a means of engaging with *Vogue India*'s ongoing efforts to negotiate a Western modern luxury brand with India's heritage and traditions, in this case their Mughal past. As expressed by Priya Tanna, managing editor of the magazine, "We'll bring fashion from runways like Milan and New York to them in a language they relate to."[74] The choice of a Mughal protagonist (the princess "it girl"), technique, and style of painting also establishes a link between India's heritage and contemporary luxury culture, generally associated with the West. That is, the Mughal period represents an earlier epoch of South Asian luxury culture, one that predates Europe's arrival to the subcontinent (and upon which Europe's rise would never have happened) and India's embrace of a Western form of neo-liberalism in the 1990s.[75] Indeed, as Tanna made clear at the time of *Vogue India*'s launch, "Indians have been surrounded by a certain sense of luxury for a long time, so it's not a cultural revolution that's been thrust upon us."[76] "The Princess Diaries" is an affirmation of a local history of luxury and elitism, the latter updated and reinforced by commissioning an international contemporary artist for the "shoot."

Over the last forty years, the emergence of editions of *Vogue* outside America and Europe offered some sign of a given country's economic arrival.[77] Today, the arrival of indigenous editions of *Vogue* in "non-Western" countries is "a barometer of the emergence of an affluent middle class" and marks new luxury markets to be targeted by luxury industries.[78] Japan, Korea, and Taiwan launched their own editions of *Vogue* in the 1990s, while China and India launched theirs in the first decade of the twenty-first century. In addition to marking surplus wealth, *Vogue*'s circulation in Asian, Middle Eastern, and Latin American countries signals local imperatives for publications that reflect their own, indigenous ideals of beauty and style, with each edition of *Vogue* reflecting the national character of the respective country, at least in theory.[79] At the time of its launch Alex Kuruvilla, managing director of *Vogue*'s parent company Condé Nast India, affirmed that

> *Vogue India* has been completely created for the Indian woman. We have very carefully syndicated some material. It is a mix but it is primarily Indian content. . . . There are more than a million *Vogue* women in India, each with high awareness of international luxury, fashion and beauty brands. . . . It's not going to be an either/or situation. The Indian affluent woman is going to have a hybrid—she's going to have the best of both worlds.[80]

As articulated in another interview, Kuruvilla specified that "Indian women's wardrobes are still dominated by Indian brands, but what is changing dramatically are their accessories, and that's where international brands are making rapid inroads."[81]

At the same time, given that all of these editions share Condé Nast's brand name, each edition of *Vogue* must conform to certain brand values and expectations still set by the West. Thus, a separate department in Condé Nast's London headquarters guides the launches of all editions of their magazine. When *Vogue India*, for example, was introduced, the Indian team was overseen by the deputy director of British *Vogue*, Anna Harvey, who ensured that the voice of the local brand was consistent with that of the mother brand.

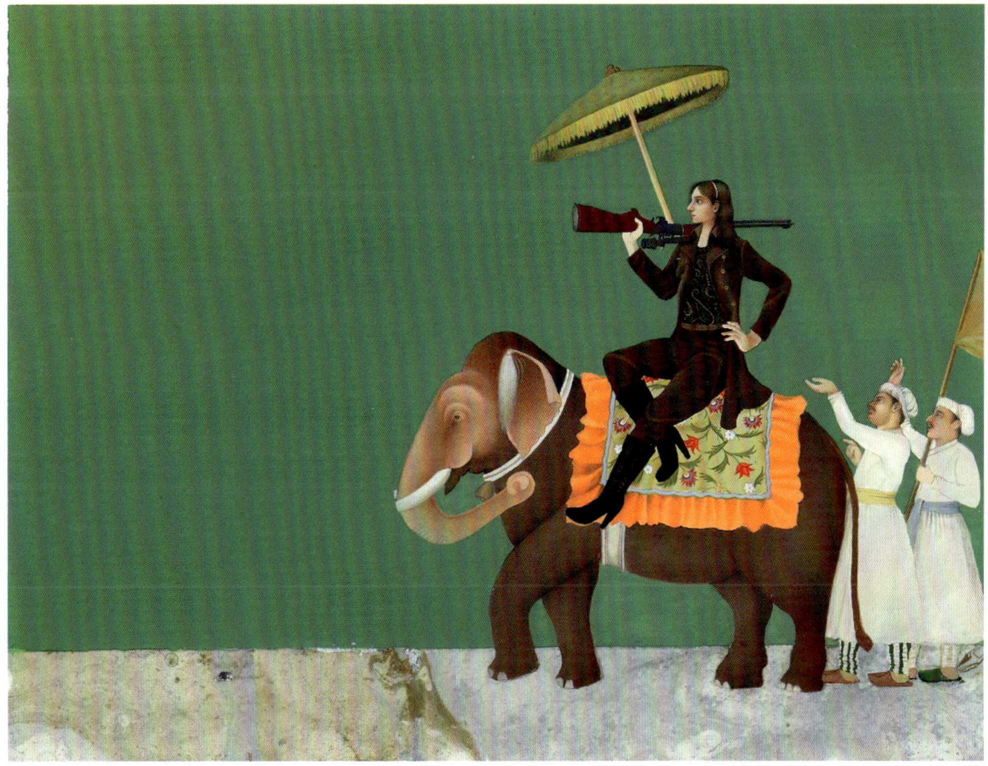

Figure 9.7. Saira Wasim, "*On the Prowl:* Round up the elephants—it's a glorious day for an old-fashioned hunt, and a military-style Ferragamo ensemble is a killer choice. Silk and brocade blouse, cashmere wool cape, wool trousers; al Salvatore Ferragamo. 'Lady Troop' boots, Cristian Louboutin." First painting in "The Princess Diaries," *Vogue India*, 5th anniversary issue, October 2012. Image courtesy of the artist.

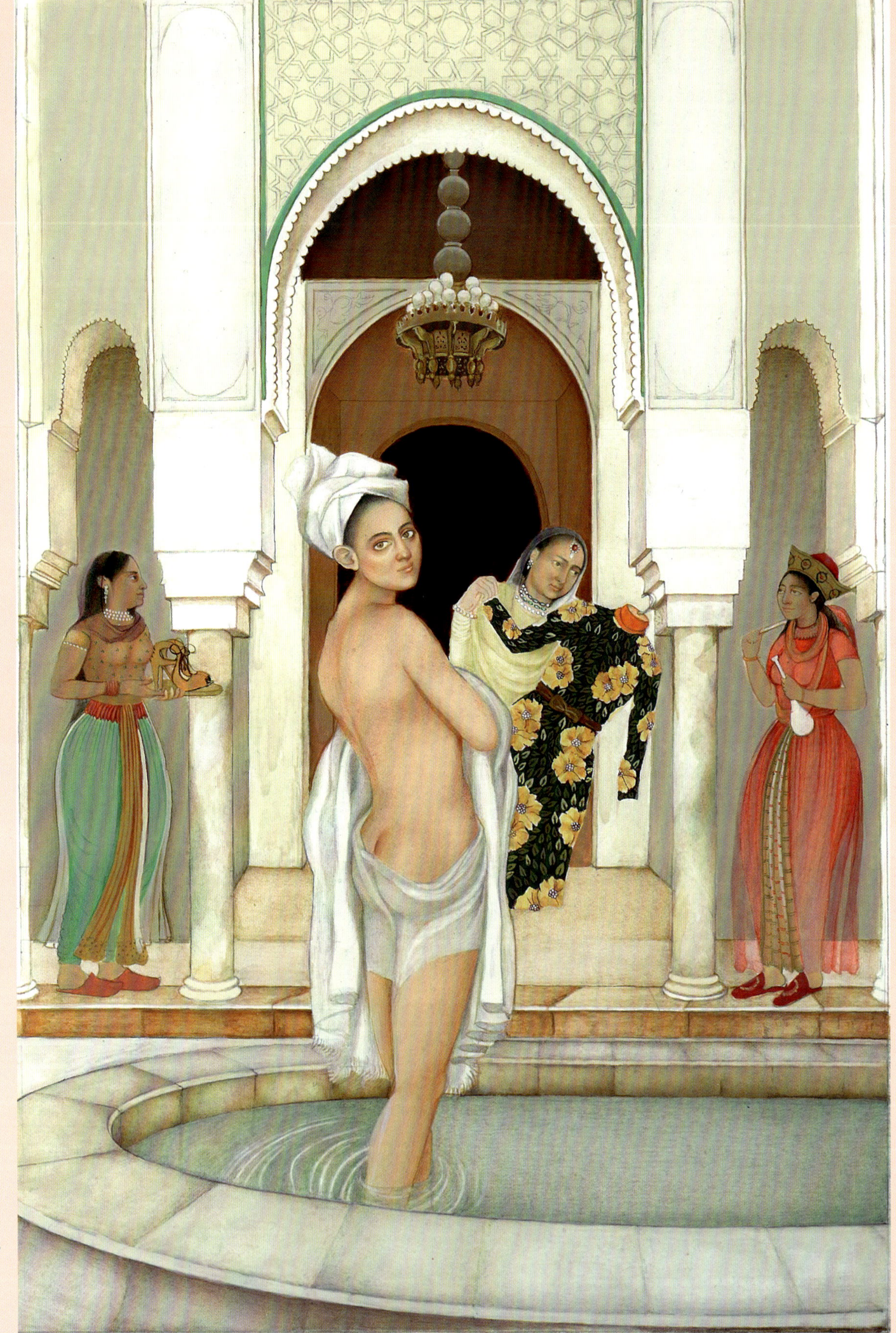

Figure 9.8. Saira Wasim, "*Rise, Shine:* Any lady-in-waiting worth her salt knows the power of Burberry. All our princess needs to do is enjoy the hammam. Cotton and silk stone-embroidered dress, bow belt; both Burberry Prorsum. 'Bolero' suede sandals. Gianvito Rossi." Second painting in "The Princess Diaries," *Vogue India*, 5th anniversary issue, October 2012. Image courtesy of the artist.

As the Indian team learned about and adhered to the mother brand's values, and as their expertise grew, Harvey's role correspondingly diminished.[82] This process ensures that the voice of each international edition remains consistent throughout all of its imprints and with that of the mother brand (namely, highest quality production values and writing, and a voice of expertise), thus linking New York's edition to China's. Moreover, *Vogues* everywhere feature prominent European and American designers and models, whereas local ones are by contrast featured in local editions only.[83] It is not surprising that two studies (Yan and Bissell; Han and Rudd) confirmed that *Vogue* magazine contributes to the Westernization of ideals of beauty and attractiveness around the world.[84]

Even ideological definitions of and criteria for what constitutes fashion—that is, a sense of constant innovation and novelty—are tied to the West. Intersecting with Western definitions of art, fashion as defined by the West emphasizes "a forward-looking, albeit inherently cyclical, process of invention and re-invention that is marked by the constant re-interpretation, rather than pure imitation, of the past."[85] This is in contrast to the ways in which Western commentators describe non-Western dress, stressing "the perceived timelessness and tradition of such clothing (or 'costume,' as it tended to be described) and its aesthetic adherence to the past."[86] Thus, in addition to being influenced by Western ideals of body type and beauty, Western ideas of what it means to be a modern, elite woman—including being up to date on what is currently in style—have altered local attitudes toward clothing.

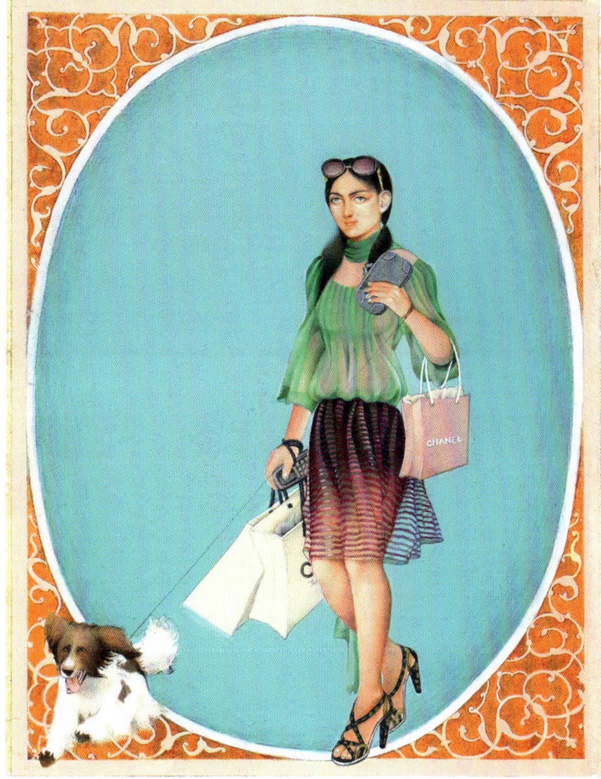

Figure 9.9. Saira Wasim, "*Talking Shop:* An afternoon of treasure-hunting in the local bazaars calls for breezy style. She sets off with her favourite companion—the palace pooch (who has some free time before his evening walk with the royal corgis). Muslin blouse, embroidered lace skirt; both Chanel. Sandals, Giambattista Valli. Sunglasses, Tom Ford. 'Intreciato' oxidized silver know clutch, Bottega Veneta." Third painting in "The Princess Diaries," *Vogue India*, 5th anniversary issue, October 2012. Image courtesy of the artist.

These tensions come to bear in the fashion story created by Wasim for *Vogue India*'s fifth anniversary. Wasim explains her concept behind the fashion story: "I was asked to paint a fashion story for their high-end fashion brands, for instance, Gucci, Prada and Chanel etc. . . . The story revolves around Mughal Princess, who begins her day with a bath, and then cycles through a series of contemporary haute couture outfits and luxury designer accessories." The model for her Mughal princess represents an amalgamation of representations of Mughal women over time, although it more closely resembles the imaginary representations of Mughal women found on a multitude of nineteenth-century portrait miniatures (fig. 9.2), made by local artists for the tourist market. The Mughal princess wears clothing and accessories that were featured on the catwalks of Europe and America that season. This means that the fashions depicted in this shoot are actual facsimiles, since like everything else featured in *Vogue India*, they would be available in designer boutiques in India.[87] Wasim's reputation for "exquisite quality" and "beautiful detail" thus was appropriate for depicting couture fashion, and in keeping with the brand's high-quality image.

As noted above, Wasim's use of the Mughal painting technique/style was a means of speaking to a national heritage, a recognition of the place of Mughal heritage in Indian culture, and an assertion of local links to a history of luxury culture. Intriguingly, this fashion story featured only clothing and accessories by Western designers as chosen by *Vogue India*'s fashion editorial team. This creates a division between heritage, represented by the Mughal princess protagonist and the medium (Mughal style and technique) of the painting on one side, and fashion, represented by the all Euro-American designers

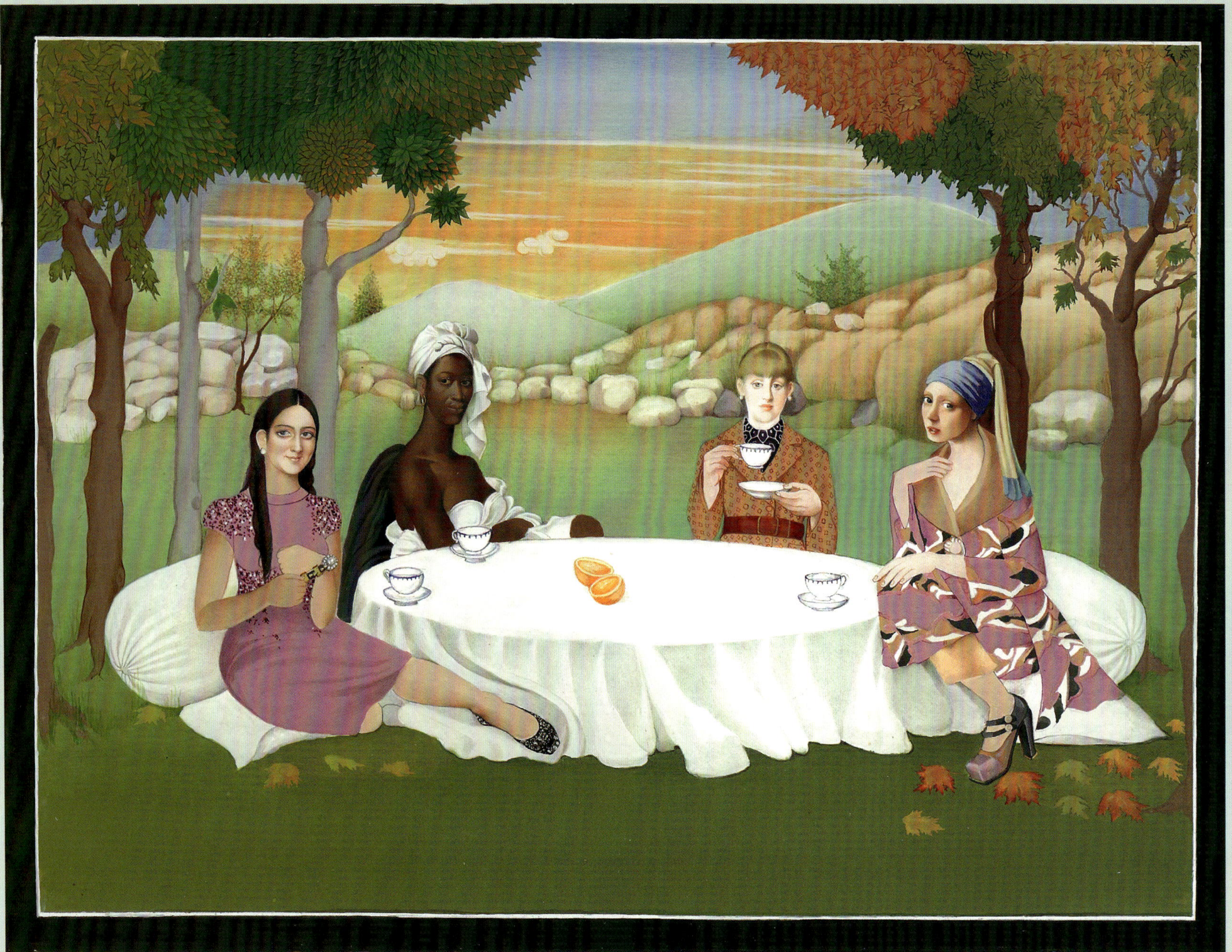

Figure 9.10. Saira Wasim, "*Garden Party:* At a picnic in the park with the muses of Benoist, Manet and Vermeer, she talks of the pressures of being an artist's inspiration. *From left to right*: Embroidered crepe dress, Bottega Veneta. 'Cosmic' glitter pumps, Jimmy Choo. Blouse, printed coat, belt; all Prada. Embellished coat, trousers, shoes; all Louis Vuitton." Fourth painting in "The Princess Diaries," *Vogue India*, 5th anniversary issue, October 2012. Image courtesy of the artist.

and designs. This decision to contrast the "contemporary western silhouettes . . . with an obviously South Asian aesthetic" was made in order to make the fashion stand out. In other words, if the Mughal princess had been dressed in Indian designer wear, for example a *lehngha* or sari, the contrast would not have been marked and the editorial fashion team involved in the shoot feared that the story "would have lost the modern."[88] This scenario perhaps replicates the problematic construct of Western (fashion) being equated with being modern while local stands for tradition.

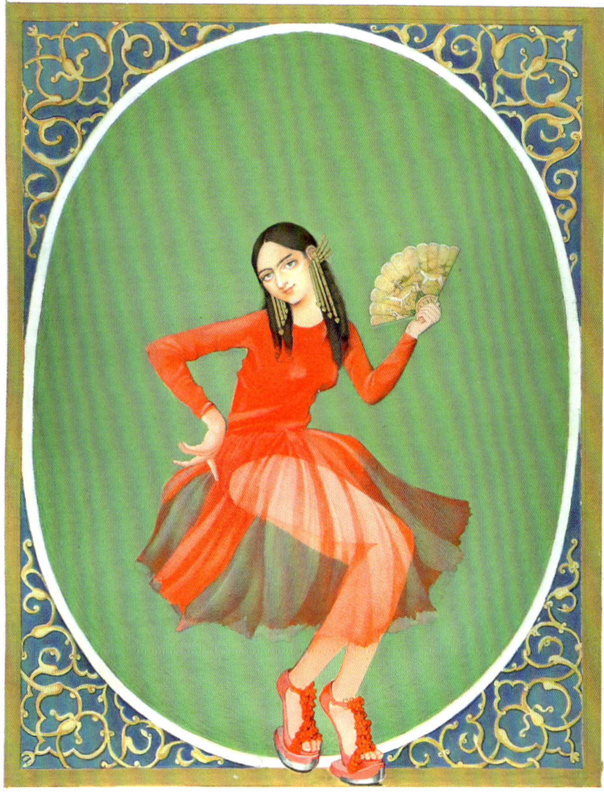

Figure 9.11. Saira Wasim, "*Dancing Queen:* Even a princess needs to unwind—slipping on a fresh-off-the-ramp Dior dress, she shakes her tulle till the wee hours. Silk dress, earrings; both Dior. Shoes, Alexander McQueen." Fifth painting in "The Princess Diaries," *Vogue India*, 5th anniversary issue, October 2012. Image courtesy of the artist.

Although Wasim was given parameters within which she needed to operate, she was also given creative license. Required to feature the chosen fashion ensembles, she was supported and encouraged to comment upon Western canons and celebrity culture in her tongue in cheek way, clearly apparent in "Garden Party" (fig. 9.10), which depicts four women in the midst of a tea party. For Wasim, the Mughal princess is the person of acclaim and status, but audiences familiar with a Western art historical canon would recognize the other three women: The girl from *Girl with a Pearl Earring* (1665) by the Dutch painter Johannes Vermeer, the bar maid in Édouard Manet's *A Bar at the Folies-Bergère* (1882), and a the woman in *Portrait d'une négresse* (1800) painted by Marie-Guilhelmine Benoist. Wasim "invited" these three women into her work to equalize class distinctions: the Mughal princess—"from her position of power" orchestrates the tea party—inviting her "close acquaintances": an enslaved woman, a working-class barmaid, and a working poor servant. In doing so, she also inverts a Western canon of art history. These three women—as depicted by Western artists and as idealizing Western standards of beauty and objectification—are icons in a Western art historical canon, one that eclipses South Asian art. At the same time, by referring to these three iconic images of women, Wasim reminds us that these are not simply "famous" or canonical paintings; rather they are images that came to be because of inequalities between races, genders, and classes. They all come together for tea—now the national drink in Pakistan and India and symbolic of hospitality—that was harvested and made popular in South Asia by and for the British. The demand for tea propelled colonization (the development of tea plantations in South Asia) and slavery (to fulfill British desires for sugar to sweeten one's tea), justified by ideological racial divisions, hierarchies, and racism. It also, by the very nature of being in an Indian edition of an international (Western) fashion magazine, cannot resist evoking another major impetus for colonization: the British desire for cotton textiles from South Asia, which eventually led the British to manufacture cotton quickly and cheaply "at home" while crippling local cotton industries in South Asia and spurring the drive to capitalize on consumer desire for clothing through constructions of "fashion." Indeed, the fact that *Vogue* targets countries with the economic capabilities of supporting Euro-American luxury markets uncomfortably reminds one of the marketing of Western commodities to Indian consumers during British colonialism, when the British inundated local markets in South Asia with British goods.

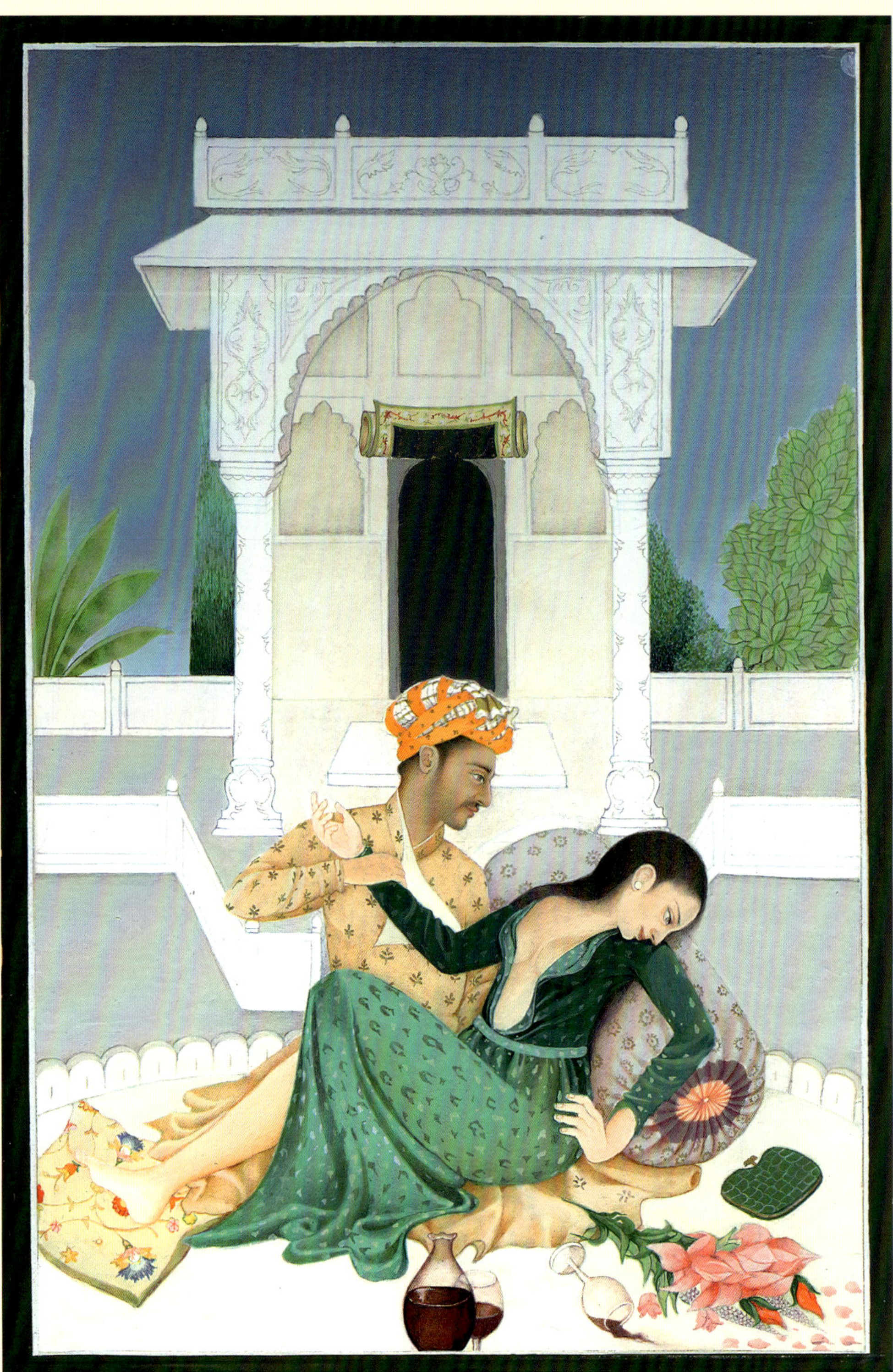

Figure 9.12. Saira Wasim, "*True Romance I:* She hides a blush from the amorous gaze of her suitor. A Gucci dress bares her décolletage as he bares his heart. Printed velvet gown, Gucci. 'Giano' suede minaudiere, Fendi." Sixth painting in "The Princess Diaries," *Vogue India*, 5th anniversary issue, October 2012. Image courtesy of the artist.

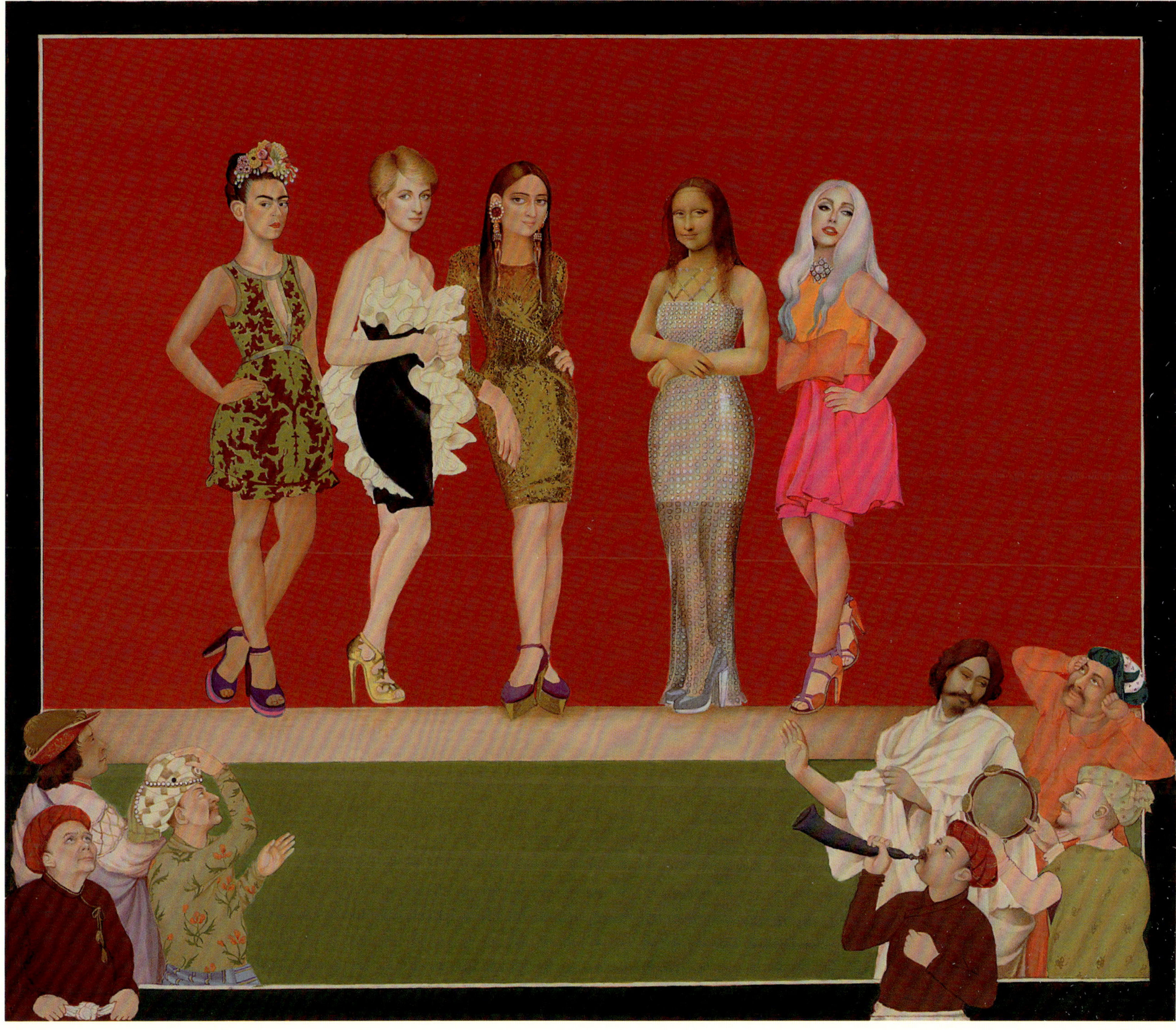

Figure 9.13. Saira Wasim, "*Blue Blood:* No soiree could be stuffy when you have your girls by your side. A vision in Bottega Veneta, our pretty princess poses with Frida, Di, Mona and Gaga as they welcome the likes of Valmiki. *From left*: Embellished dress, Roberto Cavalli. 'Levi' sandals, Jimmy Choo. Ruffled dress, Lanvin. Sandals, Rupert Sanderson. Python applique cross-front drape dress, Tom Ford. Velvet sandals, Nicholas Kirkwood. Spike and cabochon pearl earrings, Mawi. Chain-mail gown, Versace. Pumps, Yves Saint Laurent. Dress, Giorgio Armani. Shoes, Pierre Hardy. Necklace, Bottega Veneta." Seventh painting in "The Princess Diaries," *Vogue India*, 5th anniversary issue, October 2012. Image courtesy of the artist.

Conclusion

When the "miniature" practice was reclaimed and reinvented toward the end of the twentieth century, the prior feminization of the practice would enable its transformation from an elite male activity to one where women proliferated. The interwoven discursive threads of craft, ornament, decoration, detail, feminine, and the "East"—all constructed as lesser forms of practice—were used in the fabric of Western patriarchal, colonial control over women and the colonized. These threads, however, would be unraveled and reconstituted by female neo-miniaturists to fashion postcolonial pennants of resistance and subversion.

Analogous to how a male artistic practice associated with the courts of South Asia has been altered to be seen as and equated with contemporary female artistic production, we must reframe the ways in which we conceptualize, perceive, define, and discuss modernity and its supporting constructs—including art, development, democracy, and so on. As is the case for the neo-miniature genre generally and Saira Wasim's paintings in particular, altered and reconstituted frameworks advocate for political dissent, social change, and empowerment. Just as the decorative and feminine are generally dismissed as lesser and nonthreatening, they have simultaneously inspired significant, impactful transformations. Wasim's playfully subversive works are able to gain access and provide poignant critiques from within the very institutions she seeks to challenge and change.

Notes

1. This component of the article was born out of a set of conversations with Saira Wasim and Iona Fergusson, the conceptual designer and point of contact for "The Princess Diaries" series in *Vogue India*. These interviews were conducted on April 23, April 27, and May 11, 2020 (Saira Wasim), and May 1, 2020 (Iona Fergusson). I would like to express my heartfelt appreciation for their generosity, time, and insights.

2. Although the term "Indo-Persian" typically refers to the Persianate courts of South Asia, I am using this term more broadly, that is to refer to the courts of South Asia *and* Persia, as well as to the hybrid courts of South Asia, which included Muslim and Hindu patrons and artists.

3. "Portrait Miniatures," Victoria and Albert Museum website, accessed December 1, 2020, https://www.vam.ac.uk/articles/portrait-miniatures. "A History of the Portrait Miniature," Victoria and Albert Museum website, accessed December 1, 2020, http://www.vam.ac.uk/content/articles/h/a-history-of-the-portrait-miniature/. For more expansive coverage from the V&A curator, see Katherine Coombs, *The Portrait Miniature in England* (London: V&A Publications, 1998).

4. "A History of the Portrait Miniature." Italics mine.

5. "Portrait Miniatures."

6. Such prejudiced approaches to the history of Indo-Persian painting resulted in the devaluation of Indo-Persian painting practices, which more recent scholars have sought to remedy. I mention two authors here as points of departure into a rich and growing body of scholarship: David Roxburgh, "Micrographia: Toward a Visual Logic of Persianate Painting," *Res: Anthropology and Aesthetics* 43 (Spring 2003), 12–30; a *Muqarnas* edition devoted to the arts of the book and study of painting in the Islamic world (vol. 17, 2000) by David Roxburgh and Molly Emma Aitken, eds., *The Intelligence of Tradition in Rajput Court Painting* (New Haven, CT: Yale University Press, 2010).

7. The miniaturists John Smart, Ozias Humphry, and Diana Hill independently undertook the six-month journey by sea to India in the late eighteenth century. Their sitters included local dignitaries, British East India Company employees, and their families. Their presence in India facilitated the affordable and relatively easy exchange of portraits between family members and other loved ones separated by the considerable distance between Britain and India, "A History of the Portrait Miniature."

8. Roxburgh, "Micrographia," 16.

9. B. W. Robinson in Roxburgh, "Micrographia," 13–15.

10. Robinson in Roxburgh, "Micrographia," 11, 13, 15.

11. Roxburgh, 11, 13, 15.

12. Gary Shteyngart, "The Whole World Is Watching," *New York Times*, July 13, 2003, https://www.nytimes.com/2003/07/13/arts/art-architecture-the-whole-world-is-watching.html. My emphasis.

13. Debbie Lisle, "Benevolent Patriotism: Art, Dissent and 'The American Effect,'" *Security Dialogue* 38, no. 2 (June 2007): 246.

14. Virginia Whiles, *Art and Polemic: Cultural Politics and Tradition in Contemporary Miniature Painting* (London: Tauris Academic Studies, 2010), 105. Even today in India, where "miniaturists" are regarded as craftsmen, one still hears of miniaturists hired to decorate walls. For a recent example, please see Ligasha Mishan, "In Jaipur, a Clothing Designer's Vibrant and Wonderfully Imperfect Home," *New York Times Style Magazine* November 28, 2018, https://www.nytimes.com/2018/11/28/t-magazine/caroline-weller-banjanan-jaipur-india-home.html.

15. Murad Khan Mumtaz, "Miniature Painting in Pakistan: Divergences between Traditional and Contemporary Practice," *Guggenheim Blogs*, February 4, 2013, https://www.guggenheim.org/blogs/map/miniature-painting-in-pakistan-divergences-between-traditional-and-contemporary-practice; Whiles, *Art and Polemic*, 100; Salima Hashmi, "Spinning Stories," in *A Thousand and One Days: Pakistani Women Artists*, ed. Duccio K. Marignoli and Enrico Mascelloni (Milan: Silvana Editorale, 2005), 24. Catalog of an exhibition held at the Honolulu Academy of Arts, October 13–December 11, 2005.

16. Hashmi, "Spinning Stories," 24.

17. Salima Hashmi, *Unveiling the Visible: Lives and Works of Women Artists of Pakistan* (Islamabad: Salima Hashmi and ActionAid, 2002), 15.

18. Virginia Whiles, "Karkhana: Revival or Re-Invention?" in *Karkhana: A Contemporary Collaboration*, ed. Hammad Nasar (London: Aldrich Contemporary Art Museum, 2005) 30–31.

19. Hashmi, "Spinning Stories," 25; Salima Hashmi, "Radicalising Tradition: Painting in Pakistan," *Artlink* 20, no. 2 (2000): 33; Salima Hashmi and Yashodhara Dalmia, eds., *Memory, Metaphor, Mutations: Contemporary Art of India and Pakistan* (New Delhi: Oxford University Press, 2007) 74; Walter Mignolo et al., "Decolonial Aesthetics I," TDI + Transnational Decolonial Institute, May 22, 2011, https://transnationaldecolonialinstitute.wordpress.com/decolonial-aesthetics/.

20. Hashmi, "Spinning Stories," 25.

21. Hashmi, 25, 30.

22. Vishakha Desai and Shahzia Sikander, "Intertwined Identities: Shahzia Sikander in Conversation with Vishakha Desai," *ArtAsiaPacific* 85 (September–October 2013), http://li367-91.members.linode.com/Magazine/85/IntertwinedIdentities.

23. Ian Berry, "Nemesis: A Dialogue with Shahzia Sikander," in *Opener 6: Shahzia Sikander—Nemesis*, ed. Ian Berry and Jessica Hough (Ridgefield, CT: Tang, copublished with the Aldrich Contemporary Art Museum, 2004), 7.

24. Personal communication with Saira Wasim, April 23, 2020.

25. Marignoli and Mascelloni, *Thousand and One Days: Pakistani Women Artists*, 13–14. Emphasis in the original.

26. Hashmi, "Spinning Stories," 25; Hashmi, "Radicalising Tradition," 33–34; Hashmi, *Memory, Metaphor, Mutations*, 73.

27. Hashmi, "Radicalising Tradition," 33; Hashmi, *Memory, Metaphor, Mutations*, 74; Mignolo et al., "Decolonial Aesthetics I," 2011.

28. Juliana Cerqueira Leite, "Beyond the Page—Hammad Nasar on Contemporary Pakistani Art," *Naked Punch*, last updated September 19, 2010, http://www.nakedpunch.com/articles/40.

29. Whiles, *Art and Polemic*, 211.

30. Whiles, 211.

31. Moira Vincentelli, *Women and Ceramics: Gendered Vessels* (Manchester: Manchester University Press, 2000), 77. One infamous example is Adolf Loos's "Ornament and Crime" (1908); see also Naomi Schor's book *Reading in Detail: Aesthetics and the Feminine* (New York: Methuen, 1987).

32. Vincentelli, *Women and Ceramics*, 77.

33. Bridget Elliot and Janice Heiland, "Introduction," in *Women Artists and the Decorative Arts 1880–1935: The Gender of Ornament*, 1–14, ed. Bridget Elliot and Janice Heiland (Burlington, VT: Ashgate, 2002).

34. Schor, *Reading in Detail*, 1987, cited in p. 4 in Elliot and Heiland, "Introduction," iii.

35. Katlijne Van der Stighelen and Lisa Heer, "Amateur Artists," in *Concise Dictionary of Women Artists*, ed. Delia Gaze (New York: Routledge, 2001), 59–60.

36. Van der Stighelen and Heer, "Amateur Artists," 59.

37. "Publisher's Note," in *By a Woman's Hand: Illustrators of the Golden Age*, ed. Mary Carolyn Waldrep (Mineoloa, NY: Dover Publications Inc., 2010), vi.

38. Elliot and Heiland, "Introduction," vi.

39. For example, Shahzia Sikander, Talha Rathore, and Saira Wasim—three of the most prominent neo-miniaturists—all attended a convent school. Of her early education at the Convent of Jesus and Mary, Wasim has commented: "It's a missionary school being run by the nuns. It's based on British colonial educational system, we were taught Victorian literature; the curriculum and the textbooks were by [*sic*] Oxford and Cambridge." Jeremy Adkins, "Saira Wasim Interview," Asian American Art Oral History Project, 2010, https://via.library.depaul.edu/oral_his_series/26.

40. Hashmi, *Unveiling the Visible*, 7. Anna Molka Ahmed was the first appointee to the fine arts department at Punjab University.

41. Hashmi, 7.

42. Hashmi, 7.

43. Hashmi, *Memory, Metaphor, Mutations*, 37, 39; Hashmi, *Unveiling the Visible*, 7–8.

44. Hashmi, *Unveiling the Visible*, 7.

45. Hashmi, "Spinning Stories," 27.

46. Hashmi, *Memory, Metaphor, Mutations*, 92.

47. Hashmi, "Spinning Stories," 31.

48. Hashmi, *Memory, Metaphor, Mutations*, 91–92.

49. Hashmi, "Spinning Stories," 27; Hashmi, *Memory, Metaphor, Mutations*, 92.

50. Louis Werner, "Reinventing the Miniature Painting," *Aramco World* 60, no. 4 (2009), https://archive.aramcoworld.com/issue/200904/reinventing.the.miniature.painting.htm.

51. Hashmi, "Radicalising Tradition," 33; Hashmi, *Memory, Metaphor, Mutations*, 77.

52. Hashmi, *Memory, Metaphor, Mutations*, 77.

53. Murtaza Vali, "Pakistan Goes Global! Essays: State of the Art," *ArtAsiaPacific* 56 (November–December 2007), http://li367-91.members.linode.com/Magazine/56/StateOfTheArtPakistanGoesGlobal.

54. Shazia Sikander and Sadia Abbas, "Dialogue," *Aleph Review* 4 (2020): 27, 29.

55. Anna Sloan, "Embodied Space: The Miniature as Attitude," in *Beyond the Page: Contemporary Art from Pakistan: An Exhibition Presented by Asia House in Partnership with Manchester Art Gallery and Shisha*, ed. Anita Dawood and Hammad Nasar (London: Asia House and Green Cardamom, 2006), between figures 28 and 29.

56. Toril Moi, "Marginality and Subversion: Julia Kristeva," *Sexual/Textual Politics: Feminist Literary Theory*, 2nd ed. (London and New York: Routledge, 2002), 163.

57. Saira Wasim, Official Website, accessed December 1, 2020, https://www.sairawasim.com/.

58. Editors, "Mughal Magical Realism," *Himal South Asian*, July 2003, https://www.himalmag.com/round-up-of-regional-news-42/.

59. Zahir Janhomamed, "Artist Saira Wasim: The Imagery of Clowns," *altmuslim*, October 23, 2006, https://www.patheos.com/blogs/altmuslim/2006/10/the_imagery_of_clowns/.

60. Painters of Pakistan (website), accessed September 19, 2022, https://paintersofpakistan.wordpress.com/tag/saira-wasim/.

61. Gauruv Sood, "Interview with Saira Wasim," *Goji Berries*, August 13, 2008, http://gbytes.gsood.com/2008/08/13/interview-with-saira-wasim/.

62. "11 Influential South Asian Neo-Miniaturists," *Art Radar*, January 2, 2014, https://artradarjournal.com/2014/01/02/10-influential-south-asian-neo-miniaturists/.

63. Virginia Whiles, "The Role of Portraiture in Pakistani Contemporary Miniature Painting: The 'Mughal Connection,'" *Portraiture in South Asia Since the Mughals: Art, Representation and History*, edited by Crispin Branfoot (London, New York: I.B. Tauris, 2018), 233–34; Anna Sloan, "A Divine Comedy of Errors: Political Paintings of Saira Wasim," in *Transcendent Contemplations: Paintings by Hasnat Mehmood and Saira Wasim*, ed. Anita Dawood and Hammad Nasar (London: Green Cardamom, 2004), 5; Adkins, "Saira Wasim Interview."

64. "James Gillray: The Art of Caricature," Tate Britain exhibition, June 5–September 2, 2001, https://www.tate.org.uk/whats-on/tate-britain/exhibition/james-gillray-art-caricature.

65. "James Gillray."

66. Roberta Smith, "A Mélange of Asian Roots and Shifting Identities," *New York Times* September 8, 2006, https://www.nytimes.com/2006/09/08/arts/design/08asia.html.

67. Janhomamed, "Artist Saira Wasim."

68. Sloan, "A Divine Comedy of Errors," 5.

69. Saira Wasim, Official Website, accessed December 1, 2020, https://saira-sairawasim-com.artcall.org/a-1-silent-plea.

70. Most (if not all) fashion lifestyle magazines include features that explore different fashion trends over a number of pages.

71. It is worth noting that although the Mughal period is conceived as part of India's heritage, this is in marked contrast to debates surrounding the "foreignness" of Mughal miniatures during the struggle for independence and ongoing efforts by the Hindu right to recognize Mughal contributions—as representative of a Muslim empire—to India's cultural landscape.

72. This project is so different from what Wasim is known for that she expressed some surprise when I told her I was interested in writing about this series.

73. Werner, "Reinventing the Miniature Painting."

74. "Vogue India Launches," *Forbes*, September 18, 2007, https://www.forbes.com/2007/09/18/vogue-india-interview-markets-equity-cx_rd_0917markets13.html.

75. The current state of affairs is a far cry from Gandhi's vision of a self-sustaining village-model of the nation as well as Nehru's socialist vision for the state.

76. "Vogue India Launches."

77. *Vogue* was founded in New York in 1892 and became a glamorous lifestyle magazine when Condé Nast became its publisher in 1909. European editions soon followed (e.g., Britain in 1916 and France in 1920), with each country producing their own editions. Mary E. Davis, "Vogue," in *Classic Chic: Music, Fashion, and Modernism* (Berkeley: University of California Press, 2006), 203.

78. According to journalist Rebecca Voight, "India's luxury expansion really took off in January 2006, when the government began to allow foreign direct investment of as much as 51 percent in single-brand retail operations." Rebecca Voight, "India: Another Emerging Luxury Market,"

New York Times, November 27, 2007, https://www.nytimes.com/2007/11/27/style/27iht-remerge.1.8498149.html.

79. Jess Cartner-Morley, "From Thailand to Ukraine: A Country's in Vogue When It Has Its Own Vogue," *Guardian*, December 19, 2002, https://www.theguardian.com/world/2012/dec/19/fashion-vogue-magazine-thailand-ukraine.

80. Stephen Brook, "Vogue Thinks Big for Indian Launch," *Guardian*, September 20, 2007, https://www.theguardian.com/media/2007/sep/20/pressandpublishing.fashion.

81. "Vogue India Launches."

82. Personal communication with Iona Fergusson, May 1, 2020. The Mughal concept for the fashion story was Iona Fergusson's, as was the artist review and selection process. As the commissioning editor, Fergusson was Wasim's primary contact at *Vogue India*.

83. Personal communication with Iona Fergusson, May 1, 2020.

84. Tim Hankert, "Vogue: Still Spreading Western Beauty Ideals?" *Diggit Magazine*, November 20, 2019, https://www.diggitmagazine.com/articles/vogue-western-beauty-ideals; Tae Im Han and Nancy A. Rudd, "Images of Beauty: Sex, Race, Age, and Occupational Analysis of Fashion Magazine Covers," *Journal of Global Fashion Marketing* 6, no. 1 (2015); Yan Yan and Kim Bissell, "The Globalization of Beauty: How Is Ideal Beauty Influenced by Globally Published Fashion and Beauty Magazines?" *Journal of Intercultural Communication Research* 43, no. 3 (2014).

85. Tara Mayer, "From Craft to Couture: Contemporary Indian Fashion in Historical Perspective," *South Asian Popular Culture* 16, no. 2–3 (2019): 184. This definition of fashion and the focus on invention and reinvention is in service of capitalist modes of production.

86. Tara Mayer, "From Craft to Couture," 184.

87. Personal communication with Iona Fergusson, May 1, 2020.

88. Personal communication with Iona Fergusson, May 1, 2020.

Bibliography

Aitken, Molly Emma. *The Intelligence of Tradition in Rajput Court Painting*. New Haven, CT: Yale University Press, 2010.

Berry, Ian. "Nemesis: A Dialogue with Shahzia Sikander." In *Opener 6: Shahzia Sikander—Nemesis*, edited by Ian Berry and Jessica Hough, 5–19. Ridgefield, CT: Tang and the Aldrich Contemporary Art Museum, 2004.

Coombs, Katherine. *The Portrait Miniature in England*. London: V&A Publications, 1998.

Davis, Mary E. "Vogue." In *Classic Chic: Music, Fashion, and Modernism*, 202–54. Berkeley: University of California Press, 2006.

Desai, Vishakha, and Shahzia Sikander. "Intertwined Identities: Shahzia Sikander in Conversation with Vishakha Desai." *ArtAsiaPacific* 85 (September–October 2013): http://li367-91.members.linode.com/Magazine/85/IntertwinedIdentities.

Elliot, Bridget, and Janice Heiland. "Introduction." In *Women Artists and the Decorative Arts 1880–1935: The Gender of Ornament*, edited by Bridget Elliot and Janice Heiland, 1–14. Burlington, VT: Ashgate, 2002.

Han, Tae Im, and Nancy A. Rudd. "Images of Beauty: Sex, Race, Age, and Occupational Analysis of Fashion Magazine Covers." *Journal of Global Fashion Marketing* 6, no. 1 (2015): 47–59.

Hashmi, Salima. "An Intelligent Rebellion: Women Artists of Pakistan." *India International Centre Quarterly* 24, nos. 2–3 (1997): 228–38.

———. "Radicalising Tradition: Painting in Pakistan." *Artlink* 20, no. 2 (2000): 33–35.

———. *Unveiling the Visible: Lives and Works of Women Artists of Pakistan*. Islamabad: Salima Hashmi and ActionAid, 2002.

Hashmi, Salima, and Yashodhara Dalmia, eds. *Memory, Metaphor, Mutations: Contemporary Art of India and Pakistan.* New Delhi: Oxford University Press, 2007.
Lisle, Debbie. "Benevolent Patriotism: Art, Dissent and 'The American Effect.'" *Security Dialogue* 38, no. 2 (June 2007): 233–50.
Marignoli, Duccio K., and Enrico Mascelloni, eds. *A Thousand and One Days: Pakistani Women Artists.* Catalogue of an exhibition held at the Honolulu Academy of Art, October 13–December 11, 2005. Milan: Silvana Editorale, 2005.
Mayer, Tara. "From Craft to Couture: Contemporary Indian Fashion in Historical Perspective." *South Asian Popular Culture* 16, nos. 2–3 (2019): 183–98.
Moi, Toril. "Marginality and Subversion: Julia Kristeva." In *Sexual/Textual Politics: Feminist Literary Theory*, 149–72. London and New York: Routledge, 2002.
Nasar, Hammad, ed. *Karkhana: A Contemporary Collaboration.* London: Aldrich Contemporary Art Museum, 2005.
"Publisher's Note." In *By a Woman's Hand: Illustrators of the Golden Age*, edited by Mary Carolyn Waldrep, v–viii. Mineola, NY: Dover, 2010.
Robinson, B. W. *Drawings of the Masters: Persian Drawings from the 14th through the 19th Century.* New York: Shorewood, 1965.
Roxburgh, David. "Micrographia: Toward a Visual Logic of Persianate Painting." *Res: Anthropology and Aesthetics* 43 (Spring 2003): 12 30.
Sikander, Shazia, and Sadia Abbas. "Dialogue." *Aleph Review* 4 (2020): 19–41.
Sloan, Anna. "A Divine Comedy of Errors: Political Paintings of Saira Wasim." In *Transcendent Contemplations: Paintings by Hasnat Mehmood and Saira Wasim*, edited by Anita Dawood and Hammad Nasar, n.p. London: Green Cardamom, 2004.
———. "Embodied Space: The Miniature as Attitude." In *Beyond the Page: Contemporary Art from Pakistan: An Exhibition Presented by Asia House in Partnership with Manchester Art Gallery and Shisha*, edited by Anita Dawood and Hammad Nasar, 26–44. London: Asia House and Green Cardamom, 2006.
Van der Stighelen, Katlijne, and Lisa Heer. "Amateur Artists." In *Concise Dictionary of Women Artists*, edited by Delia Gaze, 50–67. New York: Routledge, 2011.
Vincentelli, Moira. *Women and Ceramics: Gendered Vessels.* Manchester and New York: Manchester University Press, 2000.
Werner, Louis. "Reinventing the Miniature Painting." *Aramco World* 60, no. 4 (2009): https://archive.aramcoworld.com/issue/200904/reinventing.the.miniature.painting.htm.
Whiles, Virginia. *Art and Polemic: Cultural Politics and Tradition in Contemporary Miniature Painting.* London: Tauris Academic Studies, 2010.
———. "Art and Polemic in Pakistan." *Art in America* 99, no. 3 (March 2011): 54–60.
———. "The Role of Portraiture in Pakistani Contemporary Miniature Painting: The 'Mughal Connection.'" In *Portraiture in South Asia since the Mughals: Art, Representation and History*, edited by Crispin Branfoot, 222–48. London and New York: I. B. Tauris, 2018.
Yan, Yan, and Kim Bissell. "The Globalization of Beauty: How Is Ideal Beauty Influenced by Globally Published Fashion and Beauty Magazines?" *Journal of Intercultural Communication Research* 43, no. 3 (2014): 194–214.

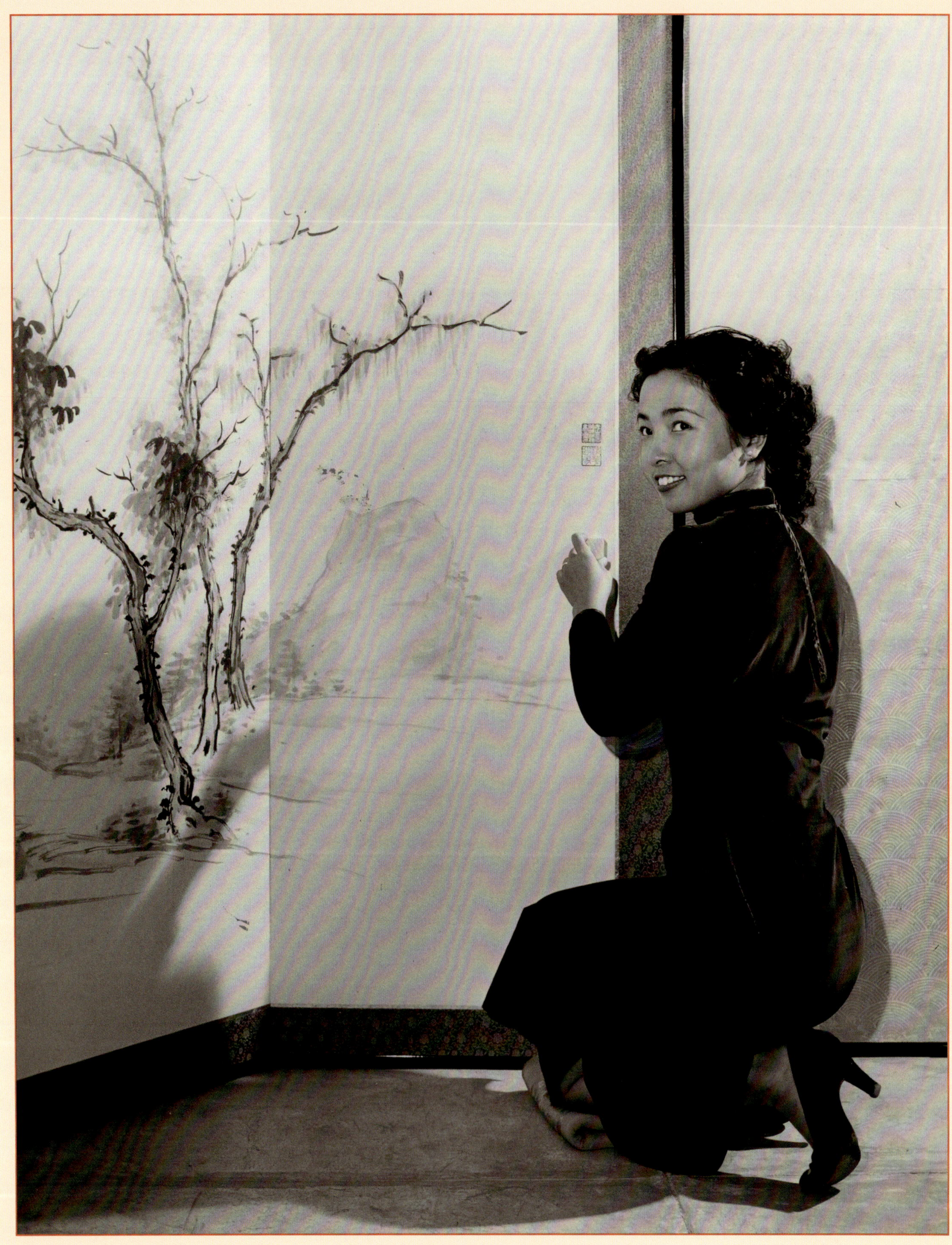

10

Tseng Yuho

Painting Her Own Path

Sati Benes Chock

> In my work, I have tried to unite many elements of the visual arts of China into one entity and give it a soul. Never underestimating the power of the unconscious and the subconscious, I believe creativity is essentially a conscious act of man. I am but a single drop of the ocean and I occasionally feel that I am at the edge of the world. Like the astronauts walking in unlimited space, I feel my creative efforts do not convey a sense of being lost, but of being found.
>
> —Tseng Yuho

Born in Beijing, the internationally acclaimed artist, author, and scholar Tseng Yuho (1925–2017) grew up in China but spent the majority of her adult life in the United States.[1] Tseng was a classically trained artist but was best known for inventing *dsui hua* (掇畫), or "assembled painting," an innovative contemporary style that layered traditional and nontraditional materials alongside multicultural symbolic references, resulting in collage-like paintings strongly imbued with meaning, and in both academic and creative fields she was lauded for her ability to bridge artistic elements in the East with those of the West.[2]

The artist dedicated her life to navigating liminal spaces and sharing discoveries with others, even as she turned more and more inward on her own metaphysical journey. Throughout her sixty years of award-winning painting and scholarship, her work celebrated tradition while testing conventions and, in the process, challenged expectations of what painting and scholarship should be.[3]

In the first week of December 1949, the young Tseng Yuho and her distinguished husband, Dr. Gustav Ecke (1896–1971), traveled as the only passengers on the *City of Alma*,

Figure 10.1. (*facing*) Tseng affixing seal to landscape screen, Honolulu Museum of Art Archives (1951).

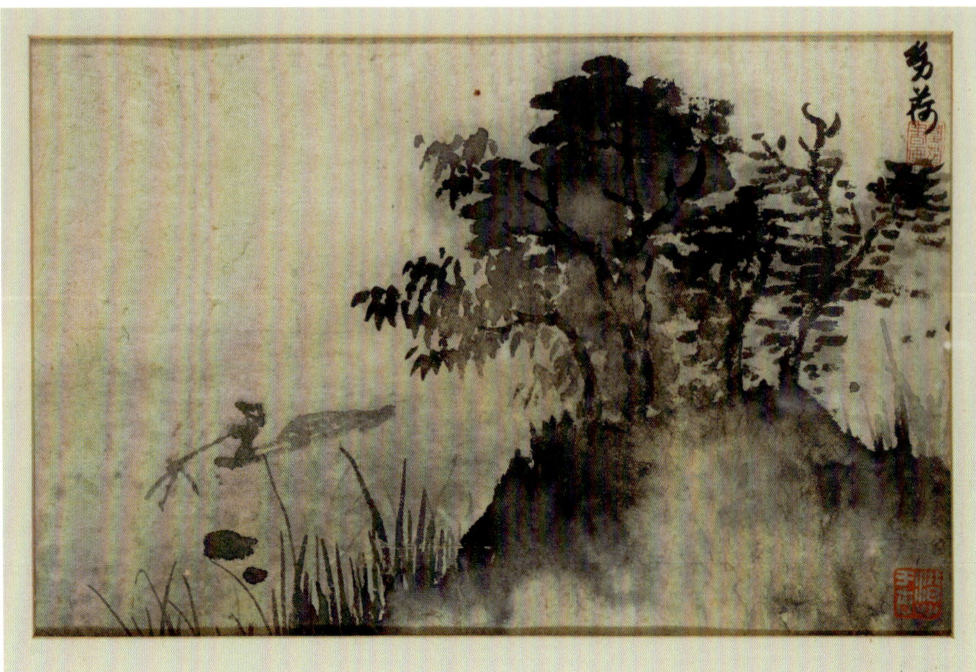

Figure 10.2. Tseng Yuho (1925–2017), *Landscape after Shih Tao* (c. 1940s), ink on paper, 7 ½ × 11 ¾ in. Anonymous Gift, 1963. Honolulu Museum of Art, © Estate of Tseng Yuho (3129.1).

a trade vessel destined for Hawai'i.[4] Ecke was to become the first curator of Asian art at the Honolulu Academy of Arts.[5] Founded by Anna Rice Cooke (1853–1934), the museum had opened its doors to the public only a couple of decades earlier, in 1927. When Tseng and Ecke arrived in Honolulu after three weeks at sea, the Academy's director, Robert Griffing, and his wife, Marjorie, were waiting for them. Griffing had secured the couple's passage with the assistance of his brother-in-law, John M. Cabot, who, as consul general of Shanghai, was the "last representative of American diplomacy in China."[6]

Beginning a new life in a foreign land during such a turbulent time must have been daunting. The People's Republic of China had been established just two months before their departure, and Ecke's employer had encouraged them to leave the country.[7] Because of the political turmoil, the artist would not see her mother again for nearly twenty-five years. This would have been difficult for most people, but it must have been especially painful for Tseng Yuho's family, who was steeped in Confucian tradition.[8] Since her childhood, Tseng's progressive parents had strongly supported education for their eldest daughter. She studied classical painting with Prince Pu Jin (1893–1966), a family friend, and was one of the first female students to attend Furen University.[9] At an early age, she mastered all of the classical painting methods, including the literati style of traditional landscape painting established centuries earlier by Dong Qichang (1555–1636), who taught that "artistic genius lay in the creative reinterpretation of tradition."[10]

The Academy's announcement of the couple's arrival in Honolulu noted that Tseng was an "accomplished painter in the Chinese style," yet her significance to the museum would not be limited to her merit as an artist. It is unlikely that anyone realized it at the time, but in welcoming Tseng and Ecke, the museum was getting two curators for the price of one, for they were an academic power couple. Ecke, a German art historian with a background in European art and philosophy, cofounded the academic journal

Monumenta Serica and was renowned for his scholarship on Chinese furniture. Tseng was a dazzling painter and art connoisseur from a prominent family that, according to Tseng, traced its lineage back to disciples of Confucius. The famed art historian and critic Michael Sullivan (1916–2013) first saw her work in London in 1946, while she was still living in China, and immediately recognized her extraordinary talent. For the rest of his life, he remained one of her strongest advocates.[11] Yet Tseng was starting all over again in Honolulu, which in 1949, before the advent of mass tourism, was still quite remote. She moved to Hawai'i to flee chaos in her birthland and to support her husband, rather than to pursue her own career. Used to the vibrant energy of Beijing, at first Tseng felt isolated in this far-flung territory, which would not achieve statehood for another ten years.[12] However, it would not take long for her to find her own path.[13]

By March 1950, only three months after her arrival, she had installed an exhibition at Gump's Waikiki of Honolulu, an exclusive home furnishing store. The exhibition centered on earlier work completed in China and was traditional, based on classical landscapes featuring rushing rivers, craggy cliffs, and gnarled trees.[14] The following year, she completed her first significant painting in Hawai'i, the *Min River* handscroll, a thirty-four-foot-long masterwork.[15] In 1952, an exhibition titled *Paintings by Tseng Yu-ho* went on view at the Academy. This successful show would later travel to the M. H. de Young Memorial Museum in San Francisco. In 1953, the Smithsonian toured Tseng's solo exhibition *Chinese Paintings* to a number of venues in the United States. The following year, Tseng began graduate studies at the University of Hawai'i.

Something else notable happened on campus during the 1950s: a man named Mitchell Hutchinson enrolled in Ecke's Chinese painting class at the University of Hawai'i. Hutchinson's very first art purchase was Tseng's own conventional work *Two Trees*, painted

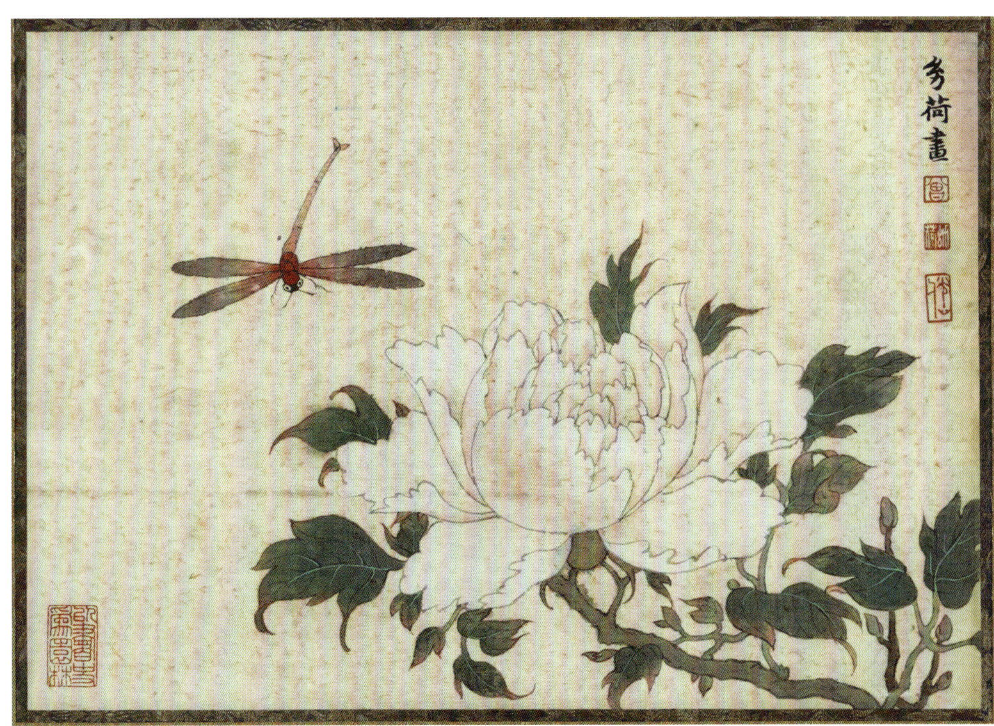

Figure 10.3. Tseng Yuho (1925–2017), *Dragonfly with Peony* (c. 1948), ink and color on paper, mounted on silk, 8 ⅝ × 12 ½ in. Gift of Ruth P. Beers in memory of her sister, Louisa F. Palmer, 1982. Honolulu Museum of Art, © Estate of Tseng Yuho (5011.1).

in the style of Wen Zhengming (1470–1559). He grew fascinated by literati painting, and although he returned to the mainland, for the next thirty years, Tseng continued to advise Hutchinson and his wife, enabling them to form a fine collection of Chinese paintings that was eventually acquired by the Academy.[16]

Around the time that Tseng was establishing herself in the United States, a number of American museums were concentrating on building strong collections of Chinese art:

> In the decades following World War II, the United States blossomed as an international hub for the study and presentation of Chinese art. International, political, economic, and social changes affected the art market, prompting a new wave of collecting, and with it, the production of new scholarship and the formation of canons of Chinese art in the United States. Exhibitions held at American museums and serious scholarly publications produced by experts living in the United States helped shape the field of Chinese art history.[17]

The Academy was one such museum, and Tseng and Ecke were two of the experts helping to shape history. Their curatorial and scholarly collaborations greatly affected Hawai'i's academic and museum worlds.[18] Tseng advised on the selection of many master Ming- and Qing-dynasty landscape paintings and works of calligraphy that compose the backbone of the museum's Chinese collection; she taught classes at the Academy Art Center, performed research, organized exhibitions, and wrote "treatises on the art of Chinese painting and calligraphy in English that have influenced generations of artists and students alike."[19] She also created, as well as exhibited, her own artwork.

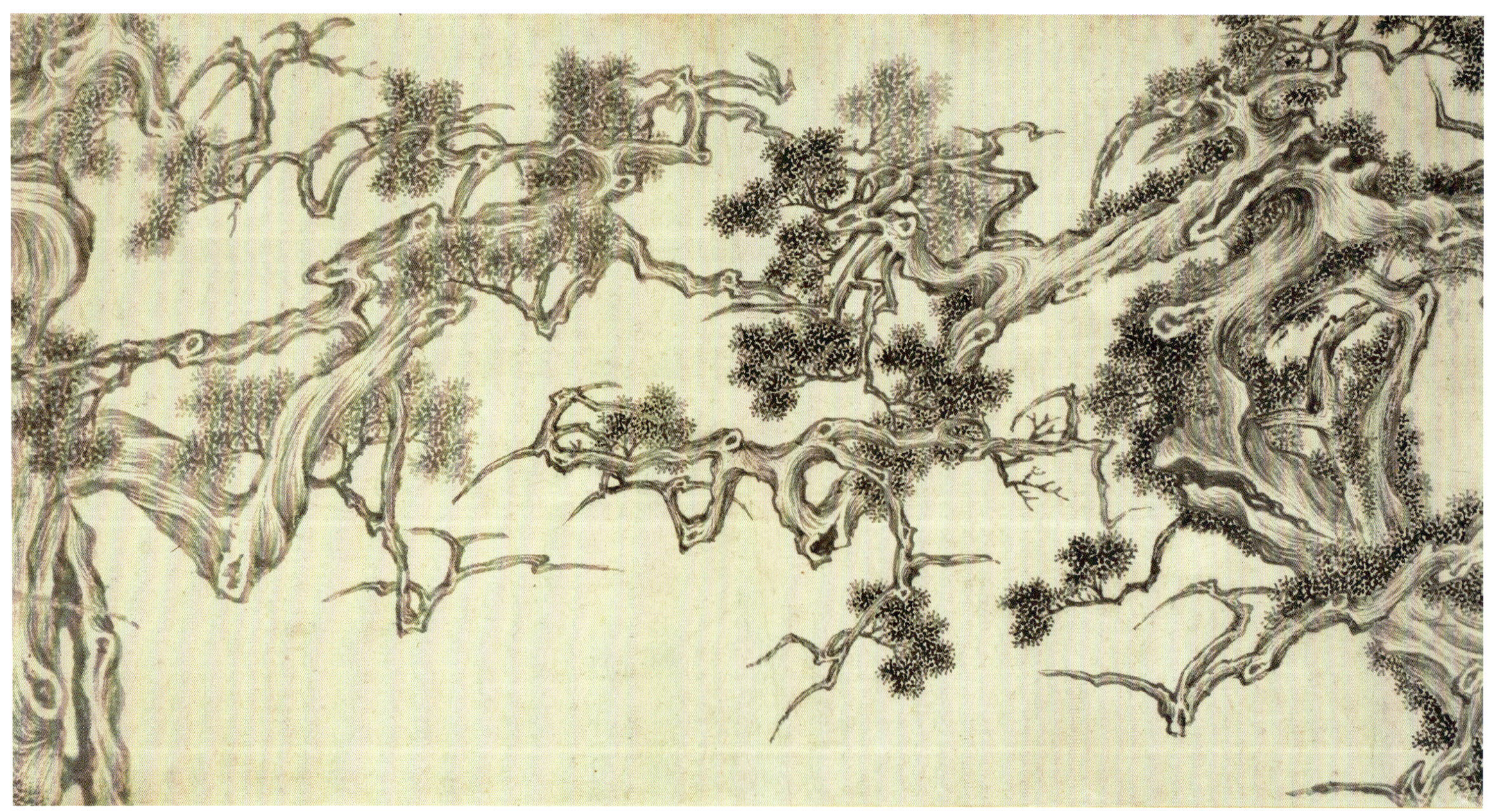

Figure 10.4. Wen Zhengming (1470–1559) (detail), *Seven Junipers*, Ming dynasty (1368–1644), dated 1532. Handscroll, ink on paper, 11 9⁄16 × 389 3⁄16 in. Gift of Mrs. Carter Galt, 1952. Honolulu Museum of Art (1666.1a).

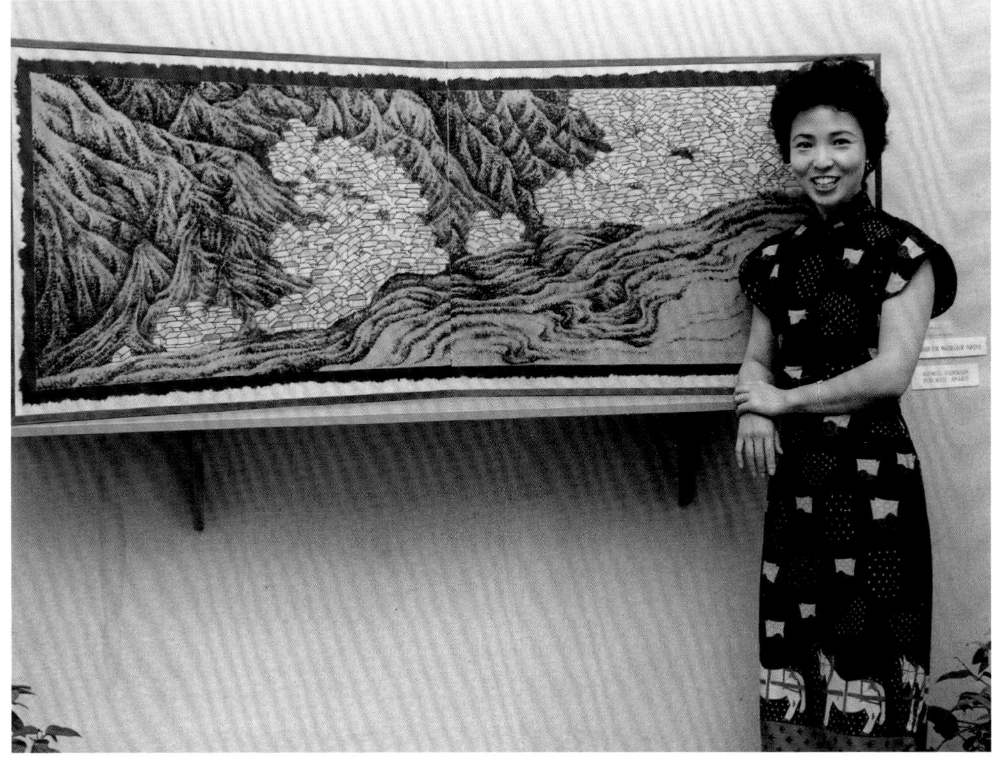

Figure 10.5. Tseng with the painting *The Settlement* in 1957. Honolulu Museum of Art Archives.

In 1965, Ecke published *Chinese Painting in Hawaii.* It was a major achievement, and he credited Tseng for much of it, asserting that without her, "this book and the Chinese collection at the Academy on which it is based would have been impossible. . . . It was her genius which brought them both about. Herself a great painter, she has a tremendous intuitive awareness of quality in art."[20]

In the 1950s and 1960s, when Tseng was most active at the Academy, the divisions between personal and business life often blurred. Like the ink wash on a Chinese landscape, professional lines were not as clearly defined as they are in today's museum world. However, thanks to these ambiguities, the institution acquired many masterpieces from Tseng and Ecke. During the 1950s, the couple sold the Academy eleven paintings, including *Seven Junipers* by Wen Zhengming (1666.1)(fig. 10.4) and *Wild Orchids* by Xue Wu (c. 1564–1637) (1667.1). In 1954, *Seven Junipers* and another of the Academy's paintings, *The Coming of Autumn* by Hongren (1610–1664) (2045.1), were included in one of the biggest exhibitions of Chinese art in the United States, Sherman E. Lee's *Chinese Landscape Painting,* which was held at the Cleveland Museum.[21]

Over the years, Tseng and Ecke donated to the Academy paintings, ceramics, jades, rubbings, textiles, and nearly thirty of Tseng's own works. Highlights of the latter include early examples of her traditional paintings, a figural painting of a Tang court lady (5691.1), stunning *dsui* works such as *Seagulls* (7049.1) and *Pregnant Hawaii* (TCM.1983.5.616) (fig. 10.14), as well as *The Settlement* (2391.1) (fig. 10.5), which foreshadowed an environmental consciousness that was not widespread at the time of its creation. Tseng also supported other Hawaiian institutions, such as the former Contemporary Museum. In the 1980s, she gave works to this museum by artists such as Jean Charlot (1898–1979) and Norman Ives (1923–1978); in the 1990s, she provided funds that allowed the

Contemporary Museum to purchase works by rising female artists, including Arabella Ark (b. 1946), Nanci Hersh (b. 1959), and Esther Shimazu (b. 1957).

In addition to her generous donations, Tseng performed pioneering research, particularly on the history of female artists such as Xue Wu: "In the annals of Chinese painting scholarship, Tseng's 1955 article on the Ming-dynasty courtesan painter Xue Wu . . . represents a breakthrough which preceded the advent of gender studies by several decades. This article sought to place Xue Wu within the social and artistic world of the Ming courtesan."[22] Regarding Xue Wu's painting *Wild Orchids* (fig. 10.6), Tseng noted:

> The orchids of Hsüeh Wu [Xue Wu] were not merely imitated from an old formula, they grew out of her own conception, her own observation of nature. The orchid handscroll . . . has been painted with great fluidity, subtle and complex, with a seriousness which hardly finds any parallel. . . . One might justly consider the Honolulu scroll as representing the orchid painting of the entire period.[23]

It is not hard to imagine how Xue Wu, a legendary artist, courtesan, and archer, would have tested societal expectations for her gender in Ming-dynasty China, or how this might have presented an irresistible field of study for Tseng—another visionary female artist determined to overcome the challenges and limitations presented by her era.[24]

Figure 10.6. Xue Wu (1564–1637) (detail), *Wild Orchids,* Ming dynasty (1368–1644), dated 1601. Handscroll, ink on paper, 12 ½ × 234 in. Purchase, 1952. Honolulu Museum of Art (1667.1).

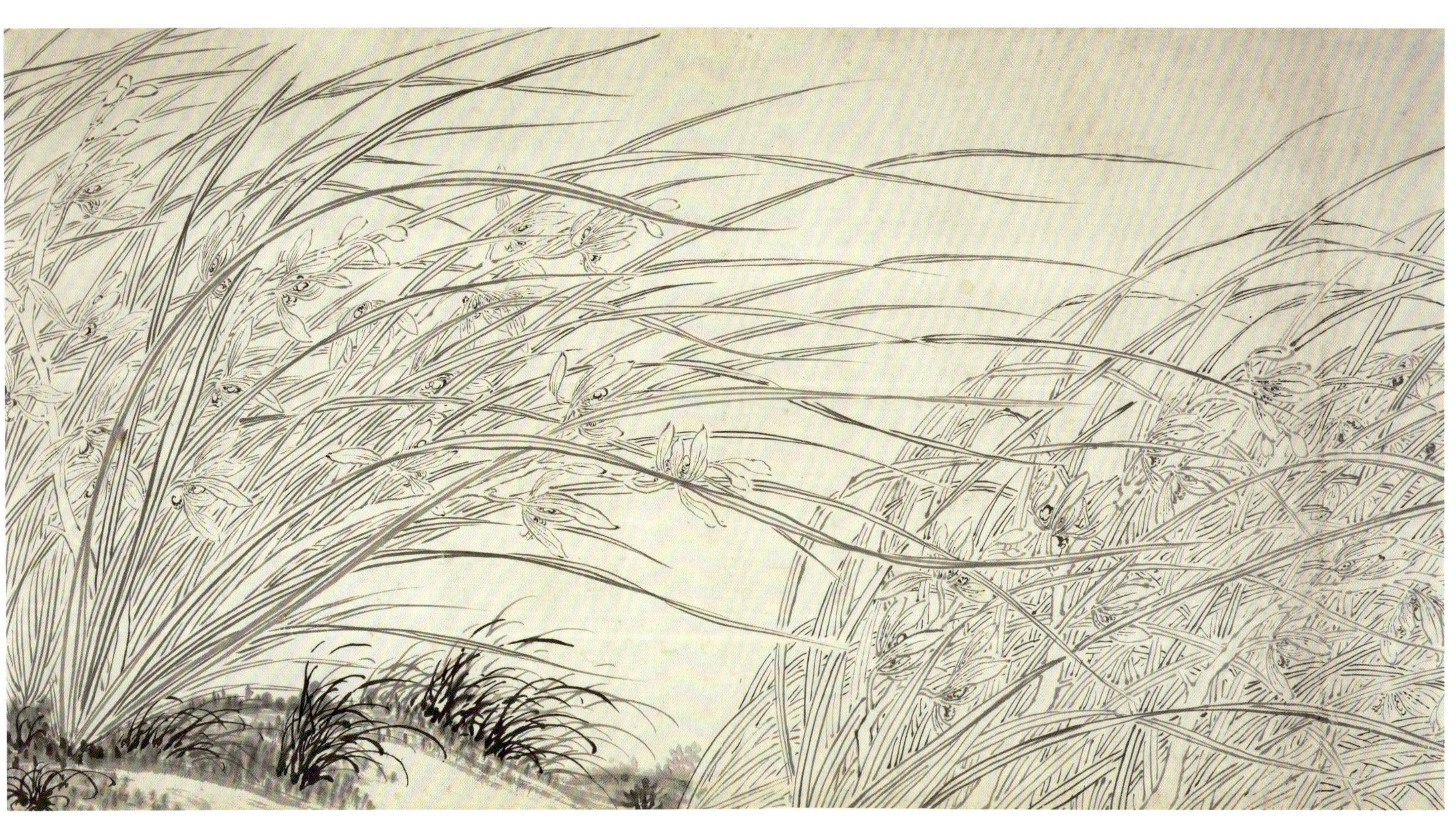

Like the quintessential figure wandering a vast Chinese landscape, Tseng was an inveterate traveler. Travel was essential to her career as an artist and as a teacher, providing fresh perspectives that allowed her to reframe and present her vision of the world to others.[25] Throughout the 1950s, she continued to exhibit on the mainland, particularly in California and New York. In 1953, Tseng and Ecke received a joint Rockefeller Foundation scholarship to visit eighteen different cities to study art. During this period, she began to invent the *dsui hua* method of assembling collage paintings that would eventually become her signature style.[26] *Dsui* took inspiration from multiple cultural sources. The material itself had roots in traditional Chinese papermaking and scroll mounting, as well as in the tapa paper found in the Pacific.[27] Stylistically, *dsui* was grounded in ancient Chinese artistic theory and subject matter but also influenced by modern Western elements of surrealism, cubism, abstraction, synchromism, and color theory.[28]

Before leaving China, Tseng spent two years in a Liulichang studio studying the mounting of traditional paintings.[29] During the mounting process, layers of paper are applied to the back of the scroll. Tseng would eventually use this idea in her *dsui* method, but with a twist: she transferred the layering process from the back to the front of the painting. While in Beijing, she collected and recycled paper from old scrolls and books to use for painting material, since it absorbed ink better than new paper. Unfortunately, she left China so quickly that she was unable to bring most of it with her.[30] When Tseng arrived in Hawai'i, she initially worked with a local Japanese mounter. However, in 1953, she began mounting her own paintings.[31] In Hawai'i, she discovered tapa, which turned out to be an excellent medium, not only as a background for a painting but also, in later works, as a decorative element. Tapa was also "the purest manifestation of Tseng's relationship to Hawaii and to her identification with regional traditions."[32]

The *dsui* technique was a lengthy procedure in which Tseng would tear and layer paper, painting the layers, allowing the "image and mood to emerge unconsciously" and organically from the process and materials.[33] Not long after she discovered this method, she began to experiment, adding in shimmering gold, silver, and other metallic colors, such as palladium and aluminum. She studied these substances as elements of Chinese religious paintings and sutras, as well as on Japanese screens and on European Christian icons. By the 1960s, her careful, planned abstraction of decorative elements had elevated her ethereal paintings to an otherworldly, mystical level.[34]

Dsui hua represented not only the transformation of Tseng's artistic style but also her personal development as a citizen of the world. According to the art historian Richard Barnhart, Tseng was "one of the preeminent Chinese painters of the 20th century," and from 1955 through the 1960s, a high point in her creative output, her paintings signified "a watershed in the history of Chinese landscape painting."[35] Tseng never relinquished her Chinese identity, yet after moving to Hawai'i, she was no longer only a Chinese artist living abroad: she had also become an international, contemporary artist.[36] As she explored Western artistic movements and applied them to the natural environment surrounding her, she began a lifelong transition for herself as well as for her painting.[37]

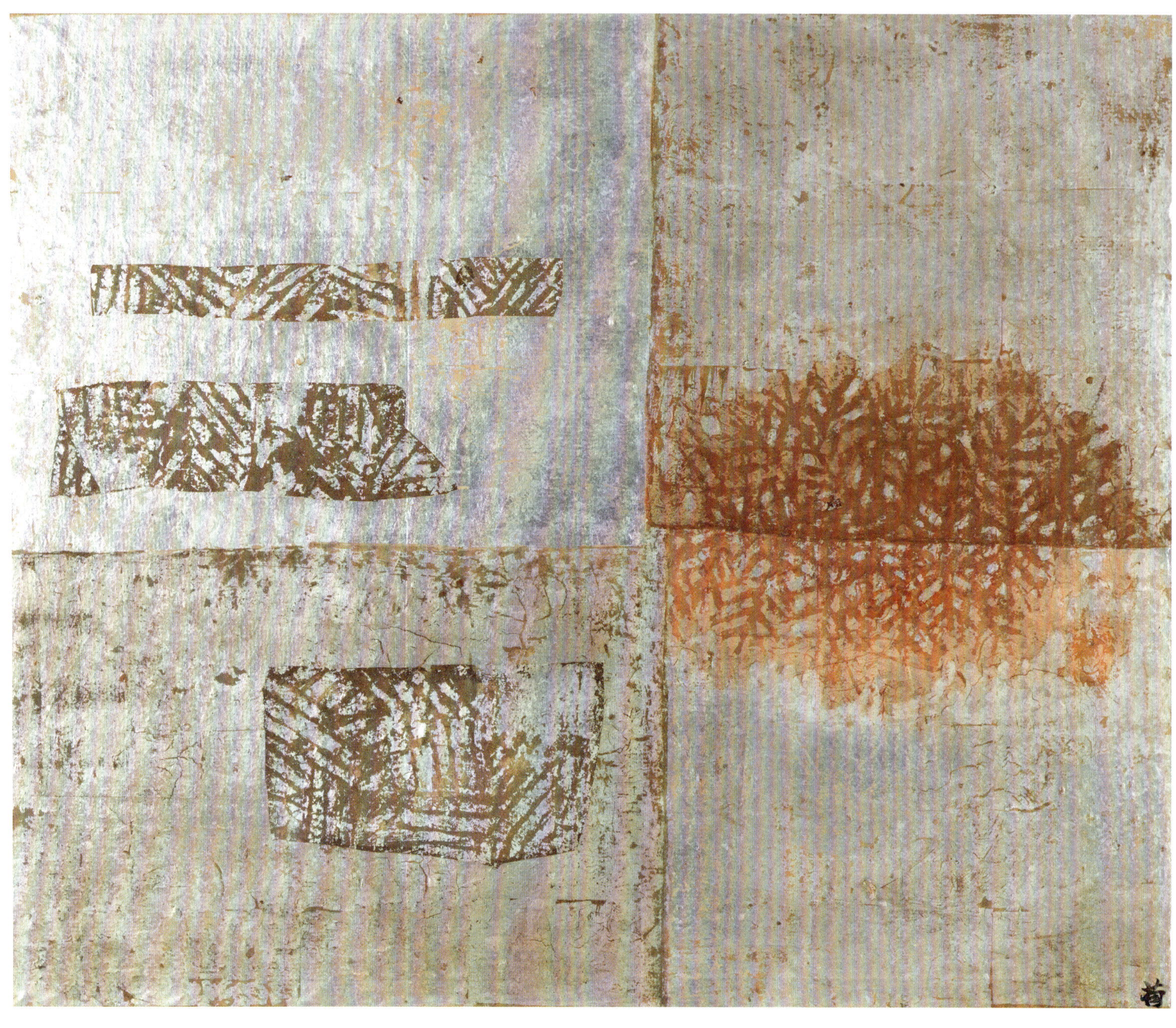

Figure 10.7. Tseng Yuho (1925–2017), *Limpidity* (1960). *Dsui* painting; ink, acrylic, aluminum, and paper, on Masonite, 30 × 36 ¼ in. Gift of Mr. and Mrs. Denny A. McLeod, 1984. Honolulu Museum of Art, © Estate of Tseng Yuho (5253.1).

In 1955, Tseng and Ecke became US citizens. They enjoyed extensive travel, but Hawai'i was now home. Chinese artists were traditionally scholars, and Tseng was no exception. Rigorously trained at an early age and skilled in calligraphy, painting, and poetry, Tseng never stopped studying.[38] She thus not only mastered proficiency in many disciplines simultaneously but also kept adding new ones, which enhanced the progression of her evocative *dsui hua* works. It was a symbiotic relationship, for her studies informed her artwork, and in turn, her art influenced her research: "My painting benefitted from my studies of the history of art by nourishing me and giving me confidence to move forward. I measured my own ability against the bold creative achievements of history. . . .

As the years went by, my work became totally introspective. I was convinced that the metaphysical approach best suited me. The more I learned, the more I realized my limitations. I also discovered that whenever I reached my own limitations, I could expand one degree beyond."[39]

When Tseng first moved to Hawai'i, she used conventional Chinese painting styles to interpret the new world around her. This is evident in the brightly colored *Scene from Oahu* (1458.1)(fig. 10.8), from 1951, and the boneless style of *Mountain Landscape* from 1956 (3116.1). However, although *Scene from Oahu* might have been rendered with traditional brushstrokes, the vivid tropical colors that illustrated her lush surroundings were a departure from the austere literati style that she favored in earlier paintings.

During the 1950s and early 1960s, Tseng's paintings retained abstract yet recognizable elements of landscape, such as trees, mountains, and rocks (see, for example, *Limpidity* [1960], fig. 10.7).[40] By the mid-1960s, as she experimented more intensively with abstraction, her paintings seemed to employ only remnants of classical Chinese techniques, with the trees, mountains, and rocks now appearing solely "as dots, squares, and grids."[41]

Figure 10.8. Tseng Yuho (1925–2017), *Scene from Oahu* (1951). Mineral colors on tapa (bark cloth), 37 × 50 ½ in. Gift of Mr. Robert Allerton, 1952. Honolulu Museum of Art, © Estate of Tseng Yuho (1458.1).

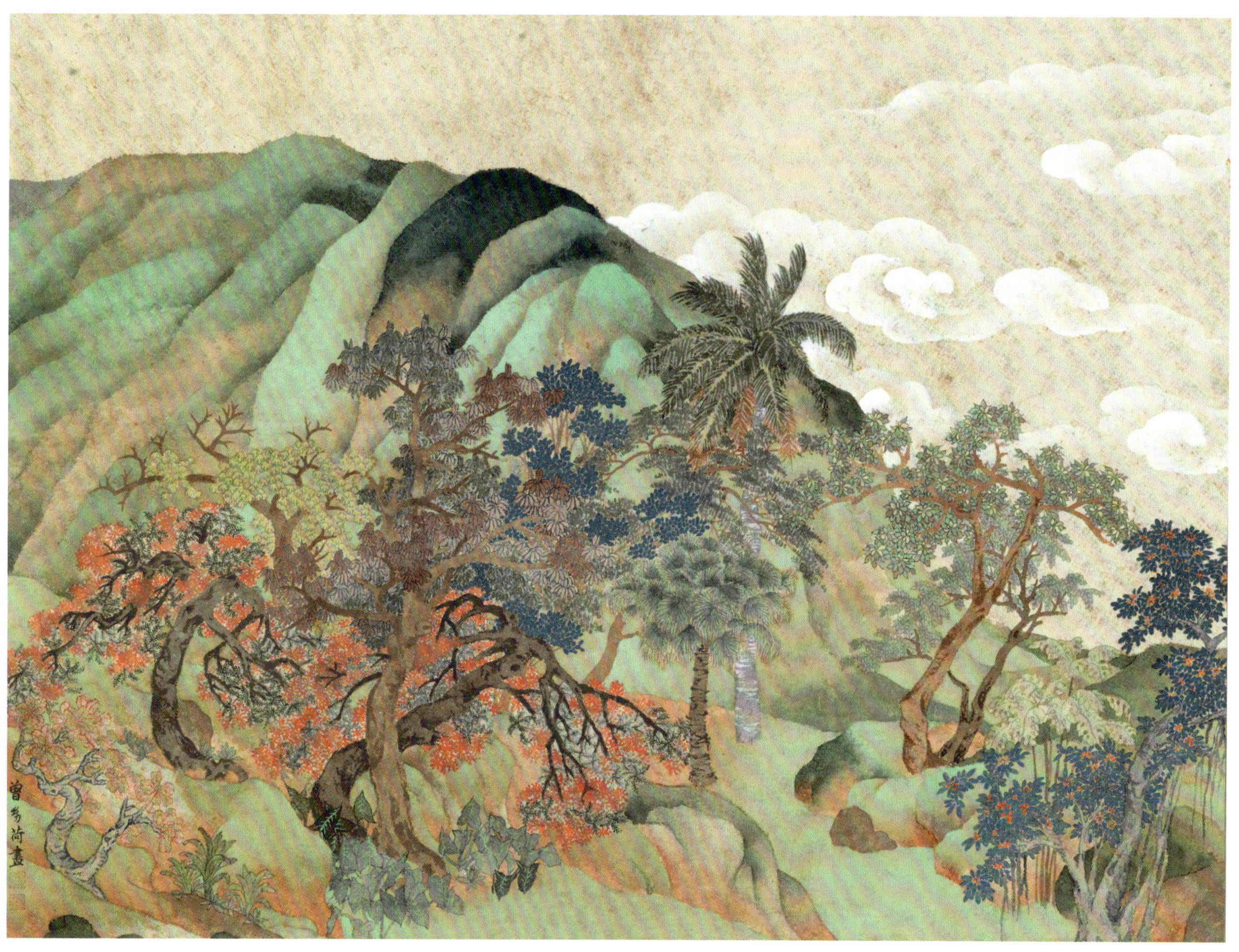

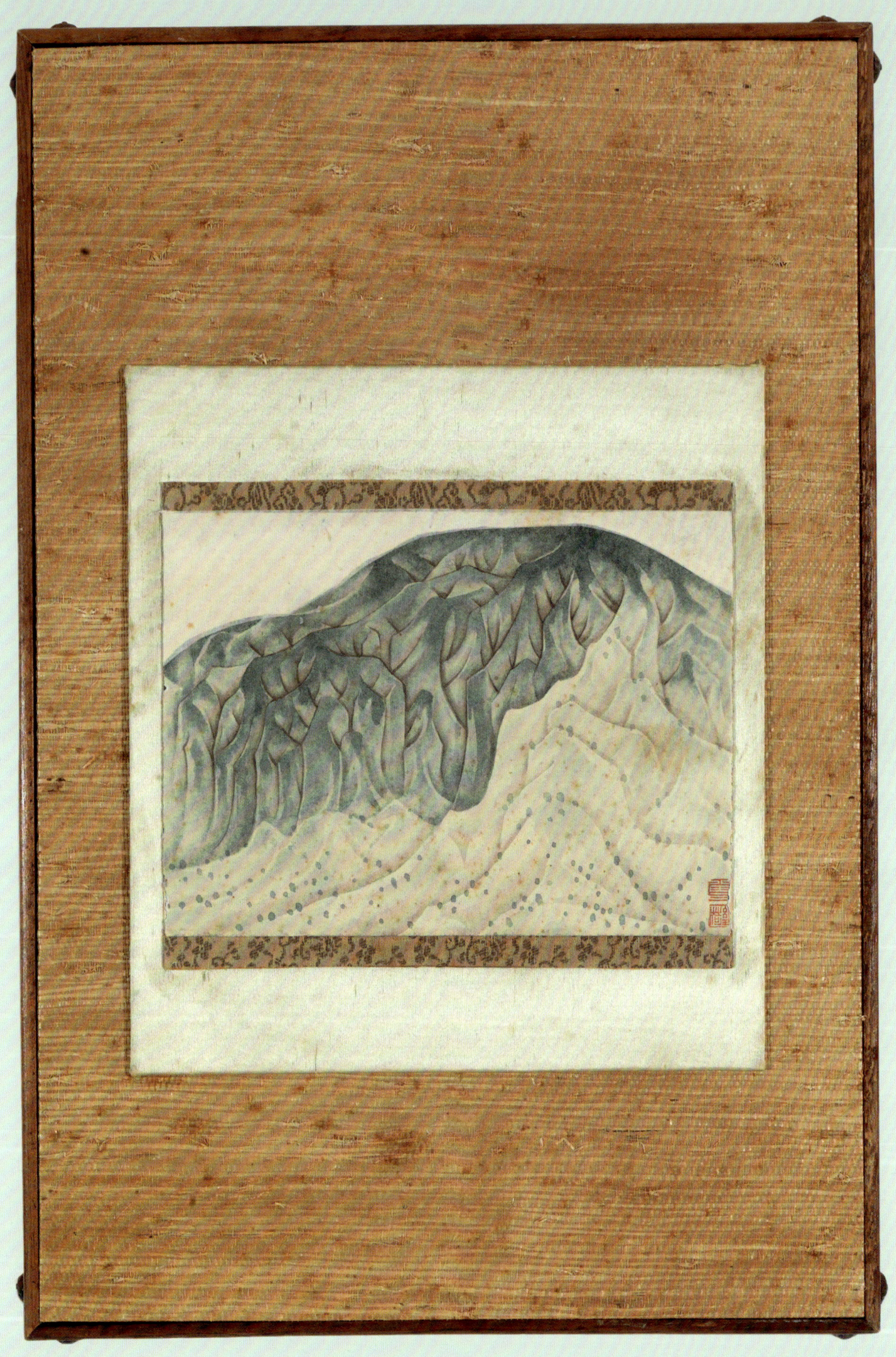

This flirtation with pure abstraction did not last, however. According to Tseng, she tried it "when everyone was in abstraction. I just wanted to make people see that I could do it."[42]

In 1957, Tseng and Ecke toured Europe, and Tseng exhibited her *dsui hua* for the first time, in a solo Paris show. Recognized in Europe by illustrious artists such as Georges Braque (1882–1963) and Max Ernst (1891–1976), Tseng acknowledged this as a huge turning point for her career. These artists strengthened her confidence by asking about her methods and sharing "their admiration for and their debt to Chinese art."[43] Ernst, a mentor whom she knew from Honolulu, bought two of her paintings.[44] This period in Europe, and later in New York, offered Tseng renewed exposure to the avant-garde art world. Her contact with modern art in Europe and the United States contributed to the evolution of her style, infusing mystery and reconfirming the primal relevance of the subconscious, which synchronized well with ancient Chinese ideologies and the belief in universal ideals, cosmic connections, and cycles.[45]

At the same time that Tseng was being celebrated in Paris, she was also thriving in the United States. In 1958, after Griffing saw her *dsui* work in a University of Hawai'i faculty show, he submitted two of her paintings to the group exhibition *American Art of the Western States* at Stanford University's art gallery. To Tseng's delight, one of them (titled *Aquarelle* [1958]) won first place.[46]

In 1959, Hawai'i became the fiftieth US state. Tseng's solo exhibition at the Academy that year traveled to Stanford and then on to the Walker Art Center in Minneapolis. The Walker's director, H. H. Arnason, who first discovered Tseng in Hawai'i, would not only become a staunch supporter but also introduce Tseng to one of her most significant connections, Edith Halpert of the Downtown Gallery.[47] Arnason felt that Tseng was "one of the most important young artists to appear from the new state of Hawai'i. Her accomplishment has been to retain the contemplative essence of the ancient Chinese tradition, and at the same time, work successfully in the mode of the complex and rapidly evolving Western aesthetic."[48]

What Arnason touched on was an aspect of Tseng's art that deepened as her work evolved: how viewing Tseng's paintings may be a spiritual, dynamic, and original experience. Her reverence for nature, the grand subject of traditional Chinese painting, remained unwavering throughout her oeuvre. She also frequently referenced calligraphy and poetry, the two other most valued arts in China. However, although classical painting theory informed the spirit, harmony, and perspective of her art, her luminous color choices for *dsui* diverged sharply from literati tradition. In her *dsui* works she often drew from the aesthetic vocabulary of ceramics, jade, and folk art rather than painting.[49] Considering this along with her unconventional use of layered paper and other materials and mounting techniques, it is unlikely that Chinese painters of the past would recognize the subjects of her more abstract works. Yet however untraditional they appeared, these delicate landscapes were filled with suggestive stylistic and thematic references to her homeland, and just as more traditional topography did for earlier Chinese artists, they continued to represent the "inner landscapes" of Tseng's "heart and mind."[50]

Figure 10.9. (*facing*) Tseng Yuho (1925–2017), *Mountain Landscape* (1956). Watercolor on paper, 5 ⅞ × 8 ⅛ in. Gift of Mrs. Cyril F. Damon, 1963. Honolulu Museum of Art, © Estate of Tseng Yuho (3116.1).

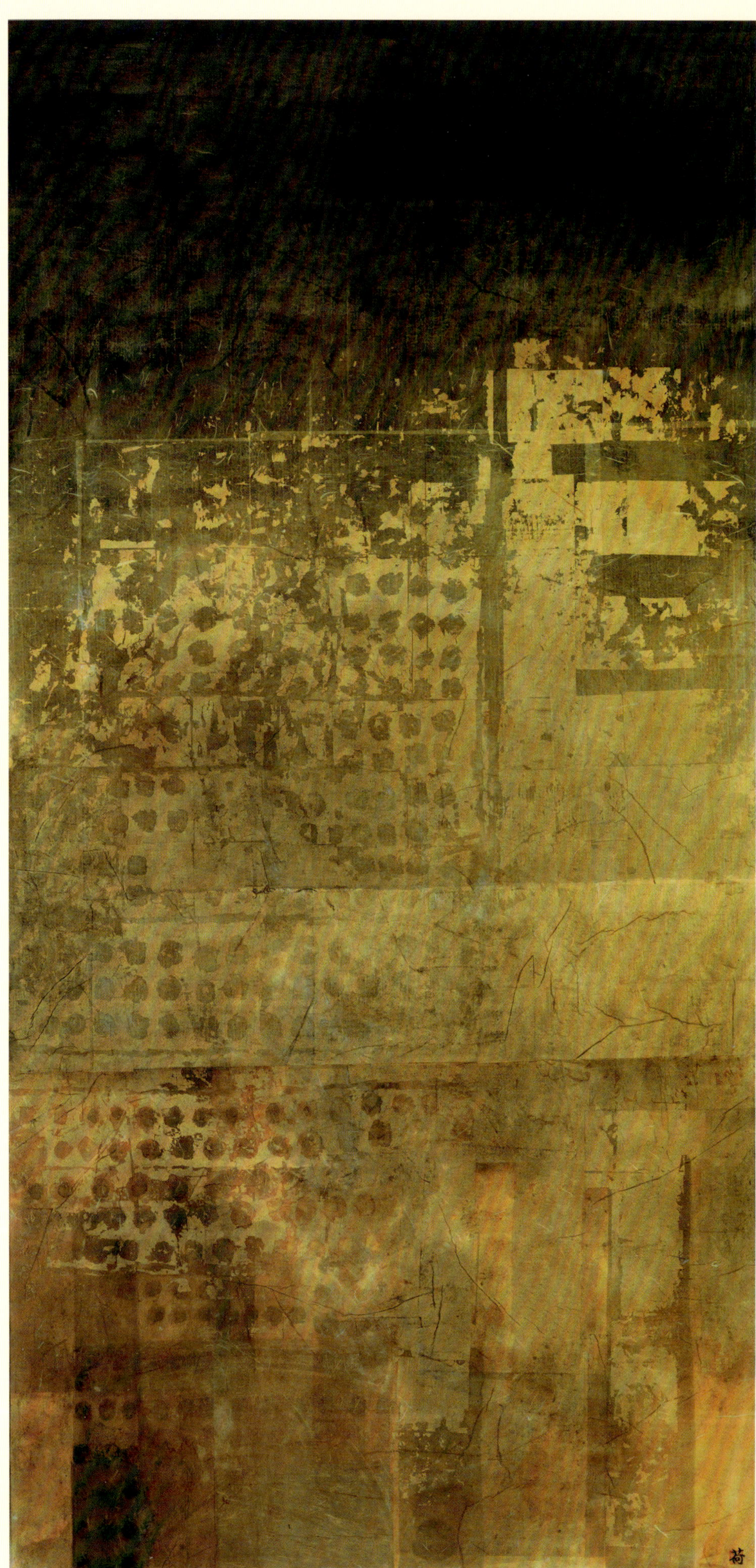

Figure 10.10. Tseng Yuho (1925–2017), *Seagulls* (1965). *Dsui* painting; gold and paper on screen. 72 × 36 ½ in. Gift of Sister Sara Kay Thompson and Philip Thompson in memory of their mother, Marie Sara Garvey Thompson, 1992. Honolulu Museum of Art, © Estate of Tseng Yuho (7049.1).

Tseng continued exploring the world and studying while steadily creating her own masterpieces. In 1960, a scholarship enabled her to travel for four months to Japan, Hong Kong, and Taiwan, where she viewed over five thousand works of Chinese painting and calligraphy. In that same year, the Downtown Gallery in New York City, which for ten years would be Tseng's exclusive representative, unveiled the first New York exhibition of her work, and in 1962, it opened her solo show *New Paintings by Tseng Yuho*. A *Time* magazine review noted that although the paintings appeared as if "composed of gossamer and mist," it was in fact this very essence of "fragility" that provided her work with "subtle strength."[51] In her own words, "A little bit of thread can express power as well as a large boulder."[52]

The *Time* article delineated the scope of Tseng's subject matter, as well as the appeal of her enigmatic paintings: "Her subjects range from the stream by her house, to a mountain top, to a wispy peek into the cosmos. Her paper world can spit fire, roar like the sea, or open up the vastness of a blue-black night. But her chief triumph is that in her work the traditional and the modern come together, not as combatants, but as companions."[53]

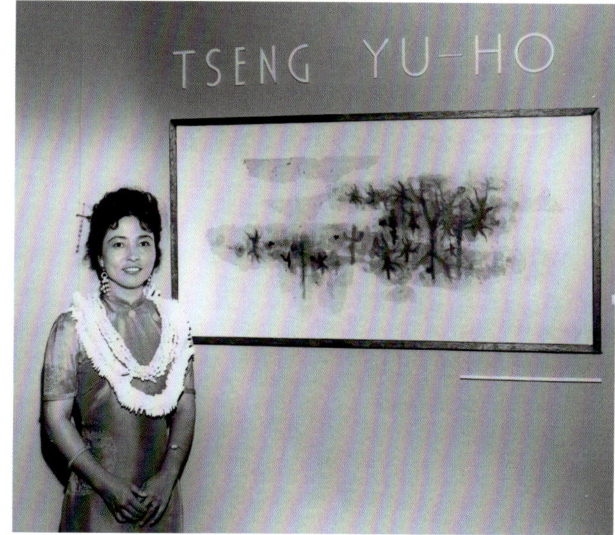

Figure 10.11. Exhibition opening in 1959 with *Nowhere*, Honolulu Museum of Art Archives.

In 1964, Golden West Savings and Loan commissioned Tseng to do a ninety-foot mural, titled *Western Frontier (Redwoods)* (fig. 10.13). A shimmering painting composed on nine panels, it contains jewel-colored shapes representing redwood trees and other landscape elements, depicted in palladium, tapa, ink, and color on Masonite. Its great size made it difficult for Tseng to find a place to work on it, but the Academy came to her rescue, and she set up in the museum basement to complete her masterpiece. The mural was temporarily on display at ʻIolani Barracks before it was shipped to San Francisco.

At one point in the 1960s, according to Tseng, she was earning nearly $50,000 a year from the Downtown Gallery's sales, which would have been an astonishingly large sum of money at the time.[54] But keeping up with gallery demand was exhausting. A great deal of energy went into the process, and she did not think that the works were ready until they were animated.[55] "While working on a painting, and when I feel the pulse emerging," she said, "the painting begins to live for me."[56] Once they were alive, she found it grueling to repeatedly part with them. Eventually, the commerciality and relentless production drained her enthusiasm, leading her back to the hallowed halls of graduate school and a renewed focus on teaching.[57]

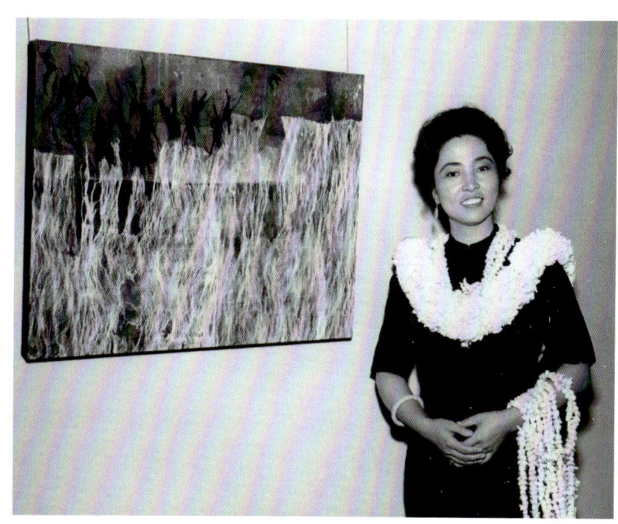

Figure 10.12. Exhibition opening in 1962 with *Mana*, Honolulu Museum of Art Archives.

In 1971, Ecke suffered a fatal heart attack in the couple's Nuʻuanu Valley residence. They had chosen this serene, pine-forested location for its resemblance to China and proximity to nature. After his death, Tseng concentrated on her studies, finishing her PhD in art history from the Institute of Fine Arts New York in 1972. Thereafter, she was offered a teaching job at Columbia University and the opportunity to permanently relocate to New York, but she declined the position. The island that had once felt so stifling was now a treasured home and peaceful respite that allowed her to fully explore her multitude of talents and to continue her artistic journey.[58]

Throughout the 1970s and 1980s, Tseng continued to be a curatorial consultant for the Academy. Her research, publications, and exhibitions centered on calligraphy, folding fans, folk art, and literati painting.[59] President Richard Nixon presented Tseng's

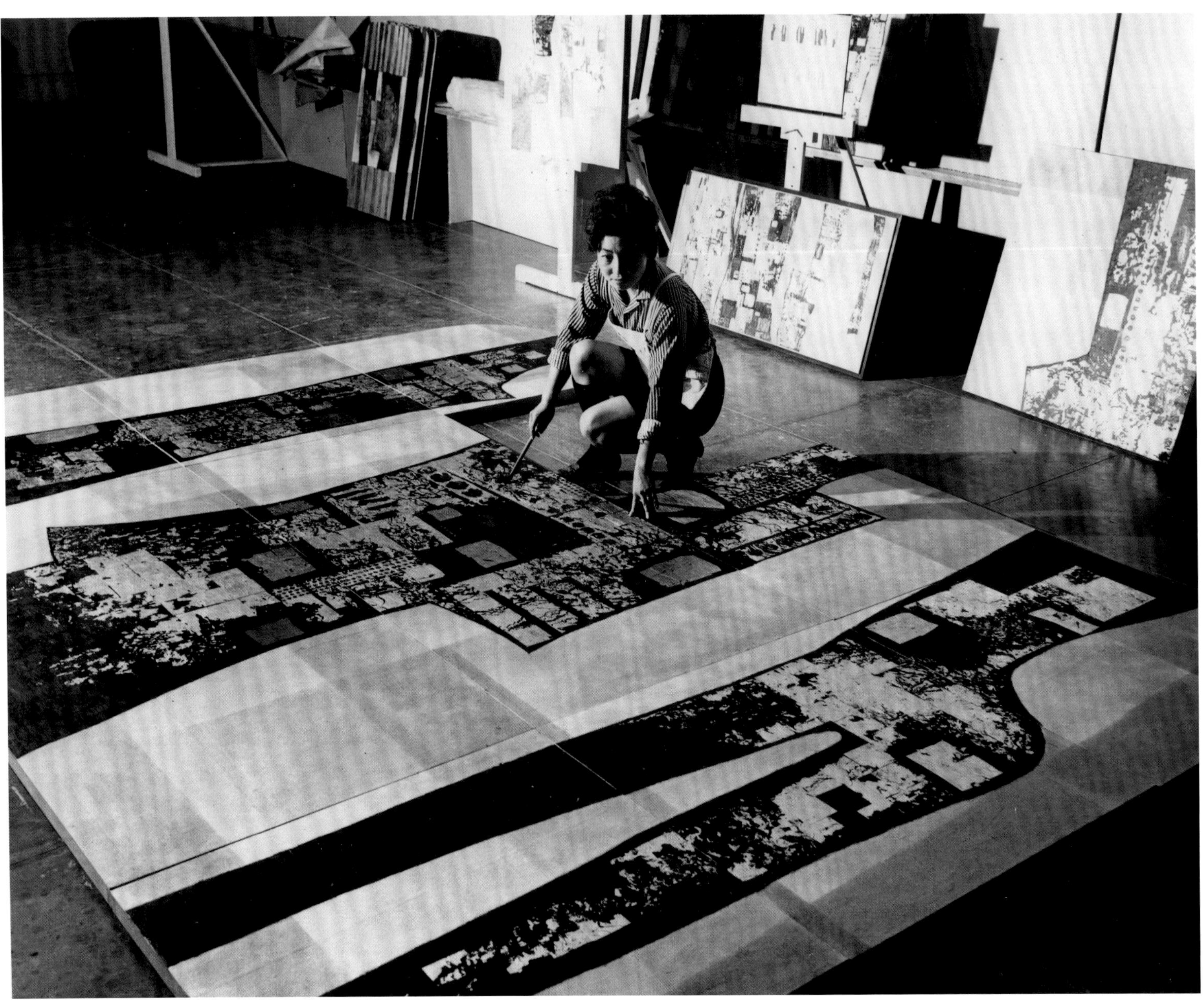

Figure 10.13. Tseng painting *Western Frontier*, 1964. Honolulu Museum of Art Archives.

comprehensive *Chinese Calligraphy* catalogue to Chairman Mao as a diplomatic gesture during his 1972 visit to China.[60] In 1984, Tseng became the Academy's part-time adjunct curator of Chinese art; the following year, she retired from the University of Hawai'i, allowing her time to focus more on painting and the Academy.[61] In 1988, she curated the exhibition *Wen-Jen Hua: Chinese Literati Painting from the Collection of Mr. and Mrs. Mitchell Hutchinson* and published an accompanying catalogue.

The year 1989 was the two hundredth anniversary of the beginning of Chinese immigration to Hawai'i. As part of the Academy's bicentennial celebration, the museum honored Tseng as one of the most celebrated Chinese immigrants to the islands by holding a special exhibition of her work titled *The Art of Tseng Yu-ho, Academy—Retrospective (1959–1989)*. In the same year, the Honpa Hongwanji Temple named Tseng a "Living

Treasure," commemorating her contributions to Hawai'i's "distinctive cultural and artistic heritage."[62]

Michael Sullivan—who by this point had been observing Tseng's career for more than forty years—well summed up the complexity of her work: "Part of the fascination of her painting is that it seems to show at work three dialectics: between past and present, between East and West, and on a purely visual level, between form and texture."[63] Sullivan further praised the maturation of her style, visible in many of her paintings from the 1980s, stating: "It is as though what she had learned and discovered of the Chinese landscape tradition, of Western contemporary art, and of the possibilities of the medium she has created, is at last distilled in a return to the ultimate source of her inspiration, which is, as it is for all Chinese artists, Nature itself."[64]

Tseng pulled apart and reassembled traditional Chinese landscape painting as original, contemporary terrain.[65] One needs no knowledge of China or of art history or theory to appreciate the visceral beauty of her work or to feel its aesthetic impact. However, when viewers recognize the inventive layers that compose her paintings, they may soar above and see the bird's-eye view, zoom in and detect dragon veins of energy humming within the ridges of powerful mountain ranges, dig deeper and discover bones of a Chinese character visible just beneath the surface, or perhaps even witness in her ethereal depictions of nature a cosmic connection not only to the past and the present but also to the future.

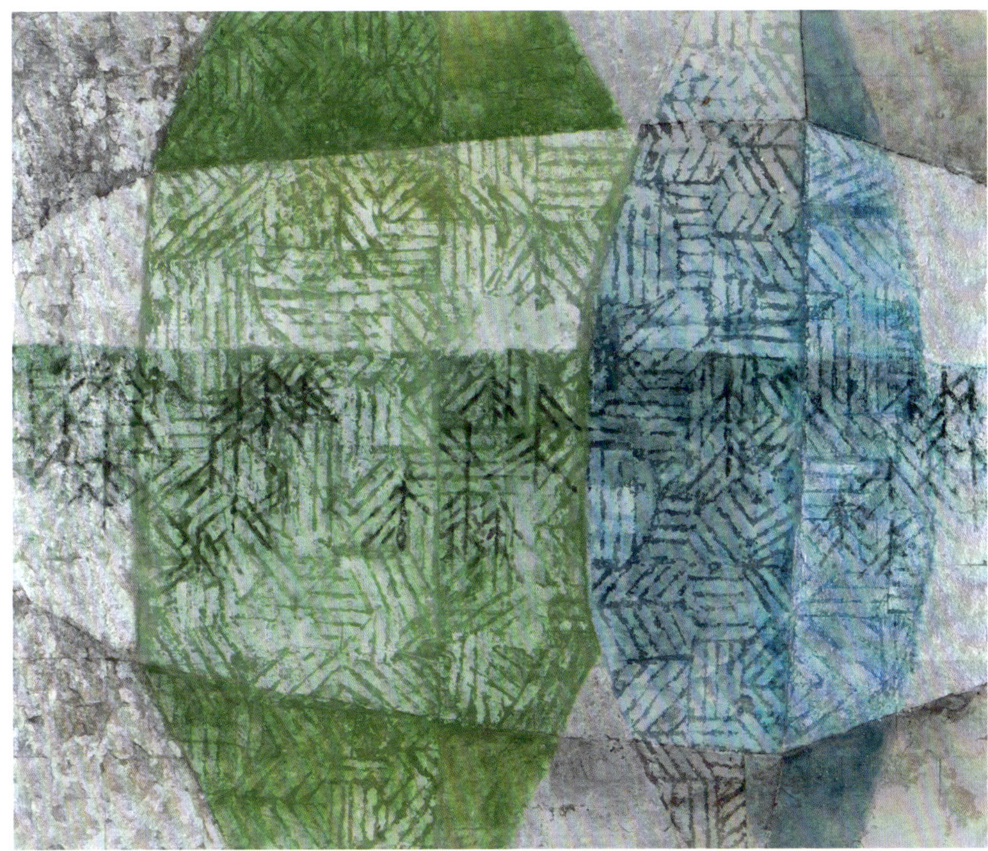

Figure 10.14. Tseng Yuho (1925–2017), *Pregnant Hawaii* (1979). *Dsui* painting; paper and wood, 33 × 39 ½ in. Gift of the Contemporary Museum, Honolulu, 2011; and gift of the Honolulu Advertiser Collection at Persis Corporation, 1983. Honolulu Museum of Art, © Estate of Tseng Yuho (TCM.1983.5.616).

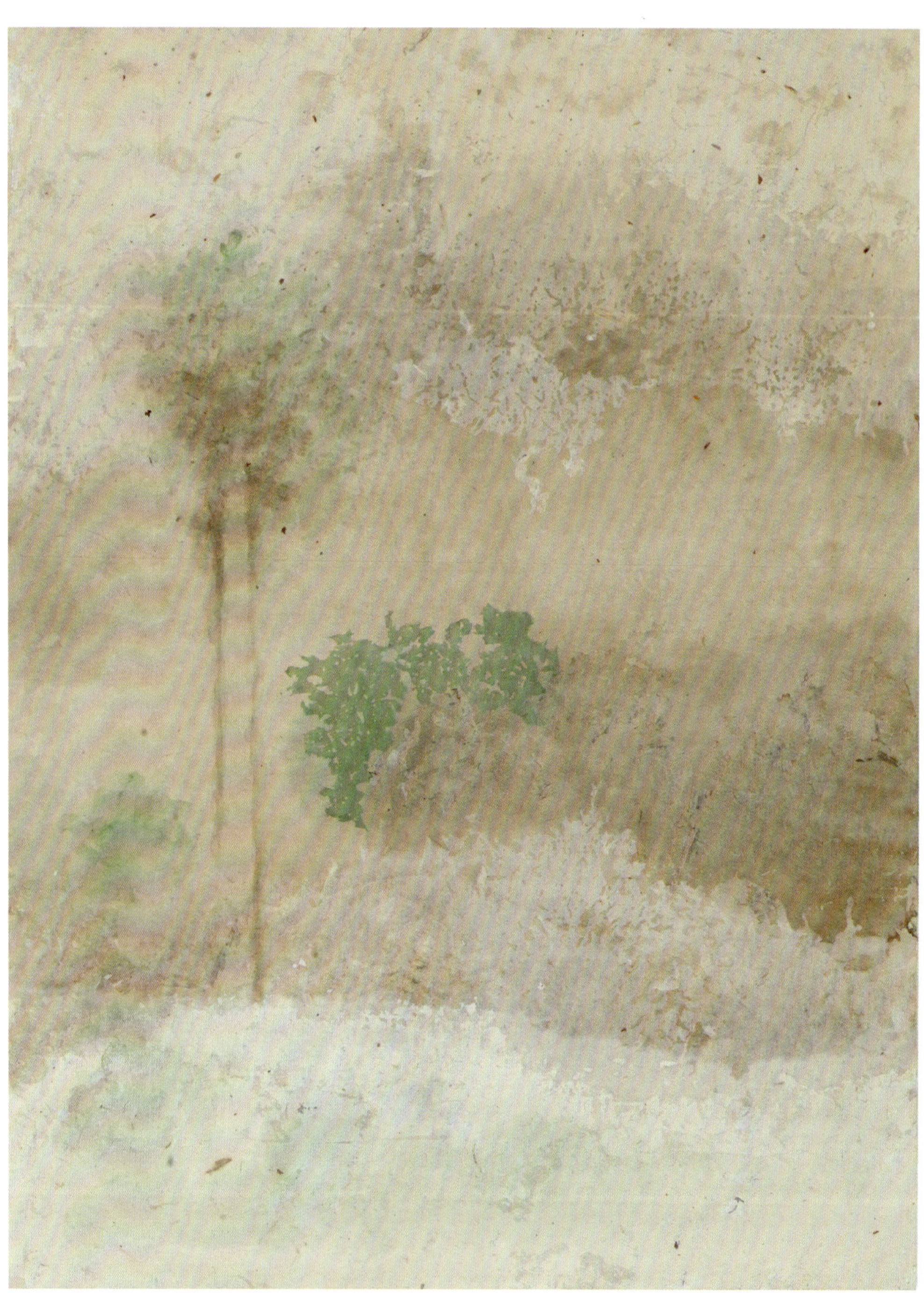

Figure 10.15. Tseng Yuho (1925–2017), *Lyric III* (1989). *Dsui* painting; acrylic and paper on Masonite, 32 × 34 in. Gift of Susan Palmore for the Estate of Betty Sterling, 2007. Honolulu Museum of Art, © Estate of Tseng Yuho (13724.1).

The Art of Tseng Yu-ho: A Retrospective Exhibition toured a number of venues in China in 1992 and went to Singapore in 1993. This historic "first major solo exhibition in the Asia region in over 40 years," was particularly meaningful because it represented a "home-coming."[66] It was the first time for many Chinese to personally experience work by an "overseas Chinese painter of international repute."[67] For one of the artists from the diaspora who left during the political turmoil and were for some time neglected, and even censured, by China, this achievement signified quite a triumph—her long-awaited acceptance and success in her birthland.[68] During the late 1990s, Tseng still visited the University of Hawai'i to create art. She looked back fondly at the many hours that she had devoted to education, declaring, "In later life my teaching and research have provided me with the satisfaction of giving something of value to others, allowing me to serve art as I would a religion."[69]

Tseng Yuho's legacy was not only innovative art that transcended boundaries but also the education of thousands of students about the art, history, and culture of China. Though she is considered "one of the preeminent Chinese painters of the 20th century," it is a testament to her dedication to education that she said of herself in 1997, "I think of myself as an educator first; second, I'm a painter."[70] Even while teaching others, she remained devoted to exploring and refining her own abilities. A lifelong learner who reveled in sharing her knowledge, she was a true master of reinvention. Like a traveler in a traditional landscape painting, she perpetually moved along her own path from the macro to the micro and back again. Yet along the way, Tseng transformed the narrative from one purely Chinese and traditional to one that was also contemporary, international, and more metaphysical: "What is inside me is formless and without bodily substance. The articulation of my ideas and feelings through art is transient. My pictorial representations are the temporary physical manifestations through which I hope to suggest the majesty of the human mind, and show my reverence for the magnitude of the cosmic world beyond. I adopt a fixed position as an artist, disclosing my individuality and circumscribing a 'suggestiveness' to evoke countless phenomena."[71]

In 2005, Tseng returned to live in China, where she remained until her death in 2017. She had prospered greatly during her fifty-six years in Hawai'i. The relaxed island lifestyle, far from the bustle of major cities such as Beijing, New York, or Paris, provided a refuge in which she could experiment and excel, eventually finding her way in a fashion that might never have been possible in her turbulent, ever-transforming homeland.[72] The islands made an indelible mark on Tseng's life and career; however, like the vermilion seals that she stamped on paintings, her imprint on Hawai'i and the art world was vivid and permanent.[73] Her visionary work ensures that we, along with future generations, may continue to explore our own inner landscapes and, like "astronauts walking in unlimited space," emerge from our experiences not lost—but found.

Notes

1. Epigraph from Tseng Yuho and Howard A. Link, *The Art of Tseng Yuho* (Honolulu: Honolulu Academy of Arts, 1987), 24. In English, Tseng's name has been published in various ways: Tseng Yu-ho, Tseng Yuho, and Zeng Youhe. In Hawai'i, she was also known as Betty Ecke, as well as Tseng Yuho Ecke. For consistency, in this essay I use the version that she preferred in later life: Tseng Yuho.

2. In 1960, Tseng coined the phrase *dsui hua* to describe her new work. Melissa Jane Thompson, "Gathering Jade and Assembling Splendor: The Life and Art of Tseng Yuho" (PhD diss., University of Washington, 2001), 112. The term *dsui* referenced multiple traditional Chinese practices: quilt work, garments styled after the robes of itinerant monks (made from donated scraps of cloth), a literati linked verse game, and, most important, the use of paper to patch old scrolls—a technique Tseng employed in her paintings. Tseng Yuho, "Dsui Hua," in *Dsui Hua: Tseng Yuho*, ed. Valerie C. Doran (Taipei: Hanart T. Z. Gallery, 1992), 24.

3. Thompson, "Gathering Jade," 112. According to Tseng, the character she chose to represent her *dsui* method (掇) was an ancient seal character with a hand radical on the left (rather than the usual silk 綴), resulting in a five-handed pictogram. Tseng Yuho, "Dsui Hua," 24.

4. See "Gustav Emil Wilhelm Ecke, 1896–1971, Collector and Art Historian," Freer Sackler Gallery, February 29, 2016, https://www.freersackler.si.edu/wp-content/uploads/2017/09//Ecke-Gustav.pdf.

5. Tseng and Link, *Art of Tseng Yuho*, 37. In 2012, the Honolulu Academy of Arts merged with the Contemporary Museum to become the Honolulu Museum of Art, as it is now known.

6. Cynthia Eyre, "Courtship in Peking," *Honolulu*, September 1966, 53.

7. Early newspapers discussed Tseng Yuho and her husband's leaving just before the rise of the Cultural Revolution. See Eyre, "Courtship in Peking," and Grace Tower Warren, "Island Hostess: Tseng Yuho, Artist and Housewife," *Paradise of the Pacific*, March 1954, 18.

8. According to Melissa Jane Thompson, Tseng was the seventy-third descendant of Zengzi, a disciple of Confucius (551–479 BCE). Thompson, "Gathering Jade," 2.

9. Thompson, 10.

10. Thompson, 3, 218–19.

11. A. A. Smyser, "Hawaii's Two Greatest Chinese Artists," *Honolulu Star-Bulletin*, May 5, 1998, http://archives.starbulletin.com/98/05/05/editorial/smyser.html.

12. Michael R. Martin, "An Interview with Tseng Yuho," *Orientations* 31, no. 5 (May 2000): 75.

13. Li Chu-tsing, "Tseng Yuho: Unusual Life, Unusual Art," in *Dsui Hua: Tseng Yuho*, ed. Valerie C. Doran (Taipei: Hanart T. Z. Gallery, 1992), 15.

14. Jean Charlot, "The Art of Tseng Yuho," *Honolulu Star-Bulletin*, July 13, 1966.

15. Thompson, "Gathering Jade," 75. The scroll includes an essay at the end, making the entire work forty-one feet long.

16. Tseng Yu-ho Ecke, *Wen-Jen Hua: Chinese Literati Painting from the Collection of Mr. and Mrs. Mitchell Hutchinson* (Honolulu: Honolulu Academy of Arts, 1988), 6.

17. Noelle Giuffrida, *Separating Sheep from Goats: Sherman E. Lee and Chinese Art Collecting in Postwar America* (Oakland: University of California Press, 2018), 1.

18. Thompson, "Gathering Jade," 6.

19. "2830: Tseng Yu-Ho, *Peaks*," *Contemporary Literati—Landscapes in Mind*, Sotheby's, accessed February 4, 2019, http://www.sothebys.com/en/auctions/ecatalogue/2014/contemporary-literati-landscapes-in-mind-hk0510/lot.2830.html.

20. "Chinese Art Expert Gustav Ecke, 75, Dies," *Honolulu Star-Bulletin*, December 20, 1971, D-6.

21. Giuffrida, *Separating Sheep*, 107.

22. Thompson, "Gathering Jade," 5.

23. Tseng Yuho, "Hsüeh Wu and Her Orchids in the Collection of the Honolulu Academy of Arts," *Arts Asiatiques* 2, no. 3 (1955): 197–98.

24. Thompson, "Gathering Jade," 200–201.

25. See Tseng Yuho chronology in Thompson, "Gathering Jade," viii–xviii.

26. Thompson, 112.

27. Also known as *kapa* in Hawai'i, tapa is a form of pounded bark cloth, usually derived from mulberry. "Kapa (Tapa) Barkcloth," Hawaiian Encyclopedia.com, accessed March 29, 2019, http://www.hawaiianencyclopedia.com/kapa-tapa-barkcloth.html.

28. Thompson, "Gathering Jade," 97–104.

29. Liulichang is a district of Beijing. Thompson, 265.

30. Thompson, 90.

31. Thompson, viii–xviii.

32. Thompson, 156.

33. Ding Xiyuan, "The Art of Tseng Yuho," in *Dsui Hua: Tseng Yuho*, ed. Valerie C. Doran (Taipei: Hanart T. Z. Gallery, 1992), 22–23.

34. Ding, "The Art of Tseng Yuho."

35. Richard Banhart, "The Artist Tseng Yuho: An Appreciation," in *Dsui Hua: Tseng Yuho*, ed. Valerie C. Doran (Taipei: Hanart T. Z. Gallery, 1992), 9, 12.

36. Li, "Tseng Yuho: Unusual Life, Unusual Art," 18.

37. It is worth noting that Tseng also strongly advocated for the recognition of abstraction as "universal in early civilization, especially in East Asia where the appearance and essence of nature was at the core of art." Thompson, "Gathering Jade," 258. For more information, see Tseng Yuho, "'Abstraction' in the Traditional Art of East Asia," in *Asian Traditions/Modern Expressions: Asian American Artists and Abstraction, 1945–1970*, ed. Jeffrey Wechsler (New York: Harry N. Abrams and Jane Voorhees Zimmerli Art Museum, 1997), 21–29.

38. For more on the role of painting, poetry, and calligraphy in China, see Michael Sullivan, *The Three Perfections: Chinese Painting, Poetry, and Calligraphy* (New York: G. Braziller, 1980).

39. Tseng, "Dsui Hua," 29.

40. Thompson, "Gathering Jade," 157.

41. Thompson, 157.

42. Thompson, 157.

43. May-ch'ing Kao, "Introductory Remarks," in *The Art of Tseng Yuho*, by Tseng Yuho and Howard A. Link (Honolulu: Honolulu Academy of Arts, 1987), 8.

44. Murry Engle, "Art, Like Love, Is a Bridge and a Bond," *Honolulu Star-Bulletin*, February 13, 1973.

45. Tseng first met and was inspired by Max Ernst and other contemporary Western artists when they visited Honolulu as part of a University of Hawai'i lecture series. Li Chu-tsing, *Trends in Modern Chinese Painting: The C. A. Drenowatz Collection* (Ascona, Switzerland: Artibus Asiae 1979), 171.

46. See Tseng Yuho chronology in Thompson, "Gathering Jade," viii–xviii, 138.

47. Li, "Tseng Yuho: Unusual Life, Unusual Art," 15.

48. H. H. Arnason, *Tseng Yu-Ho: Exhibition of Paintings in Watercolor-Collage* (New York: Downtown Gallery, 1960), n.p.

49. Tseng and Link, *Art of Tseng Yuho*, 20.

50. "Landscape Painting in Chinese Art," The Met, October 2004, accessed March 20, 2019, https://www.metmuseum.org/toah/hd/clpg/hd_clpg.htm.

51. "Painter in Paper," *Time*, January 19, 1962, 64.

52. "Painter in Paper," 64.

53. "Painter in Paper," 64.

54. Martin, "Interview," 77. An inflation calculator can be used to estimate what the equivalent amount would be today. See, for example, "CPI Inflation Calculator," Bureau of Labor Statistics, accessed March 30, 2019, https://www.bls.gov/data/inflation_calculator.htm.

55. One way in which Tseng interpreted classical Chinese painting theory was by infusing her works with "spirit resonance"; another was by incorporating stylistic and symbolic elements of nature (trees, mountains, and water regularly appeared in her works, as did calligraphic forms). However, although her starting place was Xie He's (fl. sixth century) Six Canons on painting, which codified aesthetic principles, she diverged radically from it in some aspects of her *dsui* style, especially in terms of color and object representation. "Xie He: Chinese Painter and Critic," Encyclopaedia Britannica, accessed February 28, 2019, https://www.britannica.com/biography/Xie-He; Tseng and Link, *Art of Tseng Yuho*, 15–21.

56. Tseng and Link, 15.

57. Martin, "Interview," 77.

58. Martin, 75.

59. In the 1980s, she also wrote *Poetry on the Wind: The Art of Chinese Folding Fans from the Ming and Ch'ing Dynasties* (Honolulu: Honolulu Academy of Arts, 1981), the first thorough English-language analysis of this topic, based on four significant US collections. Once again, Tseng was breaking new ground. This catalogue accompanied an Academy-organized exhibition; after opening in Honolulu, it traveled to St. Louis, Santa Barbara, and Chicago. Tseng resumed exhibiting in Asia with a show at the Taipei Municipal Art Museum in 1983, followed by the *Twentieth Century Chinese Painting* exhibition and symposium in Hong Kong in 1984.

60. Robert W. Bone, "History of Concepts," *Honolulu Advertiser*, February 10, 1972, D-1.

61. Thompson, "Gathering Jade," 226.

62. This award, now in its forty-sixth year, is for "individuals who have demonstrated excellence and high achievement in their particular field of endeavor, and who, through continuous growth, learning, and sharing, have made significant contributions towards enriching our society." It is based on Japan's Living National Treasures (Ningen Kokuho) program. "Living Treasures," Honpa Hongwanji Mission of Hawaii, accessed January 9, 2019, https://hongwanjihawaii.com/living-treasures/.

63. Michael Sullivan, "Introductory Remarks," in *The Art of Tseng Yuho*, by Tseng Yuho and Howard A. Link (Honolulu: Honolulu Academy of Arts, 1987), 6.

64. Sullivan, "Introductory Remarks," 6.

65. Chang Tsong-zung, foreword to *Dsui Hua: Tseng Yuho*, ed. Valerie C. Doran (Taipei: Hanart T. Z. Gallery, 1992), 7.

66. Chang, foreword, 7.

67. Chang Tsong-zung of Hanart Gallery, quoted in Thompson, "Gathering Jade," 255.

68. Kao, "Introductory Remarks," 8. For more information on this period, see Julia F. Andrews and Kuiyi Shen, *The Art of Modern China* (Berkeley: University of California Press, 2012), and Jeffrey Wechsler, ed., *Asian Traditions/Modern Expressions: Asian American Artists and Abstraction, 1945–1970* (New York: Harry N. Abrams and Jane Voorhees Zimmerli Art Museum, 1997).

69. Tseng Yuho, "Notes on My Life and Art," in "By Design: The Art of Tseng Yuho," special issue, *Kaikodo Journal* 16 (May 2000): 20.

70. "Dsui Hua—Tseng Yuho," Asia Art Archive, accessed January 16, 2019, https://aaa.org.hk/en/collection/search/library/dsui-hua-tseng-yuho; Thompson, "Gathering Jade," 196.

71. Tseng, "Dsui Hua," 35.

72. Thompson, "Gathering Jade," 262.

73. In addition to her contributions to the Academy of Arts and the Contemporary Museum, Tseng taught at the University of Hawai'i, donated $600,000 to the university in support of a Chinese teahouse, and was a founding member of the Society of Asian Art of Hawai'i. She was also involved with the University of Hawai'i's Council for Chinese Studies, the East West Center, and the nonprofit Friends of the Library.

Bibliography

Andrews, Julia, and Kuiyi Shen. *The Art of Modern China.* Berkeley: University of California Press, 2012.

Arnason, H. H. *Tseng Yu-Ho: Exhibition of Paintings in Watercolor-Collage.* New York: Downtown Gallery, 1960.

Dsui Hua: Tseng Yuho. Taipei: Hanart T. Z. Gallery, 1992.

Giuffrida, Noelle. *Separating Sheep from Goats: Sherman E. Lee and Chinese Art Collecting in Postwar America.* Oakland: University of California Press, 2018.

Haar, Frances, and Prithwish Neogy. *Artists of Hawaii: Nineteen Painters and Sculptors.* Honolulu: State Foundation of Culture and the Arts, 1974.

Li Chu-tsing. *Trends in Modern Chinese Painting: The C. A. Drenowatz Collection.* Ascona, Switzerland: Artibus Asiae, 1979.

Martin, Michael R. "An Interview with Tseng Yuho." *Orientations* 31, no. 5 (May 2000): 73–78.

Poon, Irene. *Leading the Way: Asian American Artists of the Older Generation.* Wenham, MA: Gordon College, 2001.

Sullivan, Michael. *The Arts of China.* Berkeley: University of California Press, 1984.

———. *The Three Perfections: Chinese Painting, Poetry, and Calligraphy.* New York: George Braziller, 1980.

Thompson, Melissa Jane. "Gathering Jade and Assembling Splendor: The Life and Art of Tseng Yuho." PhD diss., University of Washington, 2001.

Tseng Yuho. "'Abstraction' in the Traditional Art of East Asia." In *Asian Traditions/Modern Expressions: Asian American Artists and Abstraction, 1945–1970*, edited by Jeffery Wechsler, 21–29. New York: Harry N. Abrams and Jane Voorhees Zimmerli Art Museum, 1997.

———. *A History of Chinese Calligraphy.* Hong Kong: Chinese University Press, 1993.

———. "Hsüeh Wu and Her Orchids in the Collection of the Honolulu Academy of Arts." *Arts Asiatiques* 2, no. 3 (1955): 197–208.

———. "Notes on My Life and Art." In By Design: The Art of Tseng Yuho, special issue, *Kaikodo Journal* 16 (May 2000): 9–20.

———. *Some Contemporary Elements in Classical Chinese Art.* Honolulu: University of Hawai'i Press, 1963.

Tseng Yuho and Howard A. Link. *The Art of Tseng Yuho*. Honolulu: Honolulu Academy of Arts, 1987.

Tseng Yu-ho Ecke. *Chinese Folk Art in American Collections, Early 15th through Early 20th Centuries.* New York: China Institute in America, 1976.

———. *Chinese Folk Art II: In American Collections, from Early 15th Century to Early 20th Century.* Honolulu: Hawai'i Lithography/University Press of Hawai'i, 1977.

———. *Poetry on the Wind: The Art of Chinese Folding Fans from the Ming and Ch'ing Dynasties.* Honolulu: Honolulu Academy of Arts, 1981.

———. *Wen-Jen Hua: Chinese Literati Painting from the Collection of Mr. and Mrs. Mitchell Hutchinson.* Honolulu: Honolulu Academy of Arts, 1988.

Wechsler, Jeffrey, ed. *Asian Traditions / Modern Expressions: Asian American Artists and Abstraction, 1945–1970.* New York: H. N. Abrams and Jane Voorhees Zimmerli Art Museum, 1997.

Zeng Youhe. "Chinese Painting Overseas: A Personal Account of Chinese Painters Outside Chinese Society." In *Twentieth-Century Chinese Painting*, edited by Maysching Kao, 224–43. New York: Oxford University Press, 1988.

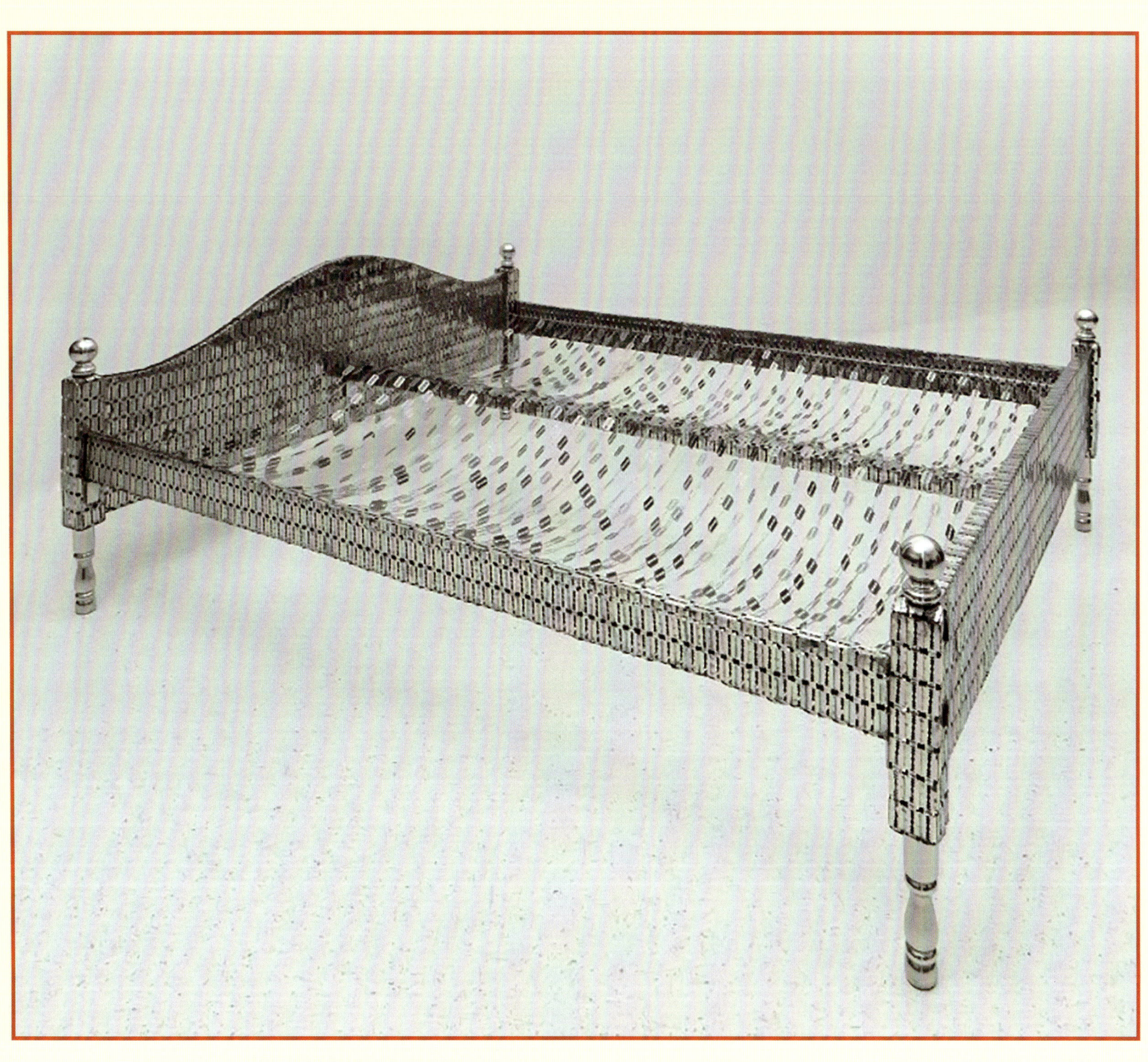

The Razor's Edge

Gender Politics and Structural Violence in the Work of Bangladeshi Artist Tayeba Begum Lipi

Melia Belli Bose

Dappled light winks and dances across the sleek silver surfaces of hundreds of enlaced stainless-steel razor blades. Strung together on delicate chains and molded into streamlined posts, a headboard, and a footboard, the blades articulate a life-size double bed (figs. 11.1, 11.2). This sculpture, *Love Bed*, now in the permanent collection of the Solomon R. Guggenheim Museum, was created in 2012 by Bangladeshi multimedia artist Tayeba Begum Lipi. Characteristic of her work, *Love Bed* and its medium are fraught with convoluted semiotics. The sculpture exposes paradoxes in the lives of rural Bangladeshi women; the bed of razors is seductive and eerily inviting, yet—by virtue of the material's potential to inflict pain and even death—dangerous. Razor blades, like the tiny golden safety pins she also uses in her works, are synecdoches anchored to key events in the artist's early childhood and young adult life. Over the course of more than a decade Lipi has created dozens of sculptures of feminine domestic objects—sewing machines, handbags, high-heeled shoes, bikinis, baby strollers—out of razor blades and safety pins to interrogate issues of gender inequality, agency, marginality, and structural violence that inform the quotidian realities of lower- and middle-class women in her country.

Lipi was born in 1969 to a lower-middle-class Muslim family in rural Gaibandha, northern Bangladesh, the eleventh of twelve children. After receiving her BFA and MFA degrees in drawing and painting from the University of Dhaka, she participated in artists' residencies and exhibited widely throughout Asia, Europe, and the United States. Her creative explorations of what it means to be a woman in a changing Bangladesh and her frank, near confessional artworks have garnered her both international acclaim and censure within her home country. Today Lipi is arguably the best-known living Bangladeshi artist in the global contemporary art world and mentor to younger Bangladeshi artists.

Figure 11.1. (*facing*) *Love Bed* (2012). Stainless steel razor blades, ready-made razor blades, and paper clips, 84 × 60 × 30 in. Image courtesy of the artist.

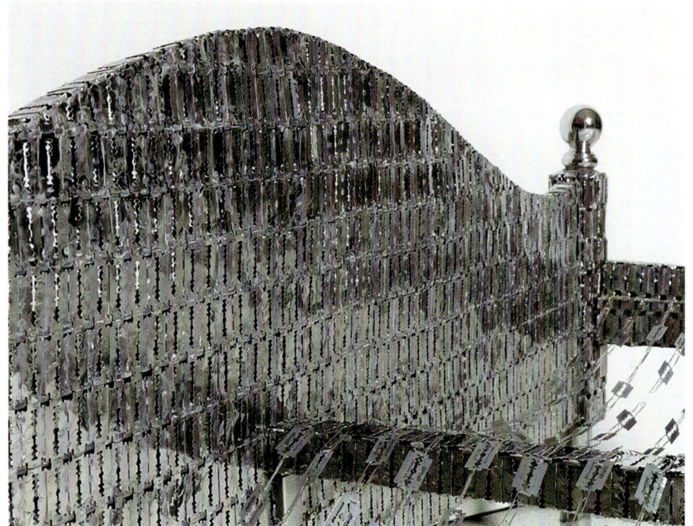

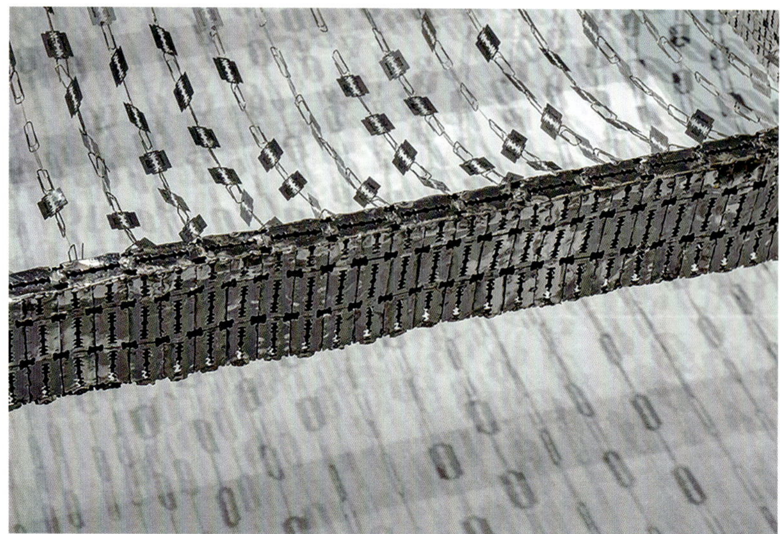

Figure 11.2. *Love Bed* (2012, details). Stainless steel razor blades, ready-made razor blades, and paper clips, 84 × 60 × 30 in. Image courtesy of the artist.

Her professional accolades include participating in numerous international group and solo exhibitions and projects at venues such as Art Basel Hong Kong, India Art Fair, the Dhaka Art Summit, and the Venice Biennale. In 2002, together with her husband, multimedia artist Mahbubur Rahman, Lipi founded Britto International Artists' Workshop, now Britto Arts Trust, the country's first artist-run nonprofit organization. In 2011 Lipi and Rahman established the first Bangladesh National Pavilion at the fifty-fourth Venice Biennale, drawing the contemporary art world's attention to their country for the first time.

Little Learner: A National Identity in Flux

The resolve required to address gender inequality in Bangladesh should not be underestimated; discussions around the body, particularly the female body, its physiology, and abuses against it are highly taboo in the country. The few women artists whose work directly engages with the female body and gendered violence are, like Lipi, routinely subjected to public rebuke and have had their exhibitions closed due to perceived threats to morality. (Two other prominent Bangladeshi women artists who confront these issues are Dilara Begum Jolly and Nazia Preema Andaleeb.[1]) In Bangladesh, notions of morality (Bangla: *lojja*, literally "shame," a term with positive associations) are formulated through the matrix of Islam.

Now divided between India and Bangladesh—yet united through a shared history and language—the region of Bengal has a long history of (largely) religious pluralism and interfaith syncretism, which is a source of pride among progressive liberal Bengalis in both nations. Although Bangladesh possesses an overwhelmingly Muslim majority population, it was founded as a secular state, as promulgated by the 1972 constitution. By the late 1970s, however, Islam was increasingly tethered to politics and widely promoted as inextricable from Bangladeshi nationalism. In 1977, references to freedom of religion were expunged from the constitution, while references to God and Islam were added. In

1988, the military dictator Muhammad Ershad declared Islam the official state religion. Although the supreme court restored the precept of secularism to the constitution in 2010, Islam remains the official state religion.[2] The waxing and waning of secularism has grave effects on religious and social minorities and remains the most definitive source of tension in Bangladeshi politics. Stakes have become exponentially higher with the growing presence of radical Islamist organizations such as the Islamic State and the local Jamaat-ul Mujahideen, which have led deadly terrorist attacks in Dhaka and other urban centers in recent years. Their targets were non-Muslims, liberal Muslims, LGBTQ rights activists, and atheist writers and bloggers, as well as nongovernmental organizations (NGOs) dedicated to family planning, women's education, and women's financial independence.[3] The majority of the country's intellectuals and artists fall into the category of liberal Muslims, making them particularly vulnerable to extremists' attention. In fact, Lipi and other artists routinely receive death threats due to the provocative content of their work.[4]

Concomitantly, over the past two decades Bangladesh has experienced greater exposure to cultural influence from Western nations through its central role in the global garment industry; the wide availability of foreign consumer goods, media, and entertainment; and the vast number of Bangladeshis traveling and migrating abroad. As I have argued elsewhere, these two disparate strands—Islamist and global secular—are colliding in contemporary Bangladesh. Artists such as Jolly, Andaleeb, and Lipi creatively examine the complexities of identity positioned at this (sometimes) uneasy intersection.[5]

In Lipi's *Little Learner* (2008), a minute-long single-channel video with sound, the artist sits across a table from herself (fig. 11.3). One of the Lipis wears a short-sleeve, knee-length red dress, her hair in a chin-length bob. In a young girl's voice, she haltingly reads aloud from a book of children's nursery rhymes in Bangla. Swathed in a shawl

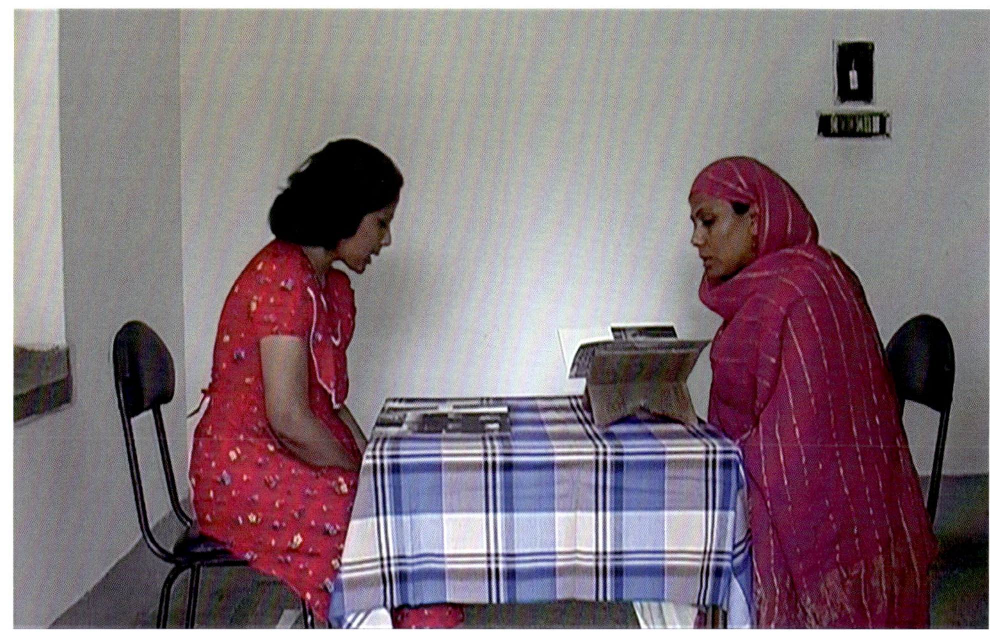

Figure 11.3. *Little Learner* (2008). Single-channel video with sound, 1:26 min. Image courtesy of the artist.

covering her head and torso, the other Lipi "reads" in Arabic from the open Koran on the stand before her in the same staccato voice. In the droning cacophony of voices only a few words are intelligible from either language. Drawn from Lipi's experience of learning to "read" the two languages as a child, this is a scenario that doubtlessly resonates with many Muslims for whom Arabic is not their mother tongue. As children, millions of non-Arabic-speaking Muslims throughout the world are taught to "read" the Koran in the sacred Islamic language of Arabic phonetically as a ritual act. As the language (and in cases like Bangla, the script) is different from their first language, often these "little learners" do not understand the semantic content of the text. The video should also be understood in the context of Bangladeshi education, in which there are two divergent streams: public or private secular schools and *mādrāsās* (Islamic religious schools). Graduates from the two streams only come together in college, where cultural antagonists frequently clash, at times with violent consequences.[6]

The veiled Lipi in the video reflects the sweeping increase in the practice of wearing the veil throughout the country. Historian of modern South Asia Willem van Schendel opines that the rising popularity of veiling in Bangladesh signals a "public adherence to the new, self-assured face of Bangladeshi Islam."[7] As with the several other artworks in which Lipi appears as contrasting cultural topoi, different possibilities of what she could be, many Bangladeshi women viewers of *Little Learner* doubtlessly identify with the two manifestations: one signifying in the Bangladeshi context global secular culture, the other Muslim.[8] Of course these two identities are not necessarily mutually exclusive, and millions of Bangladeshis within the country and abroad comfortably integrate the two strands of their identity on a daily basis. However, through her dueling droning voices, in *Little Learner* Lipi implies that they do not always comfortably coexist, fomenting what Van Schendel terms "the Bangladesh culture wars."[9]

A Silenced History of Sexual Violence

Straddling South and Southeast Asia, Bangladesh is, after East Timor, Asia's youngest country. It has undergone near constant cultural and political flux since its two independences: the first from Britain in 1947, after which it became East Pakistan, and then from Pakistan in 1971. Both partitions unfolded against a backdrop of acute violence, including sexual violence against women. Up to one million people were killed in riots and mass migrations in 1946 and 1947. Tens of thousands of families were rent apart, homes were burned down, and villages were abandoned as their former inhabitants relocated to refugee camps. In the melee an estimated seventy-five thousand women were raped, abducted, and forcibly impregnated, while countless women committed suicide to avoid such a fate and the associated stigma.[10]

The atrocities of 1947 were matched by those of the 1971 Bangladesh War of Independence, at which time Lipi was two years old. With the public sanction of influential

Muslim religious figures, Pakistani soldiers and their Bengali collaborators systematically raped and tortured between 200,000 and 400,000 East Pakistani women and girls.[11] The rapes resulted in the births of thousands of "war babies" and the ostracism (and, in many cases, suicide) of the victims, known as *Birangonas* (war heroines).[12] The magnitude of sexual violence that transpired during both partitions remains highly taboo, a national embarrassment to India, Pakistan, and Bangladesh that is seldom addressed. While on a greatly reduced scale, and far less organized, instances of structural and sexual violence against women remain commonplace throughout the subcontinent today.

Although the two are frequently imbricated, as psychologist and scholar of violence Bandy X. Lee indicates, structural violence is distinct from behavioral violence. Lee defines the former as "the avoidable limitations society places on groups of people that constrain them from achieving the quality of life that would have otherwise been possible. . . . The harm is *structural* because it is a product of the way we have organized our social world; it is *violent* because it causes injury and death."[13] Lee identifies such limitations as (but not confined to) economic, political, cultural, religious, and legal, with origins in institutions and systems that wield authority over vulnerable members of society. Akin to yet differing subtly from oppression and social injustice, structural violence may be so entrenched in a society that it becomes nearly invisible, making it all the more challenging to identify and correct. Members of a society are frequently habituated to structural violence and accept manifestations of it as unavoidable trials to be endured over the course of their own or others' lifetimes. Germane to an analysis of Lipi's art, Lee notes that structural violence frequently manifests in gender disparities, such as imbalances in education, health care, and nutrition.[14]

Other scholars explicitly identify gender-based violence, including sexual harassment—an abiding trope in Lipi's art—as a ubiquitous form of structural violence, as gender disparities are interwoven into the structural fabric of society.[15] Innumerable women and girls throughout South Asia are subjected to sexual harassment on a daily basis, with one of the most persistent forms being groping. In a survey conducted by the NGO ActionAid UK in Bangladesh, 84 percent of respondents reported having experienced sexual harassment in public (including lewd comments, advances, and being groped).[16] Rachel Jewkes, director of the UK-based NGO What Works to Prevent Violence against Women and Girls, notes that in South Asia, "gender inequality is so marked. . . . The problem of entitlement is firmly articulated by society. There is massive male sexual entitlement. . . . Public spaces are run by men. They perceive an ownership of all public places.[17] Jewkes avows that entrenched social norms embolden men to harass women, often in plain sight. As a corollary, when even public spaces are deemed unsafe, families sequester their women and girls at home, denying them education and negatively impacting their mental and physical health.[18]

Love Bed: Imbrications of Domesticity and Structural Violence

Love Bed and Lipi's other razor-blade sculptures speak directly to such practices of female sequestration and other forms of structural violence. One of the artist's earliest memories is, as a five-year-old, secretly witnessing her sister-in-law giving birth. The family lived far from a hospital and road conditions were poor, so a midwife was called to the home to perform all the family's deliveries. The sight of a stainless-steel razor blade being boiled in water and then used to sever the umbilical cord remains inscribed on Lipi's mind.[19] The incident recalls Freud's concept of the primal scene, but in this case, rather than witnessing her parents having intercourse, the artist observes the result of the act and consequently comprehends her own entry into the world. *Love Bed*'s shimmering razor-blade chains represent generations of mothers who give birth in their marital beds.

Freud described the uncanny as "that class of the terrifying which leads back to something long known to us, once very familiar."[20] Children often regard their parents' bed as a familiar refuge. However, *Love Bed*'s medium uncannily displaces the parental bed as a haven, highlighting that for rural Bangladeshi women the same bed that is a site of domesticity, intimacy, and comfort is also a locus of contestation, fraught with danger and structural violence.

The scene Lipi witnessed as a young girl is far from exceptional in rural Bangladesh, where, according to a 2016 study, 62 percent of births occur at home and 56 percent are performed by midwives or relatives rather than medical professionals. Deliveries are often conducted in unsterile conditions, greatly increasing the risk of child and maternal morbidity and mortality. (In 2010 national maternal mortality rates were reported as 194 per 100,000 live births.)[21]

Several factors account for the prevalence of home births, chief among them being the prohibitive cost of a hospital delivery. Socioreligious ideologies also contribute: delivering outside of the home is widely held to bring dishonor to both a woman and her marital family. Particularly in rural areas, where a woman's modesty is a source of cultural capital (both her own and that of her family), women are encouraged to participate in the Muslim cultural practice of "keeping purdah." Literally meaning "curtain," *purdah* refers to female sequestration within the home, or, on leaving the home, being entirely covered and shielded from the gaze of unknown men. As there are comparatively few female gynecologists in rural Bangladesh, it is likely that a hospital birth would necessitate a male doctor's seeing the mother's vagina, which for many women and their families would compromise their *lojja* and their family's status. Another deterrent of hospitals is the possibility of a cesarean delivery, which is widely held to be "unnatural" and thus disreputable.[22] The majority of rural Bangladeshi women are uninformed of the risks of home births performed by midwives with no medical training. (The literacy rate in Bangladesh is 62 percent, and in rural areas the gap between male and female literacy is 12 percent, making it more challenging for women to obtain medical information.[23]) Women who receive an education are more likely to elect to deliver in a hospital. However, irrespective of finances, for many women the decision is not theirs to make. In the joint-family household, which is the most common living arrangement in rural parts of the country, elder men are the primary decision makers, and women have little agency in decisions of where or by whom their deliveries are performed.[24]

Lipi's "Other Room": A Locus of Loss

The Dhaka Art Summit, held biannually in the capital, is one of the largest art festivals in Asia. For the 2014 summit (which attracted nearly seventy thousand visitors from Bangladesh and abroad) Lipi created the installation *A Room of My Own* (2014). In the center of the gallery, situated atop a platform and flooded by unfiltered light, Plasticine molds of the artist's hands reached for a collection of tampons and forceps in a glass tray (fig. 11.4). The walls were hung with ultrasound printouts in frames of enlaced razor blades (fig. 11.5), black-and-white photographs of the artist's face twisted in pain (fig. 11.6), a bulging pregnant midsection composed of outlines of sanitary pads each articulated by chains of golden safety pins (fig. 11.7), and vitrines filled with baby clothes (figs. 11.8a, 11.8b). An empty razor-blade stroller was parked in a corner (fig. 11.9). Although it was not displayed at the summit that year, *My Daughter's Cot* (2012), an empty baby crib made of razor blades, is part of the same, unnamed series (fig. 11.10).

A Room of My Own documented a devastating, intensely personal occurrence—the artist's late-term miscarriage of her only child, which had nearly killed her two years earlier. Over the course of several days in a government hospital, Lipi was treated for infection and severe blood loss (tampons and sanitary pads were used to absorb the blood). The photographs are self-portraits she took during the ordeal. The unworn baby clothes, including bibs bearing the phrases "Mommy loves me" and "Daddy loves me," were gifts the expectant parents received at a shower only days before the miscarriage.

Particularly when considered in light of the artist's own observation of the primal scene, the title and expository nature of *A Room of My Own* evoke what psychoanalyst Ronald Britton terms "the other room." Britton describes the concept as "the setting for the invisible primal scene of infancy"; it is a liminal, mental site of both imagination and (as the parental bedroom) a site of memory.[25] Lipi's "other room" is a site of trauma and wonder, which decades later also became a locus of loss and physical pain. As art therapists have identified, for artists, "the other room" is a "domain of contemplation," a creative mental space where the artist negotiates their relationship with their potential artwork.[26] Lipi mined her "other room" to create her controversial *A Room of My Own*.

Miscarriage (both natural and induced) is a marginalized artistic subject worldwide—Frida Kahlo, Tracey Emin, and Tabitha Moses are among the few to address their own experiences of their losses in their art. Regardless of how much each artist wanted the babies they were carrying (or not, in Emin's case) and how much physical and emotional pain they suffered, I would argue that as a Mexican woman and British women, respectively, somewhat less was at stake in their cases (at least socially) than for Lipi.

Throughout South Asia one of the first questions routinely posed to a woman is how many children does she have. Particularly in rural areas, childless women are subjected to intense scrutiny and distrust. The condition is not only widely regarded as a tragedy

Figure 11.4. *A Room of My Own* installation, Dhaka Art Summit, 2014, at the National Gallery, Bangladesh. Image courtesy of the artist.

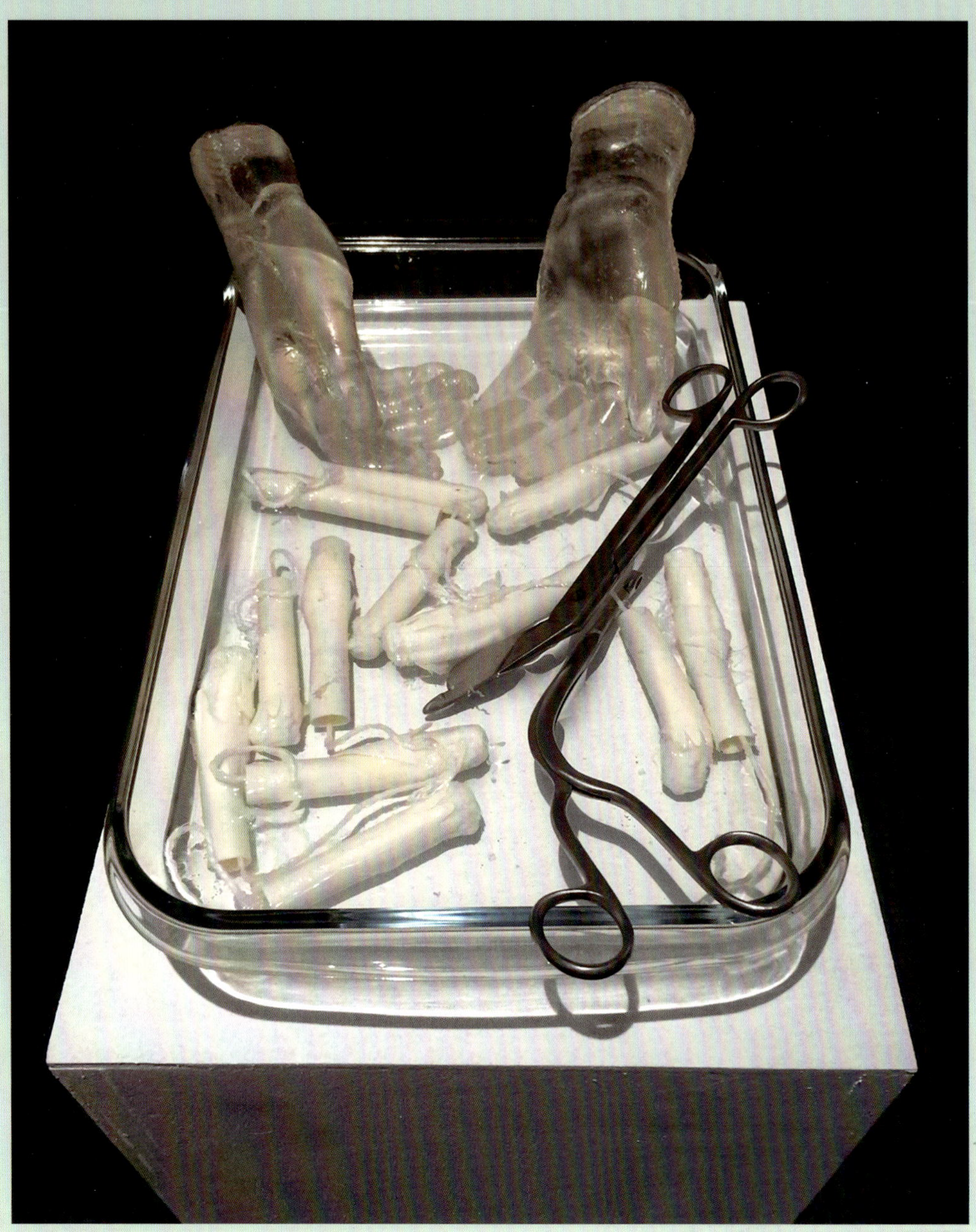

Figure 11.5. Printouts of the artist's ultrasound, razor blades (part of the solo exhibition *A Room of My Own*, Dhaka Art Summit 2014, at the National Gallery, Bangladesh). Image courtesy of the artist.

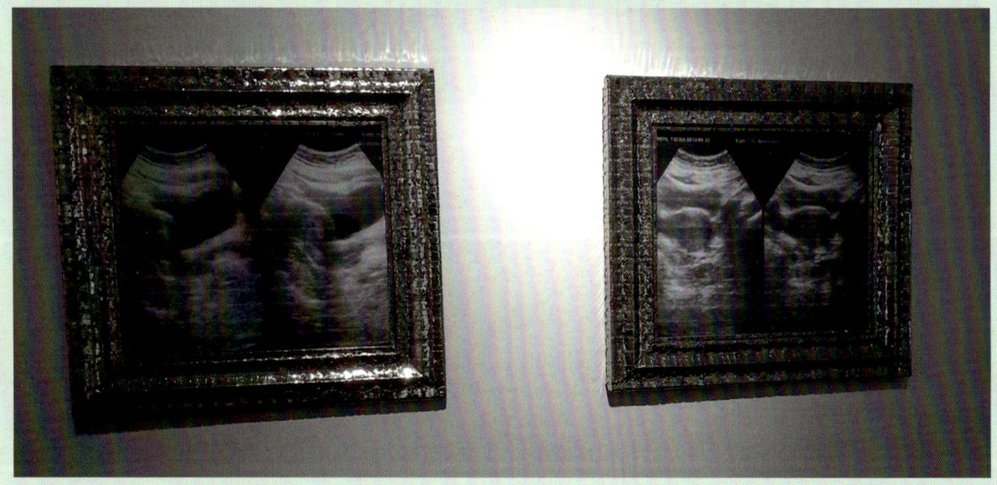

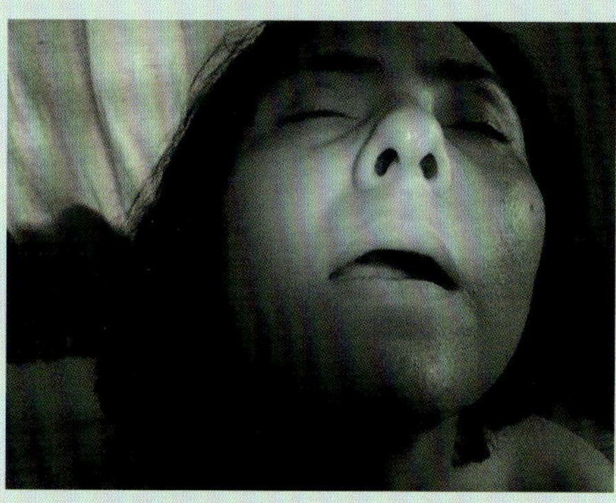

Figure 11.6. Self-portrait photograph the artist took from around the time of her miscarriage (part of the solo exhibition *A Room of My Own*, Dhaka Art Summit, 2014, at the National Gallery, Bangladesh). Photograph by Mahbubur Rahman. Image courtesy of the artist.

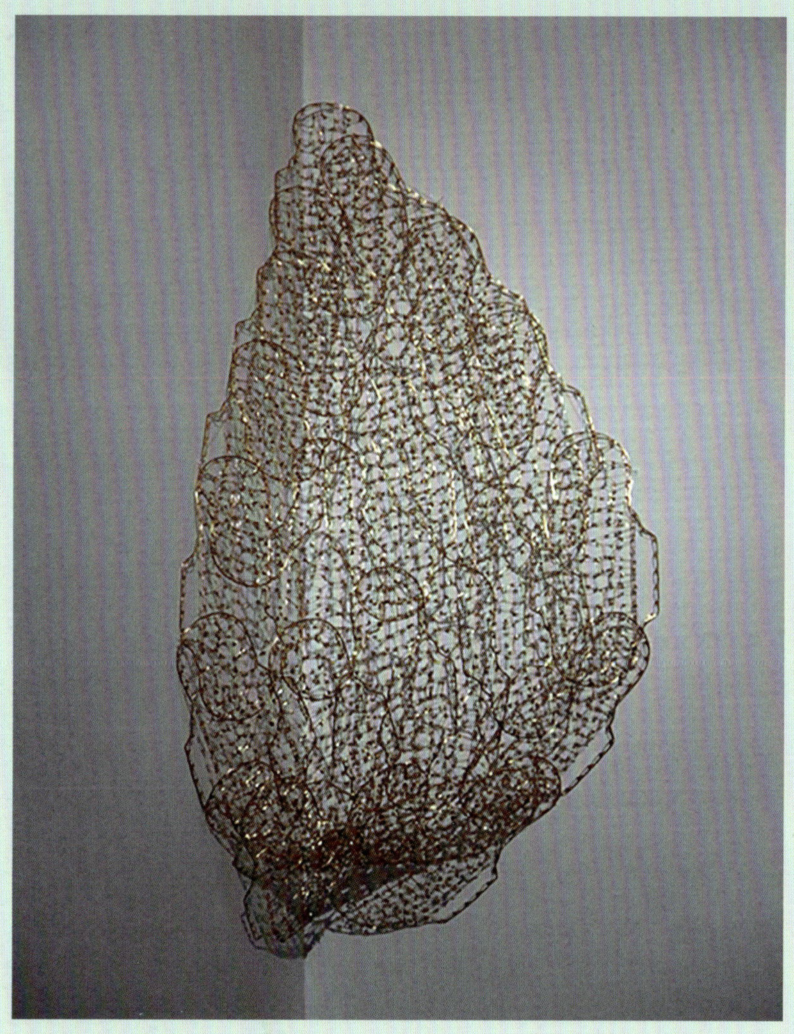

Figure 11.7. Site-specific installation sculpture, safety pins. Approx. 3 × 2 ft. (part of the solo exhibition *A Room of My Own*, Dhaka Art Summit 2014, at the National Gallery, Bangladesh). Image courtesy of the artist.

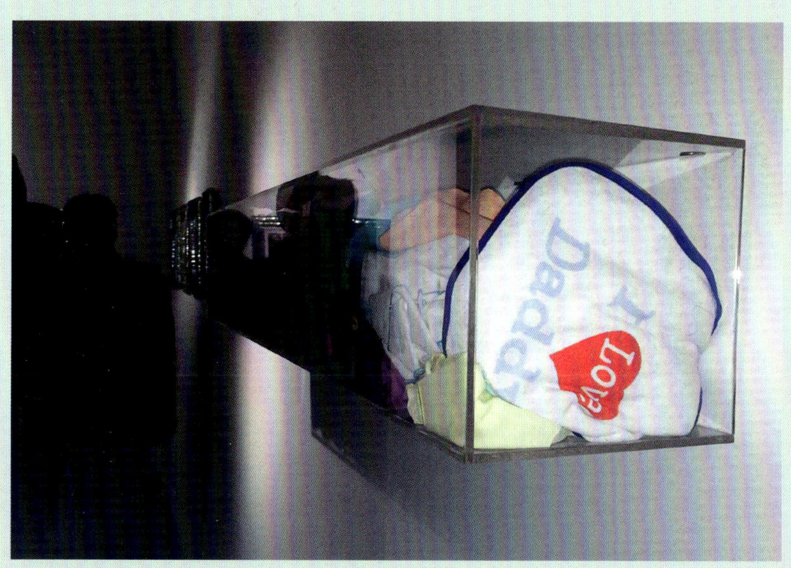

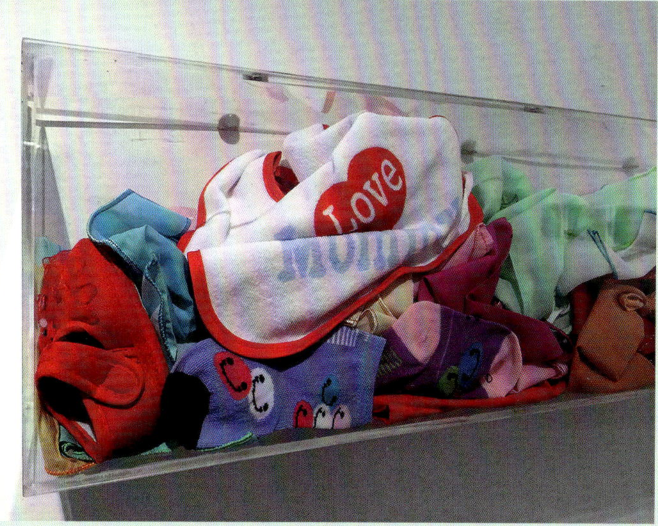

Figure 11.8. Plastic vitrine filled with unworn baby clothes (part of the solo exhibition *A Room of My Own*, Dhaka Art Summit, 2014, at the National Gallery, Bangladesh). Image courtesy of the artist.

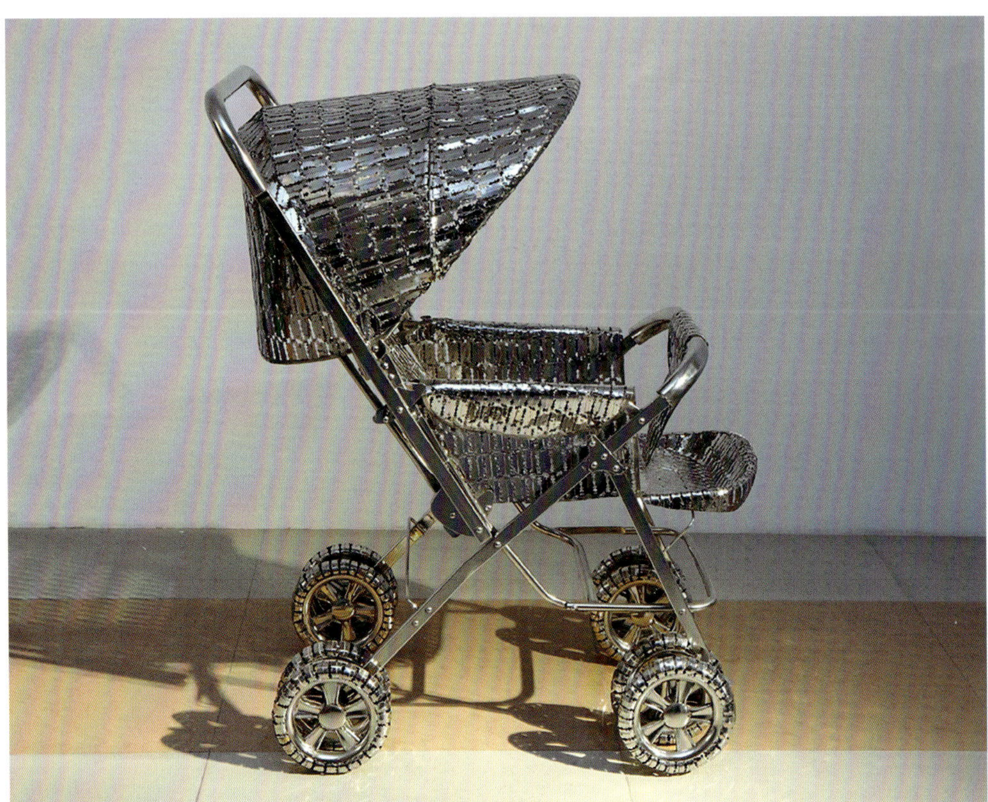

Figure 11.9. *The Stolen Dream* (2013). Stainless steel, razor blades, approx. 27 × 20 × 37 in. Image courtesy of the artist.

for a couple, but it also brings social stigma to the wife, who shoulders the brunt of the blame. In many rural Bangladeshi villages childless women are ostracized as they are popularly believed to bring ill luck. "Even a fox or a dog does not eat the dead body of a childless woman" is an oft-quoted proverb in Bangladeshi villages, which Lipi likely heard as a child.[27] In a country where, for most women, fertility is one of the only paths to symbolic capital, the concept of voluntary childlessness is incomprehensible to many. Pierre Bourdieu describes symbolic capital as "accumulated prestige"and "the acquisition of a reputation for competence and an image of respectability and honorability."[28] Motherhood is widely held to be a woman's duty to her marital family, and a mother (especially of sons) gains immense symbolic capital. The empty baby stroller and self-portraits are a public admission of the agony the artist endured, as well as a frank acknowledgment of what many Bangladeshis would consider her diminished symbolic capital.

With *A Room of My Own* Lipi brought one other gendered taboo subject into the spotlight: the tampons and sanitary pads are indexes of menstruation. Throughout South Asia menstrual blood is popularly held to be "unclean" and "polluting," and women are widely regarded as "impure" or *sharīr kharāp* (Bangla: "sick") during menstruation. Menstruating women are frequently excluded from praying, engaging in sexual intercourse, performing household tasks, and participating in community activities, and are denied protein-rich and other nutritious foods.[29] For Lipi to visually announce her miscarriage and acknowledge the index of female fertility (menstruation) in such a public venue as the Dhaka Art Summit demonstrates exceptional fortitude and audacity.

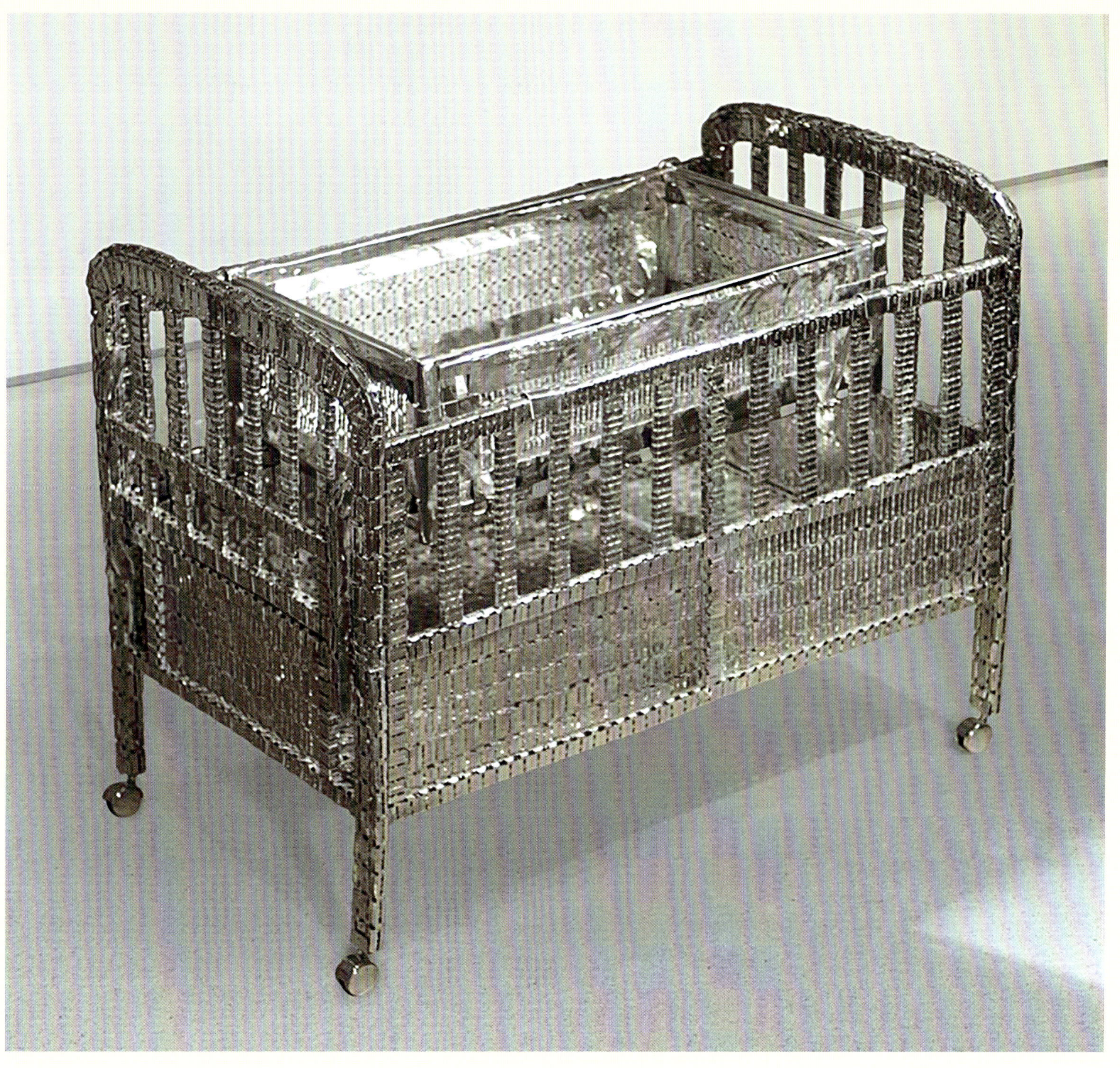

Figure 11.10. *My Daughter's Cot* (2012).
Stainless steel, razor blades, 40 × 28 × 48 in.
Image courtesy of the artist.

Comfy Bikinis: Agency and Armor in Urban Space

Lipi's installation sculpture *Comfy Bikinis* (2012) is composed of four delicate, lacelike bikinis fashioned from tiny polished golden safety pins that flicker and reflect the light as they dangle from hangers (fig. 11.11). Contrary to the associations of carefree youth and leisure most commonly assigned to bikinis, *Comfy Bikinis*, like many of the artist's works, offers an uncanny, dark social commentary through its medium. Reminiscent of Freud's notion of condensation, whereby accretions of unrelated (often threatening) concepts or experiences are signified through the same connotative sign in dreams, in Lipi's sculptures safety pins condense domesticity, sexual violence, and the possibility of women's retaliatory agency.[30]

Dhaka, the Bangladeshi capital, is one of the most densely populated cities in the world. While in rural areas sexual violence is predominantly confined to the domestic sphere, in cities throughout the subcontinent sexual predators routinely take advantage of the anonymity afforded by the tangle of limbs and lack of visibility in overcrowded buses, bazaars, and streets to grope, fondle, and even violently pinch the breasts and

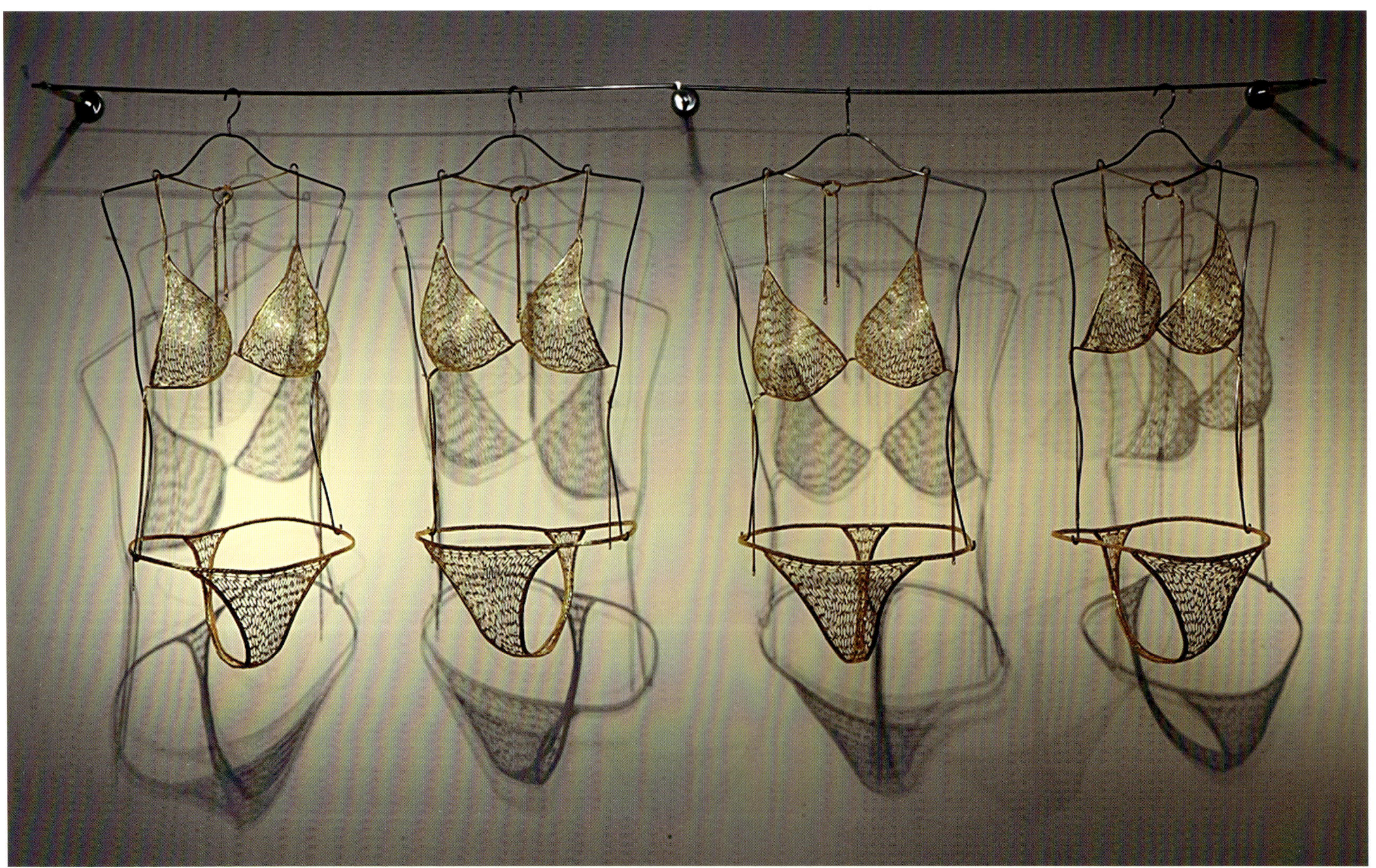

Figure 11.11. *Comfy Bikinis* (2013). Brass safety pins covered with electroless nickel, immersion gold, approx. 13 × 35 × 48 in. Image courtesy of the artist.

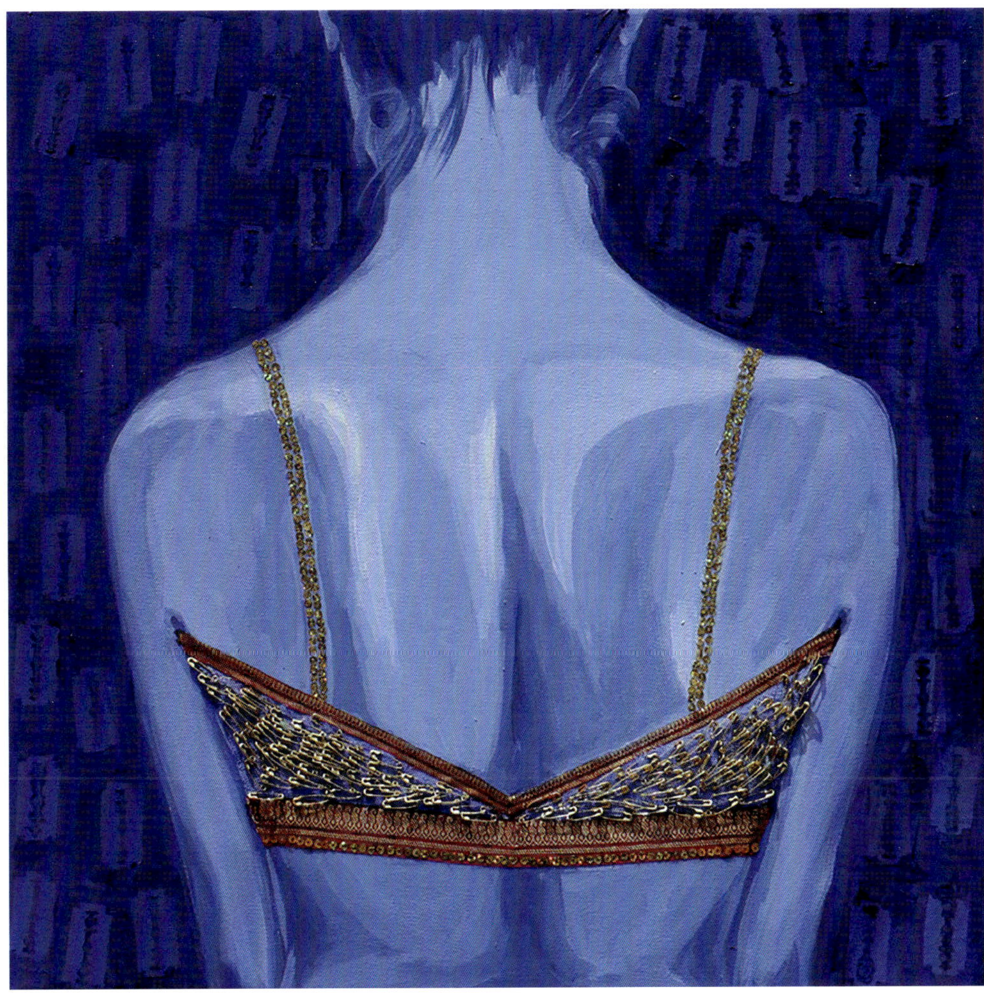

Figure 11.12. *Commodity 1* (2010). Acrylic, sequins, safety pins on canvas, approx. 19 × 19 in. Image courtesy of the artist.

buttocks of unknown women. Such behavior is particularly rampant in buses; according to ActionAid UK, half the women that researchers surveyed in Bangladesh reported being regularly groped in buses.[31]

At age nineteen Lipi moved across the country to pursue her studies in Dhaka, where she too was introduced to this manifestation of structural violence. As with other forms of structural violence and issues pertaining to the female body, public groping is a largely unacknowledged taboo subject. With no alternative means to reach work or school, women are compelled to endure this almost inevitable violation on a daily basis. Their only recourse is to arm themselves with safety pins and stab the disembodied wandering hands that assault them during the ride. The sexually harassed passengers' choice of defensive weapon is significant: safety pins are the most ubiquitous item in a Bangladeshi woman's toilet (several are required to fasten the folds of a sari, the most common garment for married and professional women).

Lipi juxtaposes razor blades and safety pins—the two synecdochical signs associated with the artist's own experiences of gendered structural violence in her art—in individual pieces from her multimedia series *Commodity* (2010). *Commodity 1* combines acrylic paint, sequins, and safety pins on canvas to articulate a slender young woman's back clad in a "comfy bikini" safety-pin top against a deluge of straight razors (fig. 11.12).

Commodity 3 offers the midsection of a young woman, wearing "comfy bikini" bottoms, against a hot-red background swirling with sperm (fig. 11.13), emphasizing the commodification of young women's bodies as objects of sexual desire available to be touched without invitation and for reproduction. Like *Love Bed*, *Comfy Bikinis* and works from the *Commodity* series entwine domesticity and structural violence in a tangled matrix of paradoxes. In Lipi's safety-pin artworks the softest and most intimate parts of the female body, associated directly with reproductivity, are enveloped in cold, sharp chain mail—the units of which are repurposed from the domestic to the defensive—to provide the requisite gendered armor for urban living in Dhaka.

Conclusion

For nearly a decade Lipi has used her art to expose persistent yet unaddressed manifestations of structural violence in her country. In her sculptures razor blades and safety pins are synecdoches connoting structural harm in the form of marginality, danger, physical pain, and assault against women. Lipi harvests her own experiences of witnessing and experiencing structural violence, but these experiences also certainly resonate with women across the Indian subcontinent and beyond.

Perhaps the greatest challenge to overturning systems of structural violence is identifying their origins and perpetrators, because, as Lee asserts, "structural violence is subtle, invisible, and accepted as a matter of course; even more difficult than detecting this type of violence is assigning culpability, for the actors are often difficult to identify."[32] By drawing attention to unnecessarily dangerous and painful deliveries, her own miscarriage, and the public groping she endured as a student (all taboo subjects, the acknowledgment of which many Bangladeshis would consider compromising to a woman's *lojja*), Lipi takes nascent yet significant steps to bring to light practices that cause physical and mental harm to women. She transforms the "subtle, invisible, and accepted as a matter of course" into life-size works of art whose delicate, light-reflective media attract the eye and provoke questions of their signification. In taking great risk by publicly acknowledging her experiences, particularly at such prestigious venues as the Dhaka Art Summit and the Guggenheim, the artist frankly gives form to these unspoken abuses, enabling them to be spoken of and ultimately (hopefully) corrected.

Acknowledgments

I am grateful to the American Institute of Bangladesh Studies and the Asian Cultural Council for supporting my research in Bangladesh in 2015. I am also indebted to Mustaque Ahmad for his support and hospitality in Dhaka. Most of all, I wish to thank Tayeba Begum Lipi and Mahbubur Rahman for sharing their art and discussing it with me over many hours.

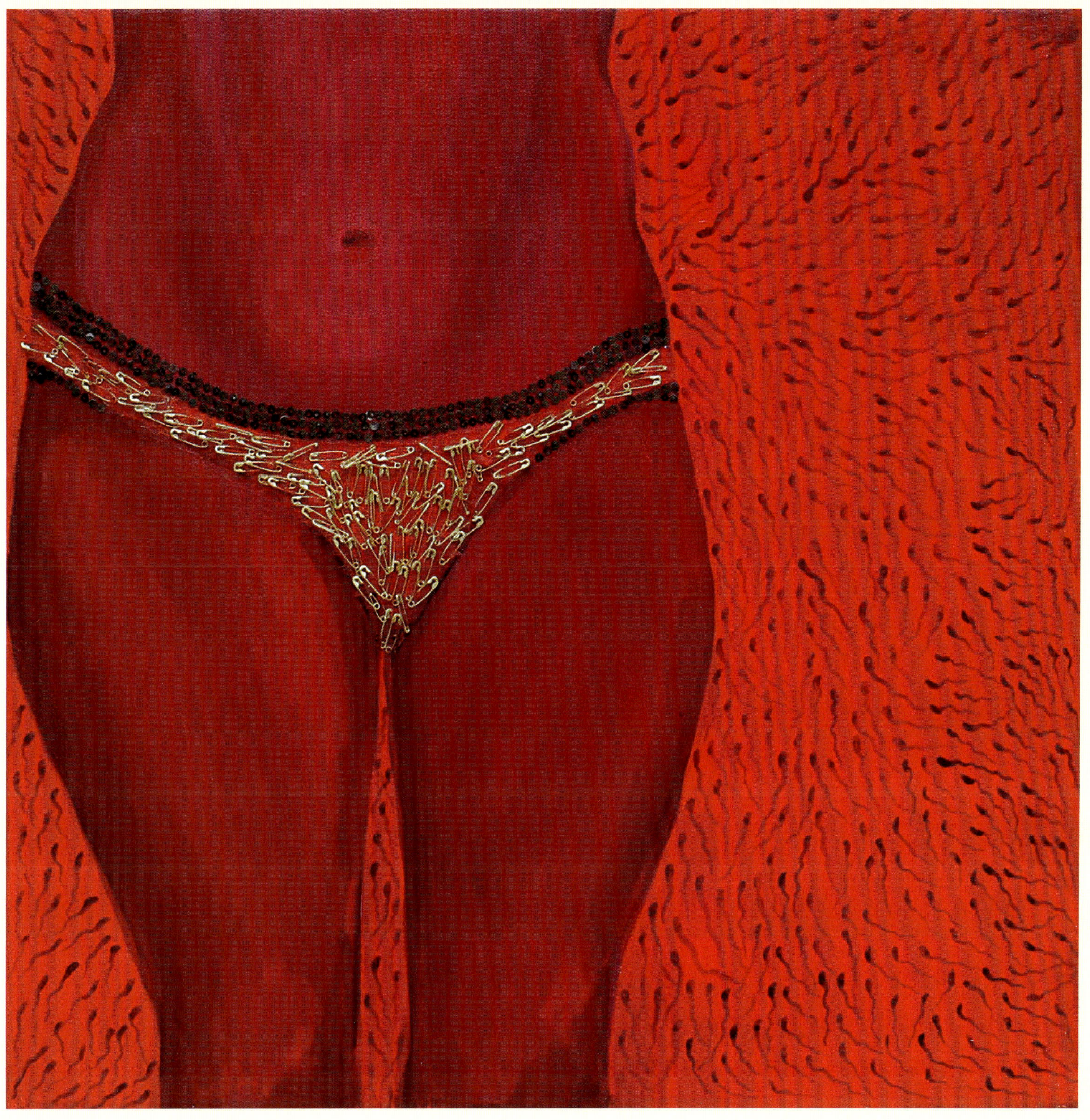

Figure 11.13. *Commodity 3* (2010). Acrylic, sequins, safety pins on canvas, approx. 19 × 19 in. Image courtesy of the artist.

Notes

1. For more on Jolly and Andaleeb's engagements with gender, the body, and sexual violence, see Melia Belli Bose, "Entangled Tensions: Bangladeshi Women Artists," *ArtAsiaPacific* 96 (November/December 2015): 88–95.

2. For a greater explication of the vicissitudes of secularism and democracy in the country, see Willem van Schendel, *A History of Bangladesh* (Cambridge: Cambridge University Press, 2009), 193–219, 251–68.

3. The devastating attack on an upscale Dhaka restaurant in which twenty-nine people were killed in 2016 is the best-known incident. Anbarasan Ethirajan, "Bangladesh Siege: Country at a Crossroads as Violence Hits Dhaka," *BBC News*, July 2, 2016, http://www.bbc.com/news/world-asia-36692741. Another internationally covered attack was the 2015 public slaying of Avijit Roy, an American Bangladeshi intellectual and atheist blogger. Roy was hacked to death with machetes at a book fair in Dhaka. Julfikar Ali Manik and Nida Najarfeb, "Avijit Roy, Bangladeshi-American Writer, Is Killed by Machete-Wielding Assailants," *New York Times*, February 27, 2015, https://www.nytimes.com/2015/02/28/world/asia/bangladeshi-american-blogger-avijit-roy-killed.html.

4. Personal communication with Tayeba Begum Lipi.

5. Belli Bose, "Entangled Tensions." See also Van Schendel, *History of Bangladesh*, 261–63.

6. In the 1990s faculty and students were killed in bloody fights between *mādrāsa*-educated Islamist and secularist student groups at several Bangladeshi universities (Van Schendel, *History of Bangladesh*, 260–63).

7. Van Schendel, *History of Bangladesh*, 255. For more on the recent increase in veiling in Bangladesh, see Shelly Feldman, "Exploring Theories of Patriarchy: A Perspective from Contemporary Bangladesh," in "Globalization and Gender," special issue, *Signs* 26, no. 4 (Summer 2001): 112–14; and Santi Rozario, "The New Burqa in Bangladesh: Empowerment or Violation of Women's Rights?" *Women's Studies International Forum* 29 (2006): 368–80. Both contend that veiling offers women the opportunity to engage with the public outside of the home while adhering to the Islamic social custom of *purdah* (female sequestration), thereby preserving their *lojja*. The increase in veiling is concomitant with the rise of women in the workforce, particularly in the garment industry, and entering into higher education.

8. There are numerous examples of women's garments that signify the wearer's Muslim identity; what Lipi wears in *Little Learner* is only one. Covering the head as she does in the video or wearing a *hijab* (headscarf) became increasingly popular in Bangladesh—as elsewhere in the Islamic world—after 9/11. Other forms of Islamic fashion, including *jilbābs* (body-covering gowns) and *niqabs* ("masks," or face coverings), have also been enjoying greater popularity in Bangladesh over the past decade. However, for much of the region's history both Hindu and Muslim women wore saris with their heads uncovered. Again, as elsewhere in the Islamic world, in Bangladesh covering the head is the most recognizable and popular way for women to become what anthropologist Emma Tarlo terms "visibly Muslim." Emma Tarlo, *Visibly Muslim: Fashion, Politics, Faith* (London: Bloomsbury Academic, 2010). See also Van Schendel, *History of Bangladesh*, 254–55, for a discussion on the recent rise in popularity of men's and women's Islamic fashion in the country.

9. Van Schendel, 261–63.

10. Urvashi Butalia, *The Other Side of Silence: Voices from the Partition of India* (Durham, NC: Duke University Press, 2000), 85–105; Barbara D. Metcalf and Thomas R. Metcalf, "The 1940s: Triumph and Tragedy," in *A Concise History of Modern India* (Cambridge: Cambridge University Press, 2011), 203–31. For a discussion of communal rape as an expression of patriarchal dominance over "the Other's woman" and constructions of modesty, see Kumar Jayawardena and Malathi De Alwis, *Embodied Violence: Communalizing Women's Sexuality in South Asia* (London: Zed Books, 1996), xvii.

11. Among others, see Bina D'Acosta, *Nationbuilding, Gender and War Crimes in South Asia* (London: Routledge, 2010), 108.

12. The honorific term *Birangona* has been controversial since Sheikh Mujibur Rahman, Bangladesh's first president, coined it to refer to the war rape victims. Several women's rights activists prefer *Mukti Bahini* ("Freedom Fighter"). *Birangona*s inhabit a liminal space in the nation's history. There have been multiple efforts to valorize and reintegrate them into society. However, numerous such women who were socially ostracized and disowned by their families have yet to be reunited with them. For many Bangladeshis, the *Birangona*s remain a taboo subject. For more on the sexual violence of the 1971 Liberation War and ongoing regard for its female victims, see Nayanika Mookherjee, *The Spectral Wound: Sexual Violence, Public Memories, and the Bangladesh War of 1971* (Durham, NC: Duke University Press, 2015).

13. Bandy X. Lee, "Causes and Cures VII: Structural Violence," *Aggression and Violent Behavior* 28 (2016): 110.

14. Lee, "Causes and Cures VII," 109–12.

15. See, for example, Joia S. Mukherjee et al., "Structural Violence: A Barrier to Achieving the Millennium Development Goals for Women," *Journal of Women's Health* 20, no. 4 (2011): 593.

16. Meera Senthilingam, "Sexual Harassment: How It Stands around the Globe," *CNN*, November 29, 2017, https://www.cnn.com/2017/11/25/health/sexual-harassment-violence-abuse-global-levels/index.html.

17. Senthilingam, "Sexual Harassment."

18. Senthilingam, "Sexual Harassment." See also Mukherjee et al., "Structural Violence."

19. Personal communication with Tayeba Begum Lipi. Lipi's sister-in-law was fortunate that her midwife used a sterile razor blade. Uninformed midwives frequently employ unsterilized household items to cut the cord, including scissors, shards of glass, kitchen instruments, bamboo strips, and stones, greatly increasing the risk of infection. Johanna Andrews and Koustuv Dalal, "Umbilical Cord–Cutting Practices and Place of Delivery in Bangladesh," *International Journal of Gynaecology and Obstetrics: The Official Organ of the International Federation of Gynaecology and Obstetrics* 114, no. 1 (July 2011): 43.

20. Bidhan Krishna Sarker et al., "Reasons for Preference of Home Delivery with Traditional Birth Attendants (TBAs) in Rural Bangladesh: A Qualitative Exploration," *PLOS ONE* 11, no. 1 (January 2016): e0146161; Ronald Britton, "Reality and Unreality in Phantasy and Fiction," in Ethel Spector Pearson, Peter Fonagy, and Sérvulo Augusto Figueira, eds., *On Freud's Creative Writers and Day-Dreaming* (New Haven, CT: Yale University Press, 1995), 19; Ronald Britton, *Sex, Death, and the Superego* (London: Karnac, 2003), 83.

21. Sarker et al., "Reasons for Preference of Home Delivery." https://doi.org/10.1371/journal.pone.0146161. As a comparison, according to the World Health Organization, in 2013 rates of maternal morbidity were 28 per 100,000 births in the United States, which has the highest rates in the developed world. Priya Agrawal, "Maternal Mortality and Morbidity in the United States of America," *Bulletin of the World Health Organization* 93, no. 3 (2015): 135, http://dx.doi.org/10.2471/BLT.14.148627.

22. Sarker et al., "Reasons for Preference of Home Delivery."

23. Sarah Cooke, "Literacy in Bangladesh: Reading between the Lines," *Daily Star*, September 8, 2013, http://www.thedailystar.net/news/literacy-in-bangladesh-reading-between-the-lines.

24. Sarker et al., "Reasons for Preference of Home Delivery."

25. Britton, "Reality and Unreality in Phantasy and Fiction," 19; Britton, *Sex, Death, and the Superego*, 83.

26. Patricia Townsend, "Making Space," in Anette Khun, ed., *Little Madnesses: Winnicott, Transitional Phenomena and Cultural Experience* (London: I. B. Tauris, 2013), 182.

27. Papreen Nahar and Annemiek Richters, "Suffering of Childless Women in Bangladesh: The Intersection of Social Identities of Gender and Class," *Anthropology & Medicine* 18, no. 3 (December 2011): 331.

28. Pierre Bourdieu, *The Field of Cultural Production* (New York: Columbia University Press, 1993), 7; Pierre Bourdieu, *Distinction: A Social Critique of the Judgement of Taste* (Cambridge, MA: Harvard University Press, 1984), 291.

29. See Janet E. Bradley et al., "Blood, Men and Tears: Keeping IUDs in Place in Bangladesh," *Culture, Health & Sexuality* 11, no. 5 (June 2009): 552–53.

30. Raymond E. Francier, *Psychoanalytic Psychology: The Development of Freud's Thoughts* (New York: W. W. Norton, 1973), 115–16.

31. Senthilingam, "Sexual Harassment."

32. Lee, "Causes and Cures VII," 110.

Bibliography

Andrews, Johanna, and Koustuv Dalal. "Umbilical Cord-Cutting Practices and Place of Delivery in Bangladesh." *International Journal of Gynecology and Obstetrics* 114, no. 1 (July 2011): 43–46.

Belli Bose, Melia. "Entangled Tensions: Bangladeshi Women Artists." *ArtAsiaPacific* 96 (November–December 2015): 88–95.

Bourdieu, Pierre. *Distinction: A Social Critique of the Judgement of Taste.* Cambridge, MA: Harvard University Press, 1984.

———. *The Field of Cultural Production.* New York: Columbia University Press, 1993.

Bradley, Janet E., Mahboob E. Alam, Fatema Shabnam, and Tara S. H. Beattie. "Blood, Men and Tears: Keeping IUDs in Place in Bangladesh." *Culture, Health and Sexuality* 11, no. 5 (June 2009): 543–58.

Butalia, Urvashi. *The Other Side of Silence: Voices from the Partition of India.* Durham, NC: Duke University Press, 2000.

D'Acosta, Bina. *Nationbuilding, Gender and War Crimes in South Asia.* New York and London: Routledge, 2010.

Feldman, Shelly. "Exploring Theories of Patriarchy: A Perspective from Contemporary Bangladesh." *Signs* 26, no. 4 (Summer 2001): 109–127.

Francier, Raymond E. *Psychoanalytic Psychology: The Development of Freud's Thoughts.* New York: W. W. Norton, 1973.

Jayawardena, Kumar, and Malathi De Alwis. *Embodied Violence: Communalizing Women's Sexuality in South Asia.* London: Zed Books, 1996.

Lee, Bandy X. "Causes and Cures VII: Structural Violence." *Aggression and Violent Behavior* 28 (2016): 100–114.

Metcalf, Barbara D., and Thomas R. Metcalf. *A Concise History of Modern India.* Cambridge, UK: Cambridge University Press, 2011.

Mookherjee, Nayanika. *The Spectral Wound: Sexual Violence, Public Memories, and the Bangladesh War of 1971.* Durham, NC: Duke University Press, 2015.

Mukherjee, Joia S., Donna J. Barry, Hind Satti, Maxi Raymonville, Sarah Marsh, and Mary Kay Smith-Fawzi. "Structural Violence: A Barrier to Achieving the Millennium Development Goals for Women." *Journal of Women's Health* 20, no. 4 (2011): 593–97.

Nahar, Papreen, and Annemiek Richters. "Suffering of Childless Women in Bangladesh: The Intersection of Social Identities of Gender and Class." *Anthropology & Medicine* 18, no. 3 (December 2011): 327–38.

Pearson, E. S., P. Fonagy, and A. S. Figueiera, eds. *On Freud's Creative Writers and Day-Dreaming.* New Haven, CT: Yale University Press, 1995.

Rozario, Santi. "The New Burqa in Bangladesh: Empowerment or Violation of Women's Rights?" *Women's Studies International Forum* 29 (2006): 368–80.

Sarkar, Bidhan Krishna, Musfikur Rahman, Tawhidur Rahman, Jahangir Hossain, Laura Reichenbach, and Dipak Kumar Mitra. "Reasons for Preference of Home Delivery with Traditional Birth Attendants (TBAs) in Rural Bangladesh: A Qualitative Exploration." *PLOS ONE* 11, no. 1 (2016): e0146161. https://doi.org/10.1371/journal.pone.0146161.

Tarlo, Emma. *Visibly Muslim: Fashion, Politics, Faith.* London: Bloomsbury Academic Press, 2010.

Townsend, Patricia. "Making Space." In *Little Madnesses: Winnicott, Transitional Phenomena and Cultural Experience,* edited by Anette Khun, 173–86. London: I. B. Tauris, 2013.

van Schendel, Willem. *A History of Bangladesh.* Cambridge, UK: Cambridge University Press, 2009.

Contributors

Melia Belli Bose is associate professor of South Asian art history at the University of Victoria, Canada. Her research focuses on South Asian art and architecture from the early modern era to present, and publications include *Royal Umbrellas of Stone: Memory, Political Propaganda, and Public Identity in Rajput Funerary Art* and the edited volumes *Women, Gender, and Art in Asia (ca. 1500–1900)*; *Intersections: Art and Islamic Cosmopolitanism*; and (forthcoming) *Gendered Threads of Globalization: 20th c. Textile Crossings in Asia.* Her monograph in progress, *Creative Interventions: Art and Cultural Activism in Bangladesh*, examines artworks that critique, help heal, and create community in a changing Bangladesh.

Sati Benes Chock attended Wheaton College in Massachusetts and taught English in Japan before getting her MA in East Asian languages and literatures from the University of Hawai'i. She currently works at the Honolulu Museum of Art, where she has been involved in many exhibitions and catalogues, including *Splendor & Serenity: Korean Ceramics from the Honolulu Museum of Art*; *Shunga: Stages of Desire*; *Masterpieces of Landscape Painting from the Forbidden City*; *Literati Modern: Bunjinga from Late-Edo to Twentieth-Century Japan*; *The Dragon's Gift: The Sacred Arts of Bhutan*; *Masterpieces of Chinese Lacquer from the Mike Healy Collection*; *Taishō Chic: Japanese Modernity, Nostalgia, & Art Deco*; and *The Sacred Treasures of Mount Kōya.*

Shana J. Brown is a specialist in modern Chinese intellectual and cultural history at the University of Hawai'i at Mānoa. Her research interests include visual culture, collecting practices, and women's history. Her book *Pastimes: From Art and Antiquarianism to Modern Chinese Historiography* (University of Hawai'i Press, 2011) discussed how nineteenth-century elite practices of collecting, representing, and studying ancient artifacts influenced historical studies in the twentieth century. She is currently completing two books, one on Chinese women as artists, art collectors, and historians, and one on leftist photography in China during World War II.

Janet C. Chen, a native of Taiwan, is an independent scholar with a bachelor's degree from National Central University, Taiwan, and a PhD in East Asian art history from the University of Kansas, where she studied both Chinese and Japanese painting and calligraphy. Her dissertation focused on depictions of talented women in late imperial China as seen through portraits of female poets and painters in the circle of the scholar Yuan Mei (1716–97). Based in Kansas City, she currently works as a translator, researcher, and consultant to an Asian art appraiser while continuing to pursue her research interests in topics related to women as artists, patrons, and artistic subjects in the history of Chinese art.

Insoo Cho is professor in the department of art theory, School of Visual Arts at Korea National University of Arts. He received a PhD in art history from the University of Kansas and was a visiting scholar at Korea Institute at Harvard University, 2011–12. He has served with the Cultural Heritage Administration of Korea as a member of the Cultural Heritage Committee since 2007. He has published articles on Korean and Chinese art, focusing on portraiture from the Joseon dynasty and images of Daoist immortals from the Ming dynasty.

Wei-Cheng Lin is associate professor in the Department of Art History at the University of Chicago. Lin specializes in the history of Chinese art and architecture with a focus on the medieval period and has published on both Buddhist and funeral art and architecture of medieval China. He has also written on topics related to traditional architecture in modern China. His first book, *Building a Sacred Mountain: Buddhist Architecture of China's Mount Wutai*, was published in 2014 by the University of Washington Press. Lin's current book project, *Performative Architecture of China*, explores architecture's performative potential through history and the meanings enacted through such architectural performance.

Ling-en Lu earned her doctoral degree in art history from the University of Kansas at Lawrence. Her research focuses on Chinese painting and Buddhist art. She has worked at the Nelson-Atkins Museum of Art at Kansas City, Missouri, since 2000. Currently she serves as curator of Chinese art. In this role, she assumes a full range of duties for the museum's collection of Chinese art, including research, exhibition, acquisition, and publication. During her tenure, she has extended her interest in the curatorship and study of furniture, textiles, lacquers, and other forms of art. Ling-en is the author of several articles on painting in Chinese and English publications.

Nick Pearce is the Richmond Chair of Fine Art at the University of Glasgow, where he specializes in the arts of China. His career has spanned both museums and universities, having held positions at the Victoria & Albert Museum, the Burrell Collection in Glasgow, and universities in Durham and Edinburgh. His research interests include photography in late-nineteenth century China and the history of collecting Chinese art, including provenance research. His recent publications include: "From Relic to Relic: A Brief History of the Skull of Confucius," *Journal of the History of Collections* (26:2, 2014), "From the Summer Palace 1860: Provenance and Politics," in L. Tythacott (ed.), *Collecting and Displaying China's Summer Palace in the West* (2018) and with Jane Milosch, *Collecting and Provenance: A Multidisciplinary Approach* (2019). With Alexander Hofmann and Christine Howald, he guest-edited *Asian Art: The Formation of Collections,* a special issue of the *Journal for Art Market Studies* (4:2, 2020).

Allysa B. Peyton served as assistant curator of Asian art at the University of Florida's Samuel P. Harn Museum of Art from 2010 to 2022. She served as chief editor for the David A. Cofrin Asian Art Manuscript Series from 2019 to 2022. Recent publications in this series include *Great Waves and Mountains: Perspectives and Discoveries in Collecting the Arts of Japan*; *Arts of South Asia: Cultures of Collecting*; and *Arts of Korea: Histories, Challenges, and Perspectives.*

Junko Uchida is associate research fellow at the Institute of History and Philology, Academia Sinica, in Taiwan. She was born in Tokyo and was trained at Kyoto University. After moving to Taipei in 2006, her work concentrated on the materials unearthed from Anyang Yinxu, which are stored at Academia Sinica. Uchida's recent scholarly work focuses on the rise and fall of the Shang dynasty and the change of social systems in one of the oldest megalopolises in Asia, including gender structure through the analysis of the archaeological materials. Publications include: "The Anyang Xibeigang Shang Royal Tombs Revisited: A Social Archaeological Approach," *Antiquity* 92, no. 363 (coauthored with Koji Mizoguchi).

Saleema Waraich is associate professor in the art history department and a faculty affiliate of the Asian studies program at Skidmore College. Previously she held postdoctoral fellowships at Massachusetts Institute of Technology and Smith College, and served as an assistant curator of South Asian art at the Asian Art Museum of San Francisco. Her research spans the early modern to the contemporary eras, focusing on Mughal material as well as its political, social, and aesthetic ties to the present.

Midori Yamamura, PhD, is associate professor of art history at CUNY Kingsborough, and the 2022–23 Alcaly-Bodian Distinguished Scholar, CUNY Graduate Center. She specializes in global contemporary art history, focusing on Asia and its diaspora, feminism, and postcolonialism. The author of *Yayoi Kusama: Inventing the Singular* (MIT Press: 2015), a critical biography of Yayoi Kusama examined through a feminist lens, and coeditor of *Visual Representation and the Cold War: Art and Postcolonial Struggles in East and Southeast Asia* (Routledge, 2021), she is currently completing a book on Japanese contemporary art. She has been exploring community-based college teaching centering on the critical issues in contemporary art. In 2022, she cocurated a pedagogical exhibition, *UuHomeless NYC* (2022), which connected classroom research, art, and the local artists and activists community.

Photograph Credits

Thanks are extended to the following institutions:

Academy of Korean Studies
Andong National University Museum
Asian Art Museum of San Francisco
Bridgeman Images
British Museum
Cheongju National Museum
Chiljangsa Temple
Chinese University of Hong Kong
Chungbuk National University Museum
Dongguk University Library
Far Eastern Library, Royal Ontario Museum
Freer Gallery of Art and Arthur M. Sackler Gallery Archives
Guerrilla Girls
Hiratsuka Museum of Art
Honolulu Museum of Art
Honolulu Museum of Art Archives
Indianapolis Museum of Art Archives
Institute of History and Philology, Academia Sinica
Kansong Art Museum
Katsumi Asaba Design Studio
Kyujanggak Institute for Korean Studies
Los Angeles County Museum of Art
Metropolitan Museum of Art
Minokamo City Museum
Museum of Fine Arts, Boston
Museum of Fine Arts, Gifu
Museum of the City of New York
National Hangeul Museum
National Museum of Korea
National Palace Museum of Korea
National Palace Museum, Taipei
National Portrait Gallery, London
Nelson-Atkins Museum of Art
Nerima Art Museum
Palace Museum, Beijing
President and Fellows of Harvard College
Maho Kubota Gallery
San Diego Museum of Art
School of Architecture, Tsinghua University
Seoul National University Museum
Sezon Museum of Art
Sotheby's
Spencer Museum of Art, University of Kansas
Taka Ishii Gallery
Tokyo Photographic Art Museum
Tsinghua University
Tsinghua University Art Museum
University of Hawai'i Library
University of Toronto Archives
Victoria & Albert Museum
Zeit-Foto

Index

Page numbers in *italics* refer to figures.

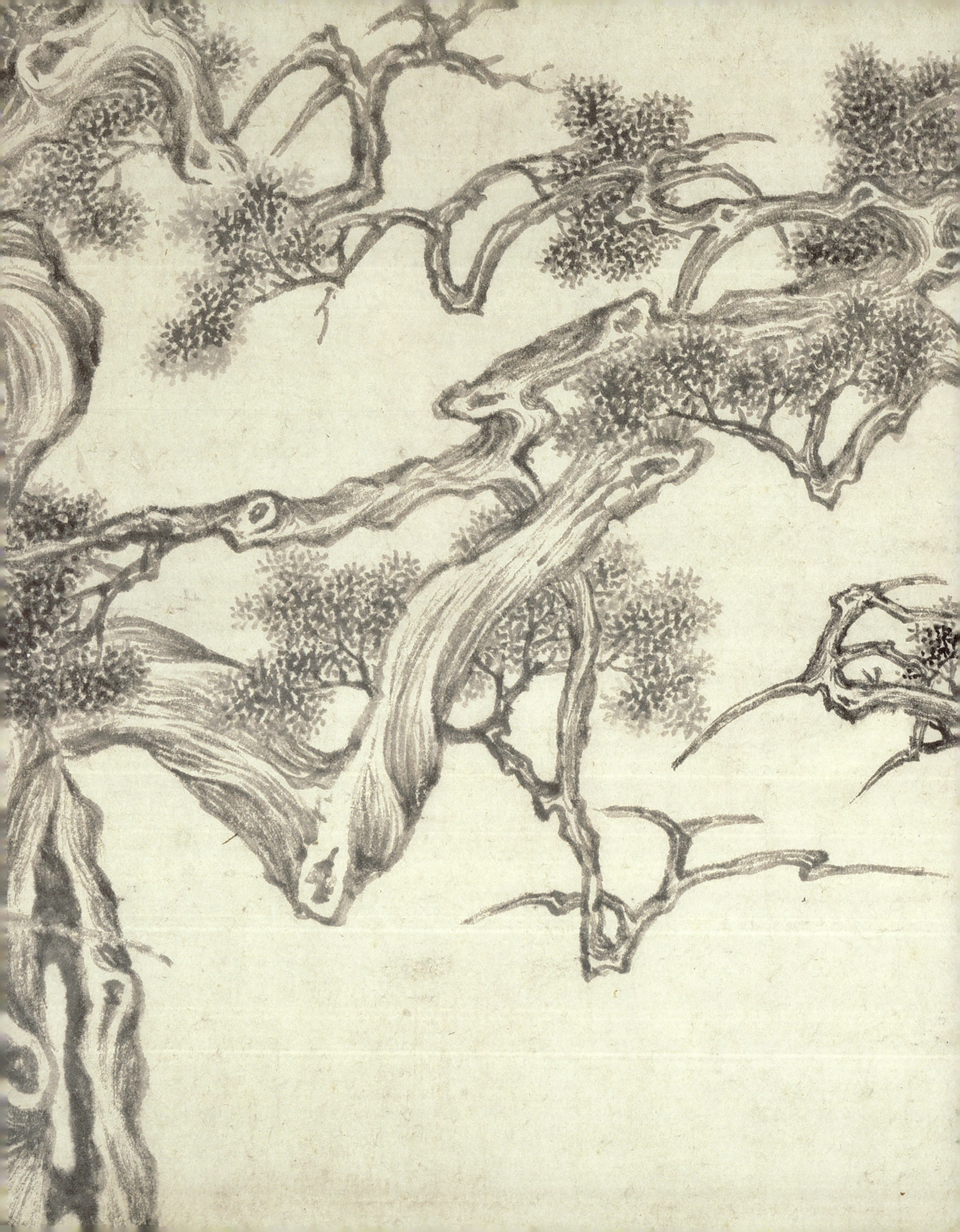